Sustainability and the Future of Work and Entrepreneurship for the Underserved

JoAnn Denise Rolle
Medgar Evers College, City University of New York, USA

Micah Crump
Medgar Evers College, City University of New York, USA

A volume in the Advances in Human Resources Management and Organizational Development (AHRMOD) Book Series

IGI Global
PUBLISHER of TIMELY KNOWLEDGE

Published in the United States of America by
IGI Global
Business Science Reference (an imprint of IGI Global)
701 E. Chocolate Avenue
Hershey PA, USA 17033
Tel: 717-533-8845
Fax: 717-533-8661
E-mail: cust@igi-global.com
Web site: http://www.igi-global.com

Library of Congress Cataloging-in-Publication Data

Names: Rolle, Jo-Ann, 1953- editor. | Crump, Micah, 1964- editor.
Title: Sustainability and the future of work and entrepreneurship for the underserved / Jo-Ann Rolle, and Micah Crump, editor.
Description: Hershey PA : Business Science Reference, [2022] | Includes bibliographical references and index. | Summary: "This book highlights marginalized labor and entrepreneurial market segments and reviews strategies used to prepare for technology changes globally with the intent to provide a series of recommendation by thought leaders that may aid in growing and sustaining a more inclusive global society"-- Provided by publisher.
Identifiers: LCCN 2022007825 (print) | LCCN 2022007826 (ebook) | ISBN 9781668443224 (hardcover) | ISBN 9781668443231 (paperback) | ISBN 9781668443248 (ebook)
Subjects: LCSH: Sustainable development. | Entrepreneurship. | Small business. | Minority business enterprises. | Income distribution. | Employees--Effect of technological innovations on. | COVID-19 Pandemic, 2020---Economic aspects. | COVID-19 Pandemic, 2020---Social aspects.
Classification: LCC HC79.E5 S86633 2022 (print) | LCC HC79.E5 (ebook) | DDC 338.9/27--dc23/eng/20220504
LC record available at https://lccn.loc.gov/2022007825
LC ebook record available at https://lccn.loc.gov/2022007826

This book is published in the IGI Global book series Advances in Human Resources Management and Organizational Development (AHRMOD) (ISSN: 2327-3372; eISSN: 2327-3380)

British Cataloguing in Publication Data
A Cataloguing in Publication record for this book is available from the British Library.

For electronic access to this publication, please contact: eresources@igi-global.com.

Advances in Human Resources Management and Organizational Development (AHRMOD) Book Series

Patricia Ordóñez de Pablos
Universidad de Oviedo, Spain

ISSN:2327-3372
EISSN:2327-3380

Mission

A solid foundation is essential to the development and success of any organization and can be accomplished through the effective and careful management of an organization's human capital. Research in human resources management and organizational development is necessary in providing business leaders with the tools and methodologies which will assist in the development and maintenance of their organizational structure.

The **Advances in Human Resources Management and Organizational Development (AHRMOD) Book Series** aims to publish the latest research on all aspects of human resources as well as the latest methodologies, tools, and theories regarding organizational development and sustainability. The **AHRMOD Book Series** intends to provide business professionals, managers, researchers, and students with the necessary resources to effectively develop and implement organizational strategies.

Coverage

- Executive Education
- Recruitment Process
- Organizational Behavior
- Job Enrichment
- E-Human Resources Management
- Succession Planning
- Employee Benefits
- Human Resources Development
- Talent Identification and Management
- Human Relations Movement

IGI Global is currently accepting manuscripts for publication within this series. To submit a proposal for a volume in this series, please contact our Acquisition Editors at Acquisitions@igi-global.com or visit: http://www.igi-global.com/publish/.

The Advances in Human Resources Management and Organizational Development (AHRMOD) Book Series (ISSN 2327-3372) is published by IGI Global, 701 E. Chocolate Avenue, Hershey, PA 17033-1240, USA, www.igi-global.com. This series is composed of titles available for purchase individually; each title is edited to be contextually exclusive from any other title within the series. For pricing and ordering information please visit http://www.igi-global.com/book-series/advances-human-resources-management-organizational/73670. Postmaster: Send all address changes to above address.

Titles in this Series

For a list of additional titles in this series, please visit: www.igi-global.com/book-series

Leadership Strategies for the Hybrid Workforce Best Practices for Fostering Employee Safety and Significance
Matthew Ohlson (University of North Florida, USA) and Lakshmi Goel (University of North Florida, USA)
Business Science Reference • © 2022 • 315pp • H/C (ISBN: 9781668434536) • US $250.00

Handbook of Research on the Complexities and Strategies of Occupational Stress
Adnan ul Haque (Yorkville University, Canada)
Business Science Reference • © 2022 • 611pp • H/C (ISBN: 9781668439371) • US $295.00

Sustainable Development of Human Resources in a Globalization Period
Erum Shaikh (The University of Modern Sciences, Pakistan) and Muhammad Nawaz Tunio (Greenwich University, Pakistan)
Business Science Reference • © 2022 • 320pp • H/C (ISBN: 9781668449813) • US $240.00

Dissecting and Dismantling Occupational Stress in Modern Organizations
Adnan ul Haque (Yorkville University, Canada)
Business Science Reference • © 2022 • 310pp • H/C (ISBN: 9781668465431) • US $240.00

Socio-Economic Disparities, Vulnerable Communities, and the Future of Work and Entrepreneurship
JoAnn Denise Rolle (Medgar Evers College, City University of New York, USA) and Micah Crump (Medgar Evers College, City University of New York, USA)
Business Science Reference • © 2022 • 335pp • H/C (ISBN: 9781668469903) • US $240.00

Transgender Discrimination in the Workplace
Zafeiris Tsiftzis (OCL Solicitors, UK)
Business Science Reference • © 2022 • 315pp • H/C (ISBN: 9781799873129) • US $195.00

Implementing Diversity, Equity, Inclusion, and Belonging Management in Organizational Change Initiatives
Abeni El-Amin (Fort Hays State University, USA)
Business Science Reference • © 2022 • 320pp • H/C (ISBN: 9781668440230) • US $215.00

Handbook of Research on Challenges for Human Resource Management in the COVID-19 Era
Paula Cristina Nunes Figueiredo (ULHT - Universidade Lusófona, Portugal) Eduardo Luís de Campos Soares Tomé (ULHT - Universidade Lusófona, Portugal) and José Carlos Dias Rouco (ULHT - Universidade Lusófona, Portugal)
Business Science Reference • © 2022 • 450pp • H/C (ISBN: 9781799898405) • US $295.00

IGI Global
PUBLISHER of TIMELY KNOWLEDGE

701 East Chocolate Avenue, Hershey, PA 17033, USA
Tel: 717-533-8845 x100 • Fax: 717-533-8661
E-Mail: cust@igi-global.com • www.igi-global.com

Editorial Advisory Board

Table of Contents

Section 2
Sociodemographic Entrepreneurship

Section 3
Industry Challenges

Section 4
National/Regional Sustainability

Section 5
Technology and Entrepreneurial Sustainability

Detailed Table of Contents

Sociological study demonstrates that any societal collective, whether large or small, is an evolving entity subject to the forces of change. Given the interdependency of industry and cultural convention, it's imperative that business strategies within a defined societal structure keep pace with technological advances and cultural shifts within the community. Over the course of time, societal constructs evolved to support and regulate environmental conditions and the interactions of people within the workplace. While some business leaders advance in real time with shifting conditions and cultural movements, many do not. As such, there has long been an existential struggle between the maintenance of traditional workplace values, or the status quo, and progressive if not revolutionary ideas. This chapter examines a new leadership paradigm intended to promote workplace democracy in an empathetic environment based on inclusion, individual growth, and opportunity for all.

The COVID-19 pandemic has created shockwaves across the globe and impacted businesses and economies. Enormous disruptive transformations have happened in the work models and systems to enable businesses to flexibly operate, sustain, and remain agile in uncertain times. The future of work, which seemed uncertain post-pandemic, has reached normalcy due to the organisational resilience and strategic responses shown by organisational leaders and small businesses. Although small businesses across the world have been impacted negatively leading to closures, financial crunches, and job losses worldwide, many have shown signs of resilience and recovery. The chapter throws light on the work transformations across economies and strategic responses to deal with them. It describes the challenges faced by various small businesses and the way they have been flexible and resilient. The chapter proposes a framework for building an inclusive economy that has been asserted to be the solution to a sustainable and resilient future in times of uncertainties and crises.

The demand for innovative, solutions-oriented approaches to closing learning competency gaps is leading to the recasting of organizations as learning and innovation-centric organizational communities. The makerspace movement is a sector where new communities are emerging to include diverse groups of entrepreneurs. The findings in this study provide insight that will assist in meeting the challenges posed by declining economic and social conditions of former industrial centers and rural communities that were part of thriving economic pipelines during the height of the industrial age. The study examines a makerspace as a solution for creating jobs, filling gaps in the supply chain, and reimagining local manufacturing. The IOC approach also possesses potential for helping to reduce equity gaps and facilitating inclusive practices. The concept of innovation-centric organizational communities, based on maximizing affective learning, is consistent with emerging 21st century workforce demands and their relationship to entrepreneurial opportunities for underserved communities.

Rapidly changing business environments and the use of inclusive systems have magnified the emerging concept of "ecosystem" for the businesses. The need of ecosystem is further amplified for entrepreneurs working in underserved marginalized communities where networks and collaborations can play a catalyst for an inclusive future characterized by sustainable business and social uplift. Underserved communities have significant potential of entrepreneurship which can be explored by being active part of the ecosystem. This chapter focuses on the need of ecosystem approach for underserved community. The chapter presents an explanation of business ecosystem, identification of key actors and their roles in the ecosystem, and the relationship among various actors. The significance of inclusive future of work and entrepreneurship for the underserved has been highlighted through a case study findings. Furthermore, the chapter presents recommendations for the government, regulators, policymakers, the supporting institutions, small business and entrepreneurs in the underserved, and academicians.

Section 2
Sociodemographic Entrepreneurship

This chapter helps define the state of Black entrepreneurship in the United States using knowledge from business, management, entrepreneurship, sociology, and economic literature. Challenges and opportunities are laid out for Black entrepreneurs to aid their success in starting and growing new businesses particularly in a post-pandemic world. Nuanced differences in Black business formalization, social networks, entrepreneurial financing, opportunity recognition, strategic planning, STEM foundation, and customer discovery and validation processes are each addressed in how they can help improve Black entrepreneurship and business ownership outcomes. Seven specific recommendations are provided and explained along with a checklist to aid primarily Black entrepreneurs to start and grow their new businesses. The chapter content can serve as a foundation for undergraduate and master's degree program Black entrepreneurship courses, and along with its reading list, as a doctoral seminar course on Black entrepreneurship.

Utilizing critical race theory as the analytical lens, this chapter explores how the Paycheck Protection Program, which did not specify preference to race of applicant, nevertheless resulted in racialized outcomes. The chapter examines the program's primary features to understand whether the appearance of race neutrality obscures a White normative standard embedded within the program. The examination reveals that the program's design was more aligned with the White small business owner experience and that policymakers failed to adequately consider the unique needs of Black small business owners in formulating the program. The author argues that the program was therefore more accessible to White small business owners, was more beneficial to them, and helped to perpetuate the White advantage in small business outcomes. The chapter concludes with the recommendation that future small business policies should follow a targeted universalism approach. Suggestions for redesigning the Paycheck Protection Program, or similar small business policy, are provided.

While Black women entrepreneurs have the highest nascent entrepreneurship rates, they also significantly underperform their White counterparts. As some scholars have argued, the primary cause of this disparity may result from differences in access to financial capital. Utilizing a stratification economics lens, this chapter analyzes the root causes of the financial capital access gap among Black women entrepreneurs. Wealth, discrimination by financial institutions, credit history, student loan debt, negative social capital, lack of support and perceptions of illegitimacy from social networks, and family structure disadvantages are identified as structural factors driving the financial capital access gap. It is further argued that the COVID-19 pandemic will exacerbate some of these conditions. Policy recommendations are made, including increased non-traditional lending models such as character-based and forgivable loans, greater transparency of race in lending through the implementation of Section 1071 of Dodd-Frank, and student loan amnesty.

The challenges of a global pandemic have placed women's business ownership and entrepreneurship at the forefront of much debate. This is an important area to pursue within scholarly arenas because women's involvement in business ownership and entrepreneurship continues to impact women's livelihoods, families, and impacts the local and global economy. There are many studies that explored challenges and barriers to women's entrepreneurship, a more specific and focused finding should be addressed to review implications presented due to COVID-19 pandemic. An examination of how ethnicity, gender, and race plays a role in women entrepreneurship process and the way women entrepreneurs' experiences were shaped during the pre- and post-pandemic era is warranted on a scholarly level.

This chapter focusses on women entrepreneurs in the informal food production sector in Mauritius. It seeks to explore the business practices of these women entrepreneurs and investigates the business and employment challenges they face, especially during the COVID-19 pandemic. The study made use of the qualitative interpretive research paradigm, specifically using unstructured interviews, to identify the challenges and opportunities these women faced as entrepreneurs, during unprecedented times. Findings were categorized using thematic analysis and were discussed in the light of the literature review conducted. Interesting themes including support from family members, access to resources, and perception of respectable femininity and domesticity emerged for the Mauritian context. Accordingly, recommendations with respect to ensuring business continuity of women entrepreneurs in the informal food production sector in Mauritius have been made.

Like many other jobs and career opportunities, entrepreneurship is frequently contingent on a variety of factors. Developing an interest in entrepreneurship as a career appears to be increasing now that entrepreneurship education is becoming more popular in universities worldwide. This is because entrepreneurs create jobs and propel the nation's economic development. Universities have numerous

of 388 volunteers and 3D printers, and two partner organizations. The study reveals best practices for establishing Lean small-scale manufacturing, developing institutional trust, community collaboration, and developing a more inclusive, agile supply chain in healthcare equipment production.

Section 4
National/Regional Sustainability

With the outbreak of the coronavirus, the economies of developing economies, which have already been plagued by youth unemployment and poverty, became more vulnerable as the virus exacerbated the situation and resulted in more job losses. Consequently, to mitigate the effect of the virus on the developing economies post COVID-19, the chapter argues that developing entrepreneurship skills in technical and vocational education and training through a multi-stakeholder partnership remains a viable strategy. Thus, through an exploratory approach, the chapter reviewed related literature on the subject under study. The findings highlighted the following multi-stakeholders, namely the training institutions, enterprises (formal and informal), government, and non-governmental organisations, among others. Thus, this chapter concludes that collaboration between these mentioned stakeholders would aid in the development of the much-needed entrepreneurship skills in TVET, thereby serving as a recovery strategy for developing economies.

The COVID-19 pandemic has coerced society to recreate the delicate balance between small business owners and the local community. Throughout Brooklyn, NY, the anguish resonates the difficulties of increasing profits. With communal solidarity serving as a central tenet, sword, and shield, technological and social researchers traversed urban Brooklyn, NY areas. Researchers conducted a series of exploratory interviews and surveys over the course of the last quarter specifically within the geographic grouping areas of the Crown Heights 11225 and Bedford Stuyvesant 11216 zip codes. Investigators identified key interventions to assist Black and Brown-owned businesses increase long-term sustainability. Focusing primarily on the triple bottom line theory and practice, investigators compiled data to suggest how businesses can become more economically diverse in client acquisition strategies.

This chapter identifies the gaps and weakness in the current Palestinian entrepreneurial ecosystem, impeding the development of economically and socially responsive, inclusive, and sustainable entrepreneurship. It seeks to determine what factors are necessary to develop an inclusive and sustainable model for these forms of entrepreneurship to thrive. This study draws on semi-structured interviews with various actors/players in the Palestinian entrepreneurial ecosystem. The chapter finds that all existing elements in the ecosystem are yet to be developed, resulting in a fragmented ecosystem. More importantly, it finds that the dependence on foreign donors and, consequently, donor agendas in terms of entrepreneurial development frameworks has generated entrepreneurship and an entrepreneurial ecosystem that is unresponsive, unsustainable, inaccessible, and far removed from the Palestinian market needs; hence, most efforts are yet to produce significant economic and social impacts.

Chapter 17
Sustainable Growth: Growth by Poverty Alleviation or Poverty Creation – The Case of Sub-Saharan Africa 334
Adem Gök, Kırklareli University, Turkey

The authors analyzed 30 countries in Sub-Saharan Africa over the period of 1996-2015 to investigate whether economic growth is sustainable, whether decreasing income inequality sustains growth, and whether economic growth alleviates or creates poverty due to decreasing or increasing income inequality, respectively. They found that growth in Sub-Saharan Africa is self-reinforcing in the sense that past levels of GDP per capita positively affect current levels of GDP per capita due to the strategic complementarity. Decrease in income inequality leads to growth due to increased consumption, higher investment in education, lower corruption, higher political stability, and more equal redistribution policies. Economic growth does not bring down income inequality in order to maximize social welfare. The authors conclude that growth is not sustainable in Sub-Saharan Africa since it only meets two of the three criteria.

Section 5
Technology and Entrepreneurial Sustainability

Chapter 18
Digital Transformation and Sustainability of Entrepreneurship for Underserved Communities in East Africa 347
Nathan Mutwiri Mwenda, Kenyatta University, Kenya
Carolyne Jebiwott Kimutai, Kenyatta University, Kenya

Digital transformations are transforming the economy and society in East Africa, and entrepreneurs need to leverage on these digital transformations to ensure the sustainability of their businesses. This chapter therefore seeks to examine the role of digital transformation on sustainability of entrepreneurship for the underserved communities in East Africa. The chapter adopts an interdisciplinary and pragmatic world view. There exist many challenges in East Africa which stifle the progress of digital adoption. For East African countries to exploit the potential of technology, they must develop the foundational building block of digital economy. Digital innovation contributes to the development of an ecosystem that revitalizes the digital economy by supporting new technology-based products and businesses. East African countries should ensure that the underserved communities receive basic education, strengthen, and integrate a multi-sectoral approach towards a regional digital and legal policy framework in order to encourage innovation and e-business.

Preface

"When we started this journey, there were few cited roadmaps or authentic voices globally from underserved communities. We wanted to develop and sustain more and better entrepreneurship and employment outcomes for underserved communities globally."

Rolle, J. D. et al., The Future of Work & Entrepreneurship for the Underserved.

The vision for this book, *Sustaining the Future of Work and Entrepreneurship for the Underserved*, is to continue to engage, empower, and enlighten voices from a diverse community of academics, industry leaders, and other stakeholders in the search for a more inclusive and equitable society. As we emerge from the COVID-19 worldwide social, health, and economic crisis, the ensuing inequities have been more visible and more devastating, and now blur lines between a once middle class and the poor.

In our original call for chapters, we set out to infuse a discussion on wealth disparity with innovations in income experiments and experiences. We also intentionally included technology as a driver for transformations in the bottom and middle workforce sectors. We wanted to include lessons learned from communities that addressed challenges to income distribution through job and entrepreneurial strategies. Finally, we hoped that the body of work could serve as a potential roadmap for collaborations between industry, academy, government, and the community to improve sustainable outcomes for the future of work and entrepreneurship for the underserved.

The answer to the call for chapters was overwhelming. Seventy abstracts and 44 full chapter manuscripts were received for the planned 15-chapter book. The sheer volume of manuscripts to be reviewed created a challenge for the editorial and peer review team. Finally, the decision was made that there was enough quality content for two books and the first book would contain 19 chapters on related topics.

The topics that emerged from the submissions include:

1. **Inclusion:** Chapters 1-4
2. **Sociodemographic Entrepreneurship:** Chapters 5-11
3. **Industry Challenges:** Chapters 12-13
4. **National/Regional Sustainability:** Chapters 14-17
5. **Technology and Entrepreneurial Sustainability:** Chapters 18-19

While our original vision for the book was broadened by the number and quality of the submissions, the target market for the book remains the same. It is our hope that scholars, researchers, policy makers, NGOs, industry and community leaders will collaborate to explore and engage in diverse and more meaningful strategies for a sustainable and inclusive worldwide workforce that yields better equitable social and economic outcomes in the future of work for the Underserved.

SIGNIFICANCE AND OVERVIEW OF CHAPTERS

Section 1: Inclusion

Chapter 1, "Leadership, Empathy, and Inclusion," provides a roadmap for the enlightened business leader and aspiring entrepreneur, with a particular focus on those in and from underserved communities who transcend a post-COVID environment. A new leadership paradigm is presented to promote workplace democracy in an empathetic environment based on inclusion, individual growth, and opportunity for all. The roadmap helps pave the way for a more inclusive and effective professional environment for all, including the underserved in both large and small format organizations.

Chapter 2, "Post-COVID-19 Transformations for Future of Work and Small Business Sustainability: Towards an Inclusive Economy," describes strategic responses used by business organizations and human resource leaders to transform the future of work in the post-COVID era. The chapter sheds light on challenging tasks faced by small business owners in both the United States and India during the COVID pandemic and describes their strategic responses to crises. The chapter proposes a framework of new directions for organizations and small businesses to address disruptive models in the future of work for inclusive economies.

Chapter 3, "Innovation-Centric Organizational Community (IOC): What Works for the Emerging Workforce," provides insights to assist in meeting the challenges posed by declining economic and social conditions. The chapter provides insights on how a makerspace can solve the problems of job creation shortages, gaps in supply chains, and needs to reimagine local manufacturing. Innovation-Centric Organizational Community is explained as an approach with potential to help reduce equity gaps and facilitate inclusive practices.

Chapter 4, "Promoting an Ecosystem Approach for Inclusive and Sustainable Entrepreneurship in Underserved Communities," argues the need for an ecosystem approach for underserved communities. The chapter explains business ecosystem, identifies its key actors and their roles in an ecosystem, and explains the relationships among various actors. Using case study findings, the chapter highlights the significance of inclusivity in the future of work and entrepreneurship for underserved communities.

Section 2: Sociodemographic Entrepreneurship

Chapter 5, "Successfully Starting and Growing Black Businesses: For Entrepreneurs and Educators," helps to define the state of black entrepreneurship in the United States. Challenges and opportunities are laid out for black entrepreneurs to aid their success in starting and growing new businesses particularly in a post-pandemic world. This chapter lays out seven specific recommendations along with a checklist to aid primarily black entrepreneurs to start and grow their new businesses. The chapter content can serve as a foundation for undergraduate and masters black entrepreneurship courses, and as a doctoral seminar course on black entrepreneurship.

Chapter 6, "Why 'Race Neutral' Policy Fails Black Small Business Owners: Lessons Learned From the Paycheck Protection Program and Mapping an Equitable Path Forward," explores how the U.S. Paycheck Protection Program resulted in racialized outcomes. The chapter examines how race neutrality within programs intended to help underserved groups such as black entrepreneurs can deliver unintended adverse impacts. The chapter provides recommendations for redesigning the Paycheck Protection Program and similar other small business policy programs and argues that small businesses should meanwhile adopt a targeted universalism approach as an alternative to such programs.

Chapter 7, "Black Women Entrepreneurs: An Exploration of the Structural Factors Driving the Financial Capital Access Gap," analyzes root causes of financial capital access gaps between black women and other women entrepreneurs. The chapter explains structural factors that create financial capital access gaps as primarily being wealth disparity, discrimination by financial institutions, credit history, student loan debt, negative social capital, lack of support and perceptions of illegitimacy from social networks, and family structure differences.

Chapter 8, "Women Entrepreneurs and Disparities During the Pre- and Post-COVID-19 Pandemic Eras," argues that the global pandemic has placed women's business ownership and entrepreneurship as an important scholarly research area to pursue with particular emphasis on implications presented by the COVID-19 pandemic. The chapter examines how ethnicity, gender, and race play a role in women entrepreneurship processes and how women entrepreneurs' experiences were shaped during the pre and post pandemic era.

Chapter 9, "Women Entrepreneurs in the Informal Food Production Sector During the COVID-19 Pandemic: Challenges and Opportunities in Mauritius," provides an understanding of the business practices women entrepreneurs in the informal food production sector in Mauritius. The chapter explains the business and employment challenges they face especially during the COVID-19 pandemic. The role played by support from family members, access to resources, and perceptions of respectable femininity and domesticity in helping to advance an underserved population are provided in how each can help ensure business continuity among these women entrepreneurs.

Chapter 10, "Emboldening the Voice of Youth in Entrepreneurship Education," argues that universities wishing to encourage increases in entrepreneurship among students must assess students' awareness and support to determine the relationship between entrepreneurial education, mindset, intentions and actions among college students. The chapter presents findings after examining the relationships among students at a university in South Africa.

Chapter 11, "Analysis of Challenges and Opportunities Faced by Youth Entrepreneurs During COVID-19 in South Africa," argues that the COVID-19 pandemic had an especially negative impact on youth entrepreneurs, leading many countries to search for strategies to mitigate pandemic-induced economic disruption. The chapter explains that while many entrepreneurs in South Africa reacted by using bootstrapping techniques, that young entrepreneurs who were not as familiar with such techniques instead digitized their businesses during the COVID-19 pandemic. The chapter argues and explains how resilience and policy measures addressing structural support are strategies that promise to sustain entrepreneurs in a post-COVID-19 world.

Section 3: Industry Challenges

Chapter 12, "An Evaluation of How Tourism Entrepreneurs Were Impacted by the COVID-19 Pandemic," provides critical insights on the devastation of the COVID-19 pandemic on tourism entrepreneurs around the world, with an emphasis on South Africa. The chapter illuminates how tourism entrepreneurs in all industry sectors have been detrimentally impacted by the global COVID-19 pandemic, causing many of these entrepreneurs to experience negative cashflows. As a result, many of them were forced to permanently close their businesses, thereby contributing to a peaking global unemployment rate.

Chapter 13, "Local Lessons During a Global Crisis: Inclusive Entrepreneurial Solutions to Supply Chain and Production Deficits," presents a case study of *Makers Unite*, a collaborative Personal Protection Equipment (PPE) production project spearheaded by *Open Works*, a makerspace in Baltimore, Maryland. The organization produced 28,270 face shields in 56 days, averaging a production rate of 496 per day, serving over 100 clients, and resulting in a contract to produce face shields for meatpacking inspectors. The project included six full-time staff members, five temporary part-time staff members, a network of 388 volunteers, 3D printers, and two partner organizations. The chapter reveals best practices for establishing lean small-scale manufacturing, developing institutional trust, community collaboration, and developing a more inclusive, agile supply chain in healthcare equipment production.

Section 4: National/Regional Sustainability

Chapter 14, "Entrepreneurship Skills Development in TVET Through Multi-Stakeholder Partnerships: Post-COVID-19 Recovery Approach for Developing Economies," argues that developing entrepreneurship skills in technical and vocational education and training (TVET), through a multi-stakeholder partnership, remains a viable strategy to mitigate adverse economic impacts induced by the COVID-19 pandemic in developing economies. Training institutions, formal and informal enterprises, government, and non-governmental organizations are presented as key stakeholders for such multi-stakeholder partnerships. The chapter makes the case that collaboration between these stakeholders are essential in developing much-needed entrepreneurial skills in TVET in such a way that serves as an economic recovery strategy for developing economies.

Chapter 15, "Creating Social Sustainability Initiatives in an Effort to Increase Profits for the Underserved," provides key interventions that can assist black-owned and brown-owned businesses to increase long term sustainability. Drawing on *triple bottom line* theory and practice, and interview data from business owners in the Crown Heights neighborhood of Brooklyn, New York City, key interventions are explained in how businesses can become more economically diverse in their client acquisition strategies.

Chapter 16, "Development of a Sustainable and Inclusive Entrepreneurship Ecosystem Model in Occupied Palestinian Territories," identifies gaps and weaknesses in the current Palestinian entrepreneurial ecosystem that impede the development of economically and socially responsive, inclusive, and sustainable entrepreneurship. Drawing on semi-structured interviews from various ecosystem actors, the chapter illuminates how existing elements in the Palestinian entrepreneurial ecosystem are underdeveloped and thereby lead to a fragmented, nonresponsive, unsustainable, inaccessible entrepreneurial ecosystem that is far removed from actual Palestinian market needs.

Chapter 17, "Sustainable Growth: Growth by Poverty Alleviation or Poverty Creation – The Case of Sub-Saharan Africa," provides finding from nearly 20 years of data on 30 countries in Sub Saharan Africa (from 1996-2015). That chapter shows that growth in Sub-Saharan Africa is self-reinforcing, and that decreases in income inequality led to GDP growth due to increased consumption, higher investment in education, lower corruption, higher political stability and more equal redistribution policies. The chapter also shows that increases in economic growth does not increase income equality which would otherwise improve social welfare. Thus, the chapter concludes that economic growth in Sub Saharan Africa in its current form is not sustainable in helping the post-COVID-19 needs of the underserved there.

Section 5: Technology and Entrepreneurial Sustainability

Chapter 18, "Digital Transformation and Sustainability of Entrepreneurship for Undeserved Communities in East Africa," examines the role of digital transformation on sustainability of entrepreneurship for underserved communities in East Africa. The chapter argues that because of challenges in East Africa that stifle progress of digital adoption, East African countries must develop foundational building blocks of digital economy in order to exploit the potential of technology available to them. The chapter also asserts that East African countries should ensure that their underserved communities receive basic education, and strengthen and integrate a multi-sectoral approach towards a regional digital and legal policy framework in order to encourage expansive adoption of innovation and e-business commerce.

Chapter 19, "Pace of Technology Changes: Need for Adaptation and Demand for Skills – Skills Adaptation for Fast Evolving Technology-Based Workplace," closes out this book by addressing how underserved communities might adapt in response to newly sought skillsets by industry hiring organizations. Given that many underserved mechanized skilled workers are being replaced with automated technologies enhanced by artificial intelligence, the chapter presents the need for job skill retooling and repositioning. The argument is addressed through an assessment of: (1) the impact of advancement in technology on the current workplace; (2) the skill set (upskill and reskill) needs that enhance employees to meet the pace of current technology advancements; and, (3) the repositioning of workforces to be relevant in the face of automation and accelerated trends in artificial intelligence.

CONCLUSION

We present authentic voices on approaches to developing what we hope will evolve into a better "normal" post COVID. We hope that this work will create further dialogue in academia, industry, and policy on how to ensure that the underserved are included in the future of work and entrepreneurship.

Rolle, J. D. et al., The Future of Work & Entrepreneurship for the Underserved

We opened the book with the topic of inclusion. Much has been written in the literature on the importance of diversity, however diversity without inclusion yields marginal change or transformation of outcomes for the underserved. It was intentional that we started the dialogue with leadership and the necessity for a paradigm shift top down in the workplace. The roadmap to the future of work requires commitment and support to evolving real and meaningful change in how leaders work, engage, and empower the future workforce. Also cited is the need for a new and effective ecosystem to support entrepreneurial growth in diverse communities. Together with transformations in leadership of the workforce and more effective systems to sustain entrepreneurial growth, inclusion can start to impact sustainable change in income gaps and disparity.

The problem of income and wealth inequity is complex and impacts different socio-economic groups in various ways. Many of the issues that created the income disparities in these socio-economic groups are structural legacies from several global economic systems designed to be a resource for cheap or free labor. Section 2 of the book addresses specific socio-economic group challenges: the continuing disparity between black and white income earners and businesses; disparities among women income earners and entrepreneurs; and the challenge of youth income earners and entrepreneurs. In this second section of the book, we present the case that "one size does not fit all." Each socio-economic group within its community with its own set of unique cultures, challenges, and opportunities requires thought leadership that is specifically tailored to address their problems. Section 3 highlights how industry can both be impacted and respond to crisis. The entrepreneurial innovations presented in re-tooling and up-skilling of human and capital resources to meet changing market demand created by the pandemic are relevant lessons learned for the future of work and entrepreneurship for the underserved. In Section 4, we present chapters that have the broad scope of sustainability of a specific region or nation as a bridge from sustainability of income of workers, entrepreneurs, communities, or specific industries. We present the challenges of sustainability from the perspective of both developed and developing countries. One of the more troubling insights in this section was that national economic growth will not, in and of itself, yield a more socially equitable society. In fact, the case has been made that the gap in income disparity can increase with economic growth as several sectors in the workforce are left further behind. This brings us to the final section of the book. Section 5 presents technology as a disrupter and transformer for socio-economic growth. Here we address the growing digital divide, citing both issues of access and opportunities in many countries. The final chapter addresses the ever-increasing pace of technology and the need for continuous upskilling and re-tooling of the labor force. The relevant issue in the future of work for the underserved is *How and who will prepare them for the needed skills of an everchanging world*? Where are the empathetic leaders that understand the future is not in leadership or labor alone but rather in a collaboration and consolidation of mindsets coming together for problems unseen and a dynamic future that is yet unknown?

It is our hope that the 19 chapters that follow will evoke a call to action of all those who dare to change the world and create a more sustainable, equitable and just global society.

JoAnn Denise Rolle
Medgar Evers College, City University of New York, USA

Micah Crump
Medgar Evers College, City University of New York, USA

Acknowledgment

We gratefully acknowledge the 34 contributing authors in 9 different countries, the 40 editorial advisory board members in 12 countries, and Mrs. Lucie Cunningham of tellthemwell.com in Glasgow, Scotland, UK for all their laborious efforts in making this timely project a reality.

Section 1
Inclusion

Chapter 1
Leadership, Empathy, and Inclusion

Eric Feigenbaum
Embrace Design, USA & VMSD Magazine, USA

ABSTRACT

Sociological study demonstrates that any societal collective, whether large or small, is an evolving entity subject to the forces of change. Given the interdependency of industry and cultural convention, it's imperative that business strategies within a defined societal structure keep pace with technological advances and cultural shifts within the community. Over the course of time, societal constructs evolved to support and regulate environmental conditions and the interactions of people within the workplace. While some business leaders advance in real time with shifting conditions and cultural movements, many do not. As such, there has long been an existential struggle between the maintenance of traditional workplace values, or the status quo, and progressive if not revolutionary ideas. This chapter examines a new leadership paradigm intended to promote workplace democracy in an empathetic environment based on inclusion, individual growth, and opportunity for all.

INTRODUCTION

The turning of the millennium and the ensuing years have brought about unimaginable conditions and circumstances that have dramatically altered our lives. The world as we knew it, from travel protocols and the way we shop, to real estate purchases, banking, and workplace dynamics, is forever changed. The events that occurred during the early years of the 21st-century, from the attacks on 911 and the financial crises in 2008, to catastrophic storms and political and social upheaval, have restructured society in enduring and, in some cases, permanent ways. Beginning in 2019, the COVID-19 pandemic created needs and challenges that we had never faced before. It is quite evident that the pandemic has fostered significant changes to all aspects of life including the workplace. Never remaining stagnant, most successful long-term business leaders will readily embrace the challenging forces of change, evolution, and transformation. As we move deeper into the ever-evolving 21st-century, corporate structures must morph from directorial organizations to grass roots organizations. A new structure will call for a bottom up

DOI: 10.4018/978-1-6684-4322-4.ch001

administration to serve all within the collective. Additionally, the turning calendar and evolving mindsets will amplify the ever-relevant need for social responsibility. Business strategies must be reimagined and reshaped as tools for facilitating social justice and environmental sustainability. New strategies must also address emerging ethical standards in the workplace. Going forward, corporate leadership must listen to and disseminate the voice of a new generation by launching diversity, equity, and inclusion policies to create a more welcoming environment for all. The overarching goal of such initiatives is to bring awareness to the business leader and entrepreneur and, in fact, to the business community as a whole, relative to these timely and important issues.

In this study, the author provides a roadmap for the enlightened business leader and aspiring entrepreneur, with particular focus on those in and from underserved communities, to help pave the way for a more inclusive and effective professional environment for all, including the underserved in both large and small format organizations.

MAIN FOCUS OF THE CHAPTER

"What lies behind us, and what lies before us are but tiny matters compared to what lies within us." —Ralph Waldo Emerson

Adapting to change can be empirical, particularly in the face of new technologies and existential provocation such as the vice-like grip of a worldwide pandemic. In order to move forward in challenging and changing times, today's successful business leaders and aspiring underserved entrepreneurs, particularly in the retail, hospitality and service sectors, must have their hand on the pulse of our society and the heartbeat of our culture. They must recognize and understand societal shifts and current events, not only in their local communities, but across the world as well. According to Duffey (2019), "Sociologists define social change as changes in human interactions and relationships that transform cultural and social institutions. These changes occur over time and often have profound and long-term consequences for society. Well-known examples of such change have resulted from social movements in civil rights, women's rights, and LBGTQ rights, to name just a few. Relationships have changed, institutions have changed, and cultural norms have changed as a result of these social change movements" (Duffy, 2019, p. 1).

A vital characteristic of today's effective and influential business leader is an understanding and appreciation of the humanities and social sciences as well as political shifts, movements, and discourse. Progressive business leaders must broaden their worldwide perspectives. They must travel domestically and internationally while creating relationships and alliances across the globe. As the world shrinks due to the all-encompassing effects of technology, today's business leaders, including aspiring underserved entrepreneurs, must have an international perspective as well as a local grounding. If they are not thinking globally, they are not thinking at all. They should endeavor to expand their horizons in every way, from visiting museums to attending the theater, going to movies, and reading poetry, the *Wall Street Journal* and the Sunday *New York Times*.

The humanities serve as a bookmark of the past and a roadmap to the future. An immersive study into a wide range of disciplines, from comparative literature and religion to philosophy and the arts, will create a worldly mindset, creative vision and, most importantly, a recognition of the shared human values and commonalities that bind us, and an openness to the differences that add richness to the human experience. These understandings are the bedrock of creativity. Traditionally, trailblazers in the business arena have been inspired by cultural movements both past and present, while anticipating the latest trends, current events, needs, wants, and aspirations of the community today and in the future.

Moreover, they have always embraced cutting-edge advances in technology. The hallmark of business success has been a quick and effective response to change with progressive new directions and strategies. It is disappointing, however, that many businesses remain stagnant in their approach to leadership, employing theories that are relics of the 1970s, 80s, and 90s. As we move deeper into the 21st-century, we are still suffering from outdated business models that are harmful to people, which in turn is bad for business.

Exacerbating these antiquated approaches of course, are the effects of the pandemic, as COVID-19 continues to affect the health, safety, and welfare of people around the world. Every aspect of our lives, from our professional activities to our personal interactions, has been impacted by COVID-19. While the overarching characteristic of the early 2020s has been dramatic change, both unimagined and expected, it must be noted that there is more change to come. In a post-pandemic pivot, it is vital that all business leaders know and understand not only the priorities of their customers, but also the priorities of their partners, suppliers, investors, associates, and employees. Going forward, leaders in the workplace must define new benchmarks and standards for the work environment. They must explore a more humanistic approach to corporate leadership in these challenging and rapidly changing times. They must seek alternative approaches to that which has long been considered the tried and true. Albert Einstein reportedly said, “We cannot solve our problems with the same thinking we used when we created them.”

Before and during the pandemic, “empathy” was the buzzword bandied about by business executives across the world. “We have to care about our customers and clients,” was the rallying cry among entrepreneurs, particularly in the retail sector, struggling to compete in a challenging environment. Though the concept of empathy is heartfelt, it is almost universally misunderstood and largely misdirected.

There is a misconception that the biggest concern for great business leaders is their customers and/or clients. The reality is, most business executives never interact with their customers or clients. Rather, they lead a team of dedicated associates who are assigned the task of interacting, servicing, and caring about the customer. Therefore, it is the responsibility of great business leaders to care about the people they have entrusted to interact with the public. An effective leader knows implicitly that it is these associates who are vital to the health and well being of their organization. Moreover, empathy should not only be directed toward customers, but also toward the partners, associates, team members, and employees who man the front lines. Leadership begins with empathy for the team members that get it done (Sinek, 2017).

Empathy is not merely a buzzword, but rather an integral part of the lifeblood of any business. Empathy means putting yourself in another’s shoes and truly identifying with their situation. It is imperative for underserved entrepreneurs to recognize the concerns of the community they serve and the people who work for them. Empathy is a term that should be mastered, understood, embraced, and employed as part of an organizational practice and culture. Going forward, organizations, whether long established or underserved entrepreneurial start-ups, should understand that business is not merely about selling, but it is also about giving. When a business leader determines what their company can contribute to the common good, not only for their customers but for their employees as well, they will find that their business will be greatly rewarded for the effort.

METHODOLOGY

This study is an examination of emerging leadership roles, ethical standards, and management styles being developed as a result of economic, social, and technological shifts that are directly impacting the business environment. To remain relevant and effective, all mainstream business leaders and aspiring entrepreneurs, regardless of their socioeconomic standing or business format, must adapt to the changes and challenges of an evolving world. To support and document a new set of leadership conventions that will provide growth opportunities to all, and in particular to the underserved, a series of in-depth interviews was conducted with prominent business leaders. In addition, the author conducted a comprehensive study of influential authorities whose vision, experience and perspectives will serve as a guideline for all aspiring business leaders. Results and recommendations were measured against the challenges and implications of several factors including heightened levels of social awareness, and the impact of external factors such as the worldwide pandemic, ever-evolving advances in technology, and social and political discourse. A qualitative analysis of all information collected was based on the author's thirty plus years as a leader in the retail sector, as well as twenty plus years as an educator and journalist.

SOLUTIONS AND RECOMMENDATIONS FOR IMPLEMENTING SOLUTIONS

When climbing the professional ladder, most up-and-coming executives reach the next rung in the corporate hierarchy because they have a solid education, they work hard, and they are good at what they do. As they are promoted to positions of leadership, they no longer do the job that brought them to their lofty responsibilities. Rather, they supervise and, hopefully, motivate and energize the people now assigned to do the job that they excelled in. Additionally, while the upwardly mobile professional knows the intricacies and nuances of the job that propelled him or her forward, many of these individuals have never been trained to be effective leaders (Sinek, 2017).

In the 1970s, renowned economist Milton Friedman (1970) argued that the only social responsibility of business is to increase its profits. He stated further that shareholder interests should be assigned first priority relative to all other corporate stakeholders (Friedman, 1970). If one follows this logic (and many do), the natural deduction is that a corporate leader works for the shareholders. It is high time for courageous business leaders to stand up for more noble causes. It is time to focus on value rather than dollars. It is time to focus on the capital of caring.

In a post-pandemic technology driven world, it is imperative that employers at every level invest in their workers from all segments of the labor force, and contribute to their communities. Not only is this a long-term strategy for success, but also it is inarguably the moral and right thing to do. The corporate purpose must be further defined to not only serve the shareholders, but to also better serve the family of company supporters, including employees, local communities, investors, suppliers and, of course, customers.

Far too many businesses, large and small, lack the vision to recognize the potential in their employees at every level of the organizational chart, especially those in middle management positions. According to Gibson (2021), "Middle management used to be the place where careers stalled, but the COVID-19 pandemic has turned that notion on its head. In fact, mid-level leaders possess more agency now than at any other time in recent history. Companies that do not tangibly show that they value their best people—by developing their skills and helping them reach their full potential—will lose them, perhaps to competitors" (Gibson, 2021, p. 1).

Middle management and sales executives have long been called on the carpet if their numbers were down, or their general performance was not quite up to expectations. Is this approach inspirational? Should not the approach be to motivate rather than intimidate? At some point in life, we all face issues that may affect our performance. Perhaps it is a sick child, an ailing parent, or marital issues. Empathy is being concerned about people in your charge, not just about their output (Sinek 2017).

Leadership is not defined by the overarching ability to criticize failure, but rather the all-encompassing capacity to create environments that foster success. Establish a sense of anticipation in the workplace rather than a sense of dread. Instead of having people hide their mistakes, create an open and free dialogue where team members are not afraid to ask for help. It is the empathetic leader who recognizes that everyone makes mistakes. That is why pencils have erasers.

Leadership is a skill that has to be cultivated and developed. It is not about winning or losing, it is about nurturing and letting one's natural talents blossom. It is about empowering people so they can rise to the occasion and perform at their inherent best. Leadership is giving credit to others when successful and accepting responsibility when unsuccessful.

In a 1965, in an article for *The Readers Digest*, President Dwight D. Eisenhower wrote, "My own conviction is that every leader should have enough humility to accept, publicly, the responsibility for the mistakes of the subordinates he has himself selected and, likewise, to give them credit, publicly, for their triumphs. I am aware that some popular theories of leadership hold that the top man must always keep his 'image' bright and shining. I believe, however, that in the long run fairness and honesty, and a generous attitude toward subordinates and associates, pay off."

President Eisenhower was talking about an organizational culture based on caring for those in his charge.

Peter Drucker, the Austrian-American management consultant, educator, and author, is reported to have said, "Culture eats strategy for breakfast." Most progressive business leaders and entrepreneurs will find this statement to be accurate. The implication is that the success of a company is based on its culture rather than the efficacy of its strategy. According to Engel (2018), "Culture is the secret sauce that keeps employees motivated and clients happy (p. 1)." In taking this concept a step further, it should be noted that a company's culture is based on a human quotient of acceptance, agreement, and support by all within the organization.

Marcos Andrade, president and CEO of Expor Mannequins, a large Brazilian mannequin manufacturing company based in São Paulo, expands on the importance of a positive company culture. "To us it's based on a strong set of family values. An integral component of our company culture is the establishment and maintenance of an environment that considers the overall well-being of our workers. We recognize that our workforce spends a large part of the day with us, so we want to provide them with a pleasant place that is healthy, comfortable, and clean. Once people recognize that you have established a very safe and comforting environment for them in the same manner that you would for your family, they will take notice." Andrade recognizes that the well-being of his employees goes far beyond a comfortable environment. "The emotional well-being of our employees is as important as their physical well-being. There are leaders and there are followers. Everyone has the capacity to be a leader, but not everyone has the desire or the opportunity to rise within the corporate structure. In one instance, a young woman on our cleaning staff, who came to us from a marginalized labor pool, saw that there was a position open for a receptionist. She applied for the job and was given the position. A few years after that, she climbed the ladder and became the assistant to the corporate sales director at Expor. We leave the door open for those who have the ambition to walk through. We are proud of the fact that anyone can rise through the ranks of our organization. We also encourage lateral movement within the organization, providing change, new activities, and new responsibilities. In addition, we encourage our employees at every level to take new courses and workshops, and we invite them to industry conferences. The thinking here is to broaden their knowledge base; allow them to learn and discover new things. This not only broadens their horizons and core competencies, but also the scope and vision of the entire organization. I strongly believe in a culture of life-long learning. There are always new things to learn" (M. Andrade, personal communication, December 19, 2021).

As the forces of change grow exponentially due in large measure to the relentless march of technology, and the deleterious impact of the pandemic, it is incumbent upon the visionary leader to build an adaptable and creative workforce. This begins with the organization and administration of a well-defined team with a well-defined hierarchy of roles and responsibilities. However, analogous to the outdated approach to leadership in the latter part of the 20th-century, the concept of "team," as developed in the 1990s, must also be updated and reconfigured to meet the challenges that we face today.

In 1990, Federated Department Stores developed a team-buying program designed to speed up its emergence from bankruptcy. The newly established, centralized, buying approach was intended to save millions of dollars while providing the opportunity to lower price points in all of its stores nationwide. The Federated team approach began at the top with the Chairman and CEOs of all divisions, to an organizational structure that continued down through the buyers and the visual merchandising directors. Barmash (1990) stated that once formalized, the program required that all top executives and many senior and mid-level managers participate. The idea was that store principals, in addition to worrying about the whole store, became experts in a specialty.

This program was highly successful, helping Federated emerge from bankruptcy while building strong team relationships and interdepartmental and interdivisional collaboration. The program further developed core competencies among all team members and subsequently among all company divisions and departments. The concept was focused upon streamlined processes from resourcing and buying to in-store presentation. A hierarchy of responsibility was developed whereby each team member was an integral part of the whole.

This managerial strategy is an excellent example of participative leadership, a concept first brought to light in the early 1970s. According to Greiner (1973), "An extroverted, sensitive leader who openly shares decisions and authority with subordinates—this is the profile that emerged when 318 executives were asked their opinions on the characteristics of participative leadership. During the past decade, vast numbers of executives have been schooled in the virtues of participative leadership. Perhaps no other management concept has received so much recent attention in management literature, in company training programs, and in the general press. Educators, in particular, have consistently admonished managers to open up their decision-making activities to their subordinates. Youthful critics of big business have also added fuel to the fire, contending that industrial organizations are too closed and undemocratic."

At its core, participative leadership gives everyone within the organization a well-defined role whereby each member is asked to oversee a vital subset of any given project. In addition to achieving institutional goals in a more effective and efficient manner, participative leadership is also a strong motivational tool that builds skill sets and unity among all team members. By empowering people, they take ownership and pride in the individual project and, subsequently, in the organization as a whole.

The analogy can be drawn between a team structured around a participative leadership approach and a highly functioning basketball team. Every player on the team, whether performing on the basketball court, in the corporate office, or in the general workforce, understands their position and their role. The five individual members of the basketball team know that the team as a whole will only succeed if each individual executes their defined responsibilities whether its shooting, rebounding or passing the ball. Teamwork is the key to success.

While participative leadership was extremely effective before the pandemic, existing conditions post-pandemic call for an updated version of this concept. As previously stated, effective leadership gives voice to the individual as a key contributor to the whole. In a post-pandemic shift, however, leadership must not only listen to each team member's ideas and contributions relative to the effective meeting of the team objectives, but also to the individual needs of each team member. According to Gulati (2021), "Many leaders see teams as collective units, but helping individual members reach their potential—personally and professionally—can open new opportunities" (p. 1).

Gulati takes the sports analogy a step further by examining the philosophy of the winning football coach of the Seattle Seahawks, Pete Carroll. "Researching Carroll and his methods, I realized that he had developed an unusual but immensely powerful approach to leadership that held promise far beyond the football field. To optimize performance, many leaders take the team or organization as the basic unit of analysis, seeking out processes and practices that will help people work better together. Carroll looks at it a bit differently. Remembering that any team is comprised of individuals, he focuses on helping each individual reach their highest potential not just as performers but as people. Do this, and the best collective results will emerge over time" (Gulati, 2021, p. 1).

In studying Carroll's leadership style, Gulati states that the visionary coach was influenced by the work of psychologist Abraham Maslow and his hypothesis that intrinsic, not just extrinsic, rewards and motivates people to excel. Based on his studies and conversations with Carroll, Gulati (2021) upheld that there are four ways to be a better coach of individuals based on his wisdom:

1. Boost Self-Confidence

Athletes can face key moments of crisis in which their self-confidence falters. These, in turn, can lead them to become more rigid, sabotaging their own performance. A coach's job is to prevent team members from lapsing into this pattern and to help them cultivate and sustain a mindset of "relaxed concentration."

2. Make it Personal

The best coaches forge personal connections with team members, but it is hard to put this simple and obvious idea into practice. Coaches must connect with the individual team member's full humanity, practicing empathy in situations when they do not share a common background or life experience with team members. Such empathy in turn generates trust and activates team members' sense of self-worth. Each of us in our own way seeks acceptance from others. When we receive it, it not only boosts our sense of self, but also increases our willingness to help others.

3. **Allow People to be Themselves**

Employees never truly bring their whole selves to work, but we can still free them to express themselves more fully within certain limits. Leaders seem to oscillate between allowing chaotic individualism on the one hand and enforcing militaristic order on the other. In truth, a middle ground exists in which individuals can be themselves without hurting the organization. When we allow for this, people become empowered and energized, and they feel a sense of ownership.

4. **Tap Into Purpose**

Many of us go through life without a clear idea about why we do what we do. When and if we find a higher purpose, we become much more focused and directed in our efforts. When a coach helps us align a personal sense of purpose with an organization's reason for being, magic happens.

Gulati (2021) adds, "Of course, Carroll also believes in rigorous practice and is obsessed with winning. His expectation that everyone will work hard and strive to perform at their best serves as a foundation for firing up intrinsic motivation among team members. But Carroll couples that expectation with a soft touch. He calls his approach 'caring leadership' and describes it as coming from a place of love. That's not a word you would normally identify with a football coach, but if Carroll's record of success is any indication, it's one that leaders in the sports world, in business, and beyond should more openly and consistently embrace" (p. 1).

As we prepare for advances in technology in a post-pandemic world, the question must be asked: "How do we create an environment that promotes a healthy and productive workplace while providing opportunities and advancement for all?" As we cast our nets forward, it becomes prudent at times to look back through the lens of history in order to move ahead. We have come a long way in terms of leadership and workplace dynamics. According to Morgan (2017), "As with anything else in the business world, things evolve and change. The evolution that we see today continues to shift organizational priorities more and more toward focusing on people and bringing humanity and experiences into our organizations" (p. 1).

In looking back, it is important to note the progress that has been made in terms of leadership and workplace health, safety, and welfare. In defining and chronicling the employee experience, we can help to establish the road to the next level of workplace awareness. As industrialization swept through the United States, Britain, and parts of continental Europe in the mid-19th-century, jobs were created for poor marginalized workers. The census rolls began to soar exponentially in major population centers around the industrialized world. The apparent upside on the surface was that as cities grew around industrialization, factories provided work, enabling people to sustain themselves, if only barely. The downside was that living conditions were cramped and overcrowded, and salaries were meager, at best. Moreover, working conditions were difficult, dangerous, and unhealthy, with confined environments and insufficient facilities to sustain a healthy workforce, both physically and mentally. Little concern or consideration was given to worker safety, as many worked in areas that had poor ventilation, dangerous machinery without safety standards, and exposure to toxic chemicals and materials. Workers were simply thought of as utilitarian, and they were thereby provided with only the minimum in terms of tools, comfort, and safe working conditions. Additionally, the work hours in most shops, whether mills, ironworks, or garment factories, were long and arduous with workers expected to toil long hours. Twelve-hour days, six days a week was the norm for many of the workers, young and old. To make matters even worse, entire families, including children, had to work in order to pay rent and put food on the table. As a result, families were often separated as they tried to survive. The only consideration for business leaders was getting the work done.

America's economy following the Civil War paved the way for a new national ethos based on desire. While the southern states relied on an agrarian economy, the northern states thrived on a newfound commercialism. Factories in America's industrial north became self-feeding machines. They produced goods in ever-increasing quantities; factory workers had jobs, they made money and bought goods. Demand and desire increased exponentially, compelling the factories to produce even more goods. The factories of industrialized countries were grinding out goods so rapidly that there was soon an abundance of merchandise available to the general public. This desire and compulsive need for acquisition continued through the beginning of the 21st-century. Moreover, as the economy continued to churn, retail continued to nourish an insatiable appetite for consumerism. Soon, people wanted more and more of everything (Leach, 1994).

This phenomenon led to the creation of the great urban department stores in industrialized cities across the world from Paris and London to New York, Philadelphia, and Chicago, to name a few. Productivity was the order of the day, as workers were compelled to work long hours to produce more goods than ever before.

Poor working conditions for the marginalized and underserved made headlines in 1911, as a horrified nation learned about the terrible conflagration at the Triangle Shirtwaist Factory, where 146 workers were killed in a sweatshop in the Greenwich Village section of New York City. This proved to be the deadliest industrial disaster in the history of New York, with many workers, mostly young women from marginalized groups, jumping to their deaths because the owners locked the fire escape exits. This tragedy sent shockwaves across the nation, leading to many workplace reforms. Soon after the horrific event, New York State introduced a series of worker protection laws. This also brought about the establishment of the International Ladies' Garment Workers' Union (ILGWU). Founded in 1900, ILGWU, among other things, advocated for education as a vital tool toward the betterment and support of the working class and the underserved.

In 1970, the Occupational Safety and Health Act created OSHA, the Occupational Safety and Health Administration. OSHA, part of the United States Department of Labor states its mission and purpose as, "To ensure safe and healthful working conditions for workers by setting and enforcing standards and by providing training, outreach, education and assistance." This important legislation came at a time when there was growing public concern and discourse over an alarming increase in the rates of on-the-job injury and death.

Now, as we endeavor to lay the groundwork for a more inclusive future for young entrepreneurs and the underserved, we must be more understanding of one another. Moving beyond the throes of a pandemic and deeper into the age of information and technology, there is a less than subtle shift in our collective consciousness. A new sense of awareness has crept into the mindset of today's business leaders and workers alike as they reevaluate egregious mistakes and wasteful ways. According to Feigenbaum (2020), those that will succeed will look introspectively into the mirror and ask, "How have we contributed to the detrimental constructs of the world? How has our desire for acquisition and drive for profit undermined the health and well being of the planet?"

FUTURE RESEARCH DIRECTIONS

In October of 2021, Vera Bradley, a leading designer and purveyor of women's handbags, travel items and accessories, opened goodMRKT in the SoHo section of New York City. The pop-up store is a curated assortment of brands dedicated to supporting and providing good works. Among the causes that the brands support are eliminating child hunger, women's empowerment, and environmental awareness. Harry Cunningham, Co-Founder and Creative Director at goodMRKT, and Vera Bradley, VP of Retail Brand Experience, said, "goodMRKT is a place where the products have a purpose. The brands that we have assembled are dedicated to building a better future with their goods that do good" (H. Cunningham, personal communication, December 19, 2021). There were two contributing factors that led to the successful launch of this innovative retail concept. One was a company culture that encouraged experimentation, and the other was Cunningham's approach to leadership. During the summer of 2020, mired within the clutches of the pandemic, Cunningham and his associates began discussing the future of retail. As they looked ahead, they wondered what would be different in a post-pandemic world. The dialogue centered on the creation of a small store, somewhat reminiscent in concept to the large department stores of a bygone era.

As their conversations ensued, a vision came into focus of a small footprint comprised of ten to twelve brands whose mission was community-based and dedicated to doing good works. When Cunningham presented the concept to the Board at Vera Bradley, he was encouraged to "experiment" with this new idea. Calling on his leadership abilities and the lessons learned in his long and distinguished career in the retail industry, most notably with Saks Fifth Avenue, Cunningham did just that. Great leaders encourage experimentation along with research and development. You have to continually innovate. If not, someone will pass you by.

According to Cunningham, the corporate culture at Vera Bradley is based on six words: kindness, integrity, tenacity, optimism, thoughtfulness, and empathy. "These six words are more important than any strategy that we may have, and they dovetail into my philosophy on leadership. Leaders must be willing to do whatever their people are asked to do. Lead with what you know parallel to what they know. Know what you know, but support what they know. Moreover, give people the opportunity that they wouldn't have had. Given the chance, more often than not, they will succeed" (H. Cunningham, personal communication, December 19, 2021).

In the same manner that there were new rules for the industrial age, there must be new rules for the age of technology and information. As we all strive to get ahead in a better world, we must be more sensitive and democratic relative to the needs, wants, and aspirations of all. Going forward, the successful business leader will be sympathetic, empathetic, and understanding toward those who work for and with them. This is not to say that this should be a one-way street. All must find the appropriate balance between their professional responsibilities and their personal lives.

We are entering a world of new realities, which will require new approaches, new philosophies, and new standards. While advanced technologies offer new solutions to enduring problems, they also create new challenges in the workplace. Business leaders must find ways to mitigate the negative effects of technology to ensure a positive and effective work environment. According Wardynski (2019), "With a modern increase in technology that serves to automate tasks and replace certain non-technological systems, personnel often do not have to interact with other workers as much as before, but often interact more with computer systems. This is even more of an issue with telecommuting and digital nomad work.

This often results in a lack of enthusiasm for work and/or a lack of commitment to projects, along with miscommunication and misunderstandings" (p. 1).

In *Plato's Republic*, written on or about the year 375 BC, the founder of Western philosophy said, "Our need will be the real creator." Over time, this was fashioned into the well-known English proverb, "Necessity is the mother of invention." History has demonstrated that innovation is a direct response to the problems and challenges faced by any societal structure. Innovation and creativity lead to invention, and together they open the door to opportunity. The future of work and entrepreneurship belongs to those with innovative ideas and creative responses to the prevailing conditions of the day. The common perception is that creativity lies within the realm of the artist, the musician, or the writer. It must be understood that there is creativity in everything, and that it will take creative vision and a creative hand to move us toward a better and more just world.

According to Franken (1998), "Creativity is defined as the tendency to generate or recognize ideas, alternatives, or possibilities that may be useful in solving problems, communicating with others, and entertaining ourselves and others." It may also be said that creativity lies in the capacity to view the world through a different lens, and respond to events, happenings, challenges, and unforeseen phenomena while generating solutions and defining new ways forward.

Inspiration is everywhere; all one has to do is open their eyes to see it. As we look toward a more inclusive world, with equity, fairness, and equal opportunity for all, aspiring and progressive business leaders, including underserved entrepreneurs, must demonstrate the capacity to ILLUMINATE: inspire, listen, learn, understand, mentor, innovate, nurture, anticipate, teach, and empower. These 10 calls to action demonstrate a nobility of character that transcends the bottom line. These 10 points are the keys to success for those seeking opportunity and well being in an ever-changing workplace.

1. Inspire

To inspire is to bring joy and self-worth to the worker at any level and from any socioeconomic background. Workers who are inspired by the example of leadership, commitment to an idea or cause, new directions, and fresh approaches will be happier, healthier, and eager to roll up their sleeves in order to move any project forward. Excite your work base and those that you serve with new and compelling concepts. This will foster a sense of purpose that will raise the level of engagement and worker fulfillment.

2. Listen

The building of a highly effective organizational team, and ultimate success, begins with listening. According to Warström (2020), "Effective listening is an undervalued skill that is unfortunately often neglected in the modern working world. Managers and business leaders are just not trained well enough to be able to listen properly, and instead they listen as a means to respond. They listen simply for the sake of it. It's so often underestimated how much of the work that takes place on a day-to-day basis is reliant on the ability to listen to someone else. Even research, such as that conducted by Zenger Folkman, a strengths-based leadership development company, suggests that leaders who exhibit a preference for listening are rated as significantly more effective than those who spend the majority of their time talking *at* their employees. There is such an enormous difference between the two" (p. 1).

Active listening is a vital skill that all leaders must develop and practice. This is particularly relevant today as greater emphasis is being focused on the workplace experience in the technology-driven, post-COVID world. Most importantly, listening builds trust. It demonstrates that the business leader cares about the needs of the workers and has an empathetic concern for the challenges that they face.

3. **Learn**

Learning follows listening. The effective leader will understand and embrace the notion that they can learn as much from their employees as their employees can learn from them. Knowledge is a key to success. Expand your touch points and platforms to the world around you. Expand your network for knowledge gathering by listening and learning from those with whom you have built a trusting relationship. The confident and secure leader will be responsive to feedback from employees and open to new ideas and new concepts.

4. **Understand**

Understanding requires an open mind and an open heart. It is not enough to listen and learn. One must place themselves in other person's position to truly understand and comprehend their challenges and their points of view. By understanding, you can develop solutions to problems that seemed insurmountable, and common ground where there was an impassable divide.

5. **Motivate**

Motivation fuels inspiration. People should not dread going to work, rather they should anticipate it and look forward to it. For too long, we have supported a culture that vilifies work as a necessary evil. In his impassioned poem, "On Work," Kahlil Gibran, the Lebanese-born author of *The Prophet* said, "Work is Love."

On Work

By Kahlil Gibran

Then a ploughman said, Speak to us of Work.

And he answered, saying:

You work that you may keep pace with the earth and the soul of the earth.

For to be idle is to become a stranger unto the

seasons, and to step out of life's procession, that

marches in majesty and proud submission towards

the infinite.

When you work you are a flute through whose

heart the whispering of the hours turns to music.

Which of you would be a reed, dumb and silent,

when all else sings together in unison?
Always you have been told that work is a curse and labour a misfortune.
But I say to you that when you work you fulfil a part of earth's furthest dream, assigned to you when the dream was born,
And in keeping yourself with labour you are in truth loving life,
And to love life through labour is to be intimate with life's inmost secret.
But if you in your pain call birth an affliction and the support of the flesh a curse written upon your brow, then I answer that naught but the sweat of your brow shall wash away that which is written.
You have been told also that life is darkness, and in your weariness you echo what was said by the weary.
And I say that life is indeed darkness save when there is urge,
And all urge is blind save when there is knowledge,
And all knowledge is vain save when there is work,
And all work is empty save when there is love;
And when you work with love you bind yourself to yourself, and to one another, and to God.
And what is it to work with love?
It is to weave the cloth with threads drawn from your heart, even as if your beloved were to wear that cloth.
It is to build a house with affection, even as if your beloved were to dwell in that house.
It is to sow seeds with tenderness and reap the harvest with joy, even as if your beloved were to eat the fruit.
It is to charge all things you fashion with a breath

of your own spirit,
And to know that all the blessed dead are standing
about you and watching.
Often have I heard you say, as if speaking in sleep,
"He who works in marble, and finds the shape of his
own soul in the stone, is nobler than he who ploughs
the soil.
And he who seizes the rainbow to lay it on a cloth
in the likeness of man, is more than he who makes the sandals for our feet.
But I say, not in sleep but in the overwakefulness
of noontide, that the wind speaks not more sweetly
to the giant oaks than to the least of all the blades of
grass;
And he alone is great who turns the voice of the
wind into a song made sweeter by his own loving.
Work is love made visible.
And if you cannot work with love but only with
distaste, it is better that you should leave your work
and sit at the gate of the temple and take alms of
those who work with joy.
For if you bake bread with indifference, you bake a
bitter bread that feeds but half man's hunger.
And if you grudge the crushing of the grapes, your
grudge distils a poison in the wine.
And if you sing though as angels, and love not the
singing, you muffle man's ears to the voices of the day
and the voices of the night.

6. Innovate

Innovation is a vital component of any organization's long-term business strategy. Henderson (2017) said that innovation is not solely represented by new devices, ideas, or methods, but also by the process of uncovering new ways to do things. It can also pertain to modifying business models and adapting to changes to achieve better products and services. Organizations that continually innovate with new solutions and approaches are more likely to achieve sustained levels of success. Furthermore, innovation will inspire and excite team members while building enthusiasm for the task at hand, and elevated levels of trust, conviction, and collegiality.

7. **Nurture**

Recognizing talent and potential is in itself a talent. Once recognized, the effective leader will nurture and cultivate that talent. Effective leaders know that everyone brings something to the table in terms of experience, knowledge, and commitment. The adroit leader will connect and develop existing employee skill sets to the appropriate component of the overall company strategy. Nurturing talent builds enthusiasm and confidence.

It is important to remember that every individual is unique, with their own set of experiences, goals, challenges, and perspectives. Challenging employees to develop their level of expertise is an important part of the nurturing process. By so doing, the employee is compelled to find new solutions to projects and tasks. This leads to the betterment of the organization and the betterment of the individual. Moreover, it compels the employee to aspire to reach the next level of the company organizational chart. This will positively impact company culture, well-being, and ultimate path to success.

8. **Anticipate**

The one constant in business is change, and business has changed more dramatically in the early years of the 21st-century than at any other point in time. As the world moves forward, stagnation is not an option for any business. Whether it is the relentless march of technology or the cruel hand of a pandemic, adjustments must be made to any business strategy. The successful business leader, however, will not merely follow the trends, but rather, be in front of the trends. This, of course, takes vision and imagination; first to recognize change, and second to creatively respond. Paul et al. (2013) state that most organizations and leaders are poor at detecting ambiguous threats and opportunities on the periphery of their business. Coors executives, famously, were late seeing the trend toward low-carb beers. Lego management missed the electronic revolution in toys and gaming. Strategic leaders, in contrast, are constantly vigilant, honing their ability to anticipate by scanning the environment for signals of change.

Anticipation begins with communication. Know your employees, your community, your suppliers, as well as your customers. Know what they are thinking and what their wants, needs, and concerns are.

9. **Teach**

Teaching is naturally a vital component of any workplace strategy. Greater emphasis has been placed on this important function over the last several decades as new technologies and new levels of awareness have found their way into the work environment. However, like anything else, teaching style, philosophies, and approaches must be updated to keep pace with the ever-changing world. According to Fuller et al. (2019), "Don't just set up training programs—create a learning culture. If companies today engage in training, they tend to do it at specific times (when on-boarding new hires, for example), to prepare workers for particular jobs (like selling and servicing certain products), or when adopting new technologies. That worked well in an era when the pace of technological change was relatively slow. But advances are happening so quickly and with such complexity today that companies need to shift to a continuous-learning model—one that repeatedly enhances employees' skills and makes formal training broadly available. Firms also need to expand their portfolio of tactics beyond online and off-line courses to include learning on the job through project staffing and team rotations. Such an approach can help companies rethink traditional entry-level barriers (among them, educational credentials) and draw from a wider talent pool" (p. 1).

As we move ever deeper into an age of technical advancement and social awareness, employee training must go beyond basic company procedures. Educational programs must be expanded to not only hone individual skill sets and digital competencies, but also to engage in thoughtful dialogue relative to social concerns and interpersonal engagement beyond digital platforms. This expanded instruction should be part of an organization's DNA and should be offered on a regular basis. When implemented strategically, companies will find that most workers are eager, willing, and ready to learn new skill sets and techniques that will further their careers, and ideas that will expand their minds.

It's important to note that there is a definable difference between learning and teaching within this context. Education, information and the sharing of knowledge in a technology driven world is an integral component of any successful workplace. A healthy professional environment should be built upon a collaborative learning and teaching process that is mutually beneficial to all. As discussed earlier, the effective leader will embrace the notion that they can learn as much from their employees as their employees can learn from them. As an example, corporate leadership must listen to the voice of today's generation of young workers by launching diversity, equity, and inclusion policies to create a more welcoming environment for all. Going forward, it is equally important to recognize that as those in leadership positions embrace the opportunity to learn from their employees, they must also fulfill their responsibility to teach.

10. **Empower**

Empowerment is the final link in the effort to ILLUMINATE (inspire, listen, learn, understand, mentor, innovate, nurture, anticipate, teach, and empower) the workplace. To empower is to pave the way to a more productive, inclusive, and positive work environment. Empowerment can only take place after all of the links in the chain are imbedded into the organizational culture. There is an old adage that says if you want it done right, do it yourself. That is of course a false narrative. When you delegate, you get a broader and richer result. When you delegate, you empower people to rise to the occasion and put their best work forward. When so empowered, workers will take ownership of a project and develop a strong sense of pride in their work and in the mission of the company.

CONCLUSION

Leadership is an art and a science. The science is collecting and analyzing data and information. The art is responding to the findings in creative ways. "Leadership is an evolving skill set. Once leadership was based on knowledge of a particular subject. In the Middle Ages, for example, people worked as apprentices where they gained knowledge and skill. This was a structured path. Once they gained the requisite knowledge, they moved on to become experts in their field and then hopefully leaders. Now as we are engaged in a world a rapid change, followers can no longer come to leaders for answers. Leaders must build the knowledge base with their team. Being a leader now means being a teacher, and being a teacher today means encouraging thinking and exploration. It means encouraging the search for the best answer. If you have a hammer, every problem is a nail. Effective leaders will encourage the search for other tools. The conductor of an orchestra chooses the right tool at the right time" (M. Andrade, personal communication, December 19, 2021).

A distinction must be drawn between leaders and managers. A manager will tell their subordinates they did it their way, and that is the right way. A leader in today's world will cultivate an inquisitive culture within the organization. While a manager will detail the way it should be done, a leader will encourage experimentation and a search for the ways that it could be done. According to Gibson (2021), "To begin exploring and cultivating a leader's mindset, organizations should shift from 'telling' to 'inquiring.' Directive dialogue teaches your direct reports about how *you* think. Inquiry creates the opportunity for your direct reports to slow down and gain insight into how *they* think. When you engage with direct reports, inquire about the beliefs that underpin their assumptions. Avoid questions that begin with 'why,' as they tend to place people on the defensive and stifle dialogue. Instead, ask questions that begin with 'how' or 'what.' For instance, 'What assumptions lead you to that conclusion?' Based on their response, continue to explore their answers from a place of curiosity, not judgment. At times, this will likely require some emotional self-regulation on your part" (p. 1).

As the world continues to evolve in unimaginable ways, well-intended management is not enough to propel business forward in keeping with the changing times. Managers rely on their authority and positions of power, while leaders accept responsibility and promote individual growth, inquisitiveness, and experimentation. Leaders empower; managers merely direct.

To be an effective leader, one must create a sense of trust and an atmosphere of cooperation. A company culture that promotes growth, inclusion, equity, and empathy will build trust and cooperation. Human resources development is an essential component of an organizational culture. In fact, it is a strategic imperative. Relate to the people in your charge. Empathy is where true leadership begins and success follows.

REFERENCES

Barmash, I. (1990, July 4). Federated's New Buying Strategy. *New York Times*.

Dunfey, T. S. (2019). *What is Social Change and Why Should We Care?* Southern New Hampshire University.

Engel, A. (2018). Why Does Culture 'Eat Strategy For Breakfast'? *Forbes*. http://www. forbes.com/sites/forbescoachescouncil/2018/11/20/why-does-culture-eat-strategy-for-breakfast

Feigenbaum, E. (2020). *A New Desire, Authenticity and transparency supersede hard-sell aspirational marketing*. VMSD Magazine.

Franken, R. E. (1998). *Human Motivation*. Books/Cole Publishing Company.

Friedman, M. (1970). The Social Responsibility Of Business Is to Increase Its Profits. *New York Times*.

Fuller, J. B., Wallenstein, J. K., Raman, M., & de Chalendar, A. (2019). Your workforce is more adaptable than you think. *Harvard Business Review*, *97*(3), 118–126.

Gibson, H., & Rochelle, S. (2021). *Want to Build Better Leaders?* Focus on Mindset, Skills, Knowledge. Op-Ed Harvard Business School.

Greiner, L. E. (1973). What managers think of participative leadership. *Harvard Business Review, 51*(2), 111–117.

Gulati, R. (2021). *Team Success Starts with the Individual—and with Love*. Op-Ed Harvard Business School.

Henderson, T. (2017). Why innovation is crucial to your organization's long-term success. *Forbes*.

Leach, W. (1994). *Land of Desire*. Penguin Random House.

Morgan, J. (2017). *The employee experience advantage: How to win the war for talent by giving employees the workspaces they want, the tools they need, and a culture they can celebrate*. John Wiley & Sons.

Paul, J.H., Shoemaker, Krupp, S., & Howland, S., X. (2013). Strategic Leadership: The Essential Skills. *Harvard Business Review*. PMID:23390746

Sinek, S. (2017). *Understanding Empathy* [Video]. YouTube. https://www.youtube.com/watch?v=RyTQ5-SQYTo

Wardynski, D. J. (2019). *What Are the Effects of Technology on Human Interaction?* Brainspire. https://www.brainspire. com/blog/what-are-the-effects-of-technology-on-human-interaction

Warström, J. (2020). *Why Leaders Must Listen*. And Not Just Hear, Forbes.

KEY TERMS AND DEFINITIONS

Alternative Approaches: A transformative of action not previously considered that differs from a more traditional approach.

Empathy: Putting yourself in another's position and truly identifying with their situation.

Humanistic Approach: A psychological perspective that focuses on the unique qualities of each individual.

Innovation: The introduction and development of a new idea, concept, mechanism, tool, or process.

Inspiration: Intellectual and emotional stimulation from an external source that promotes enthusiasm and creativity.

Intrinsic Rewards: An emotional and uplifting reward that team members attain when successfully completing an assignment or project.

Participative Leadership: A team building approach to leadership where all members of an organization, group, or department are given a particular role and responsibility relative to the successful completion of a task or project.

Social Change: The revision of social constructs based on civic and cultural movements and the reevaluation of accepted behavior, shared values, and social structures.

Chapter 2

Post-COVID-19 Transformations for Future of Work and Small Business Sustainability:
Towards an Inclusive Economy

Nitu Ghosh
https://orcid.org/0000-0002-5744-1670
REVA University, India

Pratigya Sigdyal
California State University, Bakersfield, USA

Ramya U.
REVA Business School, REVA University, India

Roohi Khursheed
Dayanand Sagar University, India

ABSTRACT

The COVID-19 pandemic has created shockwaves across the globe and impacted businesses and economies. Enormous disruptive transformations have happened in the work models and systems to enable businesses to flexibly operate, sustain, and remain agile in uncertain times. The future of work, which seemed uncertain post-pandemic, has reached normalcy due to the organisational resilience and strategic responses shown by organisational leaders and small businesses. Although small businesses across the world have been impacted negatively leading to closures, financial crunches, and job losses worldwide, many have shown signs of resilience and recovery. The chapter throws light on the work transformations across economies and strategic responses to deal with them. It describes the challenges faced by various small businesses and the way they have been flexible and resilient. The chapter proposes a framework for building an inclusive economy that has been asserted to be the solution to a sustainable and resilient future in times of uncertainties and crises.

DOI: 10.4018/978-1-6684-4322-4.ch002

INTRODUCTION

The worldwide contingency triggered by the Covid-19 pandemic has created shock waves across business organisations and entrepreneurial ventures, disbalancing their momentum and survival status. The pandemic has caused disruptions in the organizations worldwide leading to innovative and inclusive business models. Lesson imparted is that transformations can happen overnight. Digital transformations, innovations, high customer value, operational scalability, and automation application are the crucial areas where responsive actions have been taken and yet need to be implemented for sustainable businesses. Organisations and HR leaders are now accelerating actions and reinventing the flexibility and sustainability value of the post-pandemic human and digital interventions. Workforce interventions focussing on work resilience, crisis management, enterprise dexterity, and hybrid work model are rapidly re-inventing HR environment and business models. The current situation is palpable and the effect of the epidemic will be on-going. Small and medium businesses worldwide are also taking their call for sustainability by measuring the risk assessment and formulating the strategies to act accordingly.

The COVID-19 crisis disarrayed labour markets globally during 2020. Gartner (2021) discussed the future of work HR dynamics that would be followed post-covid, such as an increase in remote working organisations, change towards remote work model as well as discovering the critical capabilities of workforce and cooperate digitally to be prepared to change new workforce experience tactics. According to survey results, 16 percent of companies use technology to monitor their employees more regularly such as virtual clocking, tracking work computer usage, and monitoring employee emails or internal communications/chat. The trend towards expanding contingent workers and introducing other job models like substituting regular employees with temporary ones as a cost-cutting measure is more popular now than ever before. Employers' roles have evolved from societal safety nets to personal elements and support services such as increased sick leave, financial support, changed operating hours, and child care arrangements. Employees were encouraged to gain essential talent that might offer many opportunities for their professional advancement when critical skills and responsibilities were separated. The concept of (De-)Humanization of employees referring to creating a culture of inclusiveness is now much needed to achieve long term sustainability. The considerable shrink in the work categories mandating an inclusive economy by reimagining work, the workforce, and the workplace through focus on specialized tasks and responsibilities and applying work-automation for higher employee engagement can show a foremost role in shaping the future of work in the post-covid era. A three-phased strategy bringing together technical proficiency, adaptive methods and attitudes, and community engagement to alter adverse changing aspects in complex environments for future work has to be focused upon for inclusive growth. The pandemic has taught that human skill is not replaceable even with the adoption of technologies. Hence, it is important to empower employees by providing flexible work hours, a hybrid work model, and renowned welfare policies. Work from anywhere, hybrid work model and flexible working will increase the productivity of employees' post-pandemic.

The disruptive innovations in future of work models and systems are also simultaneously accompanied by strategic responses of small business enterprises that have been struggling hard during crisis to sustain and survive. Small businesses are the backbone of any economy and their sustainability is a major concern for global economies. These small entrepreneurial ventures face immense resource and labour shortage, finance limitations, production and supply chain hurdles during the pandemic crisis. Thus, they also need to accelerate their concentration on the local communities by understanding their needs and working with them to provide a solution that will help them sustain. Several measures have been taken by the governments of various economies to support and promote the small businesses and prevent them from insolvency amidst the pandemic crisis.

The purpose of this chapter is to describe the strategic responses of business organisations and Human resource leaders in transforming the future or work in the post-covid era. The chapter throws light on the challenging tasks faced by small business owners during the COVID pandemic and describes their strategic responses to sustain during crisis. It describes the resources and policies that benefit the small business owners as they rebuild their organizations. It proposes changes necessary across different fronts to help small businesses thrive in a post-COVID world where increased uncertainties can be considered as usual occurrence. The chapter illustrates real time cases of small business owners in different global economies: India and the United States in order to offer a comparative analysis of the transformations in future of work scenario and small businesses leading to an inclusive economy. The ultimate aim of this chapter is to illustrate how the transformations in businesses are progressing towards the building of an inclusive economy. Building and sustaining a globally inclusive economy is a major millennium development goal. This chapter throws light on strategic direction adopted by organisations and small businesses in transforming the future work models. The chapter provides recommendations in the innovations required in internal and external organizational factors to help small businesses manage their survival and success in the post-covid world with emphasis on the changing nature of business processes, systems, supply chain, and employee expectations. The chapter adopts a descriptive research design with a qualitative approach. Findings are based on secondary and primary data collected from Human resource professionals of multinational companies and small business owners from India and the USA through focus group interviews and Delphi method. The data is further analysed using content analysis technique. The findings illustrated in the chapter have immense practical relevance in showing new direction to organisations and small businesses regarding disruptive models in future of work for inclusive economy.

THEORETICAL BACKGROUND

Transformations in Global Workspace during and Post Pandemic

The coronavirus pandemic crisis that started from the culmination of 2019 has been disrupting life over last two years has underscored the role of business in knitting together the fabric of the society. The business work systems and models have gone through major changes and impacted socio-economic life dramatically. There are been substantial disruptions in labour markets and work practices globally with severe short-term consequences like furloughs, unemployment, reverse migration of labour, switching occupations, adjusting to work from home, stress and workload for frontline and essential service employees with resulting socio-psychological impacts (Lund and Madgavkar, 2021). The work trends shifted to remote and hybrid work mode with virtual assignments and meetings, flexible work schedules becoming the new normal replacing the costs of office spaces with faster adoption of automation and AI. Jobs in various professions have shifted towards complete online mode with advanced technical competency requirement on the part of the job incumbent. The trend towards technological upgradation of competencies among the workforce has been the recent trend in many professions which are characterised by higher physical proximity, owing to transformations in the nature of the job like- education, essential services, medical service and telemedicine etc. Staggered job growth has been forecasted in the low-wage jobs owing to the migrant workers transiting to other locations and professions.

Most of the organisations worldwide are still adhering to remote or hybrid work mode, while some are in the early stages of re-inventing work. The report published by International Facility Management Association (IFMA) in May 2020 presented a pandemic manual with novel pandemic survival instructions for industries to plan and rebuild their resources to restart operations post-pandemic. The pandemic manual was used to produce thorough instructions for professional facilities management specialists to follow in all types of workplace management operations in office settings. Hou et al. (2021) conducted a study which emphasizes on the overall practice of changes in workplace during the coronavirus pandemic and the related CRE management (CREM) approaches build for the new normal. The findings supported the CREM strategic alignment theory conducted through in-depth interviews. Majority of the planned and employed office workplace changes are primarily focused on two forms of risk management: administrative control and personal protection. To efficiently manage costs and staff performance, firms retort to exterior situations through re-modelling their processes and re-aligning their CRE strategies, such as portfolio reform, agile group tactics, and workplace renovation, among other things. As proactive strategies for post-pandemic work arrangements, managers are currently envisioning an office set up that they want to create for their employees when they return to offices by emphasizing on maximizing the benefits of both remote and collocated work. It includes enabling flexibility in usage of office premises, continuing to evolve virtual work engagements, provide mentoring and coaching, developing the culture of the organizations and promoting innovation and knowledge sharing in organizations (Kane et al., 2021). Most of the organizations have been able to accelerate digital transformations and complete certain initiatives that encountered resistance earlier due to covid pandemic (Anderson, et al., 2020). Based on the survey conducted for 3,450 administrators of 22 industries and 20 countries which was carried by IBM Institute for Business Value and Oxford Economics for the period of April to June 2020 it was claimed that organizations have made essential changes to cope with the effect of pandemic including shifting to more cloud-based operations, quicker process automation, malleable tactic to change management, and long-term changes to the organization's strategy which have impacted the work practices and modes. Resilience has been the key value in the post pandemic work transformations (OECD, 2020; Leach et al., 2021).

Researches reveal that the pandemic crisis has initiated a revolution in organizations in terms of transformations in the working style of employees and the reinvention of operations and schedules of work through technology and security as the important aspects during conversion progression (Ancillo et al., 2020). Carroll and Conboy (2020) argued that technology and 'tech-driven' activities are being implemented in a timely manner, normalising the new normal. Normalisation Process Theory (NPT) has its fundamental constituents of cohesiveness, intellectual engagement, mutual achievement and reflexive monitoring have been widely disseminated. Based on the use of this theory the findings were suggested which envisioned NPT to serve as a better guide for businesses in normalising technology-driven work habits in the event of a pandemic. With growth of technology driven workplace practises, such as extensive use of technology, flexible work operations and the requisite to be modernized and conversant through advanced technology, the issue of techno-stress has become more prevalent (De', Pandey and Pal, 2020). Kominers and Gonzalez (2020) highlighted the need to readjust and comprehend the role of managers in meeting the expectations of employees by focusing more emphasis on results rather than activities by becoming more flexible with teams. To deliver in depth knowledge of workplace cultures and working environment the focus relies on new characteristics of remote workforce, relevance of technology adoption and impact of technology on individuals' working life. World Economic Forum in collaboration with Mercer (2020) published a white paper in "Resetting the Future of Work Agenda: The Disruption and Renewal in a Post-COVID World which stated few transformations that organizations need to adopt post-covid like adaptive and flexible workforce, examine hybrid working solutions, pivot to remote working and redesign the workspace to transform organisation and work design. The impetus of organisational transformation process should be to - safeguard physical and mental health, enable safe return to the office, embrace technology for business transformation, while laying importance on enhancing employee listening and enabling human connections, re-emphasize diversity, equity and inclusion and building human-centric leadership culture. Watson et al. (2021) examined the digital renovation of home into a workspace and the predicament faced. The case based survey from an ethnographic sample of professionals in Sydney and the use of the digital knowledge in the home setting and adopting the Socio-material theory along with the help of domestication theory complexities due to the disruption caused was analysed. The findings highlighted the modified home in the context of digital working activities during pandemic time. Existence of pressures and flexible transformation in between work and personal life was worsened by and beyond digital activity in work environments. By addressing these issues, the results revealed the sociometrical choreographies and sense modality of existence intricate to attain the progressions of digitalised home of COVID work from home (WFM) continuously configured and managed.

Innovative Disruptions in Future of Work

Disruption is a prospect as well as a challenge. The drastic transformations in workforce market due to the pandemic crisis has accelerated the new trends of remote working by integrating AI, robotics, automation and e-commerce globally. Automation is expected to lead to ultimate changes in the future of work (Beno, 2019). Organisations are facing various challenges for better prospects to hasten the changes and move forward for a humanised future world. Over the last few years, future of work is linked to automation but pandemic has accelerated the transition of how and where workforce will work and emphasis is more towards the employer and employee relationship. Leaders in the context of a pandemic have a greater obligation to rethink organisational structures to leverage on their workers as important drivers of enduring resilience and imminent success. As a result, businesses have learned to rethink their future work schemas and pave strategically for enhanced human-centric work, workspaces and workers.

Teleworking, telecommuting, distributed work and flexible work arrangements are all terms used to describe remote working (Allen et al., 2015) integrating modern technology, location independent jobs and telecoms became de-facto during covid pandemic situation with emphasis on work from anywhere. The future of work is destined to be more heterogeneous which will be combination of working from home (Sytch & Greer, 2020), along with location-based operations and hybrid way of working. There are two reasons for moving towards hybrid mode as more work requires the physical presence due to the nature of the job, compliance of guidelines and second reason is social and mental health of workers will be ensured through the hybrid work culture (Xiao, et al., 2021). The growth of remote labour is attributable to push and pull factors, like - workers who progressively desire the freedom that gives options of work from any place, and workers who want to save expenses, broaden their talent pool, and keep their staff for longer period of time. Various trends which have been outlined below have permitted innovative disruptions in the future of work. These are as follows-

Technological Breakthrough

The proliferation of disruptive technology is reshaping the business and market across the globe. Technology has facilitated the small businesses to tap into an immense reservoir of information, skills, financing, markets and consumer base which was earlier accessible only to large organisations. Fast advances in technical innovations like automation, robotics and AI are proceeding quickly and bringing the change in the different types and range of careers available. Technology advancement are improving lives of large sections of the global population through the enhancement of collective productivity, raising the living standards and enabling persons to emphasize on their social and self-fulfillment. Digitalization supports in allocating work and also helps program technology to minimize the usage of workforce to facilitate business operations during the pandemic crisis to enable e-commerce and e-business across the globe (Chertkovskaya et al., 2020). Information technology (IT) has made possible digital supply chain, data analytics, artificial intelligence, machine learning, robotics, e-commerce, and IoT enhancing resilience and recovery in the post-pandemic times and continuity of business (Nah and Siau, 2020). Advanced technology has enabled many businesses in Asian countries like India, China, Korea to regain and recover their business operations much faster through effective tracing and testing, combining resources of industries and healthcare, sharing information and knowledge exchange (Choudhury, 2020).

Demographic Shifts

The worldwide population's varying size, dispersion, and age profile, as well as the ageing of populations in a few regions are exerting stress on enterprises, social institutions, and economies. Business models, talent objectives and pension expenditures are all being influenced by the increased life span of the workforce. To keep up with technological advancements, aged working population must learn new skills and work to remain sustainable for longer period of time extending their career timelines. In the post-pandemic and pandemic era, 're-tooling' has become the norm. The demand for automation and productivity enhancements will be fueled by a shortage of human labor in a number of increasingly ageing economies. Many industrialized countries will face labor shortages as their populations age. Countries with ageing populations face a diminishing labor supply and growing fiscal and social security pressures, putting more thrust on the economy's productivity (ILO). Various data have revealed the impact of the pandemic on the population of various countries, increasing mortality rate and vulnerability of the working population on the economic growth. Millions of younger generation working population have been impacted with negative impact on proper education and vocational skill development of the children in developing countries like India, substantially impacting its economic growth prospects in the future (Zeeshan, 2021).

Transferals in Global Economic Power

The emerging countries in the post-pandemic era particularly those with a higher proportion of ageing workforce, that adopt a corporate mentality, and strengthen their edification through rapid digitalization and innovative skill development would benefit the most. Emerging countries have the greatest challenge as technology widens the gap between them and the industrialized world. Thus, without considerable long-term investment, unemployment and migration will continue to be common challenges. The erosion of the middle class, wealth disparity and job losses due to pandemic would be increasing the level of poverty and substantially soaring the risk of social unrest in developed and developing countries (Kochhar, 2021). According to the World Bank, the global economy has decreased by 4.3 percent in 2020, a 6.8 percentage point shift that will result in deteriorating living standards around the globe. South Asia, East Asia, and the Pacific saw the greatest decline in the global middle class, putting the expansion observed in the years leading up to the pandemic to a halt. Due to job and company losses, South Asia, notably India, and Sub-Saharan Africa, accounted for the majority of the increase in poverty. However, reports have projected the shift in global economic powers away from the advanced countries like North America, Western Europe and Japan to emerging Asian economies like China and India (PWC Report, 2015).

Global Socio-Economic Polarization

Global socio-economic polarisation that is exacerbated by transformations in climate conditions, rising inequality, demographic shifts, migratory burdens, urbanisation and governmental opposition to globalisation are influencing global market patterns. The pandemic has resulted in reverse migration and social mobility of employed population to their countries of origin due to government regulatory pressure and covid-19 protocols. COVID-19 pandemic has deepened income inequality by disproportionally impacting the world's already-poor, while also aggravating socio-economic polarisation in the developed and developing economies of the world (Gu and Wang, 2021).

Rise of the Gig Economy

The 'gig economy' has quickly arisen as a manner of service delivery that upends traditional corporate structures, labor-management practises and regulatory framework (Healy et al., 2017). The development of 'just-in-time' labour delivery, referred to as gig workers on the platform, is influencing economies all around the world. The idea stems from the logical extension of the the 'software-as-a-service' model, which already dominates how we acquire software, allowing us to rent usage without having to take ownership or responsibility. Unlike freelancers and consultants, who are typically hired through third-party recruitment agencies, these new gig workers are hired as independent contractors by a platform company. They are then matched to job possibilities by the platform, which is usually in charge of the rate, service performance standards, cash collection, and payment. Every industry now appears to have a platform, ranging from generalists like Upwork, Amazon Mechanical Turk, TaskRabbit, and Fiverr to specialist niche platforms like Paws (vets), Urban Massage (masseurs), Treatwell (beautificians), Uber (transport), Deliveroo (food delivery) and expert platforms like Lexoo (lawyers), CoMatch (Management Consultants) etc. The open market in which workers and employers had to discover each other through job advertisements and recruiting agencies, is giving way to a new type of company that acts as both an agency and a market. The Covid pandemic has forced jobs to become flexible and requirement of human resources to be temporary or on just-in- time basis is becoming popular. Thus, gig economy has expanded exponentially during the pandemic due to more reliance on gig-workers owing to increasing demand of home-delivery of products and service (Henderson, 2020).

Moonlighting Among Professionals

Work from home (WFM) mode has been challenging for organisations and managers in managing and engaging their talent force effectively. Monitoring and controlling of employee attendance and performance has been the major challenge. This has led to alternative opportunities taken up by professionals in the form of 'moonlighting', especially in IT and consultancy sectors. Dealing with moonlighters in the era of remote work mode is posing challenge for IT firms, as most of the tech professionals employed full time are working on part-time projects. Increasing incidences of moonlighting has resulted into employees' withdrawal cognitions, soaring turnover, productivity loss and labour law violations. Gig economy has led to popularity of moonlighting, which is now identified as the future of work (Meister and Brown, 2020). A reason for growing rate of moonlighting in many industries is due to the popularity of boundaryless careers, where the employee's focus is shifting towards completion of task rather than building relationships with the organisation (Pan and Zhao, 2015). Virtual industry 4.0 is characterised by moonlighting and skill-based gig working that is the new normal demanding a great deal of technological platform and crowd-working (De Stefano, 2015). This has infact become the new work trend during and post-pandemic (Seema, Choudhary and Saini, 2021). Organisations across industries should acknowledge the fact that Moonlighting would impact employee engagement and long-term commitment of their workforce due to lowered relational contracts and higher awareness of their competencies, job engagement and work completion goals.

Smart Contracts

Smart contracts are self-executing digital contracts that operate on an If-This-Then-That (IFTTT) basis on a blockchain. Digital rights (music), healthcare (safe healthcare records), government (particularly in the validation of electoral ballots), financial operations (secure transactions), and professional and personal identities are only some of the applications (passports, certifications, qualifications). The Covid-19 pandemic has seen a sharp increase in the use of Blockchain Smart contracts owing to the inability to form and execute physical contracts because of the social distancing norms across the world limiting international business practices (Nwafor, 2021).

Digital Transformation

Consumers have shifted to online channels as a result of the pandemic and businesses and sectors have also responded in same lines. The fast-growing trend of communicating with clients via digital media is the current business operational trend. Digital transformations change the magnitude and witnessed the impossible become possible. Projects which took years to complete, currently took just weeks through digital interface adoption. Customers eventually adapted and selected enterprises that changed gracefully throughout the epidemic and business models that were predicated on being 'in-person' successfully shifted to being provided digitally. Digital transformation during pandemic has radically upgraded the education and knowledge transfer system in most economies leading to inclusiveness among economies and various sections of the societies (Iivari et al., 2020).

Building of Inclusive Economy

An inclusive economy provides a more complete and widened possibility for more broadly shared prosperity, particularly for those who face the greatest barriers and discriminations to enhancing their well-being (Pacetti, 2016). It involves policies and environment that promotes equal participation, equity, growth, sustainability and stability among all classes, sections, communities and nations (Schlag and

Melé, 2020). Building an inclusive economy is the sustainable development goal of every nation in the world as per the Sustainable Development Goals identified by the UNDP (UNDP Report, 2015). Any uncertainty and crisis can be mitigated more effectively through inclusive systems and policies in the governance of an economy.

Based on various research reports on the concept of inclusive economy, four distinct attributes were identified: (1) an economy that prioritises inclusion and equity, (2) an equitable distribution of economic benefits (e.g., assets, power, and value), (3) equitable access to the resources needed to participate in the economy (e.g., health and education), and (4) an economy that operates within global boundaries (Shipton et al., 2021). Governments, corporations and society as a whole have the obligation and self-interest to not only search for near-term solutions to shore up livelihoods and employment, but also to take a step back and reflect on the political and economic driving forces that led to the current crisis. Covid pandemic has forced the world economies to develop policies for inclusiveness in order to be proactive enough to address such uncertainties and crisis.

Impact of Covid Pandemic on Small Businesses in Different Economies

Small businesses throughout the world have faced considerable economic uncertainties due to the COVID-related containment measures, leading to subsequently significant drop in demand and revenues. As revealed by an US survey approximately 43% of businesses had been temporarily closed due to the pandemic induced global closure. Small businesses downsized drastically, reducing their employees by 40%. Many of the small businesses had two months or less cash in reserve as covid related containment started (Humphries, Neilson and Ulyssea, 2020). Various small businesses have been reported to show liquidity challenges and about 50 thousand companies were estimated to need liquidity support in order to survive by the end of the lockdown in Italy as per a report (Schivardi and Romano, 2020). Bankruptcy and insolvency among start-ups in OECD countries has been expected to rise post-COVID as per surveys (OECD, 2020; COFACE, 2020). The SMEs and small businesses in Asian countries like India, China, Vietnam, Bangladesh and many others were badly impacted due to closures, mass lay-offs, financial fragility, disruptions in supply chain, labour shortages, demand fluctuations, limitations in adhering to government policies and covid restrictions (Sonobe et al., 2021). However, many revived and recovered with the adoption of digitization, e-commerce, IoT based applications and digital modes of financing to connect to global customers at a larger scale.

In Nepal, Industrial Enterprise act of 2020 defines small business as an enterprise with a fixed capital of less than hundred and fifty million Nepalese Rupee (Approximately around US $1,261,781). Small businesses are typically unregistered in Nepal and fall into the informal economy. These enterprises are the largest employer of female employees and are an important part of the economy (Karki, Xheneti and Madden, 2021). The effects of the global pandemic could be felt in Nepal too. According to the survey done by the World Bank in early months of the pandemic, half of the small businesses were facing the risk of permanently closing their doors. All businesses were impacted severely by the pandemic and had suffered slump in their sales and were taking measures such as reducing employee wages, employee furlough to survive the pandemic (The World Bank, 2020).

The United States Small Business Association defines a small business as an independent business that employs less than 500 people. Based on this definition, small businesses account for 99.9% of all businesses in the United States and employ around half of the US private sector workforce. In the United States, the first COVID case was reported in Washington state on January 15, 2020. As the cases around the world and the United States continued to rise, then president of the United States, Donald Trump, declared COVID-19 as a national emergency on March 13, 2020. By late April of 2020, forty-two out of fifty states declared a stay-at-home order mandating residents to stay at home except to go to an essential job or shop basic goods (Mervosh, Lu, and Swales, 2020). Several weeks into the pandemic and before receiving government aid, many small businesses suffered from weak consumer demands and employee health concerns. In a survey of several small businesses in the United States, a team of researchers found that around 43% of the small businesses had temporarily closed from March to April 2020 (Bartik et al., 2020). The hardest-hit businesses were those in the hospitality and leisure sectors and minority-owned (Wilmoth, 2021). For instance, world-renowned New York theatres shut down, and some Broadway shows permanently closed during the pandemic (Binney and Harrison, 2021).

To lessen the adverse impact of the COVID, the US congress passed the CARES (Coronavirus Aid, Relief, and Economic Security) Act in the spring of 2020. This act allocated $2 trillion for financial relief for small businesses, individuals, and the state government. Included in this plan were components such as the paycheck protection program, stimulus packages, and changes to the business tax policy. While not all firms that needed assistance participated or received relief funds, the relief package helped many firms to mitigate the revenue loss and cut in employee hours. In the COVID-19 Small Business Survey of the National Federation of Independent Business (NFIB, 2020, August), 78% of the respondents had applied for the PPP loan, and almost everyone who applied received the loan. Among them 96% of the applicants were somewhat satisfied with the program (Kakarkaplan, 2021).

The relief and the development of vaccines brought some hope to the ailing small businesses. According to the Small Business Pulse Survey data, at the end of December of 2020, around 74.4% of the small businesses reported being negatively influenced by the pandemic. However, this percentage fell to 67.3 in July 2021. By July 4, 2021, around 67% of the population had received the vaccination, and COVID hospitalization cases had dropped. However, small businesses continue to face challenges in the face of the rise of variants like Delta and Omicron.

The Evolving Nature of the Problems for the Small Business

The nature and the impact of the problems that small businesses faced during the pandemic changed with the rate of COVID infections, government interventions in the form of PPP and other developments. For example, during the early days of the pandemic in March, the COVID impacted only a segment of the small businesses; however, by April, around 92% of the samples in the NFIB periodic small business COVID survey indicated how COVID negatively impacted their businesses. At this stage, the entrepreneurs' major problem was maintaining operations; they were facing a solid cash crunch. In addition, 80% of the small business owners reported slower sales, 31% had supply chain problems, and 23% were concerned about sick employees.

The economic conditions of the small businesses began to slightly improve in July 2020 when many states eased business restrictions and stay-at-home orders. With the re-opening of businesses and markets, securing enough personal protection equipment, including hand sanitizer and face coverings, getting back customers, and managing employees' and customers' health and safety were the major non-financial concerns facing small business owners. As the economy started opening with increased vaccination rates, customer spending started to surge. Small businesses began facing supply chain disruptions. Building materials, computer chips, batteries, plastics, and lumber were short in supply. Another challenge faced by entrepreneurs was labor shortages. According to the NFIB survey, 48% of the business owners struggled to find workers to fill their open position. The labor shortages caused loss of sales to their business. To attract applicants for open positions, business owners increased wages, increased paid time off, and offered enhanced hiring bonuses and health insurance benefits. The shortage of material, wage increases, and inflation further challenged small businesses' survival and viability.

While the damage of the COVID pandemic was felt across all sectors of the economy, the severity varied across location, industry, and demographic categories. Businesses operating in accommodation and food service, arts, entertainment, and recreation incurred a considerable loss (Dua, Ellingrud, Mahajan, and Silberg, 2020). These businesses were impacted by the social distancing guidelines and mandated operational restrictions. A business owned by a minority, including African American, Asians, and Hispanic owners, suffered the most (Fairlie, 2021). Those finance, real estate, and professional services businesses experienced lesser disruption as their employees could work remotely (Bartik et al., 2020).

Silver Lining: Increases in New Business Registrations

Although COVID led to the closure of many businesses, it did not deter entrepreneurial spirit. As expected, new business applications fell off during the early months of the pandemic. In 2020, 4.3 million new businesses registered, which was around a 25% jump from a year ago, and highest compared to the last fifteen years.

Many of the newly established business owners were employees who were laid off from their work. For instance, Ian Oestreich, the founder of Curbside Bicycles, started his mobile bicycle maintenance company after being laid off from his work at the initial stages of the coronavirus pandemic (Hauge, 2021). Typically, many of the new businesses that were filed are non-employer startups – businesses that are not likely to hire any workers.

Strategic Response of Small Businesses Post Covid Pandemic

Strategies Adopted by US Small Businesses to survive During the Pandemic

COVID pandemic drastically altered the assumptions and expectations that small business owners had in their minds. To survive and recover from this disaster, small businesses changed things on the fly and adapted their strategies and business models to suit the new environment. Business owners aimed to find a fit in the new environment by adopting strategies that created and delivered value to the customers in a new way, provided an opportunity to thrive in the pandemic, and decreased the disaster's impact (Katare, Marshall and Valdivia, 2021).

Many small business owners pivoted their plans at the beginning of the pandemic. According to the NFIB's COVID-19 impact on the small business survey conducted in April 2020, 72% of the business owners were very concerned about the impact of COVID related restrictions on their small business operations and growth prospects. They had adopted several measures to survive. These changes include modifying suppliers and vendors, delayed payments, talking with employees about sick leaves, work from home policies, flexible work arrangements, scaling down businesses, and closing down the business. The business owners also had to devise plans for keeping workers safe. Some of the decisions on the employee front included the following (Score, 2020):

- Making the transition to teleworking
- Acquiring personal protective equipment for workers (PPE)
- Revising employee policies and procedures including sick leaves, work-from-home policy.
- Providing new services to support community during the crisis
- Health screening of their employees
- Providing special accommodations for at-risk employees or caregivers
- Devising staggered schedules to maintain physical distance and limited number of workforce
- Cross training as backup in case of absence of workers
- Creating new services to support employees during the crisis

To serve the customers in a changing environment, being creative and adaptive was the mantra in the face of the crisis. For instance, Jan-le-Low, an event planner and a restaurant owner in Las Vegas, faced the new reality in March 2020. Her restaurant was shut down for two months, and event management was halted as in-person gatherings were banned. Considering those changes to her environment, she pivoted both her restaurant and her event planning business in creative ways. She converted her restaurant dining area into a food delivery hub. Rather than organizing fun face-to-face parties as used to be done pre-covid, her company consulted Asian-American businesses on navigating the Paycheck protection program. She also experimented with throwing virtual parties by virtually organizing the 10th annual Chinese New Year in the desert. Her event successfully led her to be hired to produce a virtual Japanese celebration. Using creative strategies, she could survive the pandemic when at the beginning, everything looked grim (Marte, 2021; Fox, 2021).

COVID accelerated digital technology's adoption for reaching out to customers. These connections sometimes led the small businesses to reach out to new customers who wanted service but could not commit to a place and time. For example, Lisa McCaba's dance studio business suffered in the early days of the pandemic when schools shut down and the government issued a stay-at-home mandate. Before the closure, 90% of her classes were in the preschool level. After the closure, Lisa turned to online social-networking media and resumed teaching virtual dance classes, with a free dance class for kids from 10 months old to 3 years old every week. After a few months, she began hosting a paid class for 6-10 years old. Providing free online courses early into the pandemic helped her understand target customers' needs and wants. Networking with local communities, forming partnerships, and offering free courses helped her to stay afloat (Fox, 2021). Another small business success story of the pandemic is Moriarty's Gem Art, a family-run business that ran a retail jewellery store in Indiana. The store created a two-hour live stream gem show that was aired every Wednesday. The show features Steve Moriarty, the co-founder of the retail shop, as he cuts and polishes gems and talks about his travel experiences to exotic places. The Livestream attracted customers worldwide, which has helped the company stay connected with the customers and generate tons of sales (Gurchiek, 2020).

The pandemic skyrocketed the sale of products such as masks and hand sanitizers. Some small business owners could tweak their existing product offering to meet the ever-increasing demand for face masks. Tokki, a company making sustainable gift-wraps based in Seattle (Washington), used their cotton inventory to produce face masks. Tokki was not alone in doing this, around 20,000 shops on Etsy started selling face masks during the pandemic (Score, 2021; Schlosser, 2020). Pandemic also increased the sales of other products like sanitizers and cleaners. Puneet Nanda, the CEO of Guru Nanda, decided to grab the opportunity to reach customers through their brand-new product, essential oil-based hand sanitizer and masks. His essential oils and diffusers also took off as his customers used the products in their home office to change the environment (Fox, 2021).

In essence, the pandemic created tremendous challenges and also few growth opportunities. Many small businesses could not survive and closed their door permanently. However, some companies were able to sustain better than others. Small businesses had to reexamine their business model and product offerings. Building and maintaining a personal relationship was more critical than ever before. It was necessary to understand their customers' ever-changing concerns and needs. Technological tools such as Google and Amazon analytics applications provided information on recent trends. Businesses that survived the pandemic found new ways of connecting and interacting with customers, mainly by employing social media. They were able to develop personal relationships with their clients, engage with their community, and develop their skills. Some entrepreneurs also benefitted by connecting to the ecosystem through platforms such as Kauffman foundation's 1 million cups program or local small business development center's talk programs (Liguori and Pittz, 2020).

Strategies for the US Small Businesses to Survive and Thrive in the Post-COVID World

The Post-COVID world will be different from the pre-COVID world. The adaptations made by organizations, government, society, and individuals to survive the pandemic have altered individuals' habits and behaviors besides organizations' work policies and activities. For instance, in the post-COVID era, individuals are likely to continue shopping online, and business travel is expected to see a significant decline compared to the pre-COVID world. COVID has also exacerbated the need for organizations and the government to look critically at globalization and the international supply chain. These new developments can cause changes in policies and practices that impact small businesses. In the following paragraphs, we will first describe the changes that are likely to occur across different levels of the US economy. We will then critically look at the composition mix of the small businesses in the United States and the path forward.

Post-COVID Trends

The hostility between China and the United States is likely to continue the political front. This political condition impacts the ease of doing business in China and the global supply chain. During the pandemic, the logistic difficulties had forced the companies to rethink their just-in-time supply chain strategies. Furthermore, the continuous rise in nationalism can further push US companies to localize their operations in the United States (Bremmer, 2020). These changes can bring new opportunities for small businesses in the service, manufacturing, agriculture, and real-estate sectors while also causing supply chain challenges.

On the technological front, the pandemic incentivized organizations to automate their work (Chernoff and Warman, 2020). In a McKinsey survey of 800 executives (Lund, S., Cheng, Dua, Smet, Robinson, and Sanghvi, 2020), two-thirds of the executives reported their plan to increase their investments in automation and artificial intelligence technologies. The investments in automation most likely tend to be in jobs with high human interactions. While such investments in automation can undoubtedly increase productivity, it eliminates jobs from the economy and increases inequality in society (Acemoglu and Restrepo, 2019; 2021). Currently, small businesses are operating with thin margins. They do not have the necessary workforce and the capital to automate their production process as the large organizations. This differentiation in capabilities and resources between small and large firms in the same industry can further erode the small business's market prospects. Large firms will serve the customers at a lower cost point corresponding to a lower price point. Hence, small firms must differentiate their value proposition to survive. Competing based on price can be impossible; the only way to survive and thrive would be to offer niche products, focus on hyper-local demand trends, build customer loyalty, and maintain an active engagement with the local community (Dua, Mahajan, Oyer, and Ramaswamy, 2020).

The pandemic has also digitalized the workplace and fastened the transition to remote work. A survey done by McKinsey found that organizations were planning to reduce their office space by 30%. As per the Gartner Inc's survey, 74% of the CFO revealed their companies plan to shift permanently to remote work. This trend can prompt a shift in the geography of work inviting new trends in work culture and pattern. Individuals can shift out of large cities to suburbs and small cities. This change will impact small businesses such as restaurants in the downtown area. The needs of home-bound employees are an area of opportunity for small businesses. Another shift with the remote work has been declining in the business travels. Small businesses providing services to commercial airlines and hospitality and service areas are likely to be affected by the change (Lund, Madgavkar, Manyika, Smit, Ellingrud, and Robinson, 2021).

Pandemic has also normalized online shopping. Between 2019 and 2020, e-commerce sales grew by 32.4% (Arcieri, 2021). Shoppers are now getting comfortable buying clothes online and returning them by mail. Small businesses operating as brick-and-mortar stores face additional challenges because of the shift in consumer habits. For those adopting a hybrid model, the long-term success depends on their ability to rethink and redesign the shopping experience for customers. They must critically assess and design their physical store to enhance customers' experience. Online shopping has accelerated the trend towards a cashless society.

Experts predict that COVID-19 may lose its pandemic status soon as the world continues to be vaccinated. However, it might not go away completely; it might become seasonal spiking in some months of the year (Howard, 2021). When COVID-19 spikes because of new variants such as Delta or Omicron, the government may continue to provide guidelines and pose capacity restrictions. Employers will be expected to keep their workspace safe for both employees and their customers. Inability to operate at a full capacity can deter revenue-earning prospects. For instance, guidelines that tables need to be at least six feet apart can significantly reduce the number of customers that can be served. Further, establishments such as restaurants face an increase in packaging cost and a decrease in the sale of high-margin items such as desserts and alcohol. Further, unlike large businesses that order in bulk, small businesses are less likely to qualify for bulk pricing discounts when purchasing cleaning supplies, disinfectant wipes, and other materials to lessen the spread of the virus (Dua et al., 2020).

What do these Changes mean for the US Small Businesses?

Large and small businesses alike must continue to protect the health and safety of employees and customers, adapt their business model to the evolving climate, invest in technology and people, adjust operations, staffing, and labour practices to improve efficiency. However, small businesses have much weaker financial stability than their larger counterparts. They operate under thin margins, bear higher costs, and have low working capital. Moreover, a significant portion of their cost is relatively fixed for many small business owners. For example, they have a lower bargaining power to decrease occupancy costs. In addition to the high operating costs, small businesses also have added cost of servicing their debt. According to a study by McKinsey Inc (Dua et al., 2020), in a survey of 1000 small business owners in manufacturing, the cost of servicing their debt is around 30% of their revenue.

Many small business owners operate in areas that were hardly hit by the pandemic and resulting recession. The following chart shows the percentage of small businesses' contribution to the economy in mid-June 2020. Small companies have borne the pandemic's brunt, especially in the food, hospitality industry, arts and entertainment, and recreation industry. The small transportation businesses, however, may have increased in revenue due to freight and supply chain processes of the online businesses. Experts predict that the same trend will continue in the future; customer service and food-service jobs can fall by 4.3 million, whereas transportation jobs can grow by nearly 800,000 (Lund et al., 2021).

Small businesses will have to adapt and evolve to survive in the post-covid world. Because of the differences in efficiency levels, cost of production, and other advantages that larger firms have over small businesses in terms of efficiency, small businesses will most likely not be able to compete based on price. Small businesses have to constantly learn, adapt, and reimagine new ways to meet their customers' changing needs to offer customer value. Sensing the environment to be mindful of the changes in the context will be more critical to survival than ever before. Business owners must use the new tools and analytics to understand the latest trends. They will have to keep an eye on the evolving nature of competition.

Figure 1. Small business share of sector GDP%
Source: Oxford Economics, McKinsey analysis; McKinsey Global Institute Analysis as published in an article by Dua et al., (2020)

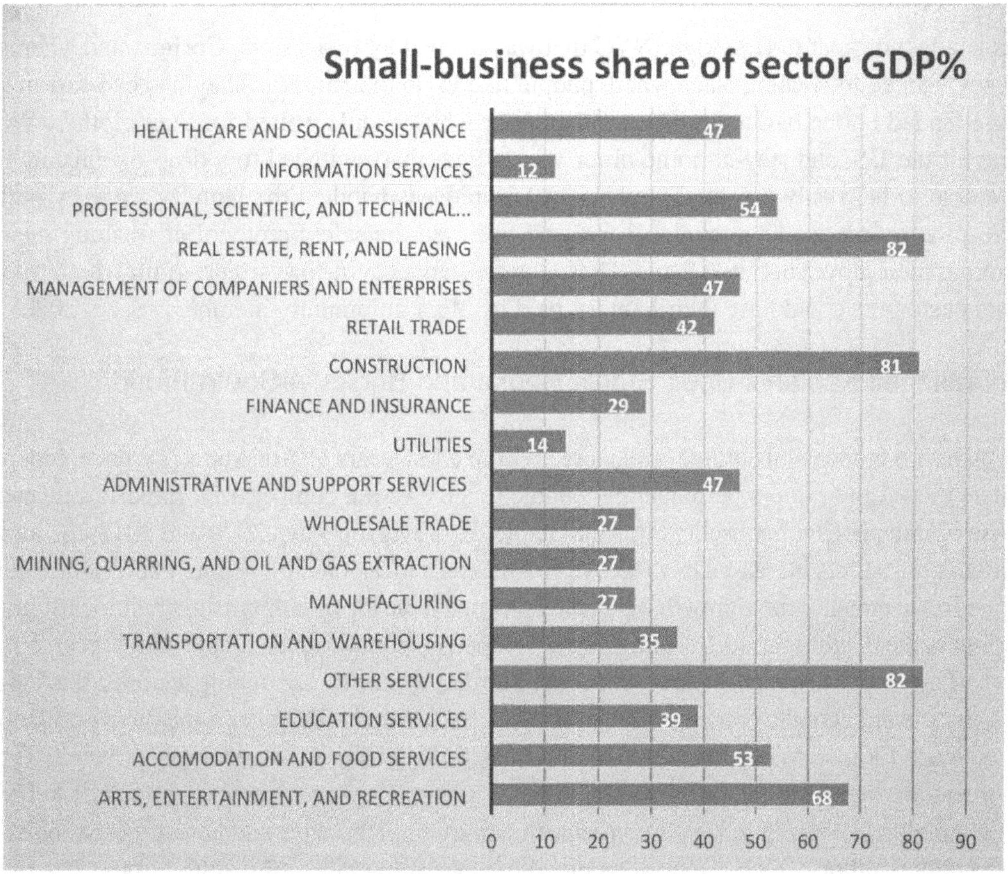

The study adopted focus group interviews and Delphi method to collect primary data from Small business owners of India and United States. Structured questionnaire was used to solicit information from selected business owners to understand the impact of covid pandemic on their business, challenges faced and the strategies adopted by them to be resilient and recover their business to normalcy. The excerpts of the interviews have been reproduced as short cases of those small businesses.

Cases of Small Business and Future of Work Transformations Post-Covid

Case of Celsious

Before the pandemic, laundromats typically operated as facilities where individuals could wash and dry their clothes without much professional help. However, the pandemic forced many small business owners to change their operations. The pandemic collapsed the business of many laundromats. Some of the losses were due to loss of commercial contracts with hotels. Before the pandemic, laundromats would get hundreds of pounds of linen from hotels. The pandemic dropped that quantity significantly, and thus the major source of their revenue was gone. Another reason for the drop in revenue was that people no longer needed to dress nicely for their office. After working from home, individuals could work in their pajamas (Cotnam, 2021).

The Successful Adaptation of Celsious

Celsious is a laundromat in Brooklyn, NYC that was opened by two sisters, Corinna and Theresa Williams. They wanted to create a place where people like to do the laundry. They had eco-fast machines, a barista-attended coffee bar, and a place to hang out while people waited for their clothes. When the pandemic hit the US, and stay-at-home order was issued, they switched to a drop-off business model and were able to help only essential workers. All employees handled the laundry work by putting on gloves, respiratory masks, and goggles. Everyone followed the safety protocol of washing their hands and changing their gloves between loads. They also created a pay-it-forward program where financially struggling customers could have their laundry paid by other community members (Saad, 2020).

Case of Mitchell Kaplan's Book Store- Books and Books in South Florida

In 1995, Amazon launched its online bookstore. Within a few years of Amazon's presence, independent booksellers closed their doors permanently, unable to survive the competition. Experts suggested that the demise of independent booksellers was inevitable. However, between 2009 and 2018, the number of independent booksellers increased by 49%. After Amazon's invasion, independent booksellers relied on three strategies to enhance their growth. First, they promoted the idea of supporting their local community by shopping in the neighborhood. Second, they developed personal connections with their customers and curated their inventory to match customers' needs. Third, they started organizing lectures, book signings, game nights, and engaging the community (Raffaelli, 2020). Mitchell Kaplan is the owner of 'Books and Books' in South Florida. When the pandemic hit the US, his business was severely affected. Typically, his customers are older and fall in the vulnerable age group. He was wise enough to shift his business to an online platform overnight. He partnered with community churches and hosted virtual book events such as meet the author, which was well received by the community and resulted in the sale of books.

Mitchell is not alone; independent bookstores faced numerous challenges during the pandemic; some closed their doors permanently. The cost of high rent and the low foot traffic to their stores forced many bookstore owners to think about creative strategies to stay afloat.

Cases of Small Businesses in India

Various small retailers, manufacturers and restaurant owners were forced to shut their business due to credit crunches and loss in demand. A Chennai-based manufacturer of air fresheners was also forced to sell his business and move to new opportunities with the lesser offline or physical setup. The owner stated that "sales turnover has been badly hit amid impact on supply chain due to Covid. While recovery is there but I want to look at other avenues where there is less hassle due to Covid-like situations and minimum physical presence."

Various primary school and kindergarten owners chose to close their business as parents are hesitant to send their children to school due to the fear of coronavirus infection. An adventure park owner in Hyderabad wants to divest his business since "it is demanding a lot of our time and finance with no customers or visitor," he said. The owner's primary business is microbreweries that was impacted during Covid. However, with the ease of lockdown restrictions and recovery in demand, the owner wants to dedicate more time to it now (Soni, 2021).

The three cases highlight the fragility of the small businesses worldwide irrespective of the state of economy and yet tell the story of how resilient owners can pivot the organization. Unlike large corporations with capital reserves, small business typically operate under a tight budget, where even small disruptions can dent the profitability and survival of the organization. COVID-19 had a jarring effect on the sustenance of the small businesses around the world. Those who were able to survive were the ones that could pivot their business models and build a sense of connection with the local community. This scenario also highlights how small business owners must be able to navigate their internal turmoil caused by the stress and uncertainty in the environment. When the external situation goes awry, the business owners must tap into their emotional intelligence and regulate their emotions and their employees emotions to a creative possibility. Given the lack of resources and capital, the best resource the business will have under their time of uncertainty will be the employees and the successful business will be the ones who will tap into the energy, emotions, and skill of their employees to do something different in the need of the hour.

Innovative Strategies and Business Models for Sustainable inclusive Economy Post Pandemic

The economic crisis brought in by the pandemic has changed the fundamental structure of collaborative action dramatically. Most of the tasks have transferred to virtual worlds, and "working from home" has become the new standard (Hwang and Höllerer, 2020). Countries like China have bounced back and United States is approaching the pre-pandemic period. Developing countries are among the hardest hit, with current growth hurdles including extreme unemployment, poverty, social unrest, low GDP and climate-related emergencies, all of which are increased by the crisis's health, economic, and social shocks. All crises bring opportunities to acquire lessons, rethink structures and sort them into more flexible and adaptable ones for enduring sustainability. The long-term visions need to be accelerated. The current challenges and disruptions necessitate an economic conversion of a magnitude and scope never seen before by contemporary generations, through upgrading industry and services in order to build a new, "green and fair" economy. Between 1990 and 2001, the overall number of people living on less than $1 per day fell from 931 to 679 million, or from 31 to 20% of a growing population in various Asian economies (Asian Development Bank Report, 2006). These achievements are linked to rapid expansion, which is fuelled in part by strong growth rates in a few nations such as China, India, and Vietnam (Asian Development Bank Report, 2006). Based on conceptual analysis of the secondary data, the authors have conceptualised a model for building inclusive economy through appropriate strategies for relief, resilience, restructuring of the businesses and economic institutions.

Figure 2. Stage-wise model for building an inclusive economy
Source: Authors' conceptualisation

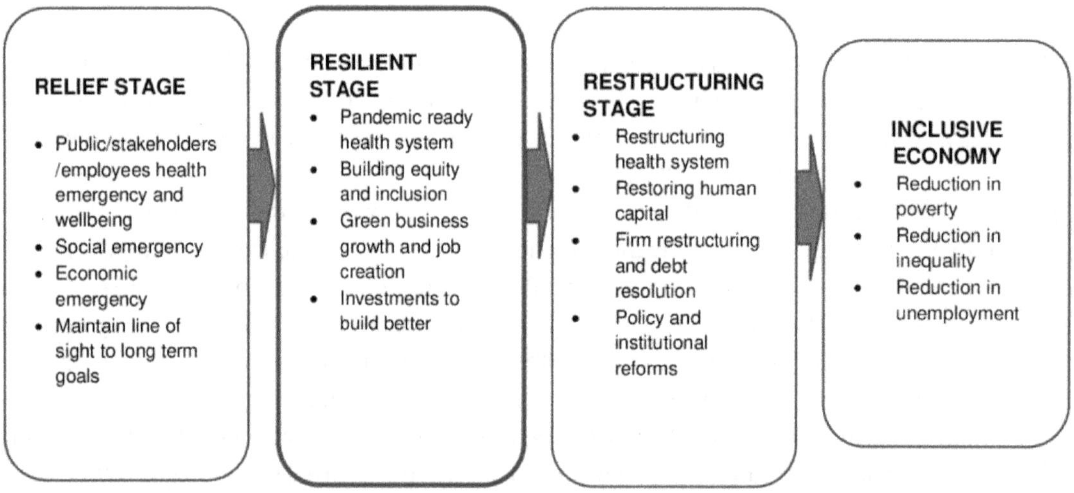

The relief stage covers various strategic responses of businesses to the pandemic's threat on health, socio-psychological impact and wellbeing of employees and other business stakeholders, as well as its immediate social, economic, and financial effects. The succeeding restructuring stage emphasizes on improving systems for crisis readiness, rebuilding human capital, and restructuring, financial recovery, and recapitalization of enterprises and economic institutions as countries bring the pandemic under control and begin reopening their economies. In a world changed by the pandemic, the robust recovery stage comprises seizing new chances to build a resilient and sustainable future through inclusive economy.

Building of Inclusive Economy

Inclusive growth is the equitable and non-discriminating financial growth between the disadvantaged and the affluent sections of the society, whether at global perspective or national (Aoyagi and Ganelli, 2015). Poverty reduction, job creation, job quality improvement, farm development, industrial growth, social sector development, regional disparities reduction, environmental preservation, and income distribution equality are some of the components (Rini and Tambunan, 2021). Among these components of Inclusive economy in both rural and urban strategies two trends – inequality and economic and political importance of the cities is fast growing across the globe (Neil Lee, 2019). The development of skill-based technological progress, strengthening the capacity of knowledge systems, globalisation and labour market shifts are crucial areas that subsidise income inequality in developed and developing nations. Economists have progressively been attentive on identifying the relations between increasing inequality and the fragility of development. Countries are working to achieve the objective to sought and achieve more inclusive equitable means of growth. Income inequality and growth are exacerbated by skill-based technical modification, education, globalisation, and labour market systems. Many economies have employed a variety of sophisticated fiscal measures to fight rising income inequality and promote inclusive growth (Heshmati, Kim and Wood, 2019). These fiscal policies are depicted in the table to highlight both distributive and inventive tactics used by various governments.

Table 1. Showing innovation strategies post-pandemic

Innovative strategies	Measures	PRACTICAL RELEVANCE	Country
Central Epidemic Command Center (CECC)	1.Eonomic dimension - bailout packages were announced social dimension 2. Social dimension-subsidies to furloughed or short-time workers and unemployment payments to those who lose jobs during the pandemic 3. Environmental dimension-Safe and healthy environment 4. Implemented special budgets as main fiscal policy responses to flexibly and quickly cope with the unprecedented pandemic	Saving lives threatened by the pandemic, Working to build a more resilient recovery	Taiwan
Growth, Inclusion, Sustainability	1.Revitalizing entrepreneurship and the small- and medium-size-business (SMB) base 2. Redoubling and scaling workforce development and reskilling 3.Investing in and tackling place-based inequalities	Protecting the poor and vulnerable Helping save jobs and businesses	United States
Government Frugal Innovation	Digital transformation, Traumatic stress has hijacked corporate strategy, Health is the key to sustainability	Cash flow and liquidity management, cost management, enterprise agility, cyber security, new market entry	India
Seondogukga	Three policy pillars—two industrial foci (i.e. digital and green industries) and one welfare focus (i.e. safety net building)	Oriented toward the development of ideology Acceleration of digital capitalism to reinforce the data frication of social world	South Korea

Source: Authors' analysis of secondary data

INNOVATION STRATEGIES POST-PANDEMIC

Practical Implications of the Study

An inclusive economy starts with growth and eradication of poverty, unemployment and inequality. Pandemic has showing and exacerbated societal discriminations, with sluggish progress on equality and poverty either crushing to a standstill or going reverse. Hence, building inclusive economy is the mandate for every nation to recover from the workforce transformations and adverse impact on small businesses due to pandemic and build a sustainable future. Practical relevance of the post-covid transformations and future of work for small business sustainability through an inclusive economy can be witnessed in the following ways-

Building the Young Generation Job Ready

The emphasis should be on how we are engaging and preparing our youth to be job ready for future market. Environment friendly careers need be at the heart of retrieval, besides with rights, societal protection, equality and inclusion. These are the fundamentals of the novel social indenture which the world needs to shape resilience at the present and for the future.

Reframing Work Model /Strategies

Pandemic has provided an opportunity for the global leaders to profoundly rethink the status- quo in relation to the share of business in the society, with larger acceptance of the notion that business actually has no other choice and stands at the forefront of addressing social and environmental implications. Business expansion and management issues post-pandemic will build additional challenges for leaders as new working models are evolving during pandemic. Small scale industries need to adapt for uncertainties with new business models and strategies for resilience and inclusivity by adopting technology, diverse workforce and strategic work models.

Investing in Resilience

It is crucial to be proactive and resilient by building roles and structures to boost agility and flexibility. By defining how processes might flex to create a more responsive organization and providing employees with a variety of roles that are adaptable and flexible so that they can be versatile. To mitigate crisis in times of disruption, organisations must focus on increasing their global diversification and investment in supplementary industries, restructure jobs and organisation with agility and manage the workforce with flexible policies and systems. Resilience can be developed with an emotionally intelligent workforce as emotionally intelligent employees and entrepreneurs have higher self-efficacy, flexibility, coping and adaptability skills than others (Ghosh & Rajaram, 2015; Ghosh, 2021).

CONCLUSION

Workforce transformation during the pandemic and post-pandemic has been an eye-opening illustration that business can never stop even though all human activities are restricted. Business organisations and management have found alternatives to such uncertainties and enabled economies to remain afloat balancing human existence during such socio-psychological calamity. HRM plays a critical role during such crises due to its crucial responsibility in relationship management with people, major stakeholders of business and strategic decisions regarding work systems and workforce management (Zagelmeyer and Gollan, 2012; Gulua, 2020). This chapter highlights the trends in workforce transformations and future of work-systems in organisations worldwide. It also describes the adversaries faced by small businesses worldwide during the pandemic and the strategic reforms that have enabled small businesses to be resilient and recover. The roadmap to sustainable future is building an inclusive economy, which has been highlighted in this chapter. It proposes a stage-wise model for building an inclusive economy. Achieving inclusiveness is the millennium development goal of all the world economies and an inclusive economy can make the future of business and work stronger and more sustainable.

REFERENCES

Acemoglu, D., & Restrepo, P. (2019). 8. Artificial Intelligence, Automation, and Work. In A. Agrawal, J. Gans, & A. Goldfarb (Eds.), *The Economics of Artificial Intelligence: An Agenda* (pp. 197–236). University of Chicago Press. doi:10.7208/9780226613475-010

Acemoglu, D., & Restrepo, P. (2021). *Tasks, Automation and the Rise in US Wage Inequality*. NBER Working Paper No. 28920. Retrieved from: https://www.nber.org/papers/w28920

Allen, T. D., Golden, T. D., & Shockley, K. M. (2015). How Effective Is Telecommuting? Assessing the Status of Our Scientific Findings. *Psychological Science in the Public Interest*, *16*(2), 40–68. doi:10.1177/1529100615593273 PMID:26403188

Anderson, C., Bieck, C., & Marshall, A. (2020). How business is adapting to COVID-19: Executive insights reveal post-pandemic opportunities. *Strategy and Leadership*. Advance online publication. doi:10.1108/SL-11-2020-0140

Aoyagi, C., & Ganelli, G. (2015). Asia's quest for inclusive growth revisited. *Journal of Asian Economics*, *40*, 29–46. doi:10.1016/j.asieco.2015.06.005

Arcieri, K. (2021, December 16). *US e-commerce sales set to maintain pandemic-fueled heights into 2022*. S&P Global Market Intelligence. Retrieved from: https://www.spglobal.com/marketintelligence/en/news-insights/latest-news-headlines/us-e-commerce-sales-set-to-maintain-pandemic-fueled-heights-into-2022-68009405

Asian Development Bank. (2006). Asian Development Outlook 2006. Author.

Asian Development Bank Outlook 2006. (2014, October 7). Retrieved from https://www.adb.org/projects/documents/asian-development-outlook-2006-tcr

Barnes, A., & Felts, T. (2020, September 26). New in KC: Why Jackie Nguyen hit the brakes on acting to open a mobile coffee café. *Startland News*. Retrieved from: https://www.startlandnews.com/2020/09/jackie-nguyen-cafe-ca-phe/

Bartik, A. W., Bertrand, M., Cullen, Z. B., Glaeser, E. L., Luca, M., & Stanton, C. (2020). The impact of COVID-19 on small business outcomes and expectations. *Proceedings of the National Academy of Sciences of the United States of America*, *117*(30), 17656–17666. doi:10.1073/pnas.2006991117 PMID:32651281

Bremmer, I. (2020). Six prominent thinkers reflect on how the pandemic has changed the world. International Monetary Fund.

C-SPAN (Producer). (2020). *Books and Books Bookstore on the continued impact of COVID-19*. Retrieved from: https://www.c-span.org/video/?474512-1/books-books-bookstore-continued-impact-covid-19

Carroll, N., & Conboy, K. (2020). Normalising the "new normal": Changing tech-driven work practices under pandemic time pressure. *International Journal of Information Management*, *55*, 102186. doi:10.1016/j.ijinfomgt.2020.102186 PMID:32836643

Chernoff, A. W., & Warman, C. (2020). *COVID-19 and Implications for Automation*. National Bureau of Economic Research Working Papers 27249. Retrieved from: https://www.nber.org/system/files/working_papers/w27249/w27249.pdf

Chertkovskaya, E., Alakavuklar, O. N., Husted, E., & Rácz, M. (2020). Reconfiguring work and organizing for post-pandemic futures. *Ephemera*, *20*(4), 1–18.

Choudhury, S. R. (2020). *How technology helped Asian countries cope in the coronavirus pandemic*. CNBC Online. https://www.cnbc.com/2020/05/13/coronavirus-mckinsey-says-technology-helping-asia-cope-better.html

Cotnam, H. (n.d.). *Wash and fold: Pandemic forcing local laundromats out of business*. CBC. Retrieved from: https://www.cbc.ca/news/canada/ottawa/covid-19-laundry-dry-cleaning-pandemic-economic-pressure-1.6027247

COVID-19 Impact and the future of small business. (2021, March 19). *SCORE Association*. Retrieved from: https://www.score.org/blog/covid-19-impact-and-future-small-business

De', R., Pandey, N., & Pal, A. (2020). Impact of digital surge during Covid-19 pandemic: A viewpoint on research and practice. *International Journal of Information Management*, *55*, 102171. https://doi.org/10.1016/j.ijinfomgt.2020.102171

de Lucas Ancillo, A., Teresa del Val Núñez, M., & Gavrila Gavrila, S. (2021). Workplace change within the COVID-19 context: A grounded theory approach. *Economic Research-Ekonomska Istraživanja*, *34*(1), 2297–2316. doi:10.1080/1331677X.2020.1862689

De Stefano, V. (2015). The rise of the just-in-time workforce: On-demand work, crowdwork, and labor protection in the gig-economy. *Comp. Lab. L. & Pol'y J.*, *37*, 471.

Dua, A., Ellingrud, K., Mahajan, D., & Silberg, J. (2020). *Which small businesses are most vulnerable to COVID-19—and when.* McKinsey & Company. Retrieved from: https://www.mckinsey.com/industries/public-and-social-sector/our-insights/us-small-business-recovery-after-the-covid-19-crisis

Dua, A., Mahajan, D., Oyer, L., & Ramaswamy, S. (2020). *US small-business recovery after the COVID-19 crisis.* McKinsey & Company. Retrieved from: https://www.mckinsey.com/industries/public-and-social-sector/our-insights/us-small-business-recovery-after-the-covid-19-crisis

Fox, M. (2021, May 19). *Here's how these small businesses pivoted to survive during the pandemic.* CNBC. https://www.cnbc.com/2021/05/19/heres-how-these-small-businesses-pivoted-to-survive-during-the-pandemic.html

Gartner Inc. (2020, April 3). *Garner CFO survey reveals 74% intend to shift some employees to remote work permanently* [Press release]. Retrieved from: https://www.gartner.com/en/newsroom/press-releases/2020-04-03-gartner-cfo-surey-reveals-74-percent-of-organizations-to-shift-some-employees-to-remote-work-permanently2

Ghosh, N. (2021). De-mystifying the Role of Emotions in Decision-making Sciences- A new HRD indicator dimension. *International Journal of Human Capital and Information Technology Professionals, 12*(4), 46–64. doi:10.4018/IJHCITP.2021100104

Ghosh, N., & Rajaram, G. (2015). Developing Emotional intelligence for Entrepreneurs: Role of entrepreneurship development programs. *South Asian Journal of Management, 22*(4), 85–100.

Gu, Y., & Wang, Z. (2021). Income Inequality and Global Political Polarization: The Economic Origin of Political Polarization in the World. *Journal of Chinese Political Science*. doi:10.1007/s11366-021-09772-1

Gulua, E. (2020). Trends. *Challenges and Orientations of HRM., 7*, 51–67. doi:10.46361/2449-2604.7.1.2020.51-67

Gurchiek, K. (2020, September 19). *Small businesses get creative to survive during the pandemic.* SHRM. https://www.shrm.org/hr-today/news/all-things-work/pages/small-businesses-get-creative-to-survive-during-the-pandemic.aspx

Hauge, R. (2021, July). Photos: In your business at Curbside Bicycles. *The Cap Times*. Retrieved from: https://captimes.com/news/local/photos-in-your-business-at-curbside-bicycles/collection_4b2ab1cb-d67b-531d-ac34-2eed086d6173.html

Healy, J., Nicholson, D., & Pekarek, A. (2017). Should we take the gig economy seriously? *Labour & Industry: A Journal of the Social and Economic Relations of Work, 27*(3), 232–248. doi:10.1080/10301763.2017.1377048

Henderson, R. (2021, December 10). *How COVID-19 Has Transformed The Gig Economy*. Retrieved from https://www.forbes.com/sites/rebeccahenderson/2020/12/10/how-covid-19-has-transformed-the-gig-economy/?sh=194140826c99

Heshmati, A., Kim, J., & Wood, J. (2019). A Survey of Inclusive Growth Policy. *Economies, 7*(3), 65. doi:10.3390/economies7030065

Home. (2020, May 20). Retrieved from https://foundation.ifma.org/

Hou, H. C., Remøy, H., Jylhä, T., & Vande Putte, H. (2021). A study on office workplace modification during the COVID-19 pandemic in The Netherlands. *Journal of Corporate Real Estate*, *23*(3), 186–202. https://doi.org/10.1108/jcre-10-2020-0051

Hou, Remøy, Jylhä, & Putte. (2021). An Investigation on Office-Based Workplace Modification During the COVID-19 Pandemic in the Netherlands. In *Proceedings of the 25th International Symposium on Advancement of Construction Management and Real Estate* (pp. 845-855). Springer.

Howard, J. (2021, December 31). *It won't be a pandemic forever. Here's what could be next.* CNN. Retrieved from: https://www.cnn.com/2021/12/31/health/covid-19-omicron-what-pandemic-end-might-look-like/index.html

Humphries, J. E., Neilson, C., & Ulyssea, G. (2020). *The Evolving Impacts of COVID-19 on Small Businesses Since the CARES Act Cowles Foundation.* Discussion Paper No. 2230, NYU Stern School of Business. Available at SSRN: https://ssrn.com/abstract=3584745

Hwang, H., & Höllerer, M. A. (2020). The COVID-19 Crisis and Its Consequences: Ruptures and Transformations in the Global Institutional Fabric. *The Journal of Applied Behavioral Science*, *56*(3), 294–300. https://doi.org/10.1177/0021886320936841

Iivari, N. (2020). Digital transformation of everyday life – How COVID-19 pandemic transformed the basic education of the young generation and why information management research should care? *International Journal of Information Management*, 55. doi:10.1016/j.ijinfomgt.2020.102183

International Facility Management Association. (2020). *Pandemic manual – planning and responding to a global health crisis for facility management professionals.* Available at: https://foundation.ifma.org/wp-content/uploads/2020/05/IFMA-Foundation-Pandemic-Manual-FINAL.pdf

Kane, G. (2019). The Technology Fallacy. *Research Technology Management*, *62*(6), 44–49. https://doi.org/10.1080/08956308.2019.1661079

Karakaplan, M. U. (2021). This time is really different: The multiplier effect of the Paycheck Protection Program (PPP) on small business bank loans. *Journal of Banking & Finance*, *133*, 106223.

Katare, B., Marshall, M. I., & Valdivia, C. B. (2021). Bend or break? Small business survival and strategies during the COVID-19 shock. *International Journal of Disaster Risk Reduction*, *61*, 102332.

Kimmons, R., & Veletsianos, G. (2016). Education scholars' evolving uses of twitter as a conference backchannel and social commentary platform. *British Journal of Educational Technology*, *47*(3), 445–464. https://doi.org/10.1111/bjet.12428

Kochhar, R. (2021, March 18). *The Pandemic Stalls Growth in the Global Middle Class, Pushes Poverty Up Sharply.* Retrieved from https://www.pewresearch.org/global/2021/03/18/the-pandemic-stalls-growth-in-the-global-middle-class-pushes-poverty-up-sharply/

Leach. (2021). Post-Pandemic transformation: How and why COVID-19 requires us to rethink development. *World Development*, 138. doi:10.1016/j.worlddev.2020.105233

Lee, N. (2018). Inclusive Growth in cities: A sympathetic critique. *Regional Studies*, *53*(3), 424–434. https://doi.org/10.1080/00343404.2018.1476753

Lee, N. (2019). Inclusive Growth in cities: A sympathetic critique. *Regional Studies*, *53*(3), 424–434. doi:10.1080/00343404.2018.1476753

Liguori, E. W., & Pittz, T. G. (2020). Strategies for small business: Surviving and thriving in the era of COVID-19. *Journal of the International Council for Small Business*, *1*(2), 106–110.

Lund, S., Madgavkar, A., Manyika, J., Smit, S., Ellingrud, K., Meaney, M., & Robinson, O. (2021). *The future of work after COVID-19.* McKinsey Global Institute.

Marte, J. (2021, April 14). *Asian-American businesses suffer outsized pandemic toll.* Reuters. https://www.reuters.com/business/finance/asian-american-businesses-suffer-outsized-pandemic-toll-2021-04-14/

Meister, J. C., & Brown, R. H. (2020). 21 HR jobs of the future. *Harvard Business Review.*

Mervosh, S., Lu, D., & Swales, V. (2020, April). See which states and cities have told residents to stay at home. *The New York Times.* Retrieved from: https://www.nytimes.com/interactive/2020/us/corona stay-at-home-order.html

Nah, F. F. H., & Siau, K. (2020). COVID-19 Pandemic – Role of Technology in Transforming Business to the New Normal. *Lecture Notes in Computer Science*, 585–600. doi:10.1007/978-3-030-60152-2_43

National Federation of Independent Business. (2020). *COVID-19 Small business survey Part 11: PPP, EIDL, unemployment, insurance, the economy.* Retrieved from: https://www.nfib.com/covid-surveys/

National Federation of Independent Business. (2020). *COVID-19 Small business survey Part 1: Impact on Small Business.* Retrieved from: https://www.nfib.com/covid-surveys/

National Federation of Independent Business. (2020). *COVID-19 Small business survey Part 2: Small Business Employers in Crisis.* Retrieved from: https://www.nfib.com/covid-surveys/

National Federation of Independent Business. (2020). *COVID-19 Small business survey Part 12: PPP, EIDL, the economy, payment deferrals.* Retrieved from: https://www.nfib.com/covid-surveys/

OECD. (2020). *OECD Policy responses to coronavirus: Building back better- a sustainable resilient recovery after COVID-19.* Retrieved from https://www.oecd.org/coronavirus/policy-responses/building-back-better-a-sustainable-resilient-recovery-after-covid-19-52b869f5/

Pacetti, E. G. (2016). *The Five Characteristics of an Inclusive Economy: Getting Beyond the Equity-Growth Dichotomy.* The Rockefeller Foundation. Retrieved from: https://www.rockefellerfoundation.org/blog/five-characteristics-inclusive-economy-getting-beyond-equity-growth-dichotomy/

Pan, J., & Zhou, W. (2015). How do employees construe their career success: An improved measure of subjective career success. *International Journal of Selection and Assessment*, *23*, 45–58. doi:10.1111/ijsa.12094

Raffaelli, R. L. (2020). *Reinventing Retail: The Novel Resurgence of Independent Bookstores.* Working paper 20-068. Harvard Business School. Retrieved from: https://www.hbs.edu/ris/Publication%20Files/20-068_c19963e7-506c-479a-beb4-bb339cd293ee.pdf

Report, P. W. C. (2015). *Will the shift in global economic power continue.* Retrieved from https://www.pwc.com/gx/en/issues/the-economy/assets/world-in-2050-february-2015.pdf

Rhyne, B. M. (2021, September). *New business applications in the US hit historic heights last year.* World Economic Forum. Retrieved from: https://www.weforum.org/agenda/2021/09/new-business-applications-in-the-us-hit-historic-highs-last-year/

Rini, D. L., & Hamonangan Tambunan, T. T. (2021). Inclusive Economic Growth of Indonesia and Its Determinants-Recent Evidence with Provincial Data. *Asian Journal of Interdisciplinary Research,* 85–100. doi:10.34256/ajir2118

Ruiz, N. G., Horowitz, J. M., & Tamir, C. (2020, July 1). *Many Black and Asian Americans say they have experienced discrimination amid the COVID-19 outbreak.* Pew Research Center. Retrieved from: https://www.pewresearch.org/social-trends/2020/07/01/many-black-and-asian-americans-say-they-have-experienced-discrimination-amid-the-covid-19-outbreak/

Saad, S. K. (2020, July 17). *How celsious, an eco-friendly laundromat, pivoted during the pandemic.* Bustle. https://www.bustle.com/life/small-business-salutes-celsious-laundromat-founders-pivot-coronavirus

Schlag, M., & Melé, D. (2020). Building Institutions for the Common Good. The Practice and Purpose of Business in an Inclusive Economy. *Humanist Manag J, 5,* 1–6. doi:10.1007/s41463-020-00092-9

Schlosser, K. (2020, April 14). *Startup founder Jane Park 'pivots with purpose' as gift wrap maker Tokki shifts to face masks.* GeekWire. https://www.geekwire.com/2020/startup-founder-jane-park-pivots-purpose-gift-wrap-maker-tokki-shifts-face-masks/

Seema, Choudhary, & Saini. (2021). Effect of Job Satisfaction on Moonlighting Intentions: Mediating Effect of Organizational Commitment. *European Research on Management and Business Economics, 27*(1). doi:10.1016/j.iedeen.2020.100137

Shipton, D. (2021). Knowing the goal: An inclusive economy that can address the public health challenges of our time. *Journal of Epidemiology and Community Health, 75*(11), 1129–1132. https://doi.org/10.1136/jech-2020-216070

Small Business Association. (2021). *What's New with Small Business?* Retrieved from: https://www.sba.gov/sites/default/files/Whats_New_With_Small_Business.pdf

Soni, S. (2021). *Covid horror: Thousands of micro, small businesses in India are on sale right now.* Financial Express. Retrieved from: https://www.financialexpress.com/industry/sme/msme-eodb-covid-horror-covid-horror-thousands-of-micro-small-businesses-in-india-are-on-sale-right-now/2339616/

Sonobe, T., Takeda, A., Yoshida, S., & Truong, H. T. (2021). *The Impacts of the COVID-19 Pandemic on Micro, Small, and Medium Enterprises in Asia and Their Digitalization Responses. ADBI Working Paper 1241.* Asian Development Bank Institute. Available https://www.adb.org/publications/impacts-covid-19-pandemic-msme-asia-their-digitalizationresponses

Steinmetz, C. (2021, September 24). Why Jackie Nguyen is planning a permanent stop, safe space for Café Cà Phê in Columbus Park. *Starland News.* Retrieved from: https://www.startlandnews.com/2021/09/cafe-ca-phe-columbus-park/

Sytch, M., & Greer, L. L. (2021, February 2). *Is Your Organization Ready for Permanent WFH?* Retrieved from https://hbr.org/2020/08/is-your-organization-ready-for-permanent-wfh

Thapa Karki, S., Xheneti, M., & Madden, A. (2021). To formalize or not to formalize: Women entrepreneurs' sensemaking of business registration in the context of Nepal. *Journal of Business Ethics*, *173*(4), 687–708.

Nwafor. (2021). The effectiveness of Blockchain Smart Contracts in Reshaping the Business landscape in Nigeria. *Business Law Review*, *42*(4), 195–200.

(2020, Winter). The Impact of COVID-19 on Small Business Owners: Evidence from the First Three Months after Social-Distancing Restrictions. *Journal of Economics & Management Strategy*, *29*(4), 727–740.

The megaphone of main street: The impact of COVID-19. (2020). *SCORE Association*. Retrieved from: https://s3.amazonaws.com/mentoring.redesign/s3fs-public/Sept2020-SCORE-Megaphone-Covid-021221.pdf

The World Bank. (2020, September). *Survey reveals extent of the fallout from the pandemic on micro, small, and medium enterprises in Nepal*. Retrieved from: https://www.worldbank.org/en/news/press-release/2020/09/23/survey-reveals-extent-of-the-fallout-from-the-pandemic-on-micro-small-and-medium-enterprises-in-nepal

United States Census Bureau. (2022). *Small Business Pulse Survey*. Retrieved from: https://portal.census.gov/pulse/data/

Watson, A., Lupton, D., & Michael, M. (2021). The COVID digital home assemblage: Transforming the home into a work space during the crisis. *Convergence (London)*, *27*(5), 1207–1221. https://doi.org/10.1177/13548565211030848

Wilmoth, D. (2021, March). *The Effects of the COVID-19 Pandemic on Small Businesses*. US Small Business Administration Office of Advocacy.

Wong, E. L. Y., Ho, K. F., Wong, S. Y. S., Cheung, A. W. L., Yau, P. S. Y., Dong, D., & Yeoh, E. K. (2020). Views on Workplace Policies and its Impact on Health-Related Quality of Life During Coronavirus Disease (COVID-19) Pandemic: Cross-Sectional Survey of Employees. *International Journal of Health Policy and Management*. doi:10.34172/ijhpm.2020.127

World Health Organization. (2020). *Coronavirus disease 2019 (COVID-19) situation report – 43*. Available at: www.who.int/docs/default-source/coronaviruse/situation-reports/20200303-sitrep43-covid-19.pdf?sfvrsn=2c21c09c_2

Xiao, Y., Becerik-Gerber, B., Lucas, G., & Roll, S. C. (2021). Impacts of Working From Home During COVID-19 Pandemic on Physical and Mental Well-Being of Office Workstation Users. *Journal of Occupational and Environmental Medicine*, *63*(3), 181–190. https://doi.org/10.1097/JOM.0000000000002097

Zagelmeyer, S., & Gollan, P. (2012). Exploring terra incognita: Preliminary reflections on the impact of the global financial crisis upon human resource management. *International Journal of Human Resource Management*, *23*, 3287-3294. . doi:10.1080/09585192.2012.689158

Zeeshan, M. (2021, March 4). *COVID-19 Threatens to Waste India's Demographic Dividend*. Retrieved from https://thediplomat.com/2021/03/covid-19-threatens-to-waste-indias-demographic-dividend/

Chapter 3
Innovation-Centric Organizational Community (IOC):
What Works for the Emerging Workforce

Ronald Coleman Williams
Coppin State University, USA

Ericka Covington
Coppin State University, USA

Clarice E. Tate
Coppin State University, USA

ABSTRACT

The demand for innovative, solutions-oriented approaches to closing learning competency gaps is leading to the recasting of organizations as learning and innovation-centric organizational communities. The makerspace movement is a sector where new communities are emerging to include diverse groups of entrepreneurs. The findings in this study provide insight that will assist in meeting the challenges posed by declining economic and social conditions of former industrial centers and rural communities that were part of thriving economic pipelines during the height of the industrial age. The study examines a makerspace as a solution for creating jobs, filling gaps in the supply chain, and reimagining local manufacturing. The IOC approach also possesses potential for helping to reduce equity gaps and facilitating inclusive practices. The concept of innovation-centric organizational communities, based on maximizing affective learning, is consistent with emerging 21st century workforce demands and their relationship to entrepreneurial opportunities for underserved communities.

DOI: 10.4018/978-1-6684-4322-4.ch003

INTRODUCTION

Building economic equity in declining urban cities is a dire need and essential in developing communities that foster job growth, commerce, and opportunities. The economic and social disparities between areas heavily populated by Black residents and White districts are astonishing and serve as barriers to equitable economic growth. Failure to address such disparities at a time of accelerating change heightened global competition, and new work paradigms are detrimental to the sustainability of national economies, national security, and the well-being of citizens who seek to improve quality of life.

It is more evident than ever before that economic disparity is deeply grounded in United States (U.S.) history and will require structural changes to address related problems. One indicator is the 2020 report produced by Citi Global Perspectives & Solutions (GPS) entitled Closing the Racial Inequality Gaps: The Economic Cost of Black Inequality in the U.S. The report placed the lost gross domestic product (GDP) caused by systemic and societal racism and discrimination faced by Black people during the first two decades of the new millennium at $16 trillion (about $49,000 per person in the US) (Citi, 2020). Despite advances since the end of chattel slavery and the displacement of Indigenous people in the U.S., the psychological impact of racism continues in social and organizational experiences.

The lagging impact of equity and inclusion efforts is evident in many public and private organizations and continues to drive statistical disparities among racial and ethnic groups. Pay inequity based between groups is common.[1] The lack of diversity at the highest levels of corporations continues to be an issue in many organizations. The lack of diversity in high revenue-generating sectors such as advanced manufacturing points to systemic inequities embedded in structural and attitudinal constructs within organizations.[2]

Such realities demand solution-oriented examination, intervention, and assessment of relational dynamics, including how relational innovations may be achieved. If the assertion made in 1982 by futurist and inventor R. Buckminster Fuller that knowledge is doubling every 12 hours is accurate and the pace of technological change (i.e., the creation of tools) is simultaneously accelerating, relational deficits witnessed in social and organizational interactions are clear indicators that affective learning has not kept pace with cognitive and psychomotor advancements. The affective learning domain is one of three domains in Bloom's Taxonomy (Bloom, et al., 1956). The domain (Krathwohl, Bloom, Masia, 1973) includes five major categories: 1. Receiving - an awareness and willingness to hear, selected attention, 2. Responding - active participation on the part of the learners, 3. Valuing - the worth or value a person attaches to a particular object, phenomenon, or behavior, 4. Organizing –arranging of values into priorities by contrasting different values, resolving conflicts between them, and creating a unique value system, and 5. Internalizing values (characterization), having a value system that controls their behavior. Relational innovation is the looming challenge of the 21st Century and will significantly influence the gains or losses resulting from advances in knowledge and technology.

The introduction of affective learning that is apparent in learning community development requires the ability to assess learning associated with that domain. The ability to assess affective learning begins with establishing appropriate learning objectives, using the appropriate behavioral or empirical verb along with the conditions and criteria associated with the objective. Assessment is addressed by researchers such as Stephens & Ormandy (2019) in the field of nursing. However, the necessity for sound assessment criteria is not restricted to a singular discipline.

As in the digital age, where networks, nodes, and links connect data, information, people, and ideas, likewise, the practice of relational innovation can be found in makerspace communities. As transformative organizations seeking to infuse entrepreneurial activity and grow enterprising influencers and innovators, IOC aspirants can learn from the makerspace examples of creating value for its members and customers through relational approaches. Such approaches align with behavioral constructs of social psychology. As community innovation hubs, makerspaces serve as settings where relational teaching, development, and assessment of individual affective behaviors take place, relational innovation techniques can be observed on interpersonal, group, organizational, and inter-organizational levels.

Formal and informal relational shifts in makerspace organizations can influence entrepreneurial network establishment, participation, and organizational acceptance by developing members who are both enterprising and skilled in using affective approaches to problem-solving. The process of sharing knowledge as a means of inspiring innovative ideas, inventions, and product solutions is enhanced when relationships are healthy.

Establishing healthy organizational community models that are grounded in a sense of belonging generated through relationally innovative practices is a potential and promising path toward developing more productive, equitable, and inclusive organizations. While there are many examples of organizational community, makerspaces have emerged since the turn of the 21st century and serve as an example of organizational community-building and innovation. Makerspaces are innovation labs that advance the democratization of production by making tools, space, and opportunities more available to internal and external stakeholders. The opportunity for the makerspace movement to provide insight into the ability of collaborative, coworking spaces to advance an inclusive entrepreneurial community is in its infancy and worthy of investigatory analysis of its potential.

The objectives of this chapter are to:

1. introduce makerspaces as a viable option for the advancement of autonomous economic development in underserved communities,
2. describe the influence of organizational community and trust in the advancement of product-based entrepreneurship in makerspaces,
3. discuss affective learning processes and practices that facilitate a sense of belonging and empowerment for underserved populations,
4. explain the value of space and access to tools in product-based entrepreneurship for underserved communities, and
5. describe affiliation and acceptance as a means of building relational cohesiveness for underserved communities.

Autonomous economic development is a form of self-determination and the desired outcome that may be achieved by the democratization of tools and other means of production.[3] Democratization is inherently an inclusive, communal process that requires relational skill. It is, therefore, necessary to develop interpersonal capabilities as a means of maximizing collaborative production. A more inclusive approach to production has the potential to accelerate entrepreneurial potential in underserved communities.

LITERATURE REVIEW

Makerspaces began as a movement to revive local, small-scale creativity and design to advance the innovation economy. The facilities are "informal sites for creative production in art, science, and engineering where people of all ages blend digital and physical technologies to explore ideas, learn technical skills, and create new products" (Sheridan, Halverson, et. al., 2014, p.505). The physical location serves as a meeting space for a "maker community" and contains the manufacturing equipment needed for the community's design activities. Such spaces are commonly community-organized with the community determining its structure, function, programming, and funding (Wilczynski, 2015). Makerspaces also provide training, certification programs, and equipment that may otherwise be too costly for individuals.

The makerspace movement was originally viewed as the next iteration of the Do-It-Yourself (DIY) culture (Anderson, 2012). When structured using a membership model, members pay membership fees for access to use the technology, which typically includes a variety of rapid prototyping equipment such as 3D printers, laser cutters, and traditional hand tools (Barrett, et al, 2015). These spaces move beyond traditional machine shops by providing meeting spaces for student design teams and integrating typical machine shop tools with a variety of rapid prototyping and low-tech building approaches (Forrest, et. al., 2014). Allowing quick, easy access to expensive equipment for a community of inspired users provides an opportunity to thrive and develop products and ideas that generate business and revenue for the surrounding community (Wilczynski, 2015).

The first academic makerspace originated at the Massachusetts Institute of Technology (MIT), where Neil Gershenfeld, of MIT's Center for Bits and Atoms, was the originator of the Fab Lab, a university course that significantly influenced the movement (Burke, 2014). Fab Labs were designed to fabricate materials using digital equipment for designing products and digitally driven tools to create them. This learning environment provided a design space and inspired a collaborative culture for students (Burke, 2014). Universities have advanced the makerspace movement by providing hands-on experience to students to support theoretical and real-world-based learning (Forrest, et al., 2014). Affording students and the surrounding university community access to makerspaces enhances broader skills including creativity, team-oriented problem solving, and multidisciplinary collaboration skills (Carlson and Sullivan 2006; Griffin and Cortes 2006). Community-embedded makerspaces provide a deeper reach into neighborhoods and are the new think tanks of the future.

Learning environments in makerspaces have no defined standard. Each makerspace space is specific to the needs of the making community and the external community where the space is located. Spaces also lower the cost barriers to business startups and help address gaps in opportunity for training, apprenticeships, and industry certifications. The value of makerspaces as incubators for business startups has increased because of the collapse of industrialized cities such as Dayton, Ohio; Detroit, Michigan; Pittsburg, Pennsylvania (Pallagst, Fleschurz, and Said, 2017). As politicians, policymakers, and community leaders struggle to find ways to rebuild declining cities, workers who once relied on factory jobs for stable income and job training are now faced with no opportunities for apprenticeships, or individualized skills training that would provide careers for economically challenged communities. Makerspaces are growing throughout the country based on the demand for access to workspaces and tools for emerging entrepreneurs.

From an organizational learning perspective, Argyris and Schon (1974) suggest that individuals and organizations maintain theories of action that they have developed about and for themselves. Organizations such as makerspaces learn from their mistakes, improve, and create best practices. Much like

Agile methods (Beck 2001) used in software development teams, organizations must move quickly and more frequently in highly innovative environments. Likewise, innovation hubs such as those created by partnerships between universities and makerspaces must be prepared to address affective, relational dynamics (Krathwohl, Bloom, Masia, 1973) due to the reality that entrepreneurial pursuits require affective responses to accelerating change (Kotter, 2012). Within makerspaces, the creation of organizational learning opportunities can spur excellence and organizational behavioral change, two pillars of the IOC framework.

The relational community that has been described in Dépelteau's relational sociology as "an open association of sociologists focusing on relations and raising our consciousness about our inescapable state of interdependency" (2018, p.7) directly addresses the value of relational affiliation. He states that "we allow ourselves to transform our experiences, to think and interact in different (relational) ways, because, for instance, the consciousness of interdependency brings to light the risks of egocentric quests for independence and freedom." Teaching and learning organically demonstrate affective behavioral competence utilizing the affective domain: receiving, responding, valuing, organizing, and characterizing (Krathwohl, Bloom, et al., 1973) information throughout daily interactions. Improving the affective competencies of today's learners is key to the thriving IOC model. Introducing affective models in underserved communities where growing entrepreneurial ecosystems exist relies on relational dynamics and shifts in the innovation actors' behaviors. Awareness of these shifts helps to shape the social trajectory and advancement of underserved interactors in a majority or non-traditional settings by increasing awareness around relational thinking (Dépelteau, 2018) as a part of the organizational culture. Within the Open Works makerspace, relational innovation includes advancing social inclusion and moving away from social generalizations that box one group in and normalize others, leading to systemic inequities for community residents.

Park and Cho state that "Wonder is the beginning of thinking creatively" (2016, p.14). As a result, the moment of wonder felt when relational affiliation and acceptance happen inspires creative thinking and collaborative drive, spurring growth and positive change. To build affective competencies, organizations must begin to operate relationally, encouraging members to act with more empathy while seeking understanding, and before characterizing select individuals and segments within the organization's domain. In this regard, IOC solution-oriented approaches activate alternative analysis by avoiding one-size-fits-all approaches to problems while developing relational intelligence.

Research regarding the need for connectedness or belongingness is not new in organizational and human relations theory. The body of knowledge has historical roots in John Bowlby's theory of attachment developed while studying the distress of infants who were separated from their parents (1969). The psychological and emotional implication is that the need to experience connectedness and belongingness begins early in life and is supported by the belongingness theory (Baumeister, DeWall, Ciarocco, & Twenge, 2005; Baumeister & Leary, 1995; Twenge, Baumeister, DeWall, Ciarocco, & Bartels, 2007). Lack of belongingness is linked to several emotional disabilities and psychological conditions, including depression (Cockshaw, et.al, 2014). Another example is Valcke et.al. (2018) findings that "inclusion (belongingness) needs and discomfort with exclusion are positively related but clearly distinct" (p.593). Those who demonstrate a need to have social relationships and who want to be included in groups show better psychological health than others who do not need social relationships and group inclusion.

Brown and McClure (2008) conducted a phenomenological study of 12 adults, ages 20 to 80, and their reported experiences ranged from their first jobs up to working for one company for over 39 years. The researchers found that belongingness at work was composed of six themes: "1. being invited and learning to be a part of a workplace, 2. connecting with colleagues and wanting to be included, 3. doing work and being recognized, 4. natural selection at work, competing and being excluded, 5. being needed and finding myself deeply involved in my profession, and 6. Reflecting on time, work and people passing" (p. 10-13). Each of the six themes represents a level of engagement throughout multiple work experiences that reflect the building of affiliation and acceptance, important components of organizational communities.

Studies during recent decades have focused on the examination of relationships between belongingness and positive workplace outcomes (Andersson & Pearson, 1999; Gkorezis, et.al. 2013; Pearson et al., 2000). This shift in research was in response to several studies that addressed relationships between negative experiences such as ostracism and the importance of belongingness (O'Reilly & Robinson, 2009; Van den Broeck et al., 2010). While the theme of literature may have been in response to diminishing workplace loyalty, corporate downsizing, rising workplace violence, incivility, and other factors that reflect a decline in belongingness, there is an increasing need to engage in learning and the production of academic artifacts that result in new learning paradigms for addressing relational deficits.

Organizations as communities is a concept with theoretical origins in social belonging theory. As described in the 2009 July-August issue of *Harvard Business Review* by Henry Mintzberg, "Community means caring about our work, our colleagues, and our place in the world, geographic and otherwise, and in turn being inspired by this caring" (p.141). The sharing of safe spaces is an intentional design incorporating the following five lessons learned by Mintzberg about developing "communityship" among managers and in organizations: 1. Community building in an organization may best begin with small groups of committed managers, 2. The sense of community takes root as the managers in these groups reflect on the experiences they have shared in the organization, 3. The insights generated by these reflections naturally trigger small initiatives that can grow into big strategies, 4. As these initial teams promote change, they become examples for other groups that spread "communityship" throughout the organization, and 5. An organization knows that "communityship" is firmly established when its members reach out in socially active, responsible, and mutually beneficial ways to the broader community (Mintzberg, 2009, p.142-143).

The Organization for Economic Co-operation and Development (OECD) is one of the quintessential international authorities on innovation. According to their 2019 publication, *Raising the Bar: Better Policies for Better Lives*, "the 60-year-old organization has been responsible for developing over 450 international standards, including conventions, recommendations, decisions, and declarations with more than 250 legal instruments in force in multiple sectoral areas" (p. 4). The OECD 2018 *Oslo Manual* is the organization's fourth edition of the 1992 publication written as an international reference guide for collecting and using data on innovation. The Oslo Manual for measuring innovation (2005, p. 47-52)) defines four types of innovation: 1. product innovation, a good or service that is new or significantly improved, 2. process innovation, a new or significantly improved production or delivery method, 3. marketing innovation, a new marketing method involving significant changes in product design or packaging, product placement, product promotion or pricing, and 4. organizational innovation, a new organizational method in business practices, workplace organization, or external relations. Our focus for this chapter is on the process and organizational innovation as defined by the 2005 *Oslo Manual.*

Recognizing the organizational definitions that are as broad as the number of theories and disciplines that address the topic of innovation, Li-Min Chuang (2007) conducted a study of organizational innovation to modify Amabile's (1988) organizational model of creativity and innovation. The study yielded three groups of factors (i.e., individual, organizational, and environmental) that influence five stages of innovations (i.e., task presentation, preparation, stage three idea generation, stage four idea generation, and outcomes assessment). It is the intersection of social levels from individual to the external environment and the stages of process innovation that inform the development of the IOC model. The researcher's efforts to develop a relational innovation model demonstrate the intersectionality of behavioral and production-oriented disciplines as well as the broad definitional constructs in both. Fløysand and Jakobsen (2011) take somewhat the same approach to integrating organizational and process innovation theory. The colleagues developed a framework for innovation studies as a relational phenomenon. They assert that "innovation systems theory defines learning knowledge creation as a key driver for entrepreneurship and innovation" (p. 341), giving credence to the convergence of disciplines.

The network that constitutes the organizational community is evident in the study of innovation-centric organizational communities such as makerspaces. Diffusion of innovation theory has been widely used to explain knowledge dissemination and mobilization required for the building of organizational and innovative community action. The stream of inquiry is evident in Gainforth et. al. (2014), a study of the role of interpersonal communication in the process of knowledge mobilization within a community-based organization. The network analysis revealed that the diffusion of innovation through relational networks is more effective when "membership in the core as opposed to the periphery is associated with knowledge mobilization" and there is a "high degree of quality" in the information being shared (p. 8). The findings are consistent with the trans-organizational pathways created by affective learning processes in the IOC network of influence.

There is a prevalent discourse in the U.S. makerspace movement about inclusion across all determinants of diversity, particularly race. Of course, there are many facilities in geographic locations where racial diversity is low, limiting the pool of prospective clientele to a homogenous racial demographic. However, as noted by the researchers in this study, a makerspace located in the heart of a majority Black city is not diverse because of the available pool of potential clients. The makerspace is racially diverse and inclusive because of a commitment to making decisions that advance inclusion and develop a sense of belonging. This is illustrated in results from the 2018 Nation of Makers' data, a national advocacy organization for the industry, that 70.2% of respondents were male and 84.7% Caucasian. While the survey also suggested that 95.2% of respondents "feel accepted, welcome, and like they belong in their space," this high feeling of acceptance is not uncommon in homogenous racial and gender groups (Williams, 2019). Indicators on all levels of industry, academia, and the public sector illustrate the need for innovation-centric organizational communities that offer climates more conducive to a sense of belonging for the emerging workforce from underserved populations.

The literature provides a foundation for descriptive, exploratory research that yields new frameworks for discussing entrepreneurial inclusion and equity for underserved communities

AN INCLUSIVE INNOVATION-CENTRIC ORGANIZATIONAL COMMUNITY (IOC)

Open Works is a state-of-the-art, 34,000 square foot facility in Baltimore, Maryland. The nonprofit has a mission is to "...make tools, technology, and the knowledge to use them accessible to all" and a long-term vision to "...rebuild the regional manufacturing economy from the grassroots up" (Open Works Baltimore, 2019).[4] In a city that experienced great population growth during the mid-20th Century and produced jobs that sustained working-class residents, Baltimore now represents leading statistics in overall poverty, child poverty, senior poverty, individuals living below 200 percent of the poverty line, residents receiving temporary cash assistance, children receiving temporary cash assistance, percentage of the population participating in food supplement programs, and the percentage of children who participate in the Free and Reduced Price Meals program (MD Alliance of the Poor, 2014). While the Covid-19 global pandemic required Open Works to change its business model, the makerspace's mission remains the same and the organization continues to serve the community and demonstrate growth. Their three-and-a-half-year pre-pandemic rapid growth demonstrates the potential of makerspaces to contribute to the local and state economies while reducing the barriers to entry for underserved communities.

At the time of data collection, the facility was equipped with a 3D printing bot farm with four Ultimaker 2 extended 3D printers, two Inventables Carvey desktop precision CNC routers, four computer workstations, and a filament recycler. The digital fabrication lab included advanced large-format machines that accurately cut through plywood, plastic, and soft metals, such as the 4'x8' Laguna Swift with vacuum bed hold-down, two 4'x8' bed ShopBot PRS Alpha CNC routers, a Tormach Personal CNC 1100 mill, two laser cutters, an 18" x 24" bed, and a laser cutter, 28" x 40" bed. The metal shop, woodworking shop, computer lab, industrial cut-and-sew studio, digital media studio, and electronics shop were equipped with an equally impressive list of tools made available through membership, education programs, special events, and collaborative community relationships. The staff at Open Works grew to 33 employees at its peak in 2020, all of whom reside in Baltimore City. Even with equipment inventory and staff adjustments required to operate during a global healthcare crisis, Open Works continues as a national model of community-embedded makerspace success.

Data was collected from the Open Works client map by city and zip code, adult class observations, adult class evaluation reports, children's class attendance records, multi-year event benchmarking reports, structured interviews with Open Works resident business owners, Open Works staff, and the general Open Works community. Qualitative analysis methodologies are based on a process of analytic induction (Angell, 1936; Lindesmith, 1947; Cressy, 1953; Bruyn, 1966) to ensure maximum generalizability of the findings and neutralize researchers' biases.

A process of analytic induction was used as the methodology for this study most because of its appropriateness when exploring the less obvious, implied aspects of organizational life when relevant variables have not been identified. While the method has been criticized for lacking rigorous scientific protocol and an inability to support scientific generalization, the criticism is addressed with the understanding that inductive, exploratory research serves a very distinct purpose; that is to search for patterns, ideas, or hypotheses regarding phenomena about which there is considerable uncertainty. It is also important to draw distinctions between the hypothesis-generating activity of inductive, exploratory research and other purposes for research activity. Analytic generalization for hypothesis generation and theory building is not a statistical (causal) generalization.

The study answers the following questions:

1. How does a large, urban, makerspace located in an underserved neighborhood build an inclusive organizational community?
2. What are the dominant relational patterns in a large, urban, makerspace located in an underserved neighborhood?
3. How is innovation encouraged by a sense of belonging developed in a large, urban, makerspace located in an underserved neighborhood?

Case Analysis

Analysis of the data yielded the following themes: 1. Trust as a Catalyst for Building Organizational Community, Focus on Affective Learning Processes and Practices, 2. The Value of Space for Playful Ingenuity and Opportunity, and 3. Advancing Inclusion through Innovation-based Affiliation and Acceptance

Trust as a Catalyst for Building Organizational Community

A communal theme is evident throughout the data. The existence of trust and perceptions of emotional safety for those using the facility contributes to a sense of belonging. The experience of affiliation and acceptance holds great value at Open Works for the diverse group of artists, entrepreneurs, machinists, and technicians. There was a degree of skepticism expressed by participants in the study about placing a facility like Open Works in an underserved community and being able to build the sustainable institutional trust required to build a welcoming, sense of belonging. This is evident in the skepticism about the institutional motives for placing a makerspace in an underserved community.

I mean, I think that an initial barrier that we faced when we opened was the perception of what a large institution was going to do, coming into a Black neighborhood and there were a lot of people from the Black creative community that was skeptical about joining membership in like...you know sort of like a certain level of distrust of institutions and organizations.

The prevalence of diversity and inclusion at Open Works cannot be completely explained by the makerspace's location in a city with a majority Black population. Open Works is diverse across all measures of diversity, whereas many organizations in the same city remain homogeneous in race, ethnicity, and gender representation. Open Works' diversity may be attributable to leadership's acknowledgment of institutional distrust resulting from the existence of historical racial discord in the U.S. and the current lack of diversity in makerspaces across the nation. The organization's national leaders in diversity may be attributed to intentional collaborations with external organizations that reflect Open Works' diversity and inclusion goals. Examples include "Moms as Entrepreneurs," which ran two 16-week cohorts of entrepreneurship training and successfully launched 18 women-owned businesses on Etsy. The Memorandum of Understanding with Coppin State University, which is the first agreement of its kind with a public, urban, Historically Black College and University (HBCU) is another example of external relationships that facilitate an internal goal to create a sense of belonging for members of underserved groups. The organization is a model for intentionally creating and maintaining a climate of institutional trust and community that facilitates transparency and cultural intelligence.

God, what's the word? ...like the quality doesn't get compromised on equipment and things like that, classes, quality of service, customer service, it's a huge one too, quality of programming. But also, if you're getting big, still helping people, giving nonprofit discounts for like the community center, the neighborhood community association can still meet here, like keeping excluded groups on the forefront.

There is evidence of intentional organizational community-building in Open Works' policies and practices. This distinction provides an opportunity for the organization to forge trust frameworks for strengthening maker communities and enabling them to serve as trust hubs and trust brokers for economic development and growth. While Open Works serves clients from 297 unique zip codes, 61% of its clientele is from Baltimore City and 34% from zip codes directly adjacent to Open Works, this local engagement provides the opportunity to build a sense of community by serving more participants in educational programs and the ability to expand community engagement through additional partnerships. As described by Open Works leadership, the organization's educational programming is "providing community access to a design-thinking pedagogy that teaches fabrication skills, practical problem-solving, and interactive design processes" (Open Works Baltimore, 2019).

Makerspace communities are "living organisms" that grow, evolve, change, and are susceptible to relational influences. Those who utilize Open Works are continuously seeking ways to achieve maximum creativity and productivity. Emerging themes indicate that trust and organizational community positively influence the culture within Open Works. This occurs despite historical distrust that may have existed between underserved, underestimated communities, and formal institutions. The effort to build an inclusive sense of community was intentional from the inception of Open Works.

So those are the two obstacles - trust and finances. Yes, and making sure that folks feel like this is a space for them. We've been designing programming that does that. And you know, keeping relationships healthy in the neighborhood is really important.

The primary way of overcoming potential barriers to success here is to continue building community.

Focus on Affective Learning Processes and Practices

Affective learning and cultural transformation occur on the individual level and group level at Open Works. This does not preclude organization-wide activities. However, for this study, organization-wide activities are considered as an amalgamation of sub-groups and teams. Standards and performance metrics for Open Works sub-groups are partially determined by the sense of belonging and trust they create. The common denominator for Open Works and its networks of external stakeholders is affective learning processes that infuse relational capital into the network.

The relational connections are also supported by the support of the major funder, The Robert W. Deutsch Foundation. The funders committed to three years of operating support for startup costs, declining every year, for education programs, capital projects, and operating expenses. This allowed Open Works to amass an impressive list of 17 partners during the first two years of operation that participate in an array of collaborative projects. The projects foster an interactive learning environment between Open Works and the external community.

Learning is a dominant theme in all activities and demonstrates the importance of distinguishing between learning domains and how each domain fosters an innovation-centric organizational community. The cognitive domain is dominant in the building of knowledge required to build relationships and foster innovation. The psycho-motor domain is dominant in demonstrating the skills required to implement collaborative, community-building programs. While these two domains are important to understanding and utilizing tools provided by the organization, it is affective learning and resulting relational innovations involving feelings, emotions, and attitudes that are the dominant psycho-social pillars of affiliation and acceptance. Affective learning innovations at Open Works emerged from the desire to build internal and external relationships between dissimilar participants. It has been the willingness to perceive, conceive, and act when challenging interpersonal exchanges occur.

The level of internal and external positive relational symbolism and protocol are reflected in the practice of never locking the main entrance doors during business hours, which may be interpreted by some as a questionable practice in a high-crime community. However, Open Works demonstrated the authenticity of its name, "Open" Works by being always open to the community, despite public safety concerns in the neighborhood. The emphasis on gathering members from dissimilar backgrounds and experiences, creating a cooperative or collaborative learning culture, and utilizing feedback to continuously improve, is the essence of developing an IOC model.

In some cases, it really does take experience and right wisdom in that area, (accepting the others), so that persons come in with that and you are able to benefit. Yes, absolutely - it contributes to the community. So, this is a shared space in education and also educational, and it's a place of business and development and self-exploration.

The Value of Space for Playful Ingenuity and Opportunity

Space is one of the major themes that emerged during research, especially regarding the ability to accommodate entrepreneurial activity and growth. The value of space and opportunity is high as a resource for entrepreneurs engaging in creative, playful ingenuity (Hewing, 2014). This type of free-wielding, collaborative engagement is integrated into each stage in the entrepreneurial process to encourage the exploration of a broad range of options for providing products and services to consumers. Dedicated space for playful ingenuity by entrepreneurs is often lacking in underserved communities. The level of the event activity, the demand for classes, and space for business expansion may appear to create competing interests and the possibility of negative conflict. However, relational innovation and competence enable Open Works to use the value of space and community as an incentive for innovation, collaboration, and strategic alliances among those with space needs.[5]

I see Open Works as a supportive space, that is actually a platform or a launchpad for bigger things. So, I hope we can continue to be a company where anybody who has a desire to be here and a desire to make things and to learn can be, and we can help them figure out how to self-start and figure out their pathway to move on and move out of this place.

The space must have a purpose that aligns with the community-focused values. Diversity and inclusion inherently bring dissimilar members into a community. Overcoming the typical in-group, out-group behaviors associated with social interactions requires relational competence that transforms the value of space and opportunity into priorities and incentives for collaboration. Conflicts regarding space or space utilization become secondary to the primary value of community cohesion. It is the value of acceptance, affiliation, and belongingness that is a catalyst for new ways of overcoming conflict in the organization.

...when you see more people using the space of all different types, I think that helped with some of the apprehension folks had before they came into the doors.

Advancing Inclusion through Innovation-based Affiliation and Acceptance

Open Works is bringing innovation to the makerspace industry. The industry's reputation for a lack of inclusive practices creates an opportunity for a large, urban makerspace organization to demonstrate inclusion in an external environment that possesses high levels of distrust due to historical racial inequity. The approach is consistent with disruptive innovation that leads to expanding, sustainable economic viability. This is evident in the failure of other large, well-funded makerspaces. Innovative disruption in the approach to affective, relational intelligence, and competence can lead to greater inclusion and enterprise sustainability. This assertion is based on the observation of a willingness to meet the defining standard of new learning, which is most often accompanied by new experiences that may have been previously resisted. It is not as if new learning cannot occur during a continuation of known information and practices. It is that learning from a continuation of known practices is less likely to be disruptive because it adheres to what is already known. Disruption is finding ways to make tools even more accessible to underserved communities when revenue is an ongoing concern.

My hope for Open Works is that we just continue to diversify, and we continue to have different options (for access), to lower the threshold. Just make it (cost) as small as possible if you want to come here.

Being an innovative disruptor in a sector that is not diverse requires relational innovation and the ability to find new methods for transcending relational barriers that lead to the exclusion of outgroups. O'Reilly and Bennis (2019) identified three stages of disruptive innovation that provide context for the Open Works approach. They are ideation, incubation, and scaling. Ideation is a process of developing prescriptive solutions to a recognized problem. There are other forms of ideation. However, the emergence of Open Works was based on the recognition of a set of problems (i.e., the lack of low-cost access to tools that could be advantageous to those in underserved communities who have entrepreneurial aspirations, and the lack of diversity and inclusion in the sector). The Open Works' commitment to innovatively disrupting the two perceived problems is a classic example of innovative disruption in the affective, relational, communal domain of learning.

I was excited about the prospect of Open Works being a place where minorities could hopefully be on the forefront of makerspace accessibility for minorities and historically excluded communities. I'm queer and have mixed ethnic heritage, and I'm so used to being in White male, older male-dominated makerspaces and feeling unsafe or harassed and may be targeted in some ways... You come in here, and it's visibly different.

The themes that emerged set forth the following hypotheses for further consideration, including:

Hypothesis One: Organizational community and belongingness advance innovative processes and practices for members of underserved populations utilizing makerspaces.

Hypothesis Two: Trust is a significant relational pillar that exists in makerspace organizations serving entrepreneurs from underserved communities

Hypothesis Three: Affective learning outcomes are a significant contributor to the perceived value of makerspaces to entrepreneurs from underserved communities.

Hypothesis Four: Space and equitable access have entrepreneurial value to underserved community members utilizing makerspaces.

Hypothesis Five: Innovation based on affiliation and acceptance leads to a more inclusive makerspace community.

SOLUTIONS AND RECOMMENDATIONS

Open Works has made a significant contribution to the entrepreneurial landscape of Baltimore and its vicinity. Its impact is also experienced beyond the region as they emerge as a national pacesetter in the maker movement. The organization exhibits a blend of mission, vision, leadership, and strategic implementation that places it on a trajectory to influence small and medium-scale manufacturing for future decades and beyond.

The analysis of Open Works and the national movement makes it clear that collaborative efforts from all stakeholders will be required to codify, interpret, and develop guiding principles and practices that will be of maximum benefit to makers and facilitate the emergence of spaces that are conducive to inclusive growth. It will also be beneficial to pursue such goals with an understanding that context matters. There is no "one size fits all" approach that will guarantee desired results when executing the mission of making tools available to as many people as possible. Assessment of the socioeconomic trajectory of the community, an ingepreneurial approach as recommended by Williams & Klugh (2017) will assist in providing context for learners and the learning process. With contextual analysis of IOC environments, the need and value of effective models of development and operation are clear.

The commitment to diversity and inclusion at Open Works is commendable in an industry that has not historically had that distinction. As much as the enterprise is dedicated to "making industrial tools available to as many people as possible," there is an opportunity to make relational tools available to as much of the industry as possible. Makerspaces are places where people of many different backgrounds and experiences come to create for creative design and production across multiple disciplines. This remains a fact regardless of the region and its cultural history. Demographic profiles may be unique; however, the need to build healthy community climates remains essential, even if the dominant difference is merely personality. Building beyond barriers in the context of IOC means much more when considering the ultimate success of Open Works and its contribution to the broader maker movement. The ability to transcend barriers is critical to creating successful pathways for underserved communities to entrepreneurial success and expansion of economic prosperity.

There is an inevitable leadership crisis once startups grow, and the need for more formal communication arises. This is an important factor in the need to infuse relational competencies into IOC-focused startups from underserved communities. While founders may be able to adjust their style, it often requires the inclusion of new people. Another crisis point is encountered as leadership becomes distanced from frontline activity. There is too much complexity in this stage to stay informed, and autonomy becomes a difficult scheme to maintain. As mid-level managers emerge, they struggle with their role as mediators, and this has the potential of eroding trust and the sense of community vital to the successful evolution of a makerspace. The growing bureaucracy also becomes problematic, and cultural tensions between creativity and structure begin to occur. There is also a point in the traditional growth cycle when further growth is difficult without collaboration with similar entities. Makerspaces such as Open Works will improve as they build effective collaboration models.

The Innovation-centric Organizational Community (IOC) model (Figure 1) aligns with the elements of "communityship" found in a large, urban, community-embedded makerspace. The framework illustrates the intersection between the internal and external environments of open systems (Morgan, 1986). Human, financial, informational, and material resources interact in internal organizational sub-systems and are catalysts for organizational responses to the external environment, output, and growth (Kast and Rosenzweig, 1973). The resources that produce organic makerspace responses to internal and external realities in the IOC model are affective learning practices and principles. Internal and external sub-systems defined by a trans-organizational, evolving community facilitate the makerspace's ability to meet the emerging needs of 21st Century entrepreneurial organizations' demand for learning readiness.

Figure 1. Innovation-centric organizational community model

The demand for learning skills represented in the IOC model is consistent with The World Economic Forum's 2020 declaration of "a reskilling emergency," recognizing that more than a billion jobs are being transformed by technology (Weforum, 2020). The affective learning process is primary in the IOC model because of its ability to determine outcomes in other learning domains. As McKinsey & Company projects that automation and artificial intelligence will take on the more routine tasks associated with work, there will be a corresponding surge in the need for social and emotional skills and declining demand for more routine, manual skills (Bughin et.al., 2018)

Process innovation is differentiated from the business model and product innovation in the IOC model. In the instance of affective learning, the methods of improving relational, cultural, or communal competence involve innovations and new ideas that are germinated and applied in an amorphous community that transcends traditional organizational boundaries. This is contrary to changing the way items are produced or services rendered in process innovation. The continuous improvement of relationships in the trans-organizational community networks is bolstered by the effective development of social and emotional skills and human affirming capabilities. Andragogical practices are more likely to render positive outcomes when aligned with best practices from social and emotional learning paradigms.

Understanding that belongingness and trust are foundational concepts in IOC affective learning constructs, external organizational community members meet community standards in less formal ways. Strategic intent is necessary for engaging external community members. They are less subject to the constraints faced by internal community members because of their more arbitrary options for disengagement. The Open Works makerspace is an excellent example of trust-inspired entrepreneurial relationships and values-inspired collaboration. The emergence of a trans-organizational, amorphous community network in the context of two affective learning processes and the application of a proven mode of production enabled Open Works to completely pivot in 10 days, produce 28,000 PPE face shields in 56 working days for over 100 clients from March 25 until June 6, 2020. The effort resulted in the acquisition of a government contract to produce face shields for meatpacking plant inspectors during the Covid-19 global pandemic.

Table 1. Evidential alignment mapping

Questions	Related Themes	Hypotheses
How does a large, urban, makerspace located in an underserved neighborhood build an inclusive organizational community?	• Trust as a Catalyst for Building Organizational Community • Focus on Affective Learning Processes and Practices	• Organizational community and belongingness advance innovative processes and practices for members of underserved populations utilizing makerspaces. • Affective learning outcomes are a significant contributor to the perceived value of makerspaces to entrepreneurs from underserved communities.
What are the dominant relational patterns in a large, urban, makerspace located in an underserved neighborhood?	• Trust as a Catalyst for Building Organizational Community	• Trust is a significant relational pillar that exists in makerspace organizations serving entrepreneurs from underserved communities
How is innovation encouraged by a sense of belonging developed in a large, urban, makerspace located in an underserved neighborhood?	• The Value of Space for Playful Ingenuity and Opportunity • Advancing Inclusion through Innovation-based Affiliation and Acceptance	• Innovation based on affiliation and acceptance leads to a more inclusive makerspace community. • Space and equitable access have entrepreneurial value to underserved community members utilizing makerspaces.

CONCLUSION

The evidence map (Table 1) provides a summary of the alignment between research questions, themes that emerged, and the resulting hypotheses. The alignment presents a foundation for conclusions and recommendations for future research.

The significance of this research has far-reaching implications for theory and practice. Evidential alignment is present in the mapping of research questions, related themes, and resulting hypotheses (Table 1). The hypotheses may be tested through nomothetic epistemological methods while raising awareness of exemplary organizations that are engaging in practices that meet the emerging needs of workers and organizations. The study also yields recommendations for practical approaches to emerging realities associated with organizational life. Solutions-oriented approaches to 21st Century organizational challenges must occur in real-time. The learning curve for organizations and individuals has been compressed by scientific and technological advancements. Organizational communities that have climates conducive to failing fast, pivoting and moving forward demonstrate that rapid learning is necessary to meet what may appear to be overwhelming demands for information processing and the development of innovative responses. The limitations of this study and others focused on the maker movement are influenced by the early-stage nature of makerspaces as engines of production democratization and economic development. Longitudinal approaches to inquiry and comprehensive research outcomes from the full spectrum of epistemological and ontological positions will mitigate the limitations of inferential, theory-building research.

FUTURE RESEARCH DIRECTIONS

This study establishes a clear need for additional research to build on the emerging hypotheses and provides a foundation for nomothetic analysis. The use of generalizations rather than specific properties supports relational innovation model adoption for the makerspace community and other innovation hubs. Centering on relational thinking supports the development of a learning culture that emphasizes people and how they think but also what they value.

Future studies may seek to explore individual and group relational development within these spaces and how they establish clear learning goals to ensure the inclusion of underserved communities within the entrepreneurial environment. Opportunities to capture innovation-centric motivations and goals can create organizational and relational priorities for addressing diverse and emerging non-traditional actors within the makerspace ecosystems. Extrapolating fundamental affective behaviors that reflect the organization's philosophy and transformation from thinking and doing to feeling and behaving with holistic frameworks for decision-making and problem-solving.

The conclusions will assist in meeting the challenges posed by declining economic and social conditions in former industrial centers and rural communities that were once part of thriving economic pipelines during the height of industrialism. Makerspaces are a viable part of the solution that will create jobs, fill gaps in the supply chain, and help expand manufacturing opportunities. This is especially true as we see the future of work rapidly changing. The "Great Resignation" and the prevailing renegotiation of social and psychological contracts associated with worker loyalty and tolerance for less satisfying work conditions are evidence of the need for affective realignment within organizational communities.[6] Makerspaces provide an opportunity to integrate the autonomy of entrepreneurial pursuits with the needs of a shifting labor market. The IOC approach also possesses the potential for facilitating the closure of organizational equity gaps and advancing inclusive practices. The concept of innovation-centric organizational communities to maximize affective learning domains is consistent with the emerging workforce demands of the mid-21st Century.

REFERENCES

Amabile, T. (1988). A model of creativity and innovation in organizations. In B. M. Staw & L. L. Cumming (Eds.), *Research in organizational behavior* (Vol. 10, pp. 123–167). JAI Press.

Anderson, C. (2012). *Makers: the new industrial revolution*. Random House.

Andersson, L. M., & Pearson, C. M. (1999). 'Tit for tat? The spiraling effect of incivility in the workplace. *Academy of Management Review, 24*(3), 452–471.

Angell, R. C. (1936). *The Family Encounters the Depression*. Scribner.

Argyris, C., & Schon, D. A. (1974). *Theory in practice: Increasing professional effectiveness*. Jossey-Bass.

Barrett, T., Pizzico, M., Levy, B. D., Nagel, R. L., Linsey, J. S., Talley, K. G., Forest, C. R., & Newsletter, W. C. (2015). *A review of university maker spaces*. Georgia Institute of Technology. doi:10.18260/p.23442

Baumeister, R. F., & Leary, M. R. (1995). The need to belong: Desire for interpersonal attachments as a fundamental human motivation. *Psychological Bulletin, 117*(3), 497–529. doi:10.1037/0033-2909.117.3.497 PMID:7777651

Baumeister, R. F., Twenge, J. M., & Nuss, C. K. (2002). Effects of social exclusion on cognitive processes: Anticipated aloneness reduces intelligent thought. *Journal of Personality and Social Psychology, 83*(4), 817–827. doi:10.1037/0022-3514.83.4.817 PMID:12374437

Baumeister, R. F., & Vohs, K. D. (2007). Self-Regulation, Ego Depletion, and Motivation. *Social and Personality Psychology Compass, 1*(1), 115–128. doi:10.1111/j.1751-9004.2007.00001.x

Beck, K. (2001). The Agile Manifesto. *Agile Alliance*. http://agilemanifesto.org/

Bowlby, J. (1969). Attachment and Loss: Vol. 1. *Attachment*. Penguin.

Bruyn, S. T. (1966). *The Human Perspective in Sociology*. Prentice-Hall.

Bughin, J. (2018). *Skill Shift: Automation and the Future of the Workforce*. McKinsey Global Institute. Retrieved online https://www.mckinsey.com/featured-insights/future-of-work/skill-shift-automation-and-the-future-of-the-workforce

Burke, J. J. (2014). *Makerspaces: a practical guide for librarians* (Vol. 8). Rowman & Littlefield.

Carlson, L. E., & Sullivan, J. F. (2006). A Multi-Disciplinary Design Environment. *ASME 2006 International Design Engineering Technical Conferences and Computers and Information in Engineering Conference, 4c*, 835–840. 10.1115/DETC2006-99148

Chuang, L.-M. (2007). The Social Psychology of Creativity and Innovation: Process Theory (Pt) Perspective. *Social Behavior and Personality, 35*(7), 875–888. doi:10.2224bp.2007.35.7.875

Citi G. P. S. Global Perspectives & Solutions (2020). *Closing the Racial Inequity Gaps: The Economic Cost of Racial Inequality in the U.S.* https://ir.citi.com/NvIUklHPilz14Hwd3oxqZBLMn1_XPqo5FrxsZD0x6hhil84ZxaxEuJUWmak51UHvYk75VKeHCMI%3D

Cockshaw, W. D., Shochet, I. M., & Obst, P. L. (2014). Depression and Belongingness in General and Workplace Contexts: A Cross-Lagged Longitudinal Investigation. *Journal of Social and Clinical Psychology, 33*(5), 448–462. doi:10.1521/jscp.2014.33.5.448

Cressey, D. R. (1953). *Other People's Money*. Free Press.

Dépelteau, F. (2018). Relational Thinking in Sociology: Relevance, Concurrence and Dissonance. In F. Dépelteau (Ed.), *The Palgrave Handbook of Relational Sociology*. Palgrave Macmillan. doi:10.1007/978-3-319-66005-9_1

Gkorezis, P., Kalampouka, P., & Petridou, E. (2013). The Mediating Role of Belongingness in the Relationship between Workplace Incivility and Thriving. *International Journal of Employment Studies, 21*(2), 63–78.

Griffin, O. H., & Cortes, S. (2006). A Learning Space of, by, and for Engineers: Virginia Tech's Joseph F. Ware, Jr. Advanced Engineering Laboratory. *ASME 2006 International Design Engineering Technical Conferences and Computers and Information in Engineering Conference*, 841–848. 10.1115/DETC2006-99205

Hewing, M. (2014). The Playful Ingenuity of Potential Users in Collaboration: Enriched Compensation and Improvisation. *Collaboration with Potential Users for Discontinuous Innovation: Experimental Research on User Creativity*, 103-149. . doi:10.1007/978-3-658-03753-6-4

Kast, F. E., & Rosenzweig, J. E. (1973). *Contingency views of organization and management*. Science Research Associates.

Kotter, J. P. (2012). Accelerate! *Harvard Business Review, 90*(11), 44–52. PMID:23155997

Krathwohl, D. R., Bloom, B. S., & Masia, B. B. (1973). *Taxonomy of Educational Objectives, the Classification of Educational Goals. In Handbook II: Affective Domain*. David McKay Co., Inc.

Lindesmith, A. R. (1947). *Opiate Addiction*. Principa.

McClure, J., & Brown, J. (2008). Belonging at work. *Human Resource Development International, 11*(1), 3–17. doi:10.1080/13678860701782261

Morgan, G. (1986). *Images of organization*. Sage Publications.

O'Reilly, C., & Binns, A. J. M. (2019). The Three Stages of Disruptive Innovation: Idea Generation, Incubation, and Scaling. *California Management Review, 61*(3), 49–71. doi:10.1177/0008125619841878

Open Works Baltimore. (2019). *About Us*. https://www.openworksbmore.org/about-us/

Pallagst, K., Fleschurz, R., & Said, S. (2017). What Drives Planning in a Shrinking City? Tales from Two German and Two American Cases. *The Town Planning Review*, *88*(1), 15–28. doi:10.3828/tpr.2017.3

Park, H. Y., & Cho, I. H. (n.d.). *Creativity and the Market for Entrepreneurs in ICT Industry*. Academic Press.

Pearson, C. M., & Porath, C. L. (2005). On the nature, consequences, and remedies of workplace incivility: No time for "nice"? Think again. *The Academy of Management Executive*, *19*(1), 7–18. doi:10.5465/ame.2005.15841946

Poor, M. A. (2014). *2014 Maryland Poverty Profile.* Retrieved from Catholic Charities of Maryland: http://www.catholiccharities-md.org/public-policy/2014-map-poverty-profiles.pdf

Sheridan, K., Halverson, E. R., Litts, B., Brahms, L., Jacobs-Priebe, L., & Owens, T. (2014). Learning in the Making: A Comparative Case Study of Three Makerspaces. *Harvard Educational Review*, *84*(4), 505–531. doi:10.17763/haer.84.4.brr34733723j648u

Valcke, B., Van Hiel, A., Van Assche, J., Van Roey, T., Onraet, E., & Roets, A. (2020). The Need for Inclusion: The relationships between Relational and Collective inclusion needs and psychological well- and ill-being. *European Journal of Social Psychology*, *50*(3), 579–596. doi:10.1002/ejsp.2641

Van den Broeck, A. (2010). Capturing autonomy, competence, and relatedness at work: Construction and initial validation of the Work-related Basic Need Satisfaction scale. *Journal of Occupational and Organizational Psychology*, *83*(4), 981–1002. doi:10.1348/096317909X481382

Wilczynski, V. (2015). Academic maker spaces and engineering design. In American Society for Engineering Education (Vol. 26, p. 1). doi:10.18260/p.23477

Williams, R. (2019). *To Know Us is to Love Us: Developing a Culture of Data-Informed Inclusivity.* https://makethedata.org/2019/12/06/to-know-us-is-to-love-us-developing-a-culture-of-data-informed-inclusivity/

Williams, R., & Klugh, E. (2017). Creating a University Driven "Ingepreneurial" Ecosystem in West Baltimore: A Strategy for Rust Belt Revitalization. *Metropolitan Universities Journal.*, *28*(2), 103–123. Advance online publication. doi:10.18060/21510

World Economic Forum. (2020). *The Reskilling Revolution: Better Skills, Better Jobs, Better Education for a Billion People by 2030.* https://www.weforum.org/press/2020/01/the-reskilling-revolution-better-skills-better-jobs-better-education-for-a-billion-people-by-2030/

ADDITIONAL READING

Avramchuk, A. S. (2017). Building Positive Organizational Communities: Communal Leadership at Work. *Graziadio Business Review*, 1-6.

Davis, A. M. L. (2018). Current Trends and Goals in the Development of Makerspaces at New England College and Research Libraries. *Information Technology and Libraries*, *37*(2), 94–117. doi:10.6017/ital.v37i2.9825

Ellinas, C., Allan, N., & Johansson, A. (2017). Dynamics of organizational culture: Individual Beliefs vs. Social Conformity. *PLoS One*, *12*(6), 1–20. doi:10.1371/journal.pone.0180193 PMID:28665960

Etzioni, A. (1996). The responsive Community: A Communitarian Perspective. *American Sociological Review*, *61*(1), 1–11. doi:10.2307/2096403

Lewis, H. (2015). *Organizational Learning: Individual Differences, Technologies and Impact of Teaching*. Nova Science Publishers, Inc.

O'Leary, M. (2018). Edelman Trust Barometer Measures World Trust Levels. *Information Today*, 14-15.

Oliver, K. (2016). Professional Development Considerations for Makerspace Leaders, Part Two: Addressing "How?". *TechTrends*, *60*(3), 211–217. doi:10.100711528-016-0050-7

Scheepers, D. S., Spears, R., Doosje, B., & Manstead, A. S. R. (2006). The Social Functions of Ingroup Bias: Creating, Confirming, or Changing Social Reality. *European Review of Social Psychology*, *17*(1), 359–396. doi:10.1080/10463280601088773

Stephens, M., & Ormandy, P. (2019). An Evidence-based Approach to Measuring Affective Domain Development. *Journal of Professional Nursing: Official Journal of the American Association of Colleges of Nursing*, *35*(3), 216–223.

Tonnies, F., & Loomis, C. P. (1957). *Community and Society.* Dover Publications, Inc.

Zakoth, D., & Mauroner, O. (2020). Industry-Specific Makerspaces: Opportunities for Collaboration and Open Innovation. *Management International / International Management / Gestión Internacional*, *24*(5), 88–99. https://doi-org.proxy-cs.researchport.umd.edu/10.7202/1075482ar

KEY TERMS AND DEFINITIONS

Affective Competence: Affective competence is the ability to effectively apply knowledge and use skills to establish and maintain psychologically and socially healthy relationships. In contrast to affective intelligence, which is the knowledge of principles, affective competence refers to the ability to apply those principles in a manner that is conducive to emotional safety and productivity.

Affective Learning Domain: The affective learning domain is one of three domains in which the process of awareness, familiarity, and mastery of information and process occurs. Learning is the process of intellectually receiving new information and may be applied as progress is made toward mastery. In contrast to the cognitive domain (knowledge) and psychomotor domain (skill), the affective learning domain is related to feelings, emotions, and psycho-social characteristics required for mentally healthy relationships.

Analytic Induction: Analytic induction is an epistemological approach to science based on an ideographic and anti-positivistic philosophical perspective. It is grounded in inductive reasoning and inferential thinking. Most often used by sociologists and those engaged in case or qualitative studies, the approach is effective for hypothesis generation and making extrapolating generalizations that make be tested by those practicing more nomothetic, positivistic approaches to science.

Innovation-Centric Organizational Community (IOC): IOC is an intra-organizational, inter-organizational, or trans-organizational group that experiences affiliation and acceptance to the extent that a sense of belonging exists based on perceived common values and beliefs. The primary characteristic of IOC is the common value of innovation. Innovation is based on ideation, strategy, incessant assessment, and organizational "double-loop" learning.

Makerspace: A makerspace is a community of creatives, technologists, and traditional tradespeople who come together to share tools and resources for innovation and production. The makerspace concept is heavily dependent on the value of share space and the democratization of access to tools.

Organizational Community: Organizational community is a group within a social organism bound by a sense of belongingness based on affiliation and acceptance.

Organizational Trust: Organizational trust is the willingness within a social organism to accept interdependence and mutual vulnerabilities. While most often used to refer to intra-organizational interdependence, it may also refer to inter-organizational or trans-organizational relationships.

Playful Ingenuity: Playful ingenuity is a term coined by researcher Martin Hewing to mean engagement in creativity without the emotional burden of production standards or expectations.

Relational Innovation: Relational innovation is the ability to find new ways of advancing collaborative, interpersonal engagement. Innovation is applied to human relationships through ideation, strategy, incessant assessment, and effective learning processes.

Social Belongingness: Social belongingness is the sense of affiliation and acceptance associated with interpersonal encounters. Belonging is an essential part of community building.

ENDNOTES

1. The United States Bureau of Labor Statistic 2021 data reveals that full-time Black workers typically earn over 21% less than the average full-time employed White worker (https://www.bls.gov/news.release/wkyeng.t03.htm).
2. The United States Bureau of Labor Statistic 2021 data reveals that Black workers constitute 4.8% of those employed in computers and electronic products manufacturing compared to 68.8% employment by White workers (https://www.bls.gov/cps/cpsaat18.htm).
3. The "makerspace movement" is a philosophical and practical attempt to increase access to tools and the means of production. Increasing the availability of the means of production is viewed as a catalyst to entrepreneurship and a stimulus for positive economic mobility.
4. Find additional information about the Open Works transition into a post-pandemic sustainability and growth model at https://www.openworksbmore.org/
5. An opportunity to engage in playful ingenuity and the provision of space is facilitated by organizational ingenuity as described by Lampel, Joseph & Honig, Benson & Drori, Israel. (2014).
6. Economists struggled to quantify the impact of the growing number of temporary, contractual, nontraditional workers (i.e., gig workers). IOC is inclusive of gig workers by their affiliation and acceptance, regardless of the time associated with the sense of belonging.

Chapter 4
Promoting an Ecosystem Approach for Inclusive and Sustainable Entrepreneurship in Underserved Communities

Aisha Ismail
https://orcid.org/0000-0003-4458-4311
University of the Punjab, Lahore, Pakistan

Sadia Farooq
University of the Punjab, Lahore, Pakistan

JoAnn D. Rolle
Medgar Evers College, City University of New York, USA

ABSTRACT

Rapidly changing business environments and the use of inclusive systems have magnified the emerging concept of "ecosystem" for the businesses. The need of ecosystem is further amplified for entrepreneurs working in underserved marginalized communities where networks and collaborations can play a catalyst for an inclusive future characterized by sustainable business and social uplift. Underserved communities have significant potential of entrepreneurship which can be explored by being active part of the ecosystem. This chapter focuses on the need of ecosystem approach for underserved community. The chapter presents an explanation of business ecosystem, identification of key actors and their roles in the ecosystem, and the relationship among various actors. The significance of inclusive future of work and entrepreneurship for the underserved has been highlighted through a case study findings. Furthermore, the chapter presents recommendations for the government, regulators, policymakers, the supporting institutions, small business and entrepreneurs in the underserved, and academicians.

DOI: 10.4018/978-1-6684-4322-4.ch004

INTRODUCTION

The recent pandemic wave has intensified income disparities in economies over the globe. Such disparities are further magnified in the economies with a large proportion of the underserved or marginalized population. Most of the countries in the world have faced disruptions in their economic, financial and social systems, resulting in both short-term and long-term consequences. These consequences are pretty severe for underserved communities that are in dire need of a sustainable solution for their livelihood. Entrepreneurs belonging to these underserved communities face challenges in accessing and using the resources[1]. These challenges can be converted into opportunities with a holistic approach of taking all stakeholders on board. For an equitable and inclusive society, there is a need to collaborate and develop fruitful networks to implement strategies effectively. A sustainable and more inclusive community will bring the underserved and marginalized segment into the mainstream and help them prepare for the technological changes that have become central to the businesses globally. Various challenges of the post-COVID era have transformed the future of work and entrepreneurship in underserved communities. An inclusive approach to businesses can help entrepreneurs and women in underserved communities attain sustainability. Therefore, there is a need for a business ecosystem approach for entrepreneurs working in underserved/marginalized communities where networks and collaborations can play a catalyst for an inclusive future characterized by sustainable business and social uplift. Women in underserved communities have significant potential for entrepreneurship which can be explored by being an active part of the ecosystem. To encourage the participation of such communities, a close collaboration among all the actors of the ecosystem is essential.

This chapter focuses on the networks of ecosystem actors and how these networks can be strengthened to make them more effective and efficient for women entrepreneurs in underserved communities. The chapter elaborates how collaboration in an ecosystem approach can offer a sustainable competitive advantage for future endeavors and promote sustainable growth, creativity, and innovation. The chapter also includes an explanation of the business ecosystem, identification of key actors and their roles in the ecosystem, and the relationship among various actors by exemplifying the ecosystem of microfinance in Pakistan for which underserved communities are the target group and have a huge potential of entrepreneurial activities if provided with financial access. The chapter further elaborates on the inter-connectedness of the ecosystem with its macro-environment based on how resources are circulated within and among the networks (internal and external). Furthermore, the chapter presents recommendations for actors, policymakers, and academicians to understand and use the ecosystem perspective in underserved communities.

BACKGROUND

The introductory chapter of the book has defined underserved communities in detail. An underserved community is a community of neglected people who face systemic neglect, racism, and structural barriers. Such a community fails to avail equal economic opportunities compared to their counterparts. Typically an underserved community has more people having low income, more women, tribal groups, and more people of color. Similarly, small businesses/ small entrepreneurs in the underserved communities traditionally face barriers to access credit, capital, and other resources necessary to grow[2]. Such communities are usually located in rural areas with more people of color, women, low income, and others.

Similar to Wang (2021), the underserved community in this chapter is defined through two dimensions. The first dimension covers gender inequality and women-owned businesses; in such a population, the disparities across gender groups adversely affect women's social, economic, and political advancement through entrepreneurship. Second, it refers to small women entrepreneurs in geographic areas with high unemployment rates, poverty, and lack of resources for entrepreneurship. Therefore, for this chapter, underserved community means the low-income group of the economy, especially women who face barriers in accessing resources like finances, education, health, shelter, etc., because of geographic location, religion, gendered identity, ethnicity, and racial population[3]. More specifically, it is the population of small women-owned businesses that covers a large proportion of the population in developing economies. Such women are small entrepreneurs who run domestic businesses and are in need of small loans that can help them in either starting or expanding their businesses.

For an inclusive future work and entrepreneurship in the post-COVID era, low-income women entrepreneurs in underserved communities can provide successful outcomes by becoming an active part of the main economic stream. The ecosystem approach will help women entrepreneurs come out of the vicious circle of poverty, improve their living standards, and positively contribute to economic growth through their income-generating activities. Women entrepreneurs, an underserved community, face many challenges that are somewhat directly linked with their financial health. For stronger community development, inequality gaps (based on income, gender identity, etc.) need to be minimized by providing a level playing field, maximizing women participation, and scaling up the social and financial capital networks that provide the foundation for inclusive work and entrepreneurship. A key concern of researchers regarding the future of entrepreneurial innovation and technology adoption for the underserved is capacity building. There is a need to create synergies for entrepreneurial activities in underserved by connecting various industry players at micro, meso and macro levels[4]. Therefore, collaborations among different players in a business ecosystem can help women entrepreneurs in underserved to sustain, grow and reduce inequalities. In the post-COVID era, for underserved economies to jump towards prosperity; a must ingredient is entrepreneurial activity supported through technology.

Financially Underserved Women Entrepreneurs

Women entrepreneurs in the underserved community face a crucial challenge of accessing small loans for their business setups; such group is referred to as financially underserved people. Common barriers for underserved women entrepreneurs include the inability to access finance, small loans with high-interest rates, and greater scrutiny requirements from financial institutions. These barriers result in underfunded business, limited growth, and a reduced likelihood of business success. Women entrepreneurs face gender disparities in terms of cultural, social, and legal barriers to participate in the financial system over the globe. In a few areas of the world, this gender disparity gap for women is huge.

According to CARE[5] international statistics, approximately 80% of women-owned businesses are either un-served or underserved for their credit needs, which create a financial gap of $1.7 trillion. Another report by CARE states that the majority of the poorest people in the world, particularly women, are financially excluded. These underserved women own small household-level businesses and participate in the economy through income-generating activities. The discrimination in accessing resources in the economy forces women to work in informal, low-income jobs and limited access to financial and non-financial services. Women entrepreneurs around the world are effectively utilizing small business opportunities to support their families and create job opportunities for the other members of the society, but approximately 70% of these are underserved by financial institutions. If these women are provided with financial access, they can benefit economies through their entrepreneurial skills. The Asia Pacific region accounts for 50 million women-owned small and medium businesses that provide employment opportunities to over 100 million people. This contribution of underserved women entrepreneurs can be increased exponentially if they are provided with equal resources. The proportion of underserved women has a recent jump because of the current pandemic wave over the globe. In most developing countries, women-owned businesses have been impacted disproportionately compared to men-owned businesses. This impact is even magnified in the absence of financial access for small businesses. The microfinance sector has tried to address the financing challenge of small businesses along with the formal financial sector, but still, there is a long way to go.

Microfinance institutions are popularly known for providing small loans to underserved low-income entrepreneurs lacking access to traditional financial services. By providing a wide range of financial and non-financial services for the underserved women entrepreneurs, microfinance can prove itself as an entry point for inclusive work and entrepreneurship. Post-COVID era is posing new challenges of limited access to finance, markets, networks, and gender-specific barriers to the sustainability of women-owned businesses. These challenges can be addressed through an inclusive future work and entrepreneurship. The underserved communities have significant potential for entrepreneurship which can be explored by being an active part of the ecosystem. To encourage the participation of such communities, close collaboration among all the actors of the ecosystem is essential. Such partnerships serve as a sustainable competitive advantage for future endeavors to promote sustainable growth, creativity, and innovation.

Need of an Ecosystem Perspective for an Inclusive and Sustainable Entrepreneurship in Underserved Communities

Despite being underserved, the inclusive approach to future work and entrepreneurship can unleash the hidden potential of people in such communities. Underserved women entrepreneurs can effectively manage their business activities in the current era of the pandemic by developing active links and networks. With active and stronger networks in a system, the survival of small businesses is easier even in the presence of a COVID-like pandemic. The presence of social capital, industry linkages, and collaborations among various community members can help in the survival of small businesses. It is difficult for businesses, especially small entrepreneurs, to survive alone in this rapidly transforming business environment. There is a need to work in a collaborative way where all players of the industry work toward a shared objective. This collaborative approach is becoming prominent in the current era where businesses are moving from standalone strategies toward a holistic approach by using an ecosystem perspective.

The business ecosystem is a term coined from the biological ecosystem; it refers to a network of actors that affect and are affected by each other's activities. For sustainable and inclusive entrepreneurship, there is a need to identify an ecosystem around underserved women entrepreneurs, key players, unique roles, and the presence of symbiotic relationships to manage the resources accordingly. If economies want to reduce the proportion of the underserved population, they have to use an ecosystem perspective where all stakeholders join hands to benefit the whole system. Devising strategies for a single player in a standalone scenario will not work for entrepreneurs in underserved communities.

The ecosystem perspective provides a holistic view of business networks, relationships among actors, interactions, and exchange of various resources (Hakala, O'Shea, Farny, & Luoto, 2020); therefore, it can help in formulating the right strategies for an inclusive future of work and entrepreneurship in underserved. If actors in an ecosystem are aware of their roles, relationships, and inter-connectedness, they can better utilize resources even in uncertain situations. This need for an ecosystem approach becomes critical for the women entrepreneurs working in underserved communities because they are deprived of resources in terms of finances, networks, knowledge, and skills. Therefore, if such underserved women entrepreneurs connect themselves through an ecosystem approach, they can better address the scarcity of resources through sharing and interactions in a productive way. The existing exacerbated disparity in various sectors of economies is leading to various social, economic, and technological challenges for the underserved. Hence, an ecosystem perspective will be a key step for a growing and sustainable, inclusive society globally.

Financially underserved women entrepreneurs are facing challenges of financial access over the globe. Although the percentage of women entrepreneurs has increased worldwide, still a majority of these women-owned businesses are restricted to micro and small business segments because of limited support of ecosystem to access finance, networks, and market linkages (Maheshwari, Gokhale, Agarwal, Makena, & Borthakur, 2019). Therefore, an inclusive approach for women entrepreneurs in the underserved will give value and voice to the most vulnerable people in society (Shahnaz, 2021).

COLLABORATIONS AND ECOSYSTEM NEED FOR SUSTAINABLE ENTREPRENEURSHIP IN UNDERSERVED COMMUNITIES

The critical part of the ecosystem approach is to identify key players, their roles and relationships, collaborations among players, and the environment so that strategies can be formulated accordingly (Marr & Tubaro, 2012; Purkayastha, Tripathy, & Das, 2020). Moreover, it is also important to explore the ecosystem and its dynamic because the actors in the ecosystem facilitate, intermediate, interact, create connections, institutionalize, and promote investment (Armstrong, Ahsan, & Sundaramurthy, 2018; Roose & Bishnoi, 2012). Apart from key players, the functioning of actors is also dependent on contextual factors, including policy, media, regulations, economic, social, and cultural conditions, administrative structure, geographic position, infrastructure, and Government support (Ledgerwood & Gibson, 2013; Purkayastha et al., 2020).

A significant contribution of the ecosystem perspective is the exploration of collaborations and interconnections, which indicate the relationships and flow of resources within an ecosystem. The interactions within an ecosystem may be cooperative and competitive because there is a co-opetition among the players in terms of exchanging knowledge, resources, and products and services (Mäkinen & Dedehayir, 2012). Moreover, it is also important for players to know the existing and expected relationships and collaborations to position themselves accordingly. Such partnerships among ecosystem players can help economies to serve the underprivileged populations with a joint effort with efficient utilization of resources at micro, meso, and macro levels. Knowing their place and roles in an ecosystem, the players need to re-engineer their processes to better serve the underserved community (Maity, Rakshit, & Ghosh, 2016). Such re-engineering of processes will help players to adopt the technological changes with the support of other players in the ecosystem.

Ecosystem Perspective for Sustainable Entrepreneurship in Underserved: A Case Study from Pakistan Microfinance Industry

This section highlights the collaborations and ecosystem needed for the growth and sustainability of small women entrepreneurs' businesses in underserved communities with the help of a case study on the "Microfinance industry of Pakistan." It further elaborates various recommendations for policymakers, small businesses and women entrepreneurs, organizations supporting underserved communities, apex institutions, government, regulators, and the other associated actors with underserved in an ecosystem. The case study is based on a qualitative research approach to explore the microfinance ecosystem in Pakistan serving one of the significant portions of the underserved community, i.e., small women-owned businesses. Based on interviews with key respondents, an ecosystem is mapped, and recommendations are various actors of the ecosystem have been presented. This identification of the ecosystem around "underserved women entrepreneurs" is critical for policymakers and other players to understand the roles and relationships among actors and develop the right strategies for the sector and target group (micro and small businesses) in the challenging environment.

In Pakistan, the microfinance industry is striving hard to serve the financially underserved people, which encompass a large proportion of the population. In order to meet the financing needs of its target group (mainly women businesses at the micro-level) industry needs a joint effort from all the players. Microfinance Providers playing an essential role in meeting the needs of underserved women entrepreneurs in Pakistan are in dire need of adopting an ecosystem framework (Ismail, Farooq, & Ahmed, 2020). Therefore, by targeting a large customer base of underserved people (specifically small women-owned businesses), the microfinance industry in Pakistan can create effective links among players to create synergies and manage uncertain situations like COVID. Although Pakistan is rated among the top industries in terms of growth, outreach, regulations, and controls6 yet its participation to lend financially underserved women is low. Women entrepreneurs in Pakistan have to struggle for loans to start and sustain their businesses because of discriminatory lending. Despite being a progressive microfinance environment in Pakistan, women entrepreneurs are not getting similar opportunities as their counterparts. Pakistan can prove itself as a global leader in microfinance by increasing its financial outreach to women (Haq & Safavian, 2013), and this is possible with an inclusive approach to the ecosystem.

Table 1. The microfinance industry in Pakistan; an overview

The microfinance industry in Pakistan; an overview
The microfinance industry showed a 24% growth over five years, i.e., 2.4 million borrowers in 2013 rise to 7.4 million active borrowers in 2018, out of which 3.8 million borrowers are women[7]. With such rapid growth, microfinance providers are serving poor clients in more than135 districts of Pakistan, with 4,230 branches lending 51% to women borrowers[8]. Most of the microfinance providers support micro and small businesses owned by women majority of which are working in rural areas. Although microfinance providers are addressing the financing needs of women entrepreneurs almost on an equal basis, but there is still a huge gap between the supply of microfinance and demand. Considering the significance of women entrepreneurs for economic growth, policymakers in Pakistan are recognizing that supporting women entrepreneurs who want to start a business or expand their existing business can be a key driver of job creation in the country. Therefore, the microfinance industry can play a pivotal role for the growth of these businesses, supporting the bulk of micro, small and medium enterprises in Pakistan and creating job opportunities for millions of underserved people. An estimate indicates that Pakistan's economy needs 1.5 to 2.5 million[9] annual jobs to meet the needs of the population, where entrepreneurship can be a key contributor to job creation, especially for women.

Table 1. presents an overview of the microfinance industry in Pakistan. The microfinance industry can play a significant role in meeting development goals, and realizing this fact; the Government has taken the microfinance industry as a critical partner in the national financial inclusion strategy. Being a key participant of national financial inclusion strategy, the microfinance sector needs effective strategies to meet the set targets. Hence, a holistic effort from the whole industry is required. In such a situation, understanding the ecosystem around its various players, their roles, and dynamics is inevitable for the microfinance industry to potentially address the financial needs of underserved people at the bottom of the pyramid.

Table 2. The microfinance ecosystem for underserved in Pakistan (Explored through qualitative study)

Microfinance Ecosystem for Underserved in Pakistan (Explored through qualitative study)
"Underserved and marginalized community" is central to the microfinance ecosystem in Pakistan. A major proportion of this underserved community comprises women who are micro-entrepreneurs who need finances either to start or to expand their businesses. Based on interviews with key informants of the industry following are the elements of the microfinance ecosystem: *"microfinance ecosystem comprises of borrowers, microfinance providers, competitors, the regulators, Government-bodies, industry-association, infrastructure that includes the technological support and payment-gateways, it also includes agent-based repayment and disbursement system, the credit information bureau and somehow the media and informal lenders that also affect microfinance working" (one of the respondents)* Based on a thematic analysis of the interviews, key elements of the microfinance ecosystem include: Clients (financially underserved communities who need microfinance and are financially excluded by commercial banks), the Government, microfinance providers (microfinance banks, microfinance intuitions, and rural support programs), credit information bureaus, wholesale lenders, regulators, industry network/association, commercial banks, technology-providers, government-bodies, national and international donor, educational institutions, insurance companies, media partners, informal lenders, rating agencies, complementary organizations, social groups in the community, training agencies, industry infrastructure, other intermediaries, payment and disbursement system, branchless-banking agents, and all others who directly or indirectly support core activities of microfinance. These are not the full and final elements and players of the microfinance ecosystem because, with the maturity of the industry and the involvement of multiple industries, the players enter and leave the ecosystem; hence, this list of elements keeps on changing.

The microfinance ecosystem in Pakistan is in its evolutionary stage as new players are entering the industry with the changes in technology and innovative products for the industry. Table 2. explains the microfinance ecosystem in Pakistan. The identified industry players have collaborations for mutual benefit; these collaborations and interactions could be more useful if established in the right way. Although industry players are sharing financial, intellectual, or informational resources to create synergies they still need to establish new relationships to meet the increasing demand for finances for the underserved community. The need for new collaborations and interactions in the industry is intensified with emerging trends and technological advancements; the players can learn from each other instead of standalone practices. Furthermore, interactions among various players of the ecosystem can help them in sharing resources for new and tailored products for underserved women entrepreneurs.

An ecosystem supports the players in many ways to perform the core operations by providing support in terms of resource mobilization, establishing strategic partnerships, funding, technical assistance, crisis management, coordination and control, supervision, capacity building of the players, networking, operational and technical support, technical and operational support, advocating interest of players, client protection rules and many others. Such functions can better support the players if there is an ecosystem in place and the players are aware of their roles, positions, and functions in the system. Moreover, the ecosystem approach can play a catalyst in achieving a sustainable solution for the underserved. If there is a collaboration between microfinance providers, government, regulators, credit information bureau, wholesale funds providers, technology partners, and the clients (underserved women entrepreneurs). In that case, it will be easier to meet the financial needs of the underserved and to adopt emerging technology.

Moreover, the findings of the study highlighted the fact that the ecosystem approach has helped the microfinance industry to survive in the COVID and post COVID era. The collaboration between government and industry players has helped to disburse funds at the grass-root level with an already established network of microfinance providers in an underserved community. Figure 1 shows the flow of various resources among players in the microfinance ecosystem in Pakistan. The different colors of arrows indicate a different resource. For example, black color is used to show the flow of financial resources between players; similarly, red dotted lines indicate the missing relationships among players. A double-sided arrow indicates a two-way flow of resources, while a single-headed arrow represents a one-way flow of resources among players.

Figure 1. Microfinance ecosystem in Pakistan
Source: (Ismail & Farooq, 2021)

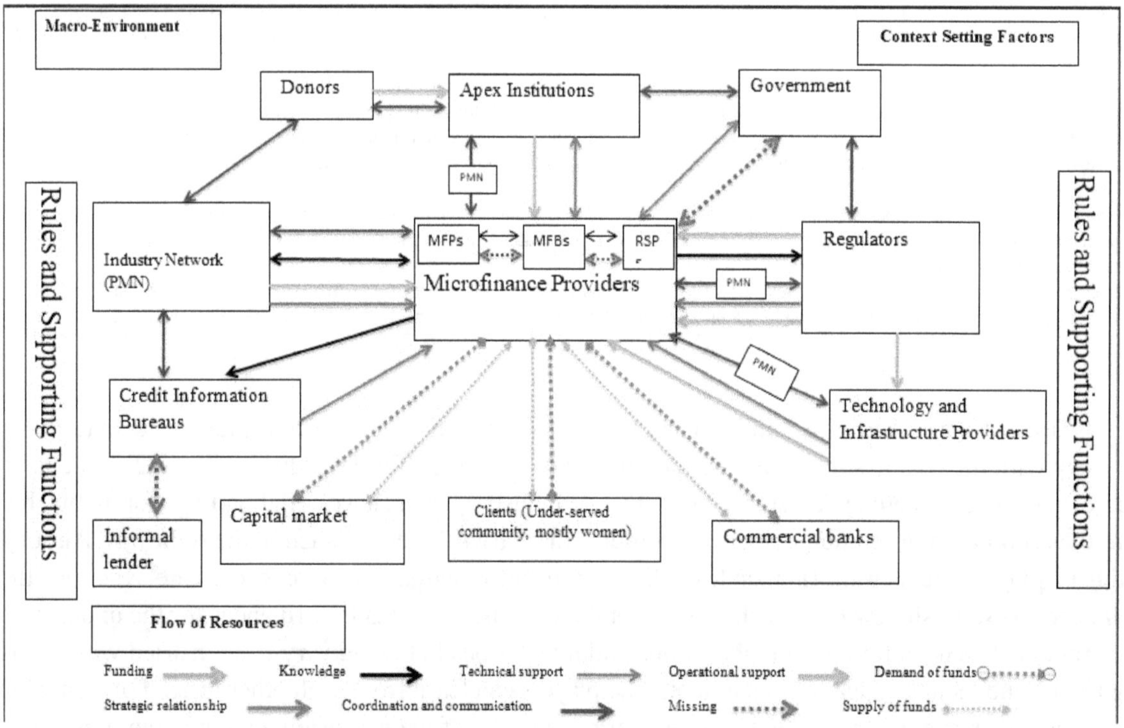

The above discussion on business ecosystem concept, its significance for underserved communities and especially for microfinance industry has raised following questions to be answered:

- Why the identification of the ecosystem players and their relationships is important?
- How the use of ecosystem perspective can help different players to improve their working and formulating effective strategies?

- How the identification of relationships among ecosystem players can help them in gauging the resources flow and to establish right collaborations?
- What could be the potential collaborations among ecosystem players to better serve the target group?
- How ecosystem players can join hands to create value for the whole system?

The recommendations section of the chapter answers the above mentioned questions.

RECOMMENDATIONS

This section presents the recommendations for various industry players for the development of the ecosystem and collaborations for sustainable entrepreneurship in the underserved community of women entrepreneurs. Based on the findings of the study conducted on the microfinance industry of Pakistan and the flow of resources among various players in Figure 1, the following are recommendations for government and policymakers, regulators, apex institutions, credit information bureaus, microfinance providers, industry association, facilitators, and for academia. These recommendations can help industry players to better utilize the available resources and to develop sustainable entrepreneurial opportunities for underserved.

Recommendations for Government, Regulators and Policy Makers

Among various stakeholders of any ecosystem, the government, regulators, and policymakers are the key ones. The role of the government and policymakers is significant for the working of any industry. The support and interventions by the government are critical for ecosystem functioning. Among various government functions, maintaining macroeconomic stability and providing an enabling environment is the prime function (Abed, 2006).

The role of the government and policymakers is pivotal institutional support and to device favorable policy for the promotion of specific sectors or specific groups. In most developing countries, microenterprises dominate the market; therefore, most of the entrepreneurship interventions by the government are focused on this group[10]. In order to reduce the financial constraint of underserved women-owned entrepreneurship, the focused intervention areas by the government include empowerment, business startup support, expansion support, micro-loans on easy terms, strengthening linkages and networks in the industry, and specialized programs (Buvinić & Furst-Nichols, 2016; Vossenberg, 2013). Other important functions performed by the government and rule makers for the underserved community are stabilizing macroeconomic-environment, providing legal and regulatory support, transferring resources, inducing special credit schemes, enforcing consumer protection laws, and enhancing supervisory capacity to strengthen the institutions (Abed, 2006; Duflos & Imboden, 2004; Ehrbeck, Pickens, & Tarazi, 2012). All these direct and indirect interventions by the government indicate how important is the role of the government in promoting resource access for the underserved.

Another important pillar of an ecosystem is the regulator; a well-regulated environment is necessary for an efficient and risk-free working of the players. The key function of regulators is to formulate rules and regulations for the working of various players. Ledgerwood and Gibson (2013) highlighted the significance of a regulatory framework for the development of industry infrastructure, a competitive environment, and the development of products are services and defining formal and informal rules. Regulations provide direction to the players to work for the benefit of the whole ecosystem. The regulations and formal rules are significant for the underserved community because these regulations help them to work in a safe environment with less exploitation and less fear of market failure. If there is an ecosystem in place, it can bring positive and friendly regulations for the players to work more confidently. The key functions of regulators include the promotion of a regulated environment, safety against various risks, unified access to resources, enhancing industry stability, strengthening industry infrastructure, improving transparency, and defining rules for new entrants (Ali, 2015; Ledgerwood, Earne, & Nelson, 2013; Ledgerwood & Gibson, 2013; Purkayastha et al., 2020). Therefore, regulators are the key players who can contribute to devising effective strategies for promoting entrepreneurship in the underserved. A well-regulated environment can become a key driver for the underserved women entrepreneurs by boosting their confidence to work, improving financial access and, to safeguard them in times of uncertainties and pandemics.

Table 3. Role of the Government, regulators, and policymakers to support underserved micro-women entrepreneurs in Pakistan

Role of the Government, regulators and policy makers to support underserved micro-women entrepreneurs in Pakistan
The efforts of Pakistan's microfinance industry have been recognized globally in terms of its regulatory environment, development of industry infrastructure, and supervisory initiatives that are backed by the Government. The industry association has highlighted the following initiatives for the microfinance industry backed by the Government and regulators: Introduction of branch-less banking, digital-payment system, M-wallets, E-money institutions, and biometric-verification, the introduction of consumer protection laws, customer-grievances mechanism, regulations for E-money institutions, establishing private credit bureau, introducing of AML/CFT framework, the establishment of the deposit-protection company, collaboration with international donors, introducing credit-lines for women and marginalized farmers, interest-free loan for youth, low-cost housing schemes, establishing investment company and, facilitating micro-enterprise-financing[11]. The findings of the study conducted in Pakistan on the microfinance ecosystem revealed that the Government and policymakers are actively participating in the growth of underserved women-owned micro-businesses through the microfinance industry. The significant supporting functions of the Government include infrastructure development, capacity building, funding facilities, resources mobilization, and crisis management policies for the microfinance industry, which provides financial access to underserved women entrepreneurs (Ismail et al., 2020). The findings also indicate the keen interest of the Government and regulators in promoting underserved women entrepreneurs through a combined effort of industry players, including regulators, apex institutions, the industry association, and infrastructure collaborations. The role of the regulator has been very supportive for the microfinance providers and their clients (underserved women entrepreneurs) in the COVID period; the regulator softened their regulations and supported the industry to survive in the post-COVID era.

According to Table 3 role of the Government, regulators, and policymakers is significant in promoting an inclusive future of work and entrepreneurship in underserved. Based on the findings of the study following are the recommendations for the Governments, regulators, and policymakers:

The Government and policymakers should understand various players' significance, roles, collaborations, and interactions to device the policies accordingly. For example, in focusing on financially underserved women-owned micro-business, the Government must know the necessary collaborations with various industries and players to enhance financial access to these underserved. Another area of focus for the Government, regulators, and policymakers is the prioritization of the "underserved" and the industry they are working in. This prioritization will lead to the formulation of focused and targeted policies. For example, there could be subsidized lending and special credit lines for financially marginalized women entrepreneurs to help them to start or expand their micro-businesses. Moreover, the

Government can also prioritize the industry that is directly linked with underserved communities. For example, the Government can support the microfinance industry by opening more funding avenues and supportive policies to promote the financing of microfinance clients. This could be an indirect contribution of the Government to promote entrepreneurial activities in the underserved, which is possible if the Government joins hands with other players i.e., use of ecosystem perspective and an inclusive approach.

The Government, regulators, and policymakers can contribute to the ecosystem through supportive policies and funding initiatives to help other players. For example, in the microfinance ecosystem, the Government can help microfinance providers to increase their customer base and outreach by providing them funding support on a priority basis. Such support can indirectly fulfill the financing needs of underserved communities through microfinance institutions. Furthermore, the Government and the regulators can play their role in inviting various stakeholders from the ecosystem to discuss issues and challenges. Such discussions can help in devising relevant policies considering the issues of players.

The role of the regulator in formulating strategies is more critical because of technological advancements over the globe. Regulators must consider various players, their roles, and interlinked industries while deciding on the regulations. For example, with the increased use of technology in the microfinance industry, new players are entering the ecosystem, new products are emerging, and there is a need for related regulations that can better safeguard the interest of all stakeholders. Furthermore, regulators can help industry players to build their capacity by arranging the right collaborations and training; such collaborations can be established if the regulators are well aware of ecosystem players and their positions. For example, the regulators in the microfinance ecosystem can devise effective policies and regulations for women entrepreneurs, arrange specific training and help in creating industry linkages to adopt technology-based business models. Moreover, the regulators can introduce flexible regulations for new players to enhance industry capacity. For example, the microfinance industry needs flexible regulations for the entry of new players so that the industry can meet the targets of reaching a large population of underserved with more players and funding solutions.

Table 4. Supporting institutions in the microfinance ecosystem for underserved women in Pakistan

Supporting institutions in microfinance ecosystem for Underserved women in Pakistan
Building upon the findings of the case study “Microfinance ecosystem in Pakistan”, the institutions supporting financially underserved women include microfinance providers, the apex, industry associations, technological partners, credit information bureaus, investors or donors, and all others who are linked with underserved women entrepreneurs. Microfinance providers, including microfinance banks, microfinance institutions, and rural support programs, are the supporting women through small loans to start or expand their businesses. These institutions are performing core functions through their financial and non-financial products for women entrepreneurs and helping them to become a part of the financial system (Ismail et al., 2020). Most of these microfinance providers are women-focused, and few have a 100% lending to women. It shows its focus on serving underserved women. Microfinance providers can increase their outreach to the underserved women’s community through collaborations with other players of the ecosystem. The other supporting institution is the apex, the wholesale fund provider in the microfinance industry of Pakistan. The Apex institution support industry and various players through their wholesale lending products, technical and operational support, and establishing collaborations with national and international donor (Ismail et al., 2020; Levy, 2002; Millis, Perez-Timermans, & Sakurai, 2018). Their major role is to meet the funding challenge of industry players. Another key supporting institution for the underserved in the microfinance ecosystem is the industry association. Industry association plays an important role in creating linkages among various players, disseminating information on various industry matters, and advocating industry issues (Ismail et al., 2020). Other players who support the functioning of the microfinance industry are credit information bureaus, national and internal donors, technology partners, and investors. These players provide technical and operational support to meet the financial needs of underserved women in Pakistan.

Recommendations for the Institutions Supporting Underserved Community

While taking an ecosystem perspective, the supporting institutions and organizations play a significant role in an underserved community. These supporting institutions are directly or indirectly linked with underserved communities for providing resources. The role of supporting institutions is critical for the smooth functioning of entrepreneurial activities of financially underserved women (Beriso, 2021; Kazumi & Kawai, 2017).

Table 4. presents the supporting institutions working in Pakistan to support the underserved. Based on the findings of the case study on the "microfinance ecosystem in Pakistan", the following are the recommendations for supporting institutions to promote entrepreneurship in underserved:

The resource providers, especially the providers of core services, should understand their clients' needs and provide need-based services. These tailored products and services can help resource providers to attain sustainability in their operations. Resource providers can establish collaborations with other industry players for efficient delivery of services and adopt technological advancements. These collaborations among industry players can create synergy for the players, and they meet the financial needs of underserved women in a more efficient way. Having cooperative relationship with other players, the resources can be pooled and utilized optimally. Similarly, the ecosystem approach also helps resource providers to use the expertise of other players in their work. Moreover, a joint effort from different players may also help resource providers mitigate risk and manage challenges with more specialized institutions instead of working alone. The ecosystem perspective can help resource providers to explore the relationship among ecosystem players; these relationships and collaborations assist them in gauging the flow of resources and device strategies accordingly.

The apex institutions working in an ecosystem for underserved can support resource providers and other players for their capacity building and funding needs. They need to develop interactions and collaborations to attract national and international donors for the industry to meet the financial needs of the underserved in a better way. The apex institutions can open new avenues for resource providers in the form of providing subsidized loans for technology adoption. These institutions can play a significant role in an ecosystem by supporting various players who are working for the unreserved community.

Industry associations also act as supporting institutions in an ecosystem; these institutions can act as an intermediary among various players to coordinate and communicate the issues. Such institutions can advocate the interest of industry players and act as industry voices at various forums; hence, they can contribute toward an inclusive approach to the underserved.

Other supporting institutions that can play their active role in an ecosystem for underserved include; the technical and operational resource providers, technological partners, donors, and investors. These institutions can join hands with other industry players to enhance their capacity and operational efficiency, digitize their operations and increase their outreach. Such institutions are becoming essential players in an ecosystem for the underserved because of technological advancements and the involvement of various industries in an ecosystem.

Recommendations for Small Businesses and Entrepreneurs in Underserved Communities

For sustainable entrepreneurship, small businesses and women entrepreneurs should understand the ecosystem around them, the key players, their roles, and relationships among various players. This understanding of the ecosystem will guide small businesses and women entrepreneurs to reach the right funding sources, establish effective collaborations, and sustain in the long run. An inclusive approach can help small businesses and women entrepreneurs to search for the right markets for their products and to enhance their business skills through relationships with other players. Moreover, the ecosystem approach can support small businesses and women entrepreneurs to meet the financial and other related challenges; these challenges can be converted into opportunities with productive collaborations.

Recommendations for Academia and Researchers

Academicians and researchers should work on small businesses and women entrepreneurs in underserved communities to identify their challenges specific to their context. This identification of challenges can help ecosystem players to formulate strategies accordingly. The researchers can become a voice for the underserved by highlighting the constraints they face in their businesses. With such an approach, researchers can put forward the issues of the underserved to the notice of concerned authorities, and a joint effort can be started for their good.

Summing up, the above-mentioned recommendation for various ecosystem players can help them know what they are doing and what they should do for the functioning of the system. A standalone strategy formulation from any of the above-mentioned players will not produce the desired results; players must put a joint effort toward the right and expected outcome.

FUTURE RESEARCH DIRECTIONS

Future research can be conducted to know the issues or the constraints the ecosystem players are facing in serving the underserved communities. Moreover, studies can be conducted to know the issues faced by small women entrepreneurs in reaching out to the financial and other resources and what alternatives they are forced to use. Researchers can also explore the use of technology and digitization for the various ecosystem players to efficiently utilize resources in underserved communities.

CONCLUSION

Underserved communities cover a large proportion of developing countries, and these communities have great potential for entrepreneurial activities. Such potential of underserved communities can be utilized through wise strategies; one of such strategies is the use of an inclusive approach, i.e., an ecosystem perspective. With the use of an inclusive approach, ecosystem players can better understand key players, their relationships, and the flow of resources and can develop effective collaborations to meet their goals. Moreover, micro-entrepreneurs working in underserved communities need a holistic effort from all relevant stakeholders to grow and sustain. Therefore, the future of work and entrepreneurship in underserved communities is the use of an inclusive approach.

REFERENCES

Abed, F. H. (2006). *Good practice guidelines for funders of microfinance*. Academic Press.

Ali, A. E. E. S. (2015). The regulatory and supervision framework of Microfinance in Kenya. *International Journal of Social Science Studies*, *3*, 123.

Armstrong, K., Ahsan, M., & Sundaramurthy, C. (2018). Microfinance ecosystem: How connectors, interactors, and institutionalizers co-create value. *Business Horizons*, *61*(1), 147–155. doi:10.1016/j.bushor.2017.09.014

Beriso, B. S. (2021). Determinants of economic achievement for women entrepreneurs in Ethiopia. *Journal of Innovation and Entrepreneurship*, *10*(1), 1–14. doi:10.118613731-020-00141-5

Buvinić, M., & Furst-Nichols, R. (2016). Promoting women's economic empowerment: What works? *The World Bank Research Observer*, *31*(1), 59–101.

Duflos, E., & Imboden, K. (2004). The role of governments in microfinance. Academic Press.

Ehrbeck, T., Pickens, M., & Tarazi, M. (2012). *Financially Inclusive Ecosystems: The roles of government today*. Academic Press.

Hakala, H., O'Shea, G., Farny, S., & Luoto, S. (2020). Re-storying the Business, Innovation and Entrepreneurial Ecosystem Concepts: The Model-Narrative Review Method. *International Journal of Management Reviews*, *22*(1), 10–32.

Haq, A., & Safavian, M. (2013). *Are Pakistan's Women Entrepreneurs Being Served by the Microfinance Sector?: Are They Being Served by the Microfinance Sector?* World Bank Publications.

Ismail, A., & Farooq, S. (2021). Business Ecosystem Framework for a Sustainable Microfinance Industry in Pakistan (PhD). University of the Punjab.

Ismail, A., Farooq, S., & Ahmed, Z. (2020). Understanding the Functions of Microfinance Ecosystem: A Perspective of Microfinance Providers in Pakistan. *Paradigms*, *14*(2), 50–64.

Kazumi, T., & Kawai, N. (2017). *Institutional support and women's entrepreneurial self-efficacy*. Asia Pacific Journal of Innovation and Entrepreneurship.

Ledgerwood, J., Earne, J., & Nelson, C. (2013). *The New Microfinance Handbook: A Financial Market System Perspective*. World Bank Publications. doi:10.1596/978-0-8213-8927-0

Ledgerwood, J., & Gibson, A. (2013). The evolving financial landscape. In J. E. J. Ledgerwood & C. Nelson (Eds.), *The New Microfinance Handbook: A Financial Market System Perspective* (pp. 15–48). World Bank Publications. doi:10.1596/9780821389270_CH01

Levy, F. (2002). *Apex institutions in microfinance*. Retrieved from https://www.cgap.org/sites/default/files/CGAP-Occasional-Paper-Apex-Institutions-in-Microfinance-Jan-2002.pdf

Maheshwari, P., Gokhale, A., Agarwal, N., Makena, A., & Borthakur, S. (2019). *The global landscape of gender lens investing*. Academic Press.

Maity, A. K., Rakshit, P., & Ghosh, C. S. (2016). *Shifting trends in the microfinance ecosystem.* Retrieved from PwC: https://www.pwc.in/publications/2016/shifting-trends-in-the-microfinance-ecosystem.html

Marr, A., & Tubaro, P. (2012). Global financial partnerships in microfinance: India, Peru and Tanzania. *Revista Iberoamericana de Estudios de Desarrollo, 1*(1), 28–57. doi:10.26754/ojs_ried/ijds.35

Millis, V., Perez-Timermans, B., & Sakurai, H. (2018). *Special Study-Credit Lines - Lending through financial intermediaries.* Retrieved from European Bank- United Kingdom file:///E:/Downloads/credit-lines.pdf

Purkayastha, D., Tripathy, T., & Das, B. (2020). Understanding the ecosystem of microfinance institutions in India. *Social Enterprise Journal, 16*(3), 243–261. doi:10.1108/SEJ-08-2019-0063

Roose, N., & Bishnoi, K. (2012). *Defining an Ecosystem for Social Finance* Master Dissertation. The FletcherSchool, TuftsUniversity.

Shahnaz, D. (2021). The Risks Not Taken: Building Inclusive Markets for Under-served Communities. In *Generation Impact.* Emerald Publishing Limited. doi:10.1108/978-1-78973-929-920200008

Vossenberg, S. (2013). Women Entrepreneurship Promotion in Developing Countries: What explains the gender gap in entrepreneurship and how to close it. *Maastricht School of Management Working Paper Series, 8*(1), 1-27.

ADDITIONAL READING

Crittenden, V. L., Crittenden, W. F., & Ajjan, H. (2019). Empowering women micro-entrepreneurs in emerging economies: The role of information communications technology. *Journal ofBusiness Research, 98*, 191–203. doi:10.1016/j.jbusres.2019.01.045

Hui, J., Toyama, K., Pal, J., & Dillahunt, T. (2018). Making a living my way: Necessity-driven entrepreneurship in resource-constrained communities. *Proceedings of the ACM on Human-Computer Interaction, 2*(CSCW), 1-24. 10.1145/3274340

Ismail, A., Farooq, S., & Ahmed, Z. (2020). Understanding the Functions of Microfinance Ecosystem: A Perspective of Microfinance Providers in Pakistan. *Paradigms, 14*(2), 50–64.

Armstrong, K., Ahsan, M., & Sundaramurthy, C. (2018). Microfinance ecosystem: How connectors, interactors, and institutionalizers co-create value. *Business Horizons, 61*(1), 147–155. doi:10.1016/j.bushor.2017.09.014

KEY TERMS AND DEFINITIONS

Business Ecosystem: A network of interconnected actors including suppliers, customers, distributors, government, competitors, and all other stakeholders who are together to create and share collective value.

Collaborations in an Ecosystem: Collaborations means arrangements among various actors of an ecosystem for mutual benefit through flow of resources.

Financially Under-Served Women-Owned Businesses: These are micro or small level businesses run by women in Under-served community with less or no financial access. These women face barriers to access finance through formal financial institutions.

Microfinance: Refers to provision of financial and non-financial services for the marginalized people who are financially excluded by the formal financial institutions. It includes a wide array of financial and non-financial services for poor.

Supporting Institutions: These are the institutions or organizations which are helping the core functions in an ecosystem.

Sustainability: Sustainability refers to the ability of a business to continue over a long period of time.

Under-Served Community: It is a community of marginalized people who are facing barriers in attaining the resources. These people face discrimination on the basis of gender, sex, ethnicity, culture etc. Majority of these include low-income group and more specifically small women-owned businesses.

ENDNOTES

1 Reaching Under-served small businesses - New Economy Initiative (neinsights.org)

2 https://www.igi-global.com/dictionary/Under-served-population/30907

3 https://www.lawinsider.com/dictionary/Under-served-populations

4 Three levels of inclusive financial system for microfinance defined by CGAP in a report" GOOD PRACTICE GUIDELINES FOR FUNDERS OF MICROFINANCE "in 2006

5 https://www.care-international.org/

6 The Economist Intelligence Unit (EIU). 2015. Global Microscope 2015: The enabling environment for financial inclusion. Sponsored by MIF/IDB, CAF, Accion and the Metlife Foundation. EIU, New York, NY

7 https://karandaaz.com.pk/wp-content/uploads/2019/12/Microfinance-Enterprise-Growth-Evidence-from-Pakistan-compressed.pdf

8 https://pmn.org.pk/wp-content/uploads/2020/11/PAKISTAN-MICROFINANCE-review-2019-10-12-Updated-Text-Oct-29.pdf

9 https://karandaaz.com.pk/wp-content/uploads/2019/12/Microfinance-Enterprise-Growth-Evidence-from-Pakistan-compressed.pdf

10 https://www.brookings.edu/blog/future-development/2020/09/16/what-types-of-interventions-promote-womens-entrepreneurship/

11 Pakistan Microfinance Reviews 2014-2019 by Pakistan Microfinance Network

Section 2

Sociodemographic Entrepreneurship

Chapter 5
Successfully Starting and Growing Black Businesses:
For Entrepreneurs and Educators

Micah E. S. Crump
Medgar Evers College, City University of New York, USA

ABSTRACT

This chapter helps define the state of Black entrepreneurship in the United States using knowledge from business, management, entrepreneurship, sociology, and economic literature. Challenges and opportunities are laid out for Black entrepreneurs to aid their success in starting and growing new businesses particularly in a post-pandemic world. Nuanced differences in Black business formalization, social networks, entrepreneurial financing, opportunity recognition, strategic planning, STEM foundation, and customer discovery and validation processes are each addressed in how they can help improve Black entrepreneurship and business ownership outcomes. Seven specific recommendations are provided and explained along with a checklist to aid primarily Black entrepreneurs to start and grow their new businesses. The chapter content can serve as a foundation for undergraduate and master's degree program Black entrepreneurship courses, and along with its reading list, as a doctoral seminar course on Black entrepreneurship.

INTRODUCTION

"Time is a most precious and limited resource that black entrepreneurs spend." David White, Queens Chamber of Commerce, New York, USA

Most people are provided 8,760 hours each year of their entire lives, and most have full discretion on how they spend their hours. But for many who struggle economically, this discretion is drastically limited. The COVID-19 pandemic at the time of writing this chapter remains particularly hard on members of the black population in the United States. Consequently, black people spend disproportionately more of their time post-pandemic than others attempting to garner economic resources to increase their economic

DOI: 10.4018/978-1-6684-4322-4.ch005

and social standings. Studies around the world repeatedly show that higher portions of black populations relative to other racial and ethnic groups actively engage in entrepreneurial activities for basic subsistence reasons. Partly owing to systemic forces such as disparate treatment of black businesses based on race, restricted access to capital, lower household assets, higher unemployment rates, lower education rates, and others, the many hours spent too often produce quantitatively and qualitatively less favorable business outcomes for these black entrepreneurs. As a result, fewer of these black entrepreneurs actually become successful and registered business owners in the United States relative to other groups.

Fortunately, some of this underrepresentation of black business ownership diminishes when the informal economy is factored into consideration. Members of all racial and ethnic groups operate in both the *formal* and the *informal* economy. Recent research suggests that once both economies are considered together, the sum of entrepreneurship rates of blacks drastically increase and likely surpass all other groups. Similarly, actual rates of black business ownership and entrepreneurship in Africa, the Caribbean, the United Kingdom, South America, and other places around the globe are likely understated.

Because the bulk of national data on entrepreneurship and business primarily reflect formal economic activity, much of black entrepreneurship remains hidden and under the radar. The hidden nature of these activities creates micro-economic and macro-economic distortions. Many otherwise successful black entrepreneurs and business owners who happen to operate in the informal economy create levels of credit worthiness, entrepreneurial experience, and business transactions that remain untraceable and unmeasurable. Yet, many of them cannot deploy or leverage these assets to generate capital and other critical resources when needed because of the hidden and undocumented state of those assets. To prospective business partners and other stakeholders, any perception that the assets do not exist is actually a distortion. When such distortions remain unchecked and uncorrected, negative consequences ensue which include prospective customers, suppliers, partners, and investors foregoing opportunities that would otherwise be provided by these types of black businesses and entrepreneurs. Additionally, policymakers, government officials, and funding institutions inadvertently divert resources elsewhere given a false premise that black populations yield comparatively lower entrepreneurial outputs and assets.

History shows that black communities are highly innovative and resourceful at solving pervasive and enduring societal problems. Members of the black population, and black women in particular, view problems and solutions from unique lenses of which society has yet to optimally capitalize. Their novel perspectives are viewed as invaluable to too few organizations. One of the major mobile phone carriers recently witnessed this firsthand when the organization sponsored a weekend long entrepreneurship hackathon competition at a major historically black college or university (HBCU). The audience and contestants were primarily black women. The market-based problems they identified, embraced, and built web- and app-based solutions for during the weekend competition were extremely novel and starkly different from typical problems embraced by young white and Asian males who more typically lead product development in tech firms.

Many black entrepreneurs in the US are extremely busy working night and day to earn income for basic survival in a post-pandemic world. A large portion work multiple jobs, attend high school or college full-time, and care for their families in the United States and often abroad. Time, as a precious commodity, is viewed and treated very differently by them. To the extent that these entrepreneurs understand how and where their time spent and actions fit within the broader scope of successful entrepreneurship is essential to increasing their business success rates.

Moreover, in the absence of resources and support from more highly resourced non-black institutions and communities, the bulk of innovations introduced by black entrepreneurs may never see the light of day. The resulting impact includes societal forfeiture of black creativity and innovation, as well as forfeiture of an opportunity to uplift disenfranchised members of the black community. The purpose of this chapter, therefore, is to share insights published by numerous entrepreneurship and business scholars that could guide post-COVID black and non-black populations to help increase the successful rates of black entrepreneurship primarily in the United States.

The next sections of this chapter begin with critical challenges that define the state of black entrepreneurship in the United States. Opportunities are then laid out as recommendations for black and other underserved entrepreneurs to aid their success in starting and running new businesses particularly in a post-pandemic world. The opportunities are presented within the context of nuanced differences in black business formalization, STEM-based business models, social networks, entrepreneurial financing, opportunity recognition, strategy development, and customer discovery and validation. Each of these topics are presented in how they can help improve black entrepreneurship and business ownership outcomes.

BACKGROUND

Black Entrepreneurship in the United States

Researchers have tracked entrepreneurship and business ownership comparisons across different racial and ethnic groups for more than a century. The product of these efforts allows people to examine differences between black entrepreneurs and non-black entrepreneurs in search of opportunities for both to learn best practices from each other. Kauffman Early-Stage Entrepreneurship Index, US Census, Panel of Study of Entrepreneurial Dynamics, Global Entrepreneurship Monitor, General Social Survey, Bureau of Labor Statistics, and many others are examples. From these, researchers have uncovered broad differences between black entrepreneurs and others including four of which are highlighted next: (1) high and low rates or entrepreneurship activity, (2) sociodemographics; (3) opportunity-based or necessity-based reasons for becoming an entrepreneur; and (4) retail scarcity activities.

1. **Black Entrepreneurship Differences**
    a. **High and Low Rates**

Of all racial and ethnic groups in the United States, blacks own the smallest proportion of registered businesses. Researchers have tracked business ownership comparisons among racial and ethnic groups for more than a century and found that only four percent of the black population owns an established business (Fairlie, 2004; 1999; Köllinger & Minniti, 2006). This compares to 12 percent among the white population (Fairlie, 2004). As a result, only 2.6 million firms are owned by members of the black population in the United States (U.S. Census 2012). Only 3.5 percent of all New York City businesses are owned by black business owners even though blacks represent 22 percent of the population there (NYC Small Business Services, 2022). In Brooklyn, New York, out of 300,000 registered businesses, only 63,000 were registered as black businesses in 2012. Moreover, only 2,000 of these businesses employed at least one employee other than the owner(s). Thus, the lion's share of black businesses registered in Brooklyn, NYC are single-person businesses (U.S. Census 2012).

Yet, many studies also show that the black population possesses the highest rates of entrepreneurial propensity in terms of entrepreneurial *interest* and *activity* (Herring, 2004; Köllinger & Minniti, 2006; Walstad & Kourilsky, 1998). Nationally, black youth have shown higher levels of entrepreneurial propensity than other groups, and prospective black entrepreneurs exhibit higher levels of optimism than other entrepreneurs (Walstad & Kourilsky, 1998; Wilson, Marlino, & Kickul, 2004; Singh & McDonald, 2004). Black people set out to start new businesses nearly three times more than whites (Köllinger & Minniti, 2006; Reynolds et al., 2004). Black women are more likely than white and Hispanic women to attempt to start a business. Black women start new businesses at 6 times the national average. Blacks are more likely to pursue new venture creation than whites and Asians. Black adults are 50 percent more likely than white adults to attempt to start a business (Reynolds et al., 2004). Collectively, these findings reveal that in spite of having the lowest established business ownership rates, black Americans have the highest *nascent* entrepreneurship rates of all other groups researched (Walstad & Kourilsky, 1998; Köllinger & Minniti, 2006; Reynolds et al., 2004; Forbes, 2016; Crump, Singh, & Wilbon, 2009; Rueben & Queen, 2015). Nascent entrepreneurs are those who are in the process of founding a venture. So, a critical question becomes *Why do so many attempt to establish a business, yet it appears that so few actually do?*

To address this question, the next section of this chapter addresses some differences between black and non-black entrepreneurship with the hope of spurring efforts to change the relationship between nascent and successful business ownership. The Summer of 2020 ushered in widespread acknowledgement that certain adverse and systemic societal forces have acted with greater constraint on blacks relative to non-blacks. These forces and their detrimental impacts have long remained salient within black communities, and have contributed to black entrepreneurs engaging in entrepreneurial activities differently than other groups. Much of what is known about these differences comes from research of black entrepreneurs who operate registered businesses in the *formal* economy. The formal economy is the economy where businesses are registered with the government, licensed, taxed and visible through various business registries.

b. Sociodemographics

Some studies show that black entrepreneurs who own established businesses often differ sociodemographically from others in education attainment (Singh & Crump, 2007; Singh & McDonald, 2004; Fairlie, 1999), family structure and the types of support they receive. On average, they are more often single, less educated, and younger than other entrepreneurs (Fairlie, 2004). Yet blacks who attain a graduate education are two to three times more likely to become an entrepreneur (Reynolds, et al., 2004). A well-established link between having an entrepreneurial father and becoming an entrepreneur does not hold for blacks. Among non-blacks, the children of entrepreneurial fathers are more likely to become entrepreneurs than the children of fathers who are not entrepreneurs (Hout & Rosen, 2000; Fairlie, 1999). Blacks differ in that having an entrepreneurial mother is a strong predictor of entrepreneurship (Singh, Crump, & Zu, 2009). Successful black families push their children to pursue wage work after first earning a quality education instead of pursuing entrepreneurship (Rhodes & Butler, 2004). Moreover, black entrepreneurs and business owners are less likely than other groups to gauge business success primarily by financial and economic metrics (Herring, 2004). Instead, black entrepreneurs gauge business success more so on the degree their business provides family support, and community involvement and support

(Brush, et al., 2006; Herring, 2004; Rhodes & Butler, 2004; Robinson, Blockson, & Robinson, 2005; Singh & McDonald, 2004).

c. Opportunity versus Necessity - Reasons for Becoming an Entrepreneur

During the 2020 George Floyd protests throughout the United States, many people confronted the uncomfortable fact that blacks have endured centuries of mistreatment, oppression and systemic racism through U.S. corporate, justice, legal and education environments. The existence of these forces has led blacks to possess lower levels of trust toward outsiders than other groups (Terrell & Terrell, 1993; Whaley, 2004; Whaley, 2001; Williams, 2001). Hence, one major reason why blacks often choose entrepreneurship over wage work is because they perceive themselves as negatively impacted by unfair practices in the labor market (Herring, 2004).

Also during the 2020 pandemic year, more people in the United States transitioned into entrepreneurship than in 2019 (Fairlie & Desai, 2021). Yet, those who became necessity-entrepreneurs grew to its highest point in 25-years (Fairlie & Desai, 2021). Necessity-entrepreneurs start businesses primarily for income subsistence. Whereas opportunity-entrepreneurs start businesses primarily because of creativity and innovation. Members of the black population experienced the second to the highest growth in necessity-based entrepreneurship, and the greatest decline in opportunity-based entrepreneurship, second only to Asian new entrepreneurs. Research shows that prospective black business people are more likely than others to decide *first* to become an entrepreneur, and only *after* that decision do they search for, discover and select a particular business opportunity that they will pursue (Singh, Knox, & Crump, 2008). Non-blacks are more likely to *first* discover some unmet need or unsolved problem, and only *afterward* do they decide to start a business. Research also shows that businesses started through opportunity-based entrepreneurship generate higher revenues and profits than those started through necessity-based entrepreneurship (Bhave, 1994; Singh & Hills, 2003). Necessity-based businesses produce lower revenues and profits because they are more often small micro-businesses that are run informally by a single business owner (DeJaeghere & Baxter, 2014; Libombo & Dinis, 2015).

Necessity-based entrepreneurship among black populations typically begins with people being resource constrained (Singh, Knox, & Crump, 2008). They first decide that they will start a business, and then search for a type of business to start. When people begin in such a resource constrained position, they perceive business opportunity options available to them as being very limited. They consider the amount of capital they can muster and the types of work skill experience and social capital that are available to them to start and run a business.

Income, education, household net worth, wealth attainment, work skill attainment, and social capital levels in resource-constrained environments are well-documented as less conducive to successful new business launch (Crump et al., 2015; Singh & Crump, 2007; Singh, Knox, Crump, 2008). Thus, global and national data show the overwhelming majority of resource-constrained startups become small microbusinesses, rarely started by more than one entrepreneur. Though self-employed, the entrepreneur is essentially starting a *job* which s/he owns rather than starting an actual self-sustaining business. Most of these startups are not registered with a city, state, or federal government. Nor are their business trade activities formally recorded, taxed, or licensed. Some may attain one or more licenses and permits, but most are not fully registered as formal businesses in what is referred to as the *formal economy*. This means that these businesses are fully or in part operating in the informal economy (Crump, 2013).

d. Retail Scarcity Activities

Retail scarcity abounds in highly urban environments. Retail scarcity is a measure of the shortage of attractive, accessible and affordable retail goods near and easily accessible to a community's residents (Porter, 2005). In many densely populated urban settings throughout the United States that house underserved communities, customers are often forced to pay highly inflated prices for goods if and when accessible. These customers often pay for substandard quality, travel far to find preferred products and services, and depend on public or fee-based transportation to access desired retail spaces compared to customers in other regions (Weiler *et al.*, 2003; Porter, 2005). This retail scarcity equates to billions of dollars of unmet consumer demand in densely populated cities throughout the United States (Weiler *et al.*, 2003; Porter & Blaxill, 1997). Many black residents in these retail scarce environments are intricately aware of these unmet consumer demands (Crump, 2013). Studies show that compared to other races, black entrepreneurs are more highly concentrated in densely populated cities compared to less densely populated cities (Sampson & Wilson, 2005). Research also suggests that black business owners in these settings are more likely to operate businesses differently than other entrepreneurs (Crump, 2013).

Collectively, all of the differences so far presented in this chapter help to illuminate why blacks are overrepresented in nascent entrepreneurship, while also being underrepresented in established business ownership. The four percent of black entrepreneurs who are mentioned earlier are those who operate primarily in the formal economy. Many of the black entrepreneurs who are very highly engaged in nascent entrepreneurship have been, contrary to empirical results, actually founding new firms. The reason why the firms are not firmly reflected in black entrepreneurship statistics is because many of these firms are established in an alternate economy that runs parallel to the formal economy. Black entrepreneurs likely operate businesses in the informal economy at significantly higher rates than other groups (Gibbs, Mahone, Crump, 2013; Crump, 2013). Thus, in order to attain a more comprehensive understanding of black entrepreneurship, one must look more closely at the *informal* economy.

2. The Informal Economy

The informal economy is extremely complex and comprises several dimensions as shown in Figure 1. This chapter focuses on the portion that relates to the trade of products and services that are legal to possess. The selling of these goods and services is considered *legitimate* activity, and would otherwise be lawful if the activities were taxed, licensed, regulated, and recorded. The informal economy is active in all countries around the world, and is growing. In many developing nations, this sector accounts for more than half of all economic output in an economy (Schneider, 2005).

To reiterate, all racial and ethnic groups conprise people who trade in the informal economy as business owners, customers, workers, or suppliers (Godfrey, 2011; Murkherjee, 2016; Schneider, 2005; Williams & Shahid, 2016). In developed economies, the percentage of any particular racial or ethnic group that engages in informal economic activities is lower than the percentage that engages in formal economic activities (Schneider, 2005). This lower percentage ratio applies to black, white, Asian, Hispanic, Indian, and other Americans as well. Hence, when interpreting and referring to this chapter, it is essential to keep the two expressions, *legitimate* and *legal,* together. This segment of the economy must be characterized using both of these terms together. Otherwise, to characterize informal economy participants as being "engaged in illegal activity" would be false and misleading.

Figure 1. Four dimensions of economies

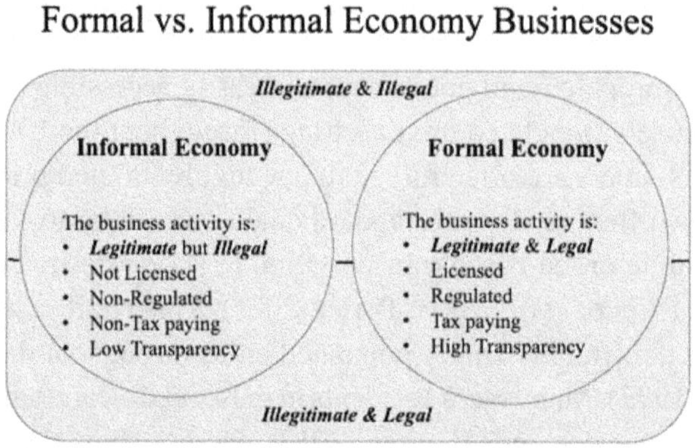

a. Why Entrepreneurs Choose the Informal Economy

There are many reasons why people all across our planet choose to operate businesses in the informal economy. Some of these include inability to find employment and sufficient income; avoidance of high and cumbersome government taxation, regulation, corruption, and administration; and low quality of public goods and infrastructure (Dreher & Schneider, 2010; Khavul, Bruton, & Wood, 2009; Maloney, 2004; Schneider, 2005; Williams & Round 2008). People with high income levels choose to run a business in the informal economy as a secondary source of income to increase their wealth, business acumen, and access to resources, as well as to exploit opportunities gained as a result of previously formal employment (Webb et al., 2009; Williams, 2008; Williams & Nadin, 2010; Williams & Round, 2008). People with middle income levels choose the informal economy because of recreational and personal interests, and to supplement their income and employment (Williams & Round, 2008). People with low incomes choose the informal economy out of necessity for income and basic survival, because of workforce discrimination, as income backup in case of demotion or dismissal from their current employment, to attain dignity and autonomy not available through formal employment, to improve their work identity such as being an unskilled laborer but also a president and CEO of one's own business, and because of recreational and personal interests (Cross, 2000; Edgcomb & Thetford, 2004; Webb et al., 2009; Williams, 2008; Williams & Nadin, 2010; Williams & Round, 2008).

Some entrepreneurs choose to operate in either the formal or the informal economy (Dreyer & Schneider, 2010). Others choose to operate in both simultaneously by formalizing some aspects of their business activities, while keeping others hidden (Guillermo, 2008). A third group of people *unwittingly* find themselves trading in a non-formal way in the informal economy, without really giving much thought to formal rules and regulations governing their trade. So, many who operate in the informal economy never make an explicitly conscious choice to do so.

b. Disadvantages Entrepreneurs Face by Remaining in the informal Economy

Entrepreneurs who operate businesses fully or primarily in the informal economy often do so unwittingly at their own peril. Informal economy businesses and customers forfeit institutional benefits and protections enjoyed by their counterparts (De Soto, 1989; Johnson, McMillan, & Woodruff, 1999). As a result, these businesses:

- remain invisible to markets of prospective customers, vendors, suppliers, investors, lenders, funders, partners, and other critical stakeholders
- are largely, and problematically, cash-based
- cannot attract corporate debt nor angel and venture capital investment because informal lending and investment structures are scant and provide little legally-backed assurances to lenders and investors
- lack access to critically needed capital for new business maintenance, growth and sustainability
- force the business owners to have unlimited liability for all business debts and financial obligations
- are blocked out of receiving government set-asides and other benefits available to their registered formal economy counterpart businesses
- stay smaller than they would if they were formalized.

Government policies aimed at addressing these shortcomings have long focused on providing workshop training, seminars, network development, business taxation relief, and improved access to business capital. In spite of the best efforts of these policies, however, lagging rates of black entrepreneurship in the formal economy relative to other racial and ethnic groups remain consistently low. As presented earlier in this chapter, the rate of black business owner participation in the U.S. formal economy remains in the low digits at around 4 percent. Throughout much of Africa, the Caribbean, and the United Kingdom, this rate of formal entrepreneurship participation is also in the low single digits (Amine & Staub, 2009; Drinkwater, Lashley, Robinson, 2018, Kiggundu, 2002; DeJaeghere and Baxter, 2014; Köllinger & Minniti, 2006; Libombo & Dinis, 2015; Rheault & Tortora, 2008; Yamoah, & Johnson, 2020). The entrepreneurship rates for other racial and ethnic groups throughout all three regions fall into the double digits, with many approaching 20 percent. Some research shows that as the portion of black populations in U.S. cities becomes increasingly dense, that the rate of black entrepreneurship participation in the formal economy there decreases (Crump, Hills, Taylor, 2017).

Studies presented thus far of black entrepreneurs can help future black entrepreneurs to more successfully start and grow their businesses especially in a post-pandemic world. For members of black communities who are underserved and may become unemployed or transition to necessity-based entrepreneurship, the next section of this chapter provides opportunities and suggestions to aid their economic relief and uplift. Opportunities are delineated from studies that relate specifically to underserved black entrepreneurs and small business owners. Each opportunity is presented as a recommended action for black entrepreneurs to supplement their existing business creation and growth strategies, if not already doing so. While the recommendations are primarily directed toward new black entrepreneurs, they may also apply to any underserved entrepreneurs who may have not yet adopted the recommendations.

METHODOLOGY

This study examined business, management, entrepreneurship, sociology and economic bodies of literature. Studies were examined that collectively contained tens of millions of data points over many decades qualitatively and quantitatively measuring black entrepreneurs' behaviors and often comparing them to others. Datasets used in those studies included US Census, Kauffman Early-Stage Entrepreneurship Index, Global Entrepreneurship Monitor, Panel Study of Entrepreneurial Dynamics, General Social Survey, Bureau of Labor Statistics and many others. The many findings that relate to black entrepreneurship and which help shed light on how to improve it particularly in a U.S. context are systematically organized and presented below to current and prospective black entrepreneurs, as well as those who educate and advise them.

FINDINGS AND RECOMMENDATIONS

Opportunities for Black Entrepreneurs

1. Benefits of Transitioning a Business into the Formal Economy

Businesses benefit more when they formally join a larger group that bestows benefits to its members. The U.S. formal economy is a group where member businesses enjoy benefits over other businesses that have not joined. In order to join the formal economy, businesses must become registered, subject their income to being taxed, and secure various types of industry-specific licenses and permits. These businesses, then, are registered, taxed, licensed, and regulated. In exchange, these businesses can grow and thrive much more easily than informal economy businesses because of the greater amounts of advantages they receive. Benefits of a business joining the formal economy include:

- enhanced legitimacy to stakeholders including customers, lenders, investors, key recruits, and government regulators
- assurances to prospective customers that if problems arise in the future, they can use a formal system for recourse purposes
- relatively safe assurances to prospective lenders and investors that their cash loaned or invested will generate attractive returns
- enhanced visibility and transparency to broader markets of potential customers, suppliers, partners, and other strategic stakeholders
- entitled access to government services and benefits such as use of national infrastructure including roads, utilities, police and fire, courts, and many others which permit reliable and efficient business trade
- access to government subsidies and incentives including procurement bids and export promotion packages
- membership in formal business associations
- access to a formal system of social security.

Because of bounded rationality, informal economy entrepreneurs may be blindsided to perceive only the benefits of trading in the informal economy. When the hidden costs of forgoing the advantages of the formal economy are factored in, a rational choice favors formalizing one's business to operate in the formal economy. Thus, in order to avoid a trap of stifling long-term business growth, black entrepreneurs should intentionally apprise themselves of these hidden costs.

2. Legal Structure Options to Formalizing One's Business

An initial step to formalizing one's business in the formal economy is to select a *legal structure* of the new business. There are several options from which business owners and founders can choose. First, the owner can establish the business as a sole proprietorship if there is only one owner. Alternatively, the owner can establish the business as a general partnership if there are two or more owners. Both of these options are easy and relatively inexpensive to set up. However, both of these choices also expose the owner(s) to unlimited liability. Unlimited liability is where one or more owners are personally liable for any and all debts or obligations their business may incur. For example, if a business is solely owned by Doodley and the business incurs $250,000 worth of obligations, but the business is worth only $100,000 then Doodley is personally liable for all outstanding debts the business owes above and beyond the $100,000 which the business is currently worth. Limited liability reduces what Doodley is responsible to pay to not exceed the current value of his ownership in the business. In this case, Doodley's liabilities for the debt would be reduced to no more than $100,000. Second, two types of partnerships, limited partnership (LP) and limited liability partnerships (LLP) are hybrids that permit one portion of the owners of a business to have limited liability and for the other portion of the owners of that business to have full liability.

Third, an additional and attractive alternative to formalize one's business is to establish the business as a separate legal entity such as a corporation (*e.g.,* a C-Corp., S-Corp, or B-Corp for benefit corporation) or limited liability company (LLC). When a business is not established as a separate legal entity, the business can be thought of as being simply a *verb* or an *action* that is accomplished by the owner(s). That is, if a business is not registered as a separate legal entity, then it is not a separate thing, nor is it a *noun*. Instead, the business is simply an action that an owner *does*. When a business remains a verb, it and the owner are one in the same. No portion of the business can be traded as equity ownership in exchange for capital when needed because no legal mechanisms exist for a business owner to sell a percentage of his *actions*. Additionally, the owner is personally and fully liable for all of the business's actions and liabilities. When an entrepreneur instead registers his/her new or existing business as a legal entity, the business becomes a *noun*, and any portion of that business (*i.e.,* the now established legal entity that is separate from the owner) can be sold or traded in exchange for equity ownership.

3. Financial Literacy for Entrepreneurs

Recent U.S. Census data show that black businesses are more often single-person businesses that generate an average of $72,154 per year in revenues (US Census, 2012). Although many exceptions exist, the majority of black owned businesses in the United States do not experience the same types of financial success as non-black businesses (Fairlie & Robb, 2007; Robb 2002). Many of them are *bootstrap* financed through paycheck, personal credit cards, and financial and labor support from family members of the owner. The businesses are classified as low-tech micro businesses, created for income subsidization. Black households contain the lowest household wealth and the highest unemployment rate among most racial groups in the U.S. (Bradford, 2003; Fairlie, 2005; 1999; Singh & McDonald, 2004; Spriggs & Williams, 2000). Blacks earn lower wages than others who have similar education attainment. With restricted capital, black entrepreneurs select business startups that can be financed by lower levels of capital that they control (Bates, 1996; Fraser, 2003; Singh & McDonald, 2004). Soon, the realization of undercapitalization kicks in and the black business owners desperately search for sources to finance their businesses to a point where they can become financially self-sustaining. Grants, micro and other business loans, government set-asides, and investor finance typically do not pan out for these entrepreneurs (Bates & Bradford, 2004; Herring, 2004; Rasheed, 2004; Rhodes & Butler, 2004; Rogers *et al.*, 2001). A major reason is because these funding mechanisms are based on formal economy parameters that do not work in informal economy settings.

In order for a business to receive a loan, the business itself, as opposed to the owner, must achieve some combination of credit worthiness, documentation of past sales and profit that demonstrate an ability to repay the loan, and collateral as a guarantee should it default on repaying the loan. A business receiving a business loan is not the same as a business owner receiving a personal loan from a bank, family member and/or friends that the owner(s) must repay. Many black business owners can receive personal loans based on how well they individually meet these thresholds. But many black-owned new businesses that are just starting cannot meet these threshold requirements and are therefore unable to attract debt financing. For more black businesses to qualify for grants, loans, and government set-asides, many new entrepreneurs must begin by making sure their businesses are banked, and that their business transactions are documented especially in financial statements such as income statements, balance sheet statements, and cash flow statements.

In order for a business to attract investment capital by an angel investor or a venture capital (VC) investor in exchange for a percentage ownership stake, typically the business must also achieve some combination of the following:

1. The business is based on some major innovation that is a candidate to disrupt (or destroy) some industry. Uber disrupted the cab industry. AirBnB disrupted the hotel industry. Digital music *destroyed* the cassette tape industry.
2. The business model contains some sustainable competitive advantage. The business must contain some rare asset that can be strategically deployed in a way that competitors cannot easily upend any projected market share. The rare asset may exist as a patented technology or new business model that cannot be easily duplicated, copyrighted files, special formula (such as Coca Cola's recipe), or other that is difficult for competitors to use.
3. The business is led by a team of highly capable co-founders. The co-founders must contain attributes that make them a potential *dream team* that other teams cannot easily outcompete even if given similar resources.
4. The business model is tech based and/or life-sciences based.
5. The business is an entrepreneurial firm. Researchers have categorized three major types of new businesses: *lifestyle firms*, *salary substitute firms*, and *entrepreneurship firms* (Barringer & Ireland, 2019). If a person loves to ski and opens a ski business, such would be a lifestyle firm. If a person earns $150,000/year from wage work and wants to quit his job while maintaining his lifestyle based on those earnings, then the business he starts or purchases is a salary substitute firm. If a person starts a business based on innovation and creativity that is likely scalable and can generate great wealth for owners, then that business is an entrepreneurial firm. A fourth type of firm can be referred to as a *salary-subsidizing* or *income-subsidizing* firm.

Unable to attract debt or investment financing, many undercapitalized black entrepreneurs must still persist in finding ways to subsidize their incomes for subsistence purposes. But uncapitalized firms do not have enough capital to pay all of their business responsibilities. Only those bare minimum expenses that keep sales going until the entrepreneur can find relief are often paid in the interim. Insurance, license and permits, warehouse, retail rent, payroll and taxes become candidates for deferral while the entrepreneur seeks more influxes of capital to cover each of these and other required business expenses. This state of undercapitalization forces many black entrepreneurs to unwittingly find themselves operating in the informal economy.

4. Entrepreneurial Social Networks

The social environment that entrepreneurs operate within can help or hurt their entrepreneurial success (Fraser, 2003; Herring, 2004; Hout & Rosen, 2000; Martin et al., 2006; Rhodes & Butler, 2004; Rogers et al., 2001; Young, 1998). Some features of entrepreneurs' social networks can be adjusted to help new black entrepreneurs improve their chances of starting and growing successful new businesses (Fraser, 2003; Young, 1998). The first of these attributes presented in this chapter is the dimension of social networks referred to as *strong-ties* versus *weak-ties* (Granovetter, 1985). Studies show that members of the black population are more likely than other groups to develop their social networks based almost entirely on strong-ties as opposed to much more so on weak-ties (Young, 1998). Their strong-ties consist of relationship connections to a relatively small core of people that remain relatively stable throughout their lives. They rely on these people for advice about major life decisions such as education and career advice, marriage, raising a family, and starting and running a business (Young, 1998). Like all racial groups, they do configure their social networks on both strong-ties and weak-ties. The difference is that they stack their networks more so with strong ties and less often with weak-ties as compared to other groups. In business however, weak-tie social network contacts lead people to discovering entrepreneurial opportunities more often than do strong-tie social network contacts (Granovetter, 1985).

The second social network attribute is *network entrepreneurs*. Network entrepreneurs are those people who discover opportunities to create new businesses along with the help of others who may also become co-founders. Network entrepreneurs recognize more opportunities than solo entrepreneurs (Hills, Lumpkin, & Singh, 1997). As explained earlier, black businesses are more often single person firms. New black entrepreneurs should expand their social networks by adding in more weak-ties. As they develop their new businesses, they should then tap into these newly configured social networks to create teams of co-founders who possess highly diverse skill sets. As network entrepreneurs, their businesses are more likely to be successful than if they proceed as solo entrepreneurs.

A third social network attribute is *structural holes*. Structural holes are non-existent connections between any two or more people in a person's social network (Burt, 1992). If two people in your social network don't know each other, then you have at least one structural hole that exists in your network until you or someone else introduces both people to each other. The two people not knowing each other constitutes a structural hole in your social network. Research shows that if you are entrepreneurial and you introduce these two people to each other, by closing this structural hole, you and those in your social network are likely to increase the amount of successful business opportunities you discover (Burt, 1992), and the levels of growth and innovation your business will achieve (Adams, Makramalla, & Miron, 2014).

New and aspiring black entrepreneurs are therefore advised to configure or reconfigure their social networks in order to increase their successful entrepreneurial outcomes. They should do this by adding more weak-ties by, for example, introducing themselves, or being introduced by acquaintances, to other people who they only casually meet such as at a conference, show, or casual outing. Additionally, they should become network entrepreneurs as opposed to solo entrepreneurs, and they should identify and remove structural holes in their social networks.

5. Entrepreneurial STEM-Void Challenge

New and aspiring black entrepreneurs should carefully select which types of businesses they start based on both their immediate and long-term needs. Of the types of businesses that entrepreneurs start, a key distinction of *entrepreneurial* firms is that they are grounded in or based on some type of high technology innovation and/or life sciences. Some creative usage of technology drives the innovation of the new business. New applications of technology are creatively deployed by enterprising individuals in such a way that provides better solutions to specific markets, while also potentially disrupting or destroying *status quo* approaches by entrenched incumbents.

Educators and policymakers have enacted various measures to address the underrepresentation of blacks in STEM education and STEM careers. Yet the disparity remains. Thus, black businesses are abundantly not anchored in a new technology created by the founders. Some businesses may be anchored in a new technology, but the entrepreneur must pay another firm in order to use the technology. In response, many of these firms are small retail or service-based businesses that are not easily scalable. This STEM-Void partially explains, in addition to systemic racism, why the portions of black businesses that attain venture capital financing have remained in the very low single digits for more than the past three decades.

To illustrate this STEM-Void, imagine two fictional people who each start a soap manufacturing firm for a market of women of color who are dissatisfied with existing soap products. Mahlanie, the first business owner, formally studied organic chemistry and has expertise with formulation. Jackie, the second business owner, formally studied business administration and has no science-based expertise. Both of these entrepreneurs manufacture bars of soap that are equally loved and purchased by women of color who view both soap bars as far superior to alternative products currently available for purchase.

Mahlanie manufactures her products in a science lab that contains state-of-the-art equipment for isolation, formulation and product validation. Mahlanie developed and patented an innovative new and much more highly efficient method of extracting essential compounds directly from readily available raw materials. Her direct manufacturing and direct labor costs are 5% of the $6 per bar price she charges. At a gross profit margin of 90%, Mahlanie's remaining indirect business expenses such as overhead, transportation, marketing, salaries, and several other expenses leave a lucrative cushion for her to produce at a bottom line, net profit margin of 40 percent of all sales. Hence, Mahlanie is operating *in the black* because her profit is a positive number. Moreover, Mahlanie's manufacturing process is scalable and outsourceable while still remaining financially viable. Mahlanie has been approached by two angel investors who want to explore becoming her investing partners. The angel investors hope to scale her business model over the next three to five years until it grows to a point where Mahlanie (and them as her new co-owners) might gain a larger venture capital investment.

Jackie manufactures her soap products from materials she purchases online and collects at various brick-and-mortar retail businesses. She mixes these products using processes she has cultivated over time from knowledge passed down to her by her mother and grandmother from their Caribbean and African heritage. Jackie's direct manufacturing and direct labor costs are 70% of the $15 per bar price she charges. Jackie's gross profit margin is 30 percent of sales, which is much lower than she would like. Thus, when Jackie computes all of her additional indirect expenses, she observes that her net profit is actually a negative number, and therefore, she is operating *in the red.*

The primary reason Jackie started her business is income-subsidization. Jackie depends on money the business produces through sales. Closing down her business even though it is not producing a net profit is not an option in Jackie's mind. Many expenses that Jackie should pay are sacrificed *for now*, and instead, only the bare bones minimum can be paid. She reasons that she will start to pay those expenses later as sales pick up or as she identifies some funding sources to help purchase ingredients and other manufacturing materials at cheaper rates. So, for now she suffices to accrue, but not pay, many of her business expenses. She hopes that she will find grant or angel investment funding to scale her operations to where the profitability of her business becomes financially sustainable, scalable and viable.

Many similar examples exist where aspiring entrepreneurs seek new businesses to create in order to subsidize their income. These necessity-based entrepreneurs often identify business opportunities that lack the types of efficiency, scalability, replicability, and disruptive innovation and leverage that STEM-based expertise can provide. These non-STEM opportunities largely consist of imitating what larger incumbents do, except by adding one or more feature enhancements, and hoping to compete by selling their products and services cheaper than incumbents do. Inadvertently, however, the cheaper prices often lead to the new business being branded in customers' minds as of lower quality and ranking. Therefore, entrepreneurs need an overarching strategy to coordinate, unify and guide many of their strategic business choices.

Having a STEM-based work and/or education background can give an entrepreneur and therefore his/her business a competitive advantage. When lead entrepreneurs do not have a STEM-based background, their businesses should recruit and bring in such talent in order to avoid having a STEM-Void and therefore lacking these types of advantages. Black businesses that are STEM-Void should decisively build co-founding teams that contain STEM knowledge, education, and experience in order to fill STEM-Voids.

When lead entrepreneurs of new startups contain expertise in a newly created technology like Bill Gates, Steve Jobs, Elon Musk, Jeff Bezos, and Mark Zuckerberg did when they founded their firms, the entrepreneurs are able to create a vision of things not yet seen, and deploy resources to enact that vision to become a reality. When entrepreneurs create a vision of a new business without the expertise to convert that vision into a reality, they must either wait until they themselves gain the expertise, which may take years or never happen at all, or they can try to hire or coopt the expertise into the fledgling firm, and then attempt to manage it.

Enormous amounts of time and resources must be spent to create an innovative solution to a market-based problem (also referred to as a "customer pain") or to create an innovation that makes a market of customers excited about using a product or service (referred to as a "customer gain"). Lead entrepreneurs who do not contain requisite technical or STEM-based expertise to lead the creation of a business built primarily on such innovations find it more difficult to build their business than lead entrepreneurs who do. The former leaders must learn and master the arduous tasks of effectively managing the ingenuity of the more tech and/or life science savvy creating experts they must retain in order to build the business.

6. Strategically Setting Initial Prices

New and aspiring black entrepreneurs should decisively and strategically make and implement their business decisions rather than making them quickly, and without intentionally aligning them to the broader long-term strategic objectives of their businesses. One component of this type of entrepreneurial strategic planning is the selecting of an optimal price point. A price point is one selected price among all possible prices for a new product or service. Much consideration should go into which price points will most effectively aid the long-term strategic objectives of the new business. There are several considerations that new black entrepreneurs should carefully weigh when setting the initial prices of the goods and services they will bring to the market to sell. Four of these considerations are: price-quality attribution, metaphorical *vitamins* versus *pain pills*, cost-based versus values-based pricing, and differentiation (Barringer & Ireland, 2019).

a. Price-Quality Attribution

Price-quality attribution is a phenomenon where customers and consumers subconsciously and automatically conclude that cheaper prices equate to cheaper quality, and that higher prices equate to higher quality (Anderson, 2010; Barringer & Ireland, 2019). Customers are those who *purchase* products, and consumers are those who *use* products. To illustrate how both psychologically associate *price* and *quality* as synonymous, think of the highest priced sunglasses, hand bags, watches, or shoes that you know of. Next, think of the lowest priced sunglasses, hand bags, watches, or shoes that you know of. If you are like most people, chances are you rank each of the highest priced items as having the highest quality, and each of the lowest priced items as having the lowest quality. Most markets of buyers and consumers similarly rank businesses in quality based on this psychological association even when the association is in reality false.

For example, the higher prices of some athletic sneakers compared to competitors' prices may simply reflect a price inflation that covers higher marketing expenses and multi-million-dollar celebrity endorsements rather than reflecting inherently greater quality. Other athletic sneaker companies might spend much less on marketing and celebrity endorsements but offer more quality than their higher priced competitors while also offering substantially lower prices because of the companies' lower costs. Based on the psychological price-quality association, many customers and consumers will assign a greater quality to the higher priced/lower-quality shoe, and will assign a lower quality to the lower priced/higher-quality shoe.

b. Dimensions of Quality of Products and Services

New and aspiring black entrepreneurs who set out to start a new business that will compete by offering higher quality products at cheaper prices should pay careful attention to the price-quality association. Imagine starting a business that manufactures laptops that are of a higher quality than Apple Inc. laptops, placing a white pear emblem on the new laptops, calling each a "Pear" and charging half the prices of Apple Inc. laptops. If you purchase two of these Pears for your middle-school age niece and nephew as Christmas gifts, they might hurl them back at you in protest as you turn and walk away. Regardless of the fact that the new Pear laptops are of superior quality, they are viewed as being "cheaper" and therefore less desirable or undesirable to the niece and nephew. In addition to perceived quality, customers and consumers internalize the **quality of products** also through seven additional dimensions as well: performance, features, reliability, conformance, durability, serviceability, and aesthetics (Garvin, 1987). They perceive the **quality of services** through five dimensions: tangibles, reliability, responsiveness, assurance, and empathy (Parasuraman, Zeithaml, & Berry, 1988).

c. Features versus Benefits of Products and Services

Many non-STEM-based necessity entrepreneurs incur elevated production costs based on the STEM-Void absence of tech-based efficiencies in production costs. They are therefore pressured to charge higher prices for their products and services in order to become financially viable. Hence, many of these entrepreneurs attempt to persuade people to buy from them by selling products and services that contain some special quality attribute that a niche-market cares much about. But, being non-STEM-based, the attributes these business owners gravitate toward are typically STEM-Void. Examples might include adding *features* such as being hand-made, homemade, serving the underserved, or containing gimmicks such as a signature or photo of the entrepreneur embedded in the product or its packaging. Yet, entrepreneurs should remain mindful that while ***features*** may be nice, what customers really care more about and more often make purchasing decisions on are ***benefits*** (Barringer & Ireland, 2019). STEM-based technology can more easily help entrepreneurs create sustainable benefits that in turn help the businesses achieve advantages over their competitors that are sustainable.

d. Differentiation and Sustainable Competitive Advantage

When these advantages are long-lasting, they are categorized as a ***sustainable competitive advantage*** (Barringer & Ireland, 2019). Entrepreneurs expend great efforts to achieve a sustainable competitive advantage which is marked by customers perceiving a unique and more desired benefit(s) by purchasing their products. A differentiation strategy is used to achieve this advantage, and this strategy consists of two approaches. The first is a ***cost-based differentiation*** approach where a business is able to profitably sell its offerings at prices much lower than competitors because the business enjoys a STEM-based low-cost production advantage over competitors (Barringer & Ireland, 2019). Or the company may have grown so large, such as Walmart Stores, Inc., that it can easily produce its offerings at a much lower cost than its competitors. The second type is a *non-cost-based differentiation* approach (often referred to simply as "***differentiation***" strategy"). Companies embracing this strategy differentiate their offerings from competitors based on some non-cost-based attributes that customers and consumers really care about (Barringer & Ireland, 2019). These attributes may consist of quality, reputation, brand appeal, attractiveness, instrumental impact, prestige, rarity and exclusivity, and other features. STEM-Void businesses find difficulty differentiating their products from competitors' in sustainable ways based on these attributes because larger competitors can easily and quickly imitate and outcompete most non-STEM-based attributes.

Competitive advantages created by STEM-based businesses are sustainable because the attributes are typically based on rare and not easily imitated technological or scientific innovations. These innovations are strategic assets that entrepreneurs should protect for privacy and security since the entrepreneurs wish to maintain the sustainable competitive advantage that these strategic assets provide. Entrepreneurs can protect these assets by registering them for legal protection as intellectual property. Intellectual property can be patents, trade secrets, copyrights, and trademarks. Other forms of rare and strategic assets can include a specific physical or virtual space, a social media following, access to key social contacts, securing a critical grant or exclusive contract, and many others that are rare and not easily imitated.

e. Economies of Scale

Cost-based differentiation that is achieved by growing production is accomplished through an *economies of scale* benefit. This type of growth could take a considerable amount of years or decades to achieve. As companies grow extremely large, many achieve a level of growth where the more items they produce, the cheaper the average cost of all of those products become. McDonald's is an example of a company which enjoys economies of scale.

If you wake up tomorrow and decide you will make a hamburger to sell, the costs you will incur to do so is exceedingly greater than the costs McDonald's incurs to produce a burger. You will need to purchase a small package of soy-based imitation meat, a small container of eggs, a package of bread, vegetables and maybe a few other items since you likely already have in your possession salt, pepper, oil, and mixing and cooking utensils. From your store-bought ingredients, you make six burgers and divide your total expenditure by six burgers. Note, because some of your costs would vary based on whether you buy ingredients to make six, twelve, or thirty burgers, those costs are referred to as your *variable costs*. Your fixed costs consist of costs you must pay each period such as per month. For example, if you rent a stove, pots and pans at $30 per month. These expenses are fixed because the monthly costs do not change based on whether you make six, twelve, thirty, or even zero burgers.

As you begin to really scale your burger production over time to large numbers approaching hundreds and thousands of burgers per day, your production costs on average will decline because you start purchasing in bulk, investing in tech-based innovation, and becoming much more efficient in your manufacturing processes. At some point, you may achieve economies of scale where your variable costs decline as you increase the quantity of units you produce. As you continue to scale up your production units per day, your variable costs on each additional item you produce will at some point begin to approach zero. McDonald's economies of scale mean that the company's costs to produce one additional burger on top of all the burgers it will produce today is close to a few pennies. Note that *cost* is the amount of money a business spends to produce the products and services it will sell. Price is the amount of money a business charges customers for those products and services.

f. STEM-based Differentiation

New entrepreneurs will find it difficult to profitably start a new business where they sell similar products and services at lower prices than competitors until they grow to achieve economies of scale and become a leader among the low-cost producers in their industry. In the meantime, new black entrepreneurs should therefore improve their business by adopting a ***STEM-based differentiation*** strategy. STEM-based expertise can be applied to any business even if it provides low technology-based business products and services such as babysitting, cooked foods, health drinks, designer apparel, jewelry, candles, cosmetics, and natural-haircare products. STEM-based adoption helps businesses leverage technology to sustainably attain high scalability, replicability, increases in efficiency, lowered cost advantages, higher profitability margins, and greater fundability by lenders and investors. The creators of AirBnB leveraged their STEM-based expertise to create a new business model to selling *rooms to rent for a day* which is a relatively low technology product. Their knowledge permitted the creators to connect millions of underused physical spaces, the owners of those spaces, and markets of people wanting to rent a space less expensively and more flexibly than a hotel room.

g. Cost-based Pricing

Cost-based pricing is a pricing strategy where a business first identifies its costs to produce its products and services (Barringer & Ireland, 2019). The company then selects some markup (such as 33% of costs, or maybe even *costs times 3*) and then simply adds that markup to the cost of the products to derive a price point. For example, if it costs a company $6 to produce a natural, fresh-squeezed 16 oz. cup of pineapple juice, then the business might select a markup of 50% of costs and then add that markup to the $6 costs of the cup of juice. So, $6 costs + (50% of $6 = $3 markup) = a price point of $9. Customers are then charged a price of $9 for one 16 oz. cup of that pineapple juice.

h. Value-based Pricing

Value-based pricing is a pricing strategy where a business first begins by building psychological value in the minds of its niche market by marketing its selected differentiation strategy (Barringer & Ireland, 2019). After building value of its products and services in niche market customers' minds, the business collects primary research data by asking many prospective customers how much they think the product is worth. Whatever general price value the niche market perceives the worth of the products to be, the business backs off of this amount just a bit in order to create a cushion of error. The slightly backed off price becomes the selected price point for the newly introduced products and services. Experts recommend entrepreneurs to use value-based pricing strategies instead of cost-based pricing strategies because they are more aligned with customers' perceptions and will indirectly lead to more sales and profits (Barringer & Ireland, 2019).

i. Metaphorical Vitamins vs. Pain Pills

Barringer and Ireland (2019) and Chesbrough (2003) explain that vitamins are inherently better for people than pain pills. But, because pain pills solve immediate and urgent crises, people will urgently stop whatever they are doing when they need a pain pill and find a 24-hour pharmacy and pay (or have their insurance pay) high amounts of money for what they perceive to be the best pain pills. Compared to one bottle of vitamin C or one bottle of vitamin D, people pay more for pain pills. Based on this distinction, if your business solves an immediate need perceived as urgent by your niche market customers, then your business is a metaphorical ***pain pill***. If your business sells primarily nice-to-have and non-urgent products and services, then your business may be a metaphorical ***vitamin***. This is not to say that metaphorical vitamin businesses are not profitable because many are indeed very profitable. The point here is that when vitamin businesses initially select an optimal price point, that optimum price point is often a lower price versus a higher one. New black entrepreneurs should always monitor, predict, and consider the prices that competitors select. Anticipating customer responses to their selected price points based on competitors' actions is critical to their business's continued success.

7. Opportunity Recognition

As prospective new and aspiring black entrepreneurs reconfigure their social networks and embrace a STEM-Void challenge, more will discover opportunities to develop new businesses that become attractive candidates in the formal economy. These processes should be executed independently of whatever is the amount of financial capital the prospective entrepreneur and his/her potential team of co-founders currently control. Startup capital is an important issue that startup founders need to overcome. Yet, many lending, investing, crowd-funding and other financing mechanisms are available to alleviate this barrier when new startup teams effectively assemble themselves and pursue the right types of new business opportunities.

a. Market-Oriented Approach to Selecting Which Business to Start

An entrepreneurial ***opportunity*** is a set of conditions that are ripe for a successful and lucrative new business to be created (Singh & Hills, 2003: Shane & Venkataraman, 2000). One of these conditions can be some major unsolved problem endured by a market of potential buyers who would likely pay substantially higher prices to any new business that solves that problem. Alternatively, an opportunity to provide some extraordinary gain to a market of potential customers might exist. Pursuing either of these two types of opportunities that begin with a group of prospective buyers and what they would like is a market-driven or ***market-oriented approach***. This approach promises a better outcome than the alternative which is called a ***product- or service-oriented approach*** (Barringer & Ireland, 2019; Farrell & Farrell, 2001). A product/service-oriented approach means an entrepreneur *first* focuses on developing some new product or service with a hope that once people are aware of how nice the new product is, they will rush to purchase it. A market-oriented approach encompasses the gaging of customers' wishes and perceptions, and subsequently making iterations and/or pivots until customer archetypes and highly valued prototypes are validated.

b. Lean Launchpad Methodology and Business Model Canvas

New black entrepreneurs should follow Steve Blank's market-oriented approach called ***Lean Launchpad Methodology*** which uses a tool called the ***Business Model Canvas***. They should master the use of this methodology and tool to more fully discover, identify, understand, and validate perceptions and desires of their niche markets prior to developing and bringing new products and services to a market. Creating effective business plans remains important to learn, but entrepreneurs should not make launching a new business dependent on first creating a business plan. In contrast, new black entrepreneurs should instead view effectively using Lean Launchpad Methodology as a necessary precondition to launch an effective new business.

FUTURE RESEARCH DIRECTIONS

Several future research opportunities are identified to help expand this work. Fist, future research should explore methods to improve existing levels of connectivity between unbanked prospective black entrepreneurs and debt and equity providers. Increasingly banking institutions are launching efforts to reach more of these populations. Research that can improve their efforts may show promise in helping to spur new black businesses. Future research might also investigate how colleges that education large numbers of black business and entrepreneurship students might increase cross-campus efforts to develop more broadly skilled black entrepreneurs. Colleges that contain autonomous and siloed academic and/or administrative units may develop entrepreneurs that more often lack broad skills. Bringing together different types of knowledge and skill development may help improve the types of successful businesses that black entrepreneurs launch. Finally, future research on how best to implement entrepreneurship incubators in partnership with industry collaborators for black entrepreneurs may likewise help to improve the rates of successful black entrepreneurship.

CONCLUSION

This chapter began with the acknowledgment that to underserved black entrepreneurs in a post-pandemic world, time is very limited and fleeting. At the time of writing this chapter, the post-COVID world is showing society that black entrepreneurship will get even worst if interventions are not made by both black entrepreneurs and those who educate and advise them. This chapter earlier explained that because of the COVID pandemic, there was a greater decrease in people becoming opportunity-entrepreneurs in the United States in 2020 than had been in the past 25 years. This change likewise corresponded to a greater increase in people becoming necessity-entrepreneurs, which yields drastically lowered economic success outcomes. But for black entrepreneurs who are more often systemically underserved in the United States, more of them became entrepreneurs out of necessity than all other races with the exception of one. The focus of this chapter, therefore, has been on seven specific actions that black entrepreneurs might take now in order to improve their post-COVID entrepreneurial success outcomes.

In order for them to efficiently and effectively spend their time, black entrepreneurs are additionally encouraged to incorporate the following 19 recommendations into their business creation and growth activities. Along with the seven opportunities delineated above, the time spent in this manner should help more black entrepreneurs to experience economic advancement through business ownership, while also improving many of society's problems through their novel creativities and innovations.

Checklist - For Black Entrepreneurs

1. Thoroughly understand the problem (pain-point) or customer gain their business will address.
2. Validate the specifics of their target market and especially their niche market – demographically, psychographically, behaviorally, and geographically.
3. Create an effective market-centered value-proposition that exceedingly solves their selected market problem or provides the right customer gain.
4. Form a new venture team of founders. Avoid a solo-entrepreneur approach.
5. Create a written founders' agreement, with legal counsel, at the right time when they know more about their business.
6. Participate in entrepreneurial bootcamps.
7. Frequent incubators, accelerators, makerspaces, shared workspaces, networking events and masterclasses.
8. Master the art and skill of effectively pitching to various types of audiences (regular customers, key customers, key recruits and partners, suppliers, government regulators, investors, lenders, sponsors, donors).
9. Start pitching their new business idea at competitions.
10. Familiarize themselves with *pro forma Numbers* and *Ratios* of their business.
11. Erect barriers of entry through intellectual property.

12. Strategize based on factors of competition specific to their industry.
13. Avoid cost-based differentiation when starting out.
14. Strategize for a STEM-based differentiation.
15. Consider the implications of "*vitamins*" versus "*pain pill*" businesses.
16. Gain entrepreneurial financial literacy.
17. Operate their business in the formal economy.
18. Embrace high-tech, blue ocean, niche-based strategies.
19. Repeatedly scan the external business environment for emerging opportunities and threats.

REFERENCES

Adams, M., Makramalla, M., & Miron, W. (2014). Down the rabbit hole: How structural holes in entrepreneurs' social networks impact early venture growth. *Technology Innovation Management Review*, *4*(9), 19–27. doi:10.22215/timreview/828

Amine, L. S., & Staub, K. M. (2009). Women entrepreneurs in Sub-Saharan Africa: An institutional theory analysis from a social marketing point of view. *Entrepreneurship and Regional Development*, *21*(2), 183–211. doi:10.1080/08985620802182144

Anderson, J. C., & Wynstra, F. (2010). Purchasing higher-value, higher-price offerings in business markets. *Journal of Business-To-Business Marketing*, *17*(1), 29–61. doi:10.1080/10517120903000363

Barringer, B. R., & Ireland, R. D. (2019). *Entrepreneurship: Successfully Launching New Ventures* (6th ed.). Pearson.

Bates, T. (1996). The financial capital needs of Black-owned businesses. *Journal of Developmental Entrepreneurship*, *1*(1), 1–15.

Bates, T., & Bradford, W. (2004). Analysis of venture-capital funds that finance minority-owned businesses. *The Review of Black Political Economy*, *32*(1), 37–46. doi:10.100712114-004-1017-z

Bhave, M. P. (1994). A process model of entrepreneurial creation. *Journal of Business Venturing*, *9*(3), 223–242. doi:10.1016/0883-9026(94)90031-0

Bradford, W. D. (2003). The wealth dynamics of entrepreneurship for black and white families in the U.S. *Review of Income and Wealth*, *49*(1), 89–116. doi:10.1111/1475-4991.00076

Brush, C., Monti, D., Gannon, A., & Ryan, A. (2006). *Inner city entrepreneurs: Building ventures and expanding community ties*. Babson College, Frontiers of Entrepreneurship Research.

Burt, R. S. (1992). *Structural holes: The social structure of competition*. Harvard University Press. doi:10.4159/9780674029095

Chesbrough, H. W. (2003). *Open Innovation*. Harvard Business Press.

Cross, J. C. (2000). Street vendors, modernity and postmodernity: Conflict and compromise in the global economy. *The International Journal of Sociology and Social Policy, 20*(1/2), 29–51. doi:10.1108/01443330010789061

Crump, M. E. S. (2013). Black entrepreneurship: Formal versus informal economy exploitation. *Washington Business Research Journal, 3*(1), 85–111.

Crump, M. E. S., Hill, N. J., & Tayor, P. G. (2017). Examining minority population and the impact of informal economy activity on collected revenues in U.S. cities. *Washington Business Research Journal, 7*(1), 6–41.

Crump, M. E. S., Singh, R. P., & Wilbon, A. D. (2009). Assessing the black entrepreneurship literature: What's known, and who's informing? *Washington Business Research Journal, 1*(1), 101–116.

Crump, M. E. S., Singh, R. P., Wilbon, A. D., & Gibbs, S. R. (2015). Socio-demographic differences of black versus white entrepreneurs. *Academy of Entrepreneurship Journal, 21*(1), 115–129.

De Soto, H. (1989). *The other path: The invisible revolution in the third world.* Tauris.

DeJaeghere, J., & Baxter, A. (2014). Entrepreneurship education for youth in sub-Saharan Africa: A capability approach as an alternative framework to neoliberalism's individualizing risks. *Progress in Development Studies, 14*(1), 61–76. doi:10.1177/1464993413504353

Dreher, A., & Schneider, F. (2010). Corruption and the shadow economy: An empirical analysis. *Public Choice, 144*(1/2), 215–238. doi:10.100711127-009-9513-0

Drinkwater, S., Lashley, J. G., & Robinson, C. (2018). Barriers to enterprise development in the Caribbean. *Entrepreneurship and Regional Development, 30*(9/10), 942–963. doi:10.1080/08985626.2018.1515821

Edgcomb, E. L., & Thetford, T. (2004). *The Informal Economy: Making it in Rural America.* Aspen Institute.

Fairlie, R., & Desai, S. (2021). *National report on early-stage entrepreneurship in the United States: 2020.* Kauffman Indicators of Entrepreneurship, Ewing Marion Kauffman Foundation.

Fairlie, R. W. (1999). The absence of the African-American owned business: An analysis of the dynamics of self-employment. *Journal of Labor Economics, 17*(1), 80–108. doi:10.1086/209914

Fairlie, R. W. (2004). Recent trends in ethnic and racial business ownership. *Small Business Economics, 23*(3), 203–218. doi:10.1023/B:SBEJ.0000032031.28403.31

Fairlie, R. W. (2005). Entrepreneurship and earnings among young adults from disadvantaged families. *Small Business Economics, 25*(3), 223–236. doi:10.100711187-003-6457-5

Fairlie, R. W., & Robb, A. M. (2007). Why are black-owned businesses less successful than white-owned businesses? The role of families, inheritances, and business human capital. *Journal of Labor Economics, 25*(2), 289–323. doi:10.1086/510763

Farrell, K., & Farrell, L. C. (2001). *Entrepreneurial Age.* Allworth Press.

Forbes. (2016). *Black women are the fastest-growing group of entrepreneurs in the U.S.* Accessed from http://www.forbes.com/sites/clareoconnor/2016/02/17/inside-one-woman-investors-plan-to-get-black-female-founders-funding/#18614f132837

Fraser, N. (2003). Social justice in the age of identity politics: Redistribution, recognition and participation. In N. Fraser & A. Honneth (Eds.), Redistribution. Academic Press.

Garvin, D. A. (1987). Competing on the eight dimensions of quality. *Harvard Business Review.*

Gibbs, S. R., Mahone, C., & Crump, M. E. S. (2013). A framework for informal economy entry: Socio-spatial, necessity-opportunity, and structural-based factors. *Academy of Entrepreneurship Journal, 20*(2), 61–85.

Granovetter, M. (1985). Economic action and social structure: The problem of embeddedness. *American Journal of Sociology, 91*(3), 481–510. doi:10.1086/228311

Guillermo, V. (2008). What is the size of the pie? Measuring the informal economy in Latin America and the Caribbean. *Money Affairs, 21*(2), 161–191.

Herring, C. (2004). Open for business in the black metropolis: Race, disadvantage, and entrepreneurial activity in Chicago's inner city. *The Review of Black Political Economy, 31*(4), 35–57. doi:10.100712114-004-1009-z

Hornaday, R., & Wheatly, W. (1986). Managerial characteristics and the financial performance of small business. *Journal of Small Business Management, 24*(2), 1–7.

Hout, M., & Rosen, H. S. (2000). Self-employment, family background, and race. *The Journal of Human Resources, 35*(4), 670–692. doi:10.2307/146367

Johnson, S., Kaufmann, D., & Zoido-Lobaton, P. (1998). Regulatory discretion and the unofficial economy. *The American Economic Review, 88*(2), 387–392.

Khavul, S., Bruton, G. D., & Wood, E. (2009). Informal family business in Africa. *Entrepreneurship Theory and Practice, 33*(6), 1219–1238. doi:10.1111/j.1540-6520.2009.00342.x

Kiggundu, M. N. (2002). Entrepreneurs and entrepreneurship in Africa: What is known and what needs to be done. *Journal of Developmental Entrepreneurship, 7*(3), 239–258.

Köllinger, P., & Minniti, M. (2006). Not for lack of trying: American entrepreneurship in black and white. *Small Business Economics, 27*(1), 59–79. doi:10.100711187-006-0019-6

Libombo, D. B., & Dinin, A. (2015). Entrepreneurship education in the context of developing countries: Study of the status and the main barriers in Mozambican higher education institutions. *Journal of Developmental Entrepreneurship, 20*(3), 1–26. doi:10.1142/S108494671550020X

Maloney, W. F. (2004). Informality revisited. *World Development, 32*(7), 1159–1178. doi:10.1016/j.worlddev.2004.01.008

Martin, W., Welch, B. A., Sandefur, J., & Pan, R. (2006). African American small business owners' attitudes toward business training. *Journal of Small Business Management, 44*(4), 577–591. doi:10.1111/j.1540-627X.2006.00192.x

Mukherjee, D. (2016). Informal economy in emerging economies: Not a substitute but a complement! *International Journal of Business & Economic Development*, *4*(3), 16–27.

New York City Small Business Services. (2022). https://www1.nyc.gov/site/sbs/businesses/black-entrepreneurs-nyc.page

Parasuraman, A., Zeithaml, V. A., & Berry, L. L. (1988). Servqual: A multiple-item scale for measuring consumer perceptions of service quality. *Journal of Retailing*, *64*(1), 12–23.

Porter, M. E. (2005). More tales of the inner city. *Inc.*, *27*(6), 86–89.

Porter, M. E., & Blaxill, M. (1997). Inner cities are the next retailing frontier. *Wall Street Journal.*

Rasheed, H. S. (2004). Capital access barriers to government procurement performance: Moderating effects of ethnicity, gender and education. *Journal of Developmental Entrepreneurship*, *9*(2), 109–126.

Reuben, L., & Queen, P. (2015). Capital constraints and industry mix implications for African-American business success. *The Review of Black Political Economy*, *42*(4), 355–378. doi:10.100712114-015-9210-9

Reynolds, P. D., Carter, N. M., Gartner, W. B., & Greene, P. G. (2004). The prevalence of nascent entrepreneurs in the United States: Evidence from the Panel Study of Entrepreneurial Dynamics. *Small Business Economics*, *23*(4), 263–284. doi:10.1023/B:SBEJ.0000032046.59790.45

Rheault, M., & Tortora, B. (2008). *Nigeria: Drivers and challenges of entrepreneurship*. www.gallup.com/poll/106345/nigeria-drivers-challenges-entrepreneurship.aspx

Rhodes, C., & Butler, J. S. (2004). Understanding self-perceptions of business performance: An examination of black American entrepreneurs. *Journal of Developmental Entrepreneurship*, *9*(1), 55–71.

Robb, A. M. (2002). Entrepreneurial performance by women and minorities: The case of new firms. *Journal of Developmental Entrepreneurship*, *7*(4), 383–398.

Robinson, J., Blockson, L., & Robinson, S. (2005). *African American women entrepreneurs and firm growth: New theoretical directions at the intersection of race, gender, and firm growth*. Babson College, Frontiers of Entrepreneurship Research.

Rogers, C. D., Gent, M. J., Palumbo, G. M., & Wall, R. A. (2001). Understanding the growth and viability of inner-city businesses. *Journal of Developmental Entrepreneurship*, *6*(3).

Sampson, R. J., & Wilson, W. J. (2005). Toward a theory of race, crime and urban inequality. In S. L. Gabbidon & H. T. Greene (Eds.), *Race, crime, and justice: A Reader*. Routledge: Taylor & Francis, Inc.

Schneider, F. (2005). The size of shadow economies in 145 countries from 1999 to 2003. *The Brown Journal of World Affairs*, *11*(2), 113–129.

Shane, S. A., & Venkataraman, S. (2000). The promise of entrepreneurship as a field of research. *Academy of Management Review*, *25*(1), 217–226. doi:10.5465/amr.2000.2791611

Singh, R. P., & Crump, M. E. S. (2007). Educational attainment: A key factor for improving the lagging rate of black entrepreneurship. *The Review of Black Political Economy*, *34*(2), 217–229. doi:10.100712114-008-9011-5

Singh, R. P., Crump, M. E. S., & Zu, X. (2009). Family matters: Examining how self-employed blacks and whites differ in having self-employed parents. In M. V. Bradshaw & P. T. Carrington (Eds.), *Entrepreneurship and its Economic Significance, Behavior and Effects* (pp. 1–20). Nova Science Publishers.

Singh, R. P., & Hills, G. E. (2003). *Recognizing opportunities vs. deciding to become an entrepreneur: A test of Bhave's model. In Research at the Marketing/Entrepreneurship Interface*. University of Illinois at Chicago.

Singh, R. P., Knox, E. L., & Crump, M. E. S. (2008). Opportunity recognition differences between black and white nascent entrepreneurs: A test of Bhave's model. *Journal of Developmental Entrepreneurship, 13*(1), 59–75. doi:10.1142/S1084946708000855

Singh, R. P., & McDonald, G. (2004). *Reasons for pursuing new venture creation: Differences between black and white nascent entrepreneurs.* 2004 Academy of Management Meeting, New Orleans, LA.

Spriggs, W., & Williams, R. (2000). What do we need to explain about African American unemployment? In R. Cherry & W. R. Rogers III, (Eds.), *Prosperity for all? The economic boom and African Americans* (pp. 188–207). Russell Sage Foundation.

Terrell, F., & Terrell, S. L. (1993). Level of cultural mistrust as a function of educational and occupational expectations among black students. *Adolescence, 28*(111), 573–578. PMID:8237544

US Census. (2012). https://www.census.gov/quickfacts/NY

Walstad, W. B., & Kourilsky, M. L. (1998). Entrepreneurial attitudes and knowledge of black youth. *Entrepreneurship Theory and Practice, 23*(2), 5–18. doi:10.1177/104225879802300201

Webb, J. W., Tihanyi, L., Ireland, R. D., & Sirmon, D. G. (2009). You say illegal, I say legitimate: Entrepreneurship in the informal economy. *Academy of Management Review, 34*(3), 492–510. doi:10.5465/amr.2009.40632826

Weiler, S., Silverstein, J., Chalmers, K., Lacey, E., Rogers, W., & Widner, B. (2003). Understanding the retail business potential of inner cities. *Journal of Economic Issues, 37*(4), 1075–1105. doi:10.1080/00213624.2003.11506643

Werbner, P. (2001). Metaphors of spatiality and networks in the plural city: A critique of the ethnic conclave economy debate. *Sociology, 35*(3), 671–693. doi:10.1177/S0038038501000347

Whaley, A. L. (2001). Cultural mistrust and mental health services for African Americans: A review and metanalysis. *The Counseling Psychologist, 29*(4), 513–531. doi:10.1177/0011000001294003

Whaley, A. L. (2004). Ethnicity/race, paranoia, and hospitalization for mental health problems among men. *American Journal of Public Health, 94*(1), 78–82. doi:10.2105/AJPH.94.1.78 PMID:14713702

Williams, C. C. (2008). Beyond necessity-driven versus opportunity-driven entrepreneurship: A study of informal entrepreneurs in England, Russia and Ukraine. *International Journal of Entrepreneurship and Innovation, 9*(3), 157–166. doi:10.5367/000000008785096647

Williams, C. C., & Nadin, S. (2010). The commonality and character of off-the-books entrepreneurship: A comparison of deprived and affluent urban neighbourhoods. *Journal of Developmental Entrepreneurship, 15*(03), 1–14. doi:10.1142/S1084946710001592

Williams, C. C., & Round, J. (2008). Retheorizing the nature of informal employment: Some lessons from Ukraine. *International Sociology, 23*(3), 367–388. doi:10.1177/0268580908088896

Williams, C. C., & Shahid, M. S. (2016). Informal entrepreneurship and institutional theory: Explaining the varying degrees of (in)formalization of entrepreneurs in Pakistan. *Entrepreneurship and Regional Development, 28*(1-2), 1–25. doi:10.1080/08985626.2014.963889

Williams, M. (2001). In whom we trust: Group membership as an effective context for trust development. *Academy of Management Review, 26*(3), 377–396. doi:10.5465/amr.2001.4845794

Wilson, F., Marlino, D., & Kickul, J. (2004). Our entrepreneurial future: Examining the diverse attitudes and motivations of teens across gender and ethnic identity. *Journal of Developmental Entrepreneurship, 9*(3), 177–197.

Yamoah, F. A., & Johnson, C. (2020). Minding the Gaps in British Ethnic Entrepreneurship and Commercial History: From the Genesis to the 21st Century. *Journal of Historical Sociology, 33*(4), 614–627. doi:10.1111/johs.12296

Young, N. (1998). *The structure and substance of African American entrepreneurial networks: Some preliminary findings*. Babson College, Frontiers of Entrepreneurship Research.

KEY TERMS AND DEFINITIONS

Financial Literacy for Entrepreneurs: Understanding how to position an entrepreneur and a new venture to attract external financing for seed, maintenance, and growth funding.

Formal Economy: A portion of a nation's economy that includes businesses that are formally registered, taxed, licensed, and regulated.

Informal Economy: A portion of a nation's economy that includes businesses that are *not* formally registered, taxed, licensed, and regulated. This segment of the economy includes the unregistered trade of both legitimate and illegitimate products and services.

Legal Structure of a Business: The selected business form to formally register a business as a sole proprietorship, general partnership, limited partnership, limited liability partnership, limited liability company, C-corporation, S-corporation, or B-corporation.

Necessity Entrepreneur: A person who primarily for income subsistence purposes decides to become an entrepreneur, and only after that decision do they search for, discover and select a particular business opportunity they will pursue.

Opportunity Entrepreneur: A person who primarily because of creativity and innovation discovers an opportunity to start a lucrative new business, and after that discovery, decides to become an entrepreneur.

Stem-Based Differentiation: A distinctive competitive feature of a successful new business where the products and services provided are based primarily on the creative use of technology and innovation. The new business uses this feature to provide more highly desired benefits to customers than competitors provide.

Strategically Setting Initial Prices: The process of methodically considering strategic factors to select a most optimal and sustainable price for all products and services a new business will introduce to a market.

Chapter 6

Why "Race Neutral" Policy Fails Black Small Business Owners:

Lessons Learned From the Paycheck Protection Program and Mapping an Equitable Path Forward

Saran Nurse
Kean University, USA

ABSTRACT

Utilizing critical race theory as the analytical lens, this chapter explores how the Paycheck Protection Program, which did not specify preference to race of applicant, nevertheless resulted in racialized outcomes. The chapter examines the program's primary features to understand whether the appearance of race neutrality obscures a White normative standard embedded within the program. The examination reveals that the program's design was more aligned with the White small business owner experience and that policymakers failed to adequately consider the unique needs of Black small business owners in formulating the program. The author argues that the program was therefore more accessible to White small business owners, was more beneficial to them, and helped to perpetuate the White advantage in small business outcomes. The chapter concludes with the recommendation that future small business policies should follow a targeted universalism approach. Suggestions for redesigning the Paycheck Protection Program, or similar small business policy, are provided.

INTRODUCTION

On March 27, 2020, the United States Congress enacted the Paycheck Protection Program (PPP) to help the nation's small businesses survive the economic fallout from the COVID -19 pandemic. While the program was lauded as a success by many, the overwhelming sentiment amongst Black small business owners has been that the PPP failed them. In the media, stories of the difficulties encountered by Black small business owners in accessing PPP funds have been ubiquitous. Andrea Power, an Atlanta-based

DOI: 10.4018/978-1-6684-4322-4.ch006

Black small business owner, applied for a PPP loan so that she could retain her ten employees. After first being told that the program had run out of money, she was then denied funding because of her poor credit history (Brooks, 2020). Dannesia Pullen, whose trucking company saw a 15-20% decline in cash flow due to the pandemic, applied for a PPP loan, and was also declined (Allam, 2020). Terrika Walker, who owns a residential care facility in Louisiana, was forced to lay off all five of her employees when she was rejected six weeks after applying for a PPP loan (Cowley, 2022). Black-owned small businesses, which are more likely to be located in highly competitive, low profitability industries, were the least likely to have the financial cushion to survive the COVID-19 pandemic. Yet, they were also least likely to receive assistance from the PPP. Meanwhile, the majority of White-owned small businesses received the PPP funds they applied for. Dr. Rich Coleman, a White veterinarian and owner of Four Paws Animal Hospital in Ohio, received a PPP loan for $206,000 within one week of applying. He stated that the loan helped him to retain his 34 employees, and allowed him to go home every night knowing that his employees could pay their rent, feed their families, and more importantly, maintain the massive amount of pets they own (Paycheck Protection Program: Loan Forgiveness and Other Challenges, 2020). The aforementioned accounts are not isolated incidents - that there were racial disparities in access to the PPP is empirically supported. According to the United States Small Business Administration (SBA), of the businesses that received PPP loans, 1.9% were Black-owned, 7% Latino-owned, while the majority - 83% - were White-owned. And, for those Black small business owners who were successful in obtaining PPP loans, their average loan amount of $24,315 was less than half of the average received by Asian-owned businesses, and merely one quarter of the average loan amount disbursed to White-owned businesses (Howell et al., 2021).

Much of the research on the experience of Black-owned small businesses with the PPP has focused on identifying racial disparities in access. The resounding conclusion of those studies is that there were indeed racial disparities. Missing from the literature, however, is a deeper exploration into the root causes of the disparities; a glaring omission that warrants further investigation. This chapter fills that void. Utilizing critical race theory as the analytical lens, the chapter explores why the PPP, which did not specify preference for race of the applicant, nevertheless resulted in racialized outcomes. Critical race theorists argue that racial inequality is maintained by policies which while appearing to be race neutral, systematically discriminate against minority groups (Bradbury, 2020). The chapter's analysis has significant policy implications. As policy-makers grapple with how to close the racial wealth gap, increasing Black entrepreneurship has been advanced as a solution. Indeed, in June 2021, the Biden-Harris Administration announced that their two areas of focus for narrowing the racial wealth gap would be home ownership and small business ownership. This study will 1) help policymakers understand the underlying causes of the racial disparities in access in the PPP 2) help policymakers to, more broadly, understand why seemingly race neutral policies have had limited impact in helping Black business owners and 3) help with the design of more racially inclusive small business policies. Regarding the latter, this chapter recommends a targeted universalism approach to small business policymaking which, as is argued herein, would ensure that future small business policies are designed to produce more equitable outcomes for Black business owners, while also gaining acceptability among the different stakeholder groups.

This chapter is organized as follows. First, to set the context, the formulation of the PPP is described and the literature on racial disparities in PPP lending is reviewed. Next, critical race theory (CRT) is presented, and the two CRT tenets most relevant to this study - the ordinariness of racism and interest convergence theory- are defined. Then, a CRT analysis of the Paycheck Protection Program is undertaken, utilizing the ordinariness of racism tenet of CRT. The chapter concludes with policy recommendations - based on CRT' s interest convergence theory - and a description of what a redesigned Paycheck Protection Program or similar small business policy should look like if it is to achieve racially equitable outcomes.

BACKGROUND

Formulation of The Paycheck Protection Program

The unexpected and unprecedented, emergence of the COVID- 19 pandemic and the attendant threat to and loss of human life, shelter at home mandates, social distancing requirements, and closure of nonessential businesses in many states was a shock to the operations of many small businesses. In less than a week of deliberation, on March 27, 2020, the U.S. Congress passed the Paycheck Protection Program, as part of the Coronavirus Aid Relief and Economic Security (CARES) Act. Initially, $350 Billion was allocated, but with demand quickly outstripping supply within thirteen days the program funds were depleted. With many small businesses left unable to access desperately needed cash, in late April 2020, an additional $329 Billion in federal funds was added to the program through a subsequent bill. In January 2021, a third round of funding provided an additional $284.5 Billion which allowed several small businesses to receive a "second draw loan". To qualify for second draw loans, businesses had to attest that they had experienced financial hardships, defined as an at least 25% decrease in any quarter's gross receipts from 2019 to 2020. In the third round of funding, modifications were made that were intended to prioritize smaller firms and minority-owned businesses. This included increased lending by Community Development Financial Institutions (CDFIs) and banks with less than $10 Billion in assets, and an advance two-week exclusive window during which CDFIs with less than $1 Billion in assets had a head-start in taking applications.

As the largest small business finance program in U.S. history, the PPP was designed with two primary goals - to provide an incentive for small businesses to retain their employees, and to help these small businesses cover some of their short-term operating expenses (Letteiri and Lyons, 2020). Given the sudden onset of the Covid-19 pandemic, the threat to the viability of small businesses and the resultant need to expeditiously provide some type of relief, policymakers rushed to design the PPP. Challenged with the determination of a policy instrument, policymakers created a program that was not innovative but similar in structure to the SBA's largest policy instrument - the 7a program. As is posited by the theory of bounded rationality, policymakers faced with constraints of resources in the decision making process - particularly constraints of time - used heuristics, familiarity and habit in designing the PPP. Public policy scholars, Howlett and Ramesh (1993) argue that the choice of policy instrument is shaped by the past experience of policymakers in dealing with the same or similar problems, and the subjective preference of the decision-makers. The PPP was therefore not a wholly new or different program. As in the traditional 7a program, the SBA utilized banks and other lending institutions to administer the federally guaranteed PPP loans to qualified businesses with up to 500 employees. The SBA compensated lenders for originating and servicing the PPP loans. Lenders received 5% for loans up to $350,000, 3% for loans between $350,000 and $2,000,000, and 1% for loans of $2,000,000 and greater. Where the PPP primarily differs from the 7a program is in the forgiveness clause. A PPP loan is forgivable, and may convert to a grant, if a business spends at least 60% of proceeds (adjusted from 75% in the initial Bill) on payroll expenses and the remainder on rent and utilities within 24 weeks (this was previously set at

8 weeks in the first bill) of disbursement. Businesses were also required to maintain payroll at least at 75% of pre-COVID-19 levels for loans to be completely forgiven. Businesses that do not qualify for forgiveness must repay the loan proceeds at a 1% interest rate within two years of the six-month grace period after disbursement (this was increased to 5 years for loans initiated after June 1, 2020).

While Section 1102 of the CARES Act specifies that the PPP should prioritize underserved markets, as well as businesses owned by socially and economically disadvantaged individuals, there was no direction initially provided to banks on how to achieve those objectives. The race of the applicant was also not an explicit factor in qualification or approval for the PPP. Program rules did not mention race or ethnicity; loan amounts were determined using calculations based, not on the applicant's race, but on the amount of the business's average monthly payroll. The Treasury Department's fact sheet for the PPP states that "all loan terms will be the same for everyone" (www.sba.com). Information on race was not even collected at all in the first round, although some limited collection of such information was done in the second round. The result was that according to the SBA, 78.6% of the total value of loans have gone to small businesses that did not report the owner's race or ethnicity. Prima facie, the PPP seemed to be race neutral in its design yet anecdotal accounts and empirical studies, have cited racial disparities in access to PPP funds.

LITERATURE REVIEW

Racial Disparities in access to the Paycheck Protection Program

Given the recency of the Covid-19 pandemic, the academic literature on the PPP is still limited. Within that body of knowledge, most studies on the experiences of Black-owned small businesses with the program have focused on identifying, and measuring, racial disparities in access. In one of the first and most cited studies on the effects of the Covid-19 pandemic on small businesses, Fairlie (2020) finds that from March to June 2020 (the first three months of the Covid-19 pandemic) Black-owned businesses were hardest hit. Black-owned businesses saw a 41% decline in business activity, compared to a 32% drop in business activity for Latinx-owned businesses, 26% for Asian-owned businesses and 17% for White-owned businesses. Building on the results of that study, in a subsequent study Fairlie and Fossen (2021) find some evidence that, while in the first round of lending, PPP funds were disproportionately disbursed to non-minority communities, in the second round funds were disproportionately disbursed to minority communities. However, it could have been that more minority business owners stipulated race in their applications during the second round (rather than there being disproportionate loan receipts by minority-owned businesses). Since it had been publicized that minority applicants were to be prioritized in the second round, more minority applicants may have indicated race in that round of applications, in the hopes that such identification would have provided them with an advantage in the application process.

Attempting to identify the source of racial disparity in loan receipts, Howell et al. (2021) point to racial discrimination by banks. They find that Black-owned small businesses were more likely to use fintech lenders to secure loans, particularly in geographic areas higher in racial animus. They postulate that automation reduces human bias and lowers the likelihood of taste-based discrimination that Black small business owners may have believed they would encounter when applying in-person at banks. They argue that their findings provide further support that automated lending processes and machine learning algorithms, could help to achieve more equitable outcomes in banking. However, as they do acknowledge, automated lending platforms still do rely on the same criteria for lending as traditional larger banks including revenues, the business owner's income and personal credit score. These criteria do have a racially biased component since Black-owned businesses tend to have lower revenues, and Black business owners are more likely to have lower assets and lower credit scores. So, while automation may reduce overt racial bias, it does not necessarily resolve the structural disadvantages Black businesses owners experience in the lending process.

Providing further evidence of racial discrimination by banks, Lederer and Oros (2020) in their matched pair audit experiment of financial institutions in Washington, DC, find that Black applicants received less encouragement and information when applying for PPP loans than did their White counterparts. Using a large sample of Florida restaurants, Chernenko and Scharfstein (2022) also point to racial discrimination by banks. They find that within the same ZIP code, Black and Hispanic-owned firms were 20.5% and 7.0% respectively, less likely than White-owned firms to receive PPP loans. And, whereas White-owned restaurants were 11.9% more likely to get a loan from a bank if they had an existing secured loan, Black-owned restaurants with existing secured loans were no more likely than those without such loans to receive PPP funding through banks. They posit that either banks did not prioritize Black-owned restaurants with which they had existing relationships, or that Black-owned businesses had weaker relationships with these banks, or that the Black restaurant owners were "discouraged borrowers" who were reluctant to apply because of previous experiences with racial discrimination. Similar to Howell et al. (2021), they also find that Black-owned firms were more likely to utilize non-bank sources (e.g. fintech lenders) for loans.

Examining whether proximity and lack of access to bank locations might be a driver of racial disparity in lending PPP outcomes, Wang and Zhang (2021) find that ZIP codes with greater percentages of Black residents had lower take-up rates of PPP loans (measure by the ratio of PPP loans to the number of establishments in a ZIP code). They posit that a lower take-up rate is related to a lower concentration of branches of PPP approved lenders in ZIP codes with more Black residents. This lower proximity to banking locations buttresses the explanation as to why Black-owned businesses were more likely to use non-traditional banking sources like fintech lenders, a theory also advanced by Erel and Liebersohn (2020) who also find that fintech lenders were disproportionately used in high minority population ZIP codes.

Atkins, Cook and Seamans (2021) find that Black-owned businesses received loans that were about 50% lower than similar White-owned businesses. They provide some evidence (although not statistically significant) that Black-White differences in PPP loan amounts decrease in areas with more commercial bank locations which provides some further support to the theory that pre-existing relationship with banks and/or proximity to bank locations is what helped to increase access to PPP funds for White-owned businesses (Erel & Liebersohn, 2020; Wang & Zhang 2021). They do find that over time the Black-White differences in loan amounts decrease, and they attribute this to increased access by Black-owned businesses to non-bank lenders such as fintech lenders. They argue that reliance on commercial banks for administering the program was the fundamental flaw in the PPP, since the design did not account for the systemic inequality that has historically been very much a part of the banking system.

But, since only ten percent of applicants reported race when applying, in most of the aforementioned studies extrapolations about race of the applicants had to be made which may not have been completely accurate. Moreover, information collected has been on the number of PPP loans disbursed rather than the percentage approved (by race) versus denied. And, as has been described above, most studies have pointed to overt forms of discrimination on the part of banking institutions as the source of racial disparities in access. However, racism is more than overt discrimination - it is also systemic and structural.

And structural racism is often the reason policies do not work for people of color (Vohra-Gupta, Kim and Cubbin, 2021).

THEORETICAL FRAMEWORK

a. Critical Race Theory

Structural racism is oftentimes difficult to identify - it is subtle and easily hides behind everyday activities, including rules and policies that claim to treat Blacks and Whites equally (Garcia, Gee and Jones, 2016). Critical race theory is a framework for detecting and analyzing structural racism. It recognizes that racial disparities do not only result from individualized prejudice or single acts of discrimination but also from "social, systemic forces that are well embedded into all major U.S. institutions and the policies that guide them" (Vohra-Gupta et al., 2021, p.1483). Critical race theory emerged from critical legal scholars who theorized that the law, institutions and systems could never be race neutral since they are shaped by the values and beliefs of those who hold power (Rocco and Gallagher, 2004). Although the Civil Rights Act of 1964 had prohibited discrimination based on race, and had provided equal protection under the law for people of color, those who were setting policy and law were guided by their subjective beliefs that Black people were still inferior and Whites superior. While racism may have been outlawed in law, it still remained embedded in norms, culture and practice so that the United States' racist past did not simply stay in the past but continued to manifest in post-civil rights laws and policies.

b. The Ordinariness of Racism Tenet

One of the most salient of CRT's perspectives is that racism is not unusual but is a normal and endemic component of our social fabric (Crenshaw, Gotanda, Peller and Thomas, 1995; Delgado and Stefancic, 2017; Bell, 2018). Indeed, what we believe to be "normal" is in fact more aligned with the White experience and White standards of normality. It is this very "normal" way of operating - the routines, practices and institutions that undergird society - that results in the oppression of people of color, and keeps them in a subordinate position (Delgado & Stefancic, 2017). Racism is often overlooked and taken for granted (Lopez, 2003) because we oftentimes fail to see the subtle ways in which it shapes our perspectives and systems, and is embedded within structures and institutions. It is often undetectable until there are egregious, racially disparate outcomes. The ordinariness of racism tenet of CRT posits that those who hold power or privilege do not realize their actions to be racist but believe those actions to be typical and consistent with the status quo (Bowman, Rocco, Peterson and Adker, 2009). Therefore, purported race neutral, or colorblind, approaches and policies are a principal means of perpetuating or maintaining racism (Gotanda, 1991; Siegel, 2020).

c. Interest Convergence Theory

Another argument of critical race theorists is that Black people only gain some progress towards social justice when their interests align with that of the White majority. According to this interest convergence theory, coined by the late Professor Derrick Bell, the dominant group permits or allows racial justice progress only when it benefits their interests (Delgado & Stefanic, 2017). And, in many instances that interest convergence does occur, progress is usually temporary since short-lived victories "slide into irrelevance as racial patterns adapt in ways that maintain White dominance" (Bell, 1992, p. 373). Interest convergence maintains that Whites are only willing to change the power differential when there is a clear benefit to them (Bowman et al., 2009). The degree of progress Blacks have made away from slavery and toward equality has depended on whether allowing Blacks more or less opportunity has best served the interests and aims of the White society (Bell, 1980). For example, the passing of the Civil Rights Act of 1964, and the end of de jure segregation were not pursued because of morality or changed ideologies of White policymakers but because they had identified that abandoning segregation would benefit the United States both economically and politically (Conyers and Fields, 2021). Because there has been insufficient convergence of interest between Blacks and White elites, efforts to eradicate racism have had minimal impact. However, many interest convergence theorists do argue that the way for Black people to advance is through joint gains rather than in cases or instances in which one group concedes while the other profits (Graham, Brown-Jeffy, Aronson, and Stephens, 2011).

METHODOLOGY AND FINDINGS

Any time we hear or assert that there are equal opportunities, CRT encourages us to dig deeper and to ask who benefits from this framing of the world? (Conyers & Fields, 2021)

A critical race theory policy analysis is useful for unmasking how policies which are believed to be equal or neutral, and not intended to be biased, result in the marginalization and oppression of communities of color (Valles and Villalpando, 2021). Following the methodological approaches used by Bradbury (2020) and Gillborn (2005; 2014), the next section of this chapter conducts a CRT policy analysis, the objective of which is to establish whether the appearance of race neutrality in the PPP may indeed obscure an embedded White standard of normality. To this end, each of the program's primary features are identified and evaluated, in turn, and the question "who is more likely to benefit from this feature?" is asked and answered. Since CRT advocates that people of color share their lived experiences with racism and oppression through storytelling, narratives, chronicles and parables (Valles & Villalpando, 2021), direct quotes from the media of Black business owners' experiences with the PPP are cited for analytical support.

a. Critical Race Theory Analysis of the Paycheck Protection Program

The primary features of the PPP have been identified as:

- Loans as the policy instrument
- Employee retention as the goal of the program
- Loan amounts calculated based on payroll costs
- Qualification linked to federal loan history
- Initial prioritizing based on the type of legal entity
- Use of banks for program implementation

1. Loans as the Policy Instrument

Policy instrument choice is one of the most important elements of policy design (Howlett, 1991). It is a systematic effort to identify the most appropriate means to solve a problem, an element of the problem or to achieve a policy target (Bali, Capano and Ramesh, 2019). In designing the PPP, policymakers chose a debt instrument (a loan) as their policy instrument. Although convertible to a grant, the PPP was essentially a loan because the applicant was required to sign a promissory note, and if the business does not meet the criteria for forgiveness, and/or does not apply for forgiveness within a specified time frame, the debt must be repaid to the Treasury.

While banks loans are the primary source of capital for many business owners (Blanchflower, Levine and Zimmerman, 2003; Cavalluzzon and Wolken, 2002), this is less so for Black business owners. Discrimination in lending has resulted in Black business owners being less likely to be approved for loans and, if approved, being required to pay higher interest rates on loans (Bates, 1997; Blanchflower et al., 2003; Bates and Robb, 2013). Fearing rejection, many Black business owners are loath to even apply for loans. As an example, a study of Black women business owners conducted by the Federal Reserve Bank of Kansas City in 2016, found that 94% of them did not apply for loans because they felt discouraged by credit opportunities (Gines, 2017). When a business challenge arose, they were more likely to respond by using personal funds, cutting payroll or downsizing operations (Gines, 2017). Conversely, White business owners have had more favorable experiences when applying for bank loans. The Center for Responsible Lending reports that 46% of White-owned businesses in the last five years accessed credit from a bank, double that of Black-owned businesses. For many Black business owners, applying for a loan through the PPP was their first time ever attempting to apply for a loan (Amato, 2020).

According to program stipulations, any part of the PPP loan that is not forgiven must be repaid within two years (for businesses loans approved prior to June 5, 2020) and within five years (for loans approved after June 5, 2020). This could pose hardship for Black small business owners who are more likely than White small business owners to operate on thin margins, and are already struggling with other forms of debt. They are more likely to be in industries such as personal services and some retail sectors which are more competitive and less profitable (Coleman 2005; Lofstrom, Bates and Parker, 2014). In aggregate 58.9% of Black-owned businesses are in the bottom twenty industries compared to only 30.6% of White-owned businesses (Myers and Chan, 2017). Of all ethnic groups, Black-owned businesses have the lowest average annual aggregate sales at $58,000 compared to $546,000 for White-owned businesses (Myers & Chan, 2017). This translates into a greater ability by White-owned businesses to absorb additional debt expense. This leads to this chapter's first proposition:

Proposition 1: *Policymakers' choice of loans as the policy instrument for the Paycheck Protection Program is more favorable to White-owned businesses because they are better able to afford debt expense (in the event that the PPP loan is not forgiven), are more likely to pursue the loan application process, and are less likely to be discouraged borrowers.*

2. Employee Retention as the Goal of the Program

Another element of an effectively designed policy is that the goals of the policy should be clear, consistent and unambiguous (Pressman and Wildavsky, 1984). As previously described, the goal of the PPP was to help small businesses survive the Covid-19 pandemic by firstly, providing an incentive for them to retain their employees, and secondly, by helping businesses to cover some of their short-term operating expenses. While 42.8% of White-owned businesses have paid staff, only 4.2% of Black-owned businesses have any staff (Myers & Chan, 2017). Black businesses are also more likely to be located in majority Black neighborhoods. In terms of rates of infection, and health outcomes, these areas have been some of the hardest hit by the pandemic (Mills and Battisto, 2020) and therefore would have experienced reduced demand due to the pandemic. Thus, even for those Black-owned businesses that do have employees, reduced demand would have made employee retention close to pre-pandemic levels unrealistic (this was the stipulated condition for loan forgiveness). Conversely, in predominantly White and other non-black neighborhoods, where most White-owned businesses are located, rates of infection have been lower and residents have not been as severely impacted by the pandemic as those in Black areas. Therefore, compared to Black-owned businesses, White-owned businesses were more likely to retain customers and, consequently, employees. Thus, while forgiveness based on employee retention may be presented as impartial, or as a race neutral criterion, it was probably less of an attainable goal for Black-owned businesses. This leads to the chapter's second proposition:

Proposition 2: *The PPP's goal of employee retention is more likely to help White-owned businesses - relative to Black-owned businesses - because White-owned businesses are more likely to have employees, less likely to have had demand disrupted by the Covid-19 pandemic and therefore more likely to retain their employees.*

3. Loan amounts Calculated Based on Payroll Costs

In the PPP, loan amounts were calculated at 2.5 times the business's average monthly payroll costs up to a maximum loan of $10 million per customer. As described above, most Black-owned businesses do not have employees, and therefore have no or low payroll costs. There is a direct correlation between the success of the business and the number of employees and/or payroll costs; businesses that are more successful would have a greater need for employees, and have higher payroll expenses. By tying loan disbursement to payroll costs, meritocracy, rather than need, was the criterion for receiving PPP funding. Critical race theorists argue that the ordinariness of racism manifests in policies that emphasize meritocracy (Gillborn, 2014). This leads to the third proposition:

Proposition 3: *The Paycheck Protection Program feature of determining loan amount based upon payroll expense is more likely to result in White-owned businesses receiving higher loan amounts because they tend to have better financial performance, more employees, and higher payroll expenses.*

4. Qualification Linked to Federal Loan History

While policymakers claimed that neither extensive credit history nor credit score were factored into determining PPP approval, if a business had previously defaulted or was delinquent on a federal loan, it was disqualified. According to the SBA, in the 7a loan program, Blacks have twice the delinquency rate as Whites (Simon and McGinty, 2014). Loan defaults and late payments are directly related to financial position. A business with greater financial resources is in a better position to repay debt, and would be less likely to default. White-owned businesses are more profitable than Black-owned businesses, and Whites also have greater wealth than Blacks. In 2016, the typical Black family's net worth, at $17,150, was a tenth the $171,000 held by White families (Dettling et al., 2017). Greater personal or familial wealth translates into better financially positioned businesses that are less likely to default on loans, and may even have less of a need for debt. Hence the next proposition:

Proposition 4: *A track record of consistent federal loan payments and no defaults as a criterion for qualification for a PPP loan would likely result in greater loan approvals of White owned-businesses, and less approvals of Black-owned businesses because these criteria are proxies for financial stability.*

5. Initial Prioritizing Based on the Type of Legal Entity

In order to quickly help the employees of businesses that may have been about to lay off workers at the onset of the pandemic, when the first set of PPP funds became available, incorporated businesses were prioritized. Independent contractors and sole proprietors were required to wait a week before applying. The assumption was that corporations were more likely to have employees. The vast majority (95%) of Black-owned small businesses are sole proprietors that do not have paid employees and were therefore not eligible to apply early in the first round. By the time many sole proprietors were eligible to apply, first round funding had been depleted. Additional funds were available in the second round of funding, and by the third round restrictions were loosened to accommodate sole proprietors. But given that as many as 58% of Black-owned businesses (compared to only 27% of White-owned businesses) were financially distressed prior to the pandemic (Atkins et al., 2021), Black-owned small businesses were in greater need of immediate access to PPP funds. Although minority businesses were prioritized in the second round of funding, by then many of these businesses had already folded. Indeed, between February and April 2020, Black-owned businesses experienced the largest rates of decline of all businesses as a result of the pandemic (Fairlie, 2020). This leads to the fifth proposition:

Proposition 5: *The prioritizing of corporations over sole proprietors in the PPP first round was more likely to ensure that White-owned businesses received funding because White-owned businesses are more likely to be corporations compared to Black-owned businesses.*

6. Use of Banks for Program Implementation

Many of the banks participating in the PPP only issued loans to existing clients. Black-owned businesses are often unbanked, and those businesses that do have banking relationships, are more likely to use smaller banks, credit unions, or community finance institutions, many of which had difficulty processing PPP applications. According to the Treasury Department, at the rollout of the PPP, only 78 of the nation's 950 community development financial institutions had the capability to process PPP loans. Major banks that offered the PPP loans, including Bank of America, JPMorgan Chase and Wells Fargo, prioritized larger loan applications in order to maximize loan-origination fees and their own profits. Financial institutions were incentivized to prioritize larger loans. Since Black-owned businesses are more likely to be small, they were less attractive to lenders, and less likely to be funded by banks. Accessing the PPP, particularly in the initial stages, also depended on the strength of the business's banking relationship and frequency of interaction with bank employees (Granja et al., 2020). As previously mentioned, the majority of

Black-owned businesses are located in majority Black neighborhoods where the higher concentration of co-ethnics tends to offer them better business opportunities. In recent years, major banks have reduced the number of their locations in majority-black neighborhoods. JPMorgan cut the number of branch locations in majority-black areas by 22.8% from 2010 to 2018, compared to a net decline of 0.2% in the rest of the U.S. Bank of America also scaled down its locations in majority-black neighborhoods by 29.1%, versus 18.4% in non-majority-black areas (Fox et al., 2019). This leads to the last proposition:

Proposition 6: *The focus on banks for implementation of the PPP, particularly in the initial rollout, increased access to the program to White-owned businesses which are more likely to be banked, are more likely to have greater physical access to banking institutions and, consequently, have had the opportunity to establish relationships necessary to help with prioritization of their PPP applications.*

b. Summary of Findings

On the surface, the PPP may have seemed to be race neutral. However, critical race theorists challenge claims of objectivity, colorblindness, race neutrality and equal opportunity (Solórzano & Yosso, 2002). Indeed, as the preceding critical race theory policy analysis has illustrated, the design of the PPP seemed to have been based on the White small business owner's experience. Each of the program's primary features seemed to have been consistent with what was tenable or "normal" for the White small business owner (see Table 1 below). Consequently, White-owned businesses were more likely to have access to the program, were more likely to be approved, to receive higher loan payouts and, overall, were more likely to benefit from the PPP. By using the White normative standard, in its design, and failing to consider the needs and experiences of Black small business owners, the PPP perpetuates racism, and the Black disadvantage in small business performance. The case of the Paycheck Protection Program also aptly illustrates how policies may inherently be designed in a racially biased manner, even without specific intent of discrimination on the part of policymakers.

RECOMMENDATIONS

As previously mentioned, the PPP was not a wholly new program but was similar in structure to the SBA's 7a loan program. In its several decades of existence, the 7a loan – which also does not stipulate preference to race of applicant - has also not been equitable in outcomes. For example, 7a program lending in majority-Black ZIP codes has been significantly lower than lending in majority-White ZIP codes. Between 2017 and 2020, more than 75% of all 7a loans went to businesses located in majority-White ZIP codes, while majority-Black ZIP codes have been consistently underserved by 7(a) programs in both the volume of loans as well as loan amounts (Simms and Robbenbolt, 2020). Given this track record of racial inequity with the 7 (a) program, and since the PPP was similarly designed, it should not be completely surprising that the PPP was also inequitable in outcome. If policymakers are to improve Black small business outcomes, a new structure and approach to policy making is needed since policies based on existing designs are likely to perpetuate racism, and the Black small business disadvantage.

Table 1. Paycheck Protection Program primary features and comparison of Black and White business owner experiences

PROGRAM FEATURE	WHITE BUSINESS OWNER EXPERIENCE	BLACK BUSINESS OWNER EXPERIENCE	WHO MORE LIKELY BENEFITS FROM THIS FEATURE?
Loans as the policy/program instrument	Are better able to afford debt expense in the event that the PPP loan is not forgiven	Less able to afford debt expense in the event that the PPP loan is not forgiven More likely to be discouraged from the loan application process.	White-owned businesses
Employee retention as the goal of the program	Less likely to have seen as sharp a decline in demand due to the pandemic as did businesses located in majority Black areas, so are more likely to be able to retain employees near pre-pandemic levels	Most do not have employees. For those businesses that did have multiple employees, sharp declines in demand due to the pandemic would have made employee retention unrealistic	White-owned businesses
Loan amounts calculated based on payroll costs	42.8% of White- owned businesses have paid staff	Only 4.2% of Black-owned businesses have any staff	White-owned businesses
Qualification linked to federal loan history	White-owned businesses have greater profitability. Whites have greater wealth and financial means and are less likely to have defaulted on previous federal loans	Black-owned businesses have lower profitability, and lower wealth, and are more likely to have defaulted on a previous federal loan	White-owned businesses
Initial prioritizing based on the type of legal entity	More likely to be corporations which were prioritized in first round funding	More likely to be sole proprietors who were unable to access first round funding when it was most needed	White-owned businesses
Use of banks as intermediaries	More likely to be located in close proximity to banking locations and to have banking relationships	Are often unbanked and in locations with fewer bank locations	White-owned businesses

a. Beyond Race Neutral Policies

Policies exist on a spectrum as regards their treatment of race (see Figure 1). On one side are race neutral policies that do not stipulate preference to race. The rationale underlying a race neutral approach, or color-blind policy, is that where race is not factored, racial discrimination cannot occur (Peery, 2011). However, as the case of the PPP aptly illustrates, a color blind policy is not race neutral in its consequences. Indeed, "color blind" policies maintain the White advantage by camouflaging themselves under the cloak of race neutrality (Bonilla-Silva, 2006). In the middle of the spectrum are race conscious policies which, while not specifically targeted at any racial group, uses tactics that are more likely to help a particular racial group. As an example, although the second round of the PPP did not specifically target Black-owned businesses, by prioritizing applications from CDFIs in the first two weeks, Black- owned businesses were more likely to be prioritized. The observation that PPP loans to Black-owned businesses may have increased in the second round of funding (Atkins et al., 2021), provides some support for the merit of a race conscious approach. On the other side of the spectrum are race based policies. Race based policies are intentional about race in their design, and do target resources at an explicitly defined racial group.

Examples include policies such as reparations and affirmative action. Race based policies face strong opposition, particularly from Whites who level charges of reverse discrimination, since these types of policies require re-distribution of resources (or opportunities) from the dominant group (Whites) to the underserved groups (such as Blacks and other people of color). However, a race based approach to policy design that does not require redistribution of resources and seeks to benefit all racial groups, may face less opposition and gain greater acceptability amongst all stakeholders. Targeted universalism is such a race based approach to policy design.

Figure 1. Range of policies regarding treatment of race

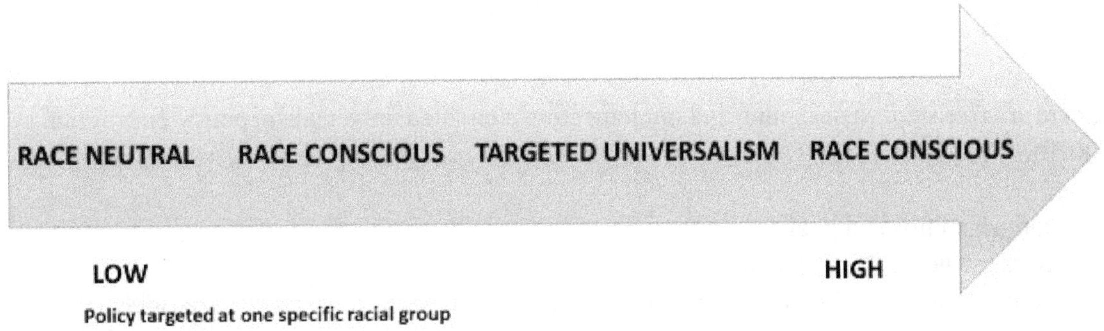

b. Targeted Universalism

"We cannot ignore and should learn from and try to recognize situations when there is a convergence of interests" (Bell 2000, p. 9)

Targeted universalism is a race based framework to developing policies that considers the unique needs of all groups while aiming to move everyone toward a universal goal (Gaynor and Wilson, 2020). This approach to policymaking considers that while a focus on disparities is important, the goal for those with less resources and power, should not simply be to achieve the same level as the majority. This is particularly salient when the majority group, although having achieved more than the minority group, still significantly underperforms. In such a situation, if the goal was simply to close a disparity between the majority group and minority group, the goal would be achieved once the minority group achieved the same level as the majority group. But this would not be the most optimal outcome for society since both groups would still only have reached sub-par levels. Under targeted universalism, the goal would be for both Blacks and Whites to achieve a lofty, universal goal but to do so utilizing different strategies that account for the unique needs of the two different groups. After establishing a universal goal, strategies would be set for each group that account for the differences in how those groups are situated. Blacks would be moved to the center in terms of societal care and attention in policymaking, at the same time that the needs of Whites are addressed (Powell, Menendian and Ake, 2019). Critical race theorists advocate for the identification of opportunities where there is convergence of interests between Blacks and Whites - where both groups jointly gain. Designing small business policy utilizing a targeted universalism approach is such an opportunity.

Figure 2. Illustration of Targeted Universalism

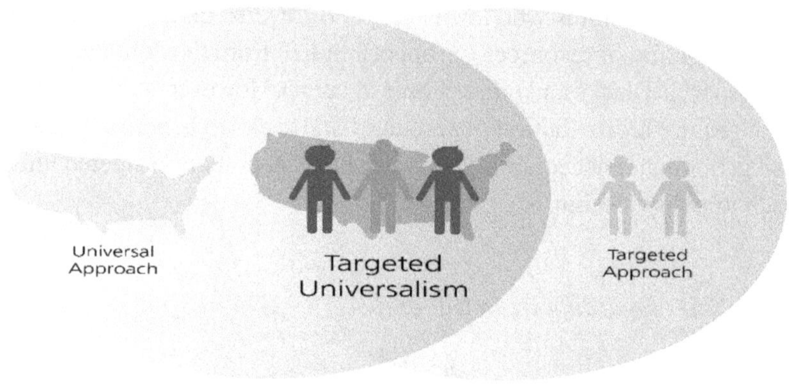

There are five steps to designing and implementing a targeted universalism policy or program (Willis, 2020).

1. Establish a universal goal.
2. Assess the general population relative to the goal.
3. Identify groups and places that are performing differently with respect to the goal and disaggregate them.
4. Assess and understand the structures that support or impede each group from achieving the universal goal. In this stage it is essential that members of each affected groups be asked to provide input.
5. Develop and implement targeted strategies for each group to reach the goal.

c. Reimagining The Paycheck Protection Program or the next Small Business Policy

A redesigned Paycheck Protection Program or other similar small business policy using targeted universalism would seek to maximize access to funds to businesses owned by people of all races. As previously discussed, participation rates in the Paycheck Protection Program were 83% and 1.9% for White and Black-owned small businesses respectively. If the goal were to simply resolve disparities in access to funding between Black and White-owned small businesses, efforts would cease once 83% of Black business owners received PPP loans. A new Paycheck Protection Program - or other program or policy to help Black-owned small businesses survive adversity using a targeted universalism approach would set a higher goal for both groups, for example, the goal may be that 100% of both Black and White-owned small businesses should have access to funding. From there, the strategies to achieve 100% access would vary based on each group's needs. For Black-owned small businesses:

- **The policy goal would be to ensure that Black-owned small businesses survive irrespective of a goal of employee retention**. This would increase access to funds for those Black-owned businesses that are sole proprietorships and partnerships that do not have employees, as well as increase access to funds for those Black-owned businesses that do have employees but are unable to retain employees due to negative demand shocks.

- **The policy instrument would be a conditional grant rather than a convertible loan.** The PPP was essentially a grant that converted to a loan if the small business owner did not meet certain requirements, and did not apply for forgiveness. Yet it was branded as a convertible loan. Given the Black business community's skepticism of, and reluctance to utilize loans, the PPP would have greater acceptability amongst the Black community if it was instead described as a grant that may be converted to a loan if the small business owner did not meet certain requirements.
- **The criteria for forgiveness would be expanded so that forgiveness is not only based on meritocracy but also on need.** Loans to Black-owned small businesses located in areas that have been the most adversely affected by the pandemic, and to businesses located in industries with lower margins (and are therefore at greatest risk of closure in turbulent economic times) would be expeditiously approved.

For all racial groups, there would be greater input from representatives from their respective groups, and greater accountability for program outcomes by ensuring that data on the race of the applicant is collected. The result would be greater overall economic benefit compared to a policy that focused specifically on Black-owned small businesses. More jobs would be created and there would be greater tax revenues collected which could be reinvested to spur further growth for all.

CONCLUSION

This goal of this chapter was to explore the root causes of the racial disparities in access observed in the Paycheck Protection Program. Utilizing critical race theory as the framework of analysis, and applying the ordinariness of racism tenet of CRT, it was found that White-owned businesses were more likely to benefit from the Paycheck Protection Program because:

1. Policymakers choice of loans as the policy instrument for the PPP is more favorable to White-owned businesses since they and are better able to afford debt expense (in the event that the PPP loan is not forgiven), are more likely to pursue the loan application process, and are less likely to be discouraged borrowers.
2. The PPP's primary goal of employee retention is more likely to help White-owned businesses - relative to Black-owned business - because White-owned businesses are more likely to have employees, not to have had their demand as greatly disrupted by the pandemic as have Black-owned businesses, and therefore more likely to retain their employees.
3. The Paycheck Protection Program feature of determining loan amount based upon payroll expense is more likely to result in White-owned businesses receiving higher loan amounts because they tend to have better financial performance, to have more employees, and to have higher payroll expenses.
4. A track record of consistent federal loan payments and no defaults as a criterion for qualification for a PPP loan would likely result in greater loan approvals of White owned-businesses, and less approvals of Black-owned businesses because these criteria are proxies for financial stability.
5. The prioritizing of corporations over sole proprietors in the PPP first round was more likely to ensure that White-owned businesses received funding since White-owned businesses are more likely to be corporations compared to Black-owned businesses.

6. The focus on banks for implementation of the PPP increased access to the program for White-owned businesses which are more likely to be banked, are more likely to have greater physical access to banking institutions and, consequently, have had the opportunity to establish relationships necessary for their PPP applications to be prioritized.

This chapter has also illuminated the utility of using a CRT policy analysis for uncovering racism, as well as for guiding the design of more equitable policies. While there has been resistance to policies that favor one racial group over another, critical race theorists argue that policies are more likely to advance when there is a convergence of Black and White interests. This chapter has proposed a targeted universalism approach to future small business policy formulation. Targeted universalism seeks to maximize the interests of all groups but is premised on the realization that groups are differently situated and have different needs. Therefore, policies should be designed to address those different needs and each group's unique characteristics.

REFERENCES

Allam, C. (2020). *Black-led businesses getting shut out of PPP loan program, owners and experts say*. Retrieved June 2, 2020, from https://www.wraltechwire.com/2020/05/22/black-led-businesses-getting-shut-out-of-ppp-loan-program-owners-and-experts-say/

Amato, N. (2020*). A tale of the PPP tape: Why relationship building matters.* Retrieved June 2, 2020 from https://www.journalofaccountancy.com/news/2020/may/ppp-loans-small-business-bank-financing-relationships.html

Atkins, R., Cook, L., & Seamans, R. (2022). Discrimination in lending? Evidence from the Paycheck Protection Program. *Small Business Economics*, *58*(2), 843–865. doi:10.100711187-021-00533-1

Bali, A. S., Capano, G., & Ramesh, M. (2019). Anticipating and designing for policy effectiveness. *Policy and Society*, *38*(1), 1–13. doi:10.1080/14494035.2019.1579502

Bates, T. (1995). Why do minority business development programs generate so little minority business development? *Economic Development Quarterly*, *9*(1), 3–14. doi:10.1177/089124249500900101

Bates, T. (1997). Unequal Qccess: Financial Institution Lending to Black-and White-Owned Small Business Start-Ups. *Journal of Urban Affairs*, *19*(4), 487–495. doi:10.1111/j.1467-9906.1997.tb00508.x

Bates, T., & Robb, A. (2013). Greater access to capital is needed to unleash the local economic development potential of minority-owned businesses. *Economic Development Quarterly*, *27*(3), 250–259. doi:10.1177/0891242413477188

Bell, D. (2018). Faces at the bottom of the well: The permanence of racism. Hachette UK.

Bell, D. A. JrBoard of Education and the Interest-Convergence Dilemma. (1980). Brown v. Board of Education and the interest-convergence dilemma. *Harvard Law Review*, *93*(3), 518–533. doi:10.2307/1340546

Bell, D. (2000). Brown v. Board of Education: Forty-five years after the fact. *Ohio NUL Rev.*, *26*, 171.

Blanchflower, D. G., Levine, P. B., & Zimmerman, D. J. (2003). Discrimination in the small-business credit market. *The Review of Economics and Statistics*, *85*(4), 930–943. doi:10.1162/003465303772815835

Bonilla-Silva, E. (2006). *Racism without racists: Color-blind racism and the persistence of racial inequality in the United States*. Rowman & Littlefield Publishers.

Bowman, L., Rocco, T. S., Peterson, E., & Adker, W. A. (2009, May). Utilizing the lens of critical race theory to analyze stories of race. In *Proceedings of the 2009 Adult Education Research Conference* (pp. 36-41). Academic Press.

Bradbury, A. (2020). A critical race theory framework for education policy analysis: The case of bilingual learners and assessment policy in England. *Race, Ethnicity and Education*, *23*(2), 241–260. doi:10.1080/13613324.2019.1599338

Brooks, K. (2020). *Few minority business owners got Paycheck Protection Program loans, survey shows*. Retrieved June 2, 2020, from https://www.cbsnews.com/news/paycheck-protection-program-black-hispanic-business-owners-shut-out-survey/

Cavalluzzo, K. S., Cavalluzzo, L. C., & Wolken, J. D. (2002). Competition, small business financing, and discrimination: Evidence from a new survey. *The Journal of Business*, *75*(4), 641–679. doi:10.1086/341638

Chernenko, S., & Scharfstein, D. S. (2022). Racial disparities in the paycheck protection program (No. w29748). National Bureau of Economic Research.

Coleman, S. (2005). The Impact of Human Capital Measures on Firm Performance: A Comparison by Gender, Race and Ethnicity. *The Journal of Entrepreneurial Finance*, *10*(2), 38–56.

Conyers, A., & Wright Fields, C. (2021). A Critical Race Theory Analysis of Institutional Racial Paralysis in Organizational Culture. *Public Integrity*, *23*(5), 484–495. doi:10.1080/10999922.2020.1832365

Cowley, S. (2022) *Little of the Paycheck Protection Program's $800 Billion Protected Paychecks*. Retrieved February 4, 2020 from, https://www.nytimes.com/2022/02/01/business/paycheck-protection-program-costs.html

Crenshaw, K., Gotanda, N., Peller, G., & Thomas, K. (1995). Critical race theory. The Key Writings that formed the Movement. Academic Press.

Delgado, R., & Stefancic, J. (2017). Critical race theory. In *Critical Race Theory* (3rd ed.). New York University Press.

Dettling, L. J. (2017). *Recent Trends in Wealth-Holding by Race and Ethnicity: Evidence from the Survey of Consumer Finances*. Retrieved November 20, 2018, from https://www.federalreserve.gov/econres/notes/feds-notes/recent-trends-in-wealth-holding-by-race-and-ethnicity-evidence-from-the-survey-of-consumer-finances-20170927.htm

Erel, I., & Liebersohn, J. (2020). Does fintech substitute for banks? evidence from the paycheck protection program (No. w27659). National Bureau of Economic Research.

Fairlie, R. W. (2020). The Impact of Covid-19 on Small Business Owners: Evidence of Early-Stage Losses from the April 2020 Current Population Survey (No. w27309). National Bureau of Economic Research.

Fairlie, R. W., & Fossen, F. (2021). Did the $660 Billion Paycheck Protection Program and $220 Billion Economic Injury Disaster Loan Program Get Disbursed to Minority Communities in the Early Stages of COVID-19? (No. w28321). National Bureau of Economic Research.

Fox, Z., Zain, T., Thomas, L., & Palicpic, C. (2019, July 25). *Bank brand closures take greatest toll on majority-black areas*. Retrieved on June 2, 2020 from, https://www.spglobal.com/marketintelligence/en/news-insights/latest-news-headlines/bank-branch-closures-take-greatest-toll-on-majority-black-areas-52872925

García, J. J., Gee, G. C., & Jones, M. (2016). A critical race theory analysis of public park features in Latino immigrant neighborhoods. *Du Bois Review*, *13*(2), 397–411. doi:10.1017/S1742058X16000187

Gaynor, T. S., & Wilson, M. E. (2020). Social vulnerability and equity: The disproportionate impact of COVID-19. *Public Administration Review*, *80*(5), 832–838. doi:10.1111/puar.13264 PMID:32836465

Gillborn, D. (2005). Education policy as an act of white supremacy: Whiteness, critical race theory and education reform. *Journal of Education Policy*, *20*(4), 485–505. doi:10.1080/02680930500132346

Gillborn, D. (2014, January). Racism as policy: A critical race analysis of education reforms in the United States and England. *The Educational Forum*, *78*(1), 26–41. doi:10.1080/00131725.2014.850982

Gines, D. (2017). *Black women business startups*. Retrieved November 20, 2018, from https://www.kansascityfed.org/~/media/40186481e0ce43a39255752080d4916b.ashx

Gotanda, N. (1991). A critique of our constitution is color-blind. *Stanford Law Review*, *44*(1), 1. doi:10.2307/1228940

Graham, L., Brown-Jeffy, S., Aronson, R., & Stephens, C. (2011). Critical race theory as theoretical framework and analysis tool for population health research. *Critical Public Health*, *21*(1), 81–93. doi:10.1080/09581596.2010.493173

Granja, J., Makridis, C., Yannelis, C., & Zwick, E. (2020). Did the Paycheck Protection Program hit the target? (No. w27095). National Bureau of Economic Research. doi:10.3386/w27095

Howell, S. T., Kuchler, T., Snitkof, D., Stroebel, J., & Wong, J. (2021). Racial Disparities in Access to Small Business Credit: Evidence from the Paycheck Protection Program (No. w29364). National Bureau of Economic Research.

Howlett, M.National Approaches to Theories of Instrument Choice. (1991). Policy instruments, policy styles, and policy implementation: National approaches to theories of instrument choice. *Policy Studies Journal: the Journal of the Policy Studies Organization*, *19*(2), 1–21. doi:10.1111/j.1541-0072.1991.tb01878.x

Howlett, M., & Ramesh, M. (1993). Patterns of policy instrument choice: Policy styles, policy learning and the privatization experience. *The Review of Policy Research*, *12*(1-2), 3–24. doi:10.1111/j.1541-1338.1993.tb00505.x

Lederer, A., & Oros, S. (2020). *Lending discrimination within the paycheck protection program*. Retrieved February 4, 2022, from http://arks.princeton.edu/ark:/88435/dsp01zk51vk84t

Letteiri & Lyons. (2020). *Understanding the Paycheck Protection Program.* Briefs and Blogs, Economic Innovation Group.

Lofstrom, M., Bates, T., & Parker, S. C. (2014). Why are some people more likely to become small-businesses owners than others: Entrepreneurship entry and industry-specific barriers. *Journal of Business Venturing*, *29*(2), 232–251. doi:10.1016/j.jbusvent.2013.01.004

Lopez, G. R. (2003). The (racially neutral) politics of education: A critical race theory perspective. *Educational Administration Quarterly*, *39*(1), 68–94. doi:10.1177/0013161X02239761

Mills, C. K., & Battisto, J. (2020). Double jeopardy: COVID-19's concentrated health and wealth effects in Black communities. Federal Reserve Bank of New York.

Myers, S., & Chan, P. (2017). *Stuck from the Start; The Financial Challenges of Low- and Moderate-Income African-American Entrepreneurs in the South.* https://prosperitynow.org/files/PDFs/07-2017_stuck_from_the_start.pdf

Paycheck Protection Program: Loan Forgiveness And Other Challenges: Hearing before the Committee On Small Business United States House Of Representatives, 116th Cong. 12 (2020) (testimony of Dr. Rich Coleman, DVM)

Peery, D. (2011). The colorblind ideal in a race-conscious reality: The case for a new legal ideal for race relations. *Nw. JL & Soc. Pol'y*, *6*, 473.

Powell, J. A., Menendian, S., & Ake, W. (2019). *Targeted universalism: Policy & practice. Haas Institute for a Fair and Inclusive Society.* University of California.

Pressman, J. L., & Wildavsky, A. (1984). *Implementation: How great expectations in Washington are dashed in Oakland; Or, why it's amazing that federal programs work at all, this being a saga of the Economic Development Administration as told by two sympathetic observers who seek to build morals on a foundation* (Vol. 708). Univ of California Press.

Rocco, T. S., & Gallagher, S. J. (2004). Discriminative justice: Can discrimination be just? *New Directions for Adult and Continuing Education*, *2004*(101), 29–41. doi:10.1002/ace.126

Siegel, M. (2020). Racial disparities in fatal police shootings: An empirical analysis informed by critical race theory. *BUL Rev.*, *100*, 1069.

Simon, R., & McGinty, T. (2014, March 14). *Loan Rebound Misses Black Businesses. Fewer SBA-Backed Loans Go To Black Borrowers.* https://www.wsj.com/articles/no-headline-available-1394831256

Sims, L., & Robbennolt, S. (2020, December). *Racial and Ethnic Inequity in SBA Lending Patterns, 2010-2020.* Retrieved on June 2, 2020, from https://prosperitynow.org/resources/racial-and-ethnic-inequity-sba-lending-patterns-2010-2020

Solórzano, D. G., & Yosso, T. J. (2002). Critical race methodology: Counter-storytelling as an analytical framework for education research. *Qualitative Inquiry*, *8*(1), 23–44. doi:10.1177/107780040200800103

Valles, B. G., & Villalpando, O. (2021). A critical race policy analysis of the school-to-prison pipeline for Chicanos. In *Handbook of critical race theory in education* (pp. 394–403). Routledge. doi:10.4324/9781351032223-34

Vohra-Gupta, S., Kim, Y., & Cubbin, C. (2021). Systemic racism and the Family Medical Leave Act (FMLA): Using critical race theory to build equitable family leave policies. *Journal of Racial and Ethnic Health Disparities*, *8*(6), 1482–1491. doi:10.100740615-020-00911-7 PMID:33211249

Wang, J., & Zhang, D. H. (2021). *The cost of banking deserts: racial disparities in access to PPP lenders and their implications.* Retrieved February 4, 2022, from https://davidzhang.scholar.harvard.edu/files/dhz/files/geographyppp.pdf

Willis, W. (2020). Take a Seat at Oregon's Kitchen Table: Adapting Targeted Universalism for Broad and Deep Civic Engagement. *National Civic Review*, *108*(4), 16–26.

KEY TERMS AND DEFINITIONS

Bounded Rationality: A theory that argues that rationality is limited when individuals make decisions because of factors such as constraints of time, budget, and mental bandwidth and cognitive ability. Decision makers see to arrive at a decision that is good enough rather than optimal.

Community Development Financial Institutions (CDFIs): Private financial institutions that are dedicated to lending financial capital and other financial services to low-income, underserved, and disadvantaged people and businesses.

Critical Race Theory (CRT): Is an intellectual movement and analytical framework emanating from legal studies. It is a useful framework for understanding how racism has shaped policy. Its core belief is that race is a social construct and that racism is not limited to individual bias or prejudice but is also structural (embedded in legal systems and policies).

FinTech Lenders: Lenders that employ the latest technologies to streamline the lending process to be able to make quick lending decisions. Examples include PayPal, and Kabbage.

Interest Convergence Theory: A theory coined by the late law professor Derrick Bell. It stipulates that Black people achieve civil rights victories only when White and Black interests converge. It is one of the tenets of Critical Race Theory.

Paycheck Protection Program (PPP): A program established by the CARES Act that provides small businesses with funds to pay up to eight weeks of payroll costs and other eligible expenses. It was intended to help small businesses survive the adverse economic effects of the Covid-19 pandemic by helping them to payroll costs and some short-term expenses.

Policy Instrument: The generic term used to encompass the various techniques at the disposal of policymakers to implement their public policy objectives. The terms policy instrument and program are used interchangeably herein.

Race Neutral: Not making distinctions, classifications, or preferences based on race. Used interchangeably with the term color blind herein.

Systemic Racism: A form of racism embedded within laws and institutions of a society or organization.

Targeted Universalism: An approach to policy making whereby universal goals are set for all groups and targeted processes to achieve those goals are pursued by each group accounting for the unique needs of each group.

Chapter 7
Black Women Entrepreneurs:
An Exploration of the Structural Factors Driving the Financial Capital Access Gap

Saran Nurse
Kean University, USA

ABSTRACT

While Black women entrepreneurs have the highest nascent entrepreneurship rates, they also significantly underperform their White counterparts. As some scholars have argued, the primary cause of this disparity may result from differences in access to financial capital. Utilizing a stratification economics lens, this chapter analyzes the root causes of the financial capital access gap among Black women entrepreneurs. Wealth, discrimination by financial institutions, credit history, student loan debt, negative social capital, lack of support and perceptions of illegitimacy from social networks, and family structure disadvantages are identified as structural factors driving the financial capital access gap. It is further argued that the COVID-19 pandemic will exacerbate some of these conditions. Policy recommendations are made, including increased non-traditional lending models such as character-based and forgivable loans, greater transparency of race in lending through the implementation of Section 1071 of Dodd-Frank, and student loan amnesty.

INTRODUCTION

During the years working as a hotel housekeeper, Kayla dreamt of having her own cleaning business (Myers and Chan, 2017). To develop her business acumen, she took classes at a local women's center where she learnt to write a business plan. She then went onto college and earned a Bachelor's degree in business administration. Kayla launched a cleaning company, left her job at the hotel, and recently celebrated five years in business. But in the past five years she has only been able to pay herself twice. Lacking sufficient financial resources, she has not been able to hire employees, nor to take on higher-paying contracts. She hopes to get a business loan to expand but without strong profits and a good credit history, her prospects seem bleak. Kayla is a Black woman and her story epitomizes the plight of many

DOI: 10.4018/978-1-6684-4322-4.ch007

Black women entrepreneurs. The last decade has seen a meteoric rise in the number of Black women pursuing entrepreneurship. This increase has been further catalyzed by the Covid-19 pandemic, as many Black women, pushed out of the mainstream labor market, have turned to self-employment as a matter of economic necessity. But while Black women have had the highest nascent entrepreneurship rates, they have also had the lowest revenues and the highest rates of failure of all women-owned businesses. There has been little research to understand why (Jackson and Sanyal, 2019).

Much of the research on gender and entrepreneurship has centered on White women, while research on race and entrepreneurship has largely focused on Black men. In the few studies that have examined the intersection of gender and race in entrepreneurship, the resounding conclusion has been that Black women entrepreneurs lack access to financial capital (e.g. Fairlie and Robb, 2008; Bates and Robb, 2013). But missing from these studies is an in-depth analysis into the root causes of this lack of access. Given this gap in knowledge, this chapter examines the structural conditions driving Black women entrepreneurs' lower access to financial capital by connecting the extant entrepreneurship literature with research from other disciplines, such as economics and sociology, where research on Black women is more developed. Utilizing stratification economics as the theoretical lens, several structural factors have been identified and illustrated in a conceptual model. It is argued that some of these factors have been exacerbated by the Covid-19 pandemic. Black women are the primary and sole providers in many Black families; when Black women succeed the effects are familial and generational (Srigley, 2005). Moreover, since Black women-owned businesses are more likely to hire Black workers, when their businesses survive and grow, they create jobs and help to reduce the high rate of unemployment that is endemic to Black communities. According to a recent report by Goldman Sachs, increased earnings from Black women could create an additional 1.2 to 1.7 million jobs in the United States, and raise the level of annual U.S. GDP by 1.4 to 2.1% each year (Struyven, George-Joseph and Milo, 2021). Improving the entrepreneurial outcomes of Black women is not only germane to economic growth and development but it is a matter of equity and social justice.

Therefore, this chapter provides insights that would help policymakers to create and refine policies and programs to reduce the financial capital access gap and increase the economic contributions of Black women entrepreneurs.

BACKGROUND

a. The State of Black Women-Owned Businesses in The United States

Over the past few decades, women have made tremendous advances in business ownership. In 1972, women-owned businesses (a total of 402,0000) accounted for 4.6% of all firms (American Express, 2018). This number has since increased to 12.3 million, and women-owned enterprises now account for 40% of all businesses in the United States. Since the mid-2000s, the growth in the number of women owned enterprises has been even more impressive. During that period, while the number of all new ventures increased by 12%, the number of women-owned start-ups increased by 58%, with Black women leading the charge. Between 2007 and 2018, the number of Black women-owned enterprises grew by an astounding 164% (American Express, 2018). Black women are now the fastest growing of all segments of entrepreneurs; they account for 20% of all women-owned businesses, and more than half of all

Black-owned firms. From all indications, Covid-19 has continued, if not accelerated, the pace of entry of Black women into entrepreneurship. This is driven by two primary factors. Firstly, Black women workers are over-represented in sectors, such as retail, hospitality and food services, as well as social services which were hardest hit by the pandemic (Holder, Jones and Masterson, 2021). Secondly, Black women are more likely to be single mothers, many of whom lacked childcare options as schools switched to remote learning (Barr, Henry-Nickie and Broady, 2021). Faced with joblessness, the financial pressure of being the primary provider for their families, and the need for greater flexibility in schedules, many Black women have turned to business ownership (Mullen, 2021).

But while Black women have had the highest rates of start-ups, their businesses have also had the lowest revenues. Whereas women-owned businesses average $143,100 in annual revenue, Black women-owned businesses only average $24,700 (American Express, 2018). The revenue gap between Black and White women-owned firms is even more profound, with White women-owned businesses averaging $212,300 (American Express, 2018).

b. What Explains the Lower Performance of Black Women Entrepreneurs?

In the studies that have examined Black Women Entrepreneurs (BWEs), the following explanations have been advanced to explain their lower business performance:

- **Cultural theory**: Originating from Max Weber's classical writings, this theory states that Black women's lower performance in business stems from cultural deficiencies - that Black culture is not conducive to successful entrepreneurship because Blacks exhibit a lower drive for achievement, have a culture of poverty, and have low expectations (Smith-Hunter and Boyd, 2004). In the same vein, Light (1980) posits that Blacks lack business acumen, have limited work ethic, and are too driven by individualism, competition, and status differentiation to overcome barriers to successful business.
- **Human capital theory:** This theory predicts that individuals or groups who possess greater levels of education, knowledge, skills and other competencies will achieve greater business performance outcomes compared to those who possess lower levels (Ployhart and Moliterno, 2011). In a study of Black workers, Bento and Brown (2021) find that respondents who indicated that they had "less than high school" education were more likely to be self-employed than their college-educated peers. According to the human capital theory since less educated Black women are more likely to start businesses, lower educational attainment may contribute to the lower financial performance of their ventures.
- **Social capital theory:** Social capital refers to the social resources available from group support networks which provide many important functions conducive to the development of business enterprises (Fratoe, 1988). Many scholars argue that social networks and relationships are critical to business formation, growth and success. As Barr (2008) states,

business relationships contribute to new economic opportunities as well as to a firm's reputation in the market. Business relationships provide opportunities for sharing business expertise, and for managerial development... (p. 146).

Entrepreneurs' social networks, which include family, organizational, and community-based ties, are known to supplement the effects of the entrepreneurs' experience, education, and financial resources (Coleman, 1994). Differences in businesses outcomes may therefore be attributed to some groups having more social capital than others. Some studies have found that, compared to other groups, Black business owners are deficient in social capital (e.g. Fratoe, 1998; Fairlie & Robb, 2008).

- **Push-pull theory**: Individuals are generally believed to be "pushed" into self-employment out of necessity or because they have limited employment options. Family-related issues and personal life changes, such as the need for more work/life balance are often labelled as push factors (Kirkwood, 2009). Pull motivators stem from internal stimuli (Singh, Knox and Crump, 2008) such as recognizing an opportunity to start a business, being drawn to the perceived allure of self-employment, and a desire for wealth, independence and autonomy. Black women are more likely to pursue entrepreneurship for push factors such as the desire to escape labor market discrimination (Gines, 2018), work-life balance and the opportunity to be better care givers (Carr, 1996). Studies have found that businesses started by entrepreneurs who experienced push motivations are less successful (financially) than those built upon pull factors (Amit and Muller, 1995).
- **Sidepreneurship theory**: Also known as the part-time entrepreneurship theory, this theory argues that, since many Black women start businesses part-time and given that the quantity of owner effort shapes business outcomes (Bates & Robb 2013), the likely lower effort from Black women entrepreneurs will produce lower financial results.

Figure 1. Barriers to success faced by Black & Latinx women entrepreneurs
Source: ProjectDiane 2020 The State of Black & Latinx Women Founders

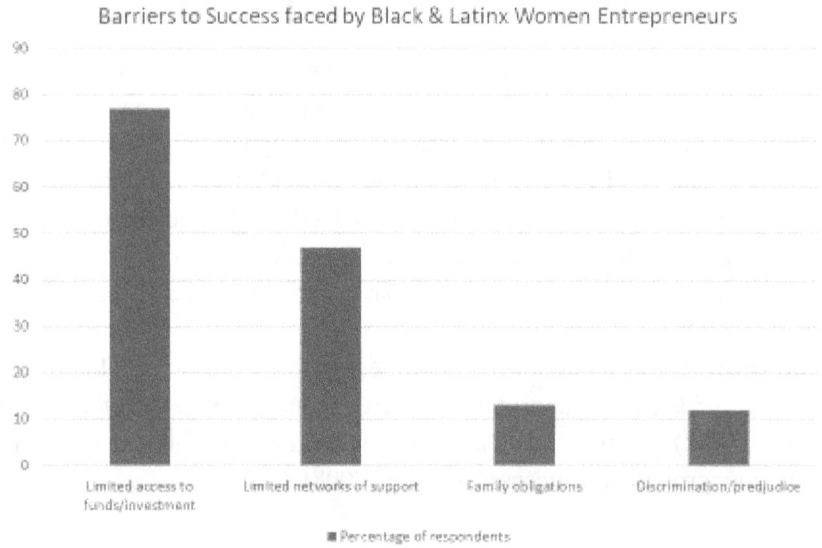

While the aforementioned are the most prominent of the theories of BWE underperformance, some of these have been refuted by scholars. For example, Inman (2016) finds that Black women entrepreneurs are equally as educated as their White counterparts. And, several scholars have debunked and railed against the cultural theory (e.g. Feagin and Imani, 1994; Bogan and Darity, 2008), arguing that the entrepreneurship literature has focused too heavily on the cultural deficiency theory without sufficient attention having been given to the role of discriminatory treatment as a causal factor in BWE under-performance. And, while there is merit to the social capital and sidepreneurship theories, the more substantive explanation seems to be that the lower performance of BWEs is really a symptom of lower access to financial capital (e.g. Bates, 1989; Bates, 2011; Fairlie, Robb and Hinson, 2010). In a recent ProjectDiane study (conducted in 2020), for the Black and Afro-Latinx women entrepreneurs surveyed, limited access to funding/investment (financial capital) was found to be the greatest barrier to success (see Figure 1). Thus, this chapter is concerned with understanding the factors affecting Black women entrepreneurs' lower access to financial capital, particularly in comparison to White women entrepreneurs.

c. Stratification Economics Theory as the Theoretical Lens

For policymakers to effectively design policies and programs to reduce disparities in financial capital access, the root causes of disparities in access must first be identified. This chapter takes a stratification economics approach to identifying the structural conditions that drive the racial/gender financial capital access gap. Generally, mainstream and orthodox economists have attributed racial and ethnic disparities to the fault of the group that is subjected to those disparities and inequalities. They argue that it is differences in individual attributes like human capital endowment, culture, motivation and tastes, that cause intergroup differences. Stratification economists takes a different view - they contend that placing the blame on the victim obscures the real factors producing intergroup inequalities (Darity, 2005). Stratification economists reject:

explanations of intergroup inequality on the basis of collective dysfunction on the part of the group burdened by comparatively negative outcomes. Correspondingly, stratification economics rejects explanations for group-linked variations in life outcomes that champion genetic or cultural-behavioral differences across groups (Darity, Hamilton and Stewart, 2015, p. 3).

Stratification economics analyses are premised on the belief that discrimination matters and its consequences and manifestations must be identified. Thus, consistent with the stratification economics perspective, this chapter looks beyond the individual traits or behaviors of BWEs - such as human capital, or cultural or character deficiencies - to understand how structural conditions that are the legacies of past discrimination, as well as current discriminatory practices, manifest in their lower access to financial capital.

FINANCIAL CAPITAL

a. Defining financial capital and its relationship to successful entrepreneurship

Financial capital refers to the money used by entrepreneurs to purchase requisite assets and cover expenses incurred in delivering products and services. As Kim, Aldrich and Keister (2006) explain, financial capital derives from two sources: personal funds and institutions. Personal funds can be viewed along two dimensions - individual and household wealth, and individual and household income. If personal and household funds are inadequate, or unavailable, entrepreneurs turn to institutions for capital - these include banks (for debt instruments such as loans) and private investors such as venture capitalists (for equity investment). Other non-traditional sources, such as crowdfunding, have also grown in prominence in recent years.

Several scholars cite financial capital as the most important factor in the establishment, expansion and growth of businesses (Bates, 1989; Fairlie, Robb & Hinson, 2010). Businesses with higher levels of start-up capital are less likely to close and do have higher profits (Bates, 1990; Fairlie & Robb, 2008). As new firms struggle to establish administrative procedures, and to learn through the process of experimentation and trial and error, and to gain credibility with customer and suppliers, greater capitalization serves as a buffer to protect start-ups from the liabilities of newness (Bates & Robb, 2013). Financial capital determines an entrepreneur's choice of business. For example, industries such as mining, construction, wholesaling and manufacturing require larger outlays of start-up funds but are also the most profitable. Sufficient levels of capital also enable firms to withstand and appropriately respond to economic shocks, environmental changes, and increased competition. Lacking an adequate buffer, poorly capitalized firms may be forced to close down during difficult periods (Bates & Robb, 2013). Sufficiently large financial resources permit operational efficiencies rooted in economies of scale (Lofstrom and Bates, 2013).

Black-owned businesses start with lower levels of capital than do White-owned firms (Smith-Hunter & Boyd, 2004; Fairlie & Robb, 2008; Shane, 2008; Bates, 2011). Accordingly, Black-owned businesses tend to be heavily concentrated in the personal services, and some retail sectors, which have lower financial requirements for entry, but are also highly competitive and provide lower returns (Coleman, 2005; Lofstrom, Bates and Parker, 2014). But regardless of size of operations, whether newly established or well-established, firms owned by Blacks have greater difficulty accessing financial capital (Fairlie & Robb 2008).

b. Factors Affecting Black Women-owned Businesses Lower Access to Financial Capital

i. Wealth

Wealth (or net worth) is determined by the sum of an individual's assets less the sum of debts. Wealth is not income; while a high income provides a greater opportunity for building wealth, income does not necessarily equal wealth. An individual with high income may have no or low wealth, for example, because that individual's debt exceeds assets or because her high debt and expenses, inhibit her ability to acquire wealth generating assets. Wealth disparity between Black and White households it at its highest level since 1989; for every dollar of wealth owned by the typical White family, the median Black family owns only five cents (Zaw et al., 2017). These disparities do not result from random misfortune nor from behavioral factors. Blacks do not have lower levels of wealth because of poor decisions or a culture of poverty (as Sowell, 1991 posits). Rather, racial wealth inequality has been structured over many generations through systematic barriers that have hampered Blacks throughout history - slavery, Jim Crow, so called de jure discrimination, and institutionalized racism (Oliver and Shapiro, 1995). At the same time, in what scholar Ira Katznelson terms "affirmative action for whites", historical government policies have helped Whites acquire the assets which are the source of today's racial wealth gap (Katznelson, 2005).

Wealth provides cash for business start-up as well as expansion. Wealth is a type of seed funding not necessarily based on individual merit or action but simply the familial position into which one is born. Since homes can be leveraged to provide cash for businesses, racial differences in home ownership rates and home equity also have important consequences for financial capital access. Less than half of Blacks own their homes, compared to three quarters of non-minorities (Fairlie & Robb 2010). The common use of personal collateral (such as a house) to obtain business loans, suggests that wealthier entrepreneurs (who tend to be White) may be able to negotiate better credit terms and obtain larger loans for their businesses, leading to more successful firms (Fairlie, 2012).

As indicated in Table 1 below, the median wealth for single Black women with children is zero (Zaw et al., 2017). Married Black women with no children have a median wealth of $45,000. This pales in comparison to the median wealth of $65,529 held by White women with children and $285,000 by White married women with no children (Zaw et al., 2017). According to a Babson College study, the cost of starting a new business can be about $20,000 to $30,000, with more lucrative businesses like construction and manufacturing requiring larger average initial investments of $98,000 and $175,000 respectively (according to the Kauffman Foundation). On the lower end, the U.S. Small Business Administration (SBA) calculates the cost of starting an at home micro-business to be $3,000 to $5,000. Since most BWEs leverage their own personal funds to start businesses (Smith-Hunter & Boyd 2004; Gines, 2018), these statistics on Black women's wealth suggest that the typical Black woman does not personally possess enough wealth to start either a micro-business or a more lucrative business that requires a larger investment. She has probably struggled to raise funds to start a business in an industry with low financial barriers to entry. Since the barriers to entry are low, the industry is quite competitive, and her business is probably not generating high revenues. Conversely, her White counterparts, possessing higher wealth, can afford to start businesses in more profitable industries like construction and manufacturing. Indeed, studies have found that Black women-owned businesses are over-represented in industries such as retail/wholesale, health, education, government and social services, all of which have lower financial barriers to entry and generate lower returns. Sixty-one percent (61%) of BWEs start businesses in these lower profit margin sectors compared to only 47% of White women (Kelley, Majbouri & Randolph, 2021).

Table 1. Median wealth of women by family structure, presence of children under 18 and race, 2013

	NO CHILDREN		WITH CHILDREN	
	BLACK	WHITE	BLACK	WHITE
Married*	$45,000	$285,000	$16,000	$65,529
Single Females	$3,000	$19,000	$0	$3,000

Source: Zaw, K, et al. 2017. Women, Race & Wealth. *Research brief series* 1

* Head of household married. Over 98% are married couple households. 1.5% are households with no "Wife" present.

Note: "With Children" refers to households with children under the age of 18.

ii. Discrimination by Financial Institutions

Lacking sufficient wealth and personal financial resources to fund their businesses, some Black women turn to financial institutions for help. While banks are the primary source of financial capital for many businesses (Blanchflower, Levine and Zimmerman, 2003; Cavalluzzo and Wolken, 2002), Black business owners are less likely to be approved for loans by banks, and, if approved, are required to pay high interest rates (Bates, 1997; Blanchflower et al., 2003; Bates & Robb, 2013). Palia (2016) found that Black small business borrowers have an approximately 30% higher rate of rejection than similarly situated White borrowers. In their audit study of small business owners seeking bank loans, Bone, Christensen and Williams (2014) found that, in the inquiry stage, in comparison to White applicants, minorities were consistently offered less assistance and subjected to greater scrutiny. The old adage that banks don't lend to people who don't have money is certainly the experience of BWEs. Banks utilize personal wealth and assets as an integral part of the credit decision (Cavalluzzo & Wolken, 2002). That BWEs have lower wealth and assets, provides a convenient excuse for banks to deny them. But studies have also found that even with the same level of collateral as Whites, Black entrepreneurs are still more likely to be denied by banks (Bates, 1997; Cavalluzzo & Wolken, 2002; Blanchard, Zhao and Yinger, 2008; Shane, 2008). Fearing rejection from banks, many BWEs do not even apply for loans. A study of women business owners conducted by the Federal Reserve Bank of Kansas City in 2016, found that 94% of BWEs did not apply for loans because they felt discouraged by credit opportunities (Gines, 2018). When a business challenge arose, they were more likely to respond by using personal funds, cutting payroll or downsizing operations (Gines, 2018).

In her study of the SBA, Nopper (2010) notes that in the past few decades, the agency has abandoned loan programs targeted specifically at Black businesses. Instead, the SBA loan program now focuses on "total minorities". The SBA also no longer lends directly to businesses but instead guarantees the majority of the loan amounts provided by private banking institutions. The result of these changes has been that BWEs receive less SBA guaranteed loans since they must now compete with all minorities, including with White women and Asian-Americans who have historically had greater access to financial capital, and consequently greater business success and track records. In 2006, Asian-Americans received twice the number of SBA guaranteed loans and larger loans amounts, than did African-Americans (Nopper, 2010). But, as Nopper further states, while Asian-Americans may now lead the "minority group" loans, White women still maintain a consistent lead among all SBA loan recipients.

iii. Credit History

As reported by the SBA, most business loans, as well as business credit cards and lines of credits, require a personal guarantee. An entrepreneur's personal credit history therefore becomes a primary determinant of approval for a small business loan. Personal debt that is incurred earlier in life may restrict an entrepreneur's credit access and have profound implications for starting and growing a business. Late payments also factor into credit score calculations which further reduce the likelihood of receiving a business loan. Credit scoring penalizes unexpected emergencies, as well as those who do not have the financial slack to address such emergencies. Since Black women have less employment security, lower income, and, overall, less financial buffers, they are more likely to fall victim to these types of emergencies that can result in missed payments that wreak havoc on credit scores. The result is that they are less likely to qualify for business loans compared to White women entrepreneurs.

iv. Student Loan Debt

As the human capital theory postulates, there is a positive relationship between educational attainment and success in entrepreneurship. Furthermore, education may also provide access to beneficial social networks - or social capital. But attaining a college degree can be a double edged sword for Black women, since they are oftentimes required to incur student debt. As a group, Black women have become the most educated but also the most student debt ridden. By graduation, Black women accumulate an average of $30,400 in student loans (Fearnow, 2018); 46% of Black women have student debt compared to only 30% of White women (Clark et al., 2021). More than three quarters of Black women entrepreneurs have at least a college degree (Kelley, Majbouri and Randolph, 2021). This means that, as the BWE is trying to establish or grow her business, she is probably also carrying a heavy student debt load and high monthly payments. This debt may impact her ability to secure business credit. Monthly student loan payments also reduce her income that could be utilized for growing the business or for just simply "staying in the game". Indeed, studies have found that the financial burden of student loan debt affects entrepreneurial decisions and outcomes (Desai, Looze and Pechenina, 2020).

Figure 2. Cumulative debt on women's undergraduate and graduate loans including principal and interest, one year after graduation by Race
Source: Deeper in Debt 2021 Update. https://www.aauw.org/app/uploads/2021/05/Deeper_In_Debt_2021.pdf

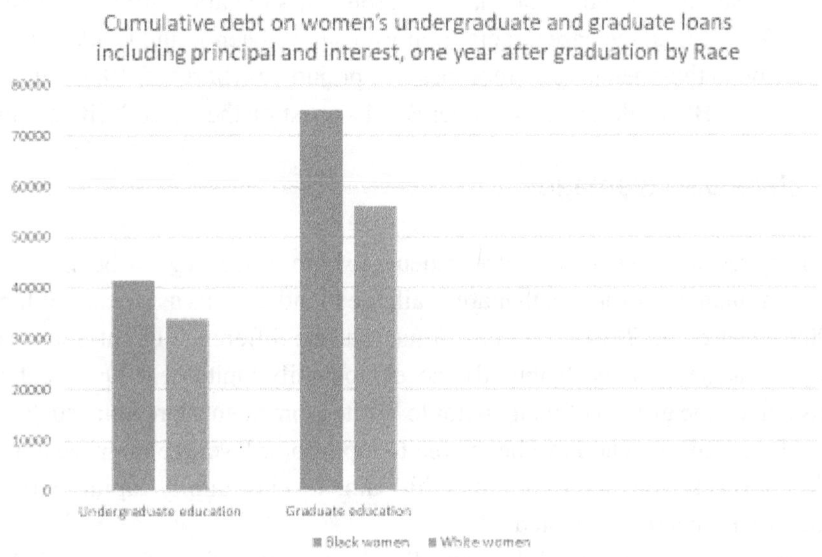

v. Negative Social Capital

While social capital is used to demarcate the positive consequences, or benefits, of group membership for the individual, the term *negative social capital* connotes the liabilities of group membership (O'Brien, 2012). Negative social capital is the pressure placed on individuals by virtue of being a part of a group which results in negative consequences to the individual, for example, in the form of lower economic capital (Portes, 1998). Having to provide financial assistance to family can be experienced as negative social capital for some Blacks (O'Brien, 2012). Some studies have suggested that Blacks are more likely than Whites to provide financial support to family and extended family (Dyer, Nenque and Hill, 2014). Black parents are more likely than White parents to expect their children to help them financially as they age (Chiteji and Hamilton, 2002); more than 80% of Black parents expect to be supported (Jones, 2017). These greater family obligations may prevent BWEs from investing their funds for their own personal advancement.

vi. Lack of Support and Perceptions of Illegitimacy From Social Networks

In addition, to being more likely to have negative social capital, the BWE may also be faced with reluctance from those within her networks who do have the ability to assist financially. Blacks with significant financial resources are sometimes hesitant to provide assistance to friends and relatives in need (Newman, 1999). They may only assist after much initial hesitation and reluctance or when they believe that there may be a future benefit to them - that is, they view their assistance as insurance should they in turn need to borrow in the future (Stack, 2008). Another reason those in the BWE's network may be unwilling to help is because they may not believe in her legitimacy as an entrepreneur. Because entrepreneurship has been dominated by White men, coupled with a lack of Black business tradition and successful track records of Black businesses, this has resulted in co-ethnics associating successful entrepreneurship with non-Blacks thus making it difficult for Black entrepreneurs to gain legitimacy even amongst their co-ethnics (Ogbolu, 2015). In some cases, racial minorities have been found to identify with dominant groups and to subscribe to their negative stereotypes and prejudices (Sarnoff, 1960). Indeed, Jackson & Sandoval (2019) state that BWEs describe that other Blacks question their credibility as business owners.

vii. Family Structure Disadvantage

Family capital is a key resource needed by entrepreneurs to both start and grow businesses. It consists of the human, social and financial resources that are available to individuals as a result of family affiliation (Danes et al., 2009; Dyer et al., 2014). Scholars argue that the difference in entrepreneurial outcomes between racial groups can be partially attributed to access to family capital (e.g. Dyer et al., 2014). Family capital is what has helped the growth of many notable White women entrepreneurs such as Kylie Jenner, Ivanka Trump and Paris Hilton, who have been able to tap into or leverage their wealthy family funds, or connections. Many Black women have not had this same level of family capital, largely because the Black family structure has been fragmented.

The past few decades has seen a precipitous decline in the proportion of married Black women. In 1970, 89% of Black females between ages 25 and 54 were ever married. By 2013, this number dropped to 51% (Caucutt, Guner and Rauh, 2016). This close to 40% decline in the percentage of Black women ever married is more than twice as high as the 15% drop in the proportion of White women ever married (see Figure 3). In their study, Caucutt et al. (2016) find that differences in incarceration and employment dynamics between Black and White men account for about 76% of the existing Black-White marriage gap. The precipitous drop in unskilled manufacturing jobs during the 1970s and 1980s was also particularly detrimental to Black men, resulting in a yawning Black-White unemployment gap that grew rapidly. By 1985, unemployment rates for Black men, aged 25–54, were two times higher than that of White men in the same age range. Among men, aged 16–24, the racial disparity was even greater, with the unemployment rate for Black men three times that of White men (Caucutt et al., 2016). Lower labor market prospects and outcomes for Black men make them more likely to be unemployed, and to be deemed "riskier spouses". Many Black women have therefore chosen not to marry. However, marriage has been found to increase entrepreneurial earnings (e.g. Sanders and Nee, 1996; Valdez 2008). Spouses provide wealth, additional income and other forms of support. Fairlie and Robb (2008) posit that lower marriage rates amongst Blacks has resulted in lower business outcomes.

Figure 3. Percentage change in Black and White women ages 25-54 ever married between 1970 and 2013
Source: Caucutt, E. M., Guner, N., & Rauh, C. (2016). Is marriage for White people? Incarceration and the racial marriage divide. Unpublished paper, Department of Economics, Western University

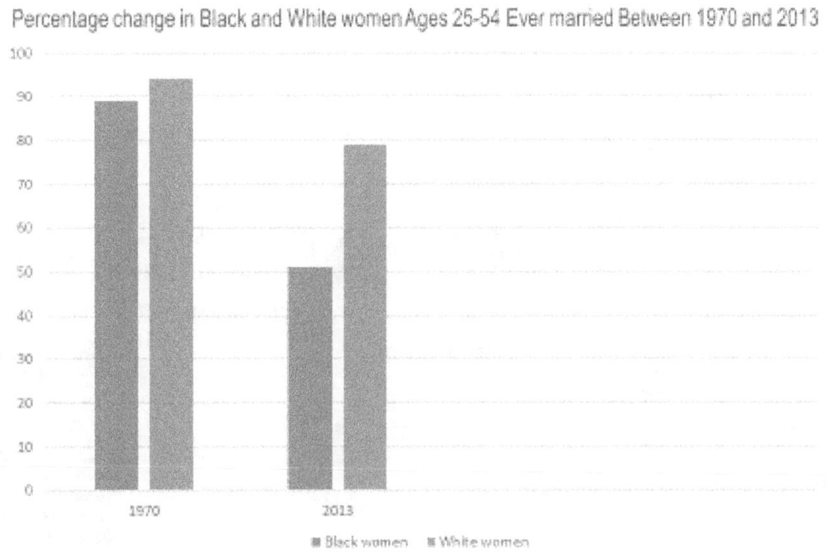

In addition to being more likely to be unmarried, a higher percentage of Black women are also more likely to be classified as single mothers; over 64% of Black mothers are reported to be single mothers (Looze and Desai, 2020). Moreover, 27% of Black entrepreneurs who are mothers stated they are sole providers, compared to 19% of Hispanic entrepreneur mothers and 23% of White entrepreneur mothers (Looze and Desai, 2020). Being the sole provider may be a factor driving Black women into entrepreneurship but it may also limit the availability of funds to commit to their ventures. Some studies have also found that women who raise children alone are held in low esteem and are more likely to be denied lending by financial institutions (Lee, 2019).

THE OUTLOOK FOR ACCESS TO FINANCIAL CAPITAL FOR BLACK WOMEN ENTREPRENEURS IN A POST COVID-19 ERA

The preceding sections have explored the structural factors affecting Black women entrepreneurs' lower access to financial capital. These factors are depicted in a conceptual model (see Figure 2) which illustrates the interconnectedness of the factors, how they lead to the financial capital access gap and, ultimately, to lower performance indicators. While, to date, there have been no published empirical studies on the effect of the Covid-19 pandemic on Black women-owned businesses, some propositions can be made from the insights provided in this chapter.

Figure 4. A conceptual model of the factors driving disparities in financial capital access between Black and White women entrepreneurs

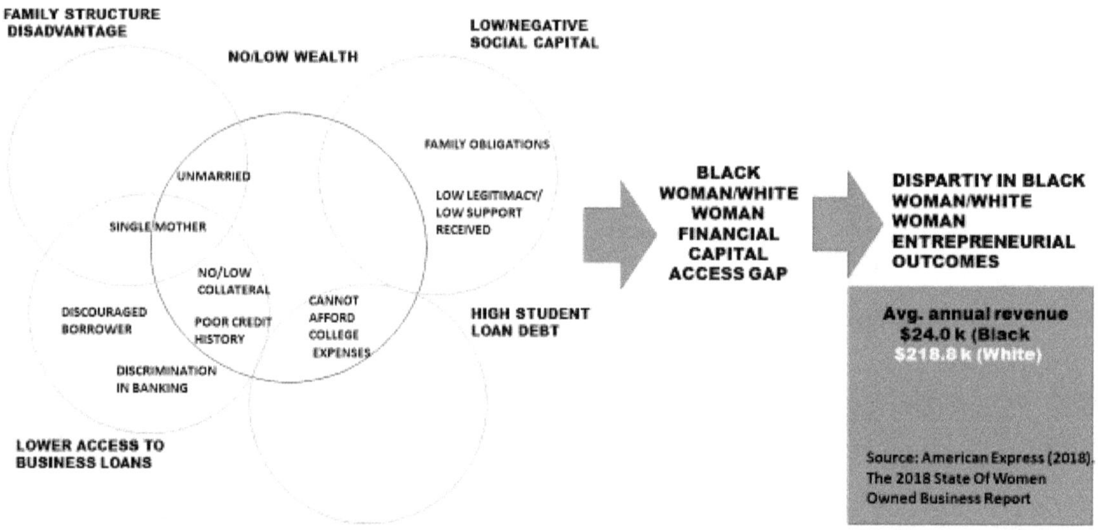

The Covid-19 pandemic has had a disproportionately negative impact on the Black population, both economically and health-wise. Since Blacks were more likely to be employed in industries such as retail and hospitality - which were the most affected by the pandemic - job loss has been prevalent amongst Black workers (Holder, Jones and Masterson, 2021). Reduced income as a result of unemployment translates into less personal financial capital that the BWE has available to invest in a business. Thus, while pandemic related unemployment may have pushed her into entrepreneurship, as previously recounted, lower availability of financial capital also relegates her to extremely competitive industries that have lower revenues and lower profit margins. Moreover, high unemployment in the Black community at large means that her social network is also less able to offer financial assistance. Thus, this chapter proposes that the disproportionate rates of unemployment amongst Blacks, due to the Covid-19 pandemic, will further reduce the Black Woman entrepreneur's access to financial.

The Covid-19 pandemic has killed 1 of every 1000 Black Americans, which is about twice the fatality rate amongst White Americans. Of the Black population, men were more likely to die than women.

The pandemic has added to the long history of disruption and separation within Black families (as has incarceration), with more Black women left as the sole providers in families. Again, this translates into lower access to financial capital, since, as the sole provider in the family, the BWE will have less unrestricted funds to invest in her business. Moreover, as previously recounted, if banks are more likely to discriminate against women who are unmarried and single mothers (Lee, 2019), the BWE's chances of receiving a bank loan will also be lower. Even in situations where family members who fell ill to Covid-19 did not succumb, many Black women, as family care givers, may face years of caring for family members suffering from long-term complications. These circumstances may also be financially taxing on the Black woman. Thus, this chapter further proposes that the higher rates of Covid-19 mortality in the Black community will result in greater disruption to the Black family, and will increase financial responsibilities for Black women who will then have less available funds to invest in their own businesses.

Some research has shown that the two major government funded programs which were to provide financial assistance to small businesses - the Paycheck Protection Program (PPP) and the Economic Injury Disaster Loan (EIDL) Program - were biased against Blacks, as well as women (Kickul, Griffiths, Robb and Gundry, 2021). Although studies have not been conducted on the experiences of Black women entrepreneurs with accessing the funding from these programs, if there was racial as well as gender bias, it should be assumed that Black women had lower access to Covid-19 relief funding. If Black women-owned businesses received lower financial assistance, then, compared to their White counterparts, their businesses are more likely to suffer declines to profitability, if not complete closure. Since profitability is a major factor considered by business lenders, lower access to PPP and EIDL may have a multiplier effect, resulting in lower access to business loans in the future. Thus this chapter's final proposition is that Black women entrepreneurs' lower access to federal Covid-19 economic relief programs will, in the short term, reduce the profitability - or viability - of their businesses. Reduced profitability will further reduce the likelihood of receiving funding from financial institutions in the future.

RECOMMENDATIONS: POLICIES TO INCREASE FINANCIAL CAPITAL ACCESS FOR BWEs

Solutions for increasing financial capital access for BWEs cannot be discussed without first acknowledging that structural racism impacts the economic opportunities of all Blacks in the United States (Pager & Shepherd, 2008), and that sweeping policy changes aimed at dismantling the effects of the historical disadvantages, and providing economic justice for all Blacks are needed. But as an immediate step, the following policy interventions specifically aimed at addressing the structural conditions outlined could be implemented:

a. Increasing Sources of Non-Traditional Funding

i. Forgivable Loans or Grants

Since BWEs are concentrated in industries with lower profit margins, they are less likely to be able to afford to repay debt. Therefore, grants or forgivable loans would be less financially burdensome. Some organizations, realizing both the plight and the economic potential of Black women entrepreneurs, have increased their financial support through funding mechanisms, such as forgivable loans and grants, which do not require repayment. Goldman Sachs, through its One Million Black Women Initiative, has made up to $100 million in philanthropic support available to Black women. Similarly, Sage and The BOSS Network have partnered to offer twenty-five $1000 grants to Black women entrepreneurs to grow their businesses.

ii. Character Based Loans

Most financial institutions utilize credit score as the proxy for an applicant's character (honesty and trustworthiness) when making lending decisions. But the emphasis on credit scores excludes many otherwise worthy business owners who may have had a single crippling financial event that negatively impacted their credit history. Realizing this, some small business lenders have utilized alternate criteria for determining trustworthiness. This new form of character based lending utilizes the borrower's actual character rather than the borrower's financial conditions as a proxy for character (Lee, 2019). Colorado Lending Source, an economic development organization based in Denver, Colorado, uses an intensive interview process in which the applicant must answer, to a committee, several questions about her business' history and prospects. They require the applicant to submit several documents and assess the degree of completion and thoroughness of the application as an indication of character. Similarly, the recently launched Brooklyn EXCELerate Loan Fund by The Social Justice Fund also eschews credit scores, instead utilizing a character based model that relies on references from community members. Repayment terms are determined by the community's support of the business. But it must also be noted that shifting from credit scoring to a more qualitative - but subjective - criteria, as in character based lending, may increase the probability of both taste and statistical discrimination by lenders. To reduce the potential for bias in character based lending, review committees should reflect the client population and must include women of color as reviewers.

b. Greater Transparency and Accountability by Implementation of Section 1071 of Dodd-Frank

Under the Equal Credit Opportunity Act (ECOA) - which sets criteria for lending - creditors are barred from even voluntarily recording the race, ethnicity and gender of small business loan applicants and borrowers. This prevents lenders from tracking their performance, and inhibits the collection of data to support federal oversight of lending institutions. Better data on lending would produce greater transparency and would be an essential step towards more equal access to credit for BWEs. There is some evidence that these disclosures have helped to increase lending in other sectors. The Home Mortgage Disclosure Act requires creditors to report on the race, ethnicity, gender and income in home mortgage lending, and is believed to have helped increase minority home ownership. Section 1071 of Dodd-Frank requires banks to report, to the federal government, lending data that includes race and gender, in order to improve transparency in the small business credit market. Its implementation would help to increase transparency and accountability in the small business lending process.

c. Student Loan Amnesty

As Black women struggle to make student loan payments while starting up and growing businesses, partial or full discharge of payments would lessen their financial burdens. Originated in 2007, the Public

Student Loan Forgiveness program (PSLF) allows certain individuals to have their loan balances forgiven after making 120 qualifying payments. Currently, people who pursue careers in the public and non-profit sectors are eligible for PSLF. Given the high rates of unemployment amongst Blacks, BWEs who establish operations in, and hire from, Black communities, help to reduce unemployment and positively impact the economy. Extending PSLF to cover BWEs who set-up businesses and consistently hire in minority communities, could provide BWEs with extra disposable income that could be injected back into the business to fuel growth and further job creation.

CONCLUSION

While Black women have had the highest nascent entrepreneurship rates, their businesses have under-performed those of women from other racial groups, and particularly those owned by White women. This chapter has outlined some theories that have been used to explain this underperformance. These are the cultural theory, human capital theory, social capital theory, push-pull theory, the sidepreneurship theory, and financial capital theory. Several scholars have argued that financial capital is the most important factor in successful entrepreneurship. But Black women face a double disadvantage in accessing financial capital on account of both gender and race. Lower financial capital access translates into lower financial gains and lower performance outcomes in entrepreneurship, which can have further far reaching economic and social consequences. This chapter has identified and analyzed the following structural factors driving the financial capital access gap: wealth, discrimination by financial institutions, credit history, student loan debt, negative social capital, lack of support and perceptions of illegitimacy from social networks, and family structure disadvantage. It has been argued that the Covid-19 pandemic will exacerbate some of these structural factors. While broader, and bolder, policies are needed to improve the economic outcomes of all Black women and, by extension, Black women entrepreneurs, some more immediate steps should be taken to help Black women entrepreneurs. These are:

- Increasing non-traditional funding instruments, such as forgivable loans and grants, as well as character based loans.
- Implementing Section 1071 of Dodd-Frank to increase transparency and accountability in business lending.
- Providing student loan amnesty by extending the Public Student Loan Forgiveness program to cover BWEs who set-up businesses and consistently hire in minority communities.

REFERENCES

American Express. (2018). *The 2018 State of Women Owned Business Report*. https://ventureneer.com/wp-content/uploads/2018/08/2018-state-of-women-owned-businesses-report_FINAL.pdf

Amit, R., & Muller, E. (1995). "Push" and "pull" entrepreneurship. *Journal of Small Business and Entrepreneurship*, *12*(4), 64–80. doi:10.1080/08276331.1995.10600505

Barr, A., Henry-Nickie, M., & Broady, K. (2021, December 8). *The November jobs report shows Black women are leaving the laborforce.* https://www.brookings.edu/blog/the-avenue/2021/12/08/the-november-jobs-report-shows-black-women-are-leaving-the-labor-force/

Barr, M. S. (2008). *Policies to expand minority entrepreneurship: Closing comments.* Academic Press.

Bates, T. (1989). The changing nature of minority business: A comparative analysis of Asian, nonminority, and black-owned businesses. *The Review of Black Political Economy, 18*(2), 25–42. doi:10.1007/BF02895231

Bates, T. (1989). Small business viability in the urban ghetto. *Journal of Regional Science, 29*(4), 625–643. doi:10.1111/j.1467-9787.1989.tb01248.x

Bates, T. (1990). Entrepreneur human capital inputs and small business longevity. *The Review of Economics and Statistics, 72*(4), 551–559. doi:10.2307/2109594

Bates, T. (1997). Unequal Access: Financial Institution Lending to Black-and White-Owned Small Business Start-Ups. *Journal of Urban Affairs, 19*(4), 487–495. doi:10.1111/j.1467-9906.1997.tb00508.x

Bates, T. (2011). Minority entrepreneurship. *Foundations and Trends in Entrepreneurship, 7*(3-4).

Bates, T., & Robb, A. (2013). Greater access to capital is needed to unleash the local economic development potential of minority-owned businesses. *Economic Development Quarterly, 27*(3), 250–259. doi:10.1177/0891242413477188

Bento, A., & Brown, T. N. (2021). Belief in systemic racism and self-employment among working blacks. *Ethnic and Racial Studies, 44*(1), 21–38. doi:10.1080/01419870.2020.1737170

Blanchard, L., Zhao, B., & Yinger, J. (2008). Do lenders discriminate against minority and woman entrepreneurs? *Journal of Urban Economics, 63*(2), 467–497. doi:10.1016/j.jue.2007.03.001

Blanchflower, D. G., Levine, P. B., & Zimmerman, D. J. (2003). Discrimination in the small-business credit market. *The Review of Economics and Statistics, 85*(4), 930–943. doi:10.1162/003465303772815835

Bogan, V., & Darity, W. Jr. (2008). Culture and entrepreneurship? African American and immigrant self-employment in the United States. *Journal of Socio-Economics, 37*(5), 1999–2019. doi:10.1016/j.socec.2007.10.010

Bone, S. A., Christensen, G. L., & Williams, J. D. (2014). Rejected, shackled, and alone: The impact of systemic restricted choice on minority consumers' construction of self. *The Journal of Consumer Research, 41*(2), 451–474. doi:10.1086/676689

Carr, D. (1996). Two paths to self-employment? Women's and men's self-employment in the United States, 1980. *Work and Occupations, 23*(1), 26–53. doi:10.1177/0730888496023001003

Caucutt, E. M., Guner, N., & Rauh, C. (2016). *Is marriage for White people? Incarceration and the racial marriage divide.* Unpublished paper, Department of Economics, Western University.

Cavalluzzo, K. S., Cavalluzzo, L. C., & Wolken, J. D. (2002). Competition, small business financing, and discrimination: Evidence from a new survey. *The Journal of Business, 75*(4), 641–679. doi:10.1086/341638

Chiteji, N. S., & Hamilton, D. (2002). Family connections and the black-white wealth gap among middle-class families. *The Review of Black Political Economy*, *30*(1), 9–28. doi:10.1007/BF02808169

Clark, R., Lusardi, A., Mitchell, O. S., & Davis, H. (2021). Factors contributing to financial well-being among Black and Hispanic women. *The Journal of Retirement*, *9*(1), 71–97. doi:10.3905/jor.2021.1.088

Coleman, J. S. (1994). *Foundations of social theory*. Harvard University Press.

Coleman, S. (2005). The impact of human capital measures on firm performance: A comparison by gender, race and ethnicity. *The Journal of Entrepreneurial Finance*, *10*(2), 38–56.

Danes, S. M., Lee, J., Amarapurkar, S., Stafford, K., Haynes, G., & Brewton, K. E. (2009). Determinants of family business resilience after a natural disaster by gender of business owner. *Journal of Developmental Entrepreneurship*, *14*(04), 333–354. doi:10.1142/S1084946709001351

Darity, W. (2005). Stratification economics: The role of intergroup inequality. *Journal of Economics and Finance*, *29*(2), 144–153. doi:10.1007/BF02761550

Darity, W. A. Jr, Hamilton, D., & Stewart, J. B. (2015). A tour de force in understanding intergroup inequality: An introduction to stratification economics. *The Review of Black Political Economy*, *42*(1-2), 1–6. doi:10.100712114-014-9201-2

Desai, S., Looze, J., & Pechenina, A. (2020). *Student Loans and Entrepreneurship: An Overview. Entrepreneurship Issue Brief. No. 5*. Ewing Marion Kauffman Foundation.

Dyer, W. G., Nenque, E., & Hill, E. J. (2014). Toward a theory of family capital and entrepreneurship: Antecedents and outcomes. *Journal of Small Business Management*, *52*(2), 266–285. doi:10.1111/jsbm.12097

Fairlie, R. W. (2012). Immigrant entrepreneurs and small business owners, and their access to financial capital. *Small Business Administration*, *396*, 1–46.

Fairlie, R. W., & Robb, A. M. (2008). Race and entrepreneurial success. Academic Press.

Fairlie, R. W., Robb, A. M., & Hinson, D. (2010). *Disparities in Capital Access Between Minority and Non-minority-owned Businesses*. US Department of Commerce, Minority Business Development Agency.

Feagin, J. R., & Imani, N. (1994). Racial barriers to African American entrepreneurship: An exploratory study. *Social Problems*, *41*(4), 562–584. doi:10.2307/3096989

Fearnow, B. (2018, July 10). *Black Women Graduate With Most U.S. Student Loan Debt, Study Says.* https://www.newsweek.com/student-loans-pay-gap-college-debt-black-women-white-men-women-gender-gap-1016776

Fratoe, F. A. (1988). Social capital of black business owners. *The Review of Black Political Economy*, *16*(4), 33–50. doi:10.1007/BF02892164

Gines, D. (2018). *Black women business startups*. The Federal Reserve Bank of Kansas City.

Holder, M., Jones, J., & Masterson, T. (2021). The early impact of COVID-19 on job losses among black women in the United States. *Feminist Economics*, *27*(1-2), 103–116. doi:10.1080/13545701.2020.1849766

Inman, K. (2016). *Women's resources in business start-up: A study of black and white women entrepreneurs*. Routledge. doi:10.4324/9781315276519

Jackson, T. M., & Sanyal, P. (2019). Struggles and strategies of Black women business owners in the US. *Journal of Business Anthropology*, *8*(2), 228–249. doi:10.22439/jba.v8i2.5850

Jones, J. (2017). *The racial wealth gap: How African-Americans have been shortchanged out of the materials to build wealth.* Economic Policy Institute. http://epi.org

Katznelson, I. (2005). *When affirmative action was white: An untold history of racial inequality in twentieth-century America.* WW Norton & Company.

Kelley, D., Majbouri, M., & Randolph, A. (2021). Black women are more likely to start a business than white men. *Harvard Business Review*.

Kickul, J., Griffiths, M. D., Robb, C. C., & Gundry, L. (2021). All for one? The Paycheck Protection Program distribution disparity. *Journal of Entrepreneurship and Public Policy*.

Kim, P. H., Aldrich, H. E., & Keister, L. A. (2006). Access (not) denied: The impact of financial, human, and cultural capital on entrepreneurial entry in the United States. *Small Business Economics*, *27*(1), 5–22. doi:10.100711187-006-0007-x

Kirkwood, J. (2009). Motivational factors in a push-pull theory of entrepreneurship. *Gender in Management*, *24*(5), 346–364. doi:10.1108/17542410910968805

Lee, W. (2019). Character-based lending for micro business development: Empirical insights into conceptualizing character. *Journal of Small Business and Entrepreneurship*, 1–16. doi:10.1080/08276331.2019.1701256

Light, I. (1980). *Ethnic Entrepreneurship in America*. University of California Press.

Lofstrom, M., & Bates, T. (2013). African Americans' pursuit of self-employment. *Small Business Economics*, *40*(1), 73–86. doi:10.100711187-011-9347-2

Lofstrom, M., Bates, T., & Parker, S. C. (2014). Why are some people more likely to become small-businesses owners than others: Entrepreneurship entry and industry-specific barriers. *Journal of Business Venturing*, *29*(2), 232–251. doi:10.1016/j.jbusvent.2013.01.004

Looze, J., & Desai, S. (2020). Economic Engagement of Mothers: Entrepreneurship, Employment, and the Motherhood Wage Penalty. *Employment, and the Motherhood Wage Penalty*.

Mullen, C. (2021, April 14). *Women of color drive new business growth during pandemic*. https://www.bizjournals.com/bizwomen/news/latest-news/2021/04/minority-women-drive-business-growth-in-pandemic.html?page=all

Myers, S., & Chan, P. (2017, July). Stuck from the Start: The Financial Challenges of Low-and Moderate-Income African-American Entrepreneurs in the South. *Prosperity Now*.

Newman, K. S. (2009). *No shame in my game: The working poor in the inner city*. Vintage.

Nopper, T. K. (2010). Colorblind racism and institutional actors' explanations of Korean immigrant entrepreneurship. *Critical Sociology*, *36*(1), 65–85. doi:10.1177/0896920509347141

O'Brien, R. L. (2012). Depleting capital? Race, wealth and informal financial assistance. *Social Forces*, *91*(2), 375–396. doi:10.1093fos132

Ogbolu, M. N. (2015). Relationship Between Legitimacy and Intended Patronage: One Size Fits All? *Journal of Business Diversity*, *15*(1).

Oliver, M. L., & Shapiro, T. M. (1995). Black Wealth/White. *Wealth: A New Perspective on.*

Pager, D., & Shepherd, H. (2008). The sociology of discrimination: Racial discrimination in employment, housing, credit, and consumer markets. *Annual Review of Sociology*, *34*(1), 181–209. doi:10.1146/annurev.soc.33.040406.131740 PMID:20689680

Palia, D. (2016). Differential access to capital from financial institutions by minority entrepreneurs. *Journal of Empirical Legal Studies*, *13*(4), 756–785. doi:10.1111/jels.12132

Ployhart, R. E., & Moliterno, T. P. (2011). Emergence of the human capital resource: A multilevel model. *Academy of Management Review*, *36*(1), 127–150. doi:10.5465/amr.2009.0318

Portes, A. (1998). Social capital: Its origins and applications in modern sociology. *Annual Review of Sociology*, *24*(1), 1–24. doi:10.1146/annurev.soc.24.1.1

ProjectDiane. (2020). *The State of Black & LatinxWomen Founders.* Digitalundivided. https://www.projectdiane.com/

Ruef, M. (2010). Entrepreneurial groups. In *Historical Foundations of Entrepreneurship Research.* Edward Elgar Publishing. doi:10.4337/9781849806947.00020

Sanders, J. M., & Nee, V. (1996). Immigrant self-employment: The family as social capital and the value of human capital. *American Sociological Review*, *61*(2), 231–249. doi:10.2307/2096333

Sarnoff, I. (1960). Psychoanalytic theory and social attitudes. *Public Opinion Quarterly*, *24*(2), 251–279. doi:10.1086/266948

Shane, S. A. (2008). *The illusions of entrepreneurship: The costly myths that entrepreneurs, investors, and policy makers live by.* Yale University Press.

Singh, R. P., Knox, E. L., & Crump, M. E. (2008). Opportunity recognition differences between black and white nascent entrepreneurs: A test of Bhave's model. *Journal of Developmental Entrepreneurship*, *13*(01), 59–75. doi:10.1142/S1084946708000855

Smith-Hunter, A. E., & Boyd, R. L. (2004). Applying theories of entrepreneurship to a comparative analysis of white and minority women business owners. *Women in Management Review*, *19*(1), 18–28. doi:10.1108/09649420410518403

Sowell, T. (1991). Cultural Diversity: A World View. *American Enterprise (Washington, D.C.)*, *2*(3), 44–55.

Srigley, K. (2005). "In case you hadn't noticed!": Race, Ethnicity, and Women's Wage-Earning in a Depression-Era City. *Labour/Le Travailleur, 55*, 69-106.

Stack, C. B. (2008). *All our kin: Strategies for survival in a black community*. Basic Books.

Struyven, D., George-Joseph, G., & Milo, D. (2021). *Black Womenomics: Investing in the Underinvested*. Goldman Sachs Research https://www.goldmansachs.com/insights/pages/black-womenomics-f/black-womenomics-report.pdf

Valdez, Z. (2008). The effect of social capital on White, Korean, Mexican and Black business owners' earnings in the US. *Journal of Ethnic and Migration Studies, 34*(6), 955–973. doi:10.1080/13691830802211265

Zaw, K., Bhattacharya, J., Price, A., Hamilton, D., & Darity Jr, W. (2017). Women, race and wealth. *Research Brief Series, 1*(1), 1-4.

KEY TERMS AND DEFINITIONS

Black Woman Entrepreneur (BWE): The term Black woman entrepreneur is used to refer to a small business owner or self-employed person who identifies as Black and woman. This research treats Black women business owners as entrepreneurs which is line with other scholars who posit that small business management requires traits that are synonymous with entrepreneurial behavior. Thus the terms *Black woman business owner* and *Black woman entrepreneur* are used interchangeably herein.

Financial Capital: The monetary assets needed by a company to provide goods or services.

Financial Capital Access Gap: In this chapter financial capital access gap refers to disparities in accessing financial capital between Black women entrepreneurs and White women entrepreneurs.

Negative Social Capital: Negative social capital is social capital that has negative results. Negative social capital is the pressure placed on individuals by virtue of being a part of a group which results in negative consequences to the individual, for example, in the form of lower economic capital (Portes, 1998).

Stratification Economics: Is a sub-field of economics that takes a systemic and empirically grounded approach to addressing intergroup inequality particularly between ethnic and racial groups. It integrates economics, sociology and social psychology.

Wealth: Also termed net worth it is the sum of an individual's assets less the sum of debts.

Woman-Owned Business: Businesses where over 50% of the owners self-identify as woman.

Chapter 8
Women Entrepreneurs and Disparities During the Pre- and Post-COVID-19 Pandemic Eras

Iris A. Billy
Medgar Evers College, City University of New York, USA

Priscilla S. Harrison
Campbellsville University, USA

Nagamani Palla
Campbellsville University, USA

ABSTRACT

The challenges of a global pandemic have placed women's business ownership and entrepreneurship at the forefront of much debate. This is an important area to pursue within scholarly arenas because women's involvement in business ownership and entrepreneurship continues to impact women's livelihoods, families, and impacts the local and global economy. There are many studies that explored challenges and barriers to women's entrepreneurship, a more specific and focused finding should be addressed to review implications presented due to COVID-19 pandemic. An examination of how ethnicity, gender, and race plays a role in women entrepreneurship process and the way women entrepreneurs' experiences were shaped during the pre- and post-pandemic era is warranted on a scholarly level.

INTRODUCTION

In 2018, University of California archaeologist Randy Haas unearthed the 9,000 – year-old remains of an adult female hunter in the Andes Mountains. The discovery challenged the assumption that gender discrimination is biologically-based due to the differences in physiology and women's role in childbirth. Gerda (1986), in her book *The Creation of Patriarchy*, suggests that female subordination arose voluntarily when humans began to settle in groups and control of reproduction resources (women) led to private

DOI: 10.4018/978-1-6684-4322-4.ch008

property ownership and class distinction. Lerner theorizes that females willingly accepted a subordinated role in exchange for male physical protection and privilege during the first periods of civilization.

During the subsequent millennia, women's status, and rights vis-a-vis that of a male, steadily declined, confined to child-raising and domestic chores with limited legal, social, or economic rights. Despite cultural barriers, females have demonstrated throughout history their capacity to overcome prejudice and discrimination in all forms of social and economic activities:

- **Politics**. The English Queens Elizabeth I, Katherine the Great, and Victoria were the equal, if not superior, to any male ruler of their times. Modern female political leaders include Golda Meir of Israel, India's Indira Gandhi, and Germany's Angela Merkel.
- **Science**. Caroline Herschel's work in astronomy in the early 1800s led to an Honorary Membership in the prestigious Royal Society more than a century before women were allowed formally into these societies. Marie Curie won two Nobel Prizes: Physics, 1903 and Radioactivity, 1911. Lise Meitner was a co-discoverer of nuclear fusions and nominated for Nobel Prizes in chemistry and physics 48 times. Fifty-eight women have won the award since 1901.
- **Business**. Eliza Lucas Pinckney (1722-1793) is considered America's first female business owner. Pinckney managed three family farms in South Carolina, she pioneered the cultivation of indigo on a commercial scale, second only to rice as South Carolina cash crop. Rebecca Lukens, the country's first female CEO, took over her deceased husband steel mill in 1925, expanding the business to become an industrial giant acquired by Bethlehem Steel in 1998. Research suggests that close to 30% of businesses in Victorian England were managed by women, including Eliza Tinsley, a widow who grew a hardware manufacturing business to 4000 employees.

There is no field of endeavor where women have not proven to be the equal of men. Nonetheless, cultural mores and traditional structures continue to impose barriers to the full equality of women as opposed to their male counterparts. Women continue to be underrepresented in starting new businesses today, unable to access resources - capital, mentoring, networks – male entrepreneurs typically enjoy in society.

History of Women Entrepreneurship

According to the study the first female-owned business in the USA was detailed in 1739 when Eliza Lucas Pinckney managed her family's estates in South Carolina as a young adult. In the 18th and 19th periods, women managed small businesses acquired from family legacy or establishing their own businesses to improve their income. In many cases, women were attempting to avoid financial hardship or were replacing the income from the demise of a spouse.

At that time, the business enterprise that these women started were not thought of as entrepreneurial enterprises, because most of these women had to focus on their domestic responsibilities. Due to time-honored and substantive barriers to educational and alternative employment opportunities, African American women were traditionally reduced to attaining low-paying jobs mostly in the field of domestic labor predominantly in the Jim Crow era of the South. As a result, African American women of the early 20th century developed entrepreneurial niches as seamstresses, hairdressers, domestic workers and as midwives.

Barriers to Entrepreneurship for Women

Lower levels of wealth, access to capital, racial discrimination and inadequate networks have been and continue to be barriers to entrepreneurship women of color experience even to date. The term entrepreneur is used to describe individuals who have ideas for products and/or services that they turn into a working business. In earlier times, this term was reserved for men who owned and managed their own business.

A recent international study found that women from low to middle income countries are more likely to enter early stage entrepreneurship when compared to those of higher-income countries. A significant factor that may play a role in this disparity can be attributed to the fact that women from low-income countries often seek additional means of income to support themselves and their families. Overall, 40 to 50 per cent of all small businesses are owned by women in developing countries. Alternatively, this may also be because in western business practices, it is not seen as beneficial to exhibit perceived feminine traits

Although female entrepreneurship and the formation of female-owned business networks are steadily rising, there are a number of challenges and obstacles that female entrepreneurs encounter. One major challenge for female entrepreneurs faces traditional gender roles that are structurally internalized by society. Entrepreneurship is considered a male-dominated field, and it may be difficult for female entrepreneurs to surpass these conventional views. Other than dealing with the dominant stereotype, female entrepreneurs are facing several obstacles related to their businesses.

Other research has shown that women entrepreneurs are already launching ambitious businesses in the high-technology industry, expanding their social networks, and making their pitches more relatable to the male-dominated venture capital industry. These expansions in businesses are despite the belief that women are not as vocal as men in the areas of venture capitalism. As a special note studies have reviewed the social networks of women entrepreneurs, showing that their networks are different from that of their male counterparts and are not overlapping as much with financial networks. An entrepreneur's social capital is defined by the networks they are able to access, and receiving private equity funding is heavily influenced by an entrepreneur's social capital and whether it overlaps with that of venture capitalists. Thus, women continue being disadvantaged in that respect upon seeking private equity funding; in general, women have lower personal financial assets than men. This means that for a given opportunity and equally capable individual, women must secure additional resources compared to men in order to exploit the opportunity; because they control less capital. The question of whether it is more difficult for women to obtain finance than men for the same business opportunity has developed into its own sub-field. One possible issue for procuring outside capital is that 96% of senior venture capitalists are men and may not be as understanding of female-centric businesses. However, the situation seems to be improving as a study by Babson College showed that in 1999, fewer than 5% of venture capital investments went to companies with a woman on the executive team. In 2011, it was 9% and in 2013 it was 18%.

A specific solution for solving women's difficulties for obtaining financing has been micro-financing. Microfinance is a financial institution that has become exceptionally popular, especially in developing economies. Female entrepreneurs have also been especially successful in getting funded through crowdfunding platforms like Kickstarter. Due to lack of funding for women in new businesses statistics show that many women founders have had to hire or create fake male profiles to act as co-founders, executives, or the face of their businesses to make progress.

In the early part of 2020, the spread of COVID-19 developed, and on March 11th, 2020, the World Health Organization declared that the virus has spread worldwide and therefore a worldwide pandemic has ensued globally. As a result, there were lockdowns on a global scale, with restrictions on worldwide travel enforced and many restaurants, hotels, and shops being closed for business. Businesses were forced to switch to remote work and employees were ask to restrict commuting to work and instead remote work was strongly encouraged on a grand scale. The phenomenon of remote work led to a decline in commuting on roadways and freeways and established businesses were affected by this sudden shift in normalcy. At the same time, opportunities and demand for new products and services emerged in many countries. These new opportunities were fueled by customer demands for online products and services such as online shopping, food deliveries, online entertainment and education, protective personal equipment and sanitizing products.

In the midst of this turmoil caused by COVID-19 pandemic, entrepreneurship and entrepreneurs have responded accordingly to the many opportunities in this climate. As an entrepreneur is not only an opportunity or a dream for many people, because there are many challenges which exist to achieve making these opportunities and dreams. Entrepreneurs have to overcome both financial and economic obstacles imposed on them by societal expectations and this is true especially for marginalized segments of the population.

Entrepreneurship and the term entrepreneur can be viewed from different angles and perspectives. According to Gupta (2019), entrepreneurship is the process where the creation of value is achieved by combining together unique and varied resources of economies for opportunities and wealth. Authors Gholami and Al Tahoo (2021, p.71) describe entrepreneurship as a process which " involves the behavior of exploiting opportunities as well as the creation of new venture, whether successful or not". Entrepreneurs often cite that one of the biggest rewards of being an entrepreneur is that of owning the decisions and choices that is made while being an entrepreneur. Accordingly, entrepreneurs have personal freedom and satisfaction to make their own business decisions and then act upon these decisions. As an entrepreneur gets a creative idea, the entrepreneur has the ability to cultivate that creative idea into action and own the aftermath good or bad for the business. This is especially true with women entrepreneurs who tend to be more passionate about their work. These women therefore become more focused and motivated as they enjoy ownership and will be passionate about their success. This passion and motivation also tends to help an entrepreneur's need to help make their community and the world a better place for all. For example, women have their own businesses want to create jobs for people and gain personal satisfaction in knowing that they are helping provide services and products needed by their community.

Conversely, entrepreneurs need to be aware of potential risks associated with being an entrepreneur, especially as marginalized business owners. One of the biggest risks is the possibility of making wrong business decisions and the time and money invested in the entrepreneurial business may not be successful. Long hours and hard work including financial insecurity at the initial start-up process are some of the other risks that entrepreneurs have to address.

COVID-19 and Women Entrepreneurs

According to Global Entrepreneurship Monitor (GEM, 2021), studies show that the proportion of women who started a new business has declined in 2020 versus their male counterpart. This could possibly be attributed to women being more focused with taking care of their family and homeschooling their children during the COVID-19 pandemic. Studies also show that women entrepreneurs and their businesses are smaller in size, produce smaller profits, and are also less successful to than are male-owned businesses (Jennings and Brush, 2013). During 2020, the effects of the pandemic were especially notable for women-owned companies, many of whom are less-well financed compared to men-owned firms. According to a study conducted by Biz2Credit a leading online credit marketplace which reviewed 40,0000 credit inquiries in the US for the entirety of 2020, revenues decreased for women-owned businesses and their earnings increased, due to a decrease in business expenses during the COVID-19 pandemic. Key findings from Biz2Credit study compared women-owned businesses versus men-owned business indicate that women-owned businesses are less likely to seek loans due to their businesses earning less than their male counterpart and therefore women-owned businesses had lower credit scores. Also, women to men business borrowing ratio was 27% for women versus 72% for men with women's credit score of 23 points lower than for men-owned business during the pandemic in 2020. Additionally, the average loan amount for women-owned businesses was 33% lower at $36,981 as compared to businesses owned by men with loan amounts of $55,061 (Rohit, 2021).

Women entrepreneurs with start-up businesses in the technology industry were in the low range of 5 to 15 percentile range over all of the total entrepreneurs in this lucrative industry segment. Studies also show that women-owned entrepreneurs develop and create their businesses offering services to their customers rather than in the creating products. With the COVID-19 pandemic, this low number of women entrepreneurs in the technology sector is especially relevant due to the industry in the country with higher level of unemployment rates in April 2020 was in the less attractive services job sector with 17.2 million new unemployed versus 2.4 million in the product producing job sector (Villaseca et al., 2021). According to a study conducted by Rohit (2021), in the 2020 more than one-quarter (25.8%) of the industry in the service sector were owned by women, with 17% in retail, 9.5% in Health Care and Social Assistance, 9.2% in Food Services, followed by 6.2% in Construction, and 5.5% in Arts, Entertainment, and Recreation sector.

Women Entrepreneurs and Financing

The impact of COVID-19 on world economies is projected to be negative even more-so than was originally anticipated and the recovery additionally is projected to be very slow. With these crises in world economies, families and the underserved or marginalized people are subjected to a high level of uncertainties in society. Studies have shown that there is a low rate of entrepreneurship among women due to this risk and uncertainty (Gompers and Wang, 2017). According to the Organization for Economic Co-operation and Development (OECD, 2017), only 16% of new business start-ups globally are by women and women given the same opportunities as men to be entrepreneurs, the global gross domestic product would be boosted by 5 trillion dollars as stated by Unnikrishnan and Blair (2019).

Female employees face many challenges and obstacles in everyday work and business landscape including overcoming the "glass ceiling" and starting a business as a woman to overcome these barriers is often seen as an attractive endeavor. The lack of ability to access finance on both the supply and demand side also showcases one of the many obstacles that female entrepreneurs encounter even to this present time. The impact of the COVID-19 crisis on women-owned entrepreneurship and the challenges of access to credit are crucial to the overall economy. The COVID-19 pandemic added a disruptive affect entrepreneurial financing issues with institutions such as banks, public and investment institutions as well as female entrepreneurs. The urgency for access to capital and financing sources is critical for business to survive during the pandemic (Alon et al., 2020).

As per Goodell, (2020) reports during the pandemic one of the main challenges of an entrepreneur is the financial fragility of obtaining sufficient cash reserves to continue operating for two weeks under COVID-19 restrictions versus smaller businesses with monthly expenses under $10,000 with sufficient cash reserves for four weeks. This fragile environment means that entrepreneurs are hard pressed and unable to obtain funding which added debt could lead to insolvency or bankruptcy. This dilemma impacted banks and investment institutions and their increasing likelihood to disapprove more funding to non-performing loans and economic losses (Goodell, 2020).

There are several forms of discrimination toward women entrepreneurs and financing. One form of discrimination is based on cultural beliefs and opinions which drives banks and investments firm's decisions to lend finance to women-owned businesses. This discriminate occurs due to prejudice against women entrepreneurs and those who are empowered to either approve or disapprove the credit and the decision to allocate financing, based in terms of economics or profit. A second form of discrimination occurs when gender dynamics is used to award credit and finance to entrepreneurs. This is based on the premise that women-owned entrepreneurs are more likely to default on their loans, and therefore lenders could use this as an average statistic to say that every women-owned business would be more likely to default and therefore is a risk. A third type of discrimination against women entrepreneurs is the implicit discrimination where women-owned businesses are discriminated even if the lender implicitly does not want to discriminate. This implicit discrimination toward women-owned businesses would decrease the likelihood of female entrepreneurs to obtain a loan or credit, not because of a rational evaluation but because of unintentional rules and attitudes not explicitly expressed towards male counterparts.

Sources of Finance for Women Entrepreneurs

Most entrepreneurs in our society have access different sources to obtain financial resources to develop or create their new businesses. Entrepreneurs in society have the ability to finance their business by borrowing from a third-party and self-funding by using their own capital is the second source of funding. Self-funding by choosing to use one's own capital and is considered a risky venture which may reduce the need for new growth and development. Self-funding has the ability to prevent future growth or opportunities or challenge the very survival of the entrepreneurial business during the COVID-19 pandemic and crises. Due to the high uncertainty during COVID-19 pandemic and the lack of accurate business and financial information, women entrepreneurs are more inclined use self-financing to fund their start-up business, and thereby avoid using third-party financing options.

1. Crowdfunding, venture capital and business angels are all external sources of financing available to women entrepreneurs. Crowdfunding is one way to obtain finance through social media where a group of like-minded individuals support a common cause and goal with contributions from group members. Studies show that there is a smaller presence of women-owned businesses that benefit from crowdfunding initiatives. According to Marom et al., (2016), in a study analyzing 80,000 projects, less than 35% of crowdfunding financing was obtained by women entrepreneurs.
2. Business angel investors are private lending institutions of consisting of investors who contribute to new businesses and enterprises and their funding with a concentrated focus on technology based projects. Business angel investors also provide entrepreneurs assistance in knowledge to manage their new start-up business. There is evidence that women entrepreneurs are underrepresented and are in the minority with only 16% participation in funding requests. This also highlights the bias evident in the business segment of the industry as women-owned businesses in the technology sector are underrepresented.

3. Venture Capital (VC) firms are lending institutions that assist new businesses in their early stages. These finance sources anticipate risks in exchange for a higher return on investment for the start-up business. Studies show that women entrepreneurs are underrepresented segment when financing via venture capital firms as opposed to their male counterparts. Entrepreneurs who finance their start-up business with the support of venture capital firms and business angel investors in their initial business development stages are more successful than those who do not have their financial support (Tinkler et al., 2015).

Women Entrepreneur, Education, and Technology

Studies conducted by the Global Entrepreneurship Monitor (GEM) in 2019 indicate that for the European Union, the ration for every ten (10) men as entrepreneurs there are six (6) women entrepreneurs. The divide is more profound in the Information Technology (IT) industry and the digital economy which is mostly dominated by men versus women. With the COVID-19 crises and pandemic, the digital economy is seen as a big contributor to overcome service disruptions. Internet sales and online shopping increased due to COVID-19 as lock-downs were imposed around the world and dramatic cultural and societal transformations occurred. Digital enterprises were created to help accommodate the needs of citizens of every country in the world. From deliveries of groceries, medicine to digital or telemedicine and remote learning for schools and universities via digital or internet services became normalized parts of our society. This digital transformation of the economy was expected to be the primary driving force for economic growth in the near future, but also has shown to herald the most disruptive enterprises. The barriers and challenges exist for women entrepreneurs even in this digital economy as evident in the low participation levels of women entrepreneurs. Women entrepreneurs can overcome these barriers and challenges by creating their own businesses with specific training and education that focuses on entrepreneurship in the digital age via mentorship, supporting and coaching each other to succeed during the COVID-19 pandemic crises.

According to Molina- López et al., (2021) women entrepreneurs in the digital economy who received external support and training felt empowered to undertake major tasks such as starting their own business. Additionally, getting entrepreneurial education helped these underserved women to be more innovative, creative and transformative by generating new businesses and enterprises. Entrepreneurial training increases self-confidence in women entrepreneurs and helps them to overcome challenges and barriers to start their own enterprises and businesses.

CASE STUDY

Our Case Study will highlight the stories of five (5) minority women entrepreneurs from various walks of life and different countries. First, the Case Study will discuss the differences in these businesses pre and post the COVID-19 pandemic. Second, the Case Study will also discuss the reason these women chose the role of entrepreneurship instead of employment with other organizations. Finally, the Case Study will include a list of insights for future women entrepreneurs from the five (5) interviewees.

Case Study #1- Carmel S

Business Joe's Mini Mart and Bar
Origin Originally from Trinidad WI (Lives in Trinidad WI).
Languages Fluent in English
***Face to face interview**

Carmel S is a 60-year-old mother of three (3) who lives in Mathura, Trinidad and Tobago located in the Caribbean. Carmel S has a high school education and although she was a good student she did not have the opportunity to earn a college education. The lack of further education and low paying menial jobs was a great motivator to starting her own business.

Carmel S has been an entrepreneur for approximately 25 years, her business consists of a local mini-mart (the equivalent of a sole proprietor grocery store) and a bar. As with most business owners in the Caribbean this store is located as part of the family's residential dwelling. Carmel S and her family reside in the upper level of her house and her business is located at the lower level. The reason for these multi-use type properties is basically to save on rental of a business property thus more profit for the business owner. A typical day for Carmel S begins at 6am and ends at 8pm as she is one of the sole mini-marts in her area. Carmel S used a combination of personal funds, loans from family members and banks to start her business. As a note the first loans were initiated by her husband however over the years Carmel S was able to obtain her own business loans from her financial institution based on her credit, funds used as collateral with the bank, and longstanding banking relationship.

The interview with Carmel S was very insightful, her business has always been profitable, and has been the sole source of income for her family especially after the death of her husband. As food is a staple to all humans the idea of a mini-mart was ideal for her small fishing village of Mathura. As entrepreneurs have realized location is very important to a business's success and as Carmel S envisioned her grocery store would be successful in her small fishing and recreation community. Not only does she serve her local community but the "out-of-towners" and tourists who visited the beaches on the weekends.

Post pandemic the business flourished and the family lived very comfortable with the earnings from the business. During the pandemic the business was open unlike many other businesses as food was deemed an essential item (bar however was closed for business as per governmental orders during the pandemic). As the pandemic continues business has been slower than Carmel S would have liked but luckily she has not misused her profits and was able to tap into her savings to ensure that the business is at an even keel.

Case Study #2 – Ruth V

Business Chicaa Rozei Boutique
Origin Originally from Colombia, South America (Has lived in the USA for 20+years).
Languages Fluent in Spanish and English
Questions and Answers

Ruth V owns Chicaa Rozei Boutique located in Plainfield New Jersey. Ruth V is Hispanic and is more fluent in Spanish than English. She is originally from Bogota Colombia and is a college graduate in her late 50s. Chicaa Rozei Boutique is a women's boutique that sells clothing, shoes, costume jewelry, belts, handbags, and hosiery. The clientele for this boutique is 99% Hispanic and this is based on statistics which shows the town is 55% Hispanic. Hereunder are the questions and Ruth Vs responses: -

1. **How the idea of opening your own business come about?**
   I have the idea that being self-employed, will give me the opportunity to manage my own time.

2. **Why did you choose a women's boutique?**
   Thinking of myself, because I like to dress well, and most of the time it's difficult to find good advice from a retail store salesperson.

3. **What was your key driving force to owning a business as opposed to working for someone else?**
   I think that it was because I wanted to control my own time, as it helps you to achieve your personal goals.

4. **How did you come up with the name for your boutique?**
   It's a French sound combination of my husband's name and mine.

5. **How did you decide where to open your boutique?**
   As I mentioned before, time is very important for me, so living close to work will help in terms of saving time.

6. **How did you raise funding for your business?**
   I used some loans and personal savings.

7. **How did you find your customers?**
   Offering good services (training personnel) and very good quality products.

8. **With the opportunity to restart your career, what would you do differently?**
   I have been happy owning and managing my business, so I will do it again, without substantial changes.

9. **How many hours a day do you work on average?**
   I wake up very early and go to bed late, and sometimes I do some work in bed. In a typical day I take care of my family (husband and kids), my house and business.

10. **How has owning your own business affected your family life in terms of time spent with growing your business?**
    We have to understand that: There is no such thing as free lunch. The best I found in terms of helping my family is owning a business to support my family and everyone working towards one goal in our own business. My husband and sons assist with the business as well. It has been idea having a family responsibility and to include or involve the family in the business.

11. **What piece of advice would you give to another female who wants to own a business?**
    I would say, "believe in yourself and do not be afraid to try and family support is fundamental".

12. **How has the COVID-19 pandemic affected your business.**
    At the beginning of the pandemic when all business was closed I was affected however my son had the idea of selling on-line and sending pictures to my clients. We posted pictures of clothing had customers order, pay with Zelle and other digital means, and deliver to their door. Although this was not the same as walk in customers we were able to maintain fairly good sales. At present with businesses reopening we have recouped but not at 100%

Case Study #3 – Jermita R

Business Jazzle Dance Studio
Origin Originally from USA with Caribbean heritage
Languages Fluent in English
Questions and Answers

Jermita R owns a dance studio in Atlanta GA. She is in her mid-30s and is a New York native who relocated to Atlanta GA in 2015 to attend Emory Healthcare's Medical Laboratory Science program. In addition to her job in laboratory science, she is a dance and youth educator and choreographer with over 15 years of experience in teaching education.

Hereunder are the questions and Jermita Rs responses: -

1. **How did the idea for opening your own business come about? Why did you choose your business?**
   I've had a passion for dance since I was 3 years old and for the first 7 years of my dance career, I taught dance (primarily tap and hip-hop) as a "paid" hobby in New York. When I moved to Georgia I procured a dance teaching position to help supplement my income while I was in Medical Technology school. At that studio I had a few dancers that were exceptional, and I felt as though their dance education and experience deserved to be expanded beyond the recreational classes they were taking. I created a competition dance company (think Dance Moms), taught more advanced choreography and we hit the stage. The first three years we lost a lot! But within 6 years we became highly decorated with 21 first place, 10 second place, 20 judges' awards and I received 3 highly coveted choreographer's awards. We outgrew our current space and it could no longer accommodate our needs. I never wanted to be a businesswoman but my spouse (who is also a creative in the field of music and film) encouraged me to expand on my own and eventually I took the leap of faith!

2. **What was your key driving force to owning a business as opposed to working for someone else?**
   The key driving force for owning my own business was space and opportunity. I felt as though my current dance company needed a bigger rehearsal space, and that I needed a bigger space to create more innovative dance routines for more students. Also, for 6 years I commuted over an hour each way to teach class and I was exhausted! I wanted to teach closer to my home.

3. **What was the inspiration for choosing the name for your business?**
   I love this story. I built my entire business in about 5 months and from the beginning I kept telling myself if I have a name and a logo everything else would fall into place. I racked my brain exclusively for 2 days trying to come up with a name that fit my vision for the studio. I desired a name that had the letter J in it (because I go by Ms. Jay in the dance world), but I didn't want it to have my whole name. I wanted it to be representative of me but not focused on me. I was on a logo creator website plugging in phrases and came across a logo that said "Razzle, Dazzle". I'm pretty dramatic so I loved the word Dazzle. Then it came to me, "Dazzle, J, JAZZLE!" After a few days of dwelling on it I decided that it was perfect. I was able to come up with so many cute slogans like "It's Time to Jazzle'' and "Razzle, Dazzle, JAZZLE". Thus, Jazzle Dance Studio was born.

4. **How did you decide where to open your business?**
   After 12+ years of long commutes in both New York and Georgia I knew that if I was going to have a business, it HAD to be very close to my house. I live in a family-oriented neighborhood in Georgia I was able to find the perfect standalone building for Jazzle where there isn't too much competition.

5. **How did you raise funding for your business? Did you use your own money, loans etc.?**
   Due to timing, I utilized personal loans for my business.

6. **How do you find your customers?**
   I find my customers through social media marketing. I run ads on Facebook, Instagram and Tik Tok.

7. **With an opportunity to start your career over again, what would you do differently? Would you prefer to own your business or work for someone else?**
   Honestly, I probably would have stuck to my guns and not have opened my own business. I love having my own dance studio but as I anticipated it's stressful, expensive and it's hard to please everyone. However, I've always played it safe in life and I think owning my studio has and will continue to afford me the opportunity to be pushed past my comfort zone, overcome adversity, and build a future beyond what I ever imagined/ expected for my family and myself. There are pros and cons to both owning my business and working for someone else, but I love the dichotomy and doing both simultaneously.

8. **How many hours a day do you work on average? Can you describe/outline your typical day?**
   In addition to owning Jazzle, I work full time as a Laboratory Scientist at a high-volume fertility clinic. A typical day includes working at the fertility clinic for 8 hours, Monday – Friday (and sometimes on the weekend). I've organized my teaching schedule by which I teach dance classes on Tuesdays, Wednesdays, Fridays for a maximum of two hours. When I'm not physically at the studio I'm working on it from my home office. Saturdays are my "dance days" and I teach anywhere from 6 to 10 hours. In total I probably work about 10-12 hours per day, including Sundays. I try to designate Thursday and Sunday evenings' as "self-care day" and I'll treat myself to a massage or allow myself to just watch television, hang out with friends or sleep!

9. **How has owning your own business affected your family life in terms of time spent with growing your business?**
Around the same time that I began Jazzle my spouse and I entered a trial separation. It wasn't due to my business, but it was a factor. Looking back, it was probably for the better that my wife nor family were privy to how much time I spent building my business because I developed some unhealthy habits. I was working within a very short time frame as I didn't finalize my lease until the middle of July, and we opened in August. Between May and December 2021, all of my time was devoted to getting everything ready for our grand opening. I spent so many early mornings working on Jazzle before heading to the clinic and stayed up to the wee hours of the night sending emails, financial planning etc. to make sure Jazzle's inception was smooth and organized. Now in 2022, because of the structure I worked extremely hard to develop, my business can run without so much of my physical attention and I have slightly more time to relax.

10. **What piece of advice would you give to another female who want to own a business?**
Before Jazzle I was a scaredy cat! Now my philosophy and what I would tell any aspiring female business owner is "if it doesn't kill you or send you to jail, go for it! Life is a journey rather than a destination so believe in gods' will and always have faith and "if you're going to do something, do it with your whole soul!

11. **How has the COVID-19 pandemic affected your business?**
The pandemic has affected my business because state and federal regulations are ever changing which affects studio policies. Many parents are hesitant to commit to classes because they are afraid that we will have to shut down. Other parents are apprehensive to send their children to class with fears that their children may contract COVID. At Jazzle we have strict COVID policies. We require dancers to wear masks from the moment they enter the facility. We also perform temperature checks and give dancers sanitizer when they enter. We have a unidirectional traffic flow that helps to mitigate reception area traffic and do not allow parents to stay in the lobby while class is in session. Thankfully we have not had any interruptions in business due to COVID.

Interview #4

Name Lynn N
Business USA Nails Texas
Origin Originally from Taiwan (Has lived in the USA for 35 years).
Languages Fluent in Taiwanese and English
Questions and Answers

1. How did the idea for opening your own business come about? Why did you choose a nail salon?
Answer: My father owned a nail salon when I was young

2. What was your key driving force to owning a business as opposed to working for someone else?
Answer: The freedom to be your own boss and I like the business.

3. What was the inspiration for the name for your business?
Answer: My husband and I talked about it and decided on the name.

4. How did you decide where to open your business?
Answer: We like the area and we also like the school district for our kids.

5. How did you raise funding for your business? Did you use your own money, loans etc.?
Answer: We had our family help with some of the money and took a business loan for the rest.

6. How do you find your customers?
Answer: We put a local advertisement in the paper and we have a big billboard that is on the street. Customers come in for service because we are a good company.

7. With an opportunity to start your career over again, what would you do differently? Would you prefer to own your business or work for someone else?
Answer: Yes, I would do the same.

8. How many hours a day do you work on average? Can you describe/outline your typical day?
Answer: 10 to 11 hrs. I usually open the store at 8:30am. I do all the office work and also take care of customers if there are more customers who need nail care.

9. How has owning your own business affected your family life in terms of time spent with growing your business?
Answer: It is very stressful because of COVID-19 however business is improving and my husband helps take care of kids which is a great assistance to me.

10. What piece of advice would you give to another female who want to own a business?
Answer: I would encourage females to be persistent and reach their goals, that there is a lot of help for women who want to start their own business. Ask you family for help too. It is the best decision I made with my husband to open this nail salon.

Interview #5

Name Magnena
Business Fabu Hair Salon Texas
Origin African American.
Languages Fluent in English
Questions and Answers

1. How did the idea for opening your own business come to fruition? Why did you choose a hair salon?
Answer: I had a friend who owned a hair salon and I worked for her for 3 years and decided I wanted my own hair salon.

2. What was your key driving force to owning a business as opposed to working for someone else?
Answer: I like to be my own boss and decide what I want to do, how I want to do with whom I want to my business with.

3. How did you come up with the name for your hair salon?
Answer: I decided on the name by myself.

4. How did you decide where to open your hair salon?
Answer: The previous owner was going to shut down her salon and a friend reached out to me and asked if I wanted to take over this business.

5. How did you raise funding for your business? Did you use your own money, loans etc.?
Answer: I had to take out a small business loan initially, however I paid it off after five years. I am doing really good right now with regard to my finances.

6. How do you find your customers?
Answer: It was mostly through friends and word of mouth and presently I have a good steady customer base with regular customers who come for their hair needs.

7. With the opportunity to restart your career, what would you do differently? Would you prefer to own your business or work for someone else?
Answer: Yes, I would do the same.

8. How many hours a day do you work on average? Can you describe/outline your typical day?
Answer: I work 10 to 11 hours per day. I am off on Mondays. Oftentimes it is very busy and some days it is not that busy however it all evens out.

9. How has owning your own business affected your family life in terms of time spent with growing your business?
Answer: Owning a business is very stressful especially, at this current time during the pandemic. Customers were not patronizing the salon and I was worried that I would have to close the doors however customers support have gotten better and back to normal.

10. What piece of advice would you give to another female who want to own a business?
Answer: This is hard work but if you want to be your own boss than you can accomplish your goals. At first it is really hard but my advice is to allow your friends and family to become your support system.

CONCLUSION

In order to increase the number of women entrepreneurs in the post COVID-19 era, several recommendations and measures are needed to help close the gender gap. Studies have shown that lack of self-confidence is one of the major setbacks that women cite for not starting their own business or enterprise. For women entrepreneurs investing in entrepreneurial education to attain the confidence and knowledge to start and create their businesses is one sure measure to undertake. The ability to obtain education instills a strong sense of self-efficacy and perception for the women entrepreneur to be innovative and be empowered in society. Additionally, it is important that the powers that be promote leadership programs that target and encourage new women entrepreneurs to undertake and learn to be leaders and role models would also empower new and up and coming female entrepreneurs.

Another recommendation is to create female networks, which generally tend to be characterized by strong network ties which are more important to build women's confidence and boost women's self-efficacy more so than men in the development of new businesses. These collaborations based on relationships that are inclusively within their selective networks with focus on empathy, trust, friends and family connections are common amongst women entrepreneurs. This support system of reliance on friendship and kinship also ties to collaboration and help with their businesses.

With the access to federal, state, and private support programs to entrepreneurial capital and resources for aspiring women entrepreneurs is one measure that needs to be pursued in the post COVID-19 pandemic era. The provision of information, research and business financing will help women to negotiate challenges and barriers in the financial sectors. Institutions such as banks, credit unions, Small Business Investment Companies (SBICs) should make access to capital easier specifically for businesses owned by women entrepreneurs. Microloans are also ideal sources for small startup businesses but do not need much capital, these loans are usually extended to by nonprofit organizations through the Small Business Administration (SBA).

COVID-19 pandemic has had a big impact on black, minority and women-entrepreneurs the challenges and barriers faced by women entrepreneurs can be mitigated by access to public or private collaborations and partnerships to entrepreneurial education, access to credit, training, and other critical resources. The aforementioned options are crucial factors for the success of women businesses and this accessibility to business prospects will increase their business sustainability. Support systems which encourage these factors can assist and influence women entrepreneur's success will can help broaden their business effectively on the global landscape in the COVID-19 pandemic era.

The role of women and their path to legal and economic equality has been slowly transformed over the centuries despite persistent cultural and gender barriers. As women are given the opportunity to consistently demonstrate leadership qualities equaling their male counterparts, especially during periods of economic and military turmoil success is imminent in their business. During the past century, the progress to entrepreneurial equality has been spurred by advances in technology, largely eliminating physical work and negating male physical advantage, while equal access to education ensured intellectual parity. The COVID-19 pandemic of 2020-2022 has decreased and, in some cases, reversed advances to full equal opportunity due to slowed economic growth, lack of childcare assistance (since women remain the primary caregivers), and the reemergence of cultural prejudice. Even as public health measures diminish the impact of the coronavirus, female advances in business and entrepreneurial activities will hopefully resume with renewed vigor and determination.

REFERENCES

Alon, T., Doepke, M., Olmstead-Rumsey, J., & Tertilt, M. (2020). *This Time it's different: the role of women's employment in a pandemic recession (no. w27660)*. National Bureau of Economic Research. doi:10.3386/w27660

Alsos, G. A., & Ljunggren, E. (2017). The Role of Gender in Entrepreneur–Investor Relationships: A Signaling Theory Approach. *Entrepreneurship Theory and Practice*, *41*(4), 567–590. doi:10.1111/etp.12226

Bhopal, R. (2004). Glossary of terms relating to ethnicity and race: For reflection and debate. *Journal of Epidemiology and Community Health*, *58*(6), 441–445. doi:10.1136/jech.2003.013466 PMID:15143107

Gawel, A., & Głodowska, A. (2021). On the relationship between economic dynamics and female entrepreneurship: Reflections for the visegrad countries. *Administrative Sciences*, *11*(3), 88. doi:10.3390/admsci11030088

Gawel, A. (2021). The gender-based attainment of education and female entrepreneurship: The European perspective. *Entrepreneurship and Sustainability Issues*, *8*(4), 403–417. doi:10.9770/jesi.2021.8.4(24)

Gerda, L. (1986). *The Creation of Patriarchy*. Oxford University Press.

Gholami, M., & Al Tahoo, L. (2021). Investigating the Influence of Entrepreneurship on Entrepreneur's Life. *International Journal of Business Ethics and Governance*, 69-95.

Global Entrepreneurship Monitor (GEM). (2019). *GEM 2018/2019 global report*. Available at: https://www.gemconsortium.org/report/gem-2018-2019-global-report

Gompers, P. A., & Wang, S. Q. (2017). *Diversity in Innovation*. National Bureau of Economic Research.

Goodell, J. W. (2020). COVID-19 and finance: Agendas for future research. *Finance Research Letters*, *35*(1). Advance online publication. doi:10.1016/j.frl.2020.101512

Gupta, S. (2019). *Investigation of the barriers affecting innovation: A qualitative comparative study of Indian start-ups operating in high and low-to medium technology sectors* (Doctoral dissertation). Brunel University London.

Hamilton, L., & De Klerk, N. (2016). Generation Y Female students' motivation towards entrepreneurship. *International Journal of Business and Management Studies*, *8*(2), 50–65.

Haas, R., Watson, J., Smith, K., Buonasera, T., Viviano, C., Southon, J., Chen, J., Noe, S., Parker, G., & Eerkens, J. (2020). Female hunters of the early Americas. *Science Advances*, *6*(45), abd0310. Advance online publication. doi:10.1126ciadv

Jennings, J. E., & Brush, C. G. (2013). Research on women entrepreneurs: Challenges to (and from) the broader entrepreneurship literature? *The Academy of Management Annals*, *7*(1), 663–715. doi:10.1080/19416520.2013.782190

Liu, Y., Lee, J. M., & Lee, C. (2020). The challenges and opportunities of a global health crisis: The management and business implications of COVID-19 from an Asian perspective. *Asian Business & Management*, *19*(3), 277–297.

Marom, D., Robb, A., & Sade, O. (2016). *Gender dynamics in crowdfunding (kickstarter): evidence on entrepreneurs, investors, deals and taste-based discrimination.* Social Science Research Network Paper 2442954.

Martínez-Rodríguez, I., Quintana-Rojo, C., & Gento, P., & Callejas-Albinana, F. E. (2021). Public policy recommendations for Promoting female entrepreneurship in Europe. *The International Entrepreneurship and Management Journal*, 1–28.

Molina-López, M., Tejeiro Koller, M., Rubio-Andrés, M., & González-Pérez, S. (2021). Never too late to learn: How education helps female entrepreneurs at overcoming barriers in the digital economy. *Sustainability, 13*(19), 11037.

OECD. (2017). *Entrepreneurship at a Glance 2017.* OECD Publishing.

Onuoha, G. (2007). Entrepreneurship, *AIST. International Journal (Toronto, Ont.), 10*(1), 20–32.

Pascoe, E. A., & Richman, L. S. (2009). Perceived discrimination and health: A meta-analytic review. *Psychological Bulletin, 135*(4), 531–554. doi:10.1037/a0016059

Rohit, A. (2021). *Credit Scores and Average Earnings of Women- Owned Businesses Rose, Yet Loan Approvals Lagged in 2020.* https://www.forbes.com/sites/rohitarora/2021/03/25/credit-scores-and-average-earnings-of-women-owned-businesses-rose-yet-loan-approvals-lagged-in-2020/?sh=bdde22b2c804

Sahlman, W. A. (1990). The structure and governance of venture-capital organizations. *Journal of Financial Economics, 27*(2), 473–521.

Schumpeter, J. A. (1965). Economic Theory and Entrepreneurial History. In H. G. Aitken (Ed.), *Explorations in enterprise.* Harvard University Press.

Tinkler, J. E., Ku, M. C., Whittington, K. B., & Davies, A. R. (2015). Gender and venture capital decision making: The effects of technical background and social capital on entrepreneurial evaluations. *Social Science Research, 51*(1), 1–16.

Unnikrishnan, S., & Blair, C. (2019). *Want to Boost the Global Economy by $5 Trillion? Support Women as Entrepreneurs.* BCG Publications.

Villaseca, D., Navío-Marco, J., & Gimeno, R. (2021). Money for female entrepreneurs does not grow on trees: Start-ups' financing implications in times of COVID-19. *Journal of Entrepreneurship in Emerging Economies, 13*(4), 698–720.

KEY TERMS AND DEFINITIONS

Capitalism: According to the Harvard Business School is often defined as an economic system where private actors are allowed to own and control the use of property in accord with their own interests, and where the invisible hand of the pricing mechanism coordinates supply and demand in markets in a way that is automatically in the best interests of society.

Discrimination: According to Pascoe (2009), "Discrimination is the unfair or prejudicial treatment of people and groups based on characteristics such as race, gender, age or sexual orientation."

Entrepreneurship: Entrepreneurship, according to Onuoha (2007), "is the practice of starting new organizations or revitalizing mature organizations, particularly new businesses generally in response to identified opportunities." Schumpeter (1965) defined "entrepreneurs as individuals who exploit market opportunity through technical and/or organizational innovation."

Ethnicity: As defined by Bhopal (2004) is "a shared culture and way of life, especially as reflected in language, folkways, religious and other institutional forms, material culture such as clothing and food, and cultural products such as music, literature, etc."

Venture Capital: Venture capital (VC) is the professional asset management activity which procures money from wealthy individuals and institutional investors ('the limited partners', LPs), invest into new ventures with risky ideas, but also with a high potential to grow (Sahlman, 1990).

Chapter 9
Women Entrepreneurs in the Informal Food Production Sector During the COVID-19 Pandemic:
Challenges and Opportunities in Mauritius

Soolakshna D. Lukea-Bhiwajee
https://orcid.org/0000-0002-4049-2594
University of Technology, Mauritius

Nitisha Purusram Dhondee
https://orcid.org/0000-0002-1138-5722
University of Technology, Mauritius

ABSTRACT

This chapter focusses on women entrepreneurs in the informal food production sector in Mauritius. It seeks to explore the business practices of these women entrepreneurs and investigates the business and employment challenges they face, especially during the COVID-19 pandemic. The study made use of the qualitative interpretive research paradigm, specifically using unstructured interviews, to identify the challenges and opportunities these women faced as entrepreneurs, during unprecedented times. Findings were categorized using thematic analysis and were discussed in the light of the literature review conducted. Interesting themes including support from family members, access to resources, and perception of respectable femininity and domesticity emerged for the Mauritian context. Accordingly, recommendations with respect to ensuring business continuity of women entrepreneurs in the informal food production sector in Mauritius have been made.

DOI: 10.4018/978-1-6684-4322-4.ch009

INTRODUCTION

On 11th March 2020, the World Health Organization (WHO) proclaimed the coronavirus (COVID-19) a pandemic (Liguori & Winkler, 2020) which, eventually caused a drastic change in the lives of many. The pandemic and all its resulting sanitary precautions and restrictions put in place in many countries also resulted in a drop in economic activities worldwide, with analysts predicting both recessions and depressions (McKibbin& Fernando, 2020).

As explained by Navarro-Garcia & Coca-Pérez (2014), during times of crisis and hardships, business continuity is heavily influenced by entrepreneurs' decision making ability which, in turn, is determined by their traits, values and entrepreneurial posture. However, given the sanitary measures put in place with the COVID-19 pandemic, the impacts are much significant in the global economy (Pantano, Pizzi, Scarpi & Dennis, 2020). Consequently, entrepreneurs have been called upon to adapt to the new situation for their own survival (Ratten, 2021).Till date, numerous studies (for example Sami, Shafiq & Afzal, 2021; Ikram, Shen, Ferasso & D'Adamo, 2021) have investigated the adverse effects which the outbreak of the pandemic has had on the economy worldwide, affecting various businesses, and more specifically, the informal economy which has been faced with a sudden decrease in demand and sales (Seetharaman, 2020).

Likewise, being among one of the major players of the informal economy, women all across the world have been affected. Lakshmi Ratan, Reover, Jhabvala & Sen (2021) argued that women in informal work, who were already in precarious situations prior to the pandemic, are now more exposed than ever to severe losses to their livelihoods, autonomy, and ability to effectively impact the communities around them. While (Kariv, 2011; Aziz & Khan, 2015) observed that primarily, the informal sector acts as an opportunity provider to those facing intricacies finding a job and those who are unemployed, Osman, Ho & Carmen Galang (2011) also pointed out that, in many cases, the informal sector or informal business activities is a solution provider for women of the lower household incomes in many developing countries (See also Franck, 2012) who are faced with the constant need of having to cope with poverty and unemployment problems.

Thus, as much anticipated by Adams-Prassl, Boneva, Golin & Rauh (2020), the present COVID-19 pandemic will adversely impact women entrepreneurs in view of their household responsibilities (International Monetary Fund [IMF], 2020), their lack of socio-economic and legal benefits (Webb, Mcquaid & Rand, 2020). In a study conducted by Women in Informal Employment: Globalizing and Organizing [WIEGO] (2020) on women in informal employment, it has been observed that during the peak COVID-19 lockdown period in different cities in India, women informal workers' earnings were only about 20 percent of their pre-COVID-19 levels as compared to men who were earning about 25 percent of their pre-pandemic earnings. According to the same study, a large percentage of women informal workers have been depleting their savings, borrowing money, and selling off their assets in order to survive in the wake of the COVID-19 pandemic.

Mauritius, a small island state in the Indian Ocean is no exception with regard to the challenges the COVID-19 pandemic brought. Like many other developing countries, Mauritius has equally not been spared by the pandemic including sanitary curfews and lockdowns imposed, causing the informal food production sector, known to primarily employ women, not to operate businesses as usual.

Of late, the informal sector in Mauritius contributed between 20 and 25 percent of the formal sector's production (IMF, 2017) thus acting as a viable social safety net, especially for women entrepreneurs. Likewise, given the low female labor force participation rate of 44.94 percent in 2019, the informal sector in Mauritius remains a vital survival mode for many retrenched or jobless Mauritian women (Kasseeah, Thoplan & Tandrayen-Ragoobur, 2014). According to latest, in 2020, the informal sector employment in Mauritius was more pronounced as compared to formal sector employment. Informal employment fell by 59 percent compared to a drop of 10 percent for formal employment during the lockdown period in 2020. By July 2020, the overall female employment declined by 6.5 percent compared to the pre-COVID-19period.

As observed by Kasseeah et al. (2014), the rising female unemployment rate in Mauritius started in 2004 with the dismantling of the Multi Fibre Agreement and the EU sugar reforms which led to the closure of many factories known to primarily employ women. This compelled women to resort to self-employment. Although few studies have looked into the women entrepreneurial community in Mauritius (Kasseeah & Tandrayen-Ragoobur, 2014; Kasseeah & Tandrayen-Ragoobur, 2016), as a Small Island Developing State, very scant research is noted in terms of women entrepreneurs in the informal sector, particularly in light of the prevailing COVID-19 pandemic.

Hence, this study aims at addressing this gap by elucidating the challenges which women engaged in the informal sector in Mauritius have been facing and are still facing because of the COVID-19 pandemic. It concentrates on women entrepreneurs involved in hot food production and has the following main objectives:

i. To explore the business practices of women in the informal food production sector in Mauritius.
ii. To investigate the business and employment challenges which these women face, especially during sanitary curfew and lock down situations, including the new normal.
iii. To identify any emerging opportunities which women entrepreneur could benefit from during the pandemic.
iv. To recommend ways to empower such women to help them continue with their businesses and innovate in their respective business practices.

LITERATURE REVIEW

The informal sector has been characterised differently by different researchers. Downing &Daniels (1992) described the sector as being one operating on a small scale, while the International Labor Office [ILO] (1972:70) opined that such businesses are "owned by family members". Chen (2012:7), on his part, forwarded that informal businesses were those which include "employment and production that takes place in unincorporated small and/or unregistered enterprises". More recently, Williams (2019) defined the sector as comprising those activities in an economy which are not supervised and controlled by the Government and which are not taxed within any legal regulatory frameworks (See also Chen, 2012; Williams & Krasniqi, 2017). However, irrespective of the meaning being given over the years, various studies (See for example Abdallah, 2017; De Wit & De Kok, 2014; Neumark, Wall & Zhang, 2011) have recognized that the informal sector is a major player which substantially contributes to a nation's economic development, especially through the job creation opportunities it provides to the unemployed.

The sector is also particularly recognized for highly contributing to growth in developing economies (Yang & Pisani 2018), offering employment outside the purview of governmental and regulatory institutions (Richardson & Pisani 2012), contributing to earnings (Jennings, 1994), helping in poverty alleviation (Bertulfo, 2011) and thus acting as a solution to the poor (Moser, 1989).

Additionally, as depicted by Bakas (2017), women entrepreneurship is a factor influencing the independence, economic prosperity, resilience and well-being of women and families globally. As indicated in the study of Melkani, Singh & Mehta (2021), most of women's entrepreneurial activities in developing and emerging nations are concentrated in the informal sectors where most women are faced with poverty and deprivation. Therefore, such women are forced to look for work outside the house, either as the primary breadwinner or to supplement male incomes. Thus, as argued by Leach (1996), when women are not working entirely in agriculture in developing nations, they are more likely to work in the informal economy. Downing & Daniels (1992), on their part, advocated that male merchants in Southern African, for example, are more likely to have large-scale manufacturing and deal with non-food products, whereas female traders are more likely to have smaller-scale production and deal primarily with food items.

Similarly, studies have emphasized the gender make-up of the female informal workforce which varies by area (See for example Tundui & Tundui, 2021; Gordon, 2000; Seshie-Nasser & Oduro, 2018). For example, almost all women in the informal sector in many African nations are either self-employed, contributing family workers, or unpaid home-based employees (Chen, 2001). Furthermore, in Africa as a whole, self-employment and women's entrepreneurship are on the rise as a method of surviving and supporting their families (Gordon, 2000).

More recently, Lakshmi, Roever, Jhabvala & Sen (2021) opined that the informality of business activities is most common for women workers in the under-developed and poorer parts of Southern Asia and the sub-Saharan Africa. It is further argued that informal jobs stimulate the sources of revenue of households and societies globally, especially among low income countries and lower-middle income countries while at the same time strengthening both the informal and the formal economy. The findings of Lakshmi et al. (2021) have also been accentuated by the International Labor Office [ILO] (2018) which shows that 89.2 percent of the employment in sub-Saharan Africa and 87.8 percent of employment in South Asia form part of the informal sector.

Although Krogh, Hansen, Wendt & Elkjaer (2009) opined that women tend to be under-represented in the formal economy and in high-value sectors in developing countries, these authors also pointed out that six out of ten women work in the informal sector in these same countries. This is also illustrated in the Mauritian context by Kasseeah &Tandrayen-Ragoobur (2014) who assert that women are over-represented in the informal sector and that they are concentrated in certain niche segments, for example the food production sector.

However, despite being the economic backbone of many countries (Jafari-Sadeghi, Dutta, Ferraris &Del Giudice, 2020), it is much anticipated that micro and small enterprises as well as entrepreneurs across the globe will be affected by the prevailing pandemic which will lead them out of business as the after-effect of the Covid-19 (Organisation for Economic Co-operation and Development [OECD], 2020). Likewise, women all across the world have been affected, particularly from low-wage jobs with few to no social and labour safeguards. A study conducted by WIEGO (2020) on women in informal employment observed that during the peak COVID-19 lockdown period in each city, women informal workers' earnings were only about 20 percent of their pre-COVID-19 levels as compared to men who were earning about 25 percent of their pre-pandemic earnings. According to the same study, a large percentage of women informal workers have been depleting their savings, borrowing money, and selling off their assets in order to survive in the wake of the COVID-19 pandemic. Very recently, a study by the All India Federation of Self-Employed Women's Association [SEWA] Bharat (2020b) across 12 Indian states, found that 78 percent of the respondents, who were women informal workers across sectors, reported a depletion of their funds.

Lakshmi et al. (2021) further argued that women in informal work, who were already in precarious situations prior to the pandemic, are now more exposed than ever to severe losses to their livelihoods, autonomy, and ability to effectively impact the communities around them. As much anticipated by Adams-Prassl et al., (2020), the present COVID-19 pandemic will adversely impact women entrepreneurs in view of their household responsibilities (IMF, 2020), their lack of socio-economic and legal benefits (Webb et al., 2020).

For instance, in the wake of the COVID-19 pandemic in Pakistan in 2020, women entrepreneurs were faced with the extreme difficulty of finding a source of capital or benefactors given that their firms were in financial jeopardy (Afshan, Shahid & Tunio, 2021). Additionally, the study of Coley, Sheshadri, Devanathan & Bhavani (2021) shows that women in India were faced with similar situations, being mostly reliant on their spouse for financial support. It is argued by Bonin, Singh, Suresh, Rashed, Uppaal, Nair & Bhavani (2021) that policies have been implemented in India to provide support to women entrepreneurs in response to the financial challenges faced by the COVID-19. However, Bonin et al. (2021) further argue these have only focused on micro-finance monetary assistance. Thus, policies have neglected other types of financial support which women entrepreneurs require, consequently accentuating access to finance in the current crisis situation.

Additionally, with regard to the gendered role of women, it is to be noted that same has been much accentuated in the current pandemic situation. For instance, the resulting lockdown of the pandemic placed an additional pressure on women's domestic chores, such as caring for children and family obligations, while simultaneously struggling to keep their businesses afloat owing to the crisis (Afshan et al, 2021). The confinement policies put in place to combat the spread of COVID-19, combined with patriarchal norms deeply embedded in developing countries, have caused negative repercussions on women's social relationships (Golesorkhi, 2022). It is being argued that women now have to perform significantly more housework and childcare demands while working remotely than they did before the pandemic, thus, resulting in career stagnation and increased "male chauvinism" (Akanji et al., 2022: 13). It is also reported that due to COVID-19, more than 1.5 billion children were out of school globally (UNESCO 2020), and childcare had to be provided by women who would otherwise be working. Having more childcare obligations than males, women responsibilities have grown during the pandemic as eldercare and daycare centers, as well as schools, were closed (Ince-Yenilmez, 2020). Consequently, caring for children at home has been a major concern for working mothers (Hickman & Saad, 2020) during the pandemic which involved having to care for children and family members while at the same time managing work (Lyttelton et al., 2020).

As pointed out by the OECD (2020), the COVID-19 pandemic therefore also exacerbated work-family conflict due to work from home policies and the closure of schools which placed additional pressure on married women in the informal sector. As a result, women in developing countries who are already in charge of family obligations must, in this present pandemic situation, manage their entrepreneurial activities from home while also caring for their families (Afshan et al., 2021). In line with Bogenhold & Klinglmair (2015), for women entrepreneurs, this inter-role duty therefore causes stress and dual responsibility patterns. Ramos (2020) points out that when both women and their spouses are confined in the house, lockdown conditions increase the likelihood of violence, exploitation, abuse, or harassment against such women. It has further been argued by Ramos (2020) that evidence from previous crises and natural catastrophes shows that confinement policies frequently result in increased or new violence against women and children.

However, despite the various challenges which they face, women opt to join the informal sector for various apparent reasons (See for example Ramadani, 2015; Ramadani, Dana, Gerguri-Rashiti & Abazi-Alili, 2015, Ratten & Dana (2017), Alom, Abdullah, Moten & Azam, 2016). These are better argued below.

Opportunities

Though it is observed that primarily, women have a tendency to shift to informal work that they self-create in order to solve the problem of unemployment and underemployment, extant researches suggest several other reasons leading women entrepreneurs to operate informally. Redundancy and dissatisfaction in formal employment, as well as responsibilities as a mother and wife, all affect women's ability to maintain full-time employment, aside from pursuing their own interests in informal economic activities (Ramadani, 2015; Ramadani et al., 2015).

For example, one of the major documented reason for women to join the informal sector is the opportunity which the sector offers to them. Known as "opportunity driven entrepreneurs", (Kasseeah & Tandrayen-Ragoobur, 2016:37) these women enter the sector by choice and seek to take advantage of the business possibilities therein. Ratten (2016) and Rezaei, Gail & Dana (2014) for instance, argue that opportunity-driven women entrepreneurs prefer informal business operations because such operations may be conducted without having to deal with the bureaucracy and legal requirements. Likewise, the study of Ratten &Dana (2017) also accentuates the choice of women entrepreneurs in Malaysia to join the informal sector given that same represents an opportunity allowing women to generate income. Thus, showing that, joining the informal sector enables women to have a better and more sustainable living status (See Alom et al., 2016) and allows them to contribute to the socioeconomic standard of living of their families.

While a good proportion of women take the business opportunities being offered by the sector, few also join same due to their low literacy. As argued by Haan (2006), because illiterate women in West Africa have limited access to formal education and formal sector work, self-employment in the informal sector is frequently their only choice for survival. Likewise as put forward by Kasseeah & Tandrayen-Ragoobur (2014), the dismantling of the Multi-Fibre Agreement and the EU Sugar Reforms in the early 2000s in Mauritius have led to the closure of several garment factories that were significant employers of female workers. As a result, such female employees have had to resort to informal employment as a means of survival, owing to their lack of skills and education, which prevented them from engaging in formal occupations that need formal training, reading and writing abilities. Thus, unlike argued by Fairlie & Fossen (2020: 256), these women have joined the sector as a "necessity driven" factor (See also for example Herrington &Kelley, 2012). Similarly, according to the conclusions of the study of Kasseeah & Tandrayen-Ragoobur (2016), women who have changed themselves into entrepreneurs, or turned to self-employment, are primarily necessity-driven entrepreneurs who were forced into entrepreneurship due to a lack of other choices available to them.

Constraints and Challenges Faced by Women Wishing to Join the Informal Sector

However, while some authors believe that female and male entrepreneurs do not differ much in terms of their capabilities and business performances (Watson, 2002; Ahl, 2006), many others argue that women entrepreneurs do differ from their male counterparts in terms of the constraints faced by these women in undertaking their business activities (See Santos, Marques &Ferreira, 2018). For instance, it is argued by Brush & Gatewood (2008) that women in the informal sector endure greater hurdles owing to societal stereotype, and social and cultural norms which lead to discrimination and increased scrutiny towards them (Santos et al., 2018; Ughettoet al., 2020)

Despite the considerable opportunities which some women have found in the informal sector, existing research also convincingly demonstrate that compared to men, women in the informal economy most often find themselves in more vulnerable employment setups such as "domestic workers, home-based workers, or contributing family workers", (ILO, 2018). As indicated in past studies (See Zainol &Al Mamun, 2018; Tundui &Tundui, 2021; Seshie-Nasser &Oduro, 2018), women entrepreneurs in the informal sector face numerous challenges in managing their businesses or ventures (Elahi &Malik, 2021). Such challenges tend to be quite the same across Asian, African, Latin American countries as well as across Small Island Developing States as further discussed in the sections which follow.

Social Constraints

Patriarchal Society

Male Attitude

A patriarchal society is one which holds men as superior to women (Rawat, 2014). It is characterized by Walby (1990) as a social system in which men has authority over women and encourages male leadership and male power. Therefore, a typical patriarchal society, accordingly to Adisa, Abdulrahem & Isiaka (2019) is one which has a system of gender distinction which allows men to dominate women in different spheres of life.

It is a known fact that women in many developing countries enjoy a weaker social status due to the prevalence of patriarchal attitudes of men in such countries(Xheneti, Karki &Adrian Madden, 2019; Tundui & Tundui, 2021; Beutell, O'Hare, Schneer & Alstete, 2019).In Pakistan, for instance, which is predominantly a patriarchal society in both the social and cultural context (Afza & Amir Rashid, 2009), women are specifically prevented from undertaking initiatives of launching their ventures which is viewed as being disrespectful towards their male spouse (Nasir, Iqbal & Akhtar, 2019). As a result, for example, Mustafa, Khursheed, Fatima & Rao (2021) have concluded that only a small number of Pakistani women are ready to initiate their own businesses and those who do take initiatives of launching their businesses normally do so under the rigorous pressure of having to cater for their own survival and for that of their households. Likewise, as indicated by Suhaimi, Al Mamun, Zainol, Nawi, Permerupan & Malarvizhi (2016), it is such patriarchal attitudes of men that also prevent Malaysian women entrepreneurs in the informal sector from successfully running their businesses, although they are able to adapt their household and entrepreneurial responsibilities to the random working hours which the informal sector entails.

Gender Roles

Women entrepreneurship is often argued to be a major driver of economic development in many societies (Morales-Alonso, Vila, Lemus-Aguilar & Hidalgo, 2020). However, at the same time, it is also argued that rural women in developing economies have to attend to a wide range of tasks, including running families, managing residences, attending to agricultural operations, caring for domestic animals, and engaging in rural artisan labor and handicrafts (Sharma, 2012). Panda (2018) advocates that women entrepreneurs in developing countries often also face stressful situations of balancing the requirements of their business activities with their household obligations, thus preventing them from further expanding or relocating their businesses.

At the same time, women's time and mobility are greatly constrained by the social and cultural norms that assign women the responsibilities of social reproduction (Ayatakshi-Endow &Steele, 2021). As with limited access to formal education, the gendered component of the informal economy also remains a crucial feature contributing to the increasing number of women in the informal sector. For example, Ramadani (2015) explains that, in transition economies such as Albania and Macedonia, gender-based obligations as a mother and wife often prohibit women from working full-time, thus having to recourse to the informal business activities and the starting up of informal micro enterprises. Such findings tend to perpetrate other developing countries such as Cambodia, Indonesia, Malaysia and Philippines, where, as reported by the UN Economic and Social Commission for Asia and the Pacific [ESCAP] (2017) on women's entrepreneurship, women of these countries share the triple gendered responsibility of having to provide for childcare, attend to their household chores and manage their jobs at the same time. As per Ayatakshi-Endow & Steele (2021), such a scenario is reiterated in Brazil where women having their own small businesses are faced with the significant challenge of managing their entrepreneurial role along with their many gendered roles. Speaking of the Nepalese context, Thapa Karki & Xheneti (2018) on their part, advocate that women entrepreneurs in the informal sector are also faced with the challenges of operating entrepreneurial activities which are in line with a women's role in their society. For instance, the entrepreneurial activities chosen by these women entrepreneurs are mostly influenced by their family members and such women are many a times forbidden from undertaking activities which are not in line with a woman's role as perceived by the Nepalese society.

Economic Constraints

Limited Access to Financial Resources

Economic freedom is the ability of individuals to engage in trade or carry out businesses of their free will and is fundamental for both the economic as well as social progress. Another important factor determining the success of a small business is the access to financial capital and resources of entrepreneurs (Omri, Frikha &Bouraoui, 2015; See also Honig, 1998; Anderson &Miller, 2003). Accordingly, the study of Omri et al. (2015) demonstrates that small firms that have better access to financial resources are more likely to engage in innovation and technology which helps them to succeed. However, it is argued by Al Mamun, Mudiady, Permarupan, Zainol &Mohamad (2016) that the lack of access to financial resources often leads to low productivity among informal female micro-entrepreneurs. Asequally observed by Fike (2017), women in many less developed and underdeveloped countries do not legally enjoy the same economic freedom as their male counterparts. It is observed that there is a tendency for male entrepreneurs to have better access to resources as their female counterparts as enumerated below.

In a study on the theory of women entrepreneurship undertaken by Greene, Hart, Gatewood &Carter (2003), women entrepreneurs have been viewed as being less creditworthy than male entrepreneurs. This is mostly attributed to that fact that women are often perceived to lack business knowledge (Ama, Mangadi & Ama, 2014), often choose to have less profitable businesses which require lesser investments (Santos et al., 2018) and have lesser time to dedicate to their business because of their gendered roles.

Consequently, this prejudice towards women entrepreneurs is accentuated in developing countries where, as indicated before, patriarchy is common (Campbell, 2010), such that many investors would largely prefer a male entrepreneur, without academic background and educational qualifications, over a female entrepreneur (Huang, 2020).In the same vein, Tandrayen-Ragoobur & Kasseeah (2012) concluded that, in Mauritius, women are compelled to remain in the informal sector due to limited access to resources which prevent them from innovating and entering new markets. This is mainly due to the fact that these women entrepreneurs lack access to finance given their low level of education and their limited negotiating skills in obtaining loans with the banks.

Speaking in the context of Ghana, Seshie-Nasser &Oduro (2018) argue that limited accesses to financing strategies prevent Ghanaian women entrepreneurs from expanding their businesses. In the same line, as pointed out by Palmer (2007), due to limited access to finance, many Ghanaian entrepreneurs in the informal sector tend to have resort to credit facilities from their family members or from informal money lenders. However, in Tanzania, also a less developed country, women find themselves being deprived of their rights to own properties which largely prevent them from owning their own businesses. Added to this constraint, is also their limited access to education. In such cases, it is observed that it is often the spouses who would provide financial assistance for the successful running of the enterprise (Fairlie &Robb, 2009). This, in turn, leads to the conclusion that in many African countries, female entrepreneurship is discouraged by marriage, given that the venture payback mostly goes to the husband rather than the woman (World Bank, 2016). This lack of access to finance and capital also remains a major factor which holds back female entrepreneurs in the UAE from undertaking entrepreneurial activities (Naguib &Jamali, 2015). For instance, the bureaucratic rules and regulations are much burdensome as regards provision of funding to women-led businesses where failure of loan repayment can lead to imprisonment or expulsion from the country for expatriates. Such fear of legal pursuits deters both expatriates and Emirati women entrepreneurs in the UAE from emerging and expanding their business activities.

The COVID-19 Pandemic and Resilience Strategies among Women Entrepreneurs

The challenges mentioned above have been accentuated during the COVID-19 pandemic. As a result, the already fragile women-led businesses are now being faced with the additional challenges of ensuring business continuity with the impact of the pandemic (See Kogut & Mejri, 2021). In such an unprecedented context, researchers have started to explore the effects of the pandemic on businesses and entrepreneurs (Shepherd, 2020).

Historically, it has been emphasized that crises, pandemics and turbulent times have sparked creativity, innovation and progress in business activities (Fineberg, 2014; Mudassir, 2020. This has been demonstrated by Ritter & Pedersen (2020) who argue that pandemics, upheavals and crises often have a significant impact on entrepreneurship, propelling some firms to succeed as opportunities and alternatives arise while forcing others out due to financial hardships (See also: Rudiger, Periz-Ortiz & Blanco-Gonzalez, 2014).

According to Korber & McNaughton (2017), the term resilience is often used interchangeably with the words readiness, perseverance, and self-efficacy to describe why certain entrepreneurs and their businesses do better than their non-resilient counterparts. Additionally, as depicted by Biggs, Westley & Carpenter (2010), entrepreneurial attributes such as cognitive and behavioral entrepreneurship are said to foster the ability of businesses to adapt to changing conditions and contribute to long-term viability through innovation.

While studies suggest that entrepreneurs experience significant levels of psychological stress during a crisis (Fowle, 2019; Freeman, Staudenmaier, Zisser& Andresen, 2018) which, in turn, can reduce their willingness to continue their business activities (Shepherd, 2020), other studies (Corner, Singh & Pavlovich, 2017; Hayward, Forster, Sarasvathy & Fredrickson, 2010) also substantiate the fact that entrepreneurs are prone to resiliency. According to Jenkins, Wiklund & Brundin (2014), as a result of crisis occurrences, entrepreneurs in fact create a form of psychological state which enables them to have higher ability to adapt to the crisis situations.

Although different entrepreneurs and businesses deal with the COVID-19 pandemic in different ways, there is evidence that having a flexible approach on part of an entrepreneur is advantageous to the business (Stephan, Zbierowski, Pérez-Luñ o& Klausen, 2021). Stephan et al. (2021) goes on to describe how, among the 5,206 entrepreneurs interviewed in 23 different countries, almost 68% of these entrepreneurs had adjusted their business strategies during the pandemic while almost 40% of the entrepreneurs recognized having had new business prospects during the pandemic.

The findings of Stephan et al. (2021) are further accentuated by Stephens, Cunningham and Kabir (2021) who emphasizes the ability and proclivity of female entrepreneurs to strive and ensure business continuity during the COVID-19 pandemic. According to Stephens et al. (2021), female entrepreneurs in Ireland have shown a strong resilience by displaying a greater propensity for business continuity during the Covid-19 pandemic and the ability to adapt to changes in their businesses activities.

However, in addition to the various challenges which have been highlighted earlier, it is clear that the present COVID-19 pandemic will continue to adversely impact women entrepreneurs (Adams-Prassl et al., 2020) in view of their household responsibilities (IMF, 2020), their lack of socio-economic and legal benefits (Webb et al., 2020). As argued by Lakshmi et al., (2021), the informal employment is neither a safety net nor a stepping stone to formal work but it has the ability to drive economic growth in the post-COVID-19 era. Thus, given the pervasiveness of entrepreneurship in today's business world, it's crucial to analyse the influence and impact of the COVID-19 on the economy (Foss, 2020), with particular attention on women entrepreneurs in the informal sector.

METHODOLOGY

Mauritius is a small island state in the Indian Ocean which has not been spared by the pandemic including sanitary curfews and lockdowns. The island was hit by a first wave in March which lasted till May 2020. After being COVID-free for nearly a year, there was a second surge of cases as from March 2021.

The Mauritian population was and is still being called upon to adapt to a "new normal", causing the informal sector not to operate businesses as usual. More so, the informal food production business cannot be ignored in Mauritius in view of the prevailing urban lifestyle. As explained earlier, during lockdown situations, this area of the informal economy is known to primarily employ ladies, often helped by other members of the family. Unfortunately, the lack of resources and awareness, coupled with quite a low level of education, made the functioning of these ladies during the confinement very difficult. Although the Government of Mauritius did not remain insensible to the situation and approved various enabling policies to help businesses, not all aspects of the informal sector, more specifically, women-led businesses in the informal food production sector of the island, have been catered for. For instance, key

Government responses included the wage subsidy to employers under the Government Wage Assistance Scheme (GWAS) and the income support under the Self-Employed Assistance Scheme (SEAS) for those employed in the informal sector or self-employed. However, since July 2020, these schemes have covered only those employed or operating in the tourism sector.

With regard to the Small and Medium Enterprise (SME) Sector, the SME COVID-19 Special Support has been introduced by the Government through the Development Bank of Mauritius, to sustain small and medium firms by providing non-guaranteed loans up to a maximum of Rs. 1M with a concessional interest rate of 0.5 percent per annum. Additionally, since the outbreak of the COVID-19 pandemic, SME Interest Free Loans of up to a maximum of Rs. 100,000, with a repayment period of eight years, are being provided as support to SMEs. However, it is observed that there has not been any specific intended policy response measure vis-à-vis women entrepreneurs operating in the informal food production sector in Mauritius post COVID-19 pandemic.

This exploratory study thus made use of the qualitative interpretive research paradigm to investigate into the business practices of women in the informal sector in Mauritius. The population for this study comprised women entrepreneurs in the informal food production sector across different regions of the island. The snowball technique was used to locate the respondents who provided rich information pertaining to the area under study. Data was collected through semi structured face-to-face and telephone interviews which were recorded in view of the sanitary protocols in force.

Data collection included women entrepreneurs operating in the informal food production sector and was carried out from 10 December 2021 to 10 January 2022.In line with Saunders, Sim, Kingstone, Baker, Waterfield, Bartlam, Burroughs &Jinks (2018), "saturation" was used as a criterion for discontinuing data collection which 'is important in any study, whether quantitative, qualitative, or mixed methods' (Fusch & Ness, 2015: 1411).Data saturation occurs when no new information is discovered in data collection, thus signaling to researchers that data collection may cease (Faulkner and Trotter, 2017). In the case of the current study, saturation was observed around the tenth interview where additional data sampling did not yield new information relevant to the research topic. Thus, data collection was ceased with a sample comprising 10 women entrepreneurs in the informal food production sector.

The researchers ensured adherence to all ethical issues, including anonymity, in the course of data collection. All the 10 respondents were involved in hot food production, thus providing catering services for weddings, parties and religious family gatherings. The demographic details of each respondent are portrayed in Table 1.

Following the interviews during which the conversations were recorded, transcripts were typed and stored in word format for further analysis. In order to obtain the exact sequence and wordings, the recordings of the interviews were played again and again (See Silverman 2006: 201) to finalise the transcripts. While Yin (2009) indicates that there are a series of computer software or assisted tools for analysing large sets of qualitative data, Creswell & Poth (2017) opines that the use of computer software in qualitative data coding and analysis is helpful with very large databases, usually with more than 500 text pages. Given that the 10 transcripts prepared had an average of around 8 to 10 pages each, the researchers did not make use of any software for the data analysis, but rather immersed themselves deeply into the transcripts, analysing the conversations line-by-line to derive meanings out of the conversations. In order to achieve same, the transcripts were carefully read several times and relevant expressions, sentences and words were underlined and notes were made to guide the researchers in line with the objectives of the study.

Table 1. Profiles of respondents

SN	Marital Status	Region (Rural/Urban)	Age of Respondent	Academic Qualification
1	Married	Urban	52 yrs	Certificate of Primary Education
2	Married	Urban	55 yrs	Form IV
3	Married	Urban	55 yrs	Certificate of Primary Education
4	Married	Urban	56 yrs	Form IV
5	Married	Urban	48 yrs	Form III
6	Married	Rural	46 yrs	School Certificate
7	Widow	Urban	57 yrs	Certificate of Primary Education
8	Widow	Urban	57 yrs	Form IV
9	Married	Urban	50 yrs	Form IV
10	Married	Rural	49 yrs	Higher School Certificate

Based on Saldana (2015), the thematic analysis process was used to analyze the coded broad themes by identifying, analysing and reporting patterns and themes within the transcripts. Thematic analysis was used to further identify the challenges, opportunities and emerging themes in the context of the informal food production sector in Mauritius. Table 2thus shows a series of challenges faced by Mauritian women entrepreneurs in the informal food production sector in the general context as well as in the context of the COVID-19 pandemic. The opportunities which the sector offered to the women entrepreneurs are also portrayed under emerging themes.

Table 2. Challenges, opportunities and emerging themes identified

<table>
<tr><td rowspan="5">Challenges</td><td>Necessity Driven</td></tr>
<tr><td>Gendered Roles
-Flexible Working Hours as a facilitator of Gendered Roles
-Gendered Roles as a barrier to business growth</td></tr>
<tr><td>Social Norms</td></tr>
<tr><td>Low Literacy and Low Autonomy</td></tr>
<tr><td>COVID-19 Related Constraints
-Need for ensuring business continuity
-Decrease in Productivity and Revenue</td></tr>
<tr><td rowspan="2">Opportunities</td><td>Support from Family Members</td></tr>
<tr><td>Non Prevalence of Economic Constraint
-Access to raw materials
-Access to Financial Resources</td></tr>
<tr><td>Emerging Theme</td><td>Perception of Respectable Femininity and Domesticity</td></tr>
</table>

Challenges of Women Entrepreneurs

Necessity Driven

In line with extant research (See: Kasseeah & Tandrayen-Ragoobur (2016), Haan (2006), Fairlie & Fossen (2020:256)), the study revealed that most, if not all respondents interviewed, joined the informal sector driven by "necessity". R1 mentions how *"money was not sufficient at all"*, R3 mentions "w*hatever my husband was earning was sometimes not enough"*.

It has been noted that most respondents had to resort to the informal employment in order to be able to cater for the financial needs of their children or to cater for their children's educational needs. For instance, many respondents revealed that they started their business when *"the children were very young" (R3, R7, R8)* or *"when the child had to go overseas for tertiary education"* (R1) and *"money was needed to finance their education" (R2)*. Furthermore, in line with Haan (2006), this study has revealed that, given their low literacy rate, joining the informal food production sector was the easiest job the respondents could find, responding by *"besides cooking, there is no other job I can do"* (R2) and *"cooking is easier, it is something which I already like doing" (R8).*

Additionally, as observed in the studies of Fineberg (2014) and Mudassir (2020), pandemics and turbulent times have often sparked creativity, innovation and progress in business activities. Although not very prevalent, the study has revealed that two of the respondents have started their business right after the first wave of the pandemic which hit the county from March to May 2020. R10, resigned from her private company to start the informal food production sector with the main business strategy of supplying *"readymade food"*, *"homemade-like hot food"* to *"people who do not have enough time to cook"*. R9, on her part, was left with no other choice than to join the informal food production, which is her passion, given that both her husband and son lost their jobs during the first wave of the pandemic.

However, even though being mostly necessity-driven entrepreneurs, it has been observed that most of the respondents have grasped the opportunity of operating their businesses informally without license or without having to undergo the rigid processes of the Government institutions. This observation is also in line with Rezaei et al., (2014) who argue that opportunity-driven women entrepreneurs prefer informal business operations because such operations may be conducted without having to deal with the bureaucracy and legal requirements.

Gendered Roles

When asked about their different roles, respondents acknowledged having multiple gendered roles. They confessed having to cater for the household chores, preparing hot meals for the family, undertaking household responsibilities while at the same time having to manage their food orders and delivery. They acknowledged having to undertake all the household responsibilities which entail *"waking up very early to be able to complete all the household chores"* (R1, R2, R3, R8) or *"having to work till late night"* (R9, R10)

One respondent, R2, indicated that she *"prefers to wake up early to be able to complete the household chores, prepare hot meals for the husband and children and when they leave for work I can then concentrate on my food orders"*

Such findings are in line with the UN ESCAP (2017), which claims that women in developing countries have to face the challenge of "the triple gendered roles" of having to provide for childcare, attend to household chores and manage their jobs at the same time.

Flexible Working Hours as a Facilitator of Gendered Roles

Interviews also revealed that all the respondents *"prefer the food production sector than any other job"* (R1, R2, R3, R5, R8, R10) and they strive to take advantage of the random working hours which their businesses entail. For example, the informal food production sector allows for *"more time to look after the household"* (R1, R4).Thus, operating their businesses require them to strike the right balance between their work and their role as a mother and wife to be able to ensure business continuity.

Gendered Roles as a Barrier to Business Growth

However, while having to undertake the multiple gendered roles, the interviews have revealed that such gendered responsibilities act as a barrier to business growth and expansion of the respondents. This is in line with Panda (2018) who advocates that women entrepreneurs in developing countries often face stressful situations of balancing the requirements of their business activities with their household obligations, thus preventing them from further expanding or relocating their businesses.

For instance, R6 highlighted that *"almost all household responsibilities are on me, thus if I take larger food orders, I won't be able to complete the household chores"*. While another respondent added, that apart from the household responsibilities, she *"is also required to look after her disabled child" (R5),* thus preventing her from further expanding her business.

The findings are therefore in line with Ramadani (2015) who observed that the gender-based obligations attributed to a woman as a mother and wife prohibit the latter from working full-time, thus having to recourse to informal businesses.

Social Norms related to Patriarchal Society

Adisa et al., (2019) define a typical patriarchal society as one which has a system of gender distinction which allows men to dominate women in different spheres of life. Although this study showed that, in the Mauritian context, the typical patriarchal society is not very prevalent, it revealed signs of the existence of a somewhat paradox attitudes from the spouses.

For R2, for instance, "my husband did not really like it that I am working". In the same line, R6 indicates that *"my husband will not like it if I do the job on a full time basis"*. For R6, this behavior of her husband is perceived as a normal behavior, indicating that *"this is normal. There are husbands who do not like their wives working [...] fearing what the society will say"*.

The prevalence of such social norms is also in line with Brush & Gatewood (2008) who argue that women in the informal sector endure greater hurdles owing to societal stereotype, and social and cultural norms.

Accordingly, for R2, she prefers to carry out all her household chores in a timely manner, fearing that *"my husband might otherwise ask me to stop the job and focus more on the house"*. Such finding is in line with Nasir et al., (2019) who depicted that women are specifically prevented from undertaking initiatives of launching their ventures which is viewed as being disrespectful towards their male spouse.

Low Literacy Rate and Low Autonomy

The study has also shown a low literacy rate among the respondents with the majority of the respondents not having fully completed the secondary level of education mainly due to early marriage. Consequently, such women have shown low self-autonomy where they have to rely greatly on their husband or family members for few of their financial transactions. For instance, R2 mentions that *"in the 18 years of my business, it is my husband who manages my banking transactions"*, while R9 mentions that her mobile financial transactions are handled by her son for online payments by her clients. Thus, during the interviews, it was noted that there is a tendency for the women entrepreneurs to resort to the tending of cash only for all their monetary transactions. Because of her low self-autonomy as regards cashless financial transactions, R5 highlights that she *"accepts cash payments only"* which saves her *"the trouble of having to recourse to banking transactions"*. R6 also shares the same response when asked about how she handles payments from her clients, emphasizing that she is more comfortable *"having cash in hand which is much easier since it does not entail having to go to the bank"*. The study also revealed a high dependency of the respondents on their spouses or children to handle their cashless monetary transactions. For example, R1 points out the she *"prefers to handle cash only"* and for any cashless transactions from her clients, it is her *son "who takes care of the online transactions through his bank account and cash same"* and gives back to his mother.

Additionally, this low literacy rate also entails a very low ICT literacy rate and a reluctance on part of the Respondents to use the ICT as a tool for their businesses. R1 indicates that *"I don't know how to use social media and have to ask my children*" while R9 relies heavily on her son who "*manages all food orders via social network which he created himself, he just tells me the orders. I have no idea how to use that"*. When asked on whether they would like to be more autonomous, many replied positively, however reiterated that *"I'm not much educated"*, *"in my old days it will be difficult to learn"* and prefer to rely on the support they have been receiving from their family members.

The above findings are thus in line with Haan (2006), who argue that because of limited access to formal education, women in developing countries and less developed countries tend to resort to self-employment in the informal sector.

COVID-19 Related Constraints

Resilience Strategies

As demonstrated by Ritter & Pedersen (2020), while pandemics propel some firms to succeed, they also force others out due to financial hardships. Although none of the respondents have indicated having been forced out of businesses, almost all of them have shared a pessimistic view of the future of their businesses: *"don't think this business will ever be like it was before"* (R2, R5), *"If the business is not ok, I will have to close down"* (R1)

All the interviewed women entrepreneurs have acknowledged their business operations to have been negatively impacted by the COVID-19 pandemic, thus, causing their businesses not to operate as usual such as *"having to adapt to food orders for fewer groups of people"* (R1), *"shifting to orders limited to individual families of 4-5 persons"* (R3) or *"from cooking for orders of 400 to 500 persons for grand events like prayers and weddings to cooking for daily lunches or dinners for households of four to five persons"* (R8). However, although the COVID-19 pandemic has greatly impacted business operations of the women entrepreneurs interviewed, the study has revealed that none of the respondents have been forced out of business or had to close down their businesses because of the pandemic. On the contrary, in line with the findings of Stephan et al. (2021), although different entrepreneurs deal with the COVID-19 pandemic in different ways, this study has shown the prevalence of strong resiliency among the women entrepreneurs in the informal food production in Mauritius during the COVID-19 pandemic through the ability to ensure business continuity and adapt to changes in their business activities. For instance, for R8 *"the Covid-19 pandemic has pushed me to scale down the business and work on smaller food orders"*. For R3, one *"should always be ready to face any hardship [...] and it is a positive mindset which can help one to ensure business continuity"*. Additionally, for R9, *"it was hard but had to quickly think of other ways to ensure business continuity"* through advertising on social media with the help of her son. The COVID-19 pandemic has led to a drastic decrease in the food orders in the informal food production sector in Mauritius. Due to sanitary restrictions limiting the hosting of grand events motivated R10 to think of a new business strategy of *"preparing food orders for individual families who are busy with having to work from home and handle the home-schooling of their kids"*. For R10, given the uncertainties of the COVID-19 pandemic, she has preferred to reinvent her business strategy and shift to more personalized food orders mostly targeting *"busy parents, thus, giving them more social time to spend with their children and family members"*. Such business strategy has also been adopted by R3 who, because of the pandemic, has chosen to focus more on *"preparing dinners for working women"* which she *"packs in disposable containers and are collected by working women after office hours"*. For R3, this new business operation ensured business continuity. She acknowledged the great help by her daughter who *"shares the photos of the packed orders on her social media or among her colleagues"*.

This shows that a major resilience strategy for women entrepreneurs in the informal food production sector in Mauritius during the COVID-19 pandemic has been to re-invent their business strategy to target more of custom-made orders. Women entrepreneurs preferred catering for individual households rather than large bulk orders and marketed same through online social media platforms with the help of family members.

Decrease in Productivity and Revenue

In line with Ratten (2021), all respondents have highlighted having been called upon to adapt their businesses to the new situation in order to survive. However, the decrease in demand and sales (Seetharaman, 2020) have been inevitable where *the "demand decreased by more than three quarter"* (R1, R2, R3) and all the respondents claiming *"not having worked at all"* during the first and the second peak of the pandemic.

The study has thus revealed that, with a considerable decrease in demand, there has been a consequent decrease in revenue where many respondents have found their savings and funds being depleted. Respondents highlighted *"I was using funds from my savings"* (R3, R5). Some of the respondents indicated that such a decline in revenue led to a loss of financial autonomy and an increased dependence on their spouses, having to rely financially on the husband to cater for their financial needs. Respondents interviewed highlighted *"my husband was giving me money"* (R1, R6) or *"my husband gave me money to pay the rent"* (R10). This is in line with Lakshmi et al. (2021) who argued that women in informal work, who were already in precarious situations prior to the pandemic, are now more exposed than ever to severe losses to their livelihoods, autonomy, and ability to effectively impact the communities around them. However, as depicted by the respondents, though being more exposed to severe losses due to the pandemic, the recurring family support received by the women entrepreneurs in Mauritius has significantly helped them to maintain business continuity.

When asked about whether they had recourse to the enabling policies put in place by the Government post COVID-19 in March 2020, some of the respondents acknowledged having benefitted from the Self-Employed Assistance Scheme (SEAS). However, it is observed that the SEAS was extended to all self-employed in the formal or informal employment from March 2020 to June 2020 only and as from July 2020, this facility was extended only to those employed or operating in the tourism sector. For R1, *"the money benefitted from the SEAS was for some months only"* and *"the amount was very less and not something you can rely on in terms of salary"* (R8). Few of the respondents highlighted not having had recourse to any of the enabling policies put in place by the Government out of fear or apprehension *"given that the business is not a registered one"* (R3). For R6, *"it was better to manage with the savings so as to avoid any hassle by the Government"*.

Opportunities

Support from Family Members

Even though there was a perceived respectful femininity and domesticity among the respondents, the study has further revealed that the respondents receive full support of their family members, namely, their spouses as well as their children in the running of their businesses.

In line with, Thapa Karki& Xheneti (2018), it has been advocated that the entrepreneurial activities chosen by women entrepreneurs are mostly influenced by their family members and such women are many a times forbidden from undertaking activities which are not in line with a woman's role as perceived by the society. However, this study revealed that all the respondents claim to receive full support from their spouses, children as well as close relatives. *"My husband is my right-hand in my business-related activities"*, claims R2 while describing how her husband fully support her in her business.

Emphasis was also laid on the encouragement received by the respondents from their husbands and children, highlighting *"he has never discouraged me"* (R1, R6), *"my husband helps me in the kitchen"*(R2, R6, R9), *"my son handles the deliveries"* (R8, R9), *"my whole family supports me"*(R1)

Non Prevalence of Economic Constraints

Access to Raw Materials

When asked about whether they faced any economic constraints in terms of having access to resources and raw materials, the respondents gave a negative response by indicating that *"it is not at all a problem to have access to resources"* (R1, R6, R10). One respondent indicated that she *"has all the contacts of suppliers and when I need something they come to deliver"* (R3) while another highlighted that *"the suppliers are just a call away and they deliver the raw materials right at my door step"* (R2).

The conversations clearly indicated that women in the informal food production sector do not face any economic constraint in terms of limited access to resources and raw materials.

These are quite different from the findings of Fike (2017) who argued that there is a tendency for male entrepreneurs to have better access to resources as their female counterparts in many less developed and underdeveloped countries where women do not legally enjoy the same economic freedom as their male counterparts. However, women interviewed in the informal food production sector in Mauritius have acknowledged not to be faced with the constraint of access to the required resources in order to carry out their businesses.

Access to Financial Resources

Likewise, the study has revealed that the respondents do not equally face any constraints with regard to having access to financial resources. None of the respondents have had recourse to any loan facility in order to start their businesses. When asked about the source of capital they invested in their businesses in the beginning, most respondents affirmed their *"husbands provided the finance"* (R1, R9, R10) to start their businesses, while the remaining affirmed having taken money from their savings to be able to start their business. For R8, she started the business with the joint money given to her by her husband and her mother: *"my mother gave me some money as well as my husband"*.

The above findings are in line with Fairlie & Robb (2009) who observed that it is often the spouses who provide financial assistance for the successful running of the female-led enterprises.

In turn, it is argued by the World Bank (2016), that in many African countries, female entrepreneurship is discouraged by marriage, given that the venture payback mostly goes to the husband rather than the woman. This argument does not reflect the findings of the study, which revealed that the paybacks derived from the business activities of the respondents, are distinct to themselves and their husbands do not interfere in their business earnings. The responses received from the Respondents when asked whether their husbands interfere in their earnings are *"my husband never takes what I earn"* (R6, R10) *"whatever I earn remains mine"* (R2)

Emerging Theme in the Mauritian Context

Perception of Respectable Femininity and Domesticity

On the other hand, according to the findings of the interviews, it has been observed that the notion of being a respectable woman recurred as respondents stated how important it is to adhere to the social norms attributing the responsibility of the household chores to women. The respondents highlighted that they *"have to complete the household chores"* (R1, R4) so as to avoid remarks such as *"the mother in law pointing out that you are focusing only on the work and neglecting the husband and the household"* (R3). For another respondent, *"it is my duty as a woman"* (R2) to complete the household chores and look after the husband failing which *"I will not feel good about it if I don't do it"*.

As shown by Radhakrishnan (2009), respectable femininity is an intellectual construct that leads to a set of behavioural standards in which women gain respectability by following certain prevalent moral principles and gendered expectations in terms of their behaviours and appearances (Skeggs, 1997). The interviews have therefore revealed that the respondents do have certain perceptions of respectable femininity as far as their role as a mother, wife and business owner is concerned.

Additionally, in line with Skeggs (1997), the interview transcripts have also revealed that the perception of domesticity, which is a component of respectable femininity where "good" women are dutiful mothers and effective housekeepers, is much prevalent among the respondents. The study revealed that there was a strong feeling among the respondents to constantly fulfill their duties as a woman, even though same is quite difficult when having to cater for their businesses at the same time.

The above is in line with the findings of Ayatakshi-Endow & Steele (2021) who have highlighted that women are greatly constrained by the social and cultural norms that assign them different gendered responsibilities such as that of social reproduction, providing child care and attending to household chores.

DISCUSSIONS OF FINDINGS AND RECOMMENDATIONS

This study has helped in gaining a deeper insight on the business practices of women in the informal food production sector in Mauritius, a small island developing state of the Indian Ocean. Data collected revealed that the challenges faced by women entrepreneurs in the informal food production in Mauritius include gendered roles, social norms related to patriarchal society, low literacy rate and low autonomy together with COVID-19 related constraints. Additionally, the study has also revealed the prevalence of strong resiliency among women entrepreneurs in the informal food production sector in the island during the pandemic, coupled with opportunities which include support from family members and the non-prevalence of economic constraints in having access to financial resources and raw materials. The perception of respectable femininity and domesticity is one factor which emerged in the course of the study for Mauritian women entrepreneurs. The following recommendations are thus proposed in view of addressing the various challenges faced by these women entrepreneurs and ensuring their business continuity.

Addressing the Need for Financial Literacy of Women Entrepreneurs

The study has shown that the majority of women entrepreneurs interviewed have sufficient literacy level for basic financial matters such as handling of cash payments from clients, managing funds for the purchase of raw materials only. This limited knowledge constrained these women entrepreneurs to rely on their spouses or family members to conduct their banking transactions which do not fully empower them.

It is a known fact that the Government, along with Non-Governmental Organizations, plays a major role in reaching out to the underprivileged and the underserved. It is thus recommended that the Government and the Non-Governmental Organizations help in sustaining women entrepreneurs in the informal food production sector in Mauritius by designing financial literacy trainings for such women entrepreneurs, including context-based trainings to enhance their long term savings and investment skills. Such trainings will not only decrease their dependency for financial transactions, but will also empower them to move from cash-only to cashless business transactions so as to enable them to adapt to the new normal in view of the COVID-19 pandemic.

ICT Literacy and Digital Skilling of Women Entrepreneurs

The study has also revealed a high level of reluctance from the women entrepreneurs in having recourse to technology on their own to carry out their business activities in view of their low level of literacy.

In today's fast growing world, the use of ICT has become almost mandatory. Additionally, the COVID-19 pandemic has increased the need for individuals to be connected to the internet on an almost permanent basis. In such an accelerated era of digitalization, there is a high need for women entrepreneurs in the informal food production sector in Mauritius to harness the use of ICT in their daily business activities.

Thus, in the longer term, the findings of this study may act as a guide for the compilation of a short course by the relevant institutions in Mauritius intended for women entrepreneurs operating in the informal food production sector who want to be better equipped to face the new normal in view of the COVID-19 pandemic, in terms of digitalization of their businesses. However, given the social norms related to patriarchal society faced by these women in the Mauritian context, the ICT courses and learning contents should be developed taking into account the needs of the women and the settings in which they live. Such courses, coupled with the already prevailing support from family members will, therefore, enable women entrepreneurs operating in the informal food production sector to outreach larger markets and innovate in their business practices, thus ensure business continuity.

LIMITATIONS AND FUTURE RESEARCH DIRECTIONS

This study has shown not only the passion which Mauritian women entrepreneur of the informal sector have for their food production business, but also the determination for business continuity despite the pandemic. None of them indicated the discontinuation or closure of their businesses despite the challenges they are facing, both on the personal and economic fronts. Rather, all of them are aware that they will have to adapt to new ways of doing business. Although few of them are quite apprehensive about the use of technology on their own, the aspect of the family support they all receive should thus be capitalized to help them advance in their respective business endeavors.

Further research could thus focus on the various ways which family members of Mauritian women entrepreneurs in the informal sector could further provide support to their mother's / wife's businesses, both in business participation and enhancing respectable femininity and domesticity. It was also observed that the findings of the study, including low general, financial and ICT literacy levels apply to women entrepreneurs in other developing countries as well. It thus becomes very important to develop better suited strategies to enhance the literacy levels of women entrepreneurs in general. For example, short, tailor-made specific programs to educate, convince and motivate women entrepreneurs to make use of technology in their businesses in view of the new normal business conditions might benefit them largely. Last but not least, it is high time to also boost the financial literacy rates of these women who have claimed that it is either their husbands or sons which handle their financial transactions in view their low literacy rates.

Additionally, while all elements of qualitative research have been embedded in the current study, the sample interviewed was limited to respondents aged between 46 and 57 years. This aroused mainly because of the snowball technique used to recruit respondents where there has been a tendency for respondents to refer the researchers to their peers of almost the same age group. Therefore, for an enhanced study pertaining to women entrepreneurs in the informal food production sector in Mauritius, it is proposed that further research could consider enlarging the age group of the sample so as to have a deeper insight of the experience of emerging women entrepreneurs as well.

CONCLUSION

This chapter used the backdrop of existing literature on women entrepreneurs in the informal sector and investigated into the challenges and opportunities which Mauritian women entrepreneurs of the informal

Chen, M. A. (2001). Women and Informality: A Global Picture, the Global Movement. *SAIS Review (Paul H. Nitze School of Advanced International Studies)*, *21*(1), 71–82. doi:10.1353ais.2001.0007

Chen, M. A. (2012), *The Informal Economy: Definitions, Theories and Policies* [Working Paper No. 1]. Women in Informal Employment: Globalizing and Organizing (WIEGO). http://www.wiego.org

Coley, C., Sheshadri, S., Devanathan, S., & Bhavani, R. R. (2021). Contextualizing women's empowerment frameworks with an emphasis on social support: A study in rural, South India. *Community Work & Family*, 1–20. doi:10.1080/13668803.2021.1879021

Corner, P., Singh, S., & Pavlovich, K. (2017). Entrepreneurial resilience and venture failure. *International Small Business Journal: Researching Entrepreneurship*, *35*(6), 687–708. doi:10.1177/0266242616685604

Creswell, J. W., & Poth, C. N. (2017). *Qualitative inquiry and research design: Choosing among five approaches*. Sage Publications.

De Wit, G., & De Kok, J. (2014). Do small businesses create more jobs? New evidence for Europe. *Small Business Economics*, *42*(2), 283–295. doi:10.100711187-013-9480-1

Downing, J., & Daniels, L. (1992). *The growth and dynamics of women entrepreneurs in Southern Africa* [GEMINI Technical Report No. 47]. United States Agency for International Development.

Economic and Social Commission for Asia and the Pacific. (2017). *Women's entrepreneurship: lessons and good practice*. United Nations Publication. https://www.unescap.org/sites/default/files/ASEAN%20women%E2%80%99s%20entrepreneurship%20case%20studies.pdf

Elahi, N., & Malik, Q. A. (2021). *Assessing the environmental and social obstacles to women entrepreneurs: a case study of Pakistan. In Women Empowerment and Well-Being for Inclusive Economic Growth*. IGI Global. doi:10.4018/978-1-7998-3737-4.ch006

Fairlie, R. W., & Robb, A. M. (2009). Gender differences in business performance: Evidence from the Characteristics of Business Owners survey. *Small Business Economics*, *33*(4), 375–395. doi:10.100711187-009-9207-5

Fairlie, R. W., & Fossen, F. M. (2020). *Defining opportunity versus necessity entrepreneurship: Two components of business creation*. Emerald Publishing Limited.

Faulkner, S. L., & Trotter, S. P. (2017). Data saturation. In J. Matthes, S. C. Davis, & R. F. Potter (Eds.), The International Encyclopedia of Communication Research Methods (pp. 1–2). doi:10.1002/9781118901731.iecrm0060

Fike, R. (2017). Adjusting for gender disparity in economic freedom and why it matters. In J. Gwartney, R. Lawson, & J. Hall (Eds.), *Economic Freedom of the World: 2017 Annual Report*. Fraser Institute.

Fineberg, H. V. (2014). Pandemic Preparedness and Response— Lessons from the H1N1 Influenza of 2009. *The New England Journal of Medicine*, *370*(14), 1335–1342. doi:10.1056/NEJMra1208802 PMID:24693893

Foss, N. J. (2020b). Behavioral Strategy and the COVID-19 Disruption. *Journal of Management*, *46*(8), 1322–1329. doi:10.1177/0149206320945015

Fowle, M. (2019). The entrepreneurial dream: Happiness, depression and freedom. *International Review of Entrepreneurship, 17*(3), 305–322.

Franck, A. K. (2012). Factors motivating women's informal micro-entrepreneurship. *International Journal of Gender and Entrepreneurship, 4*(1), 65–78. doi:10.1108/17566261211202981

Freeman, M., Staudenmaier, P., Zisser, M., & Andresen, L. (2018). The prevalence and co-occurrence of psychiatric conditions among entrepreneurs and their families. *Small Business Economics, 53*(2), 323–342. doi:10.100711187-018-0059-8

Fusch, P. I., & Ness, L. R. (2015). Are we there yet? Data saturation in qualitative research. *Qualitative Report, 20*(9), 1408–1416. doi:10.46743/2160-3715/2015.2281

Golesorkhi, L.-Z., Fortson, G., Harder, K., & Riedmann, T. (2022). Centering community in COVID-19 responses: Refugee women's livelihoods in a global pandemic. *The International Journal of Sociology and Social Policy, 42*(3/4), 289–297. doi:10.1108/IJSSP-07-2020-0332

Gordon, R. H. (2000). Taxation of capital income vs labour income: an overview. In S. Cnossen (Ed.), *Taxing Capital Income in the European Union: Issues and Options for Reform*. Oxford University Press.

Greene, P. G., Hart, M. M., Gatewood, E. J., Brush, C. G., & Carter, N. M. (2003). Women entrepreneurs: Moving front and center: An overview of research and theory. *Coleman White Paper Series, 3*(1), 1-47.

Haan, H. C. (2006). Training for Work in the Informal Micro-Enterprise Sector: Fresh Evidence from Sub-Sahara Africa. UNESCO-UNEVOC, Springer.

Handcock, M. S., & Gile, K. J. (2011). Comment: On the concept of snowball sampling. *Sociological Methodology, 41*(1), 367–371. doi:10.1111/j.1467-9531.2011.01243.x PMID:35095124

Hayward, M., Forster, W., Sarasvathy, S., & Fredrickson, B. (2010). Beyond hubris: How highly confident entrepreneurs rebound to venture again. *Journal of Business Venturing, 25*(6), 569–578. doi:10.1016/j.jbusvent.2009.03.002

Herrington, M., & Kelley, D. (2012). *Global Entrepreneurship Monitor, African Entrepreneurship, Sub-Saharan African Regional Report*. International Development Research Centre.

Honig, B. (1998). What determines success? examining the human, financial, and social capital of Jamaican microentrepreneurs. *Journal of Business Venturing, 13*(5), 371–394. doi:10.1016/S0883-9026(97)00036-0

Huang, L. (2020). *Why women get less funding: Exploring the gender gap in venture capital investing.* https://carta.com/blog/why-women-get-less-funding/

Ikram, M., Shen, Y., Ferasso, M., & D'Adamo, I. (2021). Intensifying effects of COVID-19 on economic growth, logistics performance, environmental sustainability and quality management: Evidence from Asian countries. *Journal of Asia Business Studies*. doi:10.1108/JABS-07-2021-0316

IMF Working Paper. (2017). *The Informal Economy in Sub-Saharan Africa: Size and Determinants.* https://www.imf.org

Ince-Yenilmez, M. (2020). The Role of Socioeconomic Factors on Women's Risk of Being Exposed to Intimate Partner Violence. *Journal of Interpersonal Violence*, *37*(9-10), NP6084–NP6111. doi:10.1177/0886260520966668 PMID:33047645

International Labour Office. (1972). *Employment, Incomes and Equality: A Strategy for Increasing Productive Employment in Kenya*. ILO.

International Labour Office. (2018). Women and Men in the Informal Economy: A Statistical Picture - Third edition. International Labour Office.

International Monetary Fund. (2020). *Access to Finance: Why Aren't Women Leaning In?* https://www.imf.org/external/pubs/ft/fandd/2020/03/pdf/africa-gender-gap-access-to-finance-morsy.pdf

Jafari-Sadeghi, V., Dutta, D. K., Ferraris, A., & delGiudice, M. (2020). Internationalisation business processes in an under-supported policy contexts: Evidence from Italian SMEs. *Business Process Management Journal*, *26*(5), 1055–1074. doi:10.1108/BPMJ-03-2019-0141

Jenkins, A., Wiklund, J., & Brundin, E. (2014). Individual responses to firm failure: Appraisals, grief, and the influence of prior failure experience. *Journal of Business Venturing*, *29*(1), 17–33. doi:10.1016/j.jbusvent.2012.10.006

Jennings, N. S. (1994). Small-scale mining: a labour and social perspective. In A. J. Ghose (Ed.), *Small-Scale Mining: A Global Overview* (pp. 11–18). A.A. Balkema.

Kariv, D. (2011). Entrepreneurial Orientations of Women Business Founders from a Push/Pull Perspective: Canadians versus non-Canadians—A Multinational Assessment. *Journal of Small Business and Entrepreneurship*, *24*(3), 397–425. doi:10.1080/08276331.2011.10593546

Kasseeah, H., & Tandrayen-Ragoobur, V. (2014). Women in the informal sector in Mauritius: A survival mode. *Equality, Diversity and Inclusion*, *33*(8), 750–763. doi:10.1108/EDI-04-2013-0022

Kasseeah, H., & Tandrayen-Ragoobur, V. (2016). Ex-garment female workers: A new entrepreneurial community in Mauritius. *Journal of Enterprising Communities: People and Places in the Global Economy*, *10*(1), 33–52. doi:10.1108/JEC-08-2015-0042

Kasseeah, H., Thoplan, R., & Tandrayen-Ragoobur, V. (2014). Financial crisis and informal sector women entrepreneurs in Mauritius. *International Journal of Economics and Business Research*, *8*(2), 227–243. doi:10.1504/IJEBR.2014.064123

Kogut, C. S., & Mejri, K. (2021). Female entrepreneurship in emerging markets: challenges of running a business in turbulent contexts and times. *International Journal of Gender and Entrepreneurship*. doi:10.1108/IJGE-03-2021-0052

Korber, S., & McNaughton, R. (2017). Resilience and entrepreneurship: A systematic literature review. *International Journal of Entrepreneurial Behavior & Research*, *24*(7), 1129–1154. doi:10.1108/IJEBR-10-2016-0356

Krogh, E., Hansen, T. N., Wendt, S., & Elkjaer, M. (2009). *Promoting Employment for Women as a Strategy for Poverty Reduction, Organization for Economic Cooperation and Development (OECD)*. Available at: www.oecd.org/dac/povertyreduction/43280489.pdf

Lakshmi Ratan, A., Roever, S., Jhabvala, R., & Sen, P. (2021). *Evidence Review of COVID-19 and Women's Informal Employment: A Call to Support the Most Vulnerable First in the Economic Recovery*. Bill & Melinda Gates Foundation.

Leach, F. (1996). Women in the Informal Sector: The Contribution of Education and Training. *Development in Practice*, *6*(1), 25–36. doi:10.1080/0961452961000157584

Liguori, E., & Winkler, C. (2020). From Offline to Online: Challenges and Opportunities for Entrepreneurship Education Following the COVID-19 Pandemic. *Entrepreneurship Education and Pedagogy*, *3*(4), 346–351. doi:10.1177/2515127420916738

Lyttelton, T., Zang, E., & Musick, K. (2020). *Gender Differences in Telecommuting and Implications for Inequality at Home and Work*. Yale University. doi:10.2139srn.3645561

Mayasari, Y., & Chandra, T. (2020). Social capital for knowledge management system of the creative industry. *Journal of Enterprising Communities: People and Places in the Global Economy*, *14*(4), 481–494. doi:10.1108/JEC-01-2020-0008

McKibbin, W., & Fernando, R. (2020). The economic impact of COVID-19. *Economics in the Time of COVID-19, 45*(10.1162).

Melkani, E., Singh, K., & Mehta, M. (2021). Productivity of rural women through entrepreneurship intervention. *International Journal of Education and Management Studies*, *11*(1), 7–12.

Morales-Alonso, G., Vila, G. A., Lemus-Aguilar, I., & Hidalgo, A. (2020). Data retrieval from online social media networks for defining business angels' profile. *Journal of Enterprising Communities: People and Places in the Global Economy*, *14*(1), 57–75. doi:10.1108/JEC-10-2019-0095

Moser, C. (1989). Gender planning in the Third World: Meeting practical and strategic gender needs. *World Development*, *17*(11), 1799–1825. doi:10.1016/0305-750X(89)90201-5

Mudassir, H. (2022). *COVID-19 Will Fuel the Next Wave of Innovation*. Retrieved from https://www.entrepreneur.com/article/347669

Mustafa, F., Khursheed, A., Fatima, M., & Rao, M. (2021). Exploring the impact of COVID-19 pandemic on women entrepreneurs in Pakistan. *International Journal of Gender and Entrepreneurship*, *13*(2), 187–203. doi:10.1108/IJGE-09-2020-0149

Naguib, R., & Jamali, D. (2015). Female entrepreneurship in the UAE: A multi-level integrative lens. *Gender in Management*, *30*(2), 135–161. doi:10.1108/GM-12-2013-0142

Nasir, M., Iqbal, R., & Akhtar, C. (2019). Factors affecting growth of women entrepreneurs in Pakistan. *Pakistan Administrative Review*, *3*(1), 35–50.

Navarro-García, A., & Coca-Pérez, J. L. (2014). Antecedents and Consequences of Entrepreneurial Orientation of Spanish Exporting SMEs in Time of Crisis. In *Entrepreneurship, Innovation and Economic Crisis* (pp. 21–29). Springer. doi:10.1007/978-3-319-02384-7_3

Neumark, D., Wall, B., & Zhang, J. (2011). Do Small Businesses Create More Jobs? New Evidence for the United States from the National Establishment Time Series. *The Review of Economics and Statistics*, *93*(1), 16–29. doi:10.1162/REST_a_00060

Ama, Mangadi, & Ama. (2014). Exploring the challenges facing women entrepreneurs in informal cross-border trade in Botswana. *Gender in Management*, *29*(8), 505–522. doi:10.1108/GM-02-2014-0018

OECD. (2020). *OECD policy responses to coronavirus (COVID-19) - SME policy responses – OECD overview.* Available at https://www.oecd.org/coronavirus/en/

Omri, A., Frikha, M. A., & Bouraoui, M. A. (2015). An empirical investigation of factors affecting small business success. *Journal of Management Development*, *34*(9), 1073–1093. doi:10.1108/JMD-07-2013-0088

Osman, I., Ho, T. C., & Carmen Galang, M. (2011). The relationship between human resource practices and firm performance: An empirical assessment of firms in Malaysia. *Business Strategy Series*, *12*(1), 41–48. doi:10.1108/17515631111100412

Palmer, R. (2007). Skills development, the enabling environment and informal micro-enterprise in Ghana. *Compare: A Journal of Comparative Education*, *37*(4), 565. doi:10.1080/03057920701541927

Panda, S. (2018). Constraints faced by women entrepreneurs in developing countries: Review and ranking. *Gender in Management*, *33*(4), 315–331. doi:10.1108/GM-01-2017-0003

Pantano, E., Pizzi, G., Scarpi, D., & Dennis, C. (2020). Competing during a pandemic? Retailers' ups and downs during the COVID-19 outbreak. *Journal of Business Research*, *116*, 209–213. doi:10.1016/j.jbusres.2020.05.036 PMID:32501307

Radhakrishnan, S. (2008). Examining the 'global' Indian middle class: Gender and culture in the Silicon Valley/Bangalore Circuit. *Journal of Intercultural Studies (Melbourne, Vic.)*, *29*(1), 7–20. doi:10.1080/07256860701759915

Ramadani, V. (2015). The Woman Entrepreneur in Albania: An Exploratory Study on Motivation, Problems and Success Factors. *Journal of Balkan & Near Eastern Studies*, *17*(2), 204–221. doi:10.1080/19448953.2014.997488

Ramadani, V., Dana, L., Gërguri-Rashiti, S., & Abazi-Alili, H. (2015). *The profile of female entrepreneurs in the Republic of Macedonia. In Female Entrepreneurship in Transition Economies: Trends and Challenges*. Palgrave Macmillan.

Ramos, A. G. (2020). *The New Sciences Organizations*. University of Toronto Press.

Ratten, V. (2016). Female entrepreneurship and the role of customer knowledge development, innovation outcome expectations and culture on intentions to start informal business ventures. *International Journal of Entrepreneurship and Small Business*, *27*(2/3), 262. doi:10.1504/IJESB.2016.073977

Ratten, V. (2021). Coronavirus (Covid-19) and entrepreneurship: Cultural, lifestyle and societal changes. *Journal of Entrepreneurship in Emerging Economies*, *13*(4), 747–761. doi:10.1108/JEEE-06-2020-0163

Ratten, V., & Dana, L. P. (2017). Gendered perspective of indigenous entrepreneurship. *Small Enterprise Research*, *24*(1), 62–72. doi:10.1080/13215906.2017.1289858

Rawat, P. S. (2014). Patriarchal Beliefs, Women's Empowerment, and General Well-being. *Vikalpa*, *39*(2), 43–56. doi:10.1177/0256090920140206

Rezaei, S., Goli, M., & Dana, L. P. (2014). Beyond legal entrepreneurship: The case of Austria. *International Journal of Entrepreneurship and Small Business*, *21*(2), 202. doi:10.1504/IJESB.2014.059473

Richardson, C., & Pisani, M. J. (2012). *The Informal and Underground Economy of the South Texas Border*. University of Texas Press. doi:10.7560/739277

Ritter, T., & Pedersen, C. (2020). Analyzing the impact of the coronavirus crisis on business models. *Industrial Marketing Management*, *88*, 214–224. doi:10.1016/j.indmarman.2020.05.014

Rudiger, K., Peris-Ortiz, M., & Blanco-Gonzales, A. (2014). *Entrepreneurship, Innovation and Economic Crisis, Lessons for Research, Policy and Practice*. Springer. doi:10.1007/978-3-319-02384-7

Saldaña, J. (2015). *The coding manual for qualitative researchers* (3rd ed.). Sage Publications.

Sami Ur Rehman, M., Shafiq, M. T., & Afzal, M. (2021). Impact of COVID-19 on project performance in the UAE construction industry. *Journal of Engineering, Design and Technology*, *20*(1), 245–266. doi:10.1108/JEDT-12-2020-0481

Santos, G., Marques, C. S., & Ferreira, J. J. (2018). A look back over the past 40 years of female entrepreneurship: Mapping knowledge networks. *Scientometrics*, *115*(2), 953–987. doi:10.100711192-018-2705-y

Saunders, B., Sim, J., Kingstone, T., Baker, S., Waterfield, J., Bartlam, B., Burroughs, H., & Jinks, C. (2018). Saturation in qualitative research: Exploring its conceptualization and operationalization. *Quality & Quantity*, *52*(4), 1893–1907. doi:10.100711135-017-0574-8 PMID:29937585

Seetharaman, P. (2020). Business models shifts: Impact of Covid-19. *International Journal of Information Management*, *54*, 1–4. doi:10.1016/j.ijinfomgt.2020.102173 PMID:32834338

Seshie-Nasser, H. A., & Oduro, A. D. (2018). Women-owned businesses and household welfare. *International Journal of Gender and Entrepreneurship*, *10*(4), 310–331. doi:10.1108/IJGE-01-2018-0001

Sharma, K. (2012). Role of women in informal sector in India. *Journal of the Humanities and Social Sciences*, *4*(1), 29–36. doi:10.9790/0837-0412936

Shepherd, D. A. (2020). COVID 19 and entrepreneurship: Time to pivot? *Journal of Management Studies*, *57*(8), 1750–1753. doi:10.1111/joms.12633

Silverman, D. (2006). *Interpreting Qualitative Data: Methods for Analysing Talk, Text and Interaction* (3rd ed.). Sage Publications.

Skeggs, B. (1997). *Formations of Class and Gender: Becoming Respectable*. Sage Publications.

Stephan, U., Zbierowski, P., Pérez-Luño, A., &Klausen, A., (2021). *Entrepreneurship during the Covid-19 Pandemic: A global study of entrepreneurs' challenges, resilience, and well-being*. KBS Covid-19 Research Impact Papers, No. 4.

Stephens, S., Cunningham, I., & Kabir, Y. (2021). Female entrepreneurs in a time of crisis: Evidence from Ireland. *International Journal of Gender and Entrepreneurship*, *13*(2), 106–120. doi:10.1108/IJGE-09-2020-0135

Suhaimi, N. H. B. M., Al Mamun, A., Zainol, N. R., Nawi, N. C., Permerupan, Y., & Malarvizhi, C. A. (2016). Characteristics of informal micro-entrepreneurs in Malaysia. *Mediterranean Journal of Social Sciences*, *7*(2), 128.

Tandrayen-Ragoobur, V., & Kasseeah, H. (2012b). Unveiling the profile of women entrepreneurs in the small island economy of Mauritius. *Interdisciplinary Journal of Contemporary Research in Business*, *4*(4), 437–449.

Thapa Karki, S., & Xheneti, M. (2018). Formalizing women entrepreneurs in Kathmandu, Nepal. *The International Journal of Sociology and Social Policy*, *38*(7–8), 526–541. doi:10.1108/IJSSP-12-2017-0166

Tundui, H. P., & Tundui, C. S. (2021). Marriage and business performance: The case of women-owned micro and small businesses in Tanzania. *Journal of Entrepreneurship in Emerging Economies*, *13*(5), 1287–1308. doi:10.1108/JEEE-06-2020-0202

Ughetto, E., Rossi, M., Audretsch, D., & Lehmann, E. E. (2020). Female entrepreneurship in the digital era. *Small Business Economics*, *55*(2), 305–312. doi:10.100711187-019-00298-8

UNESCO. (2020). *COVID-19 impact on education*. United Nations Educational, Scientific and Cultural Organization. Available at: https://en.unesco.org/covid19/educationresponse

Walby, S. (1990). *Theorising Patriarchy*. Blackwell.

Watson, J. (2002). Comparing the performance of male- and female-controlled businesses: Relating outputs to inputs. *Entrepreneurship Theory and Practice*, *26*(3), 91–100. doi:10.1177/104225870202600306

Webb, A., McQuaid, R., & Rand, S. (2020). Employment in the informal economy: Implications of the COVID-19 pandemic. *The International Journal of Sociology and Social Policy*, *40*(9/10), 1005–1019. doi:10.1108/IJSSP-08-2020-0371

Williams, C. C., & Krasniqi, B. (2017). Evaluating the individual- and country-level variations in tax morale. *Journal of Economic Studies (Glasgow, Scotland)*, *44*(5), 816–832. doi:10.1108/JES-09-2016-0182

Williams, C. C. (2019). Tackling undeclared work in the European Union: An evaluation of government policy approaches. *UTMS Journal of Economics (Skopje)*, *10*(2), 135–147.

Women in Informal Employment, Globalizing, and Organizing (WIEGO). (2020). *Counting the World's Informal Workers: A Global Snapshot*. WIEGO. https://www.wiego.org/sites/default/files/resources/files/WIEGO-Global-Statistics-Snapshot-Pamphlet-English-2019.pdf

World Bank. (2016). *Women, Business and the Law*. International Bank for Reconstruction and Development/The World Bank.

Xheneti, M., Karki, S. T., & Madden, A. (2019). Negotiating business and family demands within a patriarchal society – the case of women entrepreneurs in the Nepalese context. *Entrepreneurship and Regional Development*, *31*(3–4), 259–278. doi:10.1080/08985626.2018.1551792

Yang, K. M., & Pisani, M. J. (2018). When informality meets formality: Evidence from China. *Chinese Management Studies*, *12*(1), 184–201. doi:10.1108/CMS-03-2017-0055

Yin, R. K. (2009). How to do better case studies. In *The SAGE handbook of applied social research methods* (Vol. 2, pp. 254–282). Sage.

Zainol, N. R., & Al Mamun, A. (2018). Entrepreneurial competency, competitive advantage and performance of informal women micro-entrepreneurs in Kelantan, Malaysia. *Journal of Enterprising Communities: People and Places in the Global Economy*, *12*(3), 299–321. doi:10.1108/JEC-11-2017-0090

Chapter 10
Emboldening the Voice of Youth in Entrepreneurship Education

Nompumelelo Sindiswa Nqoko
University of KwaZulu-Natal, South Africa

Nigel Chiweshe
https://orcid.org/0000-0001-7757-211X
University of KwaZulu-Natal, South Africa

ABSTRACT

Like many other jobs and career opportunities, entrepreneurship is frequently contingent on a variety of factors. Developing an interest in entrepreneurship as a career appears to be increasing now that entrepreneurship education is becoming more popular in universities worldwide. This is because entrepreneurs create jobs and propel the nation's economic development. Universities have numerous opportunities to encourage student entrepreneurship. However, it is critical to assess students' awareness and support to determine the extent and effect on students. This chapter is based on an empirical study that examined the role of entrepreneurial education in fostering student entrepreneurship through students' eyes at a university in South Africa.

INTRODUCTION

Entrepreneurship education is one of the areas of business management that has received much attention over the last few decades (Lackéus, 2015; Saptono, Wibowo, Widyastuti, Narmaditya, & Yanto, 2021). According to Petersen and Kruss (2021) and Li, Pervaiz, and He (2021), universities are viewed as agents of social change and are thus encouraged to spearhead this type of collaboration. Additionally, Jena (2020) argues that the development of entrepreneurial skills and programs has become a priority for higher education to enhance the employability of graduates who will be called upon to create jobs, not seek jobs.

DOI: 10.4018/978-1-6684-4322-4.ch010

Bux and van Vuuren (2019) assert that while it is widely accepted that entrepreneurship education plays a critical role in economic development, little is known about its application until the curriculum is completed. This chapter was written to ascertain the role of entrepreneurial education in developing student entrepreneurship and comprehending students' entrepreneurial intentions. Minai, Raza, bin Hashim, Zain, and Tariq (2018) and Dana, Tajpour, Salamzadeh, Hosseini, and Zolfaghari (2021) state that the importance of entrepreneurial education cannot be overstated. Entrepreneurial education is viewed as a means of re-creating welfare and establishing and maintaining alliances between the public and private sectors by fusing market dynamism with a public interest focus. Additionally, the authors note that entrepreneurship is viewed as a solution to the global crisis exacerbated by rising youth unemployment and a recipe for economic growth.

There is a need to increase the availability and promotion of entrepreneurial talent among students to foster the development of new enterprises that contribute to job creation and thus income generation in the local economy (Aggarwal, 2018; Radebe, 2019). University-based entrepreneurship studies are structured to identify and promote entrepreneurship, creativity, and abilities; and facilitate the development of autonomous behaviour that will help students better understand business start-ups and management skills (Man, 2019; Schiuma & Carlucci, 2018).

Scholars argue that entrepreneurship educators must consider what should be taught in entrepreneurship curricula: they must have a firm grasp on how an entrepreneur should operate (Lackéus, 2015). While enrolling students in entrepreneurship preparation, it is beneficial to identify who can become an entrepreneur through study and demonstrate that students are not adequately prepared to become entrepreneurs but instead enter the labour force as workers (Forcher-Mayr & Mahlknecht, 2020).

South Africa, as a developing country, faces numerous socioeconomic challenges, including high unemployment, inequality, and poverty. The official unemployment rate in South Africa increased by 0.5 percentage points from 34.4% in the second quarter of 2021 to 34.9% in the third quarter of 2021, reaching its highest level since the QLFS began in 2008. According to the extended definition of unemployment, the unemployment rate climbed by 2.2 percentage points to 46.6% in the third quarter of 2021 compared to the second quarter (Quarterly Labour Force Survey, 2021).

As a result, both the government and higher education institutions must emphasise the value of entrepreneurship (Keeton, 2014). Researchers and policymakers agree on the importance of entrepreneurship and its impact on economic development and growth that is sustainable (Kroon, 2002; Meyer, 2017). This assertion is backed up by research which indicates that policymakers agree that additional entrepreneurial initiatives are necessary to achieve higher levels of economic innovation and development (Lackéus, 2015; Nwanko, 2005). Nwanko (2005) further adds that increased levels of entrepreneurship can be bolstered through education, particularly entrepreneurship training. It is well established that such education can be promoted and integrated into the curricula (Li et al., 2021).

Entrepreneurship education has been widely recognised as critical to economic growth (Lackéus, 2015; Tunio, Chaudhry, Shaikh, Jariko, & Brahmi, 2021). Graduates, on the other hand, are hesitant to consider entrepreneurship as a viable career path, even during periods of high unemployment. Following graduation, graduates rarely consider entrepreneurship as a viable career option (Alam, 2021; Ebewo, Rugimbana, & Shambare, 2017). Along with the more traditional economic growth and employment-related motivations for entrepreneurial education, there is a growing emphasis on the impact that entrepreneurial practices can have on students' and employees' perceived relevance, dedication, and enthusiasm in both education and work-life (Lackéus, 2015). However, there is a current decline in students' interest in business events, which calls into question the validity of this study's objective of determining the impact of entrepreneurial education on student entrepreneurship.

According to Mbuya (2022) and Koloba and Surujlal (2021) as a result of South Africa's high unemployment rate, youth entrepreneurship development plays a critical part in the formulation of government policy. According to the 2014-2015 Global Entrepreneurship Monitor (GEM) study, South African youth have the lowest entrepreneurial proclivity in Africa, at 23.3 per cent, compared to Malawi and Uganda, which have 55.2 per cent and 55.4 per cent, respectively. Additionally, the GEM research notes that South African youth entrepreneurship engagement is the lowest on the African continent, at 12.8 per cent. Although the South African government is committed to fostering and supporting young entrepreneurs in the country, new studies indicate that youth entrepreneurs face numerous obstacles when it comes to establishing successful business enterprises (Mbuya, 2022).

Entrepreneurial education is increasingly viewed as a solution to the highly globalised, chaotic, and dynamic world in which we live, which requires both individuals and organisations to be increasingly prepared with entrepreneurial skills. Indeed, the emphasis on economic success and job development has resulted in entrepreneurial education assuming a prominent role at the postsecondary level, but not as an integrated pedagogical method applicable to all students of all ages (Lackéus, 2015). Until now, the primary focus has been on elective courses and services for a select group of university students who already possess an entrepreneurial spirit and are thus self-selective in their entrepreneurial education (Meyer, 2017).

By establishing the relationship between entrepreneurial education, entrepreneurial mindset, entrepreneurial intention, and entrepreneurial action, this chapter adds to the existing literature on entrepreneurial education. Additionally, it positions entrepreneurial education as a vehicle for job creation. This chapter will contribute to the body of knowledge and will also serve as a springboard for interdisciplinarity work, in entrepreneurship, and education. The findings of this chapter are likely to shed light on entrepreneurship education and the climate at universities in South Africa and other emerging economies whose mission is to advance the role of entrepreneurial education in fostering entrepreneurship among students in general. In light of this, this chapter will provide insights to ascertain the status of entrepreneurial education in, as well as the factors influencing university students' entrepreneurial choices at this South African university.

BACKGROUND

The substantial studies exploring the entrepreneurship education-entrepreneurship intention relationship frequently overlook the relationship's influence of contingent and other mediating elements. This delusion promotes the mistaken belief that entrepreneurial intentions are immune to external forces and that the relationship between entrepreneurship education and intentions is an automated, directly linear interaction. Contrary to this premise, this chapter examines the effect of exposure to entrepreneurship education (EE), as mediated by precursors to entrepreneurial intentions on the actual entrepreneurial intentions (EI) of students at a South African University.

According to Ndofirepi (2020), concerns about the scourges of unemployment and poverty among young, particularly school leavers and college graduates, have become important topics in various emerging countries such as South Africa's economic policy discourse.

Given that the majority of contemporary social psychology theories describe EI in terms of both endogenous and exogenous elements, the authors suggest that exposure to EE can have an effect on an individual's willingness to pursue entrepreneurship as a vocation. Informed by this concept, the authors hypothesise that the EE-EI interaction is not direct and automatic since it is mediated by different individual and psychological factors (Ndofirepi, 2020).

According to Nowiński, Haddoud, Lančarič, Egerová, and Czeglédi (2019), Omer and Aljaaidi (2020) and Schimperna, Nappo, and Marsigalia (2022), entrepreneurship is widely recognised as a significant driver of economic growth by both experts and policymakers. As a result, entrepreneurial policies and educational programs have arisen. While public policy typically supports the notion that entrepreneurship education promotes entrepreneurship, research findings are not entirely conclusive. While the majority of studies establish a favourable correlation between entrepreneurial education and entrepreneurial intention, other studies demonstrate the contrary (Nowiński et al., 2019).

MAIN FOCUS OF THE CHAPTER

Issues, Controversies, Problems

Entrepreneurship education has been widely recognised as critical to economic progress. Graduates, on the other hand, are cautious about considering entrepreneurship as a viable career path, especially during periods of significant unemployment. Following graduation, graduates rarely regard entrepreneurship as a viable career option (Ebewo et al., 2017). Along with the more traditional economic growth and employment-related motivations for entrepreneurial education, there is a growing emphasis on the impact that entrepreneurial practices can have on students' and employees' perceived relevance, dedication, and enthusiasm in both education and work life.

Most of the research on the effects of entrepreneurial education is predicated on the notion that becoming an entrepreneur is a deliberate choice. The relationship between attitudes, intentions, and conduct is established using the "Theory of Planned Behaviour" (TPB) from psychology. If entrepreneurial education has a favourable effect on people's attitudes about entrepreneurship, their entrepreneurial intents will also alter, resulting in the desired entrepreneurial behaviour.

By establishing the relationship between entrepreneurial education (EE), entrepreneurial mindset (EM), entrepreneurial intention (EI), and entrepreneurial behaviour, this chapter adds to the existing literature on entrepreneurial education. This chapter also provides insights into the role of entrepreneurial education in developing student entrepreneurship, as well as ascertaining students' entrepreneurial intentions. The chapter further advocates for entrepreneurial education as a vehicle for job creation. The empirical data that underpins this chapter utilised TPB to examine the role of entrepreneurial education in promoting students' entrepreneurial development. This chapter contributes to the body of knowledge and serves as a springboard for interdisciplinarity between work, entrepreneurship, and education. The findings presented in this chapter are likely to provide light on entrepreneurship education and the climate at institutions within South Africa and beyond whose mission is to promote the role of entrepreneurial education in fostering entrepreneurship among students. Guidance on how to potentially improve the quality of entrepreneurship education at institutions of higher learning is provided within the chapter. will identify gaps in entrepreneurship studies curricula. The findings of this study may provide a foundation for future research on student entrepreneurship and entrepreneurial education at universities.

According to Ndofirepi (2020) and Radipere (2012), the terms entrepreneur and entrepreneurship are synonymous and frequently used interchangeably. An entrepreneur is sometimes referred to be a person who possesses certain characteristics, abilities, and capabilities, but entrepreneurship is a mental process associated with the development of new economic activity.

Fayolle and Gailly (2015) argue that entrepreneurship is about discovering opportunities, business advancement, self-employment, the formation of new projects and progress. This position is consistent with the broad definition of entrepreneurship of personal development and creativity, i.e., becoming entrepreneurial (Chang & Wyszomirski, 2015; Dees, 2018). Entrepreneurship as a discipline is largely established within the academic array of core subjects. Despite its academic acceptance, entrepreneurship is still young but it continues to be characterized by its rapid development especially with regard to research topics, but also with reference to the methods explaining entrepreneurial phenomena (Kuckertz, 2021).

The development of entrepreneurial competence is one of the main objectives for the progress of a society and improves the employability of citizens. Despite this interest, research has not yet found an entrepreneurial personality profile that includes both the stable and the malleable characteristics of the individual (Obschonka & Stuetzer, 2017). However, some scholars claim that entrepreneurs are born and not raised, and that it is beyond the ability of universities and business schools to train students to develop entrepreneurial skills (Obschonka & Stuetzer, 2017). This argument is contradicted by a study carried out by Bester (2017) that entrepreneurship can be taught and improved by education in entrepreneurship.

Uzunidis, Boutillier, and Laperche (2014) suggest that the possible resources of an entrepreneur can be divided into three groups: first, expertise, including schooling, secondary education, higher education, further education, and technical experience; second, financial resources, such as personal investments, bank loans, investment capital, and different types of public support; and third, connections with families, associates, professional peers and organisations are also possible opportunities for an entrepreneur.

YOUTH ENTREPRENEURSHIP

Entrepreneurship is viewed as a viable career option for young people and graduates. This is due to the increase in youth unemployment in South Africa, where entrepreneurship is now viewed as a viable choice for young people who become unemployed following the completion of their courses (Dzomonda & Fatoki, 2019). As a result of the foregoing entrepreneurship, South Africa has a low level of youth entrepreneurial activity and a high degree of so-called 'forced entrepreneurship,' a process through which young individuals establish a business due to a lack of alternative means of income (Sharma, 2018). Such a state of entrepreneurship in the economy significantly limits the scope of socioeconomic progress and the transition of the natural resource economy to a knowledge economy.

According to Bamkole and Ibeku (2020), Kluev, Bagirova, and Zabokritskaya (2017); Williams and Kluev (2014), this position provides unfavourable conditions for achieving the aims of developing an innovation-driven economy, as well as resolving issues of unemployment, social stability, and quality of life. The current situation of entrepreneurship in the world prompts the search for institutional techniques for fostering entrepreneurial environments and overcoming barriers to young people's 'anti-entrepreneur' lifestyle choices (Bamkole & Ibeku, 2020; Williams & Kluev, 2014).

Governments worldwide have recognised that youth entrepreneurship is critical for regional stability and prosperity. Promoting youth entrepreneurship will contribute to South Africa's economic development and job creation (Herrington & Coduras, 2019).

Over the past two decades, entrepreneurship has grown dramatically. This evidence is connected to the increased number of schools offering entrepreneurship education at various stages (Fayolle & Gailly, 2015; Küttim, Kallaste, Venesaar, & Kiis, 2014). The percentage of trained entrepreneurs has increased to 20% of younger and more educated entrepreneurs (Herrington & Coduras, 2019). This statistic demonstrates a sustained shift in young people's attitudes toward entrepreneurship. On the other side, the Minister of Economic Affairs has been critical of South Africa's tiny entrepreneurial population (Basuki, Widyanti, & Rajiani, 2021).

Kluev et al. (2017) hypothesised that entrepreneurship among youth and students is of critical importance. The teaching-learning process promotes the development of both knowledge and capacities, which are critical for the successful integration of young people into society. Thus, the academic status and value of entrepreneurship education become crucial in terms of encouraging skill development, a mechanism that can better prepare students for employment in entrepreneurship (Kluev et al., 2017).

According to Bux and van Vuuren (2019)'s research for the World Economic Forum's (WEF) Global Education Initiative revealed that education alone has the potential to develop latent skills in young people, which could contribute to the generation of creative thought, while also training and positioning them to solve complex challenges in the near future. Additionally, education is certainly critical to sustaining economic growth and social advancement. As a result, the world requires not only competent and successful global leaders but also a supporting educational system capable of inspiring children to pursue future entrepreneurial prospects and equipping them with the skills necessary to flourish in a changing global economy (Bux & van Vuuren, 2019).

THEORY OF PLANNED BEHAVIOUR

According to Varpio, Paradis, Uijtdehaage, and Young (2020) a theoretical framework is a coherent and rationally created collection of concepts and premises derived from one or more theories that a researcher constructs to structure a study. Additionally, the authors postulate that in order to develop a theoretical framework, the researcher must describe concepts and theories that will serve as the foundation for the research at hand, connect them logically, and tie these notions to the study being conducted (Varpio et al., 2020).

The theory of planned behaviour (TPB) has developed a strong reputation for its ability to predict and explain human behavioural intention. Individuals' behavioural intents are explained using the TPB model as a result of their attitudes, subjective norms, and perceived behavioural control (Jing, Huang, Ran, Zhan, & Shi, 2019).

The research that underpins this chapter was conducted in accordance with Ajzen's Theory of Expected Actions (TPB). This hypothesis proposes that entrepreneurial activity (EB) is a component of entrepreneurial intentions (EI) and may be conceptualised as follows: attitudes = motivation = intentions = behaviour (EA)(Ajzen, 1991, 2020). This approach recognises that entrepreneurial actions can be influenced by a variety of factors, including one's background, habits, and motivations, all of which can promote, motivate, and stimulate entrepreneurial behaviour.

This chapter determines the role of entrepreneurial education in promoting student entrepreneurship at a selected South African university, specifically in terms of the development of a particular attitude among students. This is a prerequisite for the desired outcomes of entrepreneurial education, entrepreneurial mentality, entrepreneurial intention, and entrepreneurial activity. The theory of planned behaviour is widely acknowledged as the most powerful and accurate mechanism for predicting human behaviour in applied social psychology; TPB is sometimes referred to as the most powerful and accurate mechanism for predicting human behaviour (Ajzen, 1991, 2020).

This theory was used to comprehend, investigate, and define the role of entrepreneurial education in developing student entrepreneurship. The relationship between attitudes, intentions, and conduct is depicted in Figure 1 below, based on research into the "Theory of Planned Behaviour" by (Ajzen, 2020; Bandura, 1997; La Barbera & Ajzen, 2020). If entrepreneurship education has a significant impact on students' views toward entrepreneurship, their entrepreneurial intents may change, which may lead to the desired entrepreneurial behaviour.

Figure 1. Theory of planned behaviour
Adapted:(Ajzen, 2020; Bandura, 1997)

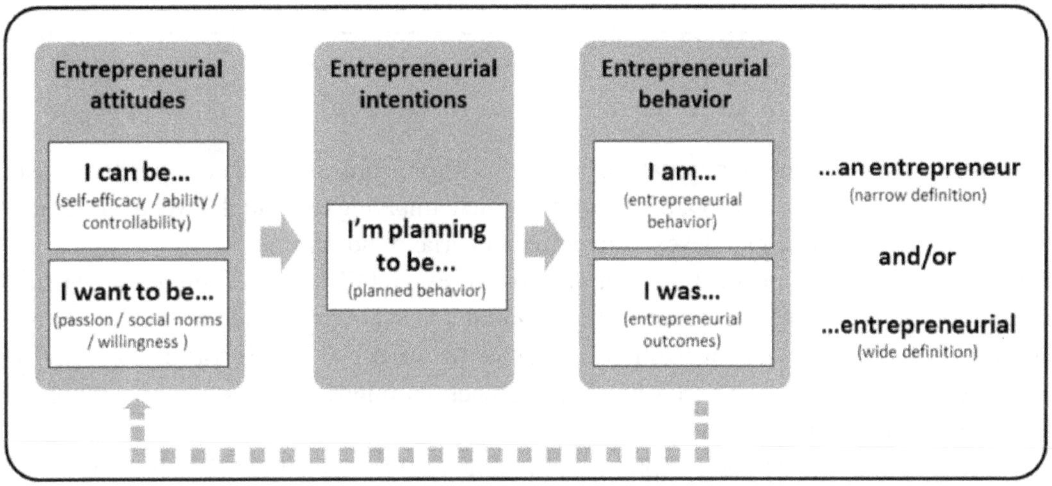

The data that informs this chapter was obtained from 169 students enrolled at a South African university at undergraduate and postgraduate levels. The study participants were purposively selected on the basis that they needed to have completed a minimum of a semester of entrepreneurship modules or were currently undertaking an entrepreneurship module. The data that informs this chapter was collected through a questionnaire.

The students who participated in the study reported that entrepreneurial education had a significant impact on the development of entrepreneurial intents and a desire in establishing a company. However, their desire to become entrepreneurs comes after they have established a stable job, indicating that it is a long-term objective. The more entrepreneurial education pupils get, the greater their entrepreneurial aspirations. The research also revealed that entrepreneurship education boosts self-efficacy, hence encouraging students to create more business proposals.

Entrepreneurial education coupled with entrepreneurial assistance such as incubators and workshops provided by universities and the government may foster entrepreneurial purpose. Students that have participated in entrepreneurial education, educational programs, and seminars show a greater level of entrepreneurial intention.

Figure 2. Pearson's product-moment correlation coefficient

Correlations				
		Entrepreneurial Education	Entrepreneurial Mindset	Entrepreneurial Intention
Entrepreneurial Education	Pearson Correlation	1		
	Sig. (2-tailed)			
	N	169		
Entrepreneurial Mindset	Pearson Correlation	.463**	1	
	Sig. (2-tailed)	.000		
	N	169	169	
Entrepreneurial Intention	Pearson Correlation	.486**	.707**	1
	Sig. (2-tailed)	.000	.000	
	N	169	169	169
**. Correlation is significant at the 0.01 level (2-tailed).				

The table above reveals that all bivariate relationships were clearly significant. A positive association between EE and EM (r =.463, n = 169, p.001) was revealed, implying that a high level of entrepreneurial education is connected with a high level of an entrepreneurial mindset.

Additionally, a moderate, positive association between EE and EI was discovered (r =.486, n = 169, p.001), demonstrating that high levels of entrepreneurial education are related to high levels of entrepreneurial intention. Furthermore, a positive association between EM and EI was discovered (r =.707, n = 169, p.001), indicating that high levels of entrepreneurial mindset are connected with high levels of entrepreneurial intention.

In the determination of the correlation between entrepreneurial intention (EI) and entrepreneurial action (EA) Figure 2 demonstrates a minor but significant positive connection between EI and EA, r =.388, n = 168, p.001, demonstrating that high levels of entrepreneurial intention are connected with high levels of entrepreneurial activity.

SOLUTIONS AND RECOMMENDATIONS

Higher education institutions would be wise to strengthen entrepreneurial education modules and make them mandatory for all credentials. When students are exposed to entrepreneurship beginning in their first year and continuing through their last year, it becomes easier for them to build profitable ventures. Entrepreneurship modules are currently only available to students enrolled in business, management, and economics-related subjects and are not available to students enrolled in other university fields. As this chapter outlines that entrepreneurial mentality is viewed as a critical component of entrepreneurial education, there must be a clear and consistent explanation of what it involves and its significance. This chapter recommends that the entrepreneurship education curriculum include modules that focus on the development of students' perceptual skills and their environment, hence promoting entrepreneurial development.

Figure 3. Pearson Correlation between EI and EA

Correlations			
		Entrepreneurial Intention	Entrepreneurial Action
Entrepreneurial Intention	Pearson Correlation	1	.388**
	Sig. (2-tailed)		.000
	N	169	168
Entrepreneurial Action	Pearson Correlation	.388**	1
	Sig. (2-tailed)	.000	
	N	168	168

**. Correlation is significant at the 0.01 level (2-tailed).

FUTURE RESEARCH DIRECTIONS

An interrogation of how cultural factors and demographic factors such as gender influence entrepreneurial intention. A large body of literature is based on studies in what could be classified as monolithic cultures. Africa is a continent rich in diversity and with this diversity, there are cultural nuances that have an impact on the desire to be an entrepreneur. Comparative studies on entrepreneurial intention in various regions of the world would allow a greater understanding of entrepreneurial intention beyond the limited western society scope.

CONCLUSION

Entrepreneurial education has encouraged students to think creatively and has honed their innovative abilities via the development of fresh and distinctive company ideas as well as novel approaches to challenges. Entrepreneurial education provides students with direction as well as the necessary skills and information to succeed as entrepreneurs. As students, the participants claimed that entrepreneurship played a variety of roles in their life, including offering them an alternative source of income, creating job chances, and promoting innovativeness and creativity. Entrepreneurial education boosts self-efficacy by assisting students in developing more strategies to establish their own businesses.

Entrepreneurial education can significantly influence students' development of entrepreneurial mindset, particularly those who have been introduced to entrepreneurship. Entrepreneurship education develops students' entrepreneurial spirit, mindset, and philosophy. Additionally, it is associated with the identification, development, and formation of enterprises; and it encourages the transfer of student entrepreneurship abilities. Entrepreneurial education research has consistently emphasized the need of developing an individual's self-efficacy. This demonstrates the critical significance of entrepreneurial education in arming individuals with the necessary entrepreneurial mindset and capacity for initiating productive intentions in the establishment of new company ventures.

REFERENCES

AggarwalA. (2018). Rural entrepreneurship development ecosystem–An emerging paradigm of rural socio-economic development. *Available at* SSRN 3184127. doi:10.2139/ssrn.3184127

Ajzen, I. (1991). The theory of planned behavior. *Organizational Behavior and Human Decision Processes*, *50*(2), 179–211. doi:10.1016/0749-5978(91)90020-T

Ajzen, I. (2020). The theory of planned behavior: Frequently asked questions. *Human Behavior and Emerging Technologies*, *2*(4), 314–324. doi:10.1002/hbe2.195

Alam, G. M. (2021). Does online technology provide sustainable HE or aggravate diploma disease? Evidence from Bangladesh—A comparison of conditions before and during COVID-19. *Technology in Society*, *66*, 101677. doi:10.1016/j.techsoc.2021.101677 PMID:34840366

Bamkole, P., & Ibeku, S. (2020). Entrepreneurial Universities: A Case Study of the Pan Atlantic University, Lagos, Nigeria. In Entrepreneurial Universities (pp. 119-141). Springer.

Bandura, A. (1997). *Self-efficacy: The exercise of control*. Freeman.

Basuki, B., Widyanti, R., & Rajiani, I. (2021). Nascent entrepreneurs of millennial generations in emerging market of Indonesia. *Entrepreneurial Business and Economics Review*, *9*(2), 151–165. doi:10.15678/EBER.2021.090210

Bester, M. (2017). Educating entrepreneurial mind-sets at a University of Technology: Curriculum enablers and constraints of selected programmes. *Journal for New Generation Sciences*, *15*(1), 188–206.

Bux, S., & van Vuuren, J. (2019). The effect of entrepreneurship education programmes on the development of self-efficacy, entrepreneurial intention and predictions for entrepreneurial activity. *Acta Commercii*, *19*(2), 1–13. doi:10.4102/ac.v19i2.615

Chang, W. J., & Wyszomirski, M. (2015). What is arts entrepreneurship? Tracking the development of its definition in scholarly journals. *Artivate*, *4*(2), 33–31. doi:10.1353/artv.2015.0010

Dana, L.-P., Tajpour, M., Salamzadeh, A., Hosseini, E., & Zolfaghari, M. (2021). The impact of entrepreneurial education on technology-based enterprises development: The mediating role of motivation. *Administrative Sciences*, *11*(4), 105. doi:10.3390/admsci11040105

Dees, J. G. (2018). The Meaning of Social Entrepreneurship 1, 2. In *Case Studies in Social Entrepreneurship and Sustainability* (pp. 22–30). Routledge. doi:10.4324/9781351278560-5

Dzomonda, O., & Fatoki, O. (2019). The role of institutions of higher learning towards youth entrepreneurship development in South Africa. *Academy of Entrepreneurship Journal*, *25*(1), 1–11.

Ebewo, P. E., Rugimbana, R., & Shambare, R. (2017). Effects of entrepreneurship education on students' entrepreneurial intentions: A case of Botswana. *Management Studies*, *5*(4), 278–289.

Fayolle, A., & Gailly, B. (2015). The Impact of Entrepreneurship Education on Entrepreneurial Attitudes and Intention: Hysteresis and Persistence. *Journal of Small Business Management*, *53*(1), 75–93. doi:10.1111/jsbm.12065

Forcher-Mayr, M., & Mahlknecht, S. (2020). Critical Entrepreneurship Education in General Education and TVET: Two Concepts of Practice in a South African Township. *Discourse and Communication for Sustainable Education*, *11*(2), 65–84. doi:10.2478/dcse-2020-0019

Herrington, M., & Coduras, A. (2019). The national entrepreneurship framework conditions in sub-Saharan Africa: A comparative study of GEM data/National Expert Surveys for South Africa, Angola, Mozambique and Madagascar. *Journal of Global Entrepreneurship Research*, *9*(1), 1–24. doi:10.118640497-019-0183-1

Jena, R. K. (2020). Measuring the impact of business management Student's attitude towards entrepreneurship education on entrepreneurial intention: A case study. *Computers in Human Behavior*, *107*, 106275. doi:10.1016/j.chb.2020.106275

Jing, P., Huang, H., Ran, B., Zhan, F., & Shi, Y. (2019). Exploring the factors affecting mode choice Intention of autonomous vehicle based on an extended theory of planned behavior—A case study in China. *Sustainability*, *11*(4), 1155. doi:10.3390u11041155

Keeton, G. (2014). Inequality in South Africa. *The Journal of the Helen Suzman Foundation*, *74*(1), 26–31.

Kluev, A., Bagirova, A., & Zabokritskaya, L. (2017). Predprinimatel'skoe obrazovanie v universitetakh stranyu: masshtabyu, vidyu programm, balans kompetentsii [Entrepreneurial education in universities of the country: scope, types of curricula, balance of competencies]. *Sovremennaya konkurenciya*, 6-20.

Koloba, H., & Surujlal, J. (2021). Influence of demographic factors on self-employment intentions of university students. *Polish Journal of Management Studies*, *24*(2), 228–241. doi:10.17512/pjms.2021.24.2.14

Kroon, J. (2002). 'n Strategie vir entrepreneurskapontwikkeling in Suid-Afrika. *Tydskrif vir Geesteswetenskappe*, *42*(3), 215–223.

Kuckertz, A. (2021). Why we think we teach entrepreneurship-and why we should really teach it. *Journal of Entrepreneurship Education*, *24*(3), 1–7.

Küttim, M., Kallaste, M., Venesaar, U., & Kiis, A. (2014). Entrepreneurship education at university level and students' entrepreneurial intentions. *Procedia: Social and Behavioral Sciences*, *110*, 658–668. doi:10.1016/j.sbspro.2013.12.910

La Barbera, F., & Ajzen, I. (2020). Control interactions in the theory of planned behavior: Rethinking the role of subjective norm. *Europe's Journal of Psychology*, *16*(3), 401–417. doi:10.5964/ejop.v16i3.2056 PMID:33680190

Lackéus, M. (2015). *Entrepreneurship in education: What, why, when, how.* Background paper.

Li, G., Pervaiz, S., & He, Q. (2021). *Can universities be a gleam of hope during COVID-19? Entrepreneurial intentions approach for academia in Pakistan.* Paper presented at the Frontiers in Education.

Man, T. W. Y. (2019). Nurturing entrepreneurial competencies through university-based entrepreneurship centers: a social constructivist perspective. In *Seminal Ideas for the Next Twenty-Five Years of Advances*. Emerald Publishing Limited. doi:10.1108/S1074-754020190000021006

Mbuya, M. J.-M. (2022). *Youth entrepreneurship in South Africa: A progress review*. Academic Press.

Meyer, N. (2017). *South Africa's youth unemployment dilemma: Whose Baby is it anyway?* Academic Press.

Minai, M. S., & Raza, S., bin Hashim, N. A., Zain, A. Y. M., & Tariq, T. A. (2018). Linking entrepreneurial education with firm performance through entrepreneurial competencies: A Proposed Conceptual framework. *Journal of Entrepreneurship Education*, *21*(4), 1–9.

Ndofirepi, T. M. (2020). Relationship between entrepreneurship education and entrepreneurial goal intentions: Psychological traits as mediators. *Journal of Innovation and Entrepreneurship*, *9*(1), 2. doi:10.118613731-020-0115-x

Nowiński, W., Haddoud, M. Y., Lančarič, D., Egerová, D., & Czeglédi, C. (2019). The impact of entrepreneurship education, entrepreneurial self-efficacy and gender on entrepreneurial intentions of university students in the Visegrad countries. *Studies in Higher Education*, *44*(2), 361–379. doi:10.1080/03075079.2017.1365359

Nwanko, S. (2005). *African Entrepreneurship in the UK. Report of the Leverhulme Study*. University of East London.

Obschonka, M., & Stuetzer, M. (2017). Integrating psychological approaches to entrepreneurship: The Entrepreneurial Personality System (EPS). *Small Business Economics*, *49*(1), 203–231. doi:10.100711187-016-9821-y

Omer, W., & Aljaaidi, K. (2020). The association of entrepreneurial education and support with entrepreneurial intention at Northern Boarder University: the case of students from College of Business Administration. *Entrepreneurship and Sustainability Issues, 8*(1), 555-572. Retrieved from https://EconPapers.repec.org/RePEc:ssi:jouesi:v:8:y:2020:i:1:p:555-572

Quarterly Labour Force Survey. (2021). *Quarterly Labour Force Survey (QLFS) – Q3:2021*. Statistics South Africa. Retrieved 10 May 2022, from https://www.statssa.gov.za/?p=14957

Petersen, I., & Kruss, G. (2021). Universities as change agents in resource-poor local settings: An empirically grounded typology of engagement models. *Technological Forecasting and Social Change*, *167*, 120693. doi:10.1016/j.techfore.2021.120693

Radebe, T. N. (2019). The challenges/barriers preventing the South African youth in becoming entrepreneurs: South African overview. *Journal of Economics and Behavioral Studies*, *11*(4 (J)), 61–70. doi:10.22610/jebs.v11i4(J).2921

Radipere, S. (2012). South African university entrepreneurship education. *African Journal of Business Management*, *6*(44), 11015–11022. doi:10.5897/AJBM12.410

Saptono, A., Wibowo, A., Widyastuti, U., Narmaditya, B. S., & Yanto, H. (2021). Entrepreneurial self-efficacy among elementary students: The role of entrepreneurship education. *Heliyon*, *7*(9), e07995. doi:10.1016/j.heliyon.2021.e07995 PMID:34585012

Schimperna, F., Nappo, F., & Marsigalia, B. (2022). Student Entrepreneurship in Universities: The State-of-the-Art. *Administrative Sciences*, *12*(1), 5. Advance online publication. doi:10.3390/admsci12010005

Schiuma, G., & Carlucci, D. (2018). Managing strategic partnerships with universities in innovation ecosystems: A research agenda. *Journal of Open Innovation*, *4*(3), 25. doi:10.3390/joitmc4030025

Sharma, L. (2018). Entrepreneurial intentions and perceived barriers to entrepreneurship among youth in Uttarakhand state of India: A cross-cultural investigation across genders. *International Journal of Gender and Entrepreneurship*, *10*(3), 243–269. doi:10.1108/IJGE-02-2018-0009

Tunio, M. N., Chaudhry, I. S., Shaikh, S., Jariko, M. A., & Brahmi, M. (2021). Determinants of the Sustainable Entrepreneurial Engagement of Youth in Developing Country—An Empirical Evidence from Pakistan. *Sustainability*, *13*(14), 7764. doi:10.3390u13147764

Uzunidis, D., Boutillier, S., & Laperche, B. (2014). The entrepreneur's 'resource potential'and the organic square of entrepreneurship: Definition and application to the French case. *Journal of Innovation and Entrepreneurship*, *3*(1), 1–17. doi:10.1186/2192-5372-3-1

Varpio, L., Paradis, E., Uijtdehaage, S., & Young, M. (2020). The distinctions between theory, theoretical framework, and conceptual framework. *Academic Medicine*, *95*(7), 989–994. doi:10.1097/ACM.0000000000003075 PMID:31725464

Williams, D., & Kluev, A. (2014). The entrepreneurial university: Evidence of the changing role of universities in modern Russia. *Industry and Higher Education*, *28*(4), 271–280. doi:10.5367/ihe.2014.0212

ADDITIONAL READING

Chiu, R. (2012). *Entrepreneurship Education in Nordic Countries: Strategy Implementation and Good Practices*. Nordic Innovation.

Chukwuma-Nwuba, E. O. (2018). The influence of Culture on Entrepreneurial Intentions: A Nigerian University Graduates' Perspective. *Business and Economic Development in Africa*, *10*(3), 213–232. doi:10.1080/19186444.2018.1507877

Díaz-García, M. C., & Jiménez-Moreno, J. (2010). Entrepreneurial intention: The role of gender. *The International Entrepreneurship and Management Journal*, *6*(3), 261–283. doi:10.100711365-008-0103-2

Gupta, V. K., Turban, D. B., Wasti, S. A., & Sikdar, A. (2009). The role of gender stereotypes in perceptions of entrepreneurs and intentions to become an entrepreneur. *Entrepreneurship Theory and Practice*, *33*(2), 397–417. doi:10.1111/j.1540-6520.2009.00296.x

Kristiansen, S., & Indarti, N. (2004). Entrepreneurial intention among Indonesian and Norwegian students. *Journal of Enterprising Culture*, *12*(01), 55–78. doi:10.1142/S021849580400004X

Liñán, F., Urbano, D., & Guerrero, M. (2011). Regional variations in entrepreneurial cognitions: Start-up intentions of university students in Spain. *Entrepreneurship and Regional Development*, *23*(3-4), 187–215. doi:10.1080/08985620903233929

Shinnar, R. S., Giacomin, O., & Janssen, F. (2012). Entrepreneurial perceptions and intentions: The role of gender and culture. *Entrepreneurship Theory and Practice*, *36*(3), 465–493. doi:10.1111/j.1540-6520.2012.00509.x

Turker, D., & Selcuk, S. S. (2009). Which factors affect entrepreneurial intention of university students? *Journal of European Industrial Training*, *33*(2), 142–159. doi:10.1108/03090590910939049

Wilson, F., Kickul, J., & Marlino, D. (2007). Gender, entrepreneurial self–efficacy, and entrepreneurial career intentions: Implications for entrepreneurship education. *Entrepreneurship Theory and Practice*, *31*(3), 387–406. doi:10.1111/j.1540-6520.2007.00179.x

KEY TERMS AND DEFINITIONS

Entrepreneurial Action: Entails the gradual development of new possibilities and businesses over time.

Entrepreneurial Education: Relates to the various educational programs that cultivate creative abilities conducive to innovation.

Entrepreneurial Intention: Refers to the proclivity for entrepreneurial action and the ambition to pursue an entrepreneurial career as the initial steps in the sometimes lengthy phase of venture growth.

Entrepreneurial Mindset: Can be described as an outgoing personality that seeks opportunities, imbibes consistency, is self-motivated, explores opportunities, and is nimble and self-regulating in personal thinking when confronted with dynamic and unexpected work situations.

Perceived Behavioural Control: Perceived behavioural control measures a respondent's confidence in his or her ability to act entrepreneurially.

Subjective Norms: Subjective norms are used to ascertain the respondent's view of what members of his or her network would say if the respondent becomes an entrepreneur. As a result, subjective standards are inextricably linked to social and societal pressure to adopt certain conduct. In this regard, the goals of friends, family, co-workers, networks, and advisors towards the desirability of entrepreneurship are critical.

Theory of Planned Behaviour: This model outlines that the behavioural intentions of individuals are explained in terms of their attitudes, subjective norms, and perceived behavioural control.

Chapter 11

Analysis of Challenges and Opportunities Faced by Youth Entrepreneurs During COVID-19 in South Africa

Luyanda Ngcongo
University of KwaZulu-Natal, South Africa

Andrisha Beharry Ramraj
University of KwaZulu-Natal, South Africa

ABSTRACT

The Coronavirus (COVID-19) has made a huge impact on the world economy. Many countries, including South Africa, are searching for strategies to mitigate the pandemic's economic disruption. The crisis seems to have had an especially negative impact on youth entrepreneurs. Most entrepreneurs have reacted by using bootstrapping techniques; however, young entrepreneurs were not familiar with these techniques and moved to rather digitise their businesses during COVID-19. Resilience and policy measures such as structural support are seen as strategies that will sustain entrepreneurs post COVID-19.

INTRODUCTION

Many countries are faced with the challenge of including young people in the economy, whether through employment or entrepreneurial activities, and the rate at which job opportunities are created is typically less than the rate of population growth (DTI, 2013). Maharaj et al (2016 indicated young entrepreneurs encounter many challenges in the day-to-day of their businesses. In addition, Mjadu (2018) indicated a few challenges faced by young entrepreneurs which are no access to funding, lack of fundamental entrepreneurial training, lack of access to business networks, and lack of education. Whereas considerable effort has recently been put in by the public and private sectors to create a more suitable environment for young entrepreneurs to establish and grow their businesses; despite this effort, young entrepreneurs

DOI: 10.4018/978-1-6684-4322-4.ch011

are still facing challenges (Mjadu, 2018). As the focus on fostering entrepreneurship grows around the world, especially among the youth, given the possibility that entrepreneurship will help the youth participate in the economy, youth entrepreneurship recently encountered a challenge due to the Coronavirus (COVID-19) pandemic (Youth Co-Lab, 2020. Most entrepreneurs have reacted by using bootstrapping techniques, however, due to their inexperience young entrepreneurs are less familiar with these techniques (OECD, 2020). This prevents the country's economic growth and places a greater strain on the government to offer social assistance. Entrepreneurship plays a critical part in any country's economic development. Although youth entrepreneurship is often regarded as a crucial factor in poverty reduction, economic development and job creation, participation in other countries is worrisome (Diraditsile and Maphula, 2018). According to the African Information 2019 Report, the number of young people (15 to 34 years old) associated with entrepreneurial activity remains incredibly low at 6%. According to OECD (2021), supporting youth in starting their enterprises is one strategy to alleviate youth unemployment in developing countries. Furthermore, young people are interested in becoming self-employed and can do so. Entrepreneurship, like other disciplines, lacks a commonly accepted definition because many researchers and writers have understood it differently based on their perspectives. Entrepreneurship, according to Hisrich (2002), is the process of creating something valuable by devoting the necessary time and effort, taking associated financial, psychological and social risks, and earning financial and personal satisfaction and independence as a result. According to Audretsch, Belitski and Desai (2015), entrepreneurship is a determining component of economic growth, social change and structural change. More constricted definitions of entrepreneurship have defined it as the designing process, launching, and running a new business, which is frequently similar to a small business (Gaddefors et al., 2001). A conclusive definition for this chapter will be, that entrepreneurship is the establishment of a new business and the expectation of the risks related to that business in exchange for profit generated from the exploitation of the market opportunities (Gutterman, 2020). Entrepreneurship has a variety of societal benefits. Entrepreneurship is encouraged for a variety of reasons, including the ability to start one's own business, be self-employed and employ others (Diraditsile and Maphula, 2018). Entrepreneurship, particularly youth entrepreneurship, plays a key role in raising the overall standard of living in society, not only by creating new jobs but also by developing and implementing new advanced knowledge and innovations that enhance the quality of life for employees, customers and other community stakeholders (Boateng et al., 2014).

Entrepreneurship and business formation are becoming more popular among young people in various economies, whose age group is frequently confronted with double-digit unemployment rates (Sambo, 2016). Youth unemployment has become one of the world's most economically and socially significant concerns in the last decade (OECD, 2020). From 2013 to 2019, the youth unemployment rate in South Africa averaged 52.43%, peaking at 56.40% in the second quarter of 2019 (Trading Economics, 2019). Even though entrepreneurship and business formation are on the rise, young entrepreneurs still face significant challenges when entering the small and medium-sized business sector (Katrodia et al., 2018). Lack of funding, unfavourable government policies, a lack of suitable capital, and lack of access to credit are some of the obstacles that young entrepreneurs encounter. According to the latest figures released by the Organisation for Economic Co-operation and Development (OECD, 2020), young entrepreneurs have been among the hardest hit by the COVID-19 crisis, with nearly 90% of youth entrepreneurs reporting a negative impact on their business, including declining customer demand, distribution disruptions and supply chain disruptions.

COVID-19 has presented new challenges and opportunities for youth entrepreneurs, forcing them to come up with strategies to keep their businesses afloat. According to a study conducted by Youth Co-Lab (2020), COVID-19 has harmed 86% of young entrepreneurs' businesses. Other young entrepreneurs have reported a significant slowdown, while others have completely stopped or placed their businesses on hold. While COVID-19 poses challenges, other young entrepreneurs recognised new business opportunities as a result of the pandemic. The online platform that was adapted by youth-led entrepreneurs helped them to find innovative ways to keep their businesses alive (OECD, 2020). Digitalisation, health and well-being, local versus global business focus, sustainability and new business models were among the opportunities (OECD, 2020). In addition, before the pandemic, few job opportunities were created by the 4th Industrial Revolution which is the fusion of the advanced Artificial Intelligent (AI), robotics, Internet of Things (IoT), and other technologies (McGinnis, 2020). Then the COVID-19 accelerated the use of the 4th Industrial Revolution so that the young entrepreneurs will stay in the business. However, young entrepreneurs who reinvented themselves will still have to face a lack of funding, unfavourable government policies, lack of suitable capital, and lack of access to credit.

An investigation into the possible challenges and opportunities to youth entrepreneurship is very vital. The objective of this chapter is to analyse the challenges and opportunities faced by youth entrepreneurs during COVID-19 in South Africa.

BACKGROUND

According to the World Health Organization (2020), COVID-19 is a global infectious disease caused by the SARS-CoV-2 virus, which can be spread through respiratory droplets from an infected person when the person coughs or sneezes. The economic fallout from COVID-19 is affecting millions of young entrepreneurs around the world. For young entrepreneurs who were already facing challenges in running their businesses, the COVID-19 crisis brought new challenges and opportunities. According to Agwa-Ejon and Mbohwa (2015), the South African micro-entrepreneurs are facing many challenges which include lack of access to finance, limited funding, lack of entrepreneurial culture, lack of access to technology, lack of management skills, and many barriers to market entry which results in a higher rate of failure for the businesses. In addition, Agwa-Ejon and Mbohwa (2015) reported that there is still a lack of government coordination of support for micro-entrepreneurs and as stated above the COVID-19 brought new challenges for young entrepreneurs. The new young entrepreneurs who were starting new businesses (start-ups) it was reported they were mostly affected by the outset of the coronavirus (OECD, 2021). The Lockdown and social isolation, lower demand, disrupted supply chains and other challenges have driven several businesses to close, while others are barely surviving (Intracen.org, 2021). The outbreak of the COVID-19 pandemic in South Africa resulted in a complete lockdown, with all businesses, particularly young entrepreneurs' enterprises and smaller businesses, having to close down except those providing necessary services (Narula, 2020). During the crisis, newer businesses had to adapt and explore new opportunities, while also utilising government assistance and harbouring growth ambitions beyond the pandemic. As a result, the highlighted problem in the literature is that researchers and other organisations such as the World Health Organization have researched and discussed how COVID-19 has affected young entrepreneurs and also what opportunities COVID-19 has offered.

As mentioned earlier, this chapter aims to address the research problem by analysing and discussing the challenges facing youth entrepreneurs during the COVID-19 pandemic in South Africa and the chapter will analyse the opportunities offered by COVID-19 to help youth entrepreneurs to remain stable and profitable during the pandemic. According to Looze and Desai (2020), the importance and complexity of challenges facing entrepreneurs might vary depending on where they are in their business journey. According to research released by the OECD in May 2020, youth-led enterprises were already vulnerable before the pandemic due to a lack of labour market experience and entrepreneurial skills. During the COVID-19 crisis, youth entrepreneurs were forced to respond to the negative consequences of COVID-19 by laying off employees or cutting hours, cancelling supplier orders and lowering wages; as a result of these activities, several businesses were forced to stop operations and close down (Youth Co-Lab, 2020). The literature examined discovered a gap in research or report finding regarding the challenges and opportunities that young entrepreneurs, as well as other entrepreneurs, faced during COVID-19. The early impact of COVID-19 on entrepreneurs and small businesses is unclear due to a lack of timely business-level statistics released by the government (Fairlie, 2020).

YOUTH ENTREPRENEURSHIP

To learn more about COVID-19 challenges and opportunities for youth entrepreneurs It is critical to define the term "youth entrepreneurship." Unfortunately, there is currently no widely accepted definition of the terms "entrepreneurship," "entrepreneur" or "youth entrepreneurship" and "youth" in the literature. To begin, the research will evaluate what defines "youth". As previously stated, defining youth is a difficult task and many researchers, institutions and organisations have come up with their definitions of who qualifies as a youth. According to Maina (2012), youth are people between the ages of 15 and 28. According to the National Youth Policy 2009-2014 (The Presidency, 2009), youth are defined as those under the age of 35. To this day, there is no universally accepted definition of youth. In the context of entrepreneurship or entrepreneur, there is no universally accepted definition because several scholars have defined it differently depending on their viewpoints. According to Sathiabama (2010), entrepreneurship is a dynamic process of making wealth by individuals or groups of individuals. According to Bungau, Borza and Aurel (2018), an entrepreneur is someone who uses limited resources to increase earnings while also providing value. According to Smith (2010), entrepreneurship is defined as the number of new businesses started during a period. According to Shrivastava and Shrivastava (2013), entrepreneurship is helpful to growing the economy because entrepreneurs establish new enterprises, which in turn create new jobs, hence contributing to the strengthening of competitiveness. Gwija et al. (2014) describe youth entrepreneurship as "young individuals with the ability to perceive an opportunity and act on it to generate value and money by starting a new or expanding an existing business." According to Kelley (2015), a youth entrepreneur is someone under the age of 35 who has entrepreneurial attitudes and skills. A study on youth entrepreneurship undertaken by Youth Business International and the Global Entrepreneurship Monitor (GEM) revealed several reasons why youth entrepreneurship is important. Young entrepreneurs are more interested in new economic prospects and developments (e.g., trends), youth entrepreneurs are more creative and regularly develop new sorts of individual work and young people are active in high-growth sectors (Herrington, 2016). Furthermore, Leshilo and Lethoko (2017) defined youth entrepreneurship as the growth of entrepreneurship attitude, abilities and chances for youth from secondary education through early adulthood. These distinct qualities of youth entrepreneurship differ from those of adult entrepreneurship. Furthermore, the World Economic Forum (2015) stated that young entrepreneurs from various countries pursue entrepreneurship as a means of combating socio-economic problems such as poverty, high unemployment and crime.

YOUTH ENTREPRENEURSHIP IN SOUTH AFRICA

Entrepreneurship has been proven to assist in economic growth, job creation and poverty reduction (Chiloane and Mmako, 2014). Youth entrepreneurship has been recognised by several countries, including South Africa, as a critical component in tackling high rates of youth unemployment (Kew, 2015). In terms of the importance of entrepreneurship, Mohamed (2020) indicated that entrepreneurship accelerates economic growth, promotes innovation and social change, promotes research and industrial development, and develops and improves existing enterprises. And in terms of youth entrepreneurship, as stated before youth entrepreneurship plays an important role in addressing the high unemployment which is about twice the adult rate (OECD, 2020). In addition, youth entrepreneurship generates job opportunities for youth and other young people they employ in their businesses. As a result, it's critical to assess the significance of the present challenges that youth entrepreneurs face. Adopting sustainable entrepreneurship development in the form of Small, Medium, and Micro Enterprises (SMMEs) is high on practically every country's policy agenda, as successful businesses may generate more jobs and contribute significantly to a country's economic growth (Cassia et al., 2012). Several countries are trying to support small and medium-sized businesses to provide job opportunities for their growing young population and to promote economic development. For example, in South Africa, different programmes are put in place to help young entrepreneurs to deal with the challenges they face in their businesses. National Youth Development Agency (NYDA) is another programme created by the South Africa Government that aim to tackle the challenges that hinder youth to be involved in entrepreneurship ventures (Radebe, 2019). Other countries such as the European Union have a programme called the European Union Fund that is used to help young entrepreneurs to deal with challenges such as lack of education, limited business networks, market challenges, and lack of awareness of entrepreneurship (OECD, 2014). Also, India has introduced the start-up India initiative to ensure job creation for youth through bank financing of their start-ups (Katrodia and Sibanda, 2018). According to Gwiji et al. (2014), entrepreneurship has been considered a global way to help in assuring the economic participation of young people. Many experts have turned their attention on youth entrepreneurship and governments have focused their policies on encouraging the youth to become entrepreneurs, owing to their difficulty to integrate themselves into the country's economy and the economy's inability to absorb them (Majola, 2017). The South African government has emphasised youth entrepreneurship as a long-term solution to young unemployment and a variety of policies and programmes have been implemented to assist this mandate (DTI, 2013). According to the GEM study for 2014-2015, South African youth entrepreneurship propensity is the lowest in Africa at 23.3%, compared to 55.2% in Malawi and 55.4% in Uganda (Diniso, 2020). Encouraging young entrepreneurship will contribute to South Africa's economic growth and labour market absorption. Furthermore, according to Fatoki and Chindonga (2011), youth entrepreneurship will help achieve economic freedom and reduce the youth's reliance on government aid. This is could be achieved by youth who have the desire and potential to be involved in entrepreneurial activities. In addition, Fatoki and Chindonga (2011), indicated that youth should be advised that they should take entrepreneurship as a career rather than depending on the government programmes.

COVID-19 CHALLENGES FOR SOUTH AFRICAN YOUTH ENTREPRENEURS

Unemployment among young people is a major global issue that appears to be considerably worse in South Africa than in other countries (Majola, 2017). Maharaj et al (2016 indicated young entrepreneurs encounter many challenges in the day-to-day activities of their businesses. Also, Majola (2017) revealed that the entrepreneurial activity in South Africa is very low which is caused by different challenges such as access to financial capital, no credit history to serve as the collateral to be able to obtain loans and lack of education and skills. In addition, Radebe (2018) also indicated the barriers that hamper youth entrepreneurship development before COVID-19 namely; access to credit, entrepreneurship education, society's attitude towards youth entrepreneurship, and entrepreneurship culture. South Africa's government looked to entrepreneurship as a solution to youth unemployment (DTI, 2013). The recent COVID-19 outbreak primarily impacted youth entrepreneurs around the world (OECD, 2020). According to research conducted by the National Youth Development Agency (NYDA, 2020), the full economic impact of COVID-19 and lockdown will be impossible to assess because it will take months or years to do so. The research also stated that other countries such as South Africa are already experiencing a severe drop in income, rising unemployment and widespread business closures, all of which affect youth-owned firms. Young entrepreneurs face numerous challenges when starting a business before COVID-19. Insufficient cash, unfavourable government policies and a lack of experience running a business are just a few of the challenges that still exist during COVID-19 (Fairlie, 2020). According to a survey conducted by McKinsey & Company (2020), the challenge that young entrepreneurs in South Africa encounter and which is limiting their business growth is funding. Youth-owned businesses have a difficult time accessing financing because of their informality and general lack of capacity to submit credit-worthy business plans and financial records and reports of their enterprises and financial institutions are not willing to offer loans or credit to businesses in such a sector. According to Kalidas et al. (2020), even if youth entrepreneurs do not qualify for funding, South African youth entrepreneurs are unaware of the opportunities or do not know where to locate the information required to apply. According to a survey performed by Catalyst for Growth (2020), most young entrepreneurs' start-ups are mostly informal, with little to no access to operational and growth funding. The severe impact of containment measures has resulted in business closures and employment. Furthermore, the lockdown regulations have affected their productivity, production capacity and transportation of goods to clients, and young entrepreneurs have reported that the COVID-19 pandemic has changed consumer behaviour, resulting in decreasing demand for their goods and services (Di Crosta et al., 2021). According to Tshabalala and Beharry-Ramraj (2021), COVID-19 harmed South African youth entrepreneurs' business confidence because demand for non-essential products fell dramatically as a result of job losses and customers prioritising essential products. As a result, young entrepreneurs had to use a variety of strategies to stay profitable, including laying-off employees or cutting hours, withdrawing supplier orders and lowering wages. Some businesses were forced to stop production and shut down as a result of these actions. Finally, according to a study conducted by Catalyst for Growth (2020), most first-time youth entrepreneurs lack the skills needed to run and build a business, which was a hurdle faced by youth entrepreneurs during the COVID-19 pandemic.

COVID-19 OPPORTUNITIES FOR SOUTH AFRICAN YOUTH ENTREPRENEURS

In South Africa, some entrepreneurs and youth entrepreneurs seized the opportunity to reposition their businesses to respond to current economic demands and restore their lost livelihoods from challenges such as rising unemployment, job loss and lockdown and unstable businesses due to cash flow or profit loss (Dladla, 2020). Despite the odds, there have been positive developments in the labour market and young entrepreneurs are one of South Africa's best hopes for resolving the job crisis. There is an increasing number of start-ups, particularly in the digital sector, that are growing quickly and could become an engine of job growth in the future (Wolfgang et al., 2021). Illingworth (2020) noted that 2020 youth have traits and skills that they should be utilising - their energy, health and digital skills - and business concepts in response to COVID-19, opportunities are there if you can provide, connect and teach. Sanitation and personal protection equipment such as marks and alcohol-based cleaning disinfectants were among the business ideas or opportunities that the youth noticed during COVID-19, as were online and digital services, education and information. In terms of online and digital services, South Africa has a large number of youths who are involved in social media and run their businesses online by becoming "influencers," "blogging," a new term used mostly by youth in social media, or doing YouTube videos, all of which are about using your audience to become an ambassador to help champion or endorse a brand or campaign to a targeted audience (SME South Africa, 2020). According to the World Economic Forum (2020), during the pandemic, some newborn entrepreneurs and start-ups were more opportunistic, turning their businesses through some type of redirection of existing knowledge, skills, people and networks to new demands that appeared. In reaction to the pandemic, for example, young entrepreneurs in South Africa had to expand their businesses into online trading and/or delivery. South African youth entrepreneurs, for example, had to adapt to the digital platform by selling their items online or through an application. Youth entrepreneurs with digital stores benefited from this, for example, Kasi Eat and Vuleka (Vaal, 2020).

MAJOR EFFECT OF COVID-19 ON GLOBAL YOUTH ENTREPRENEURIAL ACTIVITIES

In one way or another, the COVID-19 pandemic has affected practically everyone. According to the OECD (2020), the COVID-19 pandemic affected largely young entrepreneurs in terms of social crisis, economic costs and long-term consequences. Furthermore, according to the organisation (OECD), COVID-19 harmed approximately 90% of global youth entrepreneurs' ventures. Their businesses were affected due to lockdown and they were forced to close. Others had to rely on their savings to get through the pandemic. According to Youth Co-Lab (2020), the crisis had an influence on the businesses of youth entrepreneurs by disrupting supply chains and increasing the cost of production as well as limiting access to financing and investment. Furthermore, Youth Co: Lab stated that COVID-19 worsened the situation for young entrepreneurs as they were still vulnerable before the pandemic for a variety of reasons, including a lack of market experience, information/education and entrepreneurial skills. According to a report by the OECD (2020), youth entrepreneurs were forced to take measures to mitigate the negative effects of the COVID-19 pandemic, including reducing personnel and working hours, cancelling orders from suppliers and lowering wages. All of this had an impact on the businesses and some had to completely shut down. According to the United Nations Industrial Development Organization (UNIDO, 2020), the

COVID-19 pandemic had an impact on business activity, with 49% of female entrepreneurs reporting that they had to temporarily close their businesses. In addition, 51% of young entrepreneurs also reported that they had to temporarily shut down their enterprises. According to a report by the World Economic Forum (2020), the number of start-up businesses created by young entrepreneurs decreased during the COVID-19 pandemic, however, there was also an increase in youth entrepreneurial activities during the pandemic. Youth entrepreneurs all across the globe are coming up with creative methods to cope with the consequences of COVID-19 and to help the community by developing new goods and services (CIPE, 2021). For example, using technology, remote work and the app economy, young entrepreneurs all around the world are generating their own jobs.

SUSTAINABLE ENTREPRENEURSHIP POST-COVID

Around the world, the COVID-19 epidemic is affecting people's health and economic activity. According to KritiKoS (2014), entrepreneurship stimulates economic growth by offering innovative technology, products and services. Entrepreneurship also produces jobs and helps to alleviate poverty. The COVID-19 pandemic, on the other hand, has had a huge impact on the world on many levels, driving the development of cures and solutions as well as compelling the need for entrepreneurial transformation. According to Castro and Zermeno (2021), the pandemic has had a substantial impact on the world economy, particularly on entrepreneurs and small businesses. Furthermore, it was reported that the pandemic is expected to have a long-term influence on global economies (OECD, 2020). The pandemic has slowed entry into entrepreneurship, with business applications in other nations falling by 40% (UNCTD, 2020). Furthermore, the pandemic increased the gender gap, with women's entrepreneurship rates remaining low. Women and young entrepreneurs have been particularly affected by the COVID-19 pandemic. According to Castro and Zermeno (2021), entrepreneurs must be able to adapt to change and resilience will be the key to adapting to change. As a result, entrepreneurs must demonstrate resilience both throughout and after COVID-19. Resilience provides entrepreneurs with a useful framework for how their businesses should recover from crises. It was also reported that the government needs to stimulate entrepreneurship post-COVID by implementing new policies or, additionally, by improving existing policies (OECD, 2020). Governments around the world reacted to the issues faced by entrepreneurs during the pandemic by introducing supportive measures and stimuli (OECD, 2021). For example, government structural support measures aimed at helping entrepreneurs to adapt and build resilience during COVID-19 and after COVID-19 include support for start-ups, sustainability, skilled and unskilled labour and digitisation. To support entrepreneurial efforts, a variety of instruments such as vouchers, grants, employment and training programmes are used.

SUSTAINABLE TECHNOLOGICAL STRATEGIES FOR YOUTH ENTREPRENEURS

In the middle of the global pandemic, digital technologies have grabbed society's interest as a result of their ability to help us battle COVID-19 (UNESCO, 2021). COVID-19 has emphasised the importance of promoting small businesses and entrepreneurs' use of digital technology, not only to strengthen their resilience but also to find answers to the pandemic (OECD, 2021). The majority of business owners and young entrepreneurs understand that technology is a strategic tool in the business, not only a cost-cutting tool (McKinsey & Company, 2020). With increasing technological advancement there is an increasing opportunity for young entrepreneurs to better connect digital finance and business platforms. During the lockdown, the young entrepreneurs were forced to temporarily close their businesses. The entrepreneurs responded with a bootstrapping technique to deal with COVID-19, however, youth entrepreneurs were not used to this technique due to a lack of experience. During the COVID-19 pandemic, young entrepreneurs were more likely to digitise their businesses (OECD, 2020) and the use of digital technology has made it possible for young entrepreneurs to reduce their risks. According to a study conducted by Mwakilama (2021), the pandemic has educated young entrepreneurs to invest more in technology to launch and operate their businesses. The COVID-19 pandemic has encouraged the development of digital solutions that employ leverage frontier technology such as blockchain, big data and artificial intelligence to better handle crises and address a variety of socio-economic issues. Furthermore, digital technology is used not only as a long-term plan but also generates new chances for entrepreneurs and new businesses for those who were not into entrepreneurship. However, the opportunities for the youth to utilise digital technologies have been unequal, due to challenges such as infrastructure and digital skills (Pinet et al., 2021).

THEORETICAL FRAMEWORK

There are numerous theories surrounding entrepreneurship and it is the most often debated topic among professionals and the general public worldwide. Numerous titles clarify entrepreneurship theory and assessment of the business and business environment, and researchers attempt to form an understanding of entrepreneurship and perceive what entrepreneurship is and what can be expected from it based on these views and other influences (Papulová and Papula, 2015). Entrepreneurship involves the use of human capital, social capital and financial capital. Schott et al. (2015) characterise these elements as collective resources in different aspects of entrepreneurial capital from the standpoint of youth. Human capital refers to people's knowledge, skills and experience, which includes both implicit and tacit knowledge acquired via education and experience (Schtt et al., 2015). The institutional support received from an individual's relationships and networks are referred to as social capital. These relationships and networks are with persons who can help or support the other person and vice versa. Financial capital refers to "funds that a person can access to invest in the beginning, running and expanding of a business" (Schtt et al., 2015). Raising capital, whether from banks or investors, is difficult for young people who do not have a strong credit history along with a successful track record of running a business. These elements of entrepreneurial capital will be utilised to assess the challenges and opportunities given by COVID-19 among South African youth entrepreneurs in the findings.

RESEARCH METHODOLOGY

This study utilised the desktop research method where relevant literature was used to analyse challenges and opportunities faced by youth entrepreneurs during COVID-19. Desktop research refers to secondary data, where the researcher uses data previously collected for studies related to the current research. The study was also descriptive as it was trying to seek answers to questions such as what the challenges and opportunities facing youth entrepreneurs during COVID-19 were. A qualitative approach was adopted to enable the use of secondary data literature and to be able to analyse the research objectives. The study relied on reports from organisations, journal articles, government publications and other relevant sources to address study objectives. The target population for this study was South African youth entrepreneurs therefore the data collected came from sources that discuss opportunities and challenges South African youth entrepreneurs faced during the COVID-19 pandemic.

FINDINGS AND DISCUSSION

COVID-19 has posed numerous challenges for young entrepreneurs in South Africa and the effect has been devastating. According to the study, South African youth entrepreneurs face challenges such as a lack of funding, limited demand for goods and services and a lack of experience in running a business, which is still present in COVID-19. Due to the pandemic, some young entrepreneurs were forced to shut their businesses down. The study also found out that funding was a big challenge for them due to a large number of youth entrepreneurs' start-ups being in the informal sector therefore banks and other institutions are hesitant to offer loans or funding. Another reason is that youth entrepreneurs' businesses are not registered companies and have outdated financial information and other youth entrepreneurs did not meet the requirement for funding or any support. The human capital theory in this role is that people do not know about running a business or do not have skills in financial management. Also, the social capital theory involves the institutional support derived from an individual's relationships and networks. Thus, the research furthermore found that youth entrepreneurs could not reach out to customers or clients due to lockdown regulations during the pandemic and this affected their productivity, and other businesses had to shut down entirely. Some businesses had to implement new strategies to get the businesses going, for example using e-commerce to run businesses. Table 1 below tabulates the challenges entrepreneurs face.

Looking back there is a saying by Weiner (1976): "Don't waste a crisis" and the COVID-19 pandemic did not stop South African youth entrepreneurs from being innovative and creative. While there are challenges presented by COVID-19, other young entrepreneurs saw new business opportunities emerge during the pandemic. The study found that digital and new technologies were used as a strategy to improve youth entrepreneurs' businesses. In addition, these technologies created opportunities for entrepreneurs. The study found that e-commerce/online buying and selling, manufacturing of facemasks and entertainment were opportunities presented by COVID-19. Digital economy opportunities are increasing, providing new growth prospects for young people. The ability to buy and sell products and services over the internet has transformed marketplaces and, like delivery services, has been in high demand since the crisis began. The digital revolution in South Africa is boosting the creation of new types of work. This motivated other youth-owned businesses to gather information on how to use the internet and websites to sell and buy their goods and services. For example, Thuli Hlongwane, who works in the beauty industry, began focusing on services before the COVID-19 crisis but is now shifting to product sales and exploring developing and offering virtual services. Other youth entrepreneurs seized the opportunity by doing delivery businesses as many people were unable to go to shops, especially those with comorbidities, others manufactured face masks and sold them to members of their communities. Other youth entrepreneurs who are in the music or entertainment industry used their talent online through Facebook, Twitter and YouTube to keep the country entertained and, in this regard, the findings found Donald Moatshe who is a Platinum-selling, award-winning South African soul artist and former season

13 SA Idols mentor, created a platform that will be used by people to showcase their talents and this was loved by many people in South Africa. Other youth entrepreneurs gained knowledge about funding procedures and the advantage of applying for funding. In terms of human capital, the study found that other youth entrepreneurs were able to gain knowledge and skills through social media on how to advertise their businesses and sell their products.

Table 1. Challenges faced by South African youth entrepreneurs

Authors	Challenges
Catalyst for Growth (2020)	The study found that South African youth entrepreneurs suffered a loss of income as there was limited funding. In addition, youth entrepreneurs have been having difficulties in accessing funding before COVID-19. This prove that this is still a major challenge faced by youth entrepreneurs. Furthermore, the majority of youth entrepreneurs in South Africa have small businesses, making it difficult to access retained earnings from previous profits. Youth entrepreneurs found it difficult to obtain credit from financial institutions and capital from current or prospective investors to help them survive during this period this is because youth entrepreneurs do not have track records and financial institutions do not assist small businesses due to their failure in early stages of growth. Then Youth entrepreneurs in South Africa had to rely on friends and family for support but family and friends during COVID-19 faced challenges such as job loss and financial troubles.
McKinsey & Company (2020)	According to the report, youth entrepreneurs in South Africa were reported to have limited access to funding, which hindered their business growth. Furthermore, only 6% of youth entrepreneurs surveyed obtained government support, while only 9% received funding from private sources (own funds). In addition to funding, the study discovered that even when capital (funding) is provided, a lack of knowledge of opportunities and financial understanding are major obstacles for young entrepreneurs seeking help. In addition, the study found that youth entrepreneurs face slow demand, leading them to downsize their expansion plans and seek out new ways to sell their items online or through a website. However, selling online have been a trend before COVID-19, COVID-19 accelerated the trend and help those who were not selling online
Centre of Development Enterprise (2020)	According to a survey of 233 youth entrepreneurs in South Africa, 86% of respondents do not know where to go for emergency funding and 50% of them do not think their business would survive. Lack of knowledge in terms of getting funding have been a major problem for youth entrepreneurs before COVID-19 and this is because the source of funding or when the funding is published do not reach youth entrepreneurs easily.
NYDA (2020)	The organisation conducted a survey on youth-owned businesses and interviewed 54 youth entrepreneurs, establishing that none of the respondents had received any other government or private-sector funding during the lockdown, this is supported by the above statement that lack of knowledge about how to get funding is a major challenge for youth entrepreneurs. In addition, the survey discovered that because of the lockdown, youth entrepreneurs were unable to contact their clients and there was lower demand and this resulted the business not to progress and made no profit.
Lang (2020)	According to the survey, the main challenges faced by youth entrepreneurs in South Africa during lockdown included a lack of access to relief funds, a lack of cash reserves, the incapacity to operate during the lockdown and outdated financial information. According to the report, 42.7% of firms surveyed closed within the first five months of the pandemic, 43% applied for relief funds and 99.9% of those who applied were denied owing to weak consumer credit scores.

Table 2. Opportunities faced by South African youth entrepreneurs

Authors	Opportunities
Business Tech (2020)	According to the study, some young entrepreneurs took advantage of opportunities and refocused their businesses to respond to the COVID-19 pandemic by starting delivery businesses because many people, especially those with comorbidities, were unable to go to shops, others manufactured face masks and sold them to members of their communities and others used online entertainment platforms to adhere to the lockdown regulations. Online-entertainment have been a tool for youth entrepreneurs to sell and buy their goods and services before COVID-19 and COVID-19 accelerated the use of social media to help youth entrepreneurs to stay in the business.
Shoba (2020)	According to the findings, other youth entrepreneurs were heavily affected by the shutdown but many found creative ways to keep their businesses running during this trying time. For example, Lusanda Worsely, managing director of Empire Experiential Marketing, said that her team was heavily affected by the pandemic, but they started SFG (Swipe, F***, Ghost) as a method to keep their sanity during COVID-19, but it blossomed into a profitable initiative.
SABC News (2020)	The SABC reported that young musicians and artists have been using social media to interact with fans since the national lockdown. An example of such is Donald Moatshe, who is a Platinum-selling, award-winning South African soul artist and former season 13 SA Idols mentor. After the national lockdown was extended, Donald started a talent show to find new musicians and the winner will record a song with Donald and possibly be signed to his own record label.
UNDP (2020)	The UNDP undertook a study to ascertain how young entrepreneurs are coping with the pandemic. The research interviewed Thuli Hlongwane, who is the founder and Managing Director of Prim-U, an easy-to-use App platform that makes appointment processes effortless and transparent for both customers and stylists. She indicated that like many other industries, the beauty industry has been hugely affected by the COVID-19 crisis, so her business started focusing on services before the COVID-19 crisis and is now shifting into product sales and exploring developing and offering virtual services.
IDCRC-CRDI (2020)	The study found that youth entrepreneurs now see and recognise the advantages of registering their activities to benefit from the safety nets and financial incentives put in place by governments.
UNCDF (2021)	A study found that youth entrepreneurs used many digital solutions and technologies, including resource planning and digital platforms, for marketing, selling and business operations.

RECOMMENDATIONS

The economic fallout from COVID-19 has affected millions of young entrepreneurs around the world (World Economic Forum, 2020). Young entrepreneurs faced new challenges and opportunities as a result of the COVID-19 crisis. As a result, young entrepreneurs must conduct a study on the challenges that businesses have faced and how youth entrepreneurs can overcome these challenges. In addition, as the saying goes, one must not waste a crisis; youth entrepreneurs need to research the opportunities provided by the COVID-19 in their businesses. COVID-19 harmed young entrepreneur start-ups since some youth entrepreneurs lacked the necessary skills to develop and manage a business. Most entrepreneurs have reacted by using bootstrapping methods, however, due to their inexperience young entrepreneurs are less familiar with these methods (OECD, 2020). As a result, young entrepreneurs must identify market gaps rather than just by buying or starting a business where there is none. COVID-19 has harmed youth-owned enterprises, forcing several to close, therefore it is important to develop strategies to keep the enterprise sustainable and profitable. Being an entrepreneur involves a variety of skills, including creativity and risk tolerance, so it's critical to develop solutions and accept any challenges you face. According to GEM (2013), youth entrepreneurs are important because they are more adaptable to new economic opportunities and trends. As there are youth entrepreneurs who were denied funding for the reasons stated above (findings and discussion), it is recommended that youth entrepreneurs should try to learn more about funding procedures and find out where youth entrepreneurs can get funding if they want to, as that is another factor that has affected youth entrepreneurs' opportunity to secure funding. Also, when it comes to funding, there must be clear communication about the nature of the support. If it is a loan, the conditions and potential implications for the organisation should be highlighted and the numerous funding options should be centralised and widely publicised. It has also been stated that during a disaster there are opportunities (Weiner, 1976). Some youth-owned businesses seized the opportunities presented during the lockdown. Other youth entrepreneurs used an online platform to advertise or sell and buy goods and services. The information and technology sector has been a lifeline during the COVID-19 crisis (Kalidas et al., 2020). Online digital platforms, new technologies and innovations created new opportunities for small businesses. Adopting this change will enable youth entrepreneurs to stay in business and be profitable.

FUTURE RESEARCH

Future research should focus on funding a study utilizing primary research to discover the challenges youth entrepreneurs face. In addition, future research could find out more about the strategies that youth entrepreneurs should implement if they are faced with challenges. Furthermore, future research can focus on what development programmes and strategies the South African government should put in place to develop youth entrepreneurs' capabilities bearing in mind COVID-19. Also, future research should examine the importance of the digital economy as it is increasing worldwide and because for youth entrepreneurs to be profitable in business and to make the standard of living better, they need technology. Future research should also be focused on how the Fourth Industrial Revolution (4IR) will benefit young entrepreneurs and what are the setbacks for youth entrepreneurs who want to benefit from it.

CONCLUSION

The focus of this chapter was to analyse the challenges and opportunities that COVID-19 presents to South African youth entrepreneurs. The COVID-19 pandemic had an impact on human health and economic well-being all around the world. The crisis had a particularly negative impact on young entrepreneurs. Given the potential for entrepreneurship to encourage economic involvement of the youth, the focus on fostering youth entrepreneurship is expanding in other countries, including South Africa, and youth entrepreneurship recently encountered a major challenge due to COVID-19. As a result, the COVID-19 pandemic has brought new challenges as well as opportunities for young entrepreneurs, forcing them to devise strategies to keep their businesses afloat. Many countries, including South Africa, went into lockdown and had to adhere to COVID-19 regulations which had a significant impact on the businesses of youth entrepreneurs. Some had to close down and others had to devise strategies to stay in business while others saw opportunities during COVID-19. This research, therefore, intended to analyse challenges youth entrepreneurs encountered as well as opportunities they discovered during COVID-19.

According to the findings above, COVID-19 presented challenges to youth entrepreneurs in South Africa. According to the findings, South African youth entrepreneurs face challenges such as a lack of funding, low demand for goods and services and a lack of experience running a business, all of which persisted during COVID-19. The study also found that funding was a big challenge for them due to a large number of youth entrepreneurs' start-ups being in the informal sector and some youth entrepreneurs did not know where to get funding. Another challenge the study found was that youth entrepreneurs encountered obstacles in reaching customers or clients which was a challenge persisting over previous years. The study also found out that some youth entrepreneurs rose above the situation, were creative and were able to start other businesses from these challenges; this enabled their businesses to stay open and operate. The study found out that e-commerce/online, manufacturing of face masks and entertainment were opportunities presented by COVID-19. In South Africa, the number of youth entrepreneurs is on the increase as youth have found opportunities during COVID-19. The study found that some youth entrepreneurs started delivery businesses and others manufactured masks and sold them to their communities. The study found that the greatest opportunity created by COVID-19 was the digital economy as people used technology to promote their goods and services and others used social media to entertain.

In addition, it is important for youth entrepreneurs to research challenges that businesses had to deal with and how youth entrepreneurs managed to survive those challenges. Also, youth entrepreneurs are encouraged to research opportunities the COVID-19 pandemic presented for their businesses, urging them not to waste a crisis. As the study discovered, funding is a problem and the government must deliver a clear communication on the type of funding that can be provided to youth entrepreneurs. If it is a loan, the conditions and potential implications for the organisation should be emphasised and the various funding options should be centralised and well-publicised.

REFERENCES

Agwa-Ejon, J., & Mbohwa, C. (2015). Financial challenges faced by SMMES in Gauteng South Africa. In *International Association for Management of Technology IAMOT 2015 Conference Proceedings* (pp. 520-534). Academic Press.

Audretsch, D. B., Belitski, M., & Desai, S. (2015). Entrepreneurship and economic development in cities. *The Annals of Regional Science*, 1–28.

Boateng, G. O., Boateng, A. A., & Bampoe, H. S. (2014). Barriers to youthful entrepreneurship in rural areas of Ghana. *Global Journal of Business Research*, *8*(3), 109-119.

Bungau, C., Borza, A., & Aurel, C. A. U. S. (2018). Comparative studies of indicators defining entrepreneurship culture in Romania. *Acta Technica Napocensis-Series: Applied Mathematics. Mechanical Engineering*, *61*(3).

BusinessTech. (2020). *Ramaphosa on large vs small companies in South Africa, and how entrepreneurs are finding success in Covid-19*. Available from: https://businesstech.co.za/news/business/417795/ramaphosa-on-large-vs-small-companies-in-south-africa-and-how-entrepreneurs-are-finding-success-in-covid-19/

Cassia, L., & Minola, T. (2012). Hyper-growth of SMEs: Toward a reconciliation of entrepreneurial orientation and strategic resources. *International Journal of Entrepreneurial Behaviour & Research*, *18*(2), 179–197. doi:10.1108/13552551211204210

Catalyst for Growth. (2020). *The impact of Covid-19 on African SMMES operations*. Available from: https://www.goethe.de/resources/files/pdf208/c4g-the-impact-of-covid-19-on-african-smmes-operations-online.pdf

Centre of Development Enterprise. (2020). *Impact of COVID-19 on small, medium and micro enterprises since lockdown*. Available from: http://www.nyda.gov.za/Portals/0/downloads/Impact%20of%20 COVID_19%20on%20SMMEs_1000_Businesses_100Days%202020_10_01.pdf

Chiloane-Tsoka, G. E., & Mmako, N. M. (2014). Effects of migration and immigration on SMMEs: The case study of Diepsloot informal settlement, South Africa. *Problems and Perspectives in Management*, *12*(4), 377–383.

CIPE. (2021). *Effects of COVID-19 on Youth Entrepreneurs*. Available from: https://www.cipe.org/blog/2021/07/22/effects-of-covid-19-on-youth-entrepreneurs/

Di Crosta, A., Ceccato, I., Marchetti, D., La Malva, P., Maiella, R., Cannito, L., Cipi, M., Mammarella, N., Palumbo, R., Verrocchio, M. C., Palumbo, R., & Di Domenico, A. (2021). Psychological factors and consumer behavior during the COVID-19 pandemic. *PLoS One*, *16*(8), e0256095. doi:10.1371/journal.pone.0256095 PMID:34398916

Diniso, C. (2020). *Youth entrepreneurship in South Africa: A progressive review*. Available from: https://www.researchgate.net/publication/351249747_YOUTH_ENTREPRENEURSHIP_IN_SOUTH_AFRICA_A_PROGRESS_REVIEW

Diraditsile, K., & Maphula, P. (2018). Entrepreneurship as a mechanism for addressing youth unemployment in Botswana: A reality or idealism? *International Journal of Development and Sustainability*, *7*(3), 836–847.

Dladla, L. G. (2020). The Economics of the Covid-19 Pandemic and its Effects on Small Businesses in South Africa. *Asian Journal of Social Sciences Review*, *2*(2).

DTI. (2013). *Youth Enterprise Development Strategy*. Available from: https://www.ilembechamber.co.za/wp-content/uploads/2017/12/Youth-Enterprise-Development-Strategy-2013-2023.pdf

DTI. (2013). *Youth Enterprise Development Strategy*. Available from: https://www.ilembechamber.co.za/wp-content/uploads/2017/12/Youth-EnterpriseDevelopment-Strategy-2013-2023.pdf

Fairlie, R. (2020). The impact of COVID-19 on small business owners: Evidence from the first three months after widespread social-distancing restrictions. *Journal of Economics & Management Strategy*, *29*(4), 727–740. doi:10.1111/jems.12400 PMID:32904856

Fatoki, O., & Chindoga, L. (2011). An investigation into the obstacles to youth entrepreneurship in South Africa. *International Business Research*, *4*(2), 161–169. doi:10.5539/ibr.v4n2p161

GuttermanA. (2020). Definitions and Types of Entrepreneurships. Available at SSRN. doi:10.2139/ssrn.3930375

Gwija, S., Eresia-Eke, C., & Iwu, C. (2014). Challenges and Prospects of Youth Entrepreneurship Development in a Designated Community in the Western Cape, South Africa. *The Journal of Behavioral Economics*, *6*, 10–20.

Herrington, M., & Kew, P. (2016). *Global Entrepreneurship Monitor (GEM): South African Report 2015/16 – Is South Africa heading for an economic meltdown?* Available from: https://www.gemconsortium.org/news/Is%20South%20Africa%20headed%20for%20economic%20meltdown?

Hisrich, R. D., & Peters, M. P. (2002). Entrepreneurship (5th ed.). McGraw Hill/Irvin, Higher Education.

IDCRC-CRDI. (2020). *Boosting youth employment in Africa during and after the COVID-19 pandemic.* Available from: https://www.idrc.ca/en/research-in-action/boosting-youth-employment-africa-during-and-after-covid-19-pandemic

Intracen.org. (2021). *Lifting Ghana's youth entrepreneurs through the Ye! Boost Programme*. Available from: https://www.intracen.org/news/Lifting-Ghana-youth-entrepreneurs-through-the-Ye-Boost-Programme/

Intracen.org. (2021). *COVID-19: The Great Lockdown and its Impact on Small Business - SMECO 2020 Executive Summary*. Available from: https://www.intracen.org/publication/SMECO2020/Ex-Summary

Kalidas, S., Magwentshu, N., & Rajagopaul, A. (2020). *How South African SMEs can survive and thrive post COVID-19*. Academic Press.

Katrodia, A., & Sibanda, R. (2018). Challenges experienced by young entrepreneurs entering the small and medium enterprise sector (SME) in Rajkot region, Gujarat-India. *Academy of Entrepreneurship Journal*, *24*(4), 1–14.

Kelley, D., Brush, C., Greene, P., Herrington, M., Ali, A., & Kew, P. (2014). *Special report: Women's Entrepreneurship*. Global Entrepreneurship Monitor.

Kew, J. (2015). *Africa's Young Entrepreneurs: Unlocking the Potential for a Brighter Future*. University of Cape Town, Development Unit for New Enterprise.

KritiKoS. (2014). *Entrepreneurs and their impact on jobs and economic growth*. IZA World of Labor. Available from: https://wol.iza.org/articles/entrepreneurs-and-their-impact-on-jobs-and-economic-growth/long

Lang, J. (2020). *Covid-19 crisis a potential breeding ground for youth entrepreneurship in SA*. Available from: https://www.news24.com/citypress/voices/covid-19-crisis-a-potential-breeding-ground-for-youth-entrepreneurship-in-sa-20200611

Leshilo, A., & Lethoko, M. (2017). The contribution of youth in Local Economic Development and entrepreneurship in Polokwane municipality, Limpopo Province. *Skills at Work: Theory and Practice Journal*, *8*(1), 45–58.

Looze, J., & Desai, L. (2020). *Challenges along the Entrepreneurial Journey: Considerations for Entrepreneurship Supporters*. Ewing Marion Kauffman Foundation.

Maina, S. W. (2012). *Factors influencing the development of youth entrepreneurship in Ongata Rongai Township, Kajiado County, Kenya* (Doctoral dissertation). University of Nairobi, Kenya.

Majola, J. E. P. (2017). *The impact of entrepreneurial capital on the performance of youth-owned enterprises in South Africa* (Doctoral dissertation).

McGinnis, D. (2020). *What Is the Fourth Industrial Revolution?* Available from: https://www.salesforce.com/blog/what-is-the-fourth-industrial-revolution-4ir/

McKinsey & Company. (2020). *How South African SMEs can survive and thrive post COVID-19.* Available from: https://www.mckinsey.com/featured-insights/middle-east-and-africa/how-south-african-smes-can-survive-and-thrive-post-covid-19

Mjadu, G. (2018). *How to address common entrepreneurial challenges in SA.* Available from: https://www.news24.com/citypress/voices/how-to-address-common-entrepreneurial-challenges-in-sa-20180626

Mohamed, N. (2020). *Top 5 Takeaways on the importance of entrepreneurship.* Available from: https://dcid.sanford.duke.edu/importance-of-entrepreneurship/

Mwakilama, E. P. (2021). *Support more students with innovative business ideas.* Available from: https://www.universityworldnews.com/post.php?story=20210926110903106

Narula, R. (2020). Policy opportunities and challenges from the COVID-19 pandemic for economies with large informal sectors. *Journal of International Business Policy*, *3*(3), 302–310. doi:10.105742214-020-00059-5

NYDA. (2020). *COVID-19 crisis funding support for South Africa businesses.* Available from: http://www.nyda.gov.za/Portals/0/Downloads/Covid%20Funding%20Resources%20for%20SA%20Businesses%207-4-2020.pdf

OECD. (2020). *Supporting Young Entrepreneurs through the COVID-19 Crisis: What's Next?* Available from: https://www.oecd.org/cfe/leed/OECD_Webinar_Youth_Entrepreneurship_Policy_and_COVID-19_SUMMARY.pdf

OECD. (2021). An in-depth analysis of one year of SME and entrepreneurship policy responses to COVID-19: lessons learned for the path to recovery. In *OECD SME and Entrepreneurship Papers*. OECD Publishing.

OECD. (2021). *OECD Policy Responses to Coronavirus (COVID-19), One year of SME and entrepreneurship policy responses to COVID-19: Lessons learned to "build back better"*. Available from: https://www.oecd.org/coronavirus/policy-responses/one-year-of-sme-and-entrepreneurship-policy-responses-to-covid-19-lessons-learned-to-build-back-better-9a230220/

Papulová, Z., & Papula, J. (2015). Entrepreneurship in the Eyes of the Young Generation. *Procedia Economics and Finance*, *34*, 514–520. doi:10.1016/S2212-5671(15)01662-7

Pinet, M., Phiona, S., & Youn, A. (2021). *Advancing youth-centred digital ecosystems in Africa in a post-Covid-19 world. ODI Working paper*. ODI. https://odi.org/en/publications/advancing-youth-centred-digital-ecosystems-in-africa-in-a-post-covid-19-world/

Portuguez Castro, M., & Gómez Zermeño, M. G. (2021). Being an entrepreneur post-COVID-19 – resilience in times of crisis: A systematic literature review. *Journal of Entrepreneurship in Emerging Economies*, *13*(4), 721–746. doi:10.1108/JEEE-07-2020-0246

SABC News. (2020). *SA musician finds innovative ways to engage supporters*. Available from: https://www.sabcnews.com/sabcnews/sa-musician-finds-innovative-ways-to-engage-supporters/

Sambo, W. (2016). Factors affecting youth entrepreneurship development in Kibera district, Kenya. *Problems and Perspectives in Management*, *14*(3), 154–161. doi:10.21511/ppm.14(3-1).2016.02

Sathiabama, K. (2010). *Rural Women Empowerment and Entrepreneurship Development*. esocialsciences.com

Schøtt, T., Kew, P., & Cheraghi, M. (2015). *Future Potential: A GEM perspective on youth entrepreneurship*. Available from: https://portal.findresearcher.sdu.dk/en/publications/future-potential-a-gem-perspective-on-youth-entrepreneurship

Shoba, S. (2020). *How young entrepreneurs are surviving the pandemic*. Available from: https://www.dailymaverick.co.za/article/2020-07-23-how-young-entrepreneurs-are-surviving-the-pandemic/

Shrivastava, S., & Shrivastava, R. (2013). Role of entrepreneurship in economic development: With special focus on necessity entrepreneurship and opportunity entrepreneurship. *International Journal of Management and Social Sciences Research*, *2*(2), 1–5.

Sindabiwe, P., & Mbabazi, D. (2014). Triad Problematic of Youth Entrepreneurship. *Voices from University Students*, *1*(6), 463.

Smith, D. (2010). The Role of Entrepreneurship in Economic Growth. *Undergraduate Economic Review*, *6*(1). Available from: https://digitalcommons.iwu.edu/cgi/viewcontent.cgi?article=1064&context=uer

South Africa, S. M. E. (2020). *The best time to start a business is now - 10 plus business ideas for youth*. Available from: https://smesouthafrica.co.za/10-plus-business-ideas-for-youth/

Trading Economics. (2019). *South Africa Youth Unemployment Rate*. Available from: https://tradingeconomics.com/south-africa/youth-unemployment-rate

Tshabalala, M., & Beharry-Ramraj, A. (2021). Examining the 4th Industrial Revolution and South Africa Youth Entrepreneurship Linkage to Covid 19: Opportunities and Challenges. *Gender & Behaviour*, *19*(1), 17204–17218.

UNCDF. (2020). *Youth Entrepreneurs Engaging in the Digital Economy: The Next Generation*. Available from: https://www.undp.org/publications/youth-entrepreneurs-engaging-digital-economy-next-generation

UNDP. (2020). *Youth Entrepreneurs and COVID-19*. Available from: https://www.za.undp.org/content/south_africa/en/home/presscenter/articles/2020/youth-entrepreneurs-and-covid-19.html

UNESCO. (2021). *Fighting COVID-19 through digital innovation and transformation*. Available from: https://en.unesco.org/covid19/communicationinformationresponse/digitalinnovation

Vaal University. (2020). *Uber who? Kasi catering to the townships*. Available from: https://www.vut-research.ac.za/uber-who-kasi-catering-to-the-townships/

Wolfgang, F., Francoise, M.-N., Indermit, G., Benedecte, B., & Facundo, P. (2021). *South Africa accelerating job creation.* Available from: https://blogs.worldbank.org/africacan/south-africa-after-covid-19-accelerating-job-creation

World Economic Forum. (2020). *Discovering the real impact of COVID-19 on entrepreneurship*. Available from: https://www.weforum.org/agenda/2020/06/how-covid-19-will-change-entrepreneurial-business/

World Health Organization (WHO). (2020). *Coronavirus disease (COVID-19).* Available from: https://www.who.int/health-topics/coronavirus#tab=tab_1

Youth Co. Lab. (2020). *Impact of COVID-19 on Youth Entrepreneurs in Indonesia.* Available from: https://www.unicef.org/indonesia/media/8236/file

Section 3
Industry Challenges

Chapter 12
An Evaluation of How Tourism Entrepreneurs Were Impacted by the COVID-19 Pandemic

Nondumiso Maphumulo
University of KwaZulu-Natal, South Africa

Andrisha Beharry Ramraj
University of KwaZulu-Natal, South Africa

ABSTRACT

The Coronavirus (Covid-19) pandemic has had a devastating impact on tourism entrepreneurs around the world. Tourism is South Africa has been at a temporary standstill since March 2020. The harsh effects of the pandemic have affected economies all over the world, resulting in a significant increase in global unemployment. Before the COVID-19 pandemic, the tourism industry was one of the fastest-growing industries in the world, contributing 10.48% to the global gross domestic product (GDP).

INTRODUCTION

According to Camilleri (2017), tourism can be defined as particular activities that are undertaken by people out of their usual environment for not more than one consecutive year. It can be for leisure or business-related. Tourism entrepreneurship defines any type of business that offers tourist products and services. The products and services may include business activities such as eateries, accommodation, transport, shops, entertainment, and many others. The tourism sector is one of the largest sectors in the world, contributing 10. 48% of the world's GDP (Loss, 2019). Camilleri (2017) added that the tourism sector is crucial in the economies of countries across the world because it boosts economic growth, develops infrastructures, creates millions of jobs, and creates a sense of cultural exchange between citizens and foreigners. For these reasons, many governments across the world have constantly increased their investment in the tourism industry which includes advertising the most attractive destinations in their

DOI: 10.4018/978-1-6684-4322-4.ch012

relative countries. According to Loss (2019) tourism is the major key to South Africa's economy and the employment of its citizens. The sector has a gigantic contribution to the South African economy where it contributes 9% to the GDP. Not only does the tourism industry create revenue and cultural wealth for the country, but it also contributes significantly to enterprise development opportunities.

The Covid-19 pandemic that surfaced in December 2019, has caused undeniable suffering in the tourism industry all over the world. By June 2020, the pandemic spread to over 200 countries, infecting over 10 million people. Governments across the world responded by closing their borders to visitors and tourists. As a result, international tourism was suspended. Domestic tourism was also at a standstill because of the lockdowns and strict restrictions that were being implemented by governments all over the world. This left tourism entrepreneurs devasted because of the loss of revenue. Thus, the pandemic showed that tourism entrepreneurs need to be able to sustain themselves in cases of unforeseen events. This chapter examined different ways that sustainability can be achieved in the tourism industry.

The COVID-19 pandemic has caused incontrovertible devastations in all parts of the world. This chapter seeks to evaluate how this pandemic has caused suffering for tourism entrepreneurs in the world, and then narrow it down to South Africa. Thus, the research objectives of this chapter are to discuss how tourism entrepreneurs have been impacted by COVID-19 and to discuss the strategies that these entrepreneurs can use to recover and remain competitive and successful in the market. In essence, the chapter will also show the different ways that tourism entrepreneurs can sustain themselves in the industry. This study is important in academia because it gives insights into the magnitudinous role of the tourism sector in the economy. Discussing the challenges that tourism entrepreneurs have faced and offering strategies for their recovery can potentially fast-track the tourism industry to continue its significant contribution to the global GDP as it did before the pandemic.

BACKGROUND

Tourism is crucial for the success of many economies across the world. This sector boosts economic growth, develops infrastructures, and creates millions of jobs around the world. In 2019, the travel and tourism sector contributed 10.4% to the global Gross Domestic Product (GDP) (Abbas, Mubeen, & Terhemba, 2021). Before the pandemic, the tourism sector accounted for 10% of all jobs in the world. The novel COVID-19 pandemic emerged in 2019 in Wuhan, China, and caused undeniable global suffering. In March 2020, the World Health Organization (WHO) declared COVID-19 a pandemic (Abbas et al., 2021). To fight this pandemic, governments across the world made efforts to protect their populations by implementing strict restrictions. The President of South Africa, Cyril Ramaphosa, had his first address on the Covid-19 pandemic on 15 March 2020. On this day, the president declared a national state of disaster in terms of the Disaster Management Act. The number of COVID-19 cases was sharply increasing and there was no sign of a vaccine. Thus, the South African government authorities and health system made a drastic decision of implementing a national lockdown. This lockdown was a way to curb the spread of the virus and included restricting all travelling, banning large social gatherings, and combating non-essential businesses from operating. This meant that businesses in the tourism industry could not operate for some time because they were not classified as essential businesses. This dried up the revenue of most tourism businesses yet fixed costs remained (Abbas et al., 2021).

Before the COVID-19 pandemic, tourism was one of the fastest-growing industries and a major contributor to global economic growth but has presently become the most vulnerable industry due to the pandemic. This chapter will elaborate on the problems that were faced in the economic growth, hotel industry, transportation industry as well as restaurant industry that were infiltrated by the pandemic. These problems or challenges led to tourism entrepreneurs experiencing financial difficulties and threats to close down their businesses permanently. Finally, the chapter will offer recommendations to help tourism entrepreneurs recover from the harsh effects of the pandemic and continue being competitive in their market.

TOURISM ENTREPRENEURS

According to Camilleri (2017), tourism can be defined as particular activities that are undertaken by people out of their usual environment for not more than one consecutive year. It can be for leisure or business-related. A tourism entrepreneur is a person who undertakes a risk to start their own business in the tourism industry. The entrepreneur undertakes this risk in hopes of making profits. Tourism entrepreneurs are essentially interested in the tourism market and apply their knowledge, skills, and competencies to a tourism-related idea (Luke, 2020).

ECONOMIC IMPACT OF TOURISM IN SOUTH AFRICA

Tourism is vital for the success of many economies around the world. This sector boosts economic growth, develops infrastructures, and creates millions of jobs around the world. In 2019, the travel and tourism sector contributed 10.4% to the global Gross Domestic Product (GDP) and provided 330 million jobs around the world (Abbas, Mubeen, & Terhemba, 2021). According to Lock (2021), the travel and tourism industry's contribution to global GDP was approximately US$ 4.7 trillion.

Tourism plays a very important role in the South African economy because it contributes 9% to the GDP (gross domestic product) and contributes immensely to job creation. In 2018, the tourism sector made a direct contribution of R130,1 billion to the GDP. It also contributed to 4,5% of total employment in the country. This shows the magnitude of the tourism industry and how important tourism entrepreneurs are to South Africa. However, the COVID-19 pandemic emerged and caused disruptions in the tourism markets. According to Sperka (2020), for each day that the South African tourism sector remains under lockdown, R748 million is lost through tourism expenditure. This leads to more job losses and a wider inequality gap. It is estimated that 50 000 businesses have closed down due to this pandemic (Sperka, 2020). This has led to almost 600 000 job losses. Moreover, an estimated R54,2 billion in output is believed to have been lost between mid-March and the end of May.

CHANGES IN GLOBAL GROSS DOMESTIC PRODUCT

COVID-19 affected the GDPs of countries worldwide. The impact on GDP in Fig1 on the next page shows a significant reduction in international tourism. The restrictions that came with lockdown measures led to a national decrease in the demand and supply for exports. This, in turn, resulted in negative effects on the economic standings of many countries. Figure 1 below shows that Jamaica (-11%) is the most affected country. The pandemic had an overwhelming impact on Jamaica's economy because of the country's heavy reliance on the tourism sector. Portugal experienced a GDP change of -6%, which was mainly caused by an unprecedented decline in revenues from tourism. The main tourist attraction in Portugal is their capital city, Lisbon, and the closure of borders meant that tourists could not come to this city. Moreover, the researcher gathered that countries that are most dependent on tourism have small economies with small domestic markets, As a result, they tend to be vulnerable to external shocks. This is why tourism was one of the most affected industries by the COVID-19 pandemic.

Figure 1. Changes in GDP
Source: UNITAD (2020)

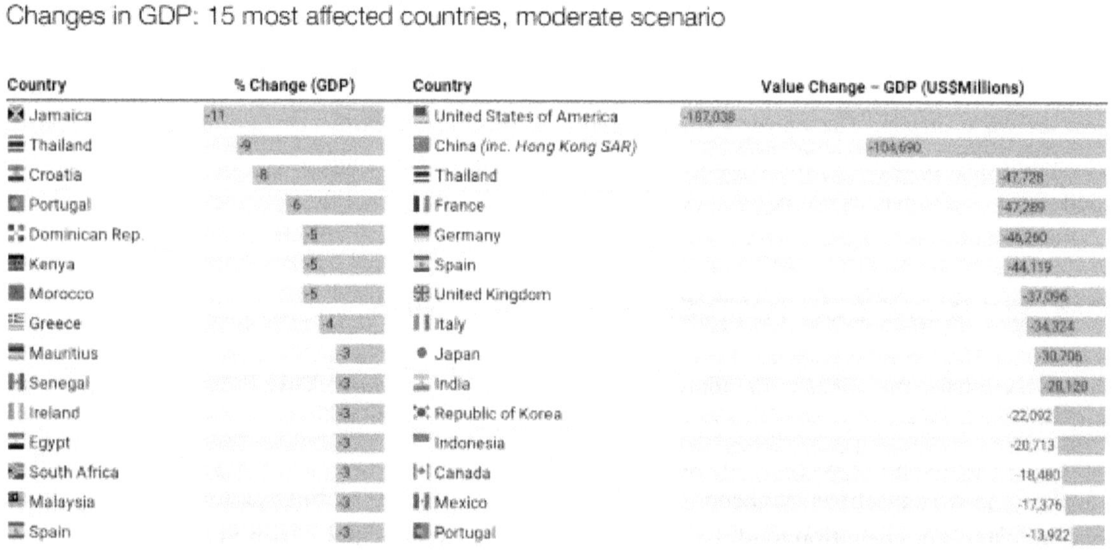

The COVID-19 pandemic has caused noteworthy increases in the unemployment rates of numerous countries. There is a net loss to the economies in many countries due to unemployed labor and capital. Many workers in the tourism industry are jobless because businesses faced negative cashflows and were unable to pay for salaries and wages. It emerged through the discussion that tourism serves as a gateway to employment for women, youth, and rural populations. Thus, these people are left jobless and the chances of them finding employment in other sectors are slim because of the economic downturns. Decreases in employment rates and negative effects on wages are high in countries that rely on the tourism sector.

The transportation sector was equally affected by the pandemic and has been experiencing a reduced travel demand. The transport sector is likely to experience financial challenges in the future due to the reduced travel demand. It emerged through the discussion that consumers still have a fear of travelling abroad and this influences why there is reduced travel demand. Figure 2 below shows the dramatic drop in revenue in the aviation industry as a result of COVID-19. As the virus continued to spread at the beginning of 2020, passenger traffic dropped by 94% compared to 2019 (IATA, 2020). The borders of countries closed at a time when the aviation industry was already losing billions of money. The substantial decline in demand for passenger air transport due to the pandemic serves as a threat for several businesses in the air transport sector. Moreover, millions of jobs are at stake.

Figure 2. Worldwide revenue of passenger-kilometres flown annually
Source: IATA (2020)

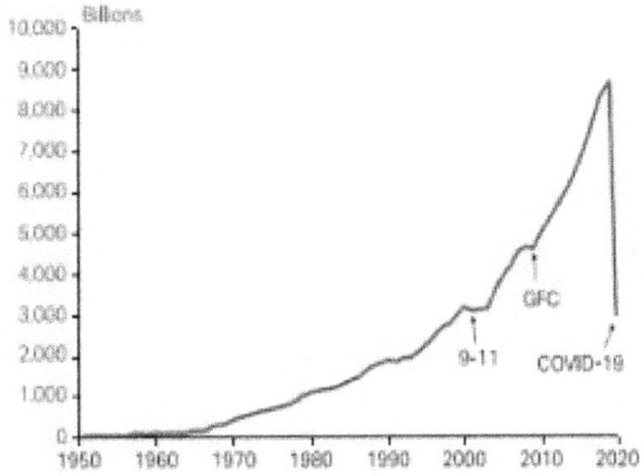

The adverse impacts of the closure of travelling activities due to the COVID-19 pandemic can be seen in the hospitality industry too. Tourism entrepreneurs that operate in the hospitality industry have experienced declines in the demand for their businesses due to the effects of lockdown measures. Entrepreneurs in the hotel sector experienced very little to no revenue during the lockdown period but they continued to face maintenance costs and other expenditures. Thus, these entrepreneurs struggled to pay the salaries of workers, which resulted in several layoffs. Moreover, restaurants were also deeply affected by Covid-19 because they had to temporarily close meaning that no revenue was coming in.

THE IMPACT OF COVID-19 ON TOURISM ENTREPRENEURS

Tourism entrepreneurs in the hotel industry, transportation sector, and restaurant industry were significantly affected by the Covid-19 pandemic. The travel restrictions and the closure of borders that were implemented by governments all over the world led to a 74% decline in international travel in 2020 compared to 2019 (UNWTO, 2021). This decline in international travel contributed to the loss of approximately USD 1.3 trillion in export revenues. Moreover, the Covid-19 pandemic has put between 100 and 120 million direct tourism jobs at risk, many of them in small and medium-sized enterprises. The severance of the impact of Covid-19 on tourism entrepreneurs will be further elaborated.

Hotel Industry

The hotel industry in the world is dealing with an unprecedented crisis due to the novel Covid-19 pandemic (Thornton, 2021). Tourism entrepreneurs that owned hotels could not operate for the longest time. The massive cancellations of hotel reservations due to government protocols resulted in a global decline in hotel occupancy rates and average room rates (Thornton, 2021). This led to the hotel industry losing billions of money worldwide. This has affected the unemployment rate in the hotel industry. According to Aharon, Jacobi, Cohen, Tzur & Qadan (2021), hoteliers currently have less than 68% of their typical employees working full time. With no further assistance from the government, employers will have to further layoff workers.

In South Africa, 32% of booking cancellations occurred before the start of the lockdown and 67.4% of booking cancellations occurred during the lockdown (Sucheran, 2021). By late March 2020, there was a 50% decline in hotel occupancy. During status level 5 lockdown, occupancy declined to under 5% (Statistics South Africa, 2020). Tourism entrepreneurs in the hotel industry faced a significant decline in revenue because the hotels were not operating. This led to the difficulty of paying the salaries and wages of workers. As a result, businesses had to make the tough decision of retrenching workers. Tsogo Sun, a South African hotel, gaming, and entertainment group, confirmed to close 36 hotels in March and April 2020. This was a result of the travel bans that were imposed by the government which caused a total collapse in demand. Moreover, the Covid-19 pandemic resulted in the closure of three well-known hotels in South Africa, Marriott International's Mount Grace Country House and Spa, the Protea Hotel by Marriott Durban Edward, and the Protea Hotel (Wilson, 2020).

Sucheran (2021) reveals that not all hotels were closed during the lockdown. Some hotels continued to operate by serving as quarantine sites for essential workers. These rooms were available at 40% less than the normal hotel rate and were vigorously cleaned and sanitized. Other hotels had to remain open to serve people from other countries who could not go back to their native countries for various reasons. Entrepreneurs in the hotel industry are experiencing revenue losses and recurrent expenditure but legislative payments still have to be made. Bama & Nyikana (2021) argue that the fear of travelling and maintaining social distancing will not fade away after the pandemic is over. This means that the hotel industry will no longer be the same post-Covid-19. Several hotels are currently facing bankruptcy which is widening the unemployment rates in the country. This pandemic has left a long-term bruise on the hotel industry in South Africa.

Transportation Sector

Tourism businesses in the transportation sector were also impacted by the Covid-19 pandemic because they had to take the necessary precautions to sustain local and international mobility (Sucheran, 2017). From rickshaw pullers and tour bus drivers to airlines, tourism entrepreneurs have been economically impacted by this pandemic. Travel and contagious diseases are linked. According to (Trapper, 2013), International travel is considered to be a fast spreader of contagious diseases because it allows people from different populations and different animal species to come into contact and share the same environments. Governments from all over the world have to make the tough decision of closing the borders of their countries. This restricted freedom of movement and encouraged people to stay in their homes as a way to curb the spread of the virus. The closure of borders had a devasting impact on tourism entrepreneurs because the absence of tourists coming into their designated countries meant an absence in their revenue. Essentially, businesses were at a standstill for an undetermined period.

To curb the infection rates, the South African government imposed a travel ban as part of the lockdown regulations. These regulations meant that airlines could not operate which has led to negative cash flows and the reduction of the workforce. The aviation industry of South Africa nearly experienced the collapse of British Airways (operated by Comair) due to COVID-19. The company entered into a business rescue which saw the employees of the airline being reduced from 2200 to 1800. Several people have lost their jobs in the aviation industry due to negative cash flows and the desperation of businesses to cut costs (Dube, 2021). Airlines such as Kulula and South African airways nearly went bankrupt because of the harsh effects of the lockdown. During level 4 of lockdown, airlines were allowed to operate but the prices of flight tickets had increased sharply. This led to a significant drop in customers travelling by plane. The collapse in international travel represents a loss of approximately R55 billion (Luke, 2020). Moreover, a change in consumer spending led to a significant decline in the demand for luxury goods or items that are transported by aircraft.

Restaurants Industry

The restaurant and food industry is an important dimension of tourism because involves trying new cuisines and going to different restaurants locally or internationally (Madeira, Palrao & Mendes, 2021). Tourism entrepreneurs in the restaurant sector were heavily impacted by the COVID-19 pandemic. According to Madeira et al., (2021), more than 110 000 restaurants closed down permanently in 2020 due to financial difficulties. This resulted in the global unemployment rate increased significantly to 6.47%. Madeira et al (2021) further assert that 70% of restaurants will not be able to pay salaries if there is no government intervention. The pandemic led to disruptions to the global and local food supply chains. Farm labour, processing, transport, and logistics have faced unprecedented stress and fluctuating demand. Tourism entrepreneurs in the restaurant sector around the world have struggled because many meat processing plants had to shut down. Those that continued to operate after the restrictions were eased, had to operate in a reduced capacity. Logistics was also affected because restaurants could not import some of the foods they normally import due to the closure of borders.

In South Africa, 40% of restaurants had to close down due to extremely low demands that were caused by the lockdown (Rogerson & Rogerson, 2020). At the beginning of the lockdown, the operations of restaurants were suspended because this sector is not an essential service. During the suspension, entrepreneurs were faced with trouble paying workers. This led to salary cuts and lay-offs. When restaurants continued operations in level 4, more challenges arose because of the disruptions in the supply chain. Entrepreneurs in this industry also face increases in the prices of raw materials from suppliers. Many suppliers tried to cover their expenses by increasing prices and this weighed heavy on entrepreneurs. Already entrepreneurs had additional costs of ensuring that workers are protected from the coronavirus by providing them with protective gear (gloves, masks, sanitisers, face shields, and aprons). Entrepreneurs had to ensure that the work environment adheres to the social distancing protocols because workers share the work environment and facilities. On occasions when a worker contracted the virus, the business had to hire people to sanitize the premises. This served as additional costs to businesses.

COVID-19 AND PESTLE ANALYSIS

The PESTLE analysis is a framework that is used to examine the macro-environment factors that may impact or influence the strategy of an organization (Perera, 2017). PESTLE is an acronym that denotes political, economic, socio-economic, technological, legal, and environmental. These external factors have to be analyzed thoroughly because they may impact the success and performance of an organization. Thus, this framework will be explained in detail because these factors impact tourism entrepreneurs and their businesses.

Political

Political factors refer to the extent to which the government influences the economy or industry. The political environment can affect an industry through factors such as trade tariffs and taxation (Perera, 2017). Governments across the world took drastic measures and changed regulations to protect their citizens from the coronavirus. The tourism sector was impacted by the government regulations of implementing national lockdowns that included border closures. This also halted international trade which is a crucial segment in the tourism sector.

In South Africa, the lockdown included the closure of 30 borders across the country as a strategy to curb the infection rates in the country. International travel constitutes 3% of the economy of the country so the closure of borders meant that the country was experiencing millions of losses. According to Statistics SA (2020), Cape Town is Africa's foremost tourist destination and had approximately 4 million people passing through its entry ports in 2018. Thus, tourism entrepreneurs in Cape Town lost out on making revenue for quite some time during the lockdown. Their businesses were at a standstill, some even at the risk of permanent closure.

Economic Factors

Economic factors essentially refer to the determinants of an economy's performance (Perera, 2017). These determinants generally include economic growth patterns, disposable income, interest rates, inflation rates, and exchange rates. The COVID-19 pandemic led the South African economy to enter a recession phase. This meant that there was a significant decline in economic activity accompanied by an increase in the unemployment rate. Many people were left jobless as a result of this pandemic which meant that they had very little disposable income (Rogerson, 2020). This leaves tourism entrepreneurs in an unfavourable position because people are unable to afford to travel and book hotels. Moreover, a decrease in economic growth leads to a decrease in demand for many goods and services. Tourism entrepreneurs were faced with a decrease in the demand for many tourism activities. For example, people were experiencing little disposable income, which means that they will spend money on basic needs. They are less likely to spend their money on going to restaurants and visiting tourist attraction sites. Even now that the borders for internal travel are open, many people cannot afford to travel because of unemployment.

Socio-Economic Factors

The factors examine the social environment of the market and refer to the traditions, values, attitudes, beliefs, lifestyles, and habits in a population group (Perera, 2017). COVID-19 has generated an enormous amount of fear and anxiety amongst people. This is highly going to impede the recovery of the tourism industry post-COVID-19. Bama & Nyikana (2021) support this statement by stating that the fear of travelling and maintaining social distancing will not fade away after the pandemic is over. A survey that was conducted by Rogerson (2020) revealed that approximately 60% of people are willing to travel outside of their country post-COVID-19. Even these people who are willing to travel are likely to take fewer trips than in the past. Rogerson (2020) reveals that there are two reasons why people will travel lesser than before. Firstly, affordability will continue to be a problem for many people because of unemployment. Secondly, travelling will not be as convenient as before because many airlines have still not financially recovered from the harsh effects of COVID-19. This is why airlines such as Mango are operating fewer flights each day on popular routes. This affects the business of tourism entrepreneurs because if people are scared to travel and visit the country, revenue is lost. Tourism entrepreneurs will have no choice but to accept the new normal and work on ways to adapt strategically.

Technological Factors

Technological factors refer to innovations in technology that affect industries. The innovations in technology can pose as favourable or unfavourable for the operation of a business (Rastogi & Trivedi, 2016). Automation, research development, and technological awareness are some of the elements that are crucial to consider for businesses, especially in this digital era. One of the ways that technological factors influence the tourism sector is through improved transportation. Buses, trains, and planes have become very convenient and comfortable. These systems now come with WIFI connectivity and charging ports which help consumers when travelling long distances. Technology has made travelling efficient in a way that one can buy a ticket within seconds in the comfort of their home. Smartphones have allowed for easy access to information where people can know about places through their phones. Travel blogs have also made people get information easily about certain places in different countries.

Legal Factors

Legal factors refer to the laws and regulations such as customer laws, health and safety laws, import/export laws, and copyright laws that impact businesses (Perera, 2017). Governments across the world made new regulations concerning the health and safety of workers in the COVID-19 environment. Entrepreneurs have to ensure that they prioritize the health and safety of workers at all times. They have to ensure that workers have the appropriate gear to prevent the contraction of the coronavirus. When workers contract the virus, they have the right to isolate themselves at home for 14 days. These workers should still get their salary or wage in full. Moreover, entrepreneurs have to also ensure the premises allow for social distancing measures.

Environmental Factors

Environmental factors refer to the environmental factors such as weather, climate, geographical location, and pollution that may affect the operations of businesses or industries (Perera, 2017). According to Nagaj & Zuromskaite (2021), tourism has harmed the environment for many years due to the carbon dioxide that is caused by airlines. They further state that an increase in tourist arrivals has a negative correlation with increasing carbon dioxide emissions. However, the COVID-19 pandemic has served as a positive impact on the environment in South Africa because carbon emissions and energy consumption have significantly decreased. After all, consumers are not travelling like before. Moreover, the borders of the country were closed during level 5 lockdown, which meant that airlines were not harming the environment. Nagaj & Zuromskaite (2021) assert that tourism accommodation contributes 21% to carbon emissions. Tourism accommodation is a source of pollutant emissions and contributes lots of energy consumption through the usage of air conditioners, heating, and lighting. These emissions have significantly dropped since the emergence of COVID-19.

SUSTAINABILITY OF TOURISM ENTREPRENEURS

According to Sharma, Thomas & Paul (2021) digitization is transforming the tourism business models and processes to greater heights. Sharma et al (2021) added that digitization helps with creating new opportunities for tourism entrepreneurs for them to have access to new markets and upgrade their position in global tourism. Moreover, it creates ways in which entrepreneurs can deliver tourism services which is crucial in cases of unforeseen events like the Covid-19 pandemic. Thus, tourism entrepreneurs need to leverage their digital technologies to be able to sustain themselves in the industry. For example, tourism entrepreneurs that sell jewellery and artwork can create apps that will enable customers to have a virtual experience with their products and purchase them online.

The second way that tourism entrepreneurs can sustain themselves in the industry is by redefining their products to reach new categories. The objective of this strategy is to expand the product opportunity into previously unreachable categories (Sharma et al, 2021). Through this strategy, entrepreneurs can retain existing customers while at the same time attracting new customers from another category. This also creates a competitive advantage. For example, an entrepreneur that sells fast food can create a menu that is specifically designed for vegans. This will attract vegan customers immensely because several other restaurants keep their vegan food and non-vegan food on one menu. Thus, vegan customers will feel like they are being valued and considered.

STRATEGIES FOR TOURISM ENTREPRENEURS

Tourism entrepreneurs should invest in research and development (R&D) which is essentially a set of innovative activities that are undertaken to develop new products and services and improve existing ones. R&D is vital for entrepreneurs because it accelerates the creation of products and services that optimize the needs of customers, which leads to satisfied customers and more revenue being generated. R&D will be beneficial for the businesses of tourism entrepreneurs because it will lead to cutting marginal costs, which will increase productivity and create a competitive advantage. This is because R&D facilitates the improvement of business processes such as manufacturing processes where businesses will be producing more outputs with fewer inputs. Moreover, entrepreneurs will gain a competitive advantage over their rivals by creating differentiated products that will be difficult for rivalries to imitate. This can lead to profit maximization.

Entrepreneurs also need to implement safety and health programs to improve hygiene standards in tourism sites, hotels, and restaurants. Entrepreneurs should strive to ensure that the health and safety of customers come first at all times. For instance, hotels and restaurants should have automatic soap dispensers because they create more hygienic environments and ensure that the Covid-19 virus transmission is kept at a minimum in establishments.

TECHONLOGICAL STRATGIES FOR TOURSIM ENTREPRENUERS

Tourism entrepreneurs should leverage their technological capabilities to remain successful and competitive in the tourism industry. One way that tourism entrepreneurs can achieve this would be to invest more in productivity-enhancing technologies such as cloud computing, data analytics, and revenue management software. These types of productivity-enhancing technologies are extremely beneficial for businesses because they ensure a lesser cost of production and more effective use of available resources (Loss, 2019). For instance, cloud computing allows businesses to respond to the needs of customers quicker than competitors. Moreover, cloud computing enables employees to access data whenever and wherever they are, which enables mobility and remote working.

Tourism entrepreneurs should invest in or improve their existing Information and Communication Technology (ICT), which includes all digital technology that assists businesses in using information. The development of ICT enables various aspects of the business to be performed more efficiently and successfully. ICT is crucial for tourism entrepreneurs because it can enhance communication and social networks immensely. Social media platforms such as WhatsApp, Facebook, Instagram, and Twitter enable businesses to communicate effectively with customers and advertise their products and services. These social media platforms create an effective communication channel where customers can express their concerns or challenges about certain products or services. Entrepreneurs can also use these social media networks to gain more insights into the needs of customers and work on how best to satisfy those needs. By doing this, entrepreneurs will create innovative products that add value to customers. This will create customer satisfaction and will lead to profit maximization.

GLOBAL TRANSFORMATION WITHIN THE TOURISM INDUSTRY

According to UNTWO (2021), the global transformation within the tourism sector has much to do with digitization. Loss (2019) further asserted that the tourism sector was one of the sectors to digitalize business processes on a global scale by making flight and hotel bookings online to become a digital pioneer. However, new digital transformation trends are crucial within the tourism sector since the Covid-19 disruptions. A digitalized tourism sector is extremely beneficial globally because it innovates new products and services and generates new business opportunities to ensure the continued competitiveness, growth, and sustainability of the sector. Wilson (2021) added that digitalization has the potential to boost innovation, generate economic and environmental efficiencies and increase productivity in the globalized tourism sector. The main objective is to achieve the Sustainability Development Goals of the United Nations and the global development community. Wilson (2021) asserted that the use of technologies including the 'Internet of Things (IoT), artificial intelligence, augmented and virtual reality and location-based services are changing the space of the tourism sector as it is creating more attractive, efficient, and environmentally sustainable tourism. For instance, artificial intelligence is changing the dynamic of customer service where a chatbot can deliver fast responses to the problems or queries of customers.

RECOMMENDATIONS

- Governments need to provide financial relief for businesses that are in need. This financial relief will be extremely beneficial for the businesses that were on the verge of permanent closure. It will also allow the airports to prepare the necessary technology in ensuring biosafety control at the airport. For example, contactless technology will ensure touchless travel.

- Entrepreneurs need to invest more in eco-friendly innovations. This is crucial for the environment because less energy that is consumed decreases greenhouse gas emissions that are facilitated by the accommodation facilities.
- The governments need to work with the tourism sectors to revive tourism successfully. Governments also need to rebuild tourist confidence and encourage innovation and investment for resilient and sustainable tourism.
- The tourism sector should look into accelerating digital transformation. This can be achieved through creating virtual tourism experiences where tourists can have the opportunity to experience a location through images, videos, or other multimedia.
- Entrepreneurs together with the government need to promote domestic tourism. Tourism entrepreneurs need to support their host countries now more than ever. Local businesses need to recover all the money that was once lost and operative successfully again.
- Entrepreneurs need to implement safety and health programs to improve hygiene standards in tourism sites, hotels, and restaurants. Hoteliers can invest in cloud technology for a better project management system. This type of virtual technology will help entrepreneurs operate their business from anywhere and will also assist in making food orders efficiently and contactless meal deliveries.
- Businesses can take this time to learn more about finance. Finance is one of the most important business skills that is needed by every entrepreneur. Thus, having more knowledge of finance will assist the business in managing their wealth and how to deal with financial challenges that may arise.

FUTURE RESEARCH

Future researchers should investigate the opportunities that the Covid-19 pandemic created for tourism entrepreneurs. As much as the pandemic caused incontrovertible suffering for the tourism industry, it also created some opportunities and realizations for tourism entrepreneurs. Thus, future researchers should elaborate on this field.

CONCLUSION

This chapter has fully evaluated how tourism entrepreneurs were affected by the Covid-19 pandemic. It was discovered how tourism entrepreneurs in the hotel, transportation and restaurant industries suffered from unprecedented challenges, mainly stemming from the lack of revenues. Governments across the world implemented lockdowns as a way to curb the spread of the virus. These lockdowns involved the closure of borders which created a riffling effect where the tourism industry was detrimentally affected. With no tourist activities, the tourism industry was left shattered. The global unemployment rate increased to 6.47% in 2020 as a result of the COVID-19 pandemic. Entrepreneurs were forced to lay off workers because of the inability to pay for their salaries and wages. The PESTLE analysis further illustrates the impacts of COVID-19 on tourism entrepreneurs. The chapter also discovered how tourism entrepreneurs can sustain themselves in the industry. This was important because it gave the study a different lens on how tourism entrepreneurs can improve their businesses and recover in cases of unforeseen events. Recommendations were offered to help tourism entrepreneurs recover from the effects of this pandemic and remain competitive and successful in the market. Future researchers should investigate the opportunities that the Covid-19 pandemic created for tourism entrepreneurs.

REFERENCES

Abbas, J., Mubeen, R., & Terhemba, I. (2021). Exploring the impacts of COVID-19 on tourism: transformational potential and implications for a sustainable of the travel and leisure industry. *Current Research in Behavioural Sciences, 2*, 130-210.

Aharon, D. Y., Jacobi, A., Cohen, E., Tzur, J., & Qadan, M. (2021). COVID-19, government measures and hospitality industry performance. *PLoS One*, *16*(8), 1–4. doi:10.1371/journal.pone.0255819 PMID:34358283

Bama, H. K. N., & Nyikana, S. (2021). The Effects of COVID-19 on Future Domestic Travel Intentions in South Africa: A Stakeholder Perspective. *African Journal of Hospitality, Tourism and Leisure*, *10*(1), 179–193. doi:10.46222/ajhtl.19770720-94

Camilleri, M. A. (2017). The Tourism Industry: An Overview. DOI: doi:10.1007/978-3-319-49849-21

Dube, K. (2021). Implications of COVID-19 Induced Lockdown on the South African Tourism Industry and Prospects for Recovery. *African Journal of Hospitality, Tourism and Leisure*, *10*(1), 270–287. doi:10.46222/ajhtl.19770720-99

IATA. (2020). *The impact of COVID-19 on aviation*. iata.org

Lock, S. (2021). *Global tourism industry - statistics & facts*. Retrieved November 19, 2021, from https://www.statista.com/topics/962/global-tourism/#dossierKeyfigures

Loss, L. (2019). *Tourism has generated 20% of total world employment since 2013*. Retrieved November 10, 2021, from https://www.tourism-review.com/tourism-industry-is-the-pillar-of-economy-news11210

Luke, R. (2020). The impact of COVID-2019 on transport in South Africa. *Journal of Transport and Supply Chain Management*, *14*, 1. doi:10.4102/jtscm.v14i0.545

Madeira, A., Palrao, T., & Mendes, A. S. (2021). The Impact of Pandemic Crisis on the Restaurant Business. *Sustainability*, *13*(1), 1–13. doi:10.3390u13010040

Martins, F. S. & Serra, F. A. R. (2018). Secondary Data in Research – Uses and Opportunities. *Revista Ibero-Americana de Estratégia. 17*(1), 1-4. . doi:10.5585/ijsm.v17i4.2723

Nagaj, R., & Žuromskaite, B. (2014). Tourism in the Era of Covid-19 and Its Impact on the Environment. *Energies*, *14*(7), 2000. Advance online publication. doi:10.3390/en14072000

Perera, R. (2017). *The PESTLE analysis*. Nerdynaut.

Rastogi, N. I. T. A. N. K., & Trivedi, M. K. (2016). PESTLE technique–a tool to identify external risks in construction projects. *International Research Journal of Engineering and Technology*, *3*(1), 384–388.

Rogerson, C. M. (2020). COVID-19 and Tourism Spaces of Vulnerability in South Africa. *Journal of Hospitality. Tourism and Leisure*, *9*(4), 382–401. doi:10.46222/ajhtl.19770720-26

Rogerson, C. M., & Rogerson, J. M. (2020). COVID-19 tourism impacts in South Africa: Government and industry responses. *GeoJournal of Tourism and Geosites*, *31*(3), 1083–1091. doi:10.30892/gtg.31321-544

Sharma, G. D., Thomas, A., & Paul, J. (2021). Reviving tourism industry post-COVID-19. *Tourism Management Perspectives*, *37*(1), 67–72. doi:10.1016/j.tmp.2020.100786 PMID:33391988

Statistics South Africa (STATS SA). (2020). *Tourist accommodation*. Retrieved September 7, 2021, from http://www.statssa.gov.za/publications/P6410/P6410May2020.pdf

Sucheran, R. (2021). Preliminary Economic Impact of the COVID-19 pandemic on the Hotel Sector in South Africa. *African Journal of Hospitality, Tourism and Leisure*, *10*(11), 115–130. doi:10.46222/ajhtl.19770720-90

Tapper, M. (2013). Emerging viral diseases and infectious disease risks. *Haemophilia*, *12*(1), 3–7. PMID:16445811

Thornton, G. (2021). Hotel industry: Navigating the impact of COVID-19. Surviving, adapting, and preparing for the new normal. *Japan-Hospitals*, *10*, 5–9.

United Nations Conference on Trade and Development. (2020). *COVID-19 and tourism*. Retrieved September 5, 2021, from https://unctad.org/system/files/official-document/ditcinf2020d3_en.pdf

UNTWO. (2021). *2020: Worst year in tourism history with 1 billion fewer international arrivals*. Retrieved November 19, 2021, from https://www.unwto.org/news/2020-worst-year-in-tourism-history-with-1-billion-fewer-international-arrivals

Wilson, N. (2020). *Iconic hotels Mount Grace in Magaliesburg & Durban's Edward to close: Times Live*. Retrieved September 7, 2021, from https://www.timeslive.co.za/news/southafrica/2020-06-19-marriott-international-shuts-iconic-mount-grace-hotel-inmagaliesburg/

Chapter 13
Local Lessons During a Global Crisis:
Inclusive Entrepreneurial Solutions to Supply Chain and Production Deficits

Ronald Coleman Williams
Coppin State University, USA

Will Holman
Open Works, Baltimore, USA

Jeff Fuchs
Neovista Consulting, USA

ABSTRACT

The impact of the COVID-19 global pandemic has been pervasive. From the first report by the World Health Organization (WHO) of a "mysterious pneumonia" sickening dozens in Wuhan, China to 5,680,741 deaths, every social and economic system has been challenged. This descriptive case study utilizes a process of analytic induction to examine Makers Unite, a collaborative personal protection equipment (PPE) production project spearheaded by Open Works, a makerspace in Baltimore, Maryland. The organization produced 28,270 face shields in 56 days, averaging a production rate of 496 per day, serving over 100 clients, and resulting in a contract to produce face shields for meatpacking inspectors. The project included six full-time staff members, five temporary part-time staff members, a network of 388 volunteers and 3D printers, and two partner organizations. The study reveals best practices for establishing Lean small-scale manufacturing, developing institutional trust, community collaboration, and developing a more inclusive, agile supply chain in healthcare equipment production.

DOI: 10.4018/978-1-6684-4322-4.ch013

INTRODUCTION

Lack of preparedness is one of the greatest threats to the United States' ability to mitigate the impact and recover from a public health crisis of the magnitude of the Covid-19 global pandemic. The high rates of uninsured, the high out-of-pocket costs of healthcare compared to other countries, having fewer doctors and hospital beds per capita than most other developed countries, and having a woefully inadequate stockpile of Personal Protective Equipment (PPE), "specialized clothing or equipment worn by an employee for protection against infectious materials" (United States Department of Labor, 2020) are all vulnerabilities that have been exposed by the pandemic. Critical equipment such as gloves, gowns/aprons, masks, and respirators were nearly exhausted as of April 1, 2020.

The mobilization and "permissionless innovation" demonstrated by local, small-scale manufacturers was phenomenal. Acknowledging that their efforts would be insufficient to overcome the shortage of PPE, makerspace facilities and informal volunteer networks across the nation began self-organizing to produce and distribute whatever their equipment and human resources would allow. Often, the efforts have been performed despite the threat to the financial futures of all. Their collaborative energies also demonstrated an ability to infuse agility in the PPE supply chain that was shown to be severely vulnerable to existing approaches to manufacturing and offshore dependencies. Their ability to mobilize networks of volunteers and resources, provide coordination and guidance to suppliers and healthcare organizations, and implement production protocols that meet stringent sanitation standards will provide valuable insights regarding post-pandemic industry practices and the revitalization of domestic manufacturing.

The Open Works' effort produced: 28,270 total face shields produced in56 working days, an average of 496 per day, for over 100 clients, utilizing 388 total volunteer printers.

Figure 1. Open Works PPE Production

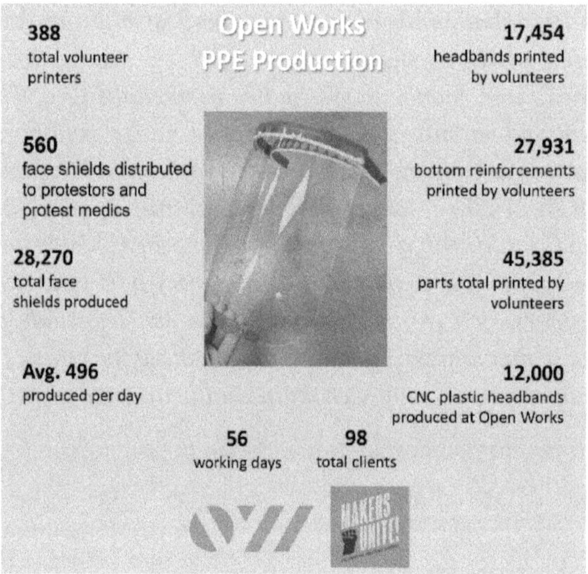

There are a lot of lessons to be learned from the global pandemic that may provide insight into how to advance the progress of entrepreneurs from underserved communities. As the means of production are made more accessible because of advancements in technology and additive manufacturing techniques such as 3D printing, there are more opportunities for participation because of cost reductions. Community-centric facilities and organizations such as makerspaces provide great potential to serve as access hubs for those who have been historically excluded from equitable, inclusive participation in the economic system.

This case study: 1. describes the relational elements present in production activities during a healthcare crisis, 2. explores the value of Lean manufacturing practices in small-scale manufacturing when experiencing supply-chain deficits, 3. examines community collaboration networks and volunteer mobilization as a means of meeting unexpected supply demands, and 4. and investigates the potential for makerspaces to serve as models of inclusion and opportunity for underserved populations.

LITERATURE REVIEW

The case Open Works response to the COVID-19 PPE shortage provides insight into small-scale, local manufacturing and the infusion of Agile practices into a product supply chain. Four streams of research literature provided the background for analyzing the case. Searches resulted in the literature on institutional trust and social cohesion, volunteerism during a societal crisis, community and placemaking, and Lean Manufacturing and supply chain management.

"Institutional trust refers to expectations that rely on formal controls, including formalized policies and practices" (Shantz et. al., 2018, p.368). Those affected by formalized policies and practice develop confidence in delivery based on consistent adherence to controls. The resulting trust facilitates collaborative potential during projects. While it may be distinguished from relational or interpersonal trust, institutional or organizational trust is part of the currency that enables stakeholders to establish the openness required to optimize collaborative efforts when urgency is required. The sense of common mission reduces relational barriers that may exist in more threatening conditions. As we face the most significant public health crisis in a century and the most devastating economic crisis since the Great Depression, the pandemic enhances the potential for mission-driven collaboration between individuals, institutions, and community partners.

There is little doubt that social conditions resulting from shifting global economies, the decline of the manufacturing base in the United States (U.S.), and a lack of viable economic drivers to replace manufacturing create conditions likely to trigger social and institutional trust deficits. Several studies have emerged describing the decline in institutional trust, the loss of "social cohesion" and social collateral, and their relationship with innovation and entrepreneurship (Andrews, Jilke, and Van de Walle, 2014; Kwon, Heflin, and Ruefc, 2013; Audretsch, Seitz, and Rouch, 2017). The analysis appears to have implications for developing effective trust frameworks for institutions of all types (e.g., political, educational, religious, community, corporate, and others). For example, the study by Andrews et al. (2014) suggests that institutional trust has a significant effect on perceptions of social cohesion in European political systems, implying that institutional trust influences tensions between different social actors and reduces confidence in the performance and policies of the government. On the other hand, Kwon et al. (2013) referenced a broader focus of analysis on the elements of social capital. Their findings question traditional assertions that social capital at an individual level, social trust, and membership in community organizations increase the probability that a community member is engaged in entrepreneurial or innovative activity. However, the relationship between entrepreneurial activities, innovation, and social trust is supported by other findings suggesting that "social trust is important" because in the tolerance-innovation relationship, "it seems that people who trust each other engage in knowledge spillover and innovation activity" (Audretsch et al. 2017).

In 2018, Strandh and Eklund utilized the Disaster Research Center (DRC) typology as an analytical tool (Brouillette & Quarantelli, 1971; Dynes, 1970; Dynes & Quarantelli, 1968) to differentiate between types of responses to disasters and different kinds of voluntary action. Recognizing the pattern in decades of research that describes volunteers in such terms as "affiliated," those associated with organizations, or "unaffiliated," those who act spontaneously and are not associated with any recognized disaster response agency (p. 330), the researchers identified four categories of volunteers: 1. established organizations such as police, ambulance, fire services, or other first responders, 2. expanding organizations such as large relief firms (e.g., Red Cross or Salvation Army), 3. extending organizations whose members generally have limited experience of disaster response, and 4. emergent organizations that did not exist before the disaster. For purposes of this study and contributing to improving supply-chain agility through local production, the focus is on the continuum between extending and emergent organizations.

Prosocial behavior is defined as the act of helping someone in need. While researchers such as Latane and Darley (1970) identified steps an individual must go through in the decision to help a stranger in need, others have also noted that assistance is more likely when actors personally know each other (Hortensius, 2018). The following are part of the thought process when volunteering to assist someone: 1. Notice what is happening, 2. Interpret the event as an emergency, 3. Experience feelings of responsibility, 4. Believe that they have the skills to help, and 5. Make a conscious choice to offer assistance. This decision-making process is consistent with other research showing that "connections to other people, in the form of psychological sense of community, are critical in predicting, if not spurring, volunteering and activism" (Omoto & Packard, 2016, p.287).

There is also a moral element to volunteerism such as that discussed by Stukas et al. (2016). The researchers reveal that "Creating a community around a moral principle or on behalf of a group that deserves assistance on moral grounds may be one way to attract and reinforce those with similar beliefs" (p. 250). Values-based community involvement is important to "building a sense of community around important issues that are intrinsically motivating to people with prosocial values and relevant attitudes and providing them with behavioral pathways for expressing them may be a more viable way to promote community involvement" (p. 249).

Volunteers, small-scale manufacturers, suppliers, customers, and other stakeholders organically build a "sense of community" (McMillan & Chavis, 1986, p. 9) that facilitates a focus on crisis response. According to the researchers, a sense of community is defined by four dimensions: "1. Membership – a feeling of belongingness or relatedness to the organization or community, 2. Influence – the feeling of making a difference in the group and mattering as a member, 3. Needs fulfillment – the perception that members will meet one another's needs, and resources will be shared through these relationships, and 4. Emotional connection – a shared emotional connection or experience, through history or common places" (Lardier et al., 2018, p. 1063). Omoto and Packard (2016) also explored psychological dynamics associated with a "sense of community" and found that "a key driver of social action appears to be perceived connections to people who share a common interest, commitment, or concern" (p. 285). Perceived common relational identity with other actors was shown to have a more significant influence on volunteerism than other motivating factors.

Womack and Jones identified five Lean manufacturing principles (i.e., value, value streams, flow, pull, and perfection) in their original work. In 2014, Herzog and Tonchia identified eight crucial areas associated with Lean thinking based on a synthesis of literature regarding assessment and measurement of the degree of Lean implementation within existing manufacturing systems. The eight areas include: "1. value concept and customers, 2. value stream mapping (VSM), 3. pull/kanban and flow (i.e., a process scheduling system that tells you what to produce, when to produce it, and how much to produce for the next phase of the production line), 4. waste elimination, 5. productive maintenance, 6. just-in-time (JIT), 7. employee involvement, and 8. the development of excellent Lean suppliers" (p. 798). With a similar emphasis on the implementation of Lean manufacturing methodologies, Anholon and Sano (2016) also identify several critical processes during the implementation of Lean projects. Their findings include: 1. procurement, 2. stakeholder, 3. communication, 4. human resources, and 5. risk management as critical in the implementation of Lean procedures. Additional value may be found in the results of the Anholon and Sano study because of their use of the Project Management Institute, Project Management Body of Knowledge (PMBoK).

While the streams of literature provide insight into the origins of intellectual inquiry associated with institutional trust and social cohesion, volunteerism during a societal crisis, community and placemaking, and Lean Manufacturing and supply chain management, there is a lack of synthesis that addresses the growing need for integrated learning paradigms. New epistemological contributions and artifacts that address learning paradigms suitable for accelerating the economic inclusion of underserved communities are needed. Systems-oriented, integrative frameworks are not new, socio-technical theory for example (Cherns, 1976; Emery, 1959; Hanna, 1988; Mohrman & Winby, 2018; Pasmore, 2001; Trist, 1981). However, there is an opportunity to integrate entrepreneurship with other discipline-specific concepts such as that done with "ingepreneurship" (Williams & Klugh, 2017). This gap in the literature may be partially closed through exploratory, descriptive analysis of models that will lead to theory-building. Opportunities are also present in producing peer-reviewed artifacts based on the synthesis of scientific, technical, entrepreneurial, social, and affective areas of study with an emphasis on improving positive economic mobility.

The literature provides an artifactual foundation for the study of local manufacturing during a healthcare crisis. The literature also establishes a context for understanding the importance of the analysis and has implications for the post-pandemic economy. The study provides answers to the following questions: 1. What is the role of trust in organizing a response to the inability to meet critical product demand during a healthcare crisis? 2. How are Lean Manufacturing principles applied in a makerspace in response to a critical product shortage during a healthcare crisis? 3. What practices during a healthcare crisis may lead to greater post-crisis supply chain agility? 4. What crisis response practices facilitate makerspace integration with the existing and emerging manufacturing sector?

LOCAL SOLUTIONS TO GLOBAL SUPPLY CHAIN PROBLEMS

Open Works is a state-of-the-art, 34,000 square foot facility in the heart of Baltimore City with a simple mission to "...make tools, technology, and the knowledge to use them accessible to all" and a long-term vision to "...rebuild the regional manufacturing economy from the grassroots up" (Open Works Baltimore, 2019). The operation has experienced growth since opening in October of 2016. Before the COVID-19 pandemic, the facility was equipped with a 3D printing bot farm with four Ultimaker 2 extended 3D printers, two Inventables Carvey desktop precision CNC routers, four computer workstations, and a filament recycler. The digital fabrication lab includes advanced large-format machines that can cut through plywood, plastic, and soft metals with hair-splitting accuracy, such as the 4'x 8' Laguna Swift with vacuum bed hold-down, two 4'x 8' bed ShopBot PRS Alpha CNC routers, a Tormach Personal CNC 1100 mill, two laser cutters, an 18" x 24" bed, and a laser cutter, 28" x 40 bed. The metal shop, woodworking shop, computer lab, industrial cut-and-sew studio, digital media studio, and electronics shop are equipped with an equally impressive list of tools made available through membership, education programs, special events, and collaborative community relationships.

The mission is supported by funders, including its primary sponsor, The Robert W. Deutch Foundation. The organization has also amassed an impressive list of 17 partners over the past two years that participate in an array of collaborative projects. The facility is 100% owned by the Baltimore Arts Realty Corporation (BARCO), a non-profit organization established in 2012 by the Robert W. Deutsch Foundation to create working spaces for Baltimore's growing community of artists, performers, makers, and artisans.

A case study method of analysis is most appropriate when researchers seek answers to "what" questions for exploratory analysis. "How" and "why" questions are best when asked about a contemporary set of events or events over which the researcher has little or no control (Yin, 2018, p.11) such as the Open Works response to the COVID-19 PPE shortage. Data was collected from multiple sources (i.e., journalistic media, social media, documentation, website content, meeting observations, and key person interviews) and organized in a database establishing a chain of evidence from the research questions through to the case study conclusions (Yin, 1989). An interview guide with open-ended questions was used to gather data from key stakeholders.

Analysis was conducted using a process of analytic induction in which hypotheses were generated from themes in the data. Iterative patterns were examined as a means of diminishing alternative explanations (Rossman, 1995).

Case Analysis

Three dominant themes emerged from the analysis of Open Works that provide insight into inclusive, entrepreneurial practices during a global healthcare crisis. The themes include Trust-Inspired Volunteerism, Leaning In — A Process for Standing Up a Crisis-Resistant Supply Chain, and Values-Inspired Mobilization.

Trust-Inspired Volunteerism

"Trust is one of the fundamental factors that affect the wealth of nations. When the interactions are improved by trust, this will make investments, financial markets, public expenditures, institutions, regulations, and firms more effective and development-friendly" (Gur 2015, p. 121). Trust involves the acceptance of mutual vulnerability and the presence or absence of trust often becomes more apparent in a time of crisis. Open Works is a trusted nonprofit in the Baltimore Greenmount West community and a facilitator of the institutional and interpersonal exchanges that prove to be valuable in a crisis as well as in more routine conditions.

The trust-inspired confidence placed in the organization contributed to the success of the response to the face shield shortage. Essentially, there was institutional trust that existed among potential volunteers before the outbreak of the virus. Since its launch in October 2016, the organization closely adhered to its mission of "...making tools, technology, and the knowledge to use them accessible to all (Open Works, 2020)." The effort to fulfill this mission required extensive outreach and the cultivation of community relationships. While the benefits of developing substantial external relationships are not always immediately realized, a crisis may cause them to become more immediately evident. The value of Open Works' external relationships was realized in the emergence of: 1. Intersubjective volunteerism, 2. Transformative volunteerism, 3. Hyper-volunteerism, and 4. Resource sharing.[1] The convergence of relationship-building practices, organizational trust among internal stakeholders, and crisis-driven opportunities resulted in volunteerism that advanced the goals of the project.

The organization is well known for being a place where people can learn, grow and practice new skills such as 3D printing, textiles work, digital fabrication, and more.

Staff from the makerspace have called on local commercial institutions, nonprofits, and hobbyists representing more than 200 3D printers to produce extra face shields for local health care organizations. As of Monday, Open Works had packed and sold 500 units of the printed and assembled shields. The University of Maryland St. Joseph Medical Center, Lorien Health Services, and Virginia Cancer Specialists have been the largest buyers so far.

Intentional, sustained outreach and relationship-building produced tangible and intangible benefits when the healthcare crisis emerged. Open Works was able to capture the momentum of intersubjective volunteerism. Intersubjectivity is a term originally coined by the philosopher Edmund Husserl (1859–1938) to describe the "interchange of thoughts and feelings, both conscious and unconscious, between two persons or subjects, as facilitated by empathy" (Cooper-White, 2014, p.17). Intersubjectivity may also be described as an agreement without a conversation.

The volunteer response represented a collective decision that expanded resources from 13 3D printers to 388 volunteers with access to almost 1,000 3D printers. Organizing organically because of the call to action, the volunteers represented a solution to a production bottleneck created by insufficient printing capacity and allowed the project to scale. This occurred on an institutional and individual level, showing evidence of inter-institutional trust as well as trust demonstrated by individuals responding to the Open Works request for assistance.

On March 21, 2020, Open Works put out a call on social media to mobilize 3D printers in Maryland to help manufacture open-source face shields for healthcare workers combatting COVID-19. Five days later, the first face shields were packaged for distribution. This extraordinary, ongoing effort relies on a remarkable crowd-sourced supply chain and strong local partners.

Dan Durand, chief innovation officer at LifeBridge Health system, said the director of technology at the Gilman School, Tye Campbell, recently reached out to him offering to donate the Baltimore institution's eight 3D printers for the health system to use. That connection led to others with private schools in the area, and now, LifeBridge has added 19 donated printers to its in-house "3D Printing Farm."

Transformative volunteerism "helps promote the incorporation of proposals for action and social transformation, which turns the volunteer into an agent of change (Ortega et al., 2018, p.34)." This type of volunteerism enables participants to reach beyond their immediate circumstances and become increasingly pro-social with a greater capacity for empathy. The trajectory of collective engagement is changed to one that promotes a cause greater than the perceived needs of individuals. The once-in-a-century threat of a global pandemic that led to the infection of millions provided an opportunity for transformative volunteerism to occur. Open Works was able to capture the growing desire to "do something" to counter the threat.

I was like this is the moment to ask not what your country can do for you but what you can do for your country. That was my moment! I was like I'm a sewer! Yes, I can do this! And I just started sewing. I've made probably about 3 dozen masks so far," said Jillian Collins, a Harford County mom and a Baltimore County teacher.

I'm hoping other people find the goodness in them to do the same thing because times of pandemic and fear bring out the best and worst in people and our country is made up of some of the best of people.

Conditions that produced a sense of collective threat also inspired volunteerism that far exceeded responses that occur during more routine conditions, a kind of hyper-volunteerism. Concerns that may prevent volunteers from participating were exceeded by the motivation to assist, and normal barriers to trust were diminished.

There was also evidence of heightened resource sharing that may be attributable to the presence of a common threat and concern for the wellbeing of the community. Creating a relationally healthy community is a core value adopted by Open Works from inception and it catalyzed transformative and hyper-volunteerism. For example, transparency is one of the trust-building practices exhibited by Open Works throughout the COVID-19 response.[2] The Maker United website evolved into a rich source of information concerning the project, including financial data, how to participate, process, design specifications, and other vital information. The degree of resource and information sharing contributed to an already high level of institutional trust. Transparency is not an unfamiliar practice for non-profit organizations such as Open Works. However, it is also acknowledged that not all makerspaces are established as non-profit organizations. Regardless of the corporate structure of the makerspace, transparency helps eliminate barriers to institutional trust and added value during the crisis by providing an outlet for intrinsically motivated volunteer vibrancy.

The response to the postings was so overwhelming that Holman needed to create a Google Form to better organize those who reached out. Within six hours of the original post, Open Works had nearly 100 volunteers that collectively had 250 printers, nearly 20 times the 13 that the maker space had on its own.

I was amazed at how quickly everyone pulled together to help with this project," said Sullivan. "In less than a week, three community members from different departments started producing face shields and utilizing Loyola's resources to aid our local health care facilities in a time of crisis. This speaks to the heart of our mission at Loyola to be people for others. The generosity of spirit, time, and talent shown by Matthew, Yanko, and Billy really captures Loyola's Jesuit values.

(Makers Unite!, 2020)

Leaning In — A Process for Creating a Crisis-Resistant Supply Chain

When there is a geographically based crisis, such as a weather event (i.e., hurricane, flood, tsunamis, etc.), there are organizations and networks of volunteers to respond. For example, disaster relief centers (DRCs) are the retailers of disaster relief supply chains. Also known as Points of Distribution (PODs), disaster relief centers are ad hoc distribution sites set up in shopping mall parking lots, schools, churches, or warehouses where relief supplies are distributed to beneficiaries. Perhaps the most significant challenge faced by DRCs is the convergence of volunteers and material resources, and the mobilization of people and supplies into affected areas following large-scale disaster events (Abualkhair, Lodree, & Davis, 2020). Supply chain scholars study beneficiary arrival and service times, donation arrival and service times, and volunteer arrival and abandonment times from food banks to faith-based warehouses (Urrea, Pedraza-Martinez, & Besiou, 2019). Organizations face high variability in volunteer experience and in volunteer arrivals, for instance, to prepare orders in storehouses. Heterogeneous volunteer experience complicates the allocation of volunteers to tasks because inexperienced volunteers can delay operations and do more harm than good in their attempts to help (Jenkin, 2015).

In the case of the Open Works COVID-19 response, there were no existing DRCs or established networks of volunteers for crisis response. The global expanse of the pandemic and the gap in the PPE supply chain were unique in scope and circumstances (i.e., the need for medical worker supplies, rather than care for disaster victims). Not only does this case consider the impact on beneficiaries of the PPE, but also how to manufacture a product in the absence of formal business networks dedicated to crisis response. Open Works, the distribution site, used Lean Manufacturing principles to quickly implement a functional continuous improvement process.

Lean Manufacturing is based on principles from Japanese culture and philosophy that influence the business practices of firms like Toyota. The company that eventually became Toyota Motor Corporation was founded in 1933 by Sakichi Toyoda who had committed 43 years to develop and perfect the production of looms (Toyota Industries Corporation, 2020). Understanding the foundational philosophy of Lean Thinking is helpful in efforts to understand the Open Works response to the COVID-19 crisis, particularly the Japanese concept of *keiretsu* which translates to mean "group" or "system" (Moffatt, 2020). The type of keiretsu most relevant to the Open Works response to the pandemic is "vertical keiretsu," or an industrial keiretsu which ties suppliers, manufacturers, and distributors of an industry together in partnership and allows all participants to detect, adjust, and respond to events such as an unexpected crisis in a short amount of time without losing focus on its mission, vision, and core values.

In the last 24 hours (two days after a call to action), we have developed sanitation protocols, written build instructions, ordered materials, printed our first prototypes, and partnered with We the Builders (wethebuilders.com) to host the build using their unique part ID system that will create a chain of custody for each part. A build instruction packet, waiver, and sign-up instructions will go out to those who have signed up later today. If you've already started printing, don't stop. If you haven't started, standby.

Y'ALL WE DID IT! 141 SHIELDS TWO DAYS AHEAD OF SCHEDULE (four days after a call to action)!! Keep the parts coming! (Hard to take a triumphant group pic while maintaining social distance.) 💪💪💪💪💪💪💪💪 Can't send us parts? Help us out at www.openworksbmore.org/support-us/ @ Open Works

Five Lean principles (i.e., value, value streams, flow, pull, and perfection) provided a framework for analysis with an emphasis on value stream development.

Open Works' supply chain created value for healthcare workers by providing supply (Livington, Desai, & Berkwits, 2020). Value was defined by customers in the context of a global pandemic and resulting shortages of life-saving equipment. The value rose as the threat increased and those who were able responded by producing what was proven valuable based on customer demand. While insufficient supply and increased demand are expected to result in higher prices according to traditional economic models, sensitivity to the crisis and the needs of current and future partners contributed to the use of pricing models more consistent with Lean Thinking "target costing" (Lean Enterprise Institute, 2020). Target costing refers to "the development and production cost that a product cannot exceed if the customer is to be satisfied with the value of the product while the manufacturer obtains an acceptable return on its investment. This was the practice developed by Toyota for its small supplier group with which it has had long-term relations. Because there is no market price available from taking bids or conducting an auction, Toyota and its suppliers determine a correct/fair cost (and price) for a supplied item by estimating what the customer thinks the item is worth and then working backward to take out cost (waste) to meet the price while preserving Toyota and supplier profit margins." As in the Open Works case, the clear objective was providing value to the customer, which had been altered by the prevailing crisis, by minimizing waste in the production process. Financial models revealed by Open Works suggest that concern for human life, the ability to provide compensation for staff members displaced by pandemic-driven closures, and a desire to provide what healthcare workers valued were priorities.

Our team and the families of our residents and the families of our staff at Arbor Place Memory Care Assisted Living in Rockville are all grateful to you; each shield you make makes a difference in the lives of many!!" -- #makersunite #getusppe #faceshield #madeatopenworks #madeinbaltimore

In the meantime, we had to lay off our entire 21 person PT staff last night due to the Governor's order closing the facility. Sterilizing, assembling, packaging, and distributing these shields will allow us to hire back some of our displaced workers. If you can donate a few dollars to help us purchase packing materials, and protective gear for our workers, and get a few shifts back online next week, we would be so grateful. We also want to be able to be in a position to reimburse volunteers for material and time at some point down the road when all of this settles down.

The value stream in Open Works' production of PPE was evident in the acquisition of raw materials, conversion of raw materials into a useful product, and the fulfillment of customer needs. The ability to efficiently meet that need was partially influenced by the ability to eliminate waste in the production process -- the goal of Lean Manufacturing. There was a need to determine how value-producing processes organically and quickly could be embedded into production. Tasks, materials, and procedures that added little or no value were eliminated. The ability to conduct a value stream analysis and move from concept to production in four days demonstrated agility that may not be as evident in the absence of a crisis. However, even after the current crisis, small and midsize manufacturers (SMMs) and suppliers such as Open Works will have demonstrated their value to supply chain agility. Organizations such as the World Economic Forum, a nonprofit foundation founded in 1971 in Geneva, Switzerland recognize the potential of SMMs. They describe the difficulty manufacturers experience when attempting to pivot due to a lack of flexibility in their supplier base (World Economic Forum, 2020). The trends of automation and small batch production were already leading some manufacturers to build a more local supply chain. The pandemic created a crisis that accelerated demonstrations of local capacity as occurred with Open Works' response to the PPE face shield shortage.

The nine-step production process mentioned earlier includes steps taken by Open Works to eliminate waste.3 Some steps were designed to eliminate waste as well as other steps that held less value but could not be avoided because of the absence of more efficient solutions. The absence of more efficient solutions may be the result of human resource limitations or insufficient production assets. The Lean Manufacturing principle of "flow" occurred as Open Works spontaneously organized a team dedicated to the production of a single item, face shields. Production assets were available to produce other PPE such as gowns and masks. However, a dedicated product team is one method of reducing production cycle time. The value of a dedicated product team was achieved while other innovations were deployed such as the invitation to the external community to print parts, sign waivers, and deliver parts to the Open Works facility. Work flowed from one value-added step to the next while minimizing stoppages, scrap, or backflows. The production milestones, the integration of external partners, and sustained demand from healthcare providers and the USDA showed the benefits of flow by eliminating threats to the continuous production flow of face shields. The results yielded over 28,270 shields in 56 working days.

Yesterday, we hit a new record of 504 assembled and packed shields in one day. Shields have been distributed to 9 clients including homeless shelters, a cancer care center, ER docs at a major hospital, and the Veteran Administration for compliance testing.

Yesterday, we ended the shift with 526 shields made, another new benchmark!

Pull is a flow control mechanism in which nothing is made or delivered by an upstream producer unless signaled by a downstream customer (Lean Enterprise Institute, 2020). A central component of Just-In-Time manufacturing, face shields were not produced without actual demand. The approach reduces design-to-delivery cycles as illustrated by Open Works' quick stand up and rapid increases in production speed. Traditional production based on pushing products to meet forecasted demand is less effective when demand rapidly increases because of an unexpected crisis. The production of tens of thousands of face shields in less than 60 days by an organization that had never produced a single face shield before the pandemic is impressive. Doing so in a manner that minimized waste by strict adherence to the emergent demand is equally impressive.

Open Works has built a reputation for excellence since its opening in 2016. Their response to the crisis and the way the organization innovatively reallocated assets is consistent with their culture. The pursuit of perfection is described in Lean Manufacturing as continuous improvement. It is a process of identifying customer value, defining value streams, facilitating flow, and allowing the pull of demand to set the pace while making perpetual steps toward perfection. The commitment to continuous improvement is as much a cultural characteristic as it is behavioral action. It is based on prevailing organizational beliefs, values, and attitudes that support continuous improvement as a collective priority.

From crisis awareness and the first call for volunteers to the conclusion of the project, there were opportunities for improvement. Opportunities emerged in part because of the spontaneous and rapid way the supply chain was created. Open Works did not have oversight of the production of face shield parts that happened outside of the facility. Quality checks following sanitation specifications and other industry requirements occurred onsite once parts were delivered. The influence was maintained by providing volunteers with clear instructions and guidance about locating resources. However, the high level of commitment and persistence among volunteers also contributed to solving production problems and continuing the flow of parts to Open Works.

Napoleon once said, "Amateurs talk tactics. Professionals talk logistics." You have helped us build a complex, beautiful, and resilient supply chain in just one week -- something experts said was impossible. Now the durability of this system will be put to the test.

Making face shields at Open Works has illustrated exactly why makerspaces are such a valuable part of any city's economic and educational vitality. From idea to testing in 90 minutes. From crisis to response in 4 days. From prototype to scalable manufacturing in a week. We can't reopen just yet. When we do, we will be ready for thousands of other crazy ideas to burst into being.

The pursuit of quality and waste reduction was exemplified by the Open Works staff. Testing, bringing on new designs, setting increasingly higher production benchmarks, meeting design standards set by demand from new clients, and repurposing production assets such as a Kraft paper dispenser occurred to continuously improve the process and increase value. Changes such as moving to a CNC-ed design to increase production speed, resolving the need for more bottom reinforcements, and providing guidance to the network of volunteer suppliers about required adjustments to their printers to accommodate the new specifications were all part of an unwavering commitment to continuously improving the production process. Open Works demonstrated the agility required to reduce effort, time, space, costs, and mistakes while delivering PPE that met all stakeholder specifications.

Rise and grind! With our second design made from CNC-cut acrylic now approved, we were able to hit a new production record of 845 shields yesterday! That brings our cumulative total to 4,415 produced and 4,360 parts collected from YOU!

View of our new hardhat design in use! Undergoing field testing with the USDA as we speak to see if it meets specs. We will be releasing it open source once we finish perfecting the files.

Values-Inspired Mobilization

The Open Works response to the COVID-19 pandemic involved several forms of mobilization to counter supply chain deficiencies in PPE production exposed by the pandemic. Mobilization is the ability to summon, organize, and deploy resources to achieve a stated objective. In this case, the objective was to contribute to a community effort to minimize the loss of life by supplying PPE to healthcare providers during the crisis. Open Works became part of a network of community partners who contributed resources and assets to achieve a common goal. Mobilization was facilitated by the alignment of values and productive capabilities that converged and became operational in a very short period.

In the face of a looming shortage, hospitals, health, and government agencies have been turning to local, small manufacturing companies to fill the void. These new partnerships are creating life-saving supplies and jobs, for those who desperately need them.

Throughout the world, healthcare professionals have struggled due to shortages of PPE, from gloves to masks to face shields. Makers have stepped up in an attempt to fill the shortage. But this attempt is one they recognize is a short-term solution for a much larger problem.

The mobilization of Open Works and its network of partners was democratic, permissionless, and knowledge-centered. Mobilization was also inspired by the concern of community actors for those who were suddenly unemployed due to closures and their desire to support frontline healthcare workers. The mobilization occurred in a manner that complied with production standards for healthcare equipment but without the sanctioning of a public or private authority. It was "grassroots" mobilization in every sense of the meaning. The threat of insufficient PPE did not allow time for an extensive feasibility analysis. The crisis demanded action and equitable opportunity to participate in solutions.

...teachers, working with school administrators, have brought printers home. He is also working with three students, using their families' 3D printers for his project. School administrators are donating filament and helping to coordinate the locations of their schools' printers. Other individuals are volunteering to gather materials and drop off the finished parts to Open Works.

Those in the position to give back have taken an all-hands-on-deck approach, diverting their attention to something impactful while social distancing. It feels great to be able to focus on something. It's why so many people have come out of the woodwork to help. This is an unprecedented national emergency. It's emotional—I'm shell shocked at the way the community has come together.

The mobilization also was enabled by information accessibility. Open source design specifications shared without intellectual property restrictions facilitated mobilization and network-building. This knowledge sharing facilitated agility that failed to materialize in the existing supply chain. Open Source Medical Supplies (OSMS) for example, which was launched in March 2020, brought together "a global network of over 70,000 makers, fabricators, community organizers, and medical professionals working together to meet the unprecedented medical supply challenges stemming from the COVID-19 pandemic" (Open Source Medical Supplies, 2020). OSMS describes its mission as:

We inform and empower makers, engineers, manufacturers, local organizers, experts, and institutions around the world working in their communities to meet supply challenges stemming from global crises.

We provide high-quality information, platforms for collaboration, and strategic support to globally-distributed local groups to facilitate rapid and effective mobilization.

We identify and collaborate closely with well-aligned strategic partners so that members of our community have a diverse ecosystem of support for their efforts.

Open Works' mobilization efforts were facilitated by the work of external partners who emerged with the same objectives during the crisis.

Makers around the world have created open-source designs that anyone with a 3D printer can download and produce. Josef Prusa at Prusa Lab in Prague, Czech Republic, devised an open-source design that was approved by the Czech Republic's Minister of Health and has been downloaded more than 40,000 times.

To make certain medical equipment, 3D-printing companies and makers may need to reverse engineer patented designs, and therefore put themselves at risk of being sued by patent owners, or gain temporary access to patented designs, which patent-holders may see as a risk to their business. 3D-printed kits might be something of a novelty in hospitals pre-COVID19, but there are niches where additive manufacturing has already taken hold.

There was a moral element to the mobilization of makers, moral in the sense that guiding principles were the catalyst for collective action. Enough community members shared the guiding principle of helping others during a crisis and mass action occurred. The morality factor also contributed to the willingness of participants to risk viral infection in the interest of protecting the broader population. The action was viewed by others as "the right thing to do" under the circumstances. The deficiencies in the supply chain were not caused by those who mobilized, but accountability for existing inadequacies was not a priority during the height of the crisis. Mobilization was the overarching goal.

In times like these, when it doesn't seem like there's much you can do and it feels like there's a lot out of your control, it's really gratifying to find something that you have a skill set for that you feel like is helping.

These charitable tinkerers provide ground for both a deeply American kind of hope—strangers doing as much as they can, wherever they can, for the good of their neighbors—and despair, at the colossal federal failure that inspired them.

The Open Works response may offer implications for the emerging manufacturing sector. Principles-based on opportunity awareness, agile performance, and continuous discovery of supply chain innovations are a few of the performance-based practices observed during the study. Practices were observed that are based on organizational learning and continuous improvement. Individual and organizational learning are capabilities that help achieve maximum production agility.

There's no way that this is more cost- or labor-efficient than making it in a giant factory, but when all the giant factories are in China and China needs all the face shields domestically, it just exposes the yawning gap in America's industrial space.

We saw on Instagram that Open Works, a studio space in Baltimore, was working on producing face shields to help with the shortage of personal protective equipment for health care workers. Open Works found an open-source design of a face shield that consists of a plastic shield that is laser cut and 3D printed parts that sit at the forehead and the bottom so the mask retains its shape.

The supply chain vulnerabilities created in part by the offshoring of manufacturing became evident during the crisis. The need for onshoring manufacturing and positioning small, local producers for crisis-ready responses was apparent. The process of awareness, response, data collection, information sharing, and quick adjustments to obstacles were critical to building on Open Works' existing institutional trust, lean approach to manufacturing, and commitment to helping address deficiencies in the PPE supply chain.

The preceding themes set forth the following hypotheses for further consideration, including:

Hypotheses One: Internal and external trust networks developed through inclusive practices will increase production in small fabrication facilities.

Hypotheses 2: Crisis mobilization practices are applicable in efforts to increase participation of underserved community members in product-based entrepreneurship.

Hypotheses Three: Intersubjective volunteerism, transformative volunteerism, hyper-volunteerism, and resource sharing are the result of effective relational practices.

Hypotheses Four: Small-scale local manufacturing will increase entrepreneurship opportunities for historically excluded underserved communities.

SOLUTIONS AND RECOMMENDATIONS

Alignment between initial questions, themes in the data, and hypotheses justify subsequent solutions and recommendations (Table 1).

Table 1. Evidential alignment mapping

Questions	Related Themes	Hypotheses
What is the role of trust in organizing a response to the inability to meet critical product demand during a healthcare crisis?	Trust-Inspired Volunteerism	Hypotheses One: Internal and external trust networks developed through inclusive practices will increase production in small fabrication facilities.
How are Lean Manufacturing principles applied in a makerspace in response to a critical product shortage during a healthcare crisis?	Leaning In (i.e., a philosophy of Lean Thinking) contributed to Creating a Crisis-Resistant Supply Chain	Hypotheses 2: Crisis mobilization practices are applicable in efforts to increase the participation of underserved community members in product-based entrepreneurship.
What practices during a healthcare crisis may lead to greater post-crisis supply chain agility?	Values-Inspired Mobilization	Hypotheses Three: Intersubjective volunteerism, transformative volunteerism, hyper-volunteerism, and resource sharing are the result of effective relational practices.
What crisis response practices facilitate makerspace integration with the existing and emerging manufacturing sector?	• Leaning In (i.e., a philosophy of Lean Thinking) contributed to Creating a Crisis-Resistant Supply Chain • Values-Inspired Mobilization	Hypotheses Four: Small-scale local manufacturing will increase entrepreneurship opportunities for historically excluded underserved communities.

The case of Open Works' response to PPE shortages during the COVID-19 pandemic led us to make the following recommendations concerning a more agile manufacturing supply chain:

Identify and Incorporate Relational Measures for Social Cohesion Factors

A recent Industry Week article (Putre, 2020) identified "trust and open and clear communications with their suppliers, as well as strong relationships built over time," as necessary for creating a post-COVID-19 economy and competitive advantage for original equipment manufacturers (OEMs). Developing a competitive advantage for manufacturers will require socio-technical approaches to production and provide strategies for maximizing volunteerism, mobilization, network development, and other elements that will help infuse agility into the supply chain and relationships with suppliers and other stakeholders. Many disruptive events are unforeseen and do not allow for the time required to establish the social and relational infrastructure required to positively influence production cycles and reduce time-to-market. Relationships, like other key collaboration factors and production assets, require testing, maintenance, and even replacement.

Utilize Data Democracy and Information Transparency to Facilitate Mobilization

Mobilization and volunteerism may be the catalysts that make agile responses viable in a crisis. These practices are most effective when they are core values in the organizational culture. Data democracy is the practice of providing all stakeholders with the ability to access, analyze, interpret, and make decisions based on available data. It requires sound data management practices and exceptional data quality. Transparency is a practice that extends beyond data and refers to a bias toward openness, which may be perceived as a negative vulnerability. However, the benefits gained from transparency far outweigh the potential negatives.

Make Value Stream Development an Important Part of your Post-COVID-19 Sustainability

Value stream development involves the identification of customer and market needs, measures that will be used to monitor and track performance relating to the generation of value, and constant processes of implementing improvement processes based on the created value. This never becomes a static process or one that has a conclusion. It is iterative by its very nature and requires constant evaluative efforts.

Prepare for a Resurgence in the Manufacturing Sector and the Key Role of Makerspaces

The discovery of supply chain vulnerabilities has revealed the need to re-shore manufacturing and train a skilled workforce that can perform well in the use of advanced technology. This will change the significance of small-scale, local manufacturing, and potential assets such as makerspaces. Once viewed as exclusive hobby spaces with no real contribution to the economy, makerspaces have proven their value to local economies and the need for agile solutions to fill gaps in the supply chain. The *2019 Turning Makerspaces into Greater Places: Organizational Assessment and Economic Impact Study of Open Works* revealed that the facility is contributing $8M annually in economic impact in Baltimore City and $9.9M annually in impact in Maryland. This level of impact will prove even more valuable in the post-COVID-19 economy, especially considering their community-centric networks.

FUTURE RESEARCH DIRECTIONS

There is a need to continue research regarding relational competencies, soft skills, and their importance in maximizing productivity in the manufacturing sector. This is especially true as it relates to trust-inspired volunteerism, values-inspired mobilization, and Lean Manufacturing. These principles have tremendous implications for demonstrating the value of inclusive practices in production. The value of greater inclusion is more evident in a crisis. However, there are benefits in the more routine needs for production as demonstrated by lingering supply chain deficiencies. The inclusion of those from under-served communities, the creation of more direct pathways into leadership and ownership opportunities in the manufacturing sector, and more localized approaches to the production of goods are all part of the pandemic story of mobilization that is demonstrated in the Open Works study and worthy of further research.

CONCLUSION

A climate of trans-institutional trust enabled Open Works and its partners to quickly and collaboratively respond when the coronavirus pandemic created a global crisis. While the crisis is global in proportion, the local response to deficient supplies of PPE for healthcare providers became critical. The impending economic threat to Open Works due to the mandated closure did not deter their leadership, staff, organizational and institutional partners, and community members from mobilizing to meet the need and produce lifesaving equipment. The selfless act of helping to save lives and the goodwill established with potential partners before the pandemic were major contributors to Open Works' ability to summon support and reach production capability in an unprecedented short amount of time. The relational collateral represented by trust-inspired volunteerism contributed to the reduction of costs and production cycle times.

The opportunity to engage in delivering collaborative solutions to a pressing need emerged from an intersubjective, unspoken agreement among collaborators that a transcendent goal was at stake, contributing to the transformative impact of their volunteerism. Not only were valuable lessons learned regarding manufacturing efficiencies, the volunteers, and the organizations in which they serve now have new data and experiences that will inform their work in the future. This is the transformative benefit of the Open Works project that may go unnoticed by those who focus totally on the quantitative measures of success. Institutional learning and societal impact are the long-term effects when the short-term purpose was to fulfill a local need while employing a skilled labor force.

The hyper-volunteerism exceeded the expectations of those who initiated the call to action. An unforeseen common threat may not always be present and should not be counted on to inspire high levels of engagement from potential partners and the community. However, the influence of a crisis on the willingness of others to join a cause has implications for elevating the importance of supply chain agility to one of collective benefit and well-being for the entire community. It is important to present supply chain agility as a means of reducing vulnerabilities for all communities. It is important to frame the threat of vulnerabilities as a condition that is ongoing and constantly critical.

Transparency and trust were factors in the mobilization of volunteers. Large volunteer responses alone are not enough to sustain a project. From the identification of open source face shield design to the publishing of financial data, openness about all phases of the process contributed to the willingness of others to join the effort. When the initial bottleneck in production was discovered at Open Works, the solution did not impede the progress of the project. Having insufficient 3D printing capabilities allowed Open Works to mobilize the collaborative goodwill and trust of the community. The call for volunteers and donations was a catalyst for mobilization driven by trust collateral that had been invested by Open Works.

Agility, resilience, and scalability are familiar terms in manufacturing. Agile manufacturing refers to the tools, techniques, and initiatives such as Lean that facilitate rapid response to their customers, the market, and innovations. The democratization of tools and production as demonstrated through a pandemic-driven crisis has the potential to provide opportunities for underserved communities.

REFERENCES

Abualkhair, H., Lodree, E. J., & Davis, L. B. (2020). Managing volunteer convergence at disaster relief centers. *International Journal of Production Economics*, *220*, 107399–107359. doi:10.1016/j.ijpe.2019.05.018

Andrews, R., Jilke, S., & Van de Walle, S. (2014). Economic strain and perceptions of social cohesion in Europe: Does institutional trust matter? *European Journal of Political Research*, *53*(3), 559–579. doi:10.1111/1475-6765.12052

Anholon, R., & Sano, A. (2016). Analysis of critical processes in the implementation of Lean manufacturing projects using project management guidelines. *International Journal of Advanced Manufacturing Technology*, *84*(9–12), 2247–2256. doi:10.100700170-015-7865-9

Audretsch, D. B., Seitz, N., & Rouch, K. M. (2018). Tolerance and innovation: the role of institutional and social trust. *Eurasian Business Review, 8*(1), 71. Available at: http://search.ebscohost.com.proxy-cs.researchport.umd.edu/login.aspx?direct=true&db=edb&AN=128333469&site=eds-live

Cherns, A. (1976). The Principles of Sociotechnical Design. *Human Relations*, *29*(8), 783–792. doi:10.1177/001872677602900806

Emery, F. (1959). *Some characteristics of sociotechnical systems*. Document # 527. London: Tavistock Institute.

Hanna, D. (1988). *Designing organizations for high performance*. Addison Wesley.

Kwon, S.-W., Heflin, C., & Ruef, M. (2013). Community Social Capital and Entrepreneurship. *American Sociological Review*, *78*(6), 980–1008. doi:10.1177/0003122413506440

Lardier, D. T., Reid, R. J., & Garcia, R. P. (2018). Validation of the Brief Sense of Community Scale among the youth of color from an underserved urban community. *Journal of Community Psychology*, *46*(8), 1062–1074. doi:10.1002/jcop.22091 PMID:30311964

Lean Enterprise Institute. (2020, July 14). *Target Cost*. Retrieved from Lean Enterprise Institute: https://www.lean.org/lexicon/target-cost

McMillan, D. W., & Chavis, D. M. (1986). Sense of Community: A Definition and Theory. *Journal of Community Psychology, 14*(1), 6–23. doi:10.1002/1520-6629(198601)14:1<6::AID-JCOP2290140103>3.0.CO;2-I

Mehta, R. K., Mehta, D., & Mehta, N. K. (2012). Lean Manufacturing Practices: Problems and Prospects. *Annals of the Faculty of Engineering Hunedoara - International Journal of Engineering, 10*(3), 119–124.

Moffatt, M. (2020, June 25). *An Economic Introduction to the Japanese Keiretsu System*. Retrieved from Thought Company: https://www.thoughtco.com/intro-to-the-japanese-keiretsu-economics-system-1148018

Mohrman, S., & Winby, S. (2018). Working toward sustainable development: Consulting to the ecosystem. In Research in organization change and development 26 (pp. 1–45). London: Emerald.

Ober, C. (2020, April 6). *Bmore Art*. Retrieved from All Masks Are Not Created Equal: Washable, Antimicrobial Masks Made in Baltimore: https://bmoreart.com/2020/04/all-masks-are-not-created-equal-washable-antimicrobial-masks-made-in-baltimore.html

Omoto, A. M., & Packard, C. D. (2016). The power of connections: Psychological sense of community as a predictor of volunteerism. *The Journal of Social Psychology, 156*(3), 272–290. doi:10.1080/00224545.2015.1105777 PMID:27064179

Open Source Medical Supplies. (2020, July 4). *Open Source Medical Supplies*. Retrieved from Open Source Medical Supplies: https://opensourcemedicalsupplies.org/?fbclid=IwAR11eW3ODq9aeBu2CwTA6pWqGNdRTLtTfhAUzQaTXYWCLv-erRKhCi95rL0

Ortega Carpio, M. L., Martinez-Cousinou, G., & Morales-Fernández, E. J. (2018). Transformative Volunteerism: An Inventory of NGDO Volunteers' Motivations. *Human Service Organizations, Management, Leadership & Governance, 42*(1), 33–52. doi:10.1080/23303131.2017.1363103

Pasmore, W. A. (2001). Action research in the workplace: The socio-technical perspective. In P. Reason & H. Bradbury (Eds.), *Handbook of action research: Participative inquiry and practice* (pp. 38–48). Sage.

Shantz, A., Wang, J., & Malik, A. (2018). Disability status, individual variable pay, and pay satisfaction: Does relational and institutional trust make a difference? *Human Resource Management, 57*(1), 365–380. doi:10.1002/hrm.21845

Strandh, V., & Eklund, N. (2018). Emergent groups in disaster research: Varieties of scientific observation over time and across studies of nine natural disasters. *Journal of Contingencies and Crisis Management, 26*(3), 329–337. doi:10.1111/1468-5973.12199

Stukas, A. A., Snyder, M., & Clary, E. G. (2016). Understanding and encouraging volunteerism and community involvement. *The Journal of Social Psychology, 156*(3), 243–255. doi:10.1080/00224545.2016.1153328 PMID:27064177

Suri, R. (2010). *It's about time: The competitive advantage of quick response manufacturing*. CRC Press. doi:10.1201/EBK1439805954

Toyota Industries Corporation. (2020, June 24). *History*. Retrieved from Toyota-Industries: https://www.toyota-industries.com/company/history/

Trist, E. L. (1981). *The evolution of socio-technical systems: A conceptual framework and an action research program*. Ontario Quality of Working Life Center, Occasional paper.

Unite, M. (2020, July 14). *FAQ*. Retrieved from Makers Unite: https://mdmakersunite.org/participate/process

United States Department of Labor. (2020, July 14). *Occupational Safety and Health Administration*. Retrieved from Personal Protective Equipment: https://www.osha.gov/personal-protective-equipment

Vujica Herzog, N., & Tonchia, S. (2014). An Instrument for Measuring the Degree of Lean Implementation in Manufacturing. *Strojniski Vestnik. Jixie Gongcheng Xuebao*, *60*(12), 797–803. https://doi-org.proxy-cs.researchport.umd.edu/10.5545/sv-jme.2014.1873

WBAL. (2020, March 24). *People with 3D printers wanted to help make face shields for hospital workers*. WBAL TV News 11. Baltimore, MD: Hearst Broadcast Group.

Williams, R., & Klugh, E. (2017). Creating a University Driven "Ingepreneurial" Ecosystem in West Baltimore: A Strategy for Rust Belt Revitalization. *Metropolitan Universities Journal.*, *28*(2), 103–123. Advance online publication. doi:10.18060/21510

ADDITIONAL READING

Habib, M. (2016). *Supply Chain Management : Applications for Manufacturing and Service Industry*. Nova Science Publishers, Inc.

Núñez-Merino, M., Maqueira-Marín, J. M., Moyano-Fuentes, J., & Martínez-Jurado, P. J. (2020). Information and digital technologies of Industry 4.0 and Lean supply chain management: A systematic literature review. *International Journal of Production Research*, *58*(16), 5034–5061. doi:10.1080/00207543.2020.1743896

Omidi, L., Moradi, G., & Sarkari, N. M. (2020). Risk of COVID-19 infection in workplace settings and the use of personal protective equipment. *Work (Reading, Mass.)*, *66*(2), 377–378. doi:10.3233/WOR-203188 PMID:32568162

Piliavin, J. A. (2009). Altruism and Helping: The Evolution of a Field: The 2008 Cooley-Mead Presentation. *Social Psychology Quarterly*, *72*(3), 209–225. doi:10.1177/019027250907200305

Ramdan, M. R., Abdullah, N. L., Isa, R. M., & Hanafiah, M. H. (2021). Organizational Ambidexterity within Supply Chain Management: A Scoping Review. *LogForum*, *17*(4), 531–546. https://doi-org.proxy-cs.researchport.umd.edu/10.17270/J.LOG.2021.618

Riglietti, G., Avatefipour, A., & Trucco, P. (2021). The impact of business continuity management on the components of supply chain resilience: A quantitative analysis. *Journal of Business Continuity & Emergency Planning*, *15*(2), 182–195. PMID:35016752

Sancha, C., Wiengarten, F., Longoni, A., & Pagell, M. (2020). The moderating role of temporary work on the performance of lean manufacturing systems. *International Journal of Production Research*, *58*(14), 4285–4305. doi:10.1080/00207543.2019.1651458

Steele, T. (2016). *Prosocial Behavior : Perspectives, Influences and Current Research.* Nova Science Publishers, Inc.

Wyrwich, M. (2019). New KIBS on the bloc: The role of local manufacturing for start-up activity in knowledge-intensive business services. *Regional Studies*, *53*(3), 320–329. doi:10.1080/00343404.2018.1478076

KEY TERMS AND DEFINITIONS

Crisis-Resistant Supply Chain: Crisis-resistant supply chain is the ability of the flow of goods and services to withstand barriers or circumstances that would reduce or end progressive movement from production to consumers.

Hyper-Volunteerism: Hyper-volunteerism is an overwhelming response to the need for volunteers, especially during a crisis. It emerges from a shared concern about catastrophic outcomes and suffering.

Intersubjective Volunteerism: Intersubjective volunteerism is an agreement by a group to assist without compensation or verbal conversation among themselves. It is volunteering with the assumption that others share the same mindset and will volunteer with you. It is also a knowledge of like-mindedness without conversational engagement.

Lean Principles: Lean Principles refer to the process of increasing value or worth with a smaller amount of resources.

Resource Sharing: The process of making a supply or means available to others, especially during a crisis.

Trust-Inspired Volunteerism: Trust-inspired volunteerism is an agreement to assist without compensation because of a willingness to sacrifice personal comfort, safety, or the convenience and accept mutual vulnerabilities.

Values-Inspired Mobilization: Values-inspired mobilization is the willingness to act and solicit the action of others by word or example. It occurs out of a shared passion, belief, or concern.

ENDNOTES

1. Building value with internal and external stakeholder groups was reported as a strategy from the inception of the organization. Opportunities for qualitative assessment of value were readily available during the crisis.
2. Transparency is observed in Open Works' willingness to welcome external examination and intentionally share information.
3. The elimination of waste is a cultural characteristic that was apparent in the data. Culture (i.e., beliefs, values, and attitudes) develop over time and are catalyzed by a crisis.

Section 4
National/Regional Sustainability

Chapter 14
Entrepreneurship Skills Development in TVET Through Multi-Stakeholder Partnerships:
Post-COVID-19 Recovery Approach for Developing Economies

Dagogo William Legg-Jack
https://orcid.org/0000-0002-6739-5575
Walter Sisulu University, South Africa

ABSTRACT

With the outbreak of the coronavirus, the economies of developing economies, which have already been plagued by youth unemployment and poverty, became more vulnerable as the virus exacerbated the situation and resulted in more job losses. Consequently, to mitigate the effect of the virus on the developing economies post COVID-19, the chapter argues that developing entrepreneurship skills in technical and vocational education and training through a multi-stakeholder partnership remains a viable strategy. Thus, through an exploratory approach, the chapter reviewed related literature on the subject under study. The findings highlighted the following multi-stakeholders, namely the training institutions, enterprises (formal and informal), government, and non-governmental organisations, among others. Thus, this chapter concludes that collaboration between these mentioned stakeholders would aid in the development of the much-needed entrepreneurship skills in TVET, thereby serving as a recovery strategy for developing economies.

INTRODUCTION

Entrepreneurship education is considered a critical component of any given nation that aims to develop the employment capacity of its youth force. This is because of its potential to address issues related to unemployment and the growth of a nation's economy (Gamede & Uleanya, 2019). In recent times,

DOI: 10.4018/978-1-6684-4322-4.ch014

poverty and youth unemployment, especially in developing economies, has undergone major debate, and the outbreak of the coronavirus (COVID-19) pandemic has exacerbated the situation. Therefore, to tackle the menace of poverty and unemployment among youth at a global level, the United Nations Educational, Scientific and Cultural Organisation (UNESCO) recommends Technical and Vocational Education and Training (TVET) as an alternative pathway by developing an entrepreneurship mindset and education (UNESCO, 2003).

TVET has been considered a system of education with the potential to combat the rising wave of poverty and unemployment, and to address the changing skills need of the workplace and rapid technological innovation at a global level. It is a department of education with the capacity to equip its recipients with skills and competencies that guarantee them either self or paid employment in the industry. However, despite this recognition accorded TVET, its provision has been marred with colossal challenges including poor funding, a dearth/shortage of qualified training personnel, lack of workshop facilities, overcrowded classrooms, insufficient classrooms and workshop buildings, obsolete curriculum, poor administration and management of TVET, and too few stakeholder partnerships, among others (Watters et al., 2013; Okwelle & Wordu, 2014; Takei, 2016).

Consequently, it is argued that one major approach to recovering from the impact of COVID-19 on the economies of developing nations is to establish robust collaboration between TVET providers and stakeholders within other sectors in the development of entrepreneurship skills. This chapter addresses one objective, namely the role of multi-stakeholders in the development of entrepreneurship skills in TVET. This objective is addressed through an exploratory qualitative approach, where data is generated through secondary sources by reviewing, *inter alia,* empirical studies, policies, and reports on the focus of the chapter.

In the following section, a brief review of related literature is presented on the coronavirus and its impact on developing economies, entrepreneurship education, TVET education, entrepreneurship education in TVET, multi-stakeholder partnership (MSP), and MSPs in TVET. Also presented is the methodology, findings and discussion, future research directions and conclusion.

REVIEW OF RELATED LITERATURE

COVID-19 and its Impact on Developing Economies

A deadly virus referred to as the novel coronavirus, and eventually COVID-19, was said to have erupted in Wuhan City, Hubei Province of China, in 2019 (Sansa, 2020). Considering the rapidity of its spread, the virus is reported to have reached Europe, America, and then Africa, having a significant impact on global economies and livelihoods (Azubuike et al., 2021; Giandhari et al., 2021). As a result, the World Health Organisation (WHO), considering the devastating impact of the virus on many countries of the world, declared it a global pandemic on January 30, 2020 (Mhlanga & Ndhlovu, 2020).

Governments across different nations in a bid to slow the spread of COVID-19 implemented regulations that require social distancing, closure of non-essential businesses, travel restrictions and, in many cases, required residents to remain in their homes (Blackman et al., 2020). According to Bottan et al. (2020), a total discouragement, restriction and prohibition was placed on all human interactions that drive the economy, such as working together in enclosed areas and enjoying entertainment activities. There has been strong compliance to these measures as well as phenomenal support of these regulations by residents (Fetzer et al., 2020; Allcott et al., 2020; Briscese et al., 2020). As argued by some scholars, these measures are necessary for public health, but evidence from developed countries suggests that they have negative economic impacts in the short run (Adams-Prassl et al., 2020; Bartik et al., 2020). For example, in countries with strong economies, such as the United Kingdom, the quarantine period is estimated to have caused a decrease in their global domestic product (GDP) by 3.0% (Nicola et al., 2020). Compliance to these measures has also led to an increase in the unemployment rate and the closure of businesses, making more evident the social inequality (Blustein et al., 2020; Nicola et al., 2020; O'Connor et al., 2020). These measures put in place can potentially broaden already existing gaps (Alon et al., 2020). These impacts could be exacerbated in developing countries with more precarious workers and firms, as well as lower levels of state capacity to face the pandemic (Bottan et al., 2020).

The current COVID-19 pandemic has been considered an unprecedented public health challenge that has distressing economic impacts for households (Bottan et., 2020). As posited by several prominent economists, inequality is the principal economic issue of our era (Stiglitz, 2013; Milanovic, 2016; Piketty et al., 2019; Zucman, 2019). This inequality was widened by recent economic slowdowns such as the Great Recession of 2008–2009 (Smeeding, 2012; Heathcote et al., 2010; Brzezinski, 2018). However, this is nothing compared to COVID-19 which has altered economic activities through different channels and on an accelerated timeline (Bottan et al., 2020).

In a study that explored 17 developing countries in Latin America and the Caribbean, it was reported that the COVID-19 pandemic has had negative economic impacts on a broad segment of the population and that these impacts are heightened for those with lower income prior to the pandemic (Bottan et al., 2020). The findings of the study further revealed that, in the overall, 45% of the respondents reported that a household member lost a job and, among households owning small family businesses, 58% of the respondents reported that a household member closed their business (Bottan et al., 2020). Economic growth in the African continent is reported to have shrunk by 2.1% in 2020 (African Development Bank, 2021). The greatest decline in economic growth amongst Africa's sub-regions was experienced by Southern Africa, the growth is estimated to have fallen by 7.0% in 2020. This precedes Central Africa (−2.7%), West Africa (−1.5%), and North Africa (−1.1%), whilst East Africa, which is least dependent on natural resources, managed an estimated 0.7% growth in 2020 (Anyanwu & Salami, 2021).

These various levels of decline, as seen above, directly lowered the GDP of nations, and hence, impacted negatively on the economy. Consequently, the starting point should be to restructure the fiscal resources for future crises, and revitalisation of economic growth is essential to enhance the fiscal position (Channing & Sherman, 2020). Thus, this chapter argues for the development of entrepreneurship skills in TVET through MSPs as a post-COVID-19 recovery approach for developing economies.

Entrepreneurship Education

Entrepreneurs play an important role in economic development (Acs, 2006; Acs & Amoros, 2008; Ribeiro & Montoro-Sánchez, 2011), and they occupy the central position in a society's economic recovery from major disruptions such as the COVID-19 pandemic (Meyer et al., 2021). Entrepreneurship is essential for the growth of both businesses and overall economies (Libecap, 2003).

There have been diverse definitions of the term "entrepreneurship" in the various professions (Igbo, 2006). Entrepreneurship is described by Key et al. (2013) as the application of enterprise skills specifically to create and grow organisations to identify and build on business opportunities. The Quality Assurance Agency (QAA) for Higher Education defined entrepreneurship as a trans-disciplinary set of skills that has a high degree of application to key issues such as employability, innovation, knowledge transfer, commercialisation, and intellectual property (QAA, 2012). In furtherance, entrepreneurship is also seen as an activity that involves the discovery, evaluation, and utilisation of opportunities to introduce new products (Shane, 2003). According to Oviawe (2010), entrepreneurship is the acquisition of skills and ideas for the sake of creating employment for one's self and others. She further asserted that entrepreneurship leads to the development of small, medium, and sometimes large-scale businesses based on creativity and innovation. Significantly, the ability to implement a business is identified as a crucial and essential factor in reaping the fruitful gains of entrepreneurship, as well as the skills acquired by those who intend to start a company (Ibrahim & Lucky, 2014), such as leadership, communication, innovation, networking, creativity and problem-solving (Liñan, 2008). These skills put together provide opportunities for practical application, job creation, and crime reduction, as posited by Oviawe (2010). In Ghana, West Africa, the integration of applied competencies, such as entrepreneurship skills, is considered an approach in the National Employment Policies to strengthen the TVET system in dealing with the employment situation and work shortages among vulnerable groups, viz. the youth, women, and persons with disability (Kissi et al., 2020). This is because TVET is perceived to increase the tendency of youth entrepreneurship in the form of self-reliance and job creation (Kissi et al., 2020).

TVET Education

The term TVET as used to refer to 'Technical and Vocational Education and Training' was recommended by UNESCO in 2004 (UNESCO, 2004). TVET as an aspect of education is described as a

[C]omprehensive term referring to those aspects of the educational process involving, in addition to general education the study of technologies and related sciences and the acquisition of practical skills, attitudes, understanding and knowledge relating to occupations in various sectors of economic and social life (UNESCO, 2010, p. 5).

In the literature, there are several concepts and constructs that have been used to describe TVET. These include, Vocational Education and Training (VTE), Career and Technical Education (CTE), Vocational Training (VT), Apprenticeship Training (AT), Technical Education (TE), Occupational Education (OE), Vocational Education (VE), Vocational and Technical Education and Training (VTET), Professional Education (PE), and Further Education and Training (FET) (Wahba, 2010; Tagicakiverta, 2012; Wang, 2012; Ladipo et al., 2013).

From the foregoing, these concepts are suggestive that TVET has a link with employability and national development (Raimi & Akhuemonkhan, 2014), and the transformative ability that guarantees the recipients of this type of education the right entry to the world of work (Maclean, 2011). Globally, TVET is seen as an instrument to combat the rising wave of poverty and unemployment, and a strategy to address the dynamic skills need of the workplace and rapid technological innovation (UNESCO, 2004; African Union [AU], 2007; McGrath, 2012). Accordingly, Alhasan and Tyabo (2013) argued that one of the major tools to fight the menace of unemployment amongst the youth is the introduction of TVET education, which will guarantee them jobs and an income, and guard them against the risk of outmodedness. It is on this premise that UNESCO, whilst addressing the need to foster an entrepreneurship mindset and the promotion of entrepreneurship education amongst the youth, recommends TVET as an alternative pathway out of poverty facing young men and women globally (UNESCO, 2003). However, it is important to mention that TVET providers were also affected by the impact of the COVID-19 pandemic (Hoftijzer et al., 2020).

In a survey conducted by the International Labour Organisation (ILO), UNESCO and World Bank, data from 1,300 respondents in 126 countries highlighted that 90% reported complete closure of TVET centres in their country, whilst 98% revealed disruption of work-based learning (Chun et al., 2021). Hindrances to the continuity of TVET programmes during the pandemic-induced lockdown period resulted from a lack of general and technological infrastructure, such as electricity, Internet, connectivity and devices (Chun et al., 2021). According to Hoftijzer et al. (2020), access to practical training was disrupted, but some institutions migrated to remote training, thereby focusing on the theoretical content of their programme with the hope of resuming practical training in the future. Although many TVET providers found it difficult to continue their practical training at the peak of the pandemic, others improvised to ensure the continuity of their programme. In such countries as Ecuador, it was reported that apprenticeship programmes continued despite the closure of schools. In such cases, students executed their practical tasks at home and sent videos and completed work for assessment to their instructors (Chun et al., 2021). Although TVET was also affected by the COVID-19 pandemic, it is argued that this system of education can play a critical role in the recovery of economies with the development of important skills required to mitigate the effect of the outbreak of the virus (Hoftijzer et al., 2020).

Entrepreneurship Education in Technical and Vocational Education and Training

Considering the popularity gained by entrepreneurship, the study of this aspect of education now spans across different training institutions (Kissi et al., 2020). The study of entrepreneurship at primary and secondary schools focuses mainly on creating the consciousness for a career option; thus, it serves as a vehicle for the development of academic skills and emphasis on the importance of school subjects (Gibb, 2008), whilst at institutions of higher learning students are imparted with entrepreneurship qualities and skills to enable them to survive in the business world (Gamede & Uleanya, 2019). The overall purpose of entrepreneurship education, according to Kissi et al. (2020), is the development of expertise as an entrepreneur, as well as the process of providing individuals with the ability to recognise business opportunities and the insight, zeal, knowledge, and the courage and skills to act on them. In conclusion, entrepreneurship is considered an important part of a country's strategy, and TVET provides a range of skills that enable individuals who go through the education process to venture into the world of business after completing their studies (Kissi et al., 2020).

TVET provides its recipients with skills for a range of occupations in diverse fields including mechanical, electrical, building, wood, computer, textile, hospitality, and business, to mention a few (Legg-Jack, 2014). In Nigeria, it is recommended in the National Policy on Education that after three years of completing a TVET programme at technical college level in any of the skilled areas listed above that such a graduate will either be employed in the industry, self-reliant, or proceed to further their education in the university (Federal Republic of Nigeria, 2013). Thus, this confirms the submission of Kissi et al. (2020) who argued that entrepreneurship education has been embedded in the TVET curriculum either directly or indirectly in many countries, such as Malaysia, to enable graduates to compete in the job market and thus create self-employment. In Malaysia, engagement in self-employment has been considered by many TVET institutions as one of the employability criterions in determining the quality of TVET graduates (Ismail et al., 2019). It is believed in most countries that the TVET system can produce skilled workers capable of creating alternative employment by encouraging students to venture into entrepreneurship by equipping them with skills like creativity, innovation, and aptitude for problem solving (Kissi et al., 2020).

However, TVET is often seen in the context of the economy and the intention to produce quality human resources who are unable to compete in the global market and other professions (Ivan & Albu, 2014). A reason for this is, because of the TVET curricular requirement of 70% practical hands-on training and 30% theory, the course structure is becoming mostly theoretical in many TVET institutions due to inadequate funding for the procurement of consumables, tools and equipment (Dzeto, 2014). Generally, TVET has faced gross neglect and little emphasis has been placed on its provision (Akanbi, 2017). This has led to evident uncertainties such as a dearth/shortage of qualified training personnel, infrastructural decay, overcrowded classrooms, misaligned curriculum, and lack of stakeholder partnerships, among others (Legg-Jack, 2018). A study conducted in the context of developing countries such as Ghana, reported that lack of industrial collaboration and readiness of the job market to absolve graduates from TVET were part of the predominant challenges faced by the TVET tutors in the delivery of entrepreneurial skill development (Kissi et al., 2020). With these challenges inherent in TVET, the goal of enlisting this aspect of education with the responsibility of increasing the number of youth and adults who are equipped with relevant skills, including technical and vocational competencies for employment, decent jobs, and entrepreneurship (UNESCO, 2016), is defeated. This highlights the need to create room for the involvement of multiple stakeholders concerned, as recommended by UNESCO (2016).

Multi-Stakeholder Partnerships

The term MSP is promoted by the World Economic Forum (WEF) within the general framework of corporate social responsibility that harnesses collaboration between a wider range of public, private, and civil society organisations (Draxler, 2008; Fennell, 2010). MSP is a collaborative governance approach that involves numerous stakeholders, such as civil society, governments, international organisations, media, and academic or research institutions in sharing their perspectives, information, technology, and financial resources to find out a shared solution (Momen, 2020). These are also considered cooperative ventures between the public, private and civil sectors, built on the proficiency of each partner that best meets clearly defined public needs for services, infrastructure, or development activities through the transfer of resources, risks and rewards between them (Vining & Boardman, 2008). The notion that underpins MSP contends that complex problems require collective action from various stakeholders (Momen, 2020). Hence, to address more multifaceted societal issues being faced by the state and other stakeholders, the MSP remains a potential framework (Momen, 2020).

The arrangement of the MSP is such that there are gains of many resources from partners involved. Promoters of MSP believe that joint learning and the creation of new knowledge is a product of collaboration between multiple partners (Dorado et al., 2009; Huxham & Hibbert, 2004). A study by Clarke and MacDonald (2019) highlighted three types of capital, namely: financial/physical capital, organisational capital, and human capital. The role of stakeholders in delivering these capitals will advance the local community in terms of better capacity, creating a new internal process and developing a new external process (Rosyadi et al., 2020). According to the authors, these three types of capital are critical for a community to address local sustainable development challenges (Rosyadi et al., 2020).

Multi-Stakeholder Partnerships in TVET

The involvement of MSPs in TVET provision is premised on the idea that delivering and sustaining a quality training programme is hinged on a broader coalition that goes beyond the involvement of the public and private sectors (Edomwonyi et al., 2016). This entails an arrangement that incorporates stakeholders from the public sector such as ministries, boards, and schools; whilst that of the public sector cuts across corporations, trade unions, and professional bodies as well as external organisations such as UNESCO, ILO, The United States Agency for International Development (USAID), and SWISS-UNIDO (Switzerland-United Nations Industrial Development Organisation), pooling their resources together to ensure quality TVET provision (Edomwonyi et al., 2016). The implication of this is that delivering a quality TVET in the context of a developing nation, as seen in the case of Nigeria, involves such stakeholders as the academia, both formal and informal enterprises, government, non-governmental organisations (NGOs), the local community, Parent-Teacher Associations (PTAs), international financing communities such as the World Bank, philanthropic individuals/organisations, and volunteers (Legg-Jack, 2018).

From the foregoing, the recommendation of TVET as an alternative way for the youth globally to escape poverty is through the development of an entrepreneurship mindset and by promoting entrepreneurship education (UNESCO, 2003), thus becomes very possible. This is because evidence as literature shows that the development of entrepreneurship skills is multidimensional, considering the resources (Gamede & Uleanya, 2019) and stakeholders involved (Sousa & Almeida, 2014). As noted, the value of partnership/s cannot be underestimated in ensuring the success of business opportunities for entrepreneurs, hence the reliance on strong stakeholder support and collaboration for success (Mpisi, 2020). For instance, a study conducted in Portugal by Galvão et al. (2020) revealed that the establishment of an entrepreneurship programme led to the reversal of the downward economic trend of high unemployment in such places as the Sabor Region of Portugal, and this was achieved through stakeholder participation. Although, the impact of stakeholder participation as revealed in the study includes the creation of jobs, competencies in municipalities, more structured and complementary businesses, partnerships between entrepreneurs, valuation of regional resources, realisation of new ideas and training courses for participants, the actors are limited to entrepreneurs, municipality personnel, and those from the industry (Galvão et al., 2020). Thus, the chapter argues that the development of entrepreneurships skills in TVET through the involvement of multiple stakeholders other than those from public and private sectors remain the panacea for a post-COVID-19 recovery approach for developing economies.

METHODOLOGY

This chapter addresses one objective, namely the role of MSPs in the development of entrepreneurship skills in TVET. An exploratory research approach was employed to address the objective of this chapter. According to George (2021), exploratory research is used when little or no data exist on the subject under study or when there is no established knowledge or paradigm with which to study it. Similarly, exploratory research is also employed when there is a need to tackle a new problem (Guragain, 2019). Although several studies have been conducted on TVET and MSPs, as well as TVET and entrepreneurship education, but none has considered these wholistically in relation to the recovery of developing economies post-COVID-19.

An exploratory approach was deemed suitable to investigate the role of MSPs in the development of entrepreneurship skills in TVET as a means for recovering developing economies post-COVID-19. The principal purpose of exploratory research is to provide a better understanding of the problem/issue and to facilitate comprehension for a more precise inquiry (Surbhi, 2017). Thus, data for this exploratory study were generated through secondary sources such as peer-reviewed and newspaper articles, policy reports, and blogs of local and international agencies on themes related to the objective of the chapter. The results and discussion are described next.

RESULTS AND DISCUSSION

This section presents the findings and discussions of the chapter on the development of entrepreneurship skills in TVET through MSPs as a key to recovering developing economies post-COVID-19. The themes outlined and discussed include training institutions, both formal and informal enterprises, government, non-governmental organisations (NGOs), the local community, international financing communities such as the World Bank, philanthropic individuals/organisations, and private individuals/role models (entrepreneurship ambassadors).

Entrepreneurship Skills Development in Technical and Vocational Education and Training Through Multi-Stakeholder Partnership: Post-COVID-19 Recovery Approach for Developing Economies

Emerging evidence from several studies have shown that the involvement of the training institutions, both formal and informal enterprises, government, NGOs, the local community, PTAs, international financing communities such as the World Bank, philanthropic individuals/organisations and volunteers (Lewis & Patrinos, 2012; Legg-Jack, 2018) improve TVET delivery. Thus, this suggests that the development of entrepreneurship skills will also leverage on these collaborative partnerships. These stakeholders and their roles are discussed below.

Training Institutions

Training institutions occupy a very prominent place amongst the stakeholders required for quality TVET provision. The responsibility of providing a conducive environment for TVET instructors and students to promote teaching and learning through the provision of the needed facilities is under the mandate of the training institution (Amankwah & Swanzy, 2011). Within the training institutions, instructors and school administrators are major stakeholders in the partnership arrangement (Rose, 2012; Billett, 2014). Therefore, in the development of entrepreneurship skills in TVET, the training institutions, through the agencies of instructors and students, have their role to play.

For instance, the building of local entrepreneurship education systems includes engaging teachers and school administrations in teaching entrepreneurship skills. Training institutions, especially entrepreneurial higher education institutions, represent important stakeholders for innovative firms, including small medium enterprises (SMEs) and start-ups, because they assist individuals to develop and update their abilities to match the evolving requirements of employers and be more resilient in the labour market (Organisation for Economic Co-operation and Development [OECD], 2019). This is done by providing trainees with an entrepreneurial mindset as well as helping universities to foster such competencies as creativity, problem-solving capacities, teamwork attitude, and other important soft skills (OECD, 2019). Evidence from research shows that academics may provide their assistance to SMEs through financial management training, which gives them access to banking financial services, as well as help SMEs obtain their intellectual property rights (Rosyadi et al., 2020).

Enterprise: Formal and Informal

Also noteworthy is the involvement of the industry stakeholder as part of the partners required for effective entrepreneurship skills development in TVET. According to Mpisi (2020), the industry stakeholder can provide inputs through the organisation of free training and support programmes, make their sites available to pilot projects executed by entrepreneurs, and most importantly, funding opportunities. Thus, Badawi (2013) recommends that TVET training institutions partner with the business sector to promote credibility of the training process in entrepreneurship education development. Additionally, not only will such partnership with industry create room for TVET trainees to secure internship opportunities and make the acquired knowledge sustainable, but it will also pool resources to promote apprenticeship among various companies. The latter will promote the employment of trainees by these companies, help them acquire the necessary skills about their trade as well as obtain occupational skills, and, moreover, provide insight on how they can turn these skills into a business opportunity.

The need to involve the industry partner in the planning, delivery, and implementation of the TVET programme cannot be overemphasised. As highlighted in a previous study (Gamede & Uleanya, 2019), industry involvement in the development of the entrepreneurship education curriculum foregrounds demand-driven training. This is in line with the call, due to increased demand, from many sectors of the economy, for greater collaboration between education and industry, as this will help stakeholders to understand what is expected of them (Bawakyillenuo et al., 2013).

Government

The role of the government is crucial in the delivery of an effective and efficient TVET programme. The latter includes the formulation of adequate and favourable policies to restructure industrial training for both staff and students; the establishment of regional training centres to build student competencies for industry; providing financial support for instructors; supplying equipment and infrastructure for the training programme; and offering inducements to encourage industry to train students through work placement (Alam & Hoque, 2010). In addition to the above, the government also gives legislative backing to national TVET policies; invests in TVET programmes; mobilises and encourages the private sector to participate in the quality delivery of TVET programmes; and also ensures the effective monitoring of TVET programmes for relevance (Aworanti, 2015). These roles, as offered by the government stakeholder, are important in the advancement of entrepreneurship programmes.

The government creates an enabling environment for the entrepreneurship ecosystem through the formulation of favourable policies that encourage the growth of entrepreneurship activities (Mason & Brown, 2014).

Non-Governmental Organisations

Another key partner in TVET provision are NGOs. NGOs represent a third sector initiative in the globalisation process in which the government is being removed from certain spheres of involvement while at the same time allowing people the freedom to initiate and choose what they want, thereby allowing them to fill the gaps left by the government in the development progression (Amutabi, 2006). It is recommended that collaborations between TVET institutions be established for the provision of funds for the proper implementation of training programmes with respect to the essential requirements of the programme. This is corroborated in a study that highlighted the need to partner with NGOs as one of the major strategies to procure facilities and equipment for TVET institutions (Umar & Ma'aji, 2010).

Community

In a developing context, the community is one of the major stakeholders in the delivery of a quality TVET provision. TVET training institutions are located in communities where members of such communities are provided with skills that benefit their immediate environment as well as other agencies, such as the industry and government, among others. Community members are the end users of the skills acquired from TVET institutions (Gagnon, 2019); thus, this makes the community a strategic stakeholder in TVET provision. According to Mertineit (2013), the model of intervention possibilities for sustainable development in qualifying vocational institutions depend on its cooperation with strategically important stakeholders such as the communities in the planning and delivery of its programmes. As reported by Legg-Jack (2018), the impact of the community transcends the provision of land by the government for the building of training institutions, serving as a protective measure for securing facilities provided by the state. The community also promotes the study of TVET by encouraging its children to be part of the training. Deductively, as seen from these scholars cited above, the community forms part of the decision-making cabinet for a successful TVET provision. However, one of the challenges of young entrepreneurs in TVET has been traced to the inability to come up innovative ideas that serve their immediate community due to the lack of proper engagement with community members who are end-users of their products and services (Gagnon, 2019).

International Donor/Financing Organisations (IFOs)

Due to the implementation of TVET programmes being capital intensive, the involvement of international organisations can help solve the problem of lack of resources needed for the implementation of TVET programmes (Edomwonyi et al., 2016). Such collaboration with international donors or financing agencies will help in the provision of well-equipped workshops and laboratories, service facilities, modern machinery, and adequate financing (Legg-Jack, 2018). Mukirae (2005) concurs that collaboration with IFOs, such as the World Bank, can assist training institutions with the provision of grants for capital development expenditure to enable them to expand their capacity and modernise their training. In his 2018 study Legg-Jack revealed the pressing need to partner with IFOs, such as the World Bank, indicating that this would help in strengthening existing partnerships for a relevant, effective and efficient TVET programme. In 2020, the World Bank approved a $104 million grant from the International Development Association (IDA) to fund skills development programmes for Mozambican youth as an investment in TVET and higher education subsystems to improve access to and the quality of educational curriculums and skills development training in response to the country's priorities and economic sectors (World Bank, 2020a). By implication, the availability of the needed facilities in TVET institutions facilitates the development of prerequisite entrepreneurship skills.

From the foregoing, it is evident that partnership with IFOs prove beneficial to the development of entrepreneurship skills/programmes in TVET. In a World Bank (2020b) report, it was revealed that the Women Entrepreneurship Development Project of Ethiopia received US$65.8 million in co-financing from Japan International Cooperation Agency (JICA) and Italian Agency for Development Cooperation (AICS). Co-financing was also received from the European Investment Bank (EIB) with a co-financing agreement signed by the World Bank. Similarly, it was also reported that the government of Eritrea implemented a project on the Support for Skills Development for Employability and Entrepreneurship in TVET, through a partnership loan from the African Development Fund (ADF) (ADF, 2015).

Private Individuals/Role Models (Entrepreneurship Ambassadors)

Partnerships with private individuals who act as role models or entrepreneurship ambassadors is well documented in contemporary research. For instance, according to the OECD (2019), the importance of role models for entrepreneurial motivation is well supported by research, as they can help develop positive collective mindsets with respect to entrepreneurship and signal that entrepreneurship is a favourable career option. The literature also shows that children of self-employed parents are more likely to become self-employed themselves (Dunn & Holtz-Eakin, 2000; Laspita et al., 2012). Role models can promote industrial transformation by helping to improve entrepreneurship cultures and encouraging innovative entrepreneurship activity for regions in industrial transition (OECD, 2019) through the role model approach as revealed in research (Lindner, 2020).

As reported by Lindner (2020) in Wales, entrepreneur role models deliver powerful curriculum sessions to make different career choices, including start-ups, a more desirable option. The latter supports the viewpoint of the OECD (2019) that exposure to direct interaction with successful entrepreneurs is one of the channels to promote entrepreneurship. This corroborates the findings of the report from the virtual conference organised by the International Centre for Technical and Vocational Education and Training (UNESCO-UNEVO), the formation of a group of career counsellors to provide virtual mentoring to link the relevance of entrepreneurial skills and mindsets to career paths, or the development of connections between students and entrepreneurial role models from different walks of life (Lindner, 2020). Thus, involving persons from this category will add more value to the development of entrepreneurship skills in TVET.

Deductions from the preceding discussion highlight the plethora of benefits associated with such partnerships in quality and efficient TVET provision. Therefore, the chapter argues that, through collaboration with key stakeholders across diverse sectors, the development of entrepreneurship skills in TVET graduates would yield a positive outcome. That is, inputs will be harnessed from all stakeholders for the planning, delivery, and implementation of entrepreneurship skills development in TVET for the purpose of recovering developing economies post-COVID-19.

FUTURE RESEARCH DIRECTIONS

Considering the exploratory approach adopted in this chapter where data was generated through secondary sources by reviewing related literature on the subject, it is obvious that the insights provided are not adjudged final. This is attributable to the reasons that primary sources of data generation such as interviews, surveys, observations and focus group discussions, among others, were not employed. Therefore, the findings in this chapter only provided insights on the need for in-depth research to be carried out at distinct educational levels with the view to explore the specific roles of each stakeholder regarding the development of entrepreneurship skills in TVET.

CONCLUSION

The chapter focused on the development of entrepreneurship skills in TVET through MSPs as a post-COVID-19 recovery strategy for developing nations. The purpose was to explore the role of MSPs in the development of entrepreneurship skills in TVET. An exploratory approach was employed to review existing and relevant literature on COVID-19 and its impact on developing economies, entrepreneurship and TVET education, entrepreneurship education in TVET, and MSPs in TVET. From the findings of the review, it was highlighted that some participants are a necessary component of the multi-stakeholders required for the development of the needed entrepreneurship in TVET. These include the training institutions, enterprises (formal and informal), government and NGOs, the community, IFOs, and private individuals who are role models/entrepreneurship ambassadors. Thus, the chapter concludes that collaboration between these stakeholders would aid in the development of the needed entrepreneurship skills in TVET, thereby serving as a recovery strategy for developing economies.

REFERENCES

Acs, Z. J. (2006). How is entrepreneurship good for economic growth? *Innovations: Technology, Governance, Globalization, 1*(1), 97–107. doi:10.1162/itgg.2006.1.1.97

Acs, Z. J., & Amoros, J. E. (2008). Entrepreneurship and competitiveness dynamics in Latin America. *Small Business Economics, 31*(3), 305–322. doi:10.100711187-008-9133-y

Adams-Prassl, A., Boneva, T., Golin, M., & Rauh, C. (2020). Inequality in the impact of the coronavirus shock: Evidence from real time surveys. *Journal of Public Economics, 189*, 104245. doi:10.1016/j.jpubeco.2020.104245

African Development Bank. (2021). African economic outlook 2021: *From debt resolution to growth: The road ahead for Africa*. African Development Bank.

African Development Fund. (2015). *Support to Skills Development for Employability and Entrepreneurship*. African Development Fund.

African Union. (2007). *Strategy to revitalize technical and vocational education and training (TVET) in Africa*. Paper presented at the Meeting of the Bureau of the Conference of Ministers of Education of the African Union (COMEDAF II+).

Akanbi, G. O. (2017). Prospects for technical and vocational education and training (TVET) in Nigeria: Bridging the gap between policy document and implementation. *International Education Journal: Comparative Perspectives, 16*(2), 1-15. https://openjournals.library.sydney.edu.au/index.php/IEJ/article/view/10668/11178

Alam, G. M., & Hoque, K. E. (2010). Who gains from" brain and body drain" business-developing/developed world or individuals: A comparative study between skilled and semi/unskilled emigrants. *African Journal of Business Management*, *4*(4), 534. doi:10.5897/AJBM.9000680

Alhasan, N. U., & Tyabo, A. (2013). Revitalizing technical and vocational education (TVET) for youth empowerment and sustainable development. *Journal of Educational and Social Research*, *3*(4), 149. doi:10.5901/jesr.2013.v3n4p149

Allcott, H., Boxell, L., Conway, J., Gentzkow, M., Thaler, M., & Yang, D. (2020). Polarization and public health: Partisan differences in social distancing during the coronavirus pandemic. *Journal of Public Economics*, *191*, 104254. doi:10.1016/j.jpubeco.2020.104254 PMID:32836504

Alon, T., Doepke, M., Olmstead-Rumsey, J., & Tertilt, M. (2020). *The impact of COVID-19 on gender equality* (No. w26947). National Bureau of Economic Research. https://www.nber.org/system/files/working_papers/w26947/w26947.pdf

Amankwah, E., & Swanzy, P. (2011). The role of stakeholders in building adequate competences in students for the job market. *International Journal of Vocational and Technical Education*, *3*(8), 107–112. doi:10.5897/IJVTE.9000038

Anyanwu, J. C., & Salami, A. O. (2021). The impact of COVID-19 on African economies: An introduction. *African Development Review*, *33*(1), 1–16. doi:10.1111/1467-8268.12531 PMID:34149237

Aworanti, O. A. (2015). *Partnership in Technical, Vocational education and training (TVET) for National Development.* A lead paper presented at the 23rd Annual International conference of the Nigeria Vocational Association held at Yaba College of Technology, Lagos.

Azubuike, O. B., Adegboye, O., & Quadri, H. (2021). Who gets to learn in a pandemic? Exploring the digital divide in remote learning during the COVID-19 pandemic in Nigeria. *International Journal of Educational Research Open*, *2*, 100022. doi:10.1016/j.ijedro.2020.100022 PMID:35059664

Badawi, A. A. (2013). TVET and entrepreneurship skills. *Revisiting global trends in TVET: Reflections on theory and practice*, 275-308.

Bartik, A. W., Bertrand, M., Cullen, Z. B., Glaeser, E. L., Luca, M., & Stanton, C. T. (2020). *How are small businesses adjusting to COVID-19? Early evidence from a survey* (No. w26989). National Bureau of Economic Research. doi:10.3386/w26989

Bawakyillenuo, S., Akoto, I. O., Ahiadeke, C., Aryeetey, E. B., & Agbe, E. K. (2013). *Tertiary education and industrial development in Ghana: Working paper.* Institute of Statistical, Social and Economic Research (ISSER): University of Ghana, Legon.

Billett, S. (2014). The standing of vocational education: Sources of its societal esteem and implications for its enactment. *Journal of Vocational Education and Training*, *66*(1), 1–21. doi:10.1080/13636820.2013.867525

Blackman, A., Ibañez, A. M., Izquierdo, A., Keefer, P., Moreira, M. M., Schady, N., & Serebrisky, T. (2020). *La política pública frente al COVID-19: recomendaciones para América Latina y el Caribe* (Vol. 810). Inter-American Development Bank.

Blustein, D. L., Duffy, R., Ferreira, J. A., Cohen-Scali, V., Cinamon, R. G., & Allan, B. A. (2020). Unemployment in the time of COVID-19: A research agenda. *Journal of Vocational Behavior*, *119*, 103436. doi:10.1016/j.jvb.2020.103436 PMID:32390656

Bottan, N., Hoffmann, B., & Vera-Cossio, D. (2020). The unequal impact of the coronavirus pandemic: Evidence from seventeen developing countries. *PLoS One*, *15*(10), e0239797. doi:10.1371/journal.pone.0239797 PMID:33027272

Briscese, G., Lacetera, N., Macis, M., & Tonin, M. (2020). *Compliance with COVID-19 social-distancing measures in Italy: the role of expectations and duration.* https://docs.iza.org/dp13092.pdf

Brzezinski, M. (2018). Income inequality and the Great Recession in Central and Eastern Europe. *Economic Systems*, *42*(2), 219–247. doi:10.1016/j.ecosys.2017.07.003

Channing, A., & Sherman, R. (2020). *Who Has Been Hit hardest by the South Africa's Lockdown: Working paper*. Braamfontein: The Conversation. https://theconversation.com/who-has-been-hit-hardest-by-south-africas-lockdown-we-found-some-answers-138481

Chun, H. K., Comyn, P., & Moreno da Fonseca, P. (2021). *Skills development in the time of COVID-19: taking stock of the initial responses in technical and vocational education and training.* https://www.ilo.org/wcmsp5/groups/public/---ed_emp/---ifp_skills/documents/publication/wcms_766557.pdf

Clarke, A., & MacDonald, A. (2019). Outcomes to partners in multi-stakeholder cross-sector partnerships: A resource-based view. *Business & Society*, *58*(2), 298–332. doi:10.1177/0007650316660534

Dorado, S., Giles, D. E. Jr, & Welch, T. C. (2009). Delegation of coordination and outcomes in cross-sector partnerships: The case of service-learning partnerships. *Nonprofit and Voluntary Sector Quarterly*, *38*(3), 368–391. doi:10.1177/0899764008316055

Draxler, A. (2008). *New Partnerships for EFA: Building on Experience*: ERIC. http://efaidnbmnnnibpcajpcglclefindmkaj/viewer.html?pdfurl=https%3A%2F%2Ffiles.eric.ed.gov%2Ffulltext%2FED499733.pdf&clen=1247609

Dunn, T., & Holtz-Eakin, D. (2000). Financial capital, human capital, and the transition to self-employment: Evidence from intergenerational links. *Journal of Labor Economics*, *18*(2), 282–305. doi:10.1086/209959

Dzeto, G. K. (2014). *Projecting Ghana into the real middle-income economy: the role of Technical, Vocational Training*. Parliamentary Briefing Paper, Friedrich Ebert Stiftung. http://library.fes.de/pdf-files/bueros/ghana/11300.pdf

Edomwonyi, J., Osasogie, H., & Olaita, E. (2016). *Actualizing Sustainable High Standard of Quality in Nigerian TVET Programme Through Multi-Stakeholders Partnership*. Academic Press.

Federal Republic of Nigeria (FRN). (2013). *National Policy on Education*. NERDC Press.

Fennell, S. (2010). Public-private partnerships and educational outcomes: New conceptual and methodological approaches. *RECOUP Working Paper, 37*(3). https://ceid.educ.cam.ac.uk/researchprogrammes/recoup/publications/workingpapers/WP37-PPP_and_Educational_Outcomes.pdf

Fetzer, T. R., Witte, M., Hensel, L., Jachimowicz, J., Haushofer, J., Ivchenko, A., ... Yoeli, E. (2020). *Global Behaviors and Perceptions at the Onset of the COVID-19 Pandemic* (No. w27082). National Bureau of Economic Research. doi:10.3386/w27082

Gagnon, P. L. (2019). *Collaborative research on community engagement in TVET*. https://unevoc.unesco.org/home/UNEVOC+Publications/lang=en/akt=detail/qs=6145

Galvão, A. R., Marques, C. S., Ferreira, J. J., & Braga, V. (2020). Stakeholders' role in entrepreneurship education and training programmes with impacts on regional development. *Journal of Rural Studies, 74*, 169–179. doi:10.1016/j.jrurstud.2020.01.013

Gamede, B. T., & Uleanya, C. (2019). Factors impacting entrepreneurship education in TVET colleges: A case of South Africa. *Journal of Entrepreneurship Education, 22*(3), 1–12. https://www.proquest.com/scholarly-journals/factors-impacting-entrepreneurship-education-tvet/docview/2331183669/se-2?accountid=36534

George, T. (2021). *Exploratory Research | Definition, Guide, & Examples* [Blog]. https://www.scribbr.com/methodology/exploratory-research/

Giandhari, J., Pillay, S., Wilkinson, E., Tegally, H., Sinayskiy, I., Schuld, M., Lourenço, J., Chimukangara, B., Lessells, R., Moosa, Y., Gazy, I., Fish, M., Singh, L., Sedwell Khanyile, K., Fonseca, V., Giovanetti, M., Carlos Junior Alcantara, L., Petruccione, F., & de Oliveira, T. (2021). Early transmission of SARS-CoV-2 in South Africa: An epidemiological and phylogenetic report. *International Journal of Infectious Diseases, 103*, 234–241. doi:10.1016/j.ijid.2020.11.128 PMID:33189939

Gibb, A. (2008). Entrepreneurship and enterprise education in schools and colleges: Insights from UK practice. *International Journal of Entrepreneurship Education, 6*(2), 1–48.

Guragain, S. (2019, October 31). *Exploratory Research Design*. https://shyamguragain.com.np/exploratory-research-design/

Heathcote, J., Perri, F., & Violante, G. L. (2010). Unequal we stand: An empirical analysis of economic inequality in the United States, 1967–2006. *Review of Economic Dynamics, 13*(1), 15–51. doi:10.1016/j.red.2009.10.010

Hoftijzer, M., Levin, V., Santos, I., & Weber, M. (2020). *TVET Systems' Response to COVID-19*. https://openknowledge.worldbank.org/bitstream/handle/10986/33759/TVET-Systems-response-to-COVID-19-Challenges-and-Opportunities.pdf?sequence=1&isAllowed=y

Huxham, C., & Hibbert, P. (2004). Collaborating to know? Interorganizational engagement and learning. *Advanced Institute of Management Research Paper*, (013). doi:10.2139/ssrn.1306956

Ibrahim, N. A., & Lucky, E. O. I. (2014). Relationship between entrepreneurial orientation, entrepreneurial skills, environmental factor and entrepreneurial intention among Nigerian students in UUM. *Entrepreneurship and Innovation Management Journal*, *2*(4), 203–213.

Igbo, C. A. (2006). Developing entrepreneurship through entrepreneurship education. *Journal of Home Economics Research*, (7), 50–54.

Ismail, A., Adnan, W. N., Masek, A., Hassan, R., Hashim, S., & Ismail, M. E. (2019). Effectiveness of entrepreneurship programmes in developing entrepreneurship skills towards quality TVET graduates. *Journal of Technical Education and Training*, *11*(1), 81–86. doi:10.30880/jtet.2019.11.01.010

Ivan, M., & Albu, R. G. (2014). A new model of Vocational Education and Training in Brasov County. *Bulletin of the Transilvania University of Brasov. Economic Sciences. Series V*, *7*(1), 77–84.

Key, M., Kenya, T., & Works, M. (2013). *Development of 21st Century Skills for Innovation and Enterprise: Exploring the role of Informal Learning Environments in the Development of Skills and Aptitudes for the Digital Creative Media Industries*. Report collated by Neil Butcher and Associates for GESCI January 2013.

Kissi, E., Ahadzie, D. K., Debrah, C., & Adjei-Kumi, T. (2020). Underlying strategies for improving entrepreneurial skills development of technical and vocational students in developing countries: Using Ghana as a case study. *Education + Training*, *62*(5), 599–614. Advance online publication. doi:10.1108/ET-11-2019-0264

Ladipo, M., Akhuemonkhan, I., & Raimi, L. (2013). *Technical Vocational Education and Training (TVET) as mechanism for Sustainable Development in Nigeria (SD): Potentials, Challenges and Policy Prescriptions*. Paper presented at the Presentation at CAPA International Conference, Banjul, Gambia.

Laspita, S., Breugst, N., Heblich, S., & Patzelt, N. (2012). Intergenerational transmission of entrepreneurial intentions. *Journal of Business Venturing*, *27*(4), 414–435. doi:10.1016/j.jbusvent.2011.11.006

Legg-Jack, D. W. (2014). *Employability skills of Technical College graduates: A case for Government Technical College (GTC) in Ahoada Rivers State Nigeria* (Masters). University of KwaZulu-Natal, Durban, South Africa. http://hdl.handle.net/10413/12688

Legg-Jack, D. W. (2018). *Technical and vocational education and training (TVET) provision in Nigerian technical colleges: exploring the relevance, effectiveness and efficiency (REE) of stakeholder partnerships using community-based participatory action research (CBPAR)* (Doctoral dissertation). University of KwaZulu-Natal, Durban, South Africa. https://researchspace.ukzn.ac.za/handle/10413/18199

Lewis, L., & Patrinos, A. H. (2012). *Impact evaluation of private sector participation in education*. The World Bank: CfBT Education Trust.

Libecap, G. D. (2003). Introduction. In G. D. Libecap (Ed.), *Issues in Entrepreneurship (Advances in the Study of Entrepreneurship, Innovation and Economic Growth, 14)* (pp. ix–xvii). Emerald Group Publishing Limited. doi:10.1016/S1048-4736(02)14010-0

Liñán, F. (2008). Skill and value perceptions: How do they affect entrepreneurial intentions? *The International Entrepreneurship and Management Journal*, *4*(3), 257–272. doi:10.100711365-008-0093-0

Lindner, J. (2020). *Entrepreneurial learning for TVET institutions: A practical guide*. UNESCO Publishing.

Maclean, R. (2011). Key Issues and Research Challenges for TVET: Bridging the gap between TVET research and the needs of policy makers. *NORRAG NEWS, Towards a New Global World of Skills Development*, 125-127.

Mason, C., & Brown, R. (2014). *Entrepreneurial ecosystems and growth-oriented entrepreneurship.* Final report to OECD. https://www.oecd.org/cfe/leed/Entrepreneurial-ecosystems.pdf

McGrath, S. (2012). Vocational education and training for development: A policy in need of a theory? *International Journal of Educational Development*, *32*(5), 623–631. doi:10.1016/j.ijedudev.2011.12.001

Mertineit, K.-D. (2013). *TVET for a Green Economy*. GIZ. https://www.enterprise-development.org/wp-content/uploads/TVET_Green_Economy.pdf

Meyer, K., Prashantham, S., & Xu, S. (2021). Entrepreneurship and the Post-COVID-19 Recovery in Emerging Economies. *Management and Organization Review*, *17*(5), 1–18. doi:10.1017/mor.2021.49

Mhlanga, D., & Ndhlovu, E. (2020). Socio-economic implications of the COVID-19 pandemic on smallholder livelihoods in Zimbabwe. doi:10.20944/preprints202004.0219.v1

Milanovic, B. (2016). Global Inequality in This Century and the Next. In *Global inequality: A new approach for the age of globalization*. Harvard University Press. doi:10.4159/9780674969797-006

Momen, M. N. (2020). Multi-stakeholder partnerships in public policy. In W. Leal Filho, A. Azul, L. Brandli, P. Özuyar, & T. Wall (Eds.), *Partnerships for the goals. Encyclopedia of the UN sustainable development goals* (pp. 1–9). Springer. doi:10.1007/978-3-319-71067-9_50-1

Mpisi, N. (2020, July 1). *The Importance of Stakeholder Relationships in Developing Business Opportunities for Entrepreneurs*. The Innovation Hub. https://www.theinnovationhub.com/press-room-media/thought-leadership-articles/innovation-articles/the-importance-of-stakeholder-relationships-in-developing-business-opportunites-for-entrepreneurs--nws682

Mukirae, S. N. (2005). *Income generating activities and their contribution to the provision of teaching-learning resources in National Polytechnics in Kenya.* Academic Press.

Nicola, M., Alsafi, Z., Sohrabi, C., Kerwan, A., Al-Jabir, A., Iosifidis, C., Agha, M., & Agha, R. (2020). The socio-economic implications of the coronavirus pandemic (COVID-19): A review. *International Journal of Surgery*, *78*, 185–193. doi:10.1016/j.ijsu.2020.04.018 PMID:32305533

O'Connor, C. M., Anoushiravani, A. A., DiCaprio, M. R., Healy, W. L., & Iorio, R. (2020). Economic recovery after the COVID-19 pandemic: Resuming elective orthopedic surgery and total joint arthroplasty. *The Journal of Arthroplasty*, *35*(7), S32–S36. doi:10.1016/j.arth.2020.04.038 PMID:32345566

Okwelle, P. C., & Wordu, C. C. R. (2014). Public-Private Partnership in Education: A Strategy for Improving Quality of Vocational-Technical Education Programme in Nigeria: A Case Study of Rivers State. *Journal of Education and Practice*, *5*(35), 180–183.

Organisation for Economic Co-operation and Development (OECD). (2019). *Regions in Industrial Transition: Policies for People and Places*. OECD Regional Development Studies, OECD Publishing. . doi:10.1787/c76ec2a1-en

Oviawe, J. I. (2010). Repositioning Nigerian youths for economic empowerment through entrepreneurship education. *European Journal of Educational Studies*, *2*(2), 113–118.

Piketty, T., Yang, L., & Zucman, G. (2019). Capital accumulation, private property, and rising inequality in China, 1978–2015. *The American Economic Review*, *109*(7), 2469–2496. doi:10.1257/aer.20170973

Quality Assurance Agency for Higher Education (QAA). (2012). *Enterprise and Entrepreneurship Education*. Guidance for UK Enterprise Education Providers.

Raimi, L., & Akhuemonkhan, I. A. I. A. (2014). Has Technical Vocational Education and Training (TVET) impactedon Employability and National Development? *The Macrotheme Review: A Multidisciplinary Journal of Global Macro Trends, 3*(2), 129-145.

Ribeiro, D., & Montoro-Sánchez, M. Á. (2011). Introduction: The challenges of defining and studying contemporary entrepreneurship. *Canadian Journal of Administrative Sciences*, *28*(3), 297–301. doi:10.1002/cjas.217

Rose, M. (2012). Rethinking remedial education and the academic-vocational divide. *Mind, Culture, and Activity*, *19*(1), 1–16. doi:10.1080/10749039.2011.632053

Rosyadi, S., Kusuma, A. S., Fitrah, E., Haryanto, A., & Adawiyah, W. (2020). The multi-stakeholder's role in an integrated mentoring model for SMEs in the creative economy sector. *SAGE Open*, *10*(4). doi:10.1177/2158244020963604

SansaN. A. (2020). Analysis for the Impact of the COVID-19 to the Petrol Price in China. doi:10.2139/ssrn.3547413

Shane, S. (2003). *A general theory of entrepreneurship: The individual-opportunity nexus*. Edward Elgar. doi:10.4337/9781781007990

Smeeding, T. (2012). *Income, wealth, and debt and the Great Recession. Report*. The Russell Sage Foundation and the Stanford Center on Poverty and Inequality.

Sousa, M. J., & Almeida, M. D. R. (2014). Entrepreneurial skills development. *Recent Advances in Applied Economics*, 135-139.

Stiglitz, J. E. (2013). Society Endangers Our Future. New York: WW Norton & Company.

Surbhi, S. (2017). Difference between exploratory and descriptive research. *Key Differences*. https://keydifferences.com/difference-between-exploratory-and-descriptive-research.html

Tagicakiverata, I. W. (2012). *TVET in Fiji: attitudes, perceptions and discourses* [Unpublished PhD Thesis]. University of Newcastle.

Takei, K. (2016). *The production of skills for the agricultural sector in Tanzania: the alignment of the provision of technical, vocational education and training with the demand for workforce skills and knowledge for rice production*. University of Sussex. http://hdl.voced.edu.au/10707/416180

Umar, I. Y., & Ma'aji, A. S. (2010). Repositioning the facilities in technical college workshops for efficiency: a case study of North Central Nigeria. *Journal of STEM Teacher Education, 47*(3), 62-85. https://ir.library.illinoisstate.edu/jste/vol47/iss3/6

UNESCO. (2003). *Implementing the UNESCO/ILO recommendations concerning technical and vocational education and training: Final report of the Sub-Regional Seminar for West Africa.* UNESCO/ILO. https://unesdoc.unesco.org/images/0014/001438/143822e.pdf

UNESCO. (2004). *UNESCO international experts meeting: Learning for work, citizenship and sustainability. Final report.* UNESCO.

UNESCO. (2010). *Guidelines for TVET Policy Review.* https://unesdoc.unesco.org/ark:/48223/pf0000187487

United Nations Educational Scientific and Cultural Organisation (UNESCO). (2016). *Unpacking Sustainable Development Goal 4: Education 2030 – Guide.* https://unesdoc.unesco.org/images/0024/002463/246300E.pdf

Vining, A. R., & Boardman, A. E. (2008). Public-private partnerships in Canada: Theory and evidence. *Canadian Public Administration, 51*(1), 9–44. doi:10.1111/j.1754-7121.2008.00003.x

Wahba, M. (2010). Vocational technical education and development. In *Vocational technical education and development.* http://www.nigerianbestforum.com/blog

Wang, S. (2012). *The Legal Frameworks of Technical and Vocational Education and Training (TVET) from International Level to National Level of China.* Academic Press.

Watters, J. J., Hay, S., Dempster, N., & Pillay, H. (2013). School industry partnerships: an innovative strategy for vocational education. *Proceedings of the ECER VETNET Conference 2013.* https://eprints.qut.edu.au/63684/

World Bank. (2020a). *World Bank Injects $104 Million to Strengthen Skills Development Programs in Mozambique.* https://www.worldbank.org/en/news/press-release/2020/09/08/world-bank-injects-104-million-to-strengthen-skills-development-programs-in-mozambique

World Bank. (2020b). *Additional Financing of the Women Entrepreneurship Development Project (WEDP).* World Bank. https://documents1.worldbank.org/curated/en/103061607914878676/text/Ethiopia-Women-Entrepreneurship-Development-Project-Additional-Financing.txt

Zucman, G. (2019). Global wealth inequality. *Annual Review of Economics, 11*(1), 109–138. doi:10.1146/annurev-economics-080218-025852

Chapter 15
Creating Social Sustainability Initiatives in an Effort to Increase Profits for the Underserved

Yosmayra Erika Reyes
City University of New York, USA

Vikiana Clement
City University of New York, USA

ABSTRACT

The COVID-19 pandemic has coerced society to recreate the delicate balance between small business owners and the local community. Throughout Brooklyn, NY, the anguish resonates the difficulties of increasing profits. With communal solidarity serving as a central tenet, sword, and shield, technological and social researchers traversed urban Brooklyn, NY areas. Researchers conducted a series of exploratory interviews and surveys over the course of the last quarter specifically within the geographic grouping areas of the Crown Heights 11225 and Bedford Stuyvesant 11216 zip codes. Investigators identified key interventions to assist Black and Brown-owned businesses increase long-term sustainability. Focusing primarily on the triple bottom line theory and practice, investigators compiled data to suggest how businesses can become more economically diverse in client acquisition strategies.

BACKGROUND

New and ongoing waves of the Coronavirus pandemic have essentially stalled foot traffic in several urban city areas. In many urban areas, businesses cannot run the way they did, at least not now with what 2022 has ushered in. 2022 has brought a new year and the presence of the Omnicron variant, resulting in another financial blow to specific industries (Haag, 2020). No longer can financial metrics of the pre-COVID 19 eras be used as indicators of overall growth, "COVID-19 totally reset everything

DOI: 10.4018/978-1-6684-4322-4.ch015

for everyone, whether you are a 30-year-old business or one that has been up for 30 seconds" (Wood, 2021). The damage the COVID-19 pandemic has inflicted on the global economy has been substantial. "The International Monetary Fund (IMF) estimates that the median global GDP dropped by 3.9% from 2019 to 2020" (World Economic Outlook, 2022). Analytically, this places the COVID-19 pandemic in place as the most destructive economic downturn since the Great Depression. Likewise, the uncertainties involved in the economic rescue of countries poses a conundrum that has provoked considerable tension in recovery efforts. These recovery efforts need to be considered in tandem with prospective courses of economic alleviating measures, vaccine roll-out, and how varying societies acclimate to the constant evolving COVID-19 pandemic variants in order to lessen both economic and communal tension (World Economic Outlook, 2022).

One sector that has felt the effects are the numerous Brooklyn hair salons and barbershops that line the streets of the Crown Heights and Bedford Stuyvesant neighborhoods. Bedford Stuyvesant and Crown Heights harbor sizable denizens of African diaspora descent. Since the late 1960s, myriads of Caribbean, African American, and African people have anointed these neighborhoods as home (Lemann, 1992). Crown Heights and Bedford Stuyvesant neighborhoods are emblematic staples of black and brown culture as well as entrepreneurship. However, black and brown-owned companies are more than simple confirmations of enterprise ownership. Black and brown-owned businesses are palimpsests with every day of operations revealing the complex levels present in chasing the American dream. A dream where market participation must coexist in an atmosphere where structural racism and discrimination serve as scaffolds (Fairlie, 2014).

Prompted by the historiographical evidence of the significance that barbers and stylists hold in black and brown culture, the researchers engaged in a quest to identify interventions that would protect such emblems of the community. Barbershops and salons provide beautification and grooming experiences. Likewise, in black and brown neighborhoods, these shops serve as a critical residence for black and brown community life (Mills, 2013). These shop owners, most of whom have been in the community for at least the last ten years prior to 2022, provide a real connection to communities often marginalized and extricated from mass media (Mills, 2013). As the time and global burden of the COVID-19 pandemic have increased, these businesses are having difficulty remaining afloat. During a recent study by the Global Entrepreneurship Monitor (GEM), an agency monitoring entrepreneurship as a driver of societal health and wealth, even amongst businesses that closed gender differences were noted with women more likely to report a business closure by 20% than their male counterpart (Lonescu, 2022). Many have taken on extra employment, lowered costs, reduced their workforce, all to report during the researchers' findings that this may very well be their last year open. Some have been ravaged by the loss of clients, family, and friends.

In the midst of researchers conversing with these businesses, any remnants of uncertainty were lifted, providing evidential certitude that these businesses serve more like communities than anything else. Observing not only the rapport with employees and the seldom customer base that was present, but also in the gathered survey responses, these shops demonstrated to be business communities (Appendix B). As such, these business communities provide a delicate social weaving to society, such that searching for a way to assist in keeping them open and self-sustainable was the only answer investigators concurrently arrived at when faced with how to resolve this current conundrum.

THEORY

Social sustainability is not a term that is easily understood and often can be oversimplified. Frequently, the social facet is the neglected atom of the element of sustainability. Sustainable evolutionary and growth dialogues constantly emphasize sustainability's environmental or economic facets (Khan, 2021). Nonetheless, all three ambits of sustainability must be grappled with to cultivate the most sustainable development potential. Social sustainability can suggest a variety of occurrences. One perspective is the construction of sustainable, prosperous establishments that encourage well-being by comprehending what individuals require from the areas where they live and work (Camilleri, 2017). Similar to a pendulum displaced from its equilibrium position and subjected to a restorative and invisible force called gravity, the social aspect within social sustainability functions as one of the invisible hands that can accelerate or decelerate businesses back into their equilibrium position.

One of the principles introduced by the triple bottom line model is that negating social value is detrimental to companies and communities in which businesses operate and serve (Henriques, 2007). The many disasters that have majorly impacted day-to-day transactions have helped companies understand that while change is inevitable, how businesses influence change can really impact the progression of society (Camilleri, 2017). In a recent webinar of the Harvard Kennedy Educator's Series, titled Promoting Social Change Through the Private Sector, Jane Nelson, Director of Corporate Social Responsibility, states that the biggest drivers of change will be local businesses (Nelson, 2020). In understanding this message, the researchers set a tremendous task of garnering a new social movement amongst this small group of entrepreneurs. Their mission, should shop owners agree, would be to increase profits through the creation of a social value for the community.

Taking more traction in accounting framework practices, the TBL has mainly been used to hold corporate organizations accountable for their varying operational sectors' mal effects on the environment (Savitz, 2014). The development of the 'p for people' in the TBL has become clearer with the addition of metrics that can be used to measure success. Growing the 'people' aspect of business has become broader and less tangible.

The triple bottom line, novel in approach in global sustainability, has evolved from inception to include a much more dynamic meaning that is not easily understood in the research findings of local black and brown businesses in the 11216 and 11225 zip codes. The triple bottom line identifies that businesses, being driven by profit alone, are at a detriment to long-term growth and sustainability. Nowhere is this more evident than during the aftermath of the first wave of the global COVID-19 pandemic. Businesses interviewed throughout this study have focused solely on monetary profit as a driver of growth. Consequently, they have found themselves at a loss as to how to function given the lack of foot traffic, and have found little impetus to create other means of growth.

METHODOLOGY

Recruitment engagement of participants for this qualitative study was done in the 11216 and 11225 zip code. Using a narrower focus in regards to region allowed researchers to delve deeply and gain critical insights into the common problems that are occurring for local black and brown businesses. A thematic analysis interpretation, in line with the Braun and Clarke outline, was used to create and identify defining themes throughout the study (Braun, 2006). The researchers conducted purposive sampling of local black and brown-owned hair and barber salons in the 11216 and 11225 zip code. The study consisted of semi-structured in-depth interviews at the place of business. Information gathered and analyzed using the COREQ qualitative interview reporting guide to ensure increasing interval validity (2006). Themes identified via extensive analysis and interpretation generated common views amongst this population that may facilitate adoption of sustainability practices in order to ensure business survivorship.

Purposive sampling size was 22 businesses, 11 participants decided not to complete questionnaires or interviews and 11 completed questionnaires and in-depth interviews. Of the 11 that decided not to complete the questionnaire, 3 were recently closing and stated that as their reason for not participating. Although outreach was made these former business owners were significantly despondent in providing meaningful feedback. Many from reports provided invested entire life savings on business ventures that fell through and were not supported by government rescue funding during the pandemic.

Data was collected at the interviewee's place of business. The setting was specifically chosen to understand the business owners in their own environment. Researchers were privy to useful knowledge, such as, assessing foot traffic and adaptive capacity for integration. Of importance to note during data collection, was the intricate relationship that had to be established requiring significant efforts in rapport building and engagement. Initially, respondents lacked engagement and motivation to take part in the study even when the time was allotted to provide education on topics addressed as well as how it may benefit the business owner. Important in helping to breach this population was the relatability of the interviewer. As noted in Nowell et al paper addressing trustworthiness in interviewing, the 'fit,' an allusive term depicting relatability between respondents and the researcher's representation of them is critical (2017). Having black and brown researchers themselves assisted in bridging cultural divides and lowering defensive responses within the interview and questionnaire. Business owners felt researchers had understood and lived their experiences. Incidentally, those that did partake of the study, once engaged, were very forthcoming with information regarding their current economic status.

Overall, semi structured interviewing provided a strong relational focus in order to establish trust and rapport. In addition, researchers felt that the semi-structured interview allowed business owners to have a platform to discuss problems not easily identified if only a survey was provided. Interviews conducted were unfolding, requiring extensive iteration between the interviewer and interviewee. The interview process involved two to three introductory attempts to understand who the owner was and coordinating logistics. After consensus was established, multiple interviews were conducted in a semi-structured format at the place of location.

Findings were extensively analyzed for the derivation of explicit themes, as well as, integrated with participant feedback during in-depth interviews. Block transcripts have been included in this report to garner the growing pains as reported directly from participants. Researchers felt it is important to include these block transcripts given the intimate nature of the questions asked and the severity of consequences experienced by owners directly from the global pandemic.

Data analysis conducted consisted of interpreting transcribed interviews made up of detailed notes, questionnaires, and assessments of the individual business adaptive capacity for change. Researchers used a thematic analysis framework, providing descriptive codes to look for patterns and themes that may assist in the adoption of social sustainability practices. Through review and quantifying of extensive feedback from businesses interviewed, the adaptive capacity for change was assessed.

Businesses were gauged for their ability to self-organize, their capacity for learning, and their understanding of diversification related to the building of clientele. With the understanding that change is actively occurring in these urban, local markets, particularly in the closure of so many businesses that were staples in the community, businesses were given a scoring card on their 'adaptiveness' to the market climate.

Efforts for increased validity were made through meticulous assessment of the business owner's adaptive capacity. Business owners were visually assessed for readiness and integration of technology in their local establishment (Appendix C). Criteria assessed include internet readiness capacity, point of sale system and e-commerce availability, to mention a few. This assessment in turn allowed the researchers to begin to understand the drivers for change by leveraging resources, learning capacity and leadership skills. Feedback on the visual assessment was not obtained by the business owners themselves, rather they were conducted by a certified software engineer in order to address any key points of intervention for technology integration.

To become immersed in the data researchers conducted weekly research meetings, reflexive writing, and journaling throughout the coding process in an effort to systematically examine reported thoughts and feelings that may have created emerging impressions. Meeting minutes were recorded in order to establish an audit trail. A temporary template to assess the data was used in order to allow for themes to emerge independently throughout the course of the work. As noted by King, in providing guidance to qualitative methods, creating a provisional template ensures validity in the coding process of themes (2004). Thematic Mindmaps were created as a visual representation of codes identified, see appendix B.

Researchers had no affiliation to businesses owners interviewed and conducted the study independently of any organization in order to provide cutting-edge research.

FINDINGS

Research conducted identified 22 barber and hair salon businesses within the 11216 and 11225 zip codes. Of the 22 that were identified 11 agreed to full interviews and assessment of adaptive capacity. To address the overall and most prevalent nuances that are being faced by shop owners in these communities, of these 11 establishments interviewed, 4 are highlighted next in (1) impressions.

Overall findings from this study grouped common themes reported among local business owners in adopting sustainable businesses practices. Of the themes identified, the idea of (2) 'being left behind,' (3) needs for targeted interventions, (4) implementation gaps and (5) adaptive capacity stand out as worthy of further discussion and will also be subsequently spotlighted.

1. Impressions

Throughout this process, significant efforts were placed in locating the owner to complete the interview. Noted by the researchers in this study, black and brown business owners identified were under substantial amounts of pressure to meet monthly finances resulting in increased efforts of engagement. Oftentimes the owner had multiple responsibilities, including for some businesses interviewed, an additional full-time job to support the running of the business. This was found to be particularly impactful with interviewees who stated this provided additional difficulties with employees who took advantage of the owner not being able to properly manage employee relations socially termed 'mind my shop' (Appendix B).

Many of the participants within this qualitative study, when asked if they ever heard of the triple bottom line model, had never heard of the theory. Likewise, when provided by the researchers with an overview of the triple bottom line model, more than 75% of the participants in the study had little to no understanding of how focusing on a social good could serve as a catalyst for more considerable proceeds and returns.

Many business owners understood sustainability as a conscious awareness of their ecology footprint, other words verbalized as the 'green movement' during interviews conducted (Appendix B). No business owner commented nor reflected on terms understood as 'social sustainability,' a concept utterly foreign to these entrepreneurs. The researchers informed business owners of data demonstrating industries that concentrated on providing a social benefit to their clientele resulting in translatable income. The akin responses from varied owners on their views provided evidence to the investigators that social sustainability received the least attention compared to the economic and environmental drivers of growth.

A.1 *Business #1: Meet Teresa*

An over 65-year-old, west Indian owner of an emblematic staple in Flatbush within the 11225 zip code area, Teresa has owned and operated her business for more than 20 years. Prior to the pandemic, her salon was operating at hustling and bustling speeds; one in which you would be lucky to receive an appointment the same week or same month of calling. Post-2020 pandemic, you would not believe however this was the same beauty salon. The salon fully empty didn't do much to quell the anxiety of a business proprietor who exhaustively feels as if this is her first merry go around in this new entrepreneurial world.

When interviewed by the researcher, and asked: 'In your own words, how have you maintained your business afloat throughout the past year?' Teresa simply answered, "We are all guessing here! I don't know what I'm doing. I come in earlier and stay later. I risk my safety, closing my shop late but I must do it. Because if my shop closes so does my safety" (Teresa, personal communication January 15, 2020). Teresa speaks to the current increase in crime that has been reported in New York and in major urban cities across the United States, as the pandemic fuels civil and economic unrest (Watkins, 2021). The increase in poverty and low-income level paying positions has been positively correlated to the increase in crime throughout New York.

Teresa's pain was palpable as she described the tremendous impact of losing her business partner, and husband, to covid. Facial gesticulations expressed the increasing demoralization endured as she fears her business will experience a similar fate: "I've lost my husband to COVID and now I'm losing my business to COVID. We, small business owners, are all feeling this loss many others have yet to feel it, they don't hear our cries but soon they will as COVID will hit them also" (Teresa, personal communication January 15, 2020). By stating businesses like hers are feeling the financial defeats brought on by the effects of a worldwide pandemic, Teresa hints at the isolation that entrepreneurs like her find themselves in. Little resources leveraged to sustain current daily activities along with no focus on practices that could sustain long term development. Unfortunately, Teresa did not expect the pandemic crisis to continue past the initial wave "Can you believe-year three of this madness? How do businesses like ours survive when customers are scared to leave their homes? It doesn't make any sense" (Teresa, personal communication January 15, 2020). Teresa bellowed a common theme echoed amongst other business owners: lack of stewardship and increase in work hours to sustain the same standard of living prior to the pandemic.

A.2 *Business #1 Technological Assessment*

Teresa's business establishment is in dire need of technological intervention. Unlike the other businesses, Teresa is unaware of the various devices available to ease transactions for her business. Neither is she aware of social media items outside of 'Whatsapp.' Currently, the Point of Sale (POS) system is extremely limited in Teresa's shop. There is a cash drawer and a credit card swipe device. However, barcode scanners, receipt printers, and contact-less register devices are not available. Likewise, the business does not have a website or social media account. Customers are not able to make appointments online or pay online. The business is predominantly operating as a cash establishment relying on foot traffic for customers.

The social media environment status for this business is currently: nonexistent. Technological suggestive changes include upgrades to hardware, software, and social media initiatives. The business establishment is in immediate need of installing a POS system that allows for contactless retail operations. Likewise, social media efforts are necessary to bring brand awareness and increase sales. Efforts in creating targeted local marketing initiatives would assist in brand development, as well as, help this owner leverage pre-existing cultural knowledge due to her long tenure as a local black and brown business owner. Online appointments and purchase capabilities should also be initiated to assist her in streamlining servicing and creating new lines for product selling. A social media strategist is urgently needed as well as a point of contact that can assist Teresa in keeping current with the constant behaviors associated with keeping the social media up and current.

B.1 *Business #2: Meet Cee*

As a full-service-grooming barbershop that serves the Brooklyn, Bedford Stuyvesant area, Cee's barbershop performs classic hot-towel shaves, facials, hair coloring, and treatments, along with razor, shear, and clipper haircuts. A central tenet to their business mission is to provide a "friendly, comfortable atmosphere where the customers can receive clean, quality, and consistent service" (Cee, personal communication January 13, 2020). Early on throughout this assessment, this establishment stood out amongst the others due to their extensive list of servicing products. Cee has managed to understand his predominantly male clientele, advertising an extensive product diversification list, that has managed to increase his value and counteract lowered foot traffic.

When asked, "in your own words, how have you maintained your business afloat throughout the past year?" Cee responded "I have a second hustle that's why. I'm a shoebox kid-I rob peter to pay paul. I build my own shop physically working construction and I save from my second hustles to make sure I can keep this shop open" (Cee, personal communication January 13, 2020). Unknowingly, Cee already adheres to the people subject under the TBL. In observation of the running of this business, the researchers noted that the owner broadened his clientele to include individuals who may require more assistance in grooming, even at the cost of charging full price. The researchers noted that this in turn allowed for community gathering amongst community members. The inclusive environment witnessed gave this business an increase in adaptive capacity. This owner was able to leverage cultural understanding of the populations he serves to create a sub list of customers that would benefit from price tiering, in which different products are created with different value pricing to attract diverse clientele.

Another important observation is the secondary employment this business owner endures to support the existing barbershop business. Contrary to other salon or barbershop owners, Cee works an outside job leaving him blindsided by what is going on in his shop when he is not there. Cee has mentioned ongoing efforts to avoid petty crime in his shop from both clients and previous employees. This owner particularly touted the ongoing pain of frequent employee turnover stating that this has specifically impacted his shop, allowing entry for poor money management.

B.2 *Business #2 Technological Assessment*

Cee's business establishment is in need of varied technological upgrades but is the only business from the pool of study not needing a severe social media intervention.

Although the Point of Sale (POS) system is limited, Cee's business does have a website and two social media accounts where clientele can make appointments and pay online.

Additionally, the business is split in operating not only as a cash establishment but also with e-commerce capabilities. Technological suggestive changes include expanding the presence and operation of the social media platform for the business. Specifically: (1) posts should be updated, most frequent post noted was 2019; (2) page and profile optimization to include more visual content such as blog banners, infographics, social media videos, and branding consistency; and (3) responsiveness to comments from followers and increase the growth of social media followers. Cee would also benefit from developing further his price tiering product values in order to provide customers with options and develop further new customer population identified throughout this year.

C.1 *Business #3: Meet Jerome*

Jerome has been operating his barbershop for 17 years, serving as a staple to the Bed-Stuy community. The Barbershop and salon have roster sheets that would make Justin Bieber jealous. The employees are treated as if they were 'family' with an average of more than 10 years working at his shop. Jerome's motto in business operation is to "be fair to my workers and to me…The pandemic has been hard on all of us. So for example this year I did not increase the rent prices of my chairs" (Jerome, personal communication January 10, 2020). The salon was notable for the inclusive language used with workers and the creation of a relaxed social environment that created added value for clients.

After hearing for the first time about the TBL theory, Jerome expressed that although he never heard of that terminology before, unknowingly, he believed that he was using the practices that fall in line with such a theory. For example, in regards to the planet, he already tries to include at his shop earth-friendly chemicals, shampoos, conditioners, and treatments for his clients. This was particularly noteworthy by the researchers, showing the entrepreneur openly leveraging culture as a way to sustain his clientele.

Jerome spoke extensively about the hair care industry and the lack of a niche market for black and brown individuals with different hair textures. The caveat, he highlighted however, is getting clients to try such products. "My clients are particular about their hair and many of them bring their own products to be used at my shop" (Jerome, personal communication January 10, 2020). The multicultural aspect of "looking good" is not a one size fits all mentality in black and brown communities, particularly where the idea of hair comes to play (Kariwo, 2013). This is a service that particularly stands amongst establishments researched in this study. "The texture, the diverse products needed, and the pressure that image brings to your hair cannot be downplayed" (Jerome, personal communication January 10, 2020).

In regards to the people aspect under the TBL, Jerome has already been involved undertaking other events that promote community relationships surrounding his shop. He understood early on, in building his star studded clientele, that he had tremendous opportunity to brand himself in the community. He has partners with Arthur Ash Downstate for about 15 years conducting workshops for the community at his shop, now on zoom, and other locations to address depression in BIPOC (black, indigenous and people of color) communities. To promote these events he has held summer block BBQs where he spreads the word by mouth to his clients.

With regards to technology integration, Jerome admitted that technologically he would love to increase his shop's social media presence and other technological advancements. Jerome identified that the biggest impediment to successful technological adoption, knowledge and understanding of integration.

C.2 *Business #3 Technological Assessment*

Jerome's business establishment is also in need of urgent technological intervention. However, Jerome is aware of the operation of social media as he has a personal social media account. He is unaware, however, of the protocols and the resources available to him or whom to contact to execute a high-end social media presence or website. He would benefit from targeted initiatives to help solidify his diverse clientele, as well as, creating a market for additional products to be sold in his shop. In regards to the POS system, Jerome's establishment would benefit highly from a POS system that would assist his operations with not just transaction processes but bookkeeping and inventory control as well. Jerome is also in need of website development services that would accommodate the other programs he is running at the shop as well, such as the mental health workshops. Jerome is successfully providing additional value to both his clients and the community. He would benefit further from developing cross-sector ties with other community agencies to assist in developing further his social value. Online appointment bookings and payment need to be added as currently, appointments are made by calling the shop.

This business is predominantly operating based on the years of relationships the shop owner has developed in the community. Jerome is actively seeing the returns of investing in a social value. He understands that the more he is connected to his clients the sooner that can translate into purchasing power. Jerome actively calls his clientele to check in with them, at least once a month, since his clients are also treated as 'family.' This act alone, can be leveraged and used with other existing businesses in order to sustain and develop further their current client list.

D.1 Business #4: Meet Maribel

Maribel is a dual citizen, born in the Dominican Republic and naturalized here in the United States. She runs a hair salon and provides servicing that includes washing, blow drying, roller sets, dyes, hair relaxers, and haircuts. Her English allows her to communicate prices with her customers as well as services. However, the language barrier presents significant impact in client diversification, as well as, business development. Maribel herself stated, during an interview conducted in her native tongue, that language barriers have been an issue in getting resources from the government throughout the pandemic both locally at community agencies and over the phone when reaching to national servicing agents.

When preparing her PPP loan application, Maribel stated the process was difficult as it required finding someone trustworthy that would assist her in translating her responses to english documentation. She reported little assistance through local business community development centers and states that going to local banks requesting additional information was not helpful. Maribel was unaware of TBL. After being given an understanding of TBL she had concerns and strong resistance as to how to incorporate the people and planet sustainability efforts into her shop. Maribel's level of distrust in government entities, a sentiment highlighted throughout many interviewees in this process, creates tremendous impediment to successful adoption. While repairing this relationship will take time, highlighted in this review are the merits of using independent agencies to mitigate the level of distrust at the communal level. These agencies can help broker services, as well as, provide guidance to businesses that are at risk of being lost in the shuffle, such as Maribel.

In regards to the people aspect under TBL Maribel states her clientele are from different ethnic backgrounds. As such, she has felt the need to adjust pricing depending on the amount of work needed for each ethnic type of hair. Maribel, although interweaving pricing tier with her clientele, has had difficulty in customer adoption with pricing. In regards to technology, she feels she can do better but is unaware of any classes that can help her understand or any workshops. Maribel stated that there are not many opportunities or resources available to small business owners like herself that can assist in brokering such cultural differences. She elaborated and disclosed that many of her professional colleagues feel the same way.

D.2 *Business #4 Technological Assessment*

Deprived of profound technological advancements, Maribel's beauty salon requires a technological makeover. Presently, the shop has an old cash register and operates specifically as a cash-only business. She needs a POS system that can assist her with tracking sales performances, inventory control, and in-store contactless retail sales. Her personal social media experience includes Whatsapp and Facebook. However, she is unaware of how to enter other social media applications or provide her business with those opportunities for exposure. Consequently, the business does not have a website or social media account. Customers are not able to make appointments online or pay online.

Maribel has been able to leverage significantly cultural sustainability tools without knowing. While she herself only speaks one language, not English, she manages to make sales predominantly to individuals who speak a different language, not English. This can be awesomely leveraged if individuals are specifically looking for servicing with the understanding that because she is Dominican she understands how to manage and protect hair to perfection'. The servicing she provides, imitative of other hair salons, is specifically sought after because of her cultural appeal. Maribel's clientele, although limited, has been consistent. Of particular use for Maribel is brokering servicing to build language of inclusion for clients, review of pricing tiers and creation of ranges for clients.

2. No One Left Behind

No business should be forgotten regarding the integration of the impacts on social change. NYC researchers noted that often black and brown businesses have become individualist in social sustainability. They have often spearheaded massive cultural movements that have opened and garnered international acclaim creating substantial local economies of scale both nationally and abroad. Contrarily this group was noted to have a limited grasp on the metrics used for measure making the applicability of this framework at a local level quite difficult. Later noted, through extensive qualitative analysis of shops interviewed, significant distrust in government has created barriers to adoption and integration. Local black and brown businesses are not confident in their interactions with the government. Many are still awaiting previously awarded funding and support from the government that for a myriad of reasons has not arrived during such a critical time.

The evolution of the TBL in accounting, particularly, in the last 10-15 years, has had a significant push in social sustainability practices. In 1997 the Global Reporting Initiative Index (GRI) was established in the United Nations who later along with the International Council for Local Environmental Initiatives ratified a list of standards for urban and community accounting making a prominent tool for public sector full cost accounting (United Nations, 2021). Other global efforts used in assessing sustainability have been the Environmental Performance Index reported under the World Economic Forum and the Genuine Progress Index both calculated at national and sub-national levels (2021). With the development of standards and guidelines, businesses have had an increasing responsibility to change and incorporate these sustainability practices. While progress has been made on international fronts, significant challenges persist in disaggregation of information at local levels. Facilitation in adoption at the local level has been a clear need identified throughout this investigative process. Local Black and Brown businesses interviewed in this study did not understand their capacity to enact impactful social change via their daily transactions believing that bigger actors, having bigger influences, should be responsible for the creation of socially impactful change.

Understanding these metrics implies that the entrepreneur must understand their clients in a more nuanced way. The eccentricities that make a person have become more complex as society evolves. One worthy data point to note was that there was no servicing tailored to the LGTBQ population. A service such as hair care, should understand their clientele very intimately and nothing is more intimate than an understanding of gender. If governmental agencies are making an effort to provide inclusive language for those who may identify as a 'they/them' then local businesses should imbibe the same practice.

3. Targeted Interventions

In the Inventors Solution, authors Christensen and Raynor, highlight a critical reality, society has created a net loss overall requiring cross-sector work and collaboration in order to drive innovation (2003). During this last year, noted as the Great Resignation, employees have exited the job market for lack of motivating and supportive work environment (Haag, 2020; Harvard, 2021; History, 2021). A strong focus has been placed in the health and wellness sector and individuals who were employed are now interested in looking for meaning in their work, work that is tied to supporting their own individualism comprised of, but not limited too, remote work option, increase in health and wellness initiatives and, equal paying opportunities for both men and women.

This modern societal revolution has the understanding that if you increase the social value of a business exchange consumers will not feel a disconnect between their purchasing power and the goods being received. Little to no consensus was found on drivers outside of increasing cash as a metric of progress. Focusing on the social impact of growth and sustainability allowed local businesses interviewed to broaden the understanding that they can in tandem influence society in a positive way and increase their profits. This involved intricate conversations on how they can leverage cultural, social, and human capital.

Cultural sustainability, a critical factor in the development of social sustainability, holds particular merit for black and brown businesses. The achievement of being a black and brown entrepreneur amidst black and brown individuals can be awesomely leveraged to create lasting ties in a community devastated by the financial toxicity of the global pandemic. Much attention has been placed on the diversification of the workforce and senior leadership in corporate agencies (Haag, 2020). During the racial turmoil that has escalated over the country in recent years, black and brown entrepreneurs can completely and utterly leverage common colloquial terms such as, 'return to black' purchasing power that has pushed major social media campaigns (Monkton, 2020).

One campaign that comes to mind is 'Blackout Tuesday" where individuals were encouraged to place a black box' on their social media platforms as a symbol of solidarity with the Black Lives Matter movement during the Summer of 2020 (Monkton, 2020).

4. Implementation Gaps

In evaluating the implementation of sustainability goals at local and communal levels significant gaps in research have been found. In depth qualitative studies such as these, are critical to drive the narrative and re-create a society that is representative of the individuals within these communities. Creating innovative research that seeks to bridge the gap and create open dialogues to perpetuate understanding are critical, particularly in assisting communities that have experienced tremendous hardships due to the global pandemic. Sponsoring field research that aims to address these gaps are critical in current market analyses.

In addition to severe economic losses faced by businesses this year, there were multiple tragedies that business owners witnessed either personally in their own families, as well as, secondary to difficulties experienced by employees. Although this information may not have directly influenced responses, owners did express ongoing feelings of low moods that may have affected them more than the interviews allowed us to interpret. In addition, amongst qualitative data interpretation, thematic analysis is not often used in comparison to other research methods, such as grounded theory or ethnography. The advantage of thematic analysis lies in the flexibility provided to a complex approach in identifying themes but requires extensive effort to ensure themes identified are cohesive and robust.

Researchers focused on the 11216 and 11225 geographical areas in an effort to address the most critical needs of black and brown business owners. The World Bank encourages the creation of resilient societies by working with those that are most fragile, residing in difficult environments (World Bank, 2020). The Crown Heights and the Bedford-Stuyvesant communities respectively, have each experienced substantial hardship in maintaining resilient communities. Along with increasing attention to systemic inequalities that have perpetuated for some time, there has also been ongoing diminishing resources that have crippled long standing black and brown businesses, such as the ones identified in this study.

The current global pandemic has created an unveiling of the multiple needs present in this community. Research such as this one conducted intends to address the biggest gaps in communities with an aim at providing sustainable long term solutions. One key highlight identified is the proposition of creating local learning communities amongst business owners in order to create innovative solutions to common concerns. These small learning communities can work towards increasing dissemination of self-sustainable solutions, such as, incentivizing technological inclusion. As well, creation of small learning communities can actively combat feelings of defeatism and apathy that continue to permeate local black and brown shop owners.

5. Adaptive Capacity

As critical as the solid foundation is to a home, so is the component of adaptive capacity to the development of social resiliency. As a critical component in building social resiliency, the application of adaptive capacity cascades to support disaster risk reduction, DRR. Disasters are a notable crisis worldwide and a serious hazard to sustainable development (Twigg, 2015). Disasters precipitate from an assortment of factors: disasters can be found in space and time, can operate in combination or separately, can result from nature or be man-made, the categories of classification and cause are boundless. Still, one métier that all disasters have in common is that they are ordinarily compartmentalized as extreme events in their scale or impact, warranting some form of external assistance (Twigg, 2015). DRR strives to ameliorate the impairments provoked by disasters via an ethic of prevention (Kocak, 2021). Under the DRR model, each determination and response positions the impacted population to become either additionally vulnerable to disasters or more resilient to them (Canlas, 2021).

Researchers in this study gathered data and insight from entrepreneurs and business owners in black and brown communities. Throughout these explorative discovery efforts data revealed associations between business ownership experience, information for sustainable development, and disaster risk reduction (DRR) teachings. These associations could be further mitigated by administering and applying an adaptive capacity lens as a shared targeted learning outcome.

Analysis of the data by the researchers took into account both the Gobet and Chassy theory of intuition and the Dreyfus model of skill acquisition. Studies of human learning by Gobet, Chassy, and Dreyfus indicate that learning various abilities is a pyramided system where people perambulate through numerous skill attainment and mastery levels (Dreyfus, 2000). The investigators categorized technological assessment into five elements of learning for adaptive capacity: "Novice, Advanced Beginner, Competent Performer, Proficient Performer, and Expert" (Dreyfus, 1980). Additionally, after gathering and reviewing the observational analysis, investigators created a post-disaster technological risk assessment (Appendix C) in line with DRR strategies and Dreyfus' mastery level categories, to relate, identify, and prevent further risk development (Twigg, 2015).

DISCUSSION

Throughout all interviewees, there were a series of consistent themes that were consistently present amongst almost all interviewees. Including:

- Distrust in government entities, particularly as it relates to small businesses
- The need for stewardship and guidance on servicing currently available in order to benefit and reap rewards to get them over this economic turbulent period
- Difficulty in establishing connections to access technical support
- Lack of activities related to mitigation of ongoing losses and transferring useful knowledge that businesses can leverage for growth

Emblematic to all owners was the inner-brow raise, one of the telltale signs of sadness that few can do on-demand. The feeling of hopelessness and longstanding grief were among the most prevalent themes. In spotlight, the sentiment that all other classifications of businesses did not partake or understand the magnitude of destitution that these service-orientated businesses had and continue to endeavor resounded throughout all interviews.

Another recurring theme highlighted throughout this investigation is the level of substantial financial toxicity experienced by business owners that have permeated

day-to-day activities. Financial institutions seem to provide black and brown businesses insufficient assistance, causing financial tools, such as attaining a Paycheck Protection Program (PPP) loan, to be neglected to these groups. Cee, the only shop owner who is a PPP recipient, stated he got the PPP loan because he knew how to "play the system." He stated, "When shit like this pandemic has come to our towns, it arrives and smashes businesses like ours because many of us were not adequately prepared to begin with all the paperwork and system operations like other businesses." … "if you ask all these shops around here, I bet you less than 50% of them won't have a traditional banking partner."

Substantial efforts have been placed by the interviewees to contain and manage the level of financial toxicity experienced. Of those interviewed, only the ones that were successful in attaining some form of government financial assistance are up to date with rent payments. All Interviewees, with the exception of one, are also awaiting the "pending" for PPP loans filed in 2021. Stated from all in their own fashion, is the structural bias that such institutions like the government have in place that do not allow shop owners like these to get the same resources as others. COVID-19 has pulled the veil on the distinctive, inequitable, business-related affairs experienced by black and brown business owners.

The research demonstrated that more programs are needed for economic development programs to be produced by the government to help produce more equitable

entrepreneurial ecosystems. Consistently resonating amongst owners was the distrust of the government to the point that owners believe they are being intentionally left behind. Unfortunately, the researchers observed this mentality causes further strife as businesses refuse to further engage with the government leaving them out of additional assistance and guidance that can be leveraged, particularly with small community business administrations, such as, for example Cypress Hill Development Corp.

In review of sentiments of government distrust, it's imperative that small business owners receive assistance in developing agency. RCS for example, a for profit company, assists local businesses who have often felt alone, displaced and poorly supported by the government broker servicing. The researchers attest that honesty and transparency from the government are key drivers for any future interactions that can allow for sustainable growth development. Companies like RSC, create professional learning communities to assist businesses improve their cross-sector expertise. For example Business owner #3 is leveraging the power of a social value by using culture to address mental health, an issue that is very sensitive for BIPOC.

'How to weather the storm' became a frequent topic of conversation throughout the investigators' extensive interviewing of black and brown-owned hair and barber salons (Jerome, personal communication January 10, 2020). These fraught, often tearful conversations, resulted in a deluge of interesting facts. Business owners fill many roles, many of which they are ill-equipped to handle due to lack of knowledge in marketing techniques, crowdsourcing, and advanced accounting practices. Owners usually are required to fill many roles. One gap that was identified is incorporating sustainability practices during these times and how to leverage sustainable practices in long-term growth development.

CONCLUSION

As the months pass with fewer and fewer foot traffic to local businesses in these neighborhoods, these epicenters rich in black and brown ownership as well as economic struggle, provided researchers with useful data that shed light on the exacerbated difficulties of making a dollar (Haag, 2020). The investigators observed that industries which have weathered the first two years of the COVID storm, require extensive assistance in developing long-term sustainable growth metrics.

Through extensive field research and rapport building with these owners, the researchers were able to identify strategies that can assist black and brown-owned tailored servicing businesses to leverage underutilized resources in an effort to increase their sustainability, in essence getting them over this economic downturn. Through the incorporation of socially sustainable business practices, businesses can redefine how they reach and keep their clientele. Lack of understanding and integration in these practices were the first barriers to adoption witnessed. Although prominent business theorists have lauded that businesses will be the biggest drivers of change in society these companies lacked the "know how" in accomplishing this (Nelson, 2020).

Society cannot afford years spent on trickle-down education. The need to actively integrate key players in order to successfully conduct cross-cultural integration research

is critical. This research effort highlights gaps in engagement, providing a framework for local businesses to flourish. In order to successfully address the social determinants of health a shift in focus needs to occur. A bigger social safety net can assist cultures' transition through stressful times, creating an infinite well of resources to choose from. Companies like RCS would seek to provide this learning framework to corporations with the understanding that cross-cultural integration is key.

We found significant barriers in adherence and slow adoption. Lack of language and application to common daily practices implies poor long term adoption. In need of increased servicing in anticipatory guidance and reasons for inclusion. Barries include, lack of communal language reflected in expenses reported, lack of awareness on how to incorporate foot initiatives and reach the targeted population.

The value framework established through this intensive qualitative study spotlights the creation of new employment in which technology is leveraged appropriately to strengthen societies. The labor force has lost a tremendous working power: millennials. The use of technology to leverage a social good has shown little merit, particularly in recent waves of government encroaching on major organizations such as Facebook, Instagram and few others. In this research technology was used as a prescriptive tool to assist black and brown businesses leverage their staying power and extend their influence. This was found to be a key dimension in the strategic planning process of using a cultural framework for adoption of sustainability practices, highlighted in SAMHSA Program Sustainability guidance (2019).

Increased funding is needed to push efforts such as these. This particular study focused primarily on addressing the financial toxicity that is extending throughout this community like a mysterious viral disease. Countless research in oncological psychosocial studies have highlighted that financial toxicity can impact health and advance the progression of cancer through the loss of a locus of control. The Social Sustainability and Inclusion Global Practice (GP) created "a new strategic direction focusing on creating more inclusive societies that fuel the empowerment of citizens, creating more resilient and peaceful environments" (World Bank, 2020). When individuals can provide self solutions, empowerment can only really exist. If this is the case then government aid should be more strategic in provisioning funds and services. Government agencies in providing funding should also provide stewardship on how to exercise each individual company's social impact and growth.

The financial burden of running a business in the last two years in the NYC area has created a substantial financial burden on local black and brown businesses. Imperative in developing a plan forward is the realization that society must move the needle forward and start tracking positive health outcomes. RCS believes that through the integration of this framework businesses can tackle problems such as, but not limited to isolation, suicide indirectly and gender equality, just to name a few.

RECOMMENDATIONS

Black and brown businesses have a tremendous number of tools in their arsenal that can be leveraged to assist in creating long term sustainability. Throughout this research, investigators noted the importance of developing relations with customers and highlighted new ways businesses can begin to market and reach additional clientele in the neighborhood. Businesses were assessed for the ability to incorporate these changes into daily business practices, as well as, their long term adoption.

Black and brown businesses have an awesome ability to leverage culture. In understanding the daily interactions of these entrepreneurs culture can be leveraged to attract new clientele. Finding new ways to attract customers and keeping them requires using this influence to provide additional services and increase value to current services provided. Local black and brown businesses should embrace the idea of adding value to the services they are already providing. Through use of technology in creating targeted marketing initiatives entrepreneurs interviewed could potentially increase local foot traffic.

Overall no businesses received additional monetary government support. The majority of the entrepreneurs interviewed stated they did not receive the PPP loan. Few understood the process of obtaining this assistance and others highlighted the tremendous amount of red tape that has been noted in local communities being able to receive funding. Owners were particularly despondent on this point as they expected more governmental assistance and hand holding. They reported feelings of abandonment termed 'left out in the cold' and 'hanging out to dry' (Appendix B).

Increasing assistance in getting and processing additional supportive funding is necessary to provide relief to the financial toxicity expressed by these owners.

Creating measurable metrics that clearly define this population is and continues to be and ongoing process. Identifying measurable metrics require further funding and investigative efforts but preliminary studies show that reintegration of customers within a block to block radius assist, creates imbibed energy in local market spending.Through engagement and brokering of services entrepreneurs identified in this study can be encouraged to create small learning communities that specifically address the creation of innovative solutions to address local common needs. Once a common language is adopted, local ground initiatives can gain substantial ground in developing long-term clientele to sustain difficulties in the market.

Increasing funding is critical, as well as, increasing the workforce that specifically addresses community integration with local businesses. Key investigative findings, highlight local businesses as strongholds for communities in place of other major infrastructures being at capacity throughout the pandemic. This potential funding and increase in manpower can assist local businesses leverage existing technology to successfully increase clientele. In turn, this repairs the trust that owners have lost in governmental systems consequently increasing dialogue and furthering opportunities to educate and increase self-sustainability.

Entrepreneurs, such as the ones interviewed in this study, require additional servicing from companies that address the idea of social sustainability. Although, a fairly new topic that requires significant traction in adoption at the local level, these companies can begin to frame this message for owners and create specific targeted marketing solutions that can assist in increasing the value attached to the services being provided. These assistive agencies can in turn provide to the government ongoing report on social adhesion and recuperation. The GEM report also cautions against the importance of focusing past diagnostics in survey findings but too trully develop longterm gains from these findings actions must be taken that are based on thorough analysis that address the gaps in entrepreneurial ecosystems (Lonescu, 2022).

The idea of informed agitation for sustainable development, a term coined by Harvard University Public Policy Professor William Clarke, is interesting in its' application to local businesses in this study. Mr. Clarke states that often business sectors needs for useful and applicable knowledge' remain unmet in order to obtain goals of sustainability. This is true in local black and brown businesses who require a certain level of stewardship in order to successfully adopt these practices (CROP secretariat, 2017). The importance of laddering their understanding in order to really profit from them is critical. Some businesses such Business #3, are already incorporating such practices and could with assistance potentially catapult into their next stage of growth. In addition increasing funding for stewardship, can potentially catalyze the recovery for the pandemic.

The President of the UN Economic and Social Council (ECOSOC) Colleen Kelapile, recently educated on this process during the 2030 Agenda for Sustainability Goals to address recovery efforts in the pandemic worldwide (CITE date ECOSOC UN 2030 agenda meeting). In this meeting attention was focused on the merits of incorporation with suggestions provided for governments to assist in aligning budgets with sustainability goals, involving engagement across all government sectors both nationally and locally. The GEM 2022 report on impacts to entrepreneurs also identifies the urgent need for sufficiency and transparency in financial supportive mechanisms in order to sustain current resuscitative developmental efforts (Lonescu, 2022). In order for disruption to be sustained and encouraged, new processes need the stepping stone of robust policy design and development in order to declare them as truly innovative.

One company highlighted in this study is Reyes Consulting Services, LLC (RCS) a company whose mission is to address the social determinants of health. RCS creates targeted initiatives that assist in increasing sustainability in communities through addressing symptoms such as isolation, gender inequality and lack of education.

Supporting companies that seek to integrate community voices in everyday practice is critical to ensuring the continual growth of society. This process highlights the importance of addressing behavioral changes in market spending and creation that ultimately can create a backbone for community development. As highlighted in GEM covid-19 response report, stewardship is required in order to support proper resource allocations for startups that can sustainably embrace a new model (Lonescu, 2022).

Entrepreneurs, particularly those interviewed in the study, cannot be given the added responsibility of educating themselves and incorporating these sustainable practices

without assistance. Partnering with agencies such as RCS can potentially assist in creating new markets and redistribution of wealth in order to assist these community staples remain in the community.

The international integrated reporting council, a value reporting foundation that seeks to facilitate sustainability integration, has provided some global recommendations that may apply here. The council identifies that full accounting cost of the life cycle of products need to include social costs. These include "promoting improvements and organizational systems that promote community well-being reduces social disturbances and increases transfer funds", known as knowledge and technology, to those who are in greatest need (McCaffry, 2014). Companies, such as RCS, address this specific infrastructural gap that exists in government servicing small businesses. Companies like RCS and others can address the ongoing process of leveraging cultural sustainability to address their own needs. Katie Wallace, in her riveting talk about the drivers of change, highlights that 'culture is curated not dictated' (TedTalks, 2016). This is important to note in order to support agencies such as RCS that seek to instill drive in culture as a method to increase growth.

REFERENCES

Bartik, A. W., Bertrand, M., Cullen, Z., Glaeser, E. L., Luca, M., & Stanton, C. (2020). The impact of COVID-19 on small business outcomes and expectations. *Proceedings of the National Academy of Sciences of the United States of America, 117*(30), 17656–17666. doi:10.1073/pnas.2006991117 PMID:32651281

Braun, V., & Clarke, V. (2006). Using thematic analysis in psychology. *Qualitative Research in Psychology, 3*(2), 77–101. doi:10.1191/1478088706qp063oa

Camilleri. (2017). Corporate sustainability and responsibility: creating value for business, society and the environment. *Asian Journal of Sustainability and Social Responsibility, 2*(1), 59–74. doi:10.1186/s41180-017-0016-5

Canlas, I. P., & Karpudewan, M. (2021). Teaching and environmentalism: A deduction from values, beliefs and norms in teaching disaster risk reduction in science. *Research in Science & Technological Education*, 1–22. doi:10.1080/02635143.2021.1978421

Christensen, C. M., & Raynor, M. E. (2003). *The Innovator's Solution: Creating and Sustaining Successful Growth*. Harvard Business School Press.

Clark, W. C., van Kerkhoff, L., Lebel, L., & Gallopin, G. C. (2016, April 26). Crafting Usable Knowledge for Sustainable Development. *Proceedings of the National Academy of Sciences of the United States of America, 113*(17), 4570–4578. doi:10.1073/pnas.1601266113 PMID:27091979

Cohen, P. J., Lawless, S., Dyer, M., Morgan, M., Saeni, E., Teioli, H., & Kantor, P. (2016). Understanding adaptive capacity and capacity to innovate in social–ecological systems: Applying a gender lens. *Ambio, 45*(S3), 309–321. doi:10.100713280-016-0831-4 PMID:27878535

Dreyfus, H., Dreyfus, S. E., & Athanasiou, T. (2000). *Mind over machine*. Simon and Schuster.

Dreyfus, H. L., & Dreyfus, H. L. (1980). *A Five-stage Model of the Mental Activities Involved in Directed Skill Acquisition*. Amsterdam University Press. doi:10.21236/ADA084551

Fairlie, R. W., & Robb, A. M. (2014). *Race and entrepreneurial success black-, asian-, and white-owned businesses in the United States*. MIT Press.

Forman, J. (2007). Damschroder L Qualitative content analysis. In *Empirical methods for bioethics: A primer* (pp. 39–62). Emerald Group Publishing Limited. doi:10.1016/S1479-3709(07)11003-7

Haag, M. (2020, August 3). *One third of New York small businesses may close be gone forever*. Retrieved December 1, 2021 from: https://www.nytimes.com/2020/08/03/nyregion/nyc-small-businesses-closing-coronaviru s.html

Harvard Kennedy Educator's Series. (2021). *Promoting Social Change through the private sector*. Retrieved January 2, 2022, from https://m.youtube.com/watch?v=W0GWqFeEu1A

History.com Editors. (2010, March 4). *The Great Migration*. History.com. Retrieved January 5, 2022, from http://www.history.com/topics/black-history/great-migration

Ionesco-Sommers, E., & Tara Wa, A. (Eds.). (2022, February 11). *Diagnosing covid-19 impacts on entrepreneurship – exploring policy remedies for recovery.* InnLab. Retrieved April 5, 2022, from https://www.upo.es/inn-lab/eventos/diagnosing-covid-19-impacts-on-entrepreneurship-e xploring-policy-remedies-for-recovery/?lang=en

Oum, S. O., & Wexler, A. (2022, February 7). *Economic impact of covid-19 on PEPFAR countries.* KFF. Retrieved February 12, 2022, from https://www.kff.org/global-health-policy/issue-brief/economic-impact-of-covid-19-on-pepf ar-countries/

Khan, N., Kakabadse, N. K.-, & Skouloudis, A. (2021). Socio-ecological resilience and environmental sustainability: case of avocado from Mexico. *International Journal of Sustainable Development & World Ecology, 28*(8), 744–758. https://doi-org.mec.ezproxy.cuny.edu/10.1080/13504509.2021.1902419

Kim, & Vachon, S. (2016). Asian journal of sustainability and social responsibility Inaugural Editorial. *Asian Journal of Sustainability and Social Responsibility, 1*(1), 57–59. doi:10.1186/s41180-016-0006-z

King, N. (2004). Using templates in the thematic analysis of text. In C. Cassell & G. Symon (Eds.), Essential guide to qualitative methods in organizational research (pp. 257–270). London, UK: Sag. doi:10.4135/9781446280119.n21

Kocak, H., Kinik, K., Caliskan, C., & Aciksari, K. (2021). The Science of Disaster Medicine: From Response to Risk Reduction. *Medeniyet Medical Journal, 36*(4), 333–342. https://doi-org.mec.ezproxy.cuny.edu/10.4274/MMJ.galenos.2021.50375

Lemann, N. (1992). *The Promised Land: The great black migration and how it changed America.* Vintage Books.

Meier, T. R. (2020). *Black Communications and learning to read: Building on children's linguistic and cultural strengths.* Routledge. doi:10.4324/9781003064442

McCaffry, R., & Topsail, N. (2014, December 12). *The Integrated Reporting System: A new ... Integrated reporting in the Public Sector.* Retrieved February 12, 2022, from https://www.researchgate.net/publication/304997679_The_integrated_reporting_system

Mills, Q. T. (2013). *Cutting along the color line: Black Barbers and Barber Shops in America.* Univ. of Pennsylvania Press.

Mohammed, A.-M., & Paleologos, E. (2021). *Social Sustainability. Social Sustainability - an overview | ScienceDirect Topics.* Retrieved January 2, 2022, from https://www.sciencedirect.com/topics/engineering/social-sustainability

Moore, M.-L., & Westley, F. (2011, January 18). *Surmountable chasms: Networks and Social Innovation for Resilient Systems. Ecology and Society.* Retrieved December 20, 2021, from https://www.ecologyandsociety.org/vol16/iss1/art5/

Monckton, P. (2021, December 10). This is why millions of people are posting black squares on Instagram. *Forbes.* Retrieved January 2, 2022, from https://www.forbes.com/sites/paulmonckton/2020/06/02/blackout-tuesday-instagram-bla ck-squares-blackouttuesday-theshowmustbepaused/?sh=7d9df7b02794

More than Green. (2016). *What's cultural sustainability? More than Green. What's cultural sustainability?* Retrieved January 2, 2022, from https://m.youtube.com/watch?v=gyIrvEZ2vXY

Nelson, J. (2020). *Promoting Social Change Through the Private Sector*. Harvard Kennedy School. https://www.hks.harvard.edu/more/about/leadership-administration/deans-office/deans-d iscussions/how-can-private-sector-promote

Nowell, L. S., Norris, J. M., White, D. E., & Moules, N. J. (2017). Thematic analysis. *International Journal of Qualitative Methods, 16*(1). doi:10.1177/1609406917733847

Nowell, L., Norris, J., White, D., & Moules, N. (2017, October 2). *Thematic Analysis: Striving to Meet the Trustworthiness Criteria*. Retrieved December 20, 2022, from https://journals.sagepub.com/doi/10.1177/1609406917733847

SAMSHA. (2018). *Sustainability Planning: Cultural Considerations*. Retrieved January 2, 2022, from https://m.youtube.com/watch?v=80POEiA-WDQ

Saeed, A., Kersten, W., & Abdelaziz, B. (2019). Sustainable product purchase: Does information about product sustainability on social media affect purchase behavior? *Asian Journal of Sustainability and Social Responsibility*, *4*(1), 1–18. https://doi.org/10.1186/s41180-019-0029-3

Shi, C., Liao, L., Li, H., & Su, Z. (2022). Which urban communities are susceptible to COVID-19? An empirical study through the lens of community resilience. *BMC Public Health*, *22*(1), 1–15. https://doi-org.mec.ezproxy.cuny.edu/10.1186/s12889-021-12419-8

TED Talks. (2016). *The Power of Culture in Driving Sustainability*. Retrieved February 11, 2022, from https://m.youtube.com/watch?v=vDZHbP_tgDY

Tong, A., Sainsbury, P., & Craig, J. (2007, December). Consolidated criteria for reporting qualitative research (COREQ): A 32-item checklist for interviews and focus groups. *International Journal for Quality in Health Care*, *19*(6), 349–357. doi:10.1093/intqhc/mzm042

Twigg, J. (2015). *Disaster Risk Reduction* (Vol. 9). Humanitarian Policy Group. http://bvpad.indeci.gob.pe/doc/pdf/esp/doc2601/doc2601-contenido.pdf

UN Dept Economic and Social Affairs. (2021, October 25). *First Global Webinar for the Voluntary National Reviews*. Retrieved February 2, 2022, from https://sustainabledevelopment.un.org/content/documents/29441Summary_First_Global _Webinar_2022_VNRs.pdf

United Nations. (2020, September). *SDG indicators*. United Nations. Retrieved December 15, 2021, from https://unstats.un.org/sdgs/report/2020/

United Nations. (2021, May 28). *Home. Sustainable development knowledge platform. Business and Industry Group Major Group - HLPF 2021 // Sectoral Paper*. Retrieved January 2, 2022, from https://sustainabledevelopment.un.org/

Watkins, A. (2021, November 8). Violent Year in New York and Across U.S. as Pandemic Fuels Crime Spike. *The New York Times*. https://www.nytimes.com/2020/12/29/nyregion/nyc-2020-crime-covid.html

World Bank Group. (2020, September 1). *Five things you need to know about social sustainability and inclusion*. World Bank.

APPENDIX 1

1. Do you know what TBP is? / Have you ever heard of TBP?
2. What do you understand by the term 'sustainable business practices?'
3. What do you understand by the term 'sustainable business practices?'
4. Have you considered the idea of 'sustainable business practices' in your company? If yes or no, why?
5. In your own words, how have you maintained your business afloat throughout the past year?
6. What services have been the most difficult to keep providing in your business?
7. What assistance could be provided to you in handling your customer(s) on a daily basis?
8. At this point in your business, what is of biggest concern to you: getting clients or keeping them?
9. Do you feel you have used technological services to the fullest advantage in your business? Why?
10. What is one thing you are keeping a focus on to meet your gains during the next quarter (3 months)?
11. Have you experienced any delay in receiving additional financial support by any state or city agencies throughout the last year?
12. Would you consider optimizing your servicing, by including wellness services for customers?

APPENDIX 2

Colloquial Terms Defined

1. *making a dollar*: making a profit
2. *business communities*: ecosystem of a business owner including personal and professional networking systems
3. *green movement*: ecological movement in sustainability
4. *métier*: specialized trade
5. *left out in the cold*: abandoned
6. *hanging out to dry*: abandoned, left in a poor condition
7. *know how*: understanding
8. *return to black*: investing in black communities
9. *mind my shop*: manage my business

Mind Map

Figure 1.

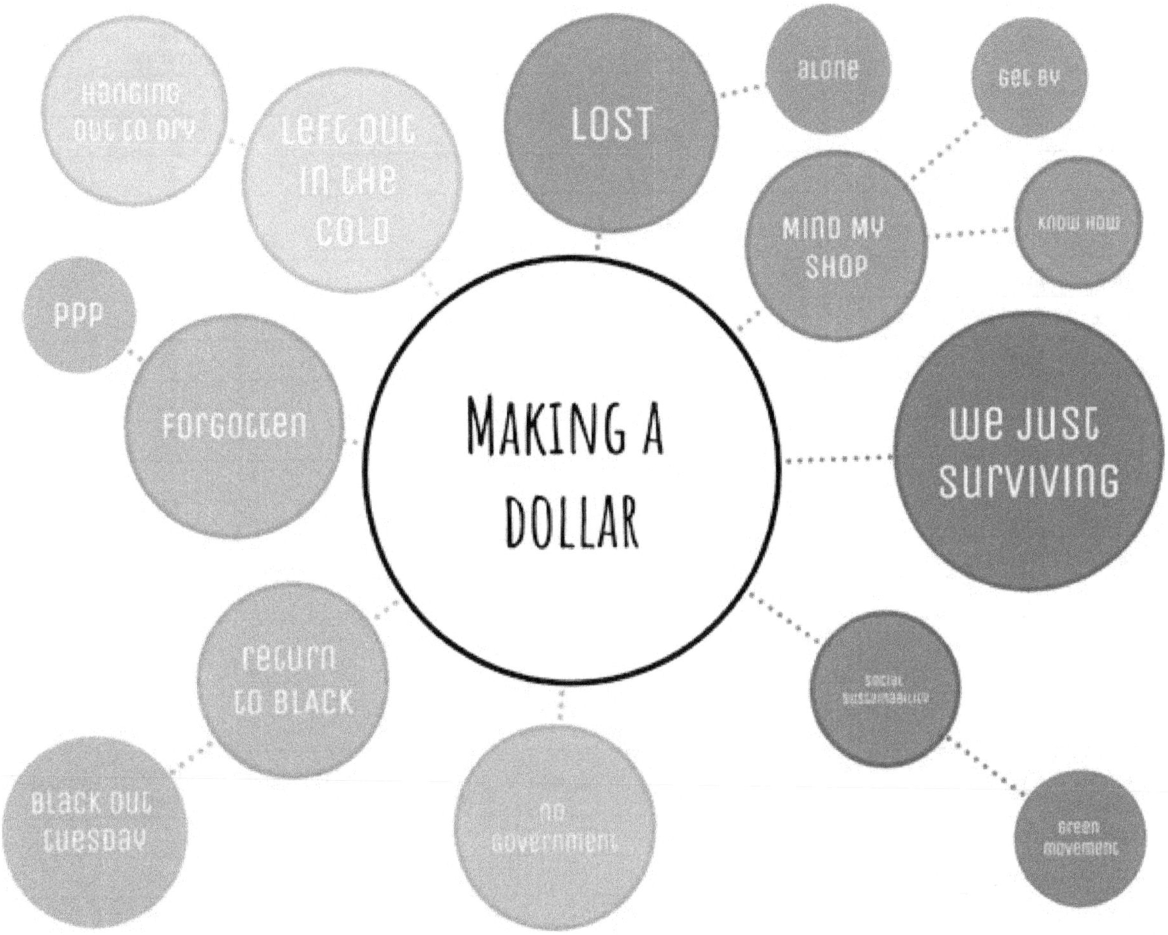

APPENDIX 3

Table 1. A. Business #1, Technological Assessment Report

	Not Applicable	Novice	Advanced Beginner	Competent Performer	Proficient Performer	Expert
Internet Ready Establishment	✔					
Retail Point of Sale Software System	✔					
Eccomerce Availability to clientele	✔					
Tracking of Real-Time Data for Sales Performance	✔					
Inventory Control Software	✔					
In-Store Contactless Retail Stands	✔					
Social Media Business Account	✔					
Social Media Business Posts	✔					
Live or Video Social Media presence	✔					
Business Website	✔					
Chatbots	✔					
Online Appointment	✔					
Online Payment	✔					

Table 2. B. Business #2, Technological Assessment Report

	Not Applicable	Novice	Advanced Beginner	Competent Performer	Proficient Performer	Expert
Internet Ready Establishment					✔	
Retail Point of Sale Software System				✔		
Eccomerce Availability to clientele					✔	
Tracking of Real-Time Data for Sales Performance				✔		
Inventory Control Software	✔					
In-Store Contactless Retail Stands	✔					
Social Media Business Account				✔		
Social Media Business Posts				✔		
Live or Video Social Media presence	✔					
Business Website						✔
Chatbots	✔					
Online Appointment						✔
Online Payment						✔

Table 3. C. Business #3, Technological Assessment Report

	Not Applicable	Novice	Advanced Beginner	Competent Performer	Proficient Performer	Expert
Internet Ready Establishment	✔					
Retail Point of Sale Software System	✔					
Eccomerce Availability to clientele	✔					
Tracking of Real-Time Data for Sales Performance	✔					
Inventory Control Software	✔					
In Store Contactless Retail Stands	✔					
Social Media Business Account		✔				
Social Media Business Posts		✔				
Live or Video Social Media presence		✔				
Business Website		✔				
Chatbots	✔					
Online Appointment		✔				
Online Payment		✔				

Table 4. D. Business #4, Technological Assessment Report

	Not Applicable	Novice	Advanced Beginner	Competent Performer	Proficient Performer	Expert
Internet Ready Establishment	✔					
Retail Point of Sale Software System	✔					
Eccomerce Availability to clientele	✔					
Tracking of Real-Time Data for Sales Performance	✔					
Inventory Control Software	✔					
In Store Contactless Retail Stands	✔					
Social Media Business Account	✔					
Social Media Business Posts	✔					
Live or Video Social Media presence	✔					
Business Website	✔					
Chatbots	✔					
Online Appointment	✔					
Online Payment	✔					

Chapter 16
Development of a Sustainable and Inclusive Entrepreneurship Ecosystem Model in Occupied Palestinian Territories

Rabeh Morrar
https://orcid.org/0000-0002-8808-3714
An-Najah National University, Palestine & Palestine Economic Policy Research Institute, Palestine

Rand Jibril Taweel
Palestine Economic Policy Research Institute, Palestine

Fuad Rayyan
Palestine Public Finance Institute, Palestine

ABSTRACT

This chapter identifies the gaps and weakness in the current Palestinian entrepreneurial ecosystem, impeding the development of economically and socially responsive, inclusive, and sustainable entrepreneurship. It seeks to determine what factors are necessary to develop an inclusive and sustainable model for these forms of entrepreneurship to thrive. This study draws on semi-structured interviews with various actors/players in the Palestinian entrepreneurial ecosystem. The chapter finds that all existing elements in the ecosystem are yet to be developed, resulting in a fragmented ecosystem. More importantly, it finds that the dependence on foreign donors and, consequently, donor agendas in terms of entrepreneurial development frameworks has generated entrepreneurship and an entrepreneurial ecosystem that is unresponsive, unsustainable, inaccessible, and far removed from the Palestinian market needs; hence, most efforts are yet to produce significant economic and social impacts.

DOI: 10.4018/978-1-6684-4322-4.ch016

INTRODUCTION

As early as 2010, the term entrepreneurship has gained traction with the Palestinian Authority (PA) and has been highlighted in government strategies as a lever for economic and social development. As a result, the number of Palestinian entrepreneurs has increased especially in the information and communication technology (ICT) sector (Morrar, 2018; Morrar et al., 2019). Formal and informal discussions among all related stakeholders began about how official bodies interact and regulate entrepreneurship to stimulate entrepreneurial activity. These efforts were reflected in a number of measures and carried out by the government and other relevant public institutions, including: the establishment of the Higher Council for Innovation and Excellence, the Ministry of Entrepreneurship and Empowerment, a draft of the new companies law, and lately a discussion about startup companies law.[1] However, there are yet to be any specific mechanisms or an integrated regulatory framework created to support entrepreneurship and develop models of sustainable and inclusive entrepreneurship able to address the needs and market demands of the Palestinian people.

Entrepreneurship in Palestine faces major challenges (legal, economic, political) in the current ecosystem in which it operates (Khatib et al., 2013; Carroll, 2014; Morrar and Abdelhadi, 2016; Morrar and Arman, 2020). The challenges include, among many others, the difficulties of interacting with foreign markets, the political instability and the economic and mobility restrictions imposed by the Israeli occupation, the lack of supportive governmental policies, and a weak legal environment. As a result, the potential positive social and economic role linked to entrepreneurship, i.e., reducing unemployment, developing services and products, and in the long term, increasing government revenues, is hampered. The prevailing and severe structural barriers to the Palestinian development negatively impact the ability of all the elements in entrepreneurial ecosystem (regulators and related public institutions, support systems for startups such as accelerators and incubators, universities, entrepreneurs, society, etc.) to adapt their services to create a business environment that is suitable the unique needs, i.e. providing growth opportunities in the context of a restricted and fragmented local market, enhancing access to foreign markets and foreign capital investment, addressing trade barriers, eliminating mobility and access barriers imposed by the Israeli occupation, introducing and implementing appropriate and effective laws and regulations, etc., the Palestinian labor market.

General governmental interventions in entrepreneurship are mainly represented in the adoption of effective policies to reform and build an ecosystem through establishing an incentive system (tax and non-tax incentives). Such incentives are intended to support the growth of the entrepreneurial class and enhance their social and economic potential (for example, stimulating innovation, creating work opportunities, increasing social welfare, accelerating economic growth). Moreover, it would contribute to the development of various actors in the surrounding environment through mutually beneficial relations. While the idea of tax incentives is receiving increasing attention from entrepreneurs, the international experience (e.g., USA, Israel, and India) has confirmed that tax incentives, or rather the application of just one form of tax incentives, is not sufficient to create an ecosystem. A mix financial and non-financial supportive policies to enhance the overall infrastructure surrounding entrepreneurs (Hoang et al.,, 2016; Sing, 2020)

The main objective of this study is to determine the forms of entrepreneurship that are needed in Palestine in light of the great economic and social challenges, and moreover, determine what factors are necessary to develop an inclusive and sustainable model for these forms of entrepreneurship to thrive. The study also aims to develop a mixed-model for the Palestinian entrepreneurship ecosystem that takes into account country-level socioeconomic and geopolitical factors. Developing an ecosystem suitable for the Palestinian context would induce a more sustainable and inclusive future of work and entrepreneurship.

This study draws on semi-structured interviews with various actors in the Palestinian entrepreneurial ecosystem to identify existing challenges and gaps in the current ecosystem hindering the development of an inclusive and sustainable Palestinian entrepreneurial environment, to deepen the understanding about the experiences of entrepreneurs in Palestine and factors key to determining their success. These interviews are compatible with the exploratory research objectives that seek to arrive at preliminary facts about the Palestinian entrepreneurial ecosystem.

The literature on the Palestinian entrepreneurial ecosystem is scarce, specifically as it relates to public institutions and their role in developing and maintaining an enabling environment. Given the scarcity of data, we employ a methodology using in-depth interviews with all relevant players in the ecosystem, which allows for a comprehensive understanding of the under-explored startup ecosystem in Palestine. This approach is also necessary given that we observe large discrepancies even in the very little data available on the ecosystem. This qualitative approach allows us to delve deeper into particular challenges and gaps and create tailored and effective policy recommendations.

In addition to archival resources, the study relies largely on semi-structured interviews to understand the specifics of the Palestinian entrepreneurial ecosystem. The interviews (26 interviews in total) included representatives of all stakeholders in the entrepreneurship ecosystem in Palestine, including government agencies and relevant public bodies (8 interviews), startups and entrepreneurs (5 interviews), accelerators and incubators (9 interviews), venture capital funds (one interview), universities and innovation centers (two interviews), and legal entities (one interview).Each interview lasted between 30 to 60 minutes, and a detailed question guide (see Appendix (1) was prepared prior to the interviews which ensured that the questions are presented in a detailed and organized manner to avoid distraction and to ensure that all factors that affect or are linked to the entrepreneurship ecosystem are addressed. The nature of the questions also varied according to the entity that would be interviewed; for example, the questions about government agencies focused more on the role of public finance in promoting entrepreneurship. The majority of interviews (all but one) were recorded to capture the data effectively and reliably. Recording the interviews allowed us to transcribe and import the data on a qualitative and mixed methods data analysis software, MAXQDA. Using MAXQDA, the interview data was organized into groups and then into pre-coded segments, allowing the authors to derive the appropriate indicators for analysis. The interview data was also used to determine the frequency of specific keywords to then identify the most prominent challenges in the ecosystem.

Along with semi-structured interviews, this research draws on extensive literature and desk research to compile the known information on the actors, institutions, and outstanding gaps within the ecosystem. First, historical and archival sources such as books, reports of international institutions and national reports were drawn upon and analyzed to develop a general understanding of the ecosystem and the institutional and regulatory environment for entrepreneurship in Palestine. These sources were mainly related to the development of the entrepreneurial sector and its ecosystem in Palestine over the past two decades, comparing this with global experiences and best practices in developing the entrepreneurship ecosystem through effective government policies and interventions (tax and non-tax incentives, institutional framework reform, etc.). The literature review informs the development of a framework that takes into account all stakeholders and players within the system and aids in understanding the best practices specific to de-developed and developing countries.

BACKGROUND

In Palestine, the infrastructure surrounding entrepreneurs is characterized by fragmentation, weakness, and immaturity (Morrar, 2019; Morrar and Arman, 2020; Morrar et al., 2021; Morrar and Baba, 2022). Therefore, it cannot be said that there is an environment surrounding entrepreneurship in the formal concept or in terms of the existence of links between all the elements that affect the emergence and success of these companies. In addition, there are still no laws or regulations concerned with entrepreneurial development whether in terms of organizing the work of public institutions in the sector or within the scope of their public financial measures (taxes, exemptions, direct and indirect support, etc.).

Discussions about the importance of a legal and legislative framework that regulates and supports entrepreneurial activities have increased over the past few years (Morrar et al., 2021). In Palestine, the government has adopted some supportive policies and measures, especially in promising economic sectors such as the information and communication technology sector (Morrar, 2019). However, there is still a paucity of public policies designed for the entrepreneurial sector, especially as it compares to the strong and conducive policies set out by the Israeli government. This may be due to the public sector's lack of awareness of the economic and social role of such policies, in addition to a limited public budget which constrains expenditures on economic development initiatives.

Entrepreneurship and innovation are mainly led by non-government organizations (NGOs) in Palestine (Morrar and Sultan, 2020; Morrar and Baba, 2022). However, NGOs in Palestine are "not sustainable due to constraints on their resources, poor ecosystems and somewhat fragile institutional environments, which do not grant them sufficient legitimacy" (Morrar and Baba, 2022). Given the persistent political and economic predicaments in Palestine, i.e., the obstacles imposed by the prolonged Israeli occupation (e.g., restricted movement of people and goods, restricted access to national resources including land, no control over international borders, etc.), the poorly regulated market economy, and the internal political fragmentation and division. Sustainable entrepreneurship requires much more than entrepreneurs being innovative and taking risks. The current Palestinian entrepreneurship ecosystem is considered one of the most challenging systems for entrepreneurs to maneuver and thrive in, especially for vulnerable groups such as Palestinian women and youth (Sadeq et al., 2011; Abdullah et al., 2014; Morrar et al., 2021). These challenges stem from Palestine's unique economic and political conditions.

The economy is characterized by its weak infrastructure, fragmented market, and mobility restrictions on goods, services, capital and people mainly due to the on-going Israeli military occupation (UNCTAD, 2012; Khalidi et al.,, 2022). These challenges resulted in limited control over economic policies, fluctuations in public revenues, difficulties in accessing regional and global markets, and high dependence on foreign aid. In fact, prospects indicate that structural factors such as: expected decline in external support (from 12% to 3.8% of GDP between 2015 and 2022); reduction of clearance revenues as a result of new Israeli legislation (a loss of 2% of GDP), the deepening of separation between Gaza and the West Bank, and the persisting uncertain climate for private sector investment are likely to cause further economic deterioration (PCBS, 2020; Khalidi et al.,, 2022).

All that is to say an ecosystem that is likely going to stimulate entrepreneurship efforts in most countries is likely ineffective and unsuitable for the Palestinian context. Still, given that the Palestinian economy is characterized by high rates of entrepreneurial activity, albeit informal and driven by necessity in the absence of wage employment opportunity (Khalidi et al.,, 2022), many believe that entrepreneurship is not only an option for economic growth in Palestine, but a necessary component of the economy in the West Bank and Gaza Strip. As a largely untapped market, as it pertains to formal economic activity and a robust modern private sector, the Palestinian economy is thirsty for a stimulating entrepreneurship environment and enabling opportunities that take into account its social, political and economic factors, allowing entrepreneurs to grow and prosper in light of the difficult reality. This is especially true given the high unemployment rates, especially amongst youth and women. Compared to 2014, the unemployment rate in 2020 (15.7% in the West Bank and 46.6% in the Gaza Strip) increased by 20.5%. Youth employment has also deteriorated in 2020, with approximately 41.7% of youth (ages 15-29) being unemployed in 2020, up from 36.1% in 2014. Moreover, over half (53%) of educated (13 years of education) women are unemployed (PCBS, 2020). The high rates of unemployment are discouraging labor force participation, calling for targeted employment and business development opportunities as well as pro-active reintegration in the labor market (Khalidi et al.,, 2022). An effective and "tailored" ecosystem, if properly utilized, contributes to promoting an inclusive labor market and economic development. A sustainable and inclusive entrepreneurship ecosystem is a key strategy for the market to absorb out of labor force females and unemployed youth and stimulate economic and social growth across the Gaza Strip and West Bank.

To encourage the development and growth of entrepreneurship, it is critical to establish a well-developed and supportive entrepreneurial ecosystem. The fundamental ideas behind entrepreneurial ecosystems emerged in the 1980s and 1990s as part of a scholarly movement to shift away from individualistic personality-based research towards a broader community perspective that incorporates the role of social, cultural, and economic forces in entrepreneurship studies (Aldrich 1990; Nijkamp, 2003; Steyaert and Katz, 2004; Stam and van de Ven, 2021). Van de Ven (1993) argued that individual entrepreneurs cannot control and command all the resources, institutions, markets, policies, and business functions that are required and necessary to develop and commercialize entrepreneurial ventures. There is extensive literature on the importance of developing a comprehensive and strong 'entrepreneurial infrastructure' to enable entrepreneurial success and growth, emphasizing the influence of regional economic and social factors over the entrepreneurship process (Pennings,1982; Dubini 1989; Gnyawali and Fogel, 1994; Van de ven, 1993; Bahrami and Evans, 1995; Claudia et al., 2019). Zahra (2007) and Zahra et al., (2014) argue that it is important to situate the entrepreneurial phenomenon in a broader context that incorporates temporal-spatial, social, organizational, and market dimensions, decentering the individual entrepreneur as the focal point of value creation.

The Palestinian Entrepreneurial Ecosystem

There is a growing interest in ecosystems as an approach for understanding the context of entrepreneurship at the macro and organization levels (Van de Ven & Stam, 2019). While scholars and practitioners do so in an attempt to improve the quantity and quality of entrepreneurial activity in the society, policymakers are increasingly concerned with economic development and finding 'levers', entrepreneurship being one of them, to encourage economic growth and job creation (Audretsch & Link, 2012). Essentially, an entrepreneurial ecosystem comprises a set of interdependent actors and factors that are governed in such a way that they enable and induce productive entrepreneurship in its various forms (Van de ven & Stam, 2019; Stam, 2015).

In recent years, there have been several attempts to analyze the Palestinian entrepreneurial ecosystem. As such, the Palestinian ecosystem remains fragmented, weak, and immature. In fact, there is no enabling environment or regulatory framework surrounding entrepreneurs in the formal sense and there are no linkages between all the elements/actors in the ecosystem (Sune, 2020). The current status of the Palestinian ecosystem, often referred to as the "activation phase" (fewer than 300 tech startups, low early-stage funding, and no high value scaleups or exits) in the literature, is comparable to other developing countries in general, and countries in the Arab region, more specifically (Kuester & Arya, 2021). Despite being comparable to developing countries in terms of progression status, unlike other ecosystems in the activation phase, Palestine, according to the comprehensive ecosystem analysis conducted by Startup Genome (2021), must focus on building a global system as global connectedness remains to be low and continues to consist a hindrance to creating a scalable business model (Kuester & Arya, 2021). Therefore, ecosystem development should focus on appropriate interventions to enhance global connectedness and market reach for entrepreneurs (currently hindered by geopolitical factors, i.e. Israeli military occupation) (Kuester & Arya, 2021).

In this section, we identity and analyze the elements and actors in the Palestinian ecosystem. An analysis as such allows for developing more tailored interventions in the ecosystem to be able to advance this important and vital sector, which, in return, can be a lever for the Palestinian economy.

Supporting Infrastructure: Incubators and Accelerators

In an ecosystem, supporting infrastructure usually refers to support systems, usually in the form of an organization, that provide services that aim to help entrepreneurs at affordable prices. Such institutions seek to increase human, social, and sometimes financial capital through providing network events, workshops, and training. These services enable knowledge transfers, provide managerial and business skills, and create spaces and opportunities for entrepreneurs to increase the frequency and quality of future business transactions and increase their awareness of industry-wide best practices (Dahl and Sorenson, 2009; Stenholm et al.,, 2013; Roebroek, 2017). Moreover, networking provides spillover opportunities to adjacent industries as experiences and knowledge are exchanged (Wenting et al.,, 2011). Overall, whether it is formal or informal, these support systems save entrepreneurs the time and cost involved in an otherwise long learning process and enables entrepreneurship to grow more quickly due to efficiency gains (Roebroek, 2017). Feldman (2014) argues that it is advantageous for entrepreneurs and entrepreneurial startups to locate within an area where an entrepreneurial ecosystem is already established and systems and knowledge are available to enable higher levels of activity and growth. In terms of the positive impact that business incubators and accelerators can have on startups and the overall business ecosystem, evidence does vary (Bone et al.,, 2019). However, in the case of developing countries, where the financing role of the government as well as the private sector is diminished, Al Mubaraki and Busler (2013) find that business incubators provide support for startup companies, increase the probability of success, and graduate companies that have a significant positive impact of economic development. Moreover, it finds that after companies graduate from incubators the positive market impact is associated with three factors, including: enhanced entrepreneurship, graduated companies, and job creation, diversifying economic growth and development (Al Mubaraki & Busler, 2013). The evidence on the positive impact business accelerators is slightly stronger than that of incubators (Bone et al.,, 2019). For example, accelerators can increase the speed of startups can raise investments (Roberts et al.,, 2016; Hallen et al.,, 2016), grow number of employees (Hallen et al.,, 2016), grow customer base (Fehder, 2015), and reduce the time it takes for the enterprises to be acquired (Hallen et al.,, 2016).

In Palestine, the first incubator, PICTI, was founded in 2004 to provide a wide range of services for tech-based entrepreneurs (PICTI, 2018). These services include workshops, training sessions, networking events, and direct financial support (Omar, 2013). Over the past two decades the number of incubators increased significantly, whether it be in the private sector (such as "Fikra" affiliated with the Palestinian Telecommunications Company) or those affiliated with universities (such as Techno Park affiliated with Birzeit University and the Korean Institute of An-Najah University), or those affiliated with and/or working as non-profits (such as Gaza Sky Geeks and Build Palestine). As for business accelerators, the first business accelerator, Fast Forward, was established by Leaders International in 2013, with the support of the Taawon Foundation. Fast Forward aims to support technology startups and help them access sustainable funding sources, especially in the early stages of their life cycle (Leaders International, 2021). According to the interviews, Fast Forward halted its local services in 2020 due to the increase in the number of accelerators in the city of Ramallah, where most accelerators are located.

Despite the increase in the number of supporting systems, the progress of business incubators and accelerators over the last two decades has been limited. This is evidenced by the limited number of success stories as well as the low socio-economic contribution of the sector. In fact, the interviews conducted for the purposes of this study revealed that there are many gaps and weaknesses in the incubator and accelerators environment. While expertise on supporting services is limited, the main weakness lies in the fact that most incubators and accelerators compete and/or are highly dependent on, an often volatile, foreign financial support, particularly aid from international development cooperation and international NGOs, to sustain their services. The almost total dependence of a large percentage of incubators, accelerators, and innovation centers on external support and, therefore, donor agendas, has contributed to the limited role and impact these institutions hold in the Palestinian ecosystem (Morrar and Baba, 2022).

A large part of the donor agenda is focused on organizing entrepreneurship-related activities, exhibitions, workshops, training courses, and some competitions, which, although important, have become the predominant activity among various local institutions, limiting the effectiveness of these institutions and their ability to provide sustainable and advanced programs. Donor support for entrepreneurship and innovation is also characterized by fluctuation and discontinuity, which contributes to the fragility of the environment for entrepreneurship and makes support systems more vulnerable to risks related to finance and funding. An expert in the field of entrepreneurship companies pointed out in the interviews that accelerators and incubators in Palestine were built as non-profit institutions, constantly seeking donor funds for continuity and sustainability.[2] This forces such institutions to either limit their support to businesses that are growing on their own or tailor the services to the agendas of donors as opposed to what the Palestinian entrepreneurs actually need in order to foster technological advancement, innovation, and economic development To build a sustainable ecosystem model, these institutions must increasingly rely on their own capabilities, develop their tools and resources, search for creative solutions, and work according to the needs and opportunities of the local market.

Additionally, the presence of an increasing number of incubators and accelerators, and the great competition and lack of coordination among them, especially in the city of Ramallah—which has been deemed by many stakeholders as a saturated environment—has created a phenomenon of "hopping around", wherein entrepreneurs jump between organizations with the aim of obtaining financing while not engaging with the other offered programming and services. Moreover, various interviewees indicated a weakness in the supervisory and regulatory framework for the ecosystem in general, and on related institutions (incubators, legislators, innovation centers, etc.) in particular. This has led to a decrease in the effectiveness of these institutions and their failure to play the role required of them in developing the sector, despite receiving significant financial and technical support over the past years. In regard to the role of government institutions in the ecosystem, there are two main bodies that act as a supporting system for entrepreneurs: The Ministry of Entrepreneurship and Empowerment and the Higher Council of Innovation and Excellence (HCIE). The Ministry of Entrepreneurship and Empowerment seeks to strengthen the legislative framework and regulatory environment surrounding entrepreneurship, enhance the role and capabilities of government institutions in supporting entrepreneurs, develop the necessary infrastructure and services, and enhance the role of education and training to foster the skills necessary for innovation (moee.pna.ps, 2022). Similarly, the HCIE seeks to play a leadership role in fostering and consolidating a culture of innovation in Palestine through strengthening the national innovation system and empowering innovators. Additionally, the HCIE provided funding, grants, and investments opportunities to some entrepreneurs (pica.pna.ps, 2022). The interviews emphasize, however, that there is a lack of clarity in the nature of the tasks and services provided by these institutions, especially the Ministry of Entrepreneurship, established only recently.

Funding Sources for Entrepreneurs

External funding sources are critical to the success and growth of entrepreneurship and the role of investors is pivotal (Singh, 2020). Roebroek (2017) defines funding and financing in the entrepreneurial ecosystem by how easily an entrepreneurial startup may receive funds for developing their business model and go through its lifespan. Interviews confirmed that there is still a great reluctance by venture capital and foreign investment funds to work in the Palestinian market. For example, one of the incubators indicated that it met with more than 11 foreign investors looking for an opportunity to convince them of the feasibility of investing in the Palestinian market, but their efforts were unsuccessful. This is mainly due to the great political and economic risks in the Palestinian market, and the obstacles related to legislation and policies when it comes to investing.

Due to the reluctance of foreign venture capital, the government and the local private sector have a greater role in bridging the financing gap for emerging enterprises. Here lies the importance of having a government guarantee fund to reduce the burden of risk on local and foreign venture capital funds. Reducing the financial risks on venture funds is likely to increase the number of available venture capital funds in Palestine. The presence of more than one risky capital investment fund enhances the efficiency of these fund and reduces monopoly. In return, this limits the phenomenon of equity dilution in the current ecosystem highlighted in the interviews. In order to attract foreign venture capital and reduce the degree of risk in the ecosystem, and with the inability to control political risks and to a lesser degree economic risks, there is an urgent need to improve the regulatory and business environment in Palestine as well as a package of incentives for entrepreneurs and investors alike.

It is also important to focus on entrepreneurs in the Gaza Strip. The Strip suffers greatly from a lack of funding and venture capital, due to the blockade imposed by the Israeli occupation for more than 15 years and the accompanying political and economic challenges. In light of the current state of division between governing political parties in the West Bank and the Gaza Strip (The PA, led by Fatah party, controls over the West Bank, why Gaza Strip is controlled by Hamas) many ecosystem stakeholders in the Gaza Strip believe that enhancing funding and the overall sustainability of the ecosystem lies on private sector to provide part of the funding necessary for entrepreneurs to grow their projects.

Institutional and Regulatory Framework

Most countries that have seen significant development in the entrepreneurial sector have had a substantial and vital government role in developing an effective ecosystem (Singh, 2020). A lack of concern for the ease of doing business for both local and foreign investors may be one of the most stifling obstacles to the growth of entrepreneurship. For entrepreneurs to operate, there must be a legal framework in place that includes legislative and regulatory rules, as well as governmental and nongovernmental regulating and supporting organizations (Roebroek, 2017). Entrepreneurial activity and startup businesses striving to develop and flourish within the ecosystem may be incentivized or hindered by these institutions and regulatory frameworks (Roebroek, 2017; Stenholm et al.,, Stephan et al.,, 2015). Incentives may include streamlined registration processes, bankruptcy laws, subsidies, or tax exemptions, whereas limits on entrepreneurs and entrepreneurial startups may include early-stage fees and taxes on investments and external financing, as well as employment standards such as minimum wages and legal restrictions (Roebroek, 2017; Stenholm et al.,, 2013; Stephen et al.,, 2015). Government incentives are critical for entrepreneurship development, growth, and survival, in addition to their critical function in maintaining fair competition among businesses (Roebroek, 2017). Numerous entrepreneurs prefer to locate their operations in a supportive regulatory environment that makes doing business easier. For example, in the United States, many Arab entrepreneurs in general, and Palestinian entrepreneurs in particular, register their entrepreneurial startups in the state of Delaware, owing to the ease of the procedures and the presence of a robust incentive structure.

The Palestinian government has lately improved the legal and regulatory framework for businesses, especially for entrepreneurial startups. As of late 2021, the Palestinian government has adopted new company legislation and begun discussing a law tailored specifically to startups. Despite this, most respondents stated that the regulatory and legal environment is one of the most significant barriers in the Palestinian economy, preventing entrepreneurship from growing. The economic and legal framework still does not support entrepreneurship and startups. Some pre-1967 laws still exist in the Palestinian territory and have not been updated by Palestinian lawmakers. In the West Bank, the Companies Law No. (12) of 1964 and its amendments apply, whereas in the Gaza Strip, the Companies Law No. (18) of 1929 and the Ordinary Companies Law No. (19) of 1930 and its revisions apply. The tax laws that apply to new businesses are the same as those that apply to existing businesses, such as the Tax Law by Decree Law No. (8) for 2011 covering income tax and its amendments, and the Jordanian system of levies on local products.

The various stakeholders in the entrepreneurial ecosystem emphasized the importance of fostering a stimulating legal environment to attract foreign investors, limit Palestinian entrepreneurs' willingness to register or invest outside of Palestine, and safeguard financial rights, particularly in the case of cross-border fund transfers in sales, exit, and acquisition transactions. Additionally, the respondents stressed the need to include entrepreneurship in the framework of investment promotion regulations. Moreover, the absence of a functioning Legislative Council and its legal and economic committees has had a detrimental effect on the entrepreneurial economic landscape during the last two decades. This is occurring at a time when entrepreneurship have made a qualitative jump on a worldwide scale because of a package of promoting and stimulating laws and regulations. Additionally, the stakeholders surveyed confirmed that the entrepreneurial ecosystem's primary flaws stem from fragmentation and a lack of integration among the ecosystem's various elements, as well as a lack of a clear governmental reference for coordinating efforts among the ecosystem's various players. Many entrepreneurs, for example, are confused about where to seek funding, support, counsel, or advice in the event of a legal dispute. Additionally, discussions with government officials indicated a lack of collaboration across the different government bodies.

In terms of procedures and policies, Palestine, like many other countries, lacks an operational definition of entrepreneurship and startups. This is evident in the paucity of precise information on entrepreneurship and their dispersion across industries, which prevents the economic and social impact of entrepreneurship from being quantified. Additionally, this significantly impairs any incentive schemes aimed at entrepreneurship or the way they are approached within the ecosystem. When the Palestinian Information and Communication Technology Incubator (PICTI) was founded in 2004 as the country's first business incubator, government agencies lacked a common concept of what startups were (Kassis, 2014), and they were classified as small and medium enterprises (SMEs). According to one of the agricultural technology entrepreneurial startups, when they applied for government registration, their business was classified as a small enterprise, not a startup. Numerous Palestinian entrepreneurs have expressed concern about the numerous regulatory and financial limitations connected with establishing and registering their entrepreneurial startup projects. Entrepreneurs also complained about exorbitant fees and business registration charges, with several reporting that they were required to spend between US $700 and $1,500 to complete the registration procedure, with a significant portion going to the lawyer and bar association (about US $1,000). While this cost might not be substantial for some entrepreneurs, having to pay fees in and of itself is discouraging to an entrepreneur seeking to materialize an idea into a service or product.

Human Capital and the Role of Universities

Studies suggest that the more qualified the individuals in the ecosystem and the better the balance between supply and demand for entrepreneurial skills, the cheaper the cost of entrepreneurial activities, which by their nature seek highly trained people in all areas (Roebroek, 2017; Wenting et al.,, 2011). Additionally, several studies (Bates, 1995; Davidsson and Honig, 2003; Kim et al.,, 2006) have demonstrated that the presence of human capital is positively correlated with an individual's likelihood of becoming an entrepreneur, implying that ecosystems with a higher level of human capital may harbor a larger number of entrepreneurs than ecosystems with a low level of human capital (Roebroek, 2017).

According to the World Bank's (2018) analysis of Palestine's technology-based entrepreneurial startups, the ecosystem suffers from a substantial shortage of expertise and skills required to establish new models that keep pace with market requirements and considerable technical advances (Mulas et al.,, 2018). Additionally, entrepreneurs have a minimal number of years of professional experience prior to founding their businesses. In this context, the director of one of the Gaza Strip's most prominent business incubators stated that the entrepreneur's prior practical expertise is critical to the project's success. This is critical, even more so in a complicated work environment such as the Palestinian one, and it assists in acquiring the tools necessary to raise the funding required for the project and to achieve sustainable entrepreneurship. He further emphasized that these abilities do not always come through training courses and workshops, but rather from the personal experiences gained from past professional encounters. He also emphasized the significance of incubators and accelerators in helping entrepreneurs establish their business systems, including marketing, management, and financial models, as well as networks and raising capital from banks and investors.

Furthermore, Palestinian entrepreneurs lack constructive professional ties with experts, mentors (Kuester & Arya, 2020), and other dynamic ecosystems throughout the world that may help them gain knowledge, skills, and experience. As a result, Palestinian entrepreneurs face a skills gap due to a lack of professional expertise. For example, in Palestine, there is an over-reliance on a small number of specialists or mentors specialized in entrepreneurship and startups (Kuester & Arya, 2020). Moreover, several business founders reported having ten or more mentors, indicating a lack of meaningful developmental relationships.

In Palestine, university enrollment has increased by nearly 200 percent in the last two decades. Most Palestinian entrepreneurs and startups founders have at least a bachelor's degree. Specifically, 55 percent have a bachelor's degree and 19 percent have a postgraduate or professional degree. However, this does not imply that the Palestinian university education environment is supportive and stimulating to entrepreneurship, or that university graduates have the skills to launch their own entrepreneurial projects.

Most Palestinian universities strive to foster an entrepreneurial culture among students and to better connect colleges to labor market demands. Most universities have built on-campus company incubators and entrepreneurship centers in recent years. Despite universities' goals, the entrepreneurial sector's lack of competence and experience is one of the primary problems facing the ecosystem, particularly in terms of developing novel and pioneering concepts that solve market needs and society's economic and social concerns. Numerous stakeholders in the entrepreneurial ecosystem note that Palestinian university graduates lack the technical and administrative abilities necessary to successfully run their entrepreneurial projects. Additionally, they lack the innovative entrepreneurial concepts key to launching new businesses. Their proposals are either traditional and replicate existing projects or are copies of successful international models that do not match the Palestinian context and market demands. Stakeholders stressed the need to initiate entrepreneurial education in the early stages of students' lives, namely during the school education stage, by including entrepreneurial elements in the curriculum. Additionally, it is necessary to employ cutting-edge teaching approaches that encourage students to think and investigate. The whole university education system and curriculum should focus on leadership and research and development (R&D), with a need for universities to provide the technical, human, and financial resources needed to support entrepreneurship. This type of entrepreneurial approach demands systemic transformation in education and ample financial resources, which most colleges lack owing to the current financial crisis. If the private sector decides this collaboration is feasible, it can provide enormous financial resources if the government spends generously on education and R&D. In industrialized economies, the private sector funds most university research initiatives and helps engage graduates in the market to commercialize products.

Obstacles Posed by the Israeli Occupation and the Labor Market in Palestine

As is the case in other sectors, it is impossible to examine the Palestinian entrepreneurial ecosystem in isolation from the hurdles and challenges posed by Israel's occupation. According to the United Nations Organization for Trade and Development's (UNCTAD) most recent study, occupation policies of closures, resource control, and other limitations resulted in economic losses of about $58 billion between 2000 and 2019. (UNCTAD, 2021). Khalidi & Taghdisi-Rad (2009) argue that the Israeli occupation policies in the West Bank and Gaza Strip, and its control over internal and external crossings, as well as the Palestinian side's compliance with the Paris Economic Agreement (Paris Protocol), have all contributed significantly to isolating the Palestinian market from the rest of the global markets (Khalidi & Taghdisi-Rad, 2009). All of this has exacerbated investment risks in the Palestinian context and significantly hampered the growth and spread of entrepreneurship both locally and globally. Additionally, it has restricted foreign venture capital investment in entrepreneurial startups.

Furthermore, the Paris Economic Agreement's restrictions hampered the growth of entrepreneurship in some key sectors. For instance, the Paris Protocol permitted the unrestricted flow of Israeli agricultural products into the Palestinian market, resulting in the sector's decline and a fall in its contribution to the Palestinian economy. This is because it is unable to compete with Israeli agricultural products, which flood Palestinian markets at affordable prices. Agriculture is one of the most strategic industries for Palestinian companies to expand and innovate (Kuester & Arya, 2021). This was also corroborated by one of the founders of an agricultural technology entrepreneurial startup, who expressed his inability to compete with agricultural companies in Israel that employ advanced technologies in the manufacturing process, especially given the government's strong backing. Numerous entrepreneurs and accelerators have raised concern about the impact of Israeli occupation-imposed limitations on their ability to compete with other Arab business ecosystems. For example, the Jordanian entrepreneurial ecosystem is similar to the Palestinian entrepreneurial ecosystem in terms of the numerous challenges and weaknesses it faces, but Jordanian entrepreneurs are distinguished by their ease of communication and accessibility to the rest of the Arab world (particularly the Gulf region) and the rest of the world.

In the Gaza Strip, the situation is more difficult due to the Israeli closure that has been in place since 2006 and the inability to interact with the outside world. According to one of the organizers of Gaza's most prominent innovation centers, "in addition to the fact that the market in Gaza is almost completely closed to the outside world, the process of transferring funds from the very limited number of international investors and supporting institutions in the field of entrepreneurship is nearly impossible due to the occupation's restrictions on the banking sector under the guise of 'security', which frustrates investors."

SOLUTIONS AND RECOMMENDATIONS

This section will discuss the weaknesses and gaps in various elements in the existing ecosystem and suggest mechanisms and policies that must be adopted to develop and stimulate a sustainable and inclusive entrepreneurship ecosystem in Palestine. It addresses gaps that, if bridged, would enable entrepreneurs to play a leading role in promoting economic growth, providing job opportunities, and addressing key societal and economic challenges such as social inclusion of marginalized groups, poverty reduction or meeting the demands of the Palestine market. The recommendations focus on ways to re-configure the current ecosystem in a way that is conducive to/allows for social entrepreneurship to develop and thrive as a model of sustainable and socially responsive entrepreneurship.

Enhancing the Regulatory and Legislative Environment

As previously stated, there are no rules or regulations for entrepreneurship in Palestine, both in terms of work organization and public financial procedures (taxes, exemptions, direct and indirect support, etc.). The necessity of a legal and legislative framework governing the entrepreneurial activities has grown in recent years. Entrepreneurship regulators must expedite and harmonize commercial and tax registration processes, which now cost entrepreneurial firms and entrepreneurs a significant amount of money and effort. This includes reducing costly licensing fees, halting the practice of forcing firms to register immediately and providing them with a retention period of six to twelve months. Against this backdrop, several entrepreneurs underlined that if these issues are not resolved, many entrepreneurs will register outside Palestine, reducing tax revenues for the state budget from these businesses. Additionally, owing to the innovative nature of entrepreneurship, strengthening the legal framework, and in particular streamlining procedures for safeguarding intellectual property are important. Public authorities must provide rapid examination and registration of patents at a low cost, as well as the necessary legal support.

Furthermore, companies in Palestine currently are regulated according to the Jordanian Companies Law No. (12) of 1964, which requires all companies in Palestine to be registered with the Companies Registrar at the Ministry of Economy and obtain an official license before operating their business. Additionally, and in accordance with Articles 2 and 3 of Income Tax Law No. (8) of 2011, individuals who engage in business or investment must register with tax authorities since all income received by an individual from any source is taxable. As a result, tax authorities treat entrepreneurial startups similarly to other enterprises.

According to Article 7 of the Income Tax Law, entrepreneurial firms and startups are not excluded from paying taxes. Therefore, they must create a tax file and pay a 15% yearly tax on net earnings, just like any other firm. However, data from the Palestinian income tax authorities shows that the contribution of small and medium-sized businesses, which include entrepreneurial startups, during their first five years is quite modest and does not contribute much to the tax revenues. This means that taxes on entrepreneurs might be temporarily reduced to achieve a variety of other economic and social goals, such as greater employment, higher personal income tax, and increased value-added tax without significantly reducing tax revenues. This might also have significant indirect implications, such as the formalization of several enterprises now operating in the informal sector.

Effective support measures for entrepreneurship require government agencies to recognize the economic, social, and financial role that entrepreneurial firms may play in the future if they are supported and reinforced. The general environment in which entrepreneurs operate, according to all those interviewed, significantly impairs their work and capacity to develop. Additionally, it restricts the economic and social impact that these businesses are meant to have, particularly considering surrounding political and economic constraints such as limited funding sources and high entrepreneurial costs. As a result, they emphasized the importance of immediate government engagement and a package of incentive measures, considering the significant hurdles posed by Covid-19. In addition, the government should incorporate an operational description of entrepreneurial firms and startups into its future legislation. The definition should reflect the Palestinian entrepreneurial environment and differentiate between entrepreneurial firms and SMEs.

To avoid fragmentation and lack of coordination within the ecosystem, there must be a single regulatory and supervisory government organization that includes all stakeholders and works with relevant government, private sector, and non-governmental bodies. It should specify the functions of various institutions in the entrepreneurial ecosystem. It should limit the tendency of owners of innovative ideas and projects to hop between accelerators and incubators in search of funding rather than benefit from their services and activities. The study recommends that a database and an electronic portal be established (by, for example, The Higher Council for Innovation and Excellence or the Ministry of Entrepreneurship and Empowerment) via which various organizations can submit their various data (activities, services, target sectors, number of working employees, available funding sources, address, etc.). This strengthens the ecosystem, assists government institutions in their regulatory and control functions, creates a space for communication between Palestinian investors and entrepreneurs and foreign venture capitalists, and enables entrepreneurs and entrepreneurial startups to connect with mentors and experts during the early stages of startup development, as well as access available funding and support. This will also minimize redundancy caused by the presence of dozens of low-impact entities supporting entrepreneurship and pave the way for integrated and more specialized entities.

Simultaneously, a national plan must be developed to address the phenomenon of entrepreneurship across a range of dimensions, including temporal, spatial, social, and organizational. It should consider the characteristics of domestic and international markets in place to avoid considering entrepreneurship in Palestine as an individual phenomenon. This plan should specify the objectives and sub-objectives, as well as the implementing agencies and funding sources. Additionally, this strategy must be aligned with other government plans, activities, and directions in this field, such as the technological cluster plan, the Supreme Council for Innovation's strategic plan, and the Ministry of Entrepreneurship and Empowerment's strategic plan.

Financing Entrepreneurs and Entrepreneurship

The political and economic challenges that Palestine is experiencing because of Israel's constraints toward the Palestinian economy, i.e., limited access to resources, mobility restrictions, continuous military attacks on the Gaza Strip, as well as the fragmented and poorly regulated markets, have resulted in real economic losses[3] and have also had a negative impact on Palestine's fiscal policy (UCTAD, 2021; World bank, 2021). The Palestinian Authority continues to face a substantial budget deficit and an inability to pay public expenditures and carry out the plans and policies it has adopted to stimulate the economy and facilitate entrepreneurship. Add to that a fragile legislative and legal environment, a lack of internal funding from the private sector and donor institutions, the vulnerability of the Palestinian economy's structure, the economic dominance of traditional service sectors, the traditional education system's structure, and the absence of entrepreneurial education. All of this has a significant impact on the government's supportive policies towards entrepreneurship (direct or indirect financial support).

Despite widespread calls from numerous stakeholders in recent years for government agencies and tax authorities to support the entrepreneurial firms through tax and non-tax incentives, there has been no defined strategy or specific procedures applied to the entrepreneurship sector. Some challenges to the creation of such policies include the disagreement and divergence of opinion among tax departments and other government agencies over the optimal strategy for dealing with entrepreneurs. Additionally, it seems impossible to determine the amount of public total expenditure on entrepreneurship and innovation due to the multitude of government entities and the overlap of their responsibilities and scope of activity. Furthermore, the effectiveness of these agencies' activities is debatable. All this creates concerns among tax authorities and policymakers about the feasibility of spending on entrepreneurship and offering tax exemptions and subsidies.

The surveyed entrepreneurial firms, business accelerators, incubators, and related parties in the public sector have consistently agreed that in order to prompt a sustainable and inclusive entrepreneurship ecosystem, government is required to offer both direct and indirect financial incentives for the entrepreneurial sector. This is because this sector can promote economic growth and alleviate high unemployment rates. This requires direct government financial assistance in addition to a variety of extra incentive measures:

1. Government agencies should begin by offering tax exemptions to entrepreneurs, which would result in a rise in the number of new businesses and employees, while also expanding their operations locally and globally. Investing in entrepreneurship and expanding the productive base is likely to positively affect government revenues in the longer run (i.e. direct and indirect increase in tax

revenues). Additionally, the government should establish funds to promote innovative ventures that have a significant social impact (social entrepreneurship), which should not be limited to the information and communication technology sector. This will assist in addressing the myriad societal difficulties that the Palestinian territories face, particularly in the aftermath of Covid-19.

2. Update and modernize laws (several respondents emphasized the need to speed up the drafting of the law on startups) and support entrepreneurial projects for young people and university graduates, as well as provide funding sources and government guarantee funds for small and medium-sized loans that pertain to high-risk projects (venture capital). Because current investment funds are limited in quantity and financial capacity, most entrepreneurs are unable to meet their criteria. These funds also demand significant percentages of the entrepreneurs' shares in exchange for small amounts of money, without properly accounting for the prospect of their development and expansion.
3. Create public funds for private venture capital funds to share risks and encourage new private investment funds to enter the market. A government fund can target underrepresented groups, economically distressed regions, and enterprises in developing and dynamic sectors like clean energy and agriculture.
4. Establishing a government research and development fund to support high-risk innovative research and development activities in entrepreneurship, which are a significant burden on these businesses in their early stages, as well as to foster collaboration between local entrepreneurs and international parties in areas where Palestine is lacking.
5. The government should appropriate sufficient funds to enable the public entities responsible for entrepreneurship (the Ministry of Entrepreneurship and Empowerment, the High Council for Innovation and Excellence, etc.) to carry out their strategic objectives aimed at developing and enhancing the role of entrepreneurship in the economy as well as supporting promising entrepreneurial projects that will develop into entrepreneurial firms.
6. To achieve an effective and sustainable entrepreneurial sector, the government must either directly support the accelerators and incubators to reduce their reliance on external financing (donor-driven model), which is frequently conditional and characterized by fluctuation, or establish public business incubators (for example, the Israel Public Technology Incubators Project) to share risk with investors in entrepreneurship. Additionally, entrepreneurial firms may be evaluated for affirmative procurement in government bids. Furthermore, supporting and fostering innovation in financial instruments specialized for funding entrepreneurial firms, rather than relying largely on venture capital funds is necessary.

Enhancing Entrepreneurial Education and Linking Universities with the Labor Market

Promoting entrepreneurship in school and university curricula, as well as embracing current educational approaches that foster entrepreneurial thinking in students as opposed to old methods is key to stimulating entrepreneurship early in the process.

The university education system should pivot towards entrepreneurial education, and research and development, with universities providing the technical, human, and financial resources necessary to drive students to lead and launch their own entrepreneurial firms. This type of entrepreneurial approach necessitates systemic reform and the provision of appropriate financial resources, which most universities are unable to deliver considering the current financial crisis. This requires generous government spending to close the gap. In addition, the government should fund universities and scientific research institutions, as well as promote and activate the cluster development plan. Additionally, the government should support the development of entrepreneurial educational curricula in order to close the gap between educational outputs and labor market needs, which has become an urgent issue due to the private and public sectors' inability to absorb large numbers of graduates and unemployed.

Strengthening collaboration between universities and the private sector can provide significant financial resources to boost R&D, bridge the skills gap between university graduates and the labor market, and provide students with new skills in entrepreneurship, creative thinking, and the establishment of entrepreneurial firms.

Enhancing Social Entrepreneurship in Palestine

Social entrepreneurship has become increasingly recognized among researchers and policymakers as a powerful global phenomenon to address social developmental challenges (Nicolls, 2008). Indeed, it has been widely used across the globe as a tool to enhance social welfare and human well-being through a model of advancing innovative approaches to solve social problems (Germak & Robinson, 2013).

Given the socioeconomic predicaments that Palestine continues to face especially in light of the political and economic vacuum, social entrepreneurship, social innovation, and social enterprises are great models to not only enhance job opportunities and innovation, but also fulfill the unmet social demands of the Palestinian people, overcome institutional voids, bring sustainable improvements to people's lives, and address key societal and economic challenges such as social inclusion of marginalized groups or poverty reduction (Akella and Eid, 2017; Morrar and Baba, 2022). However, favorable institutional and enabling conditions are crucial for the emergence and effectiveness of these models. Morrar and Baba (2022) reveal three types of barriers (traps) that social innovation face in Palestine (institutional, sustainability and effectiveness traps), which mainly relate to the extreme nature of the local institutional context. To overcome these traps requires strengthening of the institutional environment, creating an enabling environment through a cross-sectoral approach, identifying and providing local resource capacities for social innovation and social entrepreneurship to lessen their reliance on international donors and to ensure that resources can be allocated to sustainable development needs (Morrar and Baba, 2022).

These findings align with our findings from the interviews as the majority of interviewees believe that the ecosystem as a whole is built on exterior goals for social development in Palestine due to the high dependence on donor funds. In order to build an inclusive and sustainable model for entrepreneurship that seeks to fill-in the political and economic vacuum and enhance the ability of the community to find innovative approaches to dealing with complex social needs and unmet demands, it is critical to recognize that social entrepreneurship ought not to be led by donor agendas. Social entrepreneurship, by definition, must address the unmet demands of the local markets. Hence, the Palestinian private sector and governmental institutions should develop and regulate, to an extent, an ecosystem and a general entrepreneurial model that takes a market approach to develop social entrepreneurship and utilize innovative approaches to solve social problems that face the Palestinian people. In other words, a sustainable entrepreneurship model should move away from profit-oriented objectives and towards mission-oriented objectives to solve social problems that consequently return profit in the form of both capital and social welfare.

FUTURE RESEARCH DIRECTIONS

This study provides a comprehensive overview of all the existing gaps and weaknesses impeding progress towards a more sustainable, inclusive, responsive, and impactful entrepreneurial ecosystem. More specifically, it determines the factors contributing to weakness and fragmentation of the system, while also addressing the unsustainability and unattractiveness of the current entrepreneurship projects that are incompatible with the social and economic demands on the Palestinian market and instead focus on donor agendas and the foreign entrepreneurship development model. Most importantly, however, the study highlights the importance of additional future research to determine what are the exact social and economic demands and gaps in the Palestinian market that can be addressed through an entrepreneurial lens. In other words, in what areas can entrepreneurs fill in the current policy vacuum and institutional voids to bring about sustainable improvements to people's lives while addressing key societal and economic challenges. Additionally, research as such would allow current supporting systems to re-configure and re-direct their efforts and strategies to build a social entrepreneurship model that attracts more Palestinian youth, women, and vulnerable groups. Moreover, it is likely to contribute to an ecosystem that generates entrepreneurs who are able to grow their projects in a sustainable manner and respond to the unmet needs of the Palestinian people.

CONCLUSION

The research found that entrepreneurship operates in a complicated context beset by the numerous political, economic, and social challenges in Palestine. The entrepreneurial ecosystem remains fragmented, vulnerable, and immature. This is due to the lack of integration between the many elements of the ecosystem and the absence of a clear governmental framework and/or national strategy. Many entrepreneurs are unfamiliar with the governmental bodies to whom they might turn for funding, support, or counsel, as well as in the event of a legal dispute. Moreover, there are numerous regulatory and financial restraints associated with establishing and registering entrepreneurial firms, resulting in a significant impediment to their growth and their potential to produce concrete economic and social impacts. Additionally, the regulatory role in the entrepreneurial ecosystem is stunted, which has resulted in a decline in the effectiveness of its various components and a failure to play the necessary role in developing the entrepreneurship sector despite significant financial and technical support from donors in recent years.

As a result of the Israeli occupation of Palestine and the siege that has been in force on the Gaza Strip for nearly 15 years, the investment climate in Palestine is fragile, and the ecosystem of entrepreneurship is weakened and confronted by many risks. Foreign venture capital is hesitant to invest in Palestine due to the high level of risk in the entrepreneurial ecosystem and the inability to control political and, to a lesser extent, economic issues. The Paris Protocol restrictions hampered the expansion of entrepreneurship in several strategic industries. Additionally, the Israeli occupation's restrictions continue to impede the entrepreneurs' capacity to compete with the Arab region's entrepreneurial ecosystems and worldwide markets.

Moreover, the entrepreneurial ecosystem has been hindered by the excessive influence of foreign support or investment without an in-depth understanding of the market's demand and character, resulting in limited economic and social impact. External support for entrepreneurship and innovation is characterized by fluctuation and discontinuity, which contributes to the fragility of entrepreneurship, such as the risks associated with funding suspension. Together, the excessiveness, haphazardness, and volatility of foreign support have created an unsustainable and restricted ecosystem that, to a great extent, fails to meet the economic and social demands of the Palestinian labor market. Consequently, most entrepreneurial projects are unable to grow and are quick to fail due to the lack of financial sustainability and growth.

In Palestine, there are yet to be specific mechanisms or an integrated regulatory framework for dealing with entrepreneurship. Additionally, entrepreneurial firms face extra financial burdens as a result of existing taxes and fees including licensing fees, Chamber of Commerce and Industry fees, certificate renewal fees at the Ministry of Economy, and attorney fees. In addition, while there are various government agencies dedicated to stimulating, supporting, and nurturing entrepreneurship, there is lack of coordination and significant overlap in their mandates and scope of work. Additionally, the proliferation of incubators and accelerators, combined with intense competition and a lack of coordination among them, has resulted in a phenomenon in which entrepreneurs move between accelerators and incubators primarily for the purpose of obtaining funding, rather than utilizing the services and activities they provide.

In terms of skills, talent, and culture, the Palestinian educational system cannot be deemed conducive to business and entrepreneurship. Palestinian university graduates lack the technical and managerial abilities necessary to lead successful businesses, as well as the innovative entrepreneurial ideas necessary to realize new ventures.

The gaps and weaknesses in all the elements of the Palestinian entrepreneurial ecosystem have resulted in an unsustainable entrepreneurial model that is unresponsive to the economic and social needs of the Palestinian market. More specifically, the dependence on foreign donors and, consequently, donor agendas in terms of entrepreneurial development frameworks has generated entrepreneurship and an entrepreneurial ecosystem that is unresponsive, unsustainable, inaccessible, and far removed from the Palestinian market needs, hence, most efforts are yet to produce significant economic and social impacts. This existing model is obstructing the process of building an inclusive and sustainable model that is apt to develop and support social entrepreneurship efforts which seek to fill-in the governmental political and economic vacuum. It is critical to recognize that social entrepreneurship ought not to be led by donor agendas. Social entrepreneurship, by definition, must address the unmet demands of the local markets. Hence, there is a need for national strategy which focuses on creating strong interconnections and facilitating collaboration efforts between all stakeholders in the ecosystem to overcome sustainability and effectiveness traps by strengthening the institutional environment, creating an enabling environment through a cross-sectoral approach, and identifying and providing local resource capacities for social innovation and social entrepreneurship to make entrepreneurs less reliant on donor agendas.

REFERENCES

Abdullah, S., Al-Natsheh, B., & Hattawy, M. (2014). *Policies for scaling up youth entrepreneurship in the state of Palestine*. Working paper, Palestine Economic Policy Research Institute (MAS).

Akella, D., & Eid, N. (2018). Social Enterprises in Palestine: A Critical Analysis. *Journal of Enterprising Communities: People and Places in the Global Economy*.

Aldrich, H. E. (1990). Using an Ecological Perspective to Study Organizational Founding Rates. *Entrepreneurship Theory and Practice*, *14*(3), 7–24. doi:10.1177/104225879001400303

Al Mubaraki, H., & Busler, M. (2013). The Effect of Business Incubation in Developing Countries. *European Journal of Business and Innovation Research*, *1*(1), 19–25.

Bahrami, H., & Evans, S. (1995). Flexible Re-Cycling and High Technology Entrepreneurship. *California Management Review*, *37*, 62–89.

Bates, T. (1995). Self-Employment Entry Across Industry Groups. *Journal of Business Venturing*, *10*(2), 143–156. doi:10.1016/0883-9026(94)00018-P

Bone, J., Gonzalez-Uribe, J., Haley, C., & Laher, H. (2019). *The Impact of Business Accelerators and Incubators in the UK. Department for Business, Energy, and Industrial Strategy*. BEIS.

Carroll, D. (2014). *Enhancement of the Business Environment in the South Mediterranean: National Seminar for Palestine*. The European Union's project for ENP South Countries, EUROPEAID/ 133918/C/ SER/MULTI.

Cluadia, S., Maritz, A., & Nguyen, Q. (2019). Entrepreneurial Ecosystems: A Holistic and Dynamic Approach. *Journal of Industry-University Collaboration*, *1*(2), 79–95. doi:10.1108/JIUC-03-2019-0007

Dahl, M. S., & Sorenson, O. (2009). The Embedded Entrepreneur. *European Management Review*, *6*(3), 172–181. doi:10.1057/emr.2009.14

Davidsson, P., & Honig, B. (2003). The Role of Social and Human Capital Among Nascent Entrepreneurs. *Journal of Business Venturing*, *18*(3), 301–331. doi:10.1016/S0883-9026(02)00097-6

Dubini, P. (1989). The Influence of Motivations and Environment on Business Start-Ups: Some Hints For Public Policies. *Journal of Business Venturing*, *4*(1), 11–26. doi:10.1016/0883-9026(89)90031-1

Fehder, D. (2015). *Startup Accelerators and Ecosystem: Substitutes or Compliments?* Working paper. http://danielfehder. com/wpcontent/uploads/2015/10/Fehder_Accel_Ecosystem. pdf

Germak, A., & Robinson, J. A. (2013). Exploring the Motivation of Nascent Social Entrepreneurs. *Journal of Social Entrepreneurship*, *5*(1), 5–21. doi:10.1080/19420676.2013.820781

Gnyawali, D. R., & Fogel, D. S. (1994). Environments for Entrepreneurship Development: Key Dimensions and Research Implications. *Entrepreneurship Theory and Practice*, *18*(4), 43–46. doi:10.1177/104225879401800403

Hallen, B., Bingham, C., & Cohen, S. (2016). *Do Accelerators Accelerate? The role of indirect learning in New Venture Development*. Academic Press.

Kassis, L. (2014). *10 Years Forward – The Palestinian Tech Startup Scene*. LinkedIn Pulse. Retrieved from: https://www.linkedin.com/pulse/20140527081001-19548561-10-years-forward-the-palestinian-tech-startup-scene/

Hoang, C., Bernier, J., & Bard, C. (2016). How Federal, State, Local R&D Incentives Are Supporting Startups. *Chief Financial Officers (CFOs) Magazine*. Retrieved 2022, May 17 from: https://www.cfo.com/strategy/2016/07/federal-state-local-rd-incentives-supporting-startups/

Khalidi, R., & Taghdisi-Rad, S. (2009). *The Economic Dimensions of Prolonged Occupation: Continuity and Change in Israeli Policy Towards the Palestinian Economy*. UNCTAD.

Khalidi, R., Abugattas, L., Hinn, H., Hammoudah, W., Jamil, M., & Srouji. (2022). *Prospects for Development in Palestine 2021: Weathering the Storm, Mobilizing Together.* Palestine Economic Policy Research (MAS).

Khatib, I., Tsipouri, L., Bassiakos, Y., & Haj-daoud, A. (2013). Innovation in Palestinian Industries: A Necessity for Surviving the Abnormal. *Journal of the Knowledge Economy*, *4*(4), 492–510. doi:10.100713132-012-0093-8

Kim, P. H., Aldrich, H. E., & Keister, L. A. (2006). The Impact Of Financial, Human, And Cultural Capital On Entrepreneurial Entry In The United States. *Small Business Economics*, *27*(1), 5–22. doi:10.100711187-006-0007-x

Kuester, S., & Arya, P. (2021). *State of the Palestinian Startup Ecosystem.* Startup Genome & Innovative Private Sector Development.

Leaders International. (2021). *Fast Forward Accelerator Program.* Retrieved 2021, November 17 from: https://leadersinternational.org/projects/fastforward-accelerator-programme/

Morrar, R., & Abdelhadi, M. (2016). Obstacles of Innovation in Palestine. *Journal of Inspiration Economy*, *3*(2), 53–64.

Morrar, R. (2018). Development of Key Performance Indicators and Impact Assessment for Research and Development (R&D) Sector in Palestine. *Review of Economics and Business Administration*, *2*(2), 41–65.

Morrar, R. (2019). Innovation in the MENA region. *IEMed Mediterranean Yearbook 2019.*

Morrar, R., Abdeljawad, I., Jabr, S., Kisa, A., & Younis, M. Z. (2019). The Role of Information and Communications Technology (ICT) in Enhancing Service Sector Productivity in Palestine: An International Perspective. *Journal of Global Information Management*, *27*(1), 47–65. doi:10.4018/JGIM.2019010103

Morrar, R., & Arman, H. (2020). The Transformation Role of a Third Actor Within the Triple Helix Model-the Case of Palestine. *Innovation (Abingdon)*, 1–21. doi:10.1080/13511610.2020.1828045

Morrar, R., & Sultan, S. (2020). The Donor-Driven Model and Financial Sustainability: A Case Study from Palestinian Non-Government Organizations. *Cosmopolitan Civil Societies: An Interdisciplinary Journal*, *12*(2/3), 20–35. doi:10.5130/ccs.v12.i2-3.6771

Morrar, R., & Syed Zwick, H. (2021). Determinants and Wage Penalty of Qualification Mismatches: The Case of Palestine. *Journal of Education and Work*, *34*(4), 504–517. doi:10.1080/13639080.2021.1943331

Morrar, R., & Baba, S. (2022). Social Innovation in Extreme Institutional Contexts: The Case Of Palestine. Management Decision. doi:10.1108/MD-11-2020-1528

Morrar, R., Amara, M., & Syed Zwick, H. (2022). The Determinants of Self-Employment Entry of Palestinian Youth. *Journal of Entrepreneurship in Emerging Economies*, *14*(1), 23–44. doi:10.1108/JEEE-06-2020-0184

Mulas, V., Qian, K., Garza, J., & Henry, S. (2018). *Tech Startup Ecosystem in West Bank and Gaza.* The World Bank.

Nijkamp, P. (2003). Entrepreneurship in a Modern Network Economy. *Regional Studies, 37*(4), 395–405. doi:10.1080/0034340032000074424

Omar, H. (2013). *An Unlikely Setting: Hasan Omar Walks Us Through One of the Up-and-Coming*. Academic Press.

Palestine's Information and Communications Technology Incubator (PICTI). (2018). *About Us*. Retrieved 2021, December 3 from: https://picti.ps/

PCBS. (2020). *Palestinian Labour Force Survey 2020*. Retrieved from: https://www.pcbs. gov.ps/Downloads/book2562.pdf

Pennings, J. M. (1982). The Urban Quality of Life and Entrepreneurship. *Academy of Management Journal, 25*(1), 63–79.

Roebroek, S. (2017). *The Effect of Human Capital, Support Systems and cultural support of the Performance of an entrepreneurial Ecosystem: An Empirical Study on the Entrepreneurial Ecosystem in Europe*. Available at: https://scripties.uba.uva.nl/document/655274

Sadeq, T., & Hamed, M. (2011). *Policies to Promote Female Entrepreneurship in the Palestinian Territory.* Working paper, Palestine Economic Policy Research Institute (MAS).

Stam, E. (2015). Entrepreneurial Ecosystems and Regional Policy: A Sympathetic Critique. *European Planning Studies, 23*(9), 1759–1769. doi:10.1080/09654313.2015.1061484

Stenholm, P., Acs, Z. J., & Wuebker, R. (2013). Exploring Country-Level Institutional Arrangements on the Rate and Type of Entrepreneurial Activity. *Journal of Business Venturing, 28*(1), 176–193. doi:10.1016/j.jbusvent.2011.11.002

Steyaert, C., & Katz, J. (2004). Reclaiming the Space of Entrepreneurship in Society: Geographical, Discursive and Social Dimensions. *Entrepreneurship and Regional Development, 16*(3), 179–196. doi:10.1080/0898562042000197135

Sune, L. (2020). *The Palestinian Startups Scene*. LinkedIn Pulse. Retrieved from: https://www.linkedin.com/pulse/palestinian-startups-scene-laure-sune/

Singh, V. K. (2020). *Policy and Regulatory Changes for a Successful Startup Revolution: Experiences from the Startup Action Plan in India.* ADBI Working Paper 1146. Tokyo: Asian Development Bank Institute.

Stenholm, P., Acs, Z. J., & Wuebker, R. (2013). Exploring Country-Level Institutional Arrangements on the Rate and Type Of Entrepreneurial Activity. *Journal of Business Venturing, 28*(1), 176–193. doi:10.1016/j.jbusvent.2011.11.002

Stephan, U., Uhlaner, L. M., & Stride, C. (2015). Institutions and Social Entrepreneurship: The Role of Institutional Voids, Institutional Support, and Institutional Configurations. *Journal of International Business Studies, 46*(3), 308–331. doi:10.1057/jibs.2014.38

UNCTAD. (2021). *Economic Costs of the Israeli Occupation for the Palestinian People: Poverty in the West Bank Between 2000 and 2019*. UNCTAD.

United Nations Conference on Trade and Development (UNCTAD). (2012). *The Palestinian economy: Macroeconomic and trade policymaking under occupation*. UNCTAD/GDS/APP/2011/1.

Van de Ven, A., & Stam, E. (2019). Entrepreneurial Ecosystem Elements. *Small Business Economics*, *56*, 809–832.

Van De Ven, H. (1993). The Development of an Infrastructure For Entrepreneurship. *Journal of Business Venturing*, *8*(3), 211–230. doi:10.1016/0883-9026(93)90028-4

Wenting, R., Atzema, O., & Frenken, K. (2011). Urban Amenities and Agglomeration Economies? The Locational Behaviour and Economic Success of Dutch Fashion Design Entrepreneurs. *Urban Studies (Edinburgh, Scotland)*, *48*(7), 1333–1352. doi:10.1177/0042098010375992

World Bank. (2020). *Ease of Doing Business in West Bank and Gaza*. World Bank Group.

World Bank. (2021). *Economic Monitoring Report to the Ad hoc Liaison Committee*. World Bank Group.

Zahra, S. A. (2007). Contextualizing Theory Building in Entrepreneurship Research. *Journal of Business Venturing*, *22*(3), 443–452.

Zahra, S. A., Wright, M., & Abdelgawad, S. G. (2014). Contextualization and the Advancement of Entrepreneurship Research. *International Small Business Journal*, *32*(5), 479–500. doi:10.1177/0266242613519807

ENDNOTES

1. Most prominently highlighted government efforts throughout the interviews conducted for the purposes of this study.
2. Globally, there are various types of business incubators, both non-profit and for-profit institution, including: academic institutions usually run by universities; non-profit development corporations which seek to incubate enterprises to stimulate economic development and public welfare; for-profit ventures seeking to find an investment and/or develop new-technology, and venture capital-affiliated incubators which aim to invest and grow startups in exchange of equity
3. In the West bank alone, and Without the Israeli closures and military operations, the poverty rate in the West Bank in 2004 would have been one third of the observed 35% and GDP per capita in 2019 would have been 44% higher than its actual value. For more on economic losses due to the Israeli military occupation, see: https://unctad.org/system/files/official-document/a76d309_en_0.pdf

Chapter 17
Sustainable Growth:
Growth by Poverty Alleviation or Poverty Creation – The Case of Sub-Saharan Africa

Adem Gök
https://orcid.org/0000-0002-3786-2507
Kırklareli University, Turkey

ABSTRACT

The authors analyzed 30 countries in Sub-Saharan Africa over the period of 1996-2015 to investigate whether economic growth is sustainable, whether decreasing income inequality sustains growth, and whether economic growth alleviates or creates poverty due to decreasing or increasing income inequality, respectively. They found that growth in Sub-Saharan Africa is self-reinforcing in the sense that past levels of GDP per capita positively affect current levels of GDP per capita due to the strategic complementarity. Decrease in income inequality leads to growth due to increased consumption, higher investment in education, lower corruption, higher political stability, and more equal redistribution policies. Economic growth does not bring down income inequality in order to maximize social welfare. The authors conclude that growth is not sustainable in Sub-Saharan Africa since it only meets two of the three criteria.

INTRODUCTION

Although majority of the people living in high-income countries and some in the middle-income countries would enjoy unrivaled prosperity, a much larger number of the people living in low-income countries, especially in Sub Saharan Africa, continue to live in extreme poverty. Although some developing countries are experiencing rapid economic growth and poverty alleviation, most authoritarian countries in Sub Saharan Africa are struggling to implement Millennium Development Goals (MDGs) and market-oriented reforms amidst economic decline and increasing poverty (Tanzi and Chu, 1998).

DOI: 10.4018/978-1-6684-4322-4.ch017

According to MDGs, United Nations, World Bank or donor countries take all the actions to increase economic growth in Sub Saharan Africa by Official Development Assistance (ODA), official aid or through improving human capital and governance structures throughout the region for one ultimate goal; eradicating poverty or decreasing income inequality.

Deterioration of income distribution, which is proxied by increasing gini index, is taken as the creation of poverty and improvement in income distribution, which is proxied by decreasing gini index, is taken as the alleviation of poverty. Gini coefficient is used instead of other proxies such as "income share held by lowest 10%" or "income share held by lowest 20%", because of two reasons; first there are less data for these two indices than gini index, second gini index is more reliable than other indices. In other words, we refer to the relative poverty instead of absolute poverty due to the unavailability of poverty data.

Compared to other regions, Sub Saharan Africa has the lowest GDP per capita, hence lowest growth rates. There are mainly four reasons behind the lowest growth rates in the region. First reason is that the countries in Sub Saharan Africa had started with lower initial GDP per capita in the distant past. Second reason is their deficient overall governance structures due to the corrupt, unstable and authoritarian regimes. Third reason is their insufficient human capital leading to inefficient productive capacities. Final reason is higher income inequality or severe poverty that cannot be eradicated.

The main instrument to eradicate poverty or reducing income inequality is sustaining higher growth rates. But, whether higher growth rates in Sub Saharan Africa decrease poverty and income inequality is one of the key questions that the paper tries to answer. Hence, economic growth is not an end but a mean to increase the general wellbeing of the citizens.

In order to eradicate poverty or to decrease income inequality, rapid economic growth is not enough; the countries in Sub Saharan Africa need to achieve sustainable economic growth.

Aim of the study is to find out whether economic growth in countries of Sub Saharan Africa is sustainable; whether decreasing income inequality sustains higher growth rates, and whether increasing growth alleviates or creates poverty due to decreasing or increasing income inequality, respectively.

The paper contributes to the literature in the following ways. First, the paper investigates the two-way relationship between economic growth and income inequality in Sub Saharan Africa by building system of simultaneous equations with Panel Vector Auto-Regression (Panel VAR). Second, the paper offers a theoretical framework for the hypothesis of Sustainable Growth. Third, the paper analyzes whether the growth in Sub Saharan Africa is sustainable or not and why. Finally, the paper recommends policy implications for governments in Sub Saharan Africa to maintain sustainable growth.

Next section introduces literature review and brief theoretical perspective. Third section presents empirical analysis and last section presents discussion.

BACKGROUND

The literature has heavily concentrated on the one-way effect of income inequality on economic growth. Although there are studies investigating the effect of economic growth on poverty or income inequality, there is no study investigating the role of economic growth on poverty or income inequality in the broader sense for Sub Saharan Africa.

Kuznets (1955) established a systematic association between income inequality and economic growth. He argued that income inequality increases in the early stages of development, where the society shifts from rural structure to industrial structure, and it decreases when the society shits from industrial structure to modern structure, which penetrates the entire socio-economic texture of the society. An inverted U-shaped relationship between per capita income and income inequality, which is known as Kuznets Curve.

Forbes (2000) found that income inequality has a significant positive effect on subsequent economic growth, both in the short and medium run.

According to Rodrik (2000), developing countries, which have maintained sustained rapid growth in the recent past, absolute poverty has been declined supporting the fact that growth benefits the poor. High growth rates do not guarantee more equal income distribution and even income disparities between rich and poor households may grow significantly. The association between poverty and growth is altered by government policies. Government may reduce poverty or increase incomes of the poor by investing in education, health, infrastructure through redistributive policies, leading to increase in the productive capacity of the economy even economy does not grow. According to him, we focus on how and under which circumstances growth eradicates poverty instead of a meaningless debate for growth versus poverty.

By using GMM and fixed effects, Panizza (2002) could not find a positive association between economic growth and income inequality but he found a negative association between economic growth and income inequality. He concluded that the association between economic growth and income inequality is not robust due to the econometric technique used for the analysis.

By using Sachs-Warner index, Lundberg and Squire (2003) found that policies promoting economic growth may deteriorate income distribution at least in the short run, and education has negative significant effect on gini index for developing countries.

By developing a small canonical model with an extension of the basic AK model, Garcia-Penalosa and Turnovsky (2006) concluded that rapid growth has positive significant effect on income inequality.

Barro (2008) found that income inequality has a negative significant impact on economic growth and economic growth has a positive significant impact on income inequality. He concluded that the impact of income inequality on economic growth decreases as GDP per capita increases and the impact may turn to positive for the high-income countries.

By using a new inequality measures for the states, Frank (2009) concluded that there is a positive long-run relationship between economic growth and income inequality, which is principally driven by the concentration of income in the upper percentile.

Caraballo et al. (2017) estimated the association between economic growth and income inequality by using GMM for 112 emerging countries over the period of 1980-2014. They found that income inequality has a positive significant impact on economic growth for high-income countries supporting the classic theory, and a negative significant impact for low-income countries supporting the political economy approach.

Berg et al. (2018) found that net income inequality has robust negative significant impact on rapid stable growth through the channels of human capital accumulation and fertility.

Bartak and Jabłoński(2020) investigated whether income inequality impedes economic growth for OECD countries over the period of 1990–2014 by employing system GMM and to reveal whether the association between economic growth and income inequality is robust when other measures of income inequality are used. They found that income inequality has a negative impact on economic growth and using different measures of income inequality results in the altering magnitudes of coefficients.

By using a cumulative growth model, Seo et al. (2020) analyzed the impact of income inequality on economic growth for 43 countries over the period of 1991-2014 and found that income inequality has a negative effect on economic growth for developing countries.

Although there are numerous studies investigating the role of income inequality on economic growth, there are limited number of studies analyzing the role of economic growth on income inequality.

In a study for Brazil over the period of 1981-2013, Tabosa and Carvalho (2017) found that policies promoting economic growth reduces income disparities as an effective tool to combat poverty.

By using US county-level data over the period of 1990-2000, Majumdar and Partridge (2009) found that economic growth has a negative effect on income inequality since economic growth increases income for a higher number of people by creating higher investments and higher employment-generating processes. They concluded that growth decreases income inequality for urban areas since higher population density in urban areas results in more personal contacts, better networks and higher access to information, hence it increases the quantity and quality of jobs. They recommended that government should invest in educational and vocational training to generate more skilled labor force, which in turn boost economic growth and thus lead to decrease in income inequality and increase in social cohesion.

In a study of Tunisia for the period of 1984-2011, Wahiba and Weriemmi (2014) found that economic growth constitutes aggravating factors for income inequality and inequality has a negative significant effect on economic growth.

In a study for US over the period of 1953-2008, Rubin and Segal (2015) found that labor income of top percentile is more sensitive to growth compared with low percentile, hence economic growth increases income inequality.

Nolan and Maître (2008) concluded that rapid growth had no significant effect on income inequality in Ireland. Ireland still has high level of economic inequality after the Ireland's unprecedented economic boom, just as it did beforehand.

The debate for the interaction between economic growth and income inequality is still open and there is still no general consensus. As de Groot et al. (2008) stated that different conclusions are reached for the association between economic growth and income inequality in the literature due to the econometric techniques employed, the countries analyzed and the income inequality measures used for income inequality.

MAIN FOCUS OF THE CHAPTER

The hypothesis for the sustainable growth is as follows.

Growth is sustainable if it meets three conditions simultaneously:

First, growth should bring down income inequality or eradicate poverty. Economic growth should bring down income inequality in order to maximize social welfare, according to the utilitarian view. Otherwise increase in income inequality or poverty increases political instability leading to social unrest or even civil war, which harms the productive capacity of the economy.

Second, decrease in income inequality or poverty should lead growth based on four arguments. First, the marginal propensity to consume of the rich citizens is lowest. Hence an increase in income of the poorer or decrease in income of the richer increase consumption leading to growth. Second, a higher concentration of income in the hands of fewer decrease the demand of a larger share of poorer individuals, which would invest less in education and grow a sense of social and political discontent, jeopardizing human capital and political stability (Grigoli et al., 2017). Third, an economy endowed with relatively higher levels of income inequality, there is a tendency for rent-seeking, abuse of political power for self-enrichment and distrust of the incumbent government, which all contribute to corruption and political instability (Balcilar et al., 2019). Fourth, higher inequality empowers the influence of the richer people on the legislative and regulatory processes and especially motivate aggressive redistribution policies that are often blamed for slowing economic growth (Grigoli et al., 2017).

Third, growth should be self-reinforcing in the sense that past level of GDP per capita levels should be positive significant determinant of current level due to the strategic complementarity. In other words, the increase in growth should be maintained due to its structure even there is no improvement in other variables that are contributing to growth.

Present your perspective on the issues, controversies, problems, etc., as they relate to theme and arguments supporting your position. Compare and contrast with what has been, or is currently being done as it relates to the chapter's specific topic and the main theme of the book.

EMPIRICAL ANALYSIS

The paper analysis three relationships; (1) the effect of income inequality on economic growth, (2) the effect of economic growth on income inequality, (3) the effect of past levels of economic growth on current level of economic growth, in order the test the hypothesis of sustainable growth for 30 countries in Sub Saharan Africa over the period of 1996-2015. by building simultaneous system of equations with Panel VAR.

Data and Variables

Instead of analyzing just two variables; GDP per capita and gini index, we used two other control variables; governance and human capital, that are significant in the growth and income inequality regressions. Hence, we have four endogenous variables; GDP per capita for measuring growth, gini coefficient for measuring income inequality or the poverty in the broadest sense, average of scores for the six dimensions of governance for measuring overall governance performance, and school enrollment rate for measuring human capital.

We have used GDP per capita (constant 2010 US$) from WDI (2020) to proxy growth in Sub Saharan Africa since increase in GDP per capita means growth instead of using growth rates since we would be measuring the change in growth rates in that case.

We have used the estimate of gini index for income inequality from Solt (2020), which is in equivalized (square root scale) household disposable (post-tax, post-transfer) income based on Luxembourg Income Study data.

We have used the average of scores for six dimensions of governance; control of corruption, government effectiveness, political stability and absence of violence/terrorism, regulatory quality, rule of law, and voice and accountability from WGI (2020), in order to construct overall governance performance in Sub Saharan Africa.

Finally, we have used school enrollment, secondary (% gross) from WDI (2020) to proxy human capital since data for tertiary enrollment rates are unavailable for most of the countries in Sub Saharan Africa.

Less than 5% of data is either interpolated or extrapolated; by simple average or by 5-year moving average of growth, respectively.

According to the results in Table 1, there is cross-sectional independence only for governance (gov). Hence, we apply first-generation unit root test for governance (gov) and second-generation unit root test for other variables.

Table 1. Cross section dependency test

Variables	CD-Test	p-value
lngdppc	52.751	0.000
gini	2.396	0.017
gov	-1.225	0.221
humcap	69.302	0.000

Notes: Null hypothesis is the cross-section independence. P-values close to zero indicate data are correlated across panel groups.

According to the results in Table 2, only governance (gov) is stationary at the level; I(0), and other variables are stationary at their first differences; I(1). Since all variables are stationary at their first differences, we have used first differencing instead of Helmert procedure.

Table 2. Unit root tests

Levin, Lin & Chu (2002)				
	Level		**First-Difference**	
Variable	Constant	Constant & Trend	Constant	Constant & Trend
gov	-2.923***	-1.795**	-16.21***	-15.245***
Pesaran (2007)				
	Level		First-Difference	
Variable	Constant	Constant & Trend	Constant	Constant & Trend
lngdppc	-1.482	-2.122	-3.620***	-3.775***
gini	-1.117	-2.373	-3.535***	-3.945***
humcap	-1.583	-1.940	-3.217***	-3.634***

Notes: Null hypothesis for both tests is the presence of unit root. The t* values are reported for Levin, Lin & Chu, and CIPS values are reported for Pesaran (2007). ***, ** and * denote significance levels at % 1, % 5 and % 10 respectively.

Methodology

Panel Vector Auto Regression (Panel VAR) Analysis treats all variables as endogenous in order to allow unobserved individual heterogeneity (Love and Zicchino, 2006). According to the literature, governance and human capital are the most significant determinants for both growth and inequality equations, hence they were taken as control variables. Other than GDP per capita and gini coefficient, these variables are also endogenous since there exist bivariate causal relationships between them according to the Granger causality tests in the following sections, hence panel VAR was employed to build a system of four simultaneous equations.

Since we have found the optimal lag-length for the panel VAR model as one, we specify a first order panel VAR model as follows;

$$y_{it} = \Gamma_0 + \Gamma_1 y_{it-1} + f_i + d_{c,t} + e_t \quad (1)$$

where y_{it} is a vector of four-variables comprising GDP per capita, gini coefficient, human capital and governance (Love and Zicchino, 2006).

We have introduced fixed effects, f_i, and country-specific time dummies, $d_{c,t}$ to allow for individual heterogeneity and to capture aggregate country-specific macro shocks, respectively (Love and Zicchino, 2006). We have used first-differencing to eliminate fixed effects based on two reasons. First, our panel data is balanced, hence there is no need to use forward orthogonal deviation (Helmert procedure). Second, our variables are either I(0) or I(1), hence using first-differencing turns our data into stationary.

The model in first differences may be consistently estimated equation by equation by instrumenting lagged differences with differences and levels of the dependent variable vector from earlier periods by Generalized Method of Moments (GMM), which requires small *T*, large *N* (Abrigo and Love, 2016).

Panel VAR utilizes five different tools; stability test, Granger causality test, panel vector auto-regression, impulse response functions, and forecast-error variance decomposition. Panel VAR satisfies the stability condition if all the eigenvalues lie inside the unit circle according to the result of stability test. Granger causality test indicates whether the variables are endogenous or not. It can also be used to order variables more exogenous to more endogenous due to the unilateral or bilateral causal relationship between variables. Since we will use first-order panel VAR, panel vector auto-regression presents the effects of first lag of each independent variable on each of the four-variable dependent vector. The impulse-response functions present the reaction of one variable to the innovations (given shock) in another variable in the system, while holding all other shocks equal to zero. We generate confidence intervals with Monte Carlo simulations to calculate the standard errors of the impulse-response functions. Finally, we present variance decompositions to show the magnitude of the total effect. Variance decomposition shows the percent of the variation in one variable that is explained by the shock given to another variable, which is accumulated over time. We report the total effect, which is accumulated over 10 years by variance decomposition (Love and Zicchino, 2006).

We will use the stata package for the Panel VAR analysis, which is developed by Abrigo and Love (2016).

Results

Panel VAR satisfies stability condition since all the eigenvalues lie inside the unit circleaccording to the results in Table 3.

There are at least two bi-directional causal relationships between variables according to the results of Granger causality test in Table 4, which indicate that the variables are endogenous justifying to use panel VAR technique. Since there is a bi-directional causality between GDP per capita and gini coefficient, it can be concluded that a necessary but not sufficient condition is met for our hypotheses.

Table 3. Stability test

Eigenvalue		
Real	Imaginary	Modulus
0.918	0	0.918
0.557	0	0.557
0.372	0	0.372
-0.222	0	0.222

Table 4. Granger causality test

	lngdppc	gini	gov	humcap
lngdppc		0.035	0.001	0.000
gini	0.000		0.000	0.306
gov	0.142	0.002		0.000
humcap	0.000	0.000	0.011	

Notes: The numbers are the Prob > chi2 values. Null hypothesis is that the row variable does not Granger-cause column variable.

Since we have defined first-order panel VAR model, the results of Table 5 and Figure 1 are interpreted together.

The lag of the natural logarithm of GDP per capita (lngdppc_{it-1}) has positive significant effect on its current value (lngdppc_{it}) according to Table 5, or the response of the natural logarithm of GDP per capita (lngdppc_{it}) to the one standard deviation shock given to its value in the previous period (lngdppc_{it-1}) is positive significant according to Figure 1. The lag of gini coefficient (gini_{it-1}) has negative significant effect on the natural logarithm of GDP per capita (lngdppc_{it}) according to Table 5, or the response of the natural logarithm of GDP per capita (lngdppc_{it}) to the one standard deviation shock given to the lag of gini coefficient (gini_{it-1}) is negative significant according to Figure 1. The lag of governance (gov_{it-1}) has no significant effect on the natural logarithm of GDP per capita (lngdppc_{it}) according to Table 5, or the response of the natural logarithm of GDP per capita (lngdppc_{it}) to the one standard deviation shock given to the lag of governance (gov_{it-1}) is insignificant according to Figure 1. Finally, the lag of human capital (humcap_{it-1}) has positive significant effect on the natural logarithm of GDP per capita (lngdppc_{it}) according to Table 5, or the response of the natural logarithm of GDP per capita (lngdppc_{it}) to the one standard deviation shock given to the lag of human capital (humcap_{it-1}) is positive significant according to Figure 1.

The lag of the natural logarithm of GDP per capita (lngdppc_{it-1}) has positive significant effect on gini coefficient (gini_{it}) according to Table 5, or the response of gini coefficient (gini_{it}) to the one standard deviation shock given to the lag of the natural logarithm of GDP per capita (lngdppc_{it}) is positive significant according to Figure 1. The lag of governance (gov_{it-1}) has positive significant effect on gini coefficient (gini_{it}) according to Table 5, or the response of gini coefficient (gini_{it}) to the one standard deviation shock given to the lag of governance (gov_{it-1}) is positive significant according to Figure 1. Finally, the lag of human capital ($humcap_{it-1}$) has negative significant effect on gini coefficient ($gini_{it}$) according to Table 5, or the response of gini coefficient ($gini_{it}$) to the one standard deviation shock given to the lag of human capital ($humcap_{it-1}$) is negative significant according to Figure 1.

According to variance decomposition at a horizon of ten years in Table 6, forecast error variances of the natural logarithm of GDP per capita and gini coefficient are explained mostly by their own shocks; 81.85% and 76.5%, respectively. The natural logarithm of GDP per capita forecast error variance is explained by gini coefficient as 9.68%, human capital 6.5%, and governance as 1.98%. Gini coefficient forecast error variance is explained by human capital as 18.81%, governance as 2.99%, and the natural logarithm of GDP per capita as 1.7%.

Table 5. Panel vector autoregression results

	lngdppc	**gini**	**gov**	**humcap**
lngdppc (t-1)	0.4350***	0.2829**	0.3805***	22.8823***
	(0.0418)	(0.1343)	(0.1101)	(4.3568)
gini (t-1)	-0.0758***	0.9116***	0.1584***	-1.4815
	(0.0202)	(0.0469)	(0.0396)	(1.4488)
gov (t-1)	-0.0774	0.2443***	0.0061	31.0071***
	(0.0528)	(0.0782)	(0.0892)	(1.9737)
humcap(t-1)	0.0020***	-0.0078***	0.0026**	0.2726***
	(0.0004)	(0.0012)	(0.0010)	(0.0578)
No. of countries/obs				30/90

Notes: Four variable VAR model is estimated by GMM; country-time and fixed effects are removed prior to estimation. Column variables indicate dependent variables while row variables indicate independent variables. Reported numbers show the coefficients of regressing the column variables on lags of the row variables. Heteroskedasticity adjusted *z*-statistics are in parentheses. ***, ** and * denote significance levels at % 1, % 5 and % 10 respectively.

Table 6. Variance decomposition

	lngdppc	**gini**	**gov**	**humcap**
lngdppc	0.8185	0.0170	0.0714	0.1751
gini	0.0968	0.7650	0.0638	0.0446
gov	0.0198	0.0299	0.8590	0.3415
humcap	0.0650	0.1881	0.0058	0.4389

Notes: Percent of variation in the column variable (10 periods ahead) is explained by row variable.

Figure 1. Impulse response functions

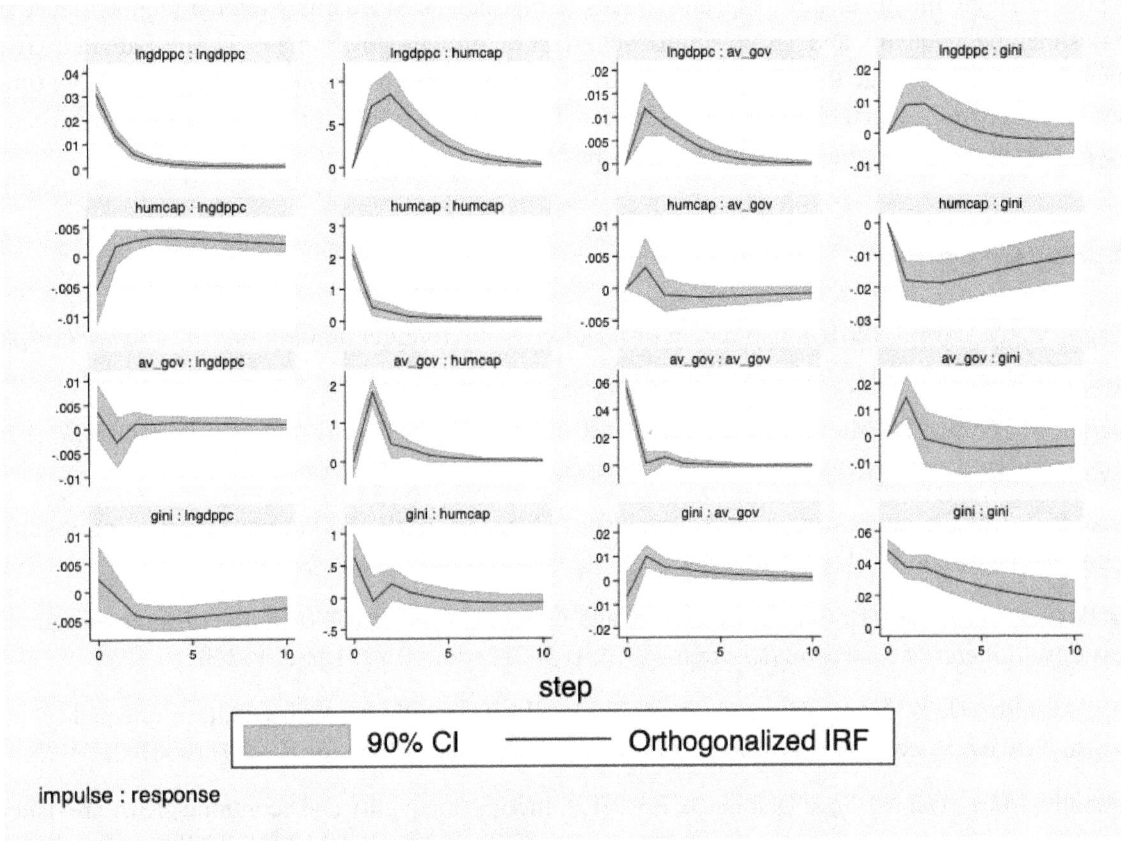

CONCLUSION

(1) Although the lag of the natural logarithm of GDP per capita has positive significant effect on its current value, and (2) gini coefficient has negative significant effect on the natural logarithm of GDP per capita, (3) the natural logarithm of GDP per capita has positive significant effect on gini coefficient. In other words, (1) growth in Sub-Saharan Africa is self-fulfilling in the sense that past levels of GDP per capita positively affecting current levels of GDP per capita due to the strategic complementarity. (2) Decrease in income inequality leads to growth in Sub Saharan Africa due to increased consumption, higher investment in education, lower corruption and higher political stability and more equal redistribution policies. (3) Economic growth does not bring down income inequality in order to maximize social welfare in Sub Saharan Africa. Instead, growth leads to social unrest or even civil wars due to the increasing number of poor households, leading to political instability, which cripples the productive capacity of the economy in a vicious cycle. Hence, economic growth creates poverty in Sub Saharan Africa. We conclude that growth is not sustainable in Sub Saharan Africa according to our hypothesis since it only meets two of the three criteria.

In order the countries in Sub Saharan Africa to have sustainable growth, we recommend the following policy implications. Since growth creates poverty in Sub Saharan Africa, governments should invest primarily in human capital, which translates into better jobs due to the higher matched skills, to decrease income inequality and poverty. But the investment in education or vocational training should first target the poor or economically disadvantaged segments of the society. Since improvement in governance increases income inequality and has no significant effect on growth, governments in Sub Saharan Africa should structurally change their governance structures, which are mostly inherited from colonial times since any improvement in their governance structures justifies the validity of their inefficient governance structures that are not leading to economic growth.

REFERENCES

Abrigo, M., & Love, I. (2016). Estimation of panel vector autoregression in Stata. *The Stata Journal, 16*(3), 778–804. doi:10.1177/1536867X1601600314

Balcilar, M., Gupta, R., Ma, W., & Makena, P. (2019). *Income inequality and economic growth: A re-examination of theory and evidence*. Working Paper. University of Pretoria.

Barro, R. J. (2008). *Inequality and growth revisited* (No. 11). ADB Working paper series on regional economic integration.

Bartak, J., & Jabłoński, Ł. (2020). Inequality and growth: What comes from the different inequality measures? *Bulletin of Economic Research, 72*(2), 185–212. doi:10.1111/boer.12220

Berg, A., Ostry, J. D., Tsangarides, C. G., & Yakhshilikov, Y. (2018). Redistribution, inequality, and growth: New evidence. *Journal of Economic Growth, 23*(3), 259–305. doi:10.100710887-017-9150-2

Caraballo, M. Á., Dabús, C., & Delbianco, F. (2017). Income inequality and economic growth revisited. A note. *Journal of International Development, 29*(7), 1025–1029. doi:10.1002/jid.3300

de Groot, H. L. F., de Dominicis, L., & Florax, R. J. G. M. (2008). Growth and Inequality: A Meta-Analysis. *Scottish Journal of Political Economy, 55*(5), 654–682. doi:10.1111/j.1467-9485.2008.00470.x

Forbes, K. J. (2000). A reassessment of the relationship between inequality and growth. *The American Economic Review, 90*(4), 869–887. doi:10.1257/aer.90.4.869

Frank, M. W. (2009). Inequality and growth in the United States: Evidence from a new state-level panel of income inequality measures. *Economic Inquiry, 47*(1), 55–68. doi:10.1111/j.1465-7295.2008.00122.x

Garcia-Penalosa, C., & Turnovsky, S. J. (2006). Growth and income inequality: A canonical model. *Economic Theory, 28*(1), 25–49. doi:10.100700199-005-0616-7

Grigoli, F., Paredes, E., & Di Bella, G. (2017). *Inequality and Growth: A Heterogeneous Approach*. International Monetary Fund.

Kuznets, S. (1955). Economic Growth and Income Inequality. *The American Economic Review, 45*(1), 1–28.

Levin, A., Lin, C. F., & Chu, C. S. J. (2002). Unit root tests in panel data: Asymptotic and finite-sample properties. *Journal of Econometrics, 108*(1), 1–24. doi:10.1016/S0304-4076(01)00098-7

Love, I., & Zicchino, L. (2006). Financial development and dynamic investment behavior: Evidence from panel VAR. *The Quarterly Review of Economics and Finance*, *46*(2), 190–210. doi:10.1016/j.qref.2005.11.007

Lundberg, M., & Squire, L. (2003). The simultaneous evolution of growth and inequality. *Economic Journal (London)*, *113*(487), 326–344. doi:10.1111/1468-0297.00127

Majumdar, S., & Partridge, M. D. (2009). *Impact of economic growth on income inequality: A regional perspective* (No. 319-2016-9872). Academic Press.

Nolan, B., & Maitre, B. (2008). Economic growth and income inequality: setting the context. In *Quality of life in Ireland* (pp. 27–41). Springer. doi:10.1007/978-1-4020-6981-9_3

Panizza, U. (2002). Income inequality and economic growth: Evidence from American data. *Journal of Economic Growth*, *7*(1), 25–41. doi:10.1023/A:1013414509803

Pesaran, M. H. (2007). A simple panel unit root test in the presence of cross-section dependence. *Journal of Applied Econometrics*, *22*(2), 265–312. doi:10.1002/jae.951

Rodrik, D. (2000). Growth versus Poverty Reduction: A Hollow Debate. *Finance & Development*, *37*(4), 8–9.

Seo, H. J., Kim, H., & Lee, Y. S. (2020). The Dynamic Relationship between Inequality and Sustainable Economic Growth. *Sustainability*, *12*(14), 5740. doi:10.3390u12145740

Solt, F. (2020). Measuring Income Inequality Across Countries and Over Time: The Standardized World Income Inequality Database. *Social Science Quarterly*, *101*(3), 1183–1199. doi:10.1111squ.12795

Tabosa, F. J. S., & de Carvalho, P. U. (2017). Brazil, 1981-2013: the effects of economic growth and income inequality on poverty. Commission for Latin America and the Caribbean, 153.

Tanzi, V., & Chu, K. Y. (Eds.). (1998). *Income distribution and high-quality growth*. Mit Press.

Wahiba, N. F., & El Weriemmi, M. (2014). The relationship between economic growth and income inequality. *International Journal of Economics and Financial Issues.*, *4*(1), 135.

WDI. (2020a). *World Development Indicators*. The World Bank.

WGI. (2020b). *Worldwide Governance Indicators*. The World Bank.

Section 5

Technology and Entrepreneurial Sustainability

Chapter 18
Digital Transformation and Sustainability of Entrepreneurship for Underserved Communities in East Africa

Nathan Mutwiri Mwenda
https://orcid.org/0000-0002-9158-320X
Kenyatta University, Kenya

Carolyne Jebiwott Kimutai
https://orcid.org/0000-0001-6199-5257
Kenyatta University, Kenya

ABSTRACT

Digital transformations are transforming the economy and society in East Africa, and entrepreneurs need to leverage on these digital transformations to ensure the sustainability of their businesses. This chapter therefore seeks to examine the role of digital transformation on sustainability of entrepreneurship for the underserved communities in East Africa. The chapter adopts an interdisciplinary and pragmatic world view. There exist many challenges in East Africa which stifle the progress of digital adoption. For East African countries to exploit the potential of technology, they must develop the foundational building block of digital economy. Digital innovation contributes to the development of an ecosystem that revitalizes the digital economy by supporting new technology-based products and businesses. East African countries should ensure that the underserved communities receive basic education, strengthen, and integrate a multi-sectoral approach towards a regional digital and legal policy framework in order to encourage innovation and e-business.

DOI: 10.4018/978-1-6684-4322-4.ch018

INTRODUCTION

Digital transformation is a comprehensive shift in the use of technology with the objective of improving business performance. Digital transformation is a key element to the sustainability of businesses; for them to remain competitive in the market, enterprises need to adopt digital innovations (Farías & Cancino, 2021). In the recent past, the world has witnessed the evolution of digital technologies, which has led to transformation in business operations, thereby necessitating changes in the entrepreneurship process. Such technologies that can boost their entrepreneurial ventures among the underserved communities include Artificial intelligence, Block chain, Robotic Process automation and Internet of things. Artificial intelligence (AI) is where learning process is applied in large data sets to make predictions and classifications. (Homi & Cohen, 2018). Therefore AI is able to learn from the past success and failure in predicting and classifying. Recent developments in the AI have helped decision makers in organizations to make critical decisions ranging from product development, customer engagements and hiring. Entrepreneurs in the underserved communities use AI to detect customer needs and develop products that meet customer expectations. The Robotic Process automation (RPA) technology mimics the human worker. It allows employees to configure computers software to capture and interpret existing applications for processing a transaction, manipulating data, trigger responses and communicate with other systems (Nair, 2018). Whereas these developments bring significant benefits to business operations, Entrepreneurs in East Africa have a long way to access and adopt them in their entrepreneurial activities because of cost and access constraints.

Block chain is a digital ledger that allows users to transfer value and track transactions in a decentralized manner, without the need for a central authority to authenticate the information assuring data transparency (Tafotie, 2020). By enabling greater financial inclusion and increasing productivity, block chain could be beneficial to underserved communities in developing economies. With the growing number of individuals owning smart phones in East Africa the block chain enables access to finance where many people do not have a bank account or the ATM services. The use of block chain to support micropayments paves the way for the creation of long-term pay-per-use services. Furthermore, KYC block chain-based systems may make it easier for banks to resolve information asymmetries and lower their cost of serving when lending money. This can help the underserved communities access cheaper credit from the financial institutions boosting the actualization of their entrepreneurial ideas.

The internet of things revolution has been witnessed in Africa and no aspect of human life will escape the revolution. By the year 2020 tens of billions of devices are connected to the internet (Okereafor & Ndubuaku, 2015). Internet of things is a worldwide infrastructure for the information society, enabling advanced services by interconnecting (physical and virtual) things based on existing and emerging interoperable information and services.

The Internet of Things, it is suggested, will allow Africa to collect massive amounts of data from connected humans, machines, and infrastructure, enhancing the ability to develop unique solutions to common problems, makes automated decisions, take real-time actions, and track the progress of society (Feyen, Frost, Gambacorta, Natarajan, & Saal, 2021). The internet of things helps the can help disadvantaged entrepreneurs deliver services to the consumers efficiently. Digital transformations are revolutionizing the economy and society in East Africa, and entrepreneurs need to leverage these digital transformations to improve the performance of their businesses and contribute to the sustainability of entrepreneurship (Kutzschenbach & Daub, 2021). One of the key contributors to United Nations Sustainable development goals is digitization. For economic and environmental challenges to be solved there ought to be transformation in business models (Bican & Brem, 2020). Global digital transformation requires entrepreneurs to develop skills about digital entrepreneurship (Ratten & Usmanij, 2021). One of the key drivers in the innovation system is digital entrepreneurship. It provides a mechanism and structure for the overall business systems affecting the entrepreneur, the entrepreneurial process and its relevant ecosystem (Satalkina & Steiner, 2020).

Globally income gaps have been a major concern for most policy makers. The IMF (2016) report, notes that despite the growth over the decades, poverty and inequality levels remain high in sub-Saharan Africa. As per the IMF report, Sub-Saharan income inequality was second globally behind Latin, while gender inequality was the highest in the world. As global wealth continues to grow at an exponential level, stagnation and rise in poverty levels at the bottom pyramid is on an increasing trend (Rolle & Kisato 2019). Underserved communities face barriers in accessing services based on their geographical location, religion, gender identity, sexual orientation, disability and poverty levels, among others. Boellstorff (2019) indicated that there is an intersection between gender and disability in the entrepreneurship domain. This compounds the exclusivity for persons who belong to these groups. Gender metrics influence the success of entrepreneurial ventures. This book chapter therefore seeks to examine the digital transformation and sustainability of entrepreneurship among the underserved communities in East Africa.

BACKGROUND

Entrepreneurship is a critical tool in poverty alleviation (Song & Yang, 2020). Digital transformation should enable the development of entrepreneurial activities, as it allows for quick adaptation of service delivery in periods of pandemic such as COVID-19. However, living in high poverty communities and areas has an influence on technological access (Jackson, 2009). Deprived economic abilities diminish the ability of the poor to adapt to digital transformations, thereby reducing their market for their entrepreneurial ventures. Whereas most of the African population lives in rural areas, East and South African city populations have been growing at an increasing speed, resulting in slums. The majority of the people in Africa live in rural areas, 82% live in extreme poverty, and they rely primarily on substance farming. According to the World Bank (2019), the levels of poverty are on an upwards trajectory rising from 55% in 2015 to a forecasted level of approximately 90% in 2030. This is a worrisome trend because it is bound to negatively affect the access and adoption of digital technologies among the underserved communities in East Africa. Youth contributes significantly to the economic development of any nation. With nearly half of the population in East Africa falling under the 18 year bracket, youth are the drivers of technological innovations and hence the region's greatest resource, (World Bank, 2020).In the recent past, the COVID-19 pandemic has weakened supply chains and jeopardized business opportunities for entrepreneurs. This has interrupted business operations across the globe. The journey towards recovery must incorporate digital anchored solutions targeting businesses owned by the underserved communities with the aim of ensuring that there is sustainable entrepreneurship.

Schaltegger and Wagner (2011) explain that a sustainable entrepreneurship typology requires the incorporation of diverse entrepreneurial approaches with the aim of meeting social goals in the market context and ensuring sustainable innovation. To capitalize on social and environmental requirements, entrepreneurs should incorporate digital technologies into their business strategies. This will ensure that their business models are anchored on a sustainable business environment, thereby ensuring the growth and development of entrepreneurial ventures (Gregori & Holzmann, 2020). George, Merrill and Schillebeeckx (2021) explored the digital technologies and the challenges businesses face to promote sustainable developments. The study explains how entrepreneurs are handling the social challenges facing communities by embracing innovative approaches. The study found that digital sustainable innovation plays a key role in spurring advances in entrepreneurial innovation, and this injects positive benefits to society.

Jawad, Naz and Maroof, (2021) agree that demographic elements such as gender affect the uptake of digital transformation since they present dynamic attributes on readiness for adoption of new technologies and innovation. Women seem to play a catch up role in embracing technology because of social, legal and cultural factors that negatively affect them.

Rolle and Kisato (2019) explored the future of technology and entrepreneurial innovation for the underserved and established that economic disparities among countries contributed to widening gaps in innovation. The study found that there is a need to strengthen weak partnerships with industry players and entrepreneurs globally. IMF (2016) found growing empirical evidence of adverse effects of income and gender inequality on economic growth in Sub-Saharan Africa. The drivers of inequality need to be factored into policy making to foster inclusive and sustainable growth of entrepreneurship. Boellstorff (2019) explored the intersect between gender and disability in the entrepreneurship domain and showed how the intersect can have negative effects on entrepreneurial growth. Orobia (2020) studied the link between entrepreneurial framework conditions and long-term company viability among young women and men. The study discovered that there are important indicators of business sustainability among youth and women entrepreneurs.

Jawad, Naz and Maroof (2021) explored how gender as a demographic attribute affects how an entrepreneur embraces digital transformation. Schaltegger and Wagner (2011) explained that for an entrepreneurial venture to be sustainable, it must address and employ an approach that addresses the social goals. This ensures that the venture is aligned with the market context while adopting sustainable innovation. The significance of digital entrepreneurship in innovation systems was investigated by Satalkina and Steiner (2020), who discovered that digital entrepreneurship is a key driver of innovation and digital transformation. According to the findings, there are three elements to innovation systems: the entrepreneur, the entrepreneurial process, and the essential ecosystems, which include the impact of external infrastructure and institutions on the development of digital entrepreneurship.

Chatterjee, Chaudhuri, Vrontis, and Basile (2021) investigated the process of digital transformation and entrepreneurship among Indian SMEs. According to the survey, small and medium businesses make a major contribution to the economy. Small and medium enterprises have to improve their ability to accept change and embrace digital transformation because it contributes to the success of businesses, ensuring sustainability. Gregori and Holzmann (2020) investigated a business model for sustainable entrepreneurship that used digital technologies. The study found that when entrepreneurs embrace digital transformations, there is a possible rise in the connectivity of the different actors within the value creation components. According to Wang and Richardson (2021), policymakers around the world have invested in the arts and cultural industries as significant drivers of economic development. They did, however, point out that race, ethnicity, gender, and inequality had not been adequately addressed. The paper studied how these factors affect the culture of entrepreneurship. According to the study, these social identities have a substantial impact on the process of starting and running innovative firms. Bailey and Ngwenyama (2013) investigated the decision making process of community members who use tele centers for entrepreneurial endeavors. The paper used a predictive model for entrepreneurial behavior and found that social demographic ties such as culture, age, education and income levels influence how individuals embrace technology in their entrepreneurial ventures.

Ratten,(2019) found that there is a need to strike a balance between open innovation and guarding against the effects of cybercrimes which is a threat to intellectual property. Entrepreneurs from underserved communities lack the capacity to protect their ideas and innovation from infringement. This is because they lack of knowhow and adequate resources. Cybercrime, has stifled development of SMES in the advent if digital transformation. Jansen et al (2016) opines that whereas technology is increasingly important for entrepreneurs, the protection of their infrastructure and data is critical because of online threats targeted at their entrepreneurial activities. Whereas the study found that entrepreneurs ought to implement protective measures against online threats, the underserved communicates in East Africa lack the resources to sufficiently protect their firms from cyber security threats

Amid the growing concerns in global, regional and national economy downturns, there are increasing efforts to create economic opportunities in developing countries (Bailey & Ngwenyama, 2013). These initiatives have acknowledged the importance of information and communication technology (ICT) in promoting social and economic development. Oestmann and Dymond (2001) argued that telecenter staff ought to use their entrepreneurial skills to build sustainable programs. The main issue confronting youth is the high rate of unemployment, which has wide-ranging economic and social consequences (Anderson & Williams, 2008). The low level of education and training makes the youth unable to find meaningful employment. Bailey and Ngwenyama,(2013) examined the role of telecenters in influencing entrepreneurship and economic development among the underserved communities. The study found that the adoption of technology is inhibited by the high poverty levels among the underserved communities.

The intersectional discrimination and substantive equality concept has been lauded as a theoretical contribution to identify recognition. It recognizes that different identity categories can coexist in the same individual. Gender reaches disability, disability wraps around economic class,and poverty intertwines with age (Clare et al, 1999).Whereas the law clings to a single axis, failing to address discrimination on multiple grounds; intersectionality is increasingly becoming a common parlance for policy makers ensuring that multiple marginalized communities are factored (Smith, 2016). However, the underserved communities may be clustered into women, youth, the disabled and the poor. It is common for entrepreneurs to identify with more than one of the clusters at the same time. This calls for the enactment of laws that ensure both formal and substantive equality thereby ensuring sustainable entrepreneurship among the underserved communities.

The sociotechnical systems theory (Trist, E. L. & Bamforth, K. W., 1951) found that the interconnected technology's nature and the social aspects of work by taking into account both the technical and social aspects that influence organizational transformation. This theory is useful for studying digital transformations, especially at a time when digital technologies cause corporate processes to be disrupted. Since advanced digital and hyperconnected technologies are at the heart of digital transformation, it necessitates a rethinking of human-technology interactions inside an organization (Mitki, Shani, & Greenbaum, 2019). As a result, digital transformation is viewed as a sociotechnical process in which social and technical aspects collaborate to achieve a common goal. (Sony & Naik, 2020)

The resource-based theory in entrepreneurship advances the boundaries of entrepreneurship. Alvrez and Busenitz (2001) extended the theory to include the cognitive ability of individual entrepreneurs. The theory postulates that new opportunities are recognized when they are identified. The desired ability to organize resources into an entity that creates heterogenous outputs that advances competitive advantage in the market is influenced by individual specific resources. The theory opines that resources are heterogeneous and immobile and values the creativity, uniqueness and entrepreneurial vision. The theory recognizes various types of resources i.e physical, reputational, organization, financial, intellectual and technological. Technology plays a critical role in businesses (Siqueira, & Bruton 2010). Caldeira and Ward, (2003) used resource-based theory to describe the benefits of information systems and information technology adoption and usage in the manufacturing sector for small and medium businesses. Technology is key in influencing the survival and performance of businesses because it plays a key role in marketing and improving efficiency and convenience for customers. The adoption of technology constrains emerging economies more than developing economies. Marginalized groups in East Africa, such as the Youth, women, the poor and the disabled, are unable to afford the requisite digital technology, which robs them the chance to fully exploit their entrepreneurial opportunities.

Technology acceptance Model (TAM) theory opines that the behavioral intention of individual technology depends on how they perceive its usefulness and its perceived ease of use (Venkatesh, 2000). Entrepreneurs will evaluate how technology will assist their business, and I have skills to adopt the technology. If the technology appears complicated, they may shy away from adopting the technology. The theory was later advanced to the Unified Theory of Acceptance and Use of Technology (UTAUT), which opines the adoption of a new technology depending on performance expectancy, effort expectancy, social influence and facilitating conditions (Venkatesh et al., 2003).The theory accesses the rate of adoption as the number of individuals who have adopted the innovation within a given time. The rate and speed of adoption rate is affected by the perceived attributes of an innovation including relative advantage, compatibility, complexity, trial-ability, observability, type of innovation decision, nature of communication channel used, nature of social system and promotional effort (Rogers, 1995).For entrepreneurs in the underserved communities to adopt a new technological innovation, they must perceive it as useful, easily adoptable and bringing efficiency in their business operations to ensure that they are sustainable.

DESIGN, METHODOLOGY AND APPROACH

The research design adopted for this study was qualitative in nature. The study employed a phenomenological and constructivist paradigm using secondary data. Phenomenology seeks to examine the structure of experiences and the implications of these lived experiences, as highlighted by Husserl and Merleau-Ponty, who were classical phenomenologists and practiced the analysis of lived experience (Zalta et al, 2021). Furthermore, it adopted an interdisciplinary and pragmatic worldview on digital transformation and sustainable entrepreneurship of the underserved communities in four East Africa countries i.e Kenya, Tanzania, Rwanda and Uganda. This engaged qualitative research by examining recent extant literature, practitioner interviews, and secondary data. The study focused on the analysis of technical reports and empirical research within the East African region. The study accessed the status of digital transformation and entrepreneurship among the undeserved communities in East Africa with a view of making policy recommendations to improve entrepreneurial success outcomes among the underserved communities.

STATUS OF DIGITAL TRANSFORMATION AND ENTREPRENEURSHIP AMONG THE UNDERSERVED COMMUNITIES IN EAST AFRICA

Globally the adoption of technologies is a powerful tool for women entrepreneurs. These technologies contribute to the sustainability of women enterprises (WEF, 2021). They are transforming how business is done and improving profitability. It provides unique opportunities for entrepreneurial women and opens up to a digital world where access to innovation, innovative business ideas and employment opportunities is guaranteed. In a world full of economic and social biases and barriers, technology and innovation play a critical role in attaining gender equality. In any nation, women entrepreneurs contribute greatly to the development of the economy. Businesses that adopt digital technologies become creative, adaptable and profitable thereby contributing to the sustainability of their businesses (Abed 2021). In most economies, digital transformations alter the way people live, work and do business, hence promoting business sustainability. The sustainability of women enterprises can be achieved through the adaptation of the tools provided by technology. Through the adoption of various technologies, entrepreneurs are changing their methods of getting information from the market. Worldwide, women are still lagging behind in the adoption of technology. As of 2018, there were 327 million fewer women who own smartphones and access the internet. Men are four times more likely to become ICT specialists (OECD, 2018), and when compared to males, women entrepreneurs obtain 23% less capital and are 30% less likely to achieve a successful exit.

African countries need to embrace digital development. With the current dynamic economic and social advancements, the expanding youth population will be denied a chance to exploit their full potential (World Bank, 2020). Digital technologies are the only hope to disrupt the trajectory and unlock new pathways and give way for rapid economic growth. However, the status is not encouraging, with access to the internet remaining out of reach. In 2017, only 22% had access to the internet and digital startups struggling to attract to attract funding. Sub-Saharan Africa is the world's poorest, most disadvantaged and most disconnected region. With a population of 1.3 billion people in Africa, 400 million are characterized as extremely poor. Africa has the highest female entrepreneurship rate in the world and has contributed to creating 54 million jobs across the continent (Herrington & Kew 2017). One of every three people in Sub-Saharan Africa is illiterate, with the majority of the illiterate being female. Access, usage, and ownership of digital tools are not gender neutral, and the benefits that digital transformation offers for many economies and societies are currently not balanced amongst social groups and genders. This can be attributed to a number of factors, including barriers to access, the cost of schooling, and a lack of technology literacy (OECD 2018d)

In the East African region, internet penetration is low, hence affecting the adoption of digital technologies by the underserved communities in East Africa. According to the International Telecommunication Union, only approximately 28% of Africans used the internet. With only 23% of the users being women (UNCTAD, 2020)

Status of Digital Transformation and Entrepreneurship among the Underserved Communities in Uganda

The Mastercard Women Entrepreneurs Index (MIWE) 2019 that tracks gender gap among business owners ranked Uganda first with 38.2%, followed by Ghana at 37.9% women owned business among the sampled African countries. This is despite Uganda having one of the poorest entrepreneurial supporting factors among the sampled countries. Uganda women, however, face many gender-specific barriers to enterprise performance, low levels of innovation, and segregation into lower-value sectors (World Bank, 2021). In the current digital age, businesses cannot thrive if they are left behind in their technological adoption. Communication access In Uganda is a key infrastructure in enabling business. The Internet is used by entrepreneurs to source and advertise items, hence enabling wider market reach. This enables businesses to expand their customer base and improve performance, thereby ensuring their sustainability. The affordability of calls and the internet is a great influence on the success of business. Similar to other studies, (Doberty, 2012, tan el al, 2010) have found that the level of information technology and communication influences business performance.

The women-owned microenterprises in Uganda generate 30% lower profits than the male owned businesses (World bank, 2019). The constrained performance is because of lower innovation levels and sector based segregation factors associated with women entrepreneurs. Women allocate fewer hours to their businesses than their male counterparts because of the demanding domestic and care responsibilities. Gender equality is a keystone to a prosperous modern economy that provides inclusive and sustainable growth. Digital transformation provides new avenues that empower women economically, ensuring greater gender equality (OECD, 2018). Komunte, M. (2015) notes that despite Uganda having a mobile penetration approximately of about 80% of its population, the usage of mobile phones among women entrepreneurs is still low. However the use of mobile phones, to some extent has helped to bridge the divide by giving the women entrepreneurs the possibility of earning additional incomes from their business. This has greatly contributed to the sustainability of their entrepreneurial ventures.

Uganda's ICT ministry is in charge of the sector's strategic and investment plan for 2015/16 to 2019/2020 and has identified priority areas for investments in ICT, infrastructure, human capacity, legal framework and financing that are necessary to facilitate youth in accessing and adopting ICTs in their businesses (UNCTAD, 2020). The major challenge as highlighted by the policy is the slow diffusion of ICTs in rural areas. The Ministry policy aims to increase access to and affordability of mobile devices and online services. Mobile phones help to increase economic participation, improve efficiency, and inspire innovation by lowering transaction costs (Mishra, Deichmann, & Goyal 2016). Disabled people can communicate through text, voice, and video thanks to technology. This aids in the reduction of knowledge gaps associated with technology adoption.

Status of Digital Transformation and Entrepreneurship among the Underserved Communities in Tanzania

In Tanzania women entrepreneurs are potential contributors to the development of the economy, job generation and poverty reduction. However, they face many challenges such as less mobility, their businesses tend to be younger than men and the cultural attitudes that prevent them from successfully operating businesses. According to Tanzania's Small and Medium Enterprise (SME) policy, access to technology is one of the seven pillars. Collaborations between technology providers and the micro, small and medium enterprises, supporting joint ventures to enable the transfer of technology are some of the efforts that have been made by the country to promote access to technology (Mori, N. 2015). Out of these initiatives; none of them specifically focuses on women-owned enterprises. The adoption of technologies by businesses has been increasing, particularly the use of mobile phones. Only 11% of women have websites, while 16% are selling their products online. Women entrepreneurs in Tanzania are increasingly adopting and using mobile phones, computers, and the internet .MIT 2012 reports that 59% of MSME owners owned a mobile phone, however, more men use ICT tools than women because they have a lot of time at their disposal to learn how to use the mobile phones as opposed to women who have little time to learn because most of their time is occupied by household chores.

In the last decade, Tanzania's digital ecosystem has grown tremendously creating a favorable environment for the adoption and use of technology by entrepreneurs from the underserved communities. Notably, more entrepreneurs are using digital services than any other time in the past. To support the immense contribution of the ICT sector in promoting socioeconomic development in Tanzania, the government launched the ICT national policy in 2016 and has also invested in fiber infrastructure across the country to support digital transformations. With these efforts, the country hopes to increase access to affordable internet among the underserved communities. This will be a milestone in ensuring that their entrepreneurial ventures will be sustainable.

Status of Digital Transformation and Entrepreneurship among the Underserved Communities in Rwanda

Rwanda is a pioneer among the East African countries on gender equality. In 2020, it was the only African country in the top 10 of the world's Economic Forums Global Gender Gap Report (EADB, 2020). The Rwandan government has been championing for women in ICT, science and technology. The proportion of women in Rwanda is 51.83% of the total population. Despite the country being at the forefront of gender equality and equity, women are still underrepresented in business, due to social customs, religion and cultural beliefs (Nsengimana, 2017). Because of their large population, successful women engagement in entrepreneurial activities has a far-reaching influence (Nsengimana, Tengeh, & Iwu, 2017).

Across various geographies and demographics there is uneven access to information and communication technologies and some geographic groups face the risk of digital exclusion with the invisibility of digital access. The inclusive internet access in Rwanda is relatively low, due to minimal access to local content. The internet user's percentage of the population has been increasing steadily from approximately 5% in 1990 to approximately 26% in January 2020 (Kemp, 2020). Whereas there has been a steady increase, only 26% of the Rwandan population has access to the internet. This percentage is quite low when compared to developed countries (World Bank, 2020). This hinders the progress of the country in achieving sustainable entrepreneurship among the underserved communities.

The Internet is often argued to be a solution to the challenges young people face. The youth have not fully benefited from its use because of nonoptimal use as a result of deprivation. The adoption and use of ICT, specifically the internet, offers a myriad of options to break the cycle of poverty and obtain access to economic and social development (Research ICT Africa, 2018).Mobile ownership forms a basis of access to digital services, and opportunities are prevalent, particularly in the older youth group between 20 and 24 years of age.In Tanzania, phone ownership among this group stood at 59% while in Rwanda, it was 47%. This is in comparison to Nigeria, where it stood at 64%. This Signifies that East African countries are behind other African countries in the West. In addition, the report indicated that East African countries youth tend to own basic phones compared to smartphones in their counterparts in Nigeria.

According to Rwanda's last census, there are more than 450,000 persons with disability representing approximately 5% of the population. Given that most of Rwanda's population lives below poverty levels, most disabled people experience extreme poverty and insecurity (Kidd and Krystle, 2019). Despite Rwanda having a comprehensive legislative and policy framework for disability, implementation and enforcement faces many challenges. The Ministry of Local Government and Community Affairs (MINALOC) and National Social Protection Strategy (NSPS) programmes have done little to address the plight of disabled people in affording the access to digital solutions. With the education levels of disabled being lower those of the abled in Rwanda, the participation of the disabled in meaningful entrepreneurial ventures is minimal.

Status of Digital Transformation and Entrepreneurship among the Underserved Communities in Kenya

The effects of digital transformation on economics and societies are offer opportunities for the growth of businesses across the world. In Kenya, however, there is a huge gender imbalance in terms of access to, use of, and ownership of technology, which limits the benefits that women entrepreneurs receive from digital transformation (OECD, 2018). In the 21st century, women are starting to take key positions in the business and the women in Kenya are not left out. In East Africa, Kenya is a regional business hub and an economic powerhouse and has constantly encouraged entrepreneurs, especially women, to embrace digital technologies for their businesses to be sustainable. Kenya made significant progress in digital technologies in 2007. MPESA was launched in Kenya as the first mobile financial service in Africa and third in the world. MPESA has enabled entrepreneurs to transfer money to one another using their mobile phones. By the time of the introduction of MPESA the financial inclusion in Kenya stood at 27%. With the success of MPESA in Africa, several competitors were encouraged within Kenya and across East Africa. Underserved communities should embrace and leverage MPESA technology to improve their operations in terms of payments to create efficiency. This will create a favorable environment, thereby improving the sustainability of these underserved communities. Through the adoption of technologies, women entrepreneurs are able to incorporate variety and advanced business practices into their businesses and are hence able to overcome the gender barriers imposed by traditions, hence achieving financial progression.

Kenya's digital economy is a key driver of the country's economic development. Between 2016 and 2019, the Information and Communication Technology (ICT) industry grew by an average of 10.8%, becoming a key source of economic development and employment creation. (World Bank, 2019). Kenya, on the other hand, has a considerable digital gap, with 44% of urban residents having internet access compared to only 17% of Kenyans living in rural regions. This is compounded by severe gaps in fundamental digital abilities, which impede digital technology use. In Kenya, women entrepreneurs face cultural biases and lack adequate support to participate in entrepreneurship or other investment activities (Mutwiri and Kimutai, 2021). While Kenya has the highest number of women entrepreneurs in East Africa, 49 percent face many barriers, such as information, time and business networks, compared to their male peers (World bank, 2018). Kenyan women entrepreneurs manage business alongside family chores preventing them from achieving their maximum output. The government has supported women and Youth through Access to Government Procurement Opportunities (AGPO), which obligates public institutions to allocate 30% of tenders to these groups. However, only large SMESs benefit from these opportunities. This is because small enterprises are unable to access these opportunities because registration and application are done digitally disadvantaging them. In addition, Cartels colludes with technocrats to include women and youths in ownerships positions as nominal heads in their businesses with no functional powers to benefit from AGPO.

The World Bank 2020 reported that approximately One billion people or 15% of the world population faces some form of disability. People with disability more often than not experience adverse economic conditions and outcomes compared to those who have no form of disabilities. In Kenya, as in other countries, the disabled face barriers that prevent them from attaining full social and economic inclusion (World Bank, 2019). These barriers include inaccessible physical environments and the unavailability of assistive devices and technologies among others. The United Nations Convention on the Rights of Persons with Disabilities (CRPD) advocates for the full integration of people with disabilities into society. According to the Kenya Integrated Household Budget Survey (KIHBS) 2015/2016, more than half of Kenyans with disability have difficulties engaging in economic activities. The Institute of development studies(IDS) 2020 report on situational analyses showed that the disabled face challenges in starting business ventures because of impending barriers such as irrelevancy and inaccurate business information services, lack of access to finance and challenges in adopting the relevant information and communication technology (ICT).The COVID 19 pandemic in Kenya has worsened the plight of disabled people because of the many restrictions the government put in place to contain the spread of the virus. However, the adoption of digital technologies such as the internet, mobile phone payment systems such as MPESA, digital marketing platform plays a big role in ensuring that the disabled as part of the underserved community are able to improve their entrepreneurial ventures, thereby ensuring that their business is sustainable in the competitive and dynamic market.

CONCLUSION, PRACTICAL IMPLICATIONS AND RECOMMENDATIONS

For East African countries to exploit the potential of technology in building an inclusive digital economy that enables sustainable entrepreneurship, they must ensure that they develop the foundational building block of the digital economy. The digital infrastructure does not only provides means for the underserved communities, business and government to get online but also link entrepreneurs to global markets and economies expanding their clientele. As a result, a reliable and economical internet connection is essential for long-term business success. Digital platforms enable the exchange of goods and services through digital channels such as computers, mobile devices and the internet, creating value for users. Digital entrepreneurship and innovation contribute to the development of an ecosystem that revitalizes the digital economy by supporting new technology-based products and businesses. This aids in the transition of existing enterprises, helps to increase net employment, and improves competitiveness and productivity. This ensures that entrepreneurial ventures owned by the underserved communities are sustainable.

Global parties and nonprofitable organizations have a great role in empowering underserved communities with digital adoption skills to enable them to embrace recent technological innovations and developments. For instance, the UNCTAD MasterClass supports the establishment of female digital entrepreneur groups in a number of nations, and advocates for more inclusive digital policymaking. The programme addresses the most pressing business needs by designing value propositions by rebooting businesses after COVID-19 and delivering them actual answers for their businesses. Gender equality must be recognized in for both genders to fully contribute to the advancement of their society and economies.

East African countries have a great opportunity to harness the digital economy as a driver for innovation. However, with weak policy guidelines and lukewarm government support, they risk failing to bridge the digital divide in their economies, which will result in isolation and stagnation, further widening the inequality gaps with developed countries. To ensure that countries keep pace with technology innovation and growth, they should support more solid digital foundations, such as new regulations and policy guidelines, to aid in digital transformation. This is because leaving the women, youth and disabled behind will only stifle the digital advancements and slow the creation of sustainable entrepreneurship undertakings in East Africa.

East African countries require a holistic approach to STI policy, design and implementation. The framework for Sustainable Development goals (SDGs) and the 2030 agenda for Sustainable Development must be factored in to ensure a synchronized and sufficient coordination of support programmes that aim at improving digital technology adoption by the youth, women and the disabled as disadvantaged populations. Technology needs assessment (TNA) should focus on the inclusive development components. This will ensure that the policies and programmes that are implemented address the core areas of need in ensuring that the youth, women and the disabled sustain their entrepreneurship ventures.

Youth play a great role in economic development. Young people have the capacity to build and grow the East African bloc, but only if they are given the skills they need to create a sustainable livelihood. This is because youth are three times more likely than adults to be unemployed. East African governments ought to invest strategically to improve the digital infrastructure. For the youth to be today's innovators, they need to be empowered with digital skills access to technology because that is critical for entrepreneurial ventures to thrive in a digitized economy.

There is a need to strengthen and integrate a multisectoral approach towards a regional digital and legal policy framework to encourage innovation and e-business. These efforts should be targeted to meet the needs of women, youth and the disabled because they are the most disfranchised by their inability to access digital services. There is a need for regulation of personal data so that they can be par with the developed nations which are significant trading partners. This creates a safer atmosphere for the Youth women and disabled to use technology in their entrepreneurial ventures, ensuring sustainability.

The East African Leaders should develop digital transformation strategies to enhance the demand and supply of online services in the region. This will scale up digital initiatives to address developmental challenges affecting East African countries. A solid, open and efficient infrastructure, including a widely accessible retail payments system, and information and communications technologies, and marketing channels is required to enable a widespread distribution of digital services to enable the underserved groups to access these services and boost their entrepreneurial operations. There is a need for Public-private Collaborations in coming up with projects geared at tapping the potential of women, Youth and the disabled. This will ensure that the whole digital transformation ecosystem, functions smoothly and seamlessly, enabling disadvantaged groups to anchor their ideas in digital platforms that will propel their entrepreneurial activities thereby creating a sustainable environment.

East African countries should ensure that the underserved communities receive basic education and literacy for them to benefit from the opportunities that technologies can offer. Training that shows women, youth and disabled entrepreneurs how to use mobile phones, computers, social media and other ICTs for their businesses. The trainings will enable these communities to build capacity and support their entrepreneurial ventures to use and integrate modern production technologies in their businesses increasing productivity and efficiency. This will go a long way in ensuring sustainable businesses by these communities.

East African countries should put more efforts and resources into improving the access of ICTs to the underserved communities. This will help bridge the current divide between these communities and other well to do groups. This can only be achieved through investments in ICT infrastructure and targeted policies to reduce the inequality in access to digital technologies. Enhancing equality and equity in access to digital services develop digital solutions and create efficiencies that provide an enabling environment for micro, small and/or medium-sized entrepreneurial ventures by the underserved communities. This environment provides a critical foundation for the sustainability of these ventures.

REFERENCES

Abed, S. S. (2021). Women Entrepreneurs' Adoption of Mobile Applications for Business Sustainability. *Sustainability, 13*(21), 11627. doi:10.3390u132111627

Alvarez, S. A., & Busenitz, L. W. (2001). The entrepreneurship of resource-based theory. *Journal of Management, 27*(6), 755–775. doi:10.1177/014920630102700609

Anderson, P., & Williams, C. (2008). *The conversation between statistics and social policy: When we listen, when we do not.* Dialogue for Development Lecture. Kingston, Jamaica: Planning Institute of Jamaica. doi:10.1080/02681102.2012.751571

Bailey, A., & Ngwenyama, O. (2013). Toward entrepreneurial behavior in underserved communities: An ethnographic decision tree model of telecenter usage. *Information Technology for Development, 19*(3), 230–248. doi:10.1080/02681102.2012.751571

Bican, P. M., & Brem, A. (2020). Digital Business Model, Digital Transformation, Digital Entrepreneurship: Is There A Sustainable "Digital"? *Sustainability, 12*(13), 5239. doi:10.3390u12135239

Boellstorff, T. (2019). The opportunity to contribute: Disability and the digital entrepreneur. *Information Communication and Society, 22*(4), 474–490. doi:10.1080/1369118X.2018.1472796

Caldeira, M. M., & Ward, J. M. (2003). Using resource-based theory to interpret the successful adoption and use of information systems and technology in manufacturing small and medium-sized enterprises. *European Journal of Information Systems, 12*(2), 127–141. doi:10.1057/palgrave.ejis.3000454

Chacha. (2019). *Kenya Economic Update: Securing Future Growth - Policies to Support Kenya's Digital Transformation.* Kenya economic update, no. 20. Washington, DC: World Bank Group. https://documents.worldbank.org/curated/en/968481572468094731/Kenya-Economic-Update-Securing-Future-Growth-Policies-to-Support-Kenya-s-Digital-Transformation

Chair and lannony. (2018). *Youth Deprivation and the Internet in Africa.* Retrieved from https://researchictafrica.net/after-access-survey papers/2018/After_Access:_youth_and_digital_inequality_in_Africa.pdf

Chatterjee, S., Chaudhuri, R., Vrontis, D., & Basile, G. (2021). Digital transformation and entrepreneurship process in SMEs of India: a moderating role of adoption of AI-CRM capability and strategic planning. *Journal of Strategy and Management.*

Clare, E. (1999). *Exile and Pride: Disability, Queerness and Liberation.* South End Press.

Deichmann, U., Goyal, A., & Mishra, D. (2016). Will digital technologies transform agriculture in developing countries? *Agricultural Economics, 47*(S1), 21–33. doi:10.1111/agec.12300

Doherty, E. (2012). *Broadband adoption and diffusion: a study of Irish SMEs* [PhD Thesis]. Ulster University Coleraine.

East Africa Development Ban. (2020). *How Rwanda is spurring a generation of women in technology.* Retrieved form https://etradeforall.org/news/adb-how-rwanda-is-spurring-a-generation-of-women-in-technology/?lang=es

Feyen, E., Frost, J., Gambacorta, L., Natarajan, H., & Saal, M. (2021). *Fintech and the digital transformation of financial services:Impliccations for market structure and Public Policy*. World Bank and BIS.

George, G., Merrill, R. K., & Schillebeeckx, S. J. (2021). Digital sustainability and entrepreneurship: How digital innovations are helping tackle climate change and sustainable development. *Entrepreneurship Theory and Practice*, *45*(5), 999–1027. doi:10.1177/1042258719899425

Gregori, P., & Holzmann, P. (2020). Digital sustainable entrepreneurship: A business model perspective on embedding digital technologies for social and environmental value creation. *Journal of Cleaner Production*, *272*, 122817. doi:10.1016/j.jclepro.2020.122817

Hakura, M. D., Hussain, M. M., Newiak, M. M., Thakoor, V., & Yang, M. F. (2016). *Inequality, gender gaps and economic growth: Comparative evidence for sub-Saharan Africa*. International Monetary Fund.

Herrington, M., & Kew, P. (2017). *Is there a change in attitude towards the small and medium business sector in South Africa?* Global Entrepreneurship Monitor. https://www.gemconsortium.org/file/open?fileId=50411

Homi, K., & Cohen, J. (2018). *Using Big data and atrificial intelligence to accelerate global development.* Academic Press.

Institute of Development Studies. (2020). *Disability inclusive development; Kenya situational analysis, June 2020 Update*. https://opendocs.ids.ac.uk/opendocs/bitstream/handle/20.500.12413/15508/DID%20Kenya%20SITAN_June%202020.pdf?sequence=1

IWEC. (2018). *Uganda leads In the ration of women doing business*. Retrieved from https://www.iwec-foundation.org/news/uganda-leads-in-ratio-of-women-doing-business/

Jackson, J. T. (2009). Capitalizing on digital entrepreneurship for low-income residents and communities. *West Virginia Law Review*, *112*, 187.

Jansen, J., Veenstra, S., Zuurveen, R., & Stol, W. (2016). Guarding against online threats: Why entrepreneurs take protective measures. *Behaviour & Information Technology*, *35*(5), 368–379.

Jawad, M., Naz, M., & Maroof, Z. (2021). Era of digital revolution: Digital entrepreneurship and digital transformation in emerging economies. *Business Strategy & Development*, *4*(3), 220–228.

Kidd & Kabare. (2019). *Social protection and Disability in Rwanda, working paper 2019, development pathways*. https://www.developmentpathways.co.uk/wp-content/uploads/2019/08/Social-Protection-and-Disability-in-Rwanda-Report-.pdf

Komunte, M. (2015). Usage of mobile technology in women entrepreneurs: A case study of Uganda. *The African Journal of Information Systems*, *7*(3), 3.

Kwagala, B., Wandera, S. O., Ndugga, P., & Kabagenyi, A. (2013). Empowerment, partner's behaviours and intimate partner physical violence among married women in Uganda. *BMC Public Health*, *13*(1), 1–10.

Mutwiri, N., & Kimutai, C. (2021). *Social-Legal Environment and Women Participation in the Securities Market in Kenya*. Academic Press.

Nsengimana, S. (2017). *Challenges to women entrepreneurship in Kigali, Rwanda* (Doctoral dissertation). Cape Peninsula University of Technology.

OECD. (2018). *Bridging the Digital gender divide, Include, Upskill, Innovate*. Retrieved form https://www.oecd.org/digital/bridging-the-digital-gender-divide.pdf

Oestmann, S., & Dymond, A. C. (2001). Telecentres – experiences, lessons and trends, in the commonwealth of learning. In Telecentre: Case studies and key issues. Vancouver, Canada: The Commonwealth of Learning.

Orobia, L. A., Tusiime, I., Mwesigwa, R., & Ssekiziyivu, B. (2020). *Entrepreneurial framework conditions and business sustainability among the youth and women entrepreneurs. Asia Pacific Journal of Innovation and Entrepreneurship.*

Otioma, C., Madureira, A. M., & Martinez, J. (2019). Spatial analysis of urban digital divide in Kigali, Rwanda. *GeoJournal*, *84*(3), 719–741.

Ratten, V., & Usmanij, P. (2021). Entrepreneurship education: Time for a change in research direction? *International Journal of Management Education*, *19*(1), 100367.

Rolle, J., & Kisato, J. (2019). The future of work and entrepreneurship for the underserved. *The Business & Management Review*, *10*(2), 224–234.

Satalkina, L., & Steiner, G. (2020). Digital entrepreneurship and its role in innovation systems: A systematic literature review as a basis for future research avenues for sustainable transitions. *Sustainability*, *12*(7), 2764.

Schaltegger, S., & Wagner, M. (2011). Sustainable entrepreneurship and sustainability innovation: Categories and interactions. *Business Strategy and the Environment*, *20*(4), 222–237.

Simon Kemp. (2018). *Digital 2020: Rwanda*. https://datareportal.com/reports/digital-2020-rwanda?rq=Rwanda%20intern

Siqueira, A. C. O., & Bruton, G. D. (2010). High-technology entrepreneurship in emerging economies: Firm informality and contextualization of resource-based theory. *IEEE Transactions on Engineering Management*, *57*(1), 39–50.

Smith, B. (2016). Intersectionality Discrimination and Substantive Equality: A comparative and Theoretical perspective. *The Equality Rights review*, (16).

Srinivasan, N. (2015). Mobile Applications: A Game Changer for Rural Women Entrepreneurs? In Unveiling Women's Leadership. Palgrave Macmillan.

Tan, K. S., Chong, S. C., Lin, B., & Eze, U. C. (2010). Internet based ICT adoption among SMEs: Demographic versus benefits, barriers, and adoption intention. *Journal of Enterprise Information Management*, *23*(1), 27–55.

Tafotie, R. (2020). *Fostering Digital Financial Services in Africa: a case of embracing*. SSRN.

UNCTAD. (2020). *Equipping East Africa women Digital entrepreneurs with skills thrive*. Retrieved form https://unctad.org/news/equipping-east-african-women-digital-entrepreneurs-skills-thrive

UNCTAD. (2020). *Uganda Science, technology & Policy review*. Retrieved from https://unctad.org/system/files/official-document/dtlstict2020d4_en.pdf

UNCTAD. (2014). *United Nations Conference on trade and development*. https://unctad.org/system/files/official-document/dtlstict2013d2_en.pdf

Venkatesh, V. (2000). Determinants of Perceived Ease of Use: Integrating Control, Intrinsic Motivation, and Emotion into the Technology Acceptance Model. *Information Systems Research*, *11*(4), 342–365.

Venkatesh, V., Morris, M., Davis, G., & Davis, F. (2003). User Acceptance of Information Technology: Toward a Unified View. *Management Information Systems Quarterly*, *27*(3), 425–478.

Venkatesh, V., Morris, M., Davis, G., & Davis, F. (2003). User Acceptance of Information Technology: Toward a Unified View. *Management Information Systems Quarterly*, *27*(3), 425–478.

Von Kutzschenbach, M., & Daub, C. H. (2021). Digital Transformation for Sustainability: A Necessary Technical and Mental Revolution. In *New Trends in Business Information Systems and Technology* (pp. 179–192). Springer.

Wang, Q., & Richardson, L. (2021). Fostering Art and Cultural Entrepreneurship in Underserved Communities: A Case of Newark, NJ. *Journal of Planning Education and Research.*

WEF. (2021). *World Economic Forum*. Retrieved from https://www.weforum.org/agenda/2021/11/digital-entrepreneurship-africa-botswana-women-gender-equality/

World Bank. (2010). *The worlds bank in Eastern and Southern Africa*. https://www.worldbank.org/en/region/afr/eastern-and-southern-africahttps://www.worldbank.org/en/region/afr/eastern-and-southern-africa

World Bank. (2021). *Unlocking the potential of women entrepreneurs in Uganda: a brief of policy interventions*. https://openknowledge.worldbank.org/bitstream/handle/10986/36220/Unlocking-the-Potential-of-Women-Entrepreneurs-in-Uganda-A-Brief-of-Policy-Interventions.pdf?sequence=1&isAllowed=y

World Bank Group. (2019). Kenya Digital Economy Assessment. Summary Report. Washington, DC: World Bank.

World Bank. (2019). *Kenya economic Update Accelerating Keya's Digital economy*. Retrieved form https://www.worldbank.org/en/country/kenya/publication/kenya-economic-update-accelerating-kenyas-digital-economy

World Bank. (2018). *The Digital Economy for Africa Initiative*. https://www.worldbank.org/en/programs/all-africa-digital-transformation

World Bank. (2019). *Accelerating Poverty reduction in Africa: In Five Charts*. https://www.worldbank.org/en/region/afr/publication/accelerating-poverty-reduction-in-africa-in-five-charts

Wu, A., Song, D., & Yang, Y. (2020). Untangling the effects of entrepreneurial opportunity on the performance of peasant entrepreneurship: The moderating roles of entrepreneurial effort and regional poverty level. *Entrepreneurship and Regional Development*, *32*(1-2), 112–133.

KEY TERMS AND DEFINITIONS

Digital Transformation: This is the inclusion of digital technology into all areas of a business that reforms business operations.

Entrepreneurship: This is the process of setting up a business venture with the aim of making profit.

Innovation: This is the creation of a new idea, method, product, or service.

Literacy: This is the ability to adopt and use technology in business operations.

Sustainability: This is the ability to sustain or continue operating entrepreneurial ventures.

Technology: This is the application of scientific knowledge for practical purposes or application in business.

Underserved Communities: These are groups of people who are marginalized in society and include women, youth and the disabled.

Chapter 19

Pace of Technology Changes, Need for Adaptation, and Demand for Skills:

Skills Adaptation for Quickly Evolving Technology-Based Workplaces

David Egbe Ola
Federal College of Education (Technical), Omoku, Nigeria

ABSTRACT

Living in the generation when it looks like the technology of the future is already here and the various shifts in technology are having profound effects on the way businesses are done and the entire labour market space, the industrial revolution has necessitated the need for changes in the nature of work and skills that meet the demands of the revolution. Currently a lot of mechanized skilled workers are being replaced with automated technologies enhanced by artificial intelligence. This has prompted the need for skillset repositioning to enable the workforce to adapt to the in-demand hot industry skills. This chapter looked at (1) the impact of advancement in technology on the current workplace, (2) the skill set (upskill and reskill) needs that enhance employee to meet the pace of the current technology advancement, and (3) repositioning of the workforce to be relevant in the face of automation and the accelerated trend of artificial intelligence.

INTRODUCTION

We are living in an era where computers are becoming more intricate part of our lives and the surge in this trend will continue to rise unabated, ranging from the field of artificial intelligence where the computers must not be explicitly programmed, but can learn with the aid of algorithms to internet of things (IoT), that connects billions of physical devices around the world that exchange data over the internet and blockchain technology that promoted immutability of transactions and smart contracts

DOI: 10.4018/978-1-6684-4322-4.ch019

among others. The take home from this reality is that evolving technology will change the nature of skills relevant to executing tasks in the workplace. Mercer (2021) lends credence to the above reality that "With the accelerating pace of technological change, many employees find themselves rushing to keep up with new software, programs and technological processes implemented in the workplace. By its very nature, technology evolves quickly, racing to address the new situations and problems created by the implementation of previous technologies, so that even young employees who enter the workplace with advanced technological skills can find themselves quickly falling behind the technological curve". These rapid transitions have placed a demand on the employee to take decisive steps to stay relevant.

Frey and Osborne (2017) estimated that approximately 47% of total employment in the United States (US) is at risk of automation in the next decade or two. That means that few highly skilled workers will be needed which emphasize the need for skill adaptation. Hamza (2021) stressed that the future of work will certainly depend on how artificial intelligence (AI), robots, and automation impact the allocation of tasks to labor and capital. This implies that artificial intelligence and robots are likely to create unemployment crises because the demand will be for the few higher-level cognitive employee that upskill to meet the need, it will also disrupt our system of educational and force the system to become a center for the acquisition of lifelong education which will not necessarily be institutional based but online for continuous education Despite the fact that this evolving workplace will need few skilled employees, new types of jobs will be created alongside with automation of routine task. though recent literature suggests that technology does not destroy jobs in the aggregate, it is clear that workers will face a transition as jobs may decline in industries where technology is adopted, but increase in other industries due to spillover effects (Autor & Salomons, 2018).

Technological advancements are demanding rapid uptake of new skills. Across the world, employers are increasingly looking for workers with advanced cognitive and socio-emotional skills. Meanwhile, demand for narrow job-specific skills wanes. Which is in agreement with UK commission for employment and skill (2015) "Greater business flexibility and incremental innovation lead to modest growth in the economy but this flexibility often results in less opportunity and weakened job security for the low skilled".

In this discourse we will consider the following very vital points as related to this work (a) The impact of advancement in technology on the current workplace (b) The skill set (upskill and reskill) needs that enhance employee to meet the pace of the current technology advancement (c) Repositioning of the workforce to be relevant in the face of automation and accelerated trend of artificial intelligence.

BACKGROUND TO THE STUDY

This study emphasized the "Pace of technology changes, need for adaptation and demand for skills" with special on focus on skills adaptation for fast evolving technology-based workplace. To guide the discussion of the subject matter, three subheadings were formulated which are summarized below.

(a) The impact of advancement in technology on the current workplace: This chapter discovered that the automation witnessed in the workplace has resulted in both positive and negative impacts; on the positive side, it has resulted in high productivity for companies, effective use of materials and resources, reduced labour, high quality products, among many others. On the other hand, automation leads to loss of jobs and displacement of workers, it also widens the inequality, because it favours the business owners more than the employees.

(b) The skill set (upskill and reskill) needs that enhance employee to meet the pace of the current technology advancement: This chapter revealed that the current and the future workplace will be highly dependent on high cognitive skills most of which are hard technology skill related such as: artificial intelligence and machine learning, big data analytics, blockchain technology, cybersecurity, video production, UX (User Experience) and UI (User Interface) design and soft skills such as critical thinking, self-management, communication skills, leadership and team management skills, collaboration and teamwork effectiveness, mental flexibility and ability to effectively build relationship with others, self-direction and motivation, integrity and discipline among others are not replaceable by automation most essentially the soft skills

(c) Repositioning of the workforce to be relevant in the face of automation and accelerated trend of artificial intelligence. Automation does not invalidate or take away jobs but rather repositioned them, and the only way the industries can catch up in carrying employees along is to reposition employee's skills in line with the new skill set in demand, the industries, educational institutions and the government should deploy more resources to enhance the gains of e-learning which is flexible and learner tailored to enable the provision of lifelong learning which will facilitate easy skill adaptation among employees.

METHODOLOGY

Mixed research method was adopted for this study; which integrate both qualitative and quantitative research approaches. This technique enables the researcher to evaluate and harmonize views of different authors from published research works, blogs and social media site such as LinkedIn and based on their perspectives from the observation of trends on the impact of technology on the in-demand skills needed at the workplace. Which enables this chapter to forecast the pace of technology changes and how it affects the workplace, also project the skills set that are most relevant and irreplaceable in the current and the future workplace.

(a)The Impact of Advancement in Technology on the Current Workplace

Advancement in technology has greatly increased productivity in the workplace, but that came with inherent demand to review the existing skills set to meet the current demand of the industrial revolution that is technology skill oriented. There is accelerated displacement of the current workforce because jobs that are normally carried out by human beings are now performed by machines which can work round the clock without getting tired and with high-level accuracy and speed. Hamllet (2019) emphasized that while technology enables business owners to reduce overhead by downsizing their workforce, individuals whose skill sets are now obsolete have limited options for employment if their current jobs are eliminated. This reality has placed new demands on the employee and our educational institutions to review the current system of learning to embrace lifelong learning and employees must diversify their skills to embrace a wide range of skills.

The pace of the current technology advancement and adoption is expected to remain unabated, cutting across almost all areas of work in organizations and companies as they continue to adopt and implement more of cloud computing, big data analytics and data encryption to enhance existing business models as e-commerce takes high precedence among business owners in addition to automation.

According to statistics from the Statistica (2021) the worldwide shipment of robots have been on the increase from 382,000 in 2019 to 435,000 in 2021 and it was projected to surge to 518,000 by 2024. This reality has revealed that today's workplace tends to favor the upward surge of automation that means that more and more jobs will be filed in the rank of automated jobs which were once manually done and to operate these new automated systems new skills will be needed. "A report from PwC estimated that robots could take up to 30 per cent of UK jobs as soon as 2030 while the Bank of England has estimated that 15 million jobs may be at risk" (Scott, 2017).

The area where this reality thrive most is occupation that perform repetitive or routine task such as machine operators, maintenance manpower and those whose job definitions are completely manual are more at risk, for instance in the banking system the ATM machines have replaced the cashier and AI enabled robots have the taken over the job of the machine operator in the industries.

The current decade will witness more of such a series of dynamic transformations that will force many employees to reskill. According to the World Economic Forum (2020) annual meeting, the following points were stressed with the conclusion that the world is facing a reskilling emergency.

- "As jobs are transformed by the technologies of the Fourth Industrial Revolution, we need to reskill more than 1 billion people by 2030.
- In the next two years – by 2022 – 42% of core skills required to perform existing jobs are expected to change.
- In addition to high-tech skills, specialized interpersonal skills will be in high demand, including skills related to sales, human resources, care and education".

The world economic forum also estimated that more than 1 billion jobs will require adaptation due to changing technology. It was also projected that more than 133 million jobs will be created to meet the need of the fourth industrial revolution. In a nutshell the evolution of work will require new skills to perform them which will lead to occupational shit which is one of the impacts of change in technology. Horda (2021) also pointed out that "Greater technology adoption will mean a change of skills across the jobs, and skills gaps will continue to be high. Those employees who stay in their roles will also witness the significant change of the core skills for their jobs. So, it is essential for both sides; companies and employees to set up a mind for the future and start preparation works".

The World Economic Forum (2020) stated that "in the absence of proactive efforts, inequality is likely to be exacerbated by the dual impact of technology and the pandemic recession. Jobs held by lower wage workers, women and younger workers were more deeply impacted in the first phase of the economic contraction. Comparing the impact of the Global Financial Crisis of 2008 on individuals with lower education levels to the impact of the COVID-19 crisis, the impact today is far more significant and more likely to deepen existing inequalities". That is in agreement with United Nation (2018) that "If the current trends continue, AI and other frontier technologies may further increase income, opportunity and impact inequalities and widen development gaps among countries and people by providing transformative opportunities to those with the requisite infrastructure, access, investments and knowledge, while those without are left further behind". In a nutshell those who will be more impacted negatively are those without access to these fourth industrial infrastructures such as internet of things (IoT) and artificial intelligence, while the economic boom rising from the smart technologies are yielding wealth to some firms it is promoting inequality between the high skill cognitive worker and those down the work ladder.

In a nutshell, the automation witnessed in the workplace has resulted in both positive and negative impacts; on the positive side, it has resulted in high productivity for companies, effective use of materials and resources, reduced labour, high quality products, among many others. On the other hand, automation leads to loss of jobs and displacement of workers, it widens the inequality, because it favors the business owners more than the employees.

(b) The Skill Set (upskill and reskill) Needs that will Enhance the Employees to Meet the Pace of the Current Technology Advancement

The World Economic forum (2018) emphasized that "the fourth industrial revolution will majorly anchor on: Artificial intelligence, Internet of Things (IoT), Quantum computing, Self-driving cars, nanotechnology, biotechnology, renewable energy". Others are blockchain technology and augmented virtual reality, the points enumerated above revealed that the world of work will depend largely on digital and technology skills which will be in hot demand across all facet of work, but that will not happen in isolation without creativity, resilience, interpersonal and communication skills among others. According to Strack et al., (2018) jobs in the world of work can be categorized into the following four groups in the order of demand.

- **Flagship jobs** are those in high demand (10,000 to 1 million postings) and still growing (up to a 20% increase in postings yearly).
- **Fast-growing jobs** also experience high demand but are growing even faster (more than 20% yearly).
- **High-growth jobs** are those that have fewer than 10,000 annual postings but are growing at an extremely high rate (more than 40%).
- **Modest-growth jobs** show the lowest demand. Because their impact is limited, we do not analyze them in detail in this report.
- **Declining jobs** are those for which demand is shrinking.

Forbes suggested ten vital skills that will be necessary to survive the dynamic transformation of the workplace, they include:

1. Technology skills
2. Diversity and cultural intelligence
3. Leadership skills
4. Interpersonal communication skills
5. Active learning with a growth mindset
6. Analytical (critical) thinking
7. Emotional intelligence (EQ)
8. Embracing change
9. Creativity
10. Judgment and decision making

The skill set needed in the economy driven largely by technology can be categorized into firstly, the "hard tech skill"; which are digital related and comprise of: computer programming, artificial intelligence and machine learning, data analytics, blockchain technology, Internet of Things (IoT), cyber security among others. Secondly, the "soft skills" which are related to people's attitude to work, these creative and interpersonal skills that are vital to all occupations they include: interpersonal and communication skills, critical and logical thinking skills, problem solving skills, positive attitude, collaboration and team work and so on. According to Tyagarajan (2019), published by Harvard Business Review, it was added that "As manual tasks become more automated and humans shift to embrace more dynamic roles, educators and business leaders alike need to constantly ask: what skills — both "hard" and "soft" — will define success in a workplace that is becoming increasingly virtual and increasingly driven by technology?", that means the success of the current and future work will depend on how companies and organization identifies and utilize these skills to achieve their set goals and objectives. Digital technology will be the driver of the skills mentioned above, the hard skills will continue to be in top demand that is why there is growing demand for IT professionals. "Digital skills make up around 70% of all fast-growing skills: those that saw more than 10,000 mentions each in 2018 online job postings and experienced, on average, more than 20% year-over-year growth in the number of mentions" (Strack et al., 2018). That was the trend in 2018, and with digital and information and communication technology gaining more and more prominence by the day the dire need for digital skills must have increased greatly. Kimberly (2021) added that "the IT industry consists of a vast range of fields related to computers and digital information. IT professionals have become some of the most in-demand members of today's labor force, as leading companies across industries continue to push for widespread adoptions of digital technologies. IT sector employment includes professionals from various sub-fields, such as technology manufacturing, telecommunications and internet services, software publishing, and many others". The chapter further gave a more detailed grouping of the in-demand skills into six groups with IT taking the front stage in table I below.

Occupation with High Demand Skills

According to Horda (2021), in a research conducted on over 200 million jobs, it was revealed the most in demand jobs that are driving businesses around the world are in the area of technology such as: artificial intelligence and machine learning, big data analytics, blockchain technology, cybersecurity, video production and UX and UI design which are discussed below:

Artificial Intelligence and Machine Learning

This involves equipping machines with the ability to mimic human intelligence by learning from experience without being explicitly programmed. While artificial intelligence enables the machine to imitate human behaviour, the subset which is machine learning enables computers to learn from data to make accurate predictions without being overtly programmed. The knowledge of Python and its machine learning libraries like TesorFlow, Keras, Pycaret Pytorch, Scikit-Learn etc. make Python programming one of the most all-time highest in-demand programming languages for delivering innovative services. Other machine learning skills that are very important to AI are natural language processing, programming with Java, C++, R, Scala, JavaScript etc.

Table 1. Hot relevant skills for the present and future workplace

TECHNOLOGY	INTERPERSONAL SKILLS
Cloud Computing	**Communication skills**
Machine learning and Artificial intelligence	Public speaking
Blockchain	Message synthesis
Big data analytics	Active listening
Virtual and augmented reality (Metaverse)	Storytelling
User Experience UX	**Mental flexibility**
DIGITAL PROFICIENCY	Adaptability
Programming knowledge	Ability to learn
Data analysis and statistics	Creativity
Digital literacy	Ability to adopt different perspective
Computational and algorithmic thinking	Translating knowledge to various contexts
Understanding of smart systems and internet of things (IoT)	**Teamwork effectiveness**
Digital ethics and cybersecurity	Collaboration
Tech enablement	Resolving conflicts
CRITICAL THINKING	Motivating different personalities
Ability to understand structured problem	Coaching
Search relevant information	Empowering people
Logical reasoning	Fostering Inclusiveness
Agile thinking	**Building Relationship**
SELF-MANAGEMENT	Inspiring trust
Understanding personal emotions and triggers	Humility
Understanding one's strength	Sociability
Self-control	Empathy
Integrity	
LEADERSHIP	
Role modelling	
Crafting and inspiring vision	
Organization awareness	
Grit and persistence	
Ability to cope with uncertainty	

Source (HRForcast, 2021) With Modifications from the Author

Big Data Analytics

Big Data refers to large and complex data sets which may come from homogenous or heterogenous sources that are impractical to manage with traditional software tools. According to Wikipedia "Big data is the term for a collection of data sets so large and complex that it becomes difficult to process it using traditional database management tools or data processing applications. The challenges include the areas of capture, curation, storage, search, sharing, transfer, analysis, and visualization of this data". Whose size can range from petabytes to exabytes that are collected from different sources over diverse online platforms such as the social media, mobile data, consumers contact center and the web, this enormous data prompts for Big Data analytic solutions, which believes that in every massive pool of data there is a hidden insight that can be extracted that can assist quick and effective decision making, risk management, product development and innovation, improved customer experience etc. There are many data analytics tools whose skills are relevant to effective analysis of big data: Hadoop, Talend, MongoDB, Cassandra, Spark, STORM and Kafka.

According to the LinkedIn (2020) survey the following are the emerging jobs and skills that are high in demand, they are listed in the order of demand from one to ten. The survey reviewed that Artificial Intelligence Specialist jobs are highest in demand in the data and AI jobs while data science skills top the list of the most in demand skills as enumerated in Table II below.

Table 2. Jobs and skills in data analytic and artificial intelligence

Emerging jobs in Data and Artificial Intelligence	Top 10 Skills in Data and AI
1 Artificial Intelligence Specialist	1 Data Science
2 Data Scientist	2 Data Storage Technologies
3 Data Engineer	3 Development Tools
4 Big Data Developer	4 Artificial Intelligence
5 Data Analyst	5 Software Development Life Cycle (SDLC)
6 Analytics Specialist	6 Management Consulting
7 Data Consultant	7 Web Development
8 Insights Analyst	8 Digital Literacy
9 Business Intelligence Developer	9 Scientific Computing
10 Analytics Consultant	10 Computer Networking

Source (LinkedIn learning, 2019)

Cloud Computing

Cloud computing according to the U.S. National Institute of Standards and Technology (NIST) can be defined as "a model for enabling ubiquitous, convenient, on-demand network access to a shared pool of configurable computing resources (e.g., networks, servers, storage, applications, and services) that can be rapidly provisioned and released with minimal management effort or service providers interaction" (Peter & Tim 2011). This has defined a new way of doing business over the internet with provision of services ranging from Platform as a service (PaaS), infrastructure as a service (IaaS), software as a service (SaaS) to data storage as a service (DSaaS). Which has to a large extent removed the burden of hardware and software provision and maintenance from an organization that is the recipient of the services, that has ushered in a new dimension of doing business with optimum flexibility. In a nutshell, "cloud computing is internet-based computing where virtual shared servers provide software, infrastructure, platform, devices and other resources and hosting to customers as a service on pay-as-you-use basis"

(Park & Ki-Woong 2011). The prominent framework and platforms for cloud computing with the most sought-after skills are Microsoft Azure, Amazon Web Services, Google Cloud, Linux Cloud Docker DevOps, and Kubernetes for cybersecurity.

Cybersecurity

One of the great risks of digitization is the proliferation of cyber-attacks. Cybersecurity is the practice of securing information systems, computer hardware and networks from attacks. The utmost goal of this flourishing sector is to be ahead of the malicious eavesdropper. According to Horda (2021), this trending sector has an annual growth rate of 30%. Kimberly (2021) further emphasized that, "The information security market which includes subsegments such as identity access management (IAM), infrastructure protection, and security services. Global security spending on identity access management is forecasted to reach almost 14 billion U.S. dollars in 2021, Spending on security services, the largest segment of the information security market, is projected to reach 72.5 billion U.S. dollars in the same year". Spending in this sector will continue to surge since organizations are expected to secure their IT infrastructures that is why skills in this area are highly sought after.

Blockchain Technology

Blockchain is a collection of digital information stored on a decentralized public or private database. The data is referred to as the block while the database is the chain of blocks. According to Ritesh (2018) Blockchain means a chain of blocks. Blockchain means having multiple blocks chained together, with each block storing transactions in a way where it is not possible to change these transactions. The first version of blockchain, version 1.0 only implemented distributed ledger technology which was used mainly for cryptocurrency transactions. Versions 2.0 and 3.0 extended the functionality of blockchain to include smart contracts and decentralized application development which blew up the usability of blockchain which has found application in industries, organizations and institutions ranging from financial to educational sector, this has hyped the need for blockchain developers around the world. Walmart, Nestle, and Unilever are just three of the large corporations that utilize blockchain tech to track and protect global supply chains (Ashley, 2021).

Video Production

The insatiable quest for video content which has found use in every facet of human existence, most predominantly in the advertising and the movie industries, has built up demand for expertise in this area. Cisco projected that video content will account 82% of global internet traffic by 2022 from 75% in 2018 (Munson, 2018).

UX and UI Design

Users experience (UX) and users' interface (UI) target making users of software have the best experience, that is what determines the usability of a hardware. While the UX designers make decisions on how users interface work and how users interact with it, the UI designers concentrate on the look and feel or the aesthetic which involve the graphic designs of the layout. UX and UI designers are in hot demand for companies that are interested in attracting customers with captivating user experience designs.

To add credence to the in-demand skills discussed above, LinkedIn learning surfed data from networks of over 660+ million professionals and 20+ million jobs. Their survey revealed the 15 most in-demand soft and hard skills as presented in Table III below:

Table 3. Hard and soft skill most needed by companies

10 Hard skills Most needed by companies in 2020	5 Soft skills Most needed by companies in 2020
1. Blockchain	1. Creativity
2. Cloud Computing	2. Persuasion
3. Analytical Reasoning	3. Collaboration
4. Artificial intelligence	4. Adaptability
5. UX design	5. Emotional Intelligence
6. Business Analysis	
7. Affiliate Marketing	
8. Sales	
9. Scientific Computing	
10. Video production	

(LinkedIn Learning, 2019)

Other Emerging Jobs and the Skills in Demand

We have established that IT will play a defining role in the transformation of skills relevant to the fourth industrial revolution workplace, to ensure a wholistic approach we also delve into other subdivision of the economy such as Caregiver, Engineering and Cloud Computing, Sales, Marketing and Content, Product Development, Green Economy, People and Culture, Data and AI. We state the emerging hot jobs in the rank of their preference and the top skills needed.

Care Economy

This is an aspect of the job market that will continue to be relevant even though it will witness progressive automation, skills and services of experts will be needed to drive this industry. According to Charlton (2021) "Almost 40% of all projected job opportunities in emerging professions will be created in the care sector between 2020 and 2023", the care economy will be second to IT in terms of emerging jobs creation. The reason is that "The growing demand for care services has the potential to generate significant job opportunities, while boosting labour force integration for informal caregivers and supporting new, more flexible ways of working".

In the Table IV below are the list of emerging jobs and skills that are most vital to the industries according to Burning Glass Technologies in care economy.

Table 4. Top jobs and skills in the care economy

Emerging Jobs in rank of preference	Top Ten Skills in care economy
Medical Transcriptionists	Respiratory Therapy
Physical Therapist Aides	Caregiving
Radiation Therapists	Sterile Procedures / Techniques Transcription
Athletic Trainers	Radiation Treatment
Medical Equipment Preparers	Medical Dosimetry
Veterinary Assistants and Laboratory Animal Caretakers	Vital Signs Measurement
Exercise Physiologists	Simulation
Recreation Workers	Advanced Cardiac Life Support (ACLS)
Personal Care Aides	Radiologic Technology
Respiratory Therapists	
Medical Assistants	
Fitness Trainers and Aerobics Instructors	
Occupational Health and Safety Technicians	
Orderlies	
Healthcare Support Workers, All Other	

(Burning Glass Technologies, 2020)

People and Culture

This sector of work will continue to be relevant, for the fact that it will enable organizations to achieve their set objectives and achieve and deliver on strategic outcomes. The people and culture jobs extend the work of the human resource from being just policy based to managing people's work culture. According to Maurer (2017) "Job seekers are most likely to choose one job over another because of the chosen employer's culture". According to Eurostat (2021) "In 2020, there were 7.2 million people in cultural employment across the EU (3.6% of total employment). That shows that the demand for Jobs and skills will grow progressively in this area. The excerpt below in Table V from LinkedIn learning (2020) reveals the emerging jobs and skills in this sector of work.

Software Engineering and Cloud Computing

It is expected that organizations will continue to subscribe to cloud computing, the demand for skills in this area will continue to surge. Programming with Python will keep playing a vital role in machine learning and data science, it will therefore continue to be relevant and those that work with the server and client-side programming skills called the full stack engineer. The details of jobs and skills most needed in this area are presented in Table VI below.

Table 5. Top jobs and skills in people and culture

Emerging Jobs	**Top needed Ten Skills**
	Recruiting
Information Technology Recruiter	Human Resources
Human Resources Partner	Business Management
Talent Acquisition Specialist	Employee Learning & Development
	Leadership
	Digital Literacy
	Project Management
	People Management
	Compensation & Benefits
	Foreign Languages

Table 6. Top jobs and skills in software engineering and cloud computing

Emerging hot Jobs Engineering and Cloud Computing	**Top Skills needed in Engineering and Cloud Computing**
Site Reliability Engineer / Cloud Computing /	Development Tools
Python Developer / Engineering /	Web Development
Full Stack Engineer / Engineering /	Data Storage Technologies
Javascript Developer / Engineering /	Software Development Life Cycle (SDLC)
Back End Developer / Engineering /	Computer Networking
Frontend Engineer / Engineering /	Human Computer Interaction
Software Developer Dotnet / Engineering/	Technical Support
Platform Engineer / Cloud Computing /	Digital Literacy
Development Specialist / Engineering /	Business Management
Cloud Engineer / Cloud Computing /	Employee Learning & Development
DevOps Engineer / Cloud Computing /	
Cloud Consultant / Cloud Computing /	
DevOps Manager / Cloud Computing /	
Technology Analyst / Engineering	

Source (LinkedIn, 2020)

Renewable (Green) Energy Sector

There are emerging jobs in this sector because the world is gearing towards renewable energy generated from natural sources such as wind, sunlight etc. This is because energy from these sources are more environmentally friendly. As stated by Rowling (2021) "The number of jobs in renewable energy worldwide increased in 2020, despite the huge economic disruptions caused by the COVID-19 pandemic, with the growing industry holding up better than fossil fuels, international agencies said 500,000 more jobs in renewable energy were made in 2020 from 2019, with a third of them being in solar power. Clean energy jobs rose to 12 million in 2020 even amid the pandemic". If global pandemics could not slow down the growth of jobs in this sector then skills in this area such as, solar photovoltaics, bioenergy, hydropower, wind energy, solar heating and cooling and the host of others will continue to be in hot demand. Other skills that are needed in this sector of are presented in Table VII below

Table 7. Top jobs and skills in renewable (green) energy sector

Most in-demand jobs	Most in-demand skills in green economy
Methane/Landfill Gas Generation System Technicians	Digital Marketing
Wind Turbine Service Technicians	Wind Turbines
Green Marketers	Landfill Gas Collection
Biofuels Processing Technicians	Social Media
Solar Energy Installation Managers	Equipment Inventory
Water Resource Specialists	Solar Installation
Wind Energy Project Managers	Health and Safety Standards
Chief Sustainability Officers	Microsoft Power BI
Refuse and Recyclable Material Collectors	Electrical Diagrams / Schematics
Sustainability Specialists	Email Marketing
Solar Photovoltaic Installers	
Water/Wastewater Engineers	
Forest Fire Inspectors and Prevention Specialists	
Fuel Cell Engineers	
Nuclear Power Reactor Operators	

Source: (Burning Glass Technologies, 2020)

Product Development

As long as new products are developed the work of the product manager will be needed. According to Gnanasambandam et al. (2017). "Product managers are the glue that bind the many functions that touch a product engineering, design, customer success, sales, marketing, operations, finance, legal, and more. They not only own the decisions about what gets built but also influence every aspect of how it gets built and launched". The task of product development is data driven such that both internal and external data becomes very vital to develop a product that satisfies the needs of the users because the relevance of any product depends on the usability. They also added that "The role of the product manager is expanding due to the growing importance of data in decision making, an increased customer and design focus, and the evolution of software-development methodologies". Software development and testing skills seems to top this area largely due to more companies tuning to software solutions for effective running of their businesses.

Table 8, below presented the emerging jobs and skills in product development.

Table 8. Op jobs and skills in product development

Emerging Jobs in Product Development	Emerging skills in Product Development
Product Owner	Software Testing
Quality Assurance Tester	Software Development Life Cycle (SDLC)
Agile Coach	Development Tools
Software Quality Assurance Engineer	Project Management
Product Analyst	Business Management
Quality Assurance Engineer	Data Storage Technologies
Scrum Master	Web Development
Digital Product Manager	Manufacturing Operations
Delivery Lead	Digital Literacy
	Leadership

Source (LinkedIn, 2020)

Sales, Marketing and Content Development

Skills in this sector of jobs will maintain steady growth since the target of companies and business outfits is to stimulate peoples' interest in their product to ensure good returns on investment. According to Hotspot (2021) "The purpose of content marketing is to create and share relevant written, downloadable, and visual media so your target audience can learn about your brand, expertise, and products or services. Content marketing statistics inform your strategy and provide insight into the ways other content marketers are solving the pain points of their target audience and generating leads". Statistics have shown that jobs in this emerging area has a promising future, according to the U.S. Bureau of Labor Statistics (2021) "Overall employment of advertising, promotions, and marketing managers is projected to grow 10 percent from 2020 to 2030, about as fast as the average for all occupations. About 31,100 openings for advertising, promotions, and marketing managers are projected each year, on average, over the decade. Many of those openings are expected to result from the need to replace workers who transfer to different occupations or exit the labor force, such as to retire".

Table 9 below gave the detail of Jobs and skill most relevant in Sales, Marketing and Content Development.

This chapter discovered in summary, that the current and the future workplace will be highly dependent on high cognitive skills most of which are hard technology skill related such as: artificial intelligence and machine learning, big data analytics, blockchain technology, cybersecurity, video production, UX and UI design and soft skills such as critical thinking, self-management, communication skills, leadership and team management skills, collaboration and team work effectiveness, mental flexibility and ability to effectively build relationship with others, self-direction and motivation, integrity and discipline among others are not replaceable by automation most essentially the soft skills.

Table 9. Emerging jobs and skills in sales, marketing and content development

Emerging Jobs in Sales, Marketing and Content	10 Emerging skills in in Sales, Marketing and Content
Social Media Assistant / Content Production /	Digital Marketing
Growth Hacker / Marketing /	Social Media
Customer Success Specialist / Sales /	Business Management
Social Media Coordinator / Content Production /	Digital Literacy
Growth Manager / Marketing /	Advertising
Sales Development Representative / Sales /	Product Marketing
Digital Marketing Specialist / Marketing /	Video
Commercial Sales Representative / Sales /	Graphic Design
Business Development Representative / Sales /	Leadership
Customer Specialist / Sales /	Writing
Content Specialist / Content Production /	
Content Producer / Content Production /	
Content Writer / Content Production /	
Partnerships Specialist / Sales /	
Digital Specialist / Marketing /	
Chief Commercial Officer / Sales /	
Ecommerce Specialist / Marketing /	
Head of Partnerships / Sales /	
Commerce Manager / Marketing /	
Head of Digital / Marketing /	
Enterprise Account Executive / Sales /	
Digital Marketing Consultant / Marketing /	
Business Development Specialist / Sales /	
Digital Marketing Manager / Marketing /	
Chief Strategy Officer / Sales /	
Creative Copywriter / Content Production / Chief	
Marketing Officer / Marketing /	
Head of Business Development / Sales /	

Source (LinkedIn, 2020)

Repositioning the Workforce to Be Relevant in The Face of Automation and The Accelerated Trend of Artificial Intelligence.

Automation is a big threat to the current workforce, both jobs that require high cognitive skilled and low skilled workers but those at a greater risk are those at the bottom of the ladder whose jobs require low cognitive skill. According to a study by Oxford University (2013), in which 700 professions were studied 12 professions have 99% chance of full automation about 8 others are likely to be automated and those whose jobs will be worse hit are low income employees at the bottom of the rung of work. Luckwaldt

(2017) added that "one possibility is superstar-biased technological change, where the benefits of technology accrue to an even smaller portion of society than just highly-skilled workers. The winner-take-most nature of information technology markets means that only a few may come to dominate markets. If labour productivity increases do not translate into wage increases, then the large economic gains brought about by AI could accrue to a select few. Instead of broadly shared prosperity for workers and consumers, this might push towards reduced competition and increased wealth inequality".

Below on the table X is the summary of the occupations that stand no chance at all in the face of automation and those that will not be affected by automation.

Table 10. Occupation at the risk of automation

Occupation taken over by Automation		Occupations with mild threat of Automation	
Position	**Chance of Automation**	**Position**	**Chance of Automation**
Telemarketer	99%	Physician	0.4%
Tax Preparer	99%	Dentist	0.4%
Insurance underwriter	99%	Computer system analyst	0.7%
Bookkeeping Clerk	98%	Registered Nurse	0.9%
Legal Secretary	98%	Teacher	1.0%
Credit Analyzer	98%	Microbiologist	1.2%
Laon Officer	98%	Pharmacist	1.2%
Real Estate Broker	97%	Sales Manager	1.3%
Payroll Clerk	97%	Engineer	1.4%
Accountant	94%	CEO	1.4%
Budget Analyst	94%	PR Manager	1.5%
Pharmacy Technician	92%	Architect	1.8%

(Visual Capitalist, 2018)

According to Luckwaldt (2017) "No industry is safe from the robot incursion, but jobs that rely on manual labour, involve repetitive work, and are relatively low-skilled are probably least secure, while those that depend on emotional labour, creative thinking, or a high level of dexterity are likely safe (at least for now)".

If the low paying routine jobs like factory machine operators, photographic process worker, library technician and accountant clerk among others are withering away to automation, then there is need for drastic steps to be taken to sustain the future of work. I don't believe that automation is completely taking our jobs but rather phasing out the old way of doing things with new methods and approach for employees to survive they need to be properly repositioned to be relevant by first understanding that the only thing that is permanent is change and those who will not be dynamic in the face of change risk losing out.

The conclusion of Frey and Osborne (2013) from their famous study conducted at Oxford University highlighted two findings as quoted below which are very essential to the future work in the face of automation. "Our model predicts a truncation in the current trend towards labour market polarization, with computerization being principally confined to low-skill and low-wage occupations. Our findings thus imply that as technology races ahead, low-skill workers will reallocate to tasks that are non-susceptible to computerization - i.e., tasks requiring creative and social intelligence. For workers to win the race, however, they will have to acquire creative and social skills." From the findings above, skill adaptation is the answer and this requires lifelong learning because automation will only whittle down the old ways of doing things and open new opportunities for those who can seize them. This also necessitates that employees of the emerging jobs should keep tune with the trend and make necessary adjustments to be relevant.

The fourth Industrial Revolution, even though it is driven by automation with the aid of artificial intelligence, the only skills that will be indispensable will be cognitive and soft skills which involves the ability to employ critical thinking to solve problems, collaborating and communicating well with others, emotional aptitude among others. According world economic forum (2018) the following skills will be indispensable to the workplace either now or in the future:

"**Complex Problem Solving**: It's true that artificial intelligence can solve problems that humans cannot – but it also goes the other way. When problem solving needs to span multiple industries or when problems are not fully defined, humans can work backwards to figure out a solution.

Critical Thinking: Machines are getting better at aspects of critical thinking, but humans are still able to connect, interpret and imagine concepts in a world full of ambiguity and nuance. A lawyer can pinpoint the exact positioning to make a case for a client, or a marketer can figure out an overarching message that can resonate with consumers.

Creativity: This requires a degree of intuitive randomness that cannot yet be imitated by AI. Why did the architect design the building a certain way, and why did the musician improvise by playing a chord out of key? It's hard to explain why to a computer – it just *feels* right.

Other important soft skills to consider are people management, coordinating with others, decision-making, negotiation, and serving others will all be important going forward as well".

In addition the points discussed above, companies and the world of business should champion the cause of reskilling and retraining those employees whose job definition ought to change as a result of automation and not laying them off because automation has taken over their jobs, that is why the world of business should make professional and job-related training available to ensure easy acclimatization to new job specifications which will enhance employee retention, in fact, if the government can make a matter of policy to ensure that before companies adopt automation reskilling the exiting employee should be a must it help in curbing automation related retrenchment.

Furthermore, our educational curriculum should not be rigid in the face of automation championed by artificial intelligence, our curriculum should spread out to incorporate trending soft and hard skills needed in the world of work which will ensure that the kind of education given by our educational institutions match the current needs of the workplace. Our educational institutions should reorient around provision of lifelong education which can be made possible largely through e-learning which is a flexible kind of education and it is learner centered and government should also increase funding for e-learning which will make lifelong learning easily accessible to all.

In summary, automation does not invalidate or take away jobs but rather repositioned them, and the only way the industries can catch up in carrying employees along is to reposition employee's skills in line with the new skill set in demand, the industries, educational institutions and the government should deploy more resources to enhance the gains of e-learning which is flexible and learner tailored to enable the provision of lifelong learning which will facilitate easy skill adaptation among employees.

CONCLUSION

Living in the era of AI powered economy, there is an urgent need to review the existing workplace skills from time to time in order to ensure an employee remains relevant. In this discourse we have looked at how AI powered automation is transforming the workplace resulting in higher productivity and at the same time putting the low skill worker out of job, we further looked at the skills set that will be necessary to survive automation most of which are hard and soft skills which are irreplaceable with automation. We also discuss how to reposition the workforce to be able to deliver the industry-based skills in hot demand and to get that achieved, the business owners and the educational institutions must collaborate to train and retrain employees and students to enable them deliver the state of art skills to drive the world economy.

REFERENCES

Ashley, M. (2021). *What are the Most In-Demand Skills for Graduates in 2021?* Retrieved from https://www.academiccourses.com/article/what-are-the-most-in-demand-skills-for-graduates-in-2021/

Autor, D. & Salomons, A. (2018). *Is Automation Labour-Displacing? Productivity Growth, Employment, and the Labour Share.* National Bureau of Economic Research.

Bernard, M. (2019). *The 10 Vital Skills You Will Need for The Future of Work.* Retrieved from https://www.forbes.com/sites/bernardmarr/2019/04/29/the-10-vital-skills-you-will-need-for-the-future-of-work/

Big Data. (2019). In *Wikipedia*. Retrieved from http:// en.wikipedia.org/ wiki/Bigdata

Technologies, B. G. (2020) *What's Trending in Jobs and Skills.* Retrieve from https:// www.burning-glass.com/ research-project/ bcg-trending-jobs-skills/

Charlton, E. (2021). *40% of all projected job opportunities will be created in this sector. And it's not technology.* World Economic Forum. Retrieved from https://www.weforum.org/ agenda/2021/05/care-economy-emerging-job-opportunities/ #:~:text=Shifting%20demographics%20are%20leading%20 to,nursing%2C%20therapy%20and%20personal%20trainers

Eurostat Statistics Explained. (2021). *Culture statistics - cultural employment.* https://ec.europa.eu/eurostat/statistics-explained/index.php?title=Culture_statistics_-_cultural_employment

Frey, C., & Osborne, M. (2017, September 17). *The future of employment: How susceptible are jobs to computerization?* Oxford Martin School, University of Oxford.

Frey, C. B., & Osborne, M. A. (2013). *The future of employment: how susceptible are jobs to computerisation?* Oxford University Engineering Sciences Department and the Oxford Martin Programme on the Impacts of Future Technology.

Gnanasambandam, C., Harrysson, M., Srivastava, S., & Wu, Y. (2017). *Product managers for the digital world.* McKinsey and Company. Retrieved from https:// www.mckinsey.com /industries /technology -media-and- telecommunications /our-insights/product-managers-for-the-digital-world

Hamza, S. (2021). *The Impact of New Technologies on Employment and the Workforce: What are the Implications for Developing Countries*. Especially in Africa.

Hamlett, C. (2019). *The Adverse Effects of Technology in the Workplace*. Retrieved from https://small-business.chron.com/adverse-effects-technology-workplace-22649.html

Horda, T. (2021). *A guide to future-oriented skills: Skills in demand to watch in the next five years.* https://hrforecast.com/a-guide-to-future-oriented-skills-skills-in-demand-to-watch-in-the-next-five-years/

Hotspot. (2021). *The Ultimate List of Marketing Statistics for 2021*. Retrieved from https://www.hubspot.com/marketing-statistics

Kimberly, M. (2021). *ICT industry full-time employment worldwide in 2019, 2020 and 2023*. Retrieved from http://www.ezwswmjk.com/statistics/1126677/it-employment-worldwide/

Kimberly, M. (2021). *Size of the cybersecurity market worldwide from 2021 to 2026 (in billion U.S. dollars).* Retrieved from https:// www.statista.com/statistics/595182/ worldwide-security-as-a-service-market-size/

Luckwaldt, J. H. (2017). *These Skills Are Most Likely to Be Automated Out of the Human Workforce* Retrieved from https:// www.payscale.com/ career-advice/skills-likely- automated-human-workforce/

Maurer, R. (2017). *Candidates Choose Jobs Because of Company Culture.* https://www.shrm.org/resourcesandtools/hr-topics/talent-acquisition/pages/candidates-choose-jobs-company-culture.aspx

Mercer, E. (2021). *How to Adapt to Changes at Work with Technology*. Retrieved from https://smallbusiness. chron.com/ adapt- changes- work-technology- 30901.html

Munson, B. (2018). *Video will account for 82% of all internet traffic by 2022, Cisco says*. https://www.fiercevideo.com/ video/video-will-account-for- 82-all-internet- traffic-by-2022-cisco-says

Park, K., & Ki-Woong, P. (2011). ACCENT: Cognitive cryptography plugged compression for SSL/TLS-based cloud computing services. *Journal of ACM Transactions on Internet Technology*, *11*(2), 7. doi:10.1145/2049656.2049659

Peter, M., & Tim, G. (2011). *The NIST Definition of Cloud Computing*. Computer Security Division Information Technology Laboratory, National Institute of Standards and Technology Gaithersburg. Retrieved from https://csrc.nist.gov/publications/detail/sp/800-145/final

Ritesh, M. (2018). Solidity Programming Essentials: A beginner's guide to build smart contracts for Ethereum and blockchain. Packt Publishing Ltd.

Rowling, M. (2021*). Research shows COVID-19 did not stop clean energy jobs from rising.* Thomson Reuters Foundation in collaboration with World Economic Forum. Retrieved from https://www.weforum.org/ agenda/ 2021/10/renewable-energy-jobs-grew-globally-2020-covid-19

Saadia, Z. (2020). *We need a global reskilling revolution – here's why.* Retrieved from https://www.weforum.org/agenda/2020/01/reskilling-revolution-jobs-future-skills/

Statista. (2021). *Worldwide installations of industrial robots from 2004 to 2020, with a forecast through 2024.* https://www.statista.com/statistics /264084/worldwide-sales-of-industrial-robots

Strack, R., Kaufman, E., Kotsis, A., Sigelman, M., Restuccia, D., & Taska, B. (2019). *What's Trending in Jobs and Skills.* Retrieved from https://www.bcg.com/publications/2019/what-is-trending-jobs-skills

Scott, P. (2017). *These are the jobs most at risk of automation according to Oxford University: Is yours one of them?* Retrieved from https:// www.telegraph.co.uk/ news/2017/09/27/jobs-risk-automation-according-oxford-university-one/

Tyagarajan, T. (2019). To Prepare for Automation, Stay Curious and Don't Stop Learning. *Harvard Business Review.* https://hbr.org/2019/10/to-prepare-for-automation-stay-curious-and-dont-stop-learning

UK Commission for Employment and Skills. (2015). *UK Commission for Employment and Skills (UKCES) annual report and accounts for financial year 2014 to 2015.* Retrieved from https://www.gov.uk/government/publications/uk-commission-for-employment-and-skills-annual-report-and-accounts-2014-to-2015

U.S. Bureau of Labour Statistics. (2021). *Advertising, Promotions, and Marketing Managers.* Retrieved from https://www.bls.gov/ooh/ management/ advertising- promotions- and- marketing- managers.htm

Van Nuys, A. (2019). *New LinkedIn Research: Upskill Your Employees with the Skills Companies Need Most in 2020.* Retrieved from https://www.linkedin.com/business/learning/blog/learning-and-development/most-in-demand-skills-2020

World Economic Forum. (2020). Jobs of Tomorrow Mapping Opportunity in the New Economy. Author.

World Economic Forum. (2018). *10 skills you'll need to survive the rise of automation.* Retrieved from https: // www. weforum.org/ agenda/ 2018/07/the-skills-needed-to- survive-the-robot-invasion-of-the-workplace

Compilation of References

(2020, Winter). The Impact of COVID-19 on Small Business Owners: Evidence from the First Three Months after Social-Distancing Restrictions. *Journal of Economics & Management Strategy*, *29*(4), 727–740.

Abbas, J., Mubeen, R., & Terhemba, I. (2021). Exploring the impacts of COVID-19 on tourism: transformational potential and implications for a sustainable of the travel and leisure industry. *Current Research in Behavioural Sciences, 2*, 130-210.

Abdallah, G. K. (2017). Differences between firms from the formal sector and the informal sector in terms of growth. *Journal of Entrepreneurship in Emerging Economies*, *9*(2), 121–143. doi:10.1108/JEEE-05-2015-0033

Abdullah, S., Al-Natsheh, B., & Hattawy, M. (2014). *Policies for scaling up youth entrepreneurship in the state of Palestine*. Working paper, Palestine Economic Policy Research Institute (MAS).

Abed, F. H. (2006). *Good practice guidelines for funders of microfinance*. Academic Press.

Abed, S. S. (2021). Women Entrepreneurs' Adoption of Mobile Applications for Business Sustainability. *Sustainability*, *13*(21), 11627. doi:10.3390u132111627

Abrigo, M., & Love, I. (2016). Estimation of panel vector autoregression in Stata. *The Stata Journal*, *16*(3), 778–804. doi:10.1177/1536867X1601600314

Abualkhair, H., Lodree, E. J., & Davis, L. B. (2020). Managing volunteer convergence at disaster relief centers. *International Journal of Production Economics*, *220*, 107399–107359. doi:10.1016/j.ijpe.2019.05.018

Acemoglu, D., & Restrepo, P. (2021). *Tasks, Automation and the Rise in US Wage Inequality*. NBER Working Paper No. 28920. Retrieved from: https://www.nber.org/papers/w28920

Acemoglu, D., & Restrepo, P. (2019). 8. Artificial Intelligence, Automation, and Work. In A. Agrawal, J. Gans, & A. Goldfarb (Eds.), *The Economics of Artificial Intelligence: An Agenda* (pp. 197–236). University of Chicago Press. doi:10.7208/9780226613475-010

Acs, Z. J. (2006). How is entrepreneurship good for economic growth? *Innovations: Technology, Governance, Globalization*, *1*(1), 97–107. doi:10.1162/itgg.2006.1.1.97

Acs, Z. J., & Amoros, J. E. (2008). Entrepreneurship and competitiveness dynamics in Latin America. *Small Business Economics*, *31*(3), 305–322. doi:10.100711187-008-9133-y

Adams, M., Makramalla, M., & Miron, W. (2014). Down the rabbit hole: How structural holes in entrepreneurs' social networks impact early venture growth. *Technology Innovation Management Review*, *4*(9), 19–27. doi:10.22215/timreview/828

Adams-Prassl, A., Boneva, T., Golin, M., & Rauh, C. (2020). Inequality in the impact of the coronavirus shock: Evidence from real time surveys. *Journal of Public Economics*, *189*, 1–33. doi:10.1016/j.jpubeco.2020.104245

Adisa, T. A., Abdulraheem, I., & Isiaka, S. B. (2019). Patriarchal hegemony. *Gender in Management, 34*(1), 19–33. doi:10.1108/GM-07-2018-0095

African Development Bank. (2021). African economic outlook 2021: *From debt resolution to growth: The road ahead for Africa*. African Development Bank.

African Development Fund. (2015). *Support to Skills Development for Employability and Entrepreneurship*. African Development Fund.

African Union. (2007). *Strategy to revitalize technical and vocational education and training (TVET) in Africa*. Paper presented at the Meeting of the Bureau of the Conference of Ministers of Education of the African Union (COMEDAF II+).

Afshan, G., Shahid, S., & Tunio, M. N. (2021). Learning experiences of women entrepreneurs amidst COVID-19. *International Journal of Gender and Entrepreneurship, 13*(2), 162–186. doi:10.1108/IJGE-09-2020-0153

Afza, T., & Amir Rashid, M. (2009). Marginalized women social well-being through enterprise development. *Journal of Chinese Entrepreneurship, 1*(3), 248–267. doi:10.1108/17561390910999533

AggarwalA. (2018). Rural entrepreneurship development ecosystem–An emerging paradigm of rural socio-economic development. *Available at* SSRN 3184127. doi:10.2139/ssrn.3184127

Agwa-Ejon, J., & Mbohwa, C. (2015). Financial challenges faced by SMMES in Gauteng South Africa. In *International Association for Management of Technology IAMOT 2015 Conference Proceedings* (pp. 520-534). Academic Press.

Aharon, D. Y., Jacobi, A., Cohen, E., Tzur, J., & Qadan, M. (2021). COVID-19, government measures and hospitality industry performance. *PLoS One, 16*(8), 1–4. doi:10.1371/journal.pone.0255819 PMID:34358283

Ahl, H. (2006). Why Research on Women Entrepreneurs Needs New Directions. *Entrepreneurship Theory and Practice, 30*(5), 595–621. doi:10.1111/j.1540-6520.2006.00138.x

Ajzen, I. (1991). The theory of planned behavior. *Organizational Behavior and Human Decision Processes, 50*(2), 179–211. doi:10.1016/0749-5978(91)90020-T

Ajzen, I. (2020). The theory of planned behavior: Frequently asked questions. *Human Behavior and Emerging Technologies, 2*(4), 314–324. doi:10.1002/hbe2.195

Akanbi, G. O. (2017). Prospects for technical and vocational education and training (TVET) in Nigeria: Bridging the gap between policy document and implementation. *International Education Journal: Comparative Perspectives, 16*(2), 1-15. https://openjournals.library.sydney.edu.au/index.php/IEJ/article/view/10668/11178

Akanji, B., Mordi, C., Ajonbadi, H., & Adekoya, O. (2022). The impact of COVID-19 on the work–life balance of working mothers: evidence from Nigerian academics. Personnel Review. doi:10.1108/PR-08-2020-0636

Akella, D., & Eid, N. (2018). Social Enterprises in Palestine: A Critical Analysis. *Journal of Enterprising Communities: People and Places in the Global Economy.*

Al Mamun, A., Muniady, R., Yukthamarani, P. P., Noor Raihani Binti, Z., & Mohamad, M. R. (2016). Micro-enterprise development initiatives and entrepreneurial competencies, innovativeness, and social capital in Malaysia. *Development in Practice, 26*(8), 1094–1110. doi:10.1080/09614524.2016.1228830

Al Mubaraki, H., & Busler, M. (2013). The Effect of Business Incubation in Developing Countries. *European Journal of Business and Innovation Research, 1*(1), 19–25.

Alam, G. M. (2021). Does online technology provide sustainable HE or aggravate diploma disease? Evidence from Bangladesh—A comparison of conditions before and during COVID-19. *Technology in Society*, *66*, 101677. doi:10.1016/j.techsoc.2021.101677 PMID:34840366

Alam, G. M., & Hoque, K. E. (2010). Who gains from" brain and body drain" business-developing/developed world or individuals: A comparative study between skilled and semi/unskilled emigrants. *African Journal of Business Management*, *4*(4), 534. doi:10.5897/AJBM.9000680

Aldrich, H. E. (1990). Using an Ecological Perspective to Study Organizational Founding Rates. *Entrepreneurship Theory and Practice*, *14*(3), 7–24. doi:10.1177/104225879001400303

Alhasan, N. U., & Tyabo, A. (2013). Revitalizing technical and vocational education (TVET) for youth empowerment and sustainable development. *Journal of Educational and Social Research*, *3*(4), 149. doi:10.5901/jesr.2013.v3n4p149

Ali, A. E. E. S. (2015). The regulatory and supervision framework of Microfinance in Kenya. *International Journal of Social Science Studies*, *3*, 123.

All India Federation of Self-Employed Women's Association (SEWA) Bharat. (2020b). *Protecting Livelihoods*. SEWA Bharat. Available at: https://sewabharatresearch.org/wp-content/uploads/2020/10/Protection-of-Livelihoods-SEWA-Data-September-2020.pdf

Allam, C. (2020). *Black-led businesses getting shut out of PPP loan program, owners and experts say*. Retrieved June 2, 2020, from https://www.wraltechwire.com/2020/05/22/black-led-businesses-getting-shut-out-of-ppp-loan-program-owners-and-experts-say/

Allcott, H., Boxell, L., Conway, J., Gentzkow, M., Thaler, M., & Yang, D. (2020). Polarization and public health: Partisan differences in social distancing during the coronavirus pandemic. *Journal of Public Economics*, *191*, 104254. doi:10.1016/j.jpubeco.2020.104254 PMID:32836504

Allen, T. D., Golden, T. D., & Shockley, K. M. (2015). How Effective Is Telecommuting? Assessing the Status of Our Scientific Findings. *Psychological Science in the Public Interest*, *16*(2), 40–68. doi:10.1177/1529100615593273 PMID:26403188

Alom, F., Abdullah, M. A., Moten, A. R., & Azam, S. M. F. (2016). Success factors of overall improvement of microenterprises in Malaysia: An empirical study. *Journal of Global Entrepreneurship Research*, *6*(1), 1–13. doi:10.118640497-016-0050-2

Alon, T., Doepke, M., Olmstead-Rumsey, J., & Tertilt, M. (2020). *The impact of COVID-19 on gender equality* (No. w26947). National Bureau of Economic Research. https://www.nber.org/system/files/working_papers/w26947/w26947.pdf

Alon, T., Doepke, M., Olmstead-Rumsey, J., & Tertilt, M. (2020). *This Time it's different: the role of women's employment in a pandemic recession (no. w27660)*. National Bureau of Economic Research. doi:10.3386/w27660

Alsos, G. A., & Ljunggren, E. (2017). The Role of Gender in Entrepreneur–Investor Relationships: A Signaling Theory Approach. *Entrepreneurship Theory and Practice*, *41*(4), 567–590. doi:10.1111/etp.12226

Alvarez, S. A., & Busenitz, L. W. (2001). The entrepreneurship of resource-based theory. *Journal of Management*, *27*(6), 755–775. doi:10.1177/014920630102700609

Ama, Mangadi, & Ama. (2014). Exploring the challenges facing women entrepreneurs in informal cross-border trade in Botswana. *Gender in Management*, *29*(8), 505–522. doi:10.1108/GM-02-2014-0018

Amabile, T. (1988). A model of creativity and innovation in organizations. In B. M. Staw & L. L. Cumming (Eds.), *Research in organizational behavior* (Vol. 10, pp. 123–167). JAI Press.

Amankwah, E., & Swanzy, P. (2011). The role of stakeholders in building adequate competences in students for the job market. *International Journal of Vocational and Technical Education, 3*(8), 107–112. doi:10.5897/IJVTE.9000038

Amato, N. (2020*). A tale of the PPP tape: Why relationship building matters.* Retrieved June 2, 2020 from https://www.journalofaccountancy.com/news/2020/may/ppp-loans-small-business-bank-financing-relationships.html

American Express. (2018). *The 2018 State of Women Owned Business Report.* https://ventureneer.com/wp-content/uploads/2018/08/2018-state-of-women-owned-businesses-report_FINAL.pdf

Amine, L. S., & Staub, K. M. (2009). Women entrepreneurs in Sub-Saharan Africa: An institutional theory analysis from a social marketing point of view. *Entrepreneurship and Regional Development, 21*(2), 183–211. doi:10.1080/08985620802182144

Amit, R., & Muller, E. (1995). "Push" and "pull" entrepreneurship. *Journal of Small Business and Entrepreneurship, 12*(4), 64–80. doi:10.1080/08276331.1995.10600505

Anderson, A. R., & Miller, C. J. (2003). Class matters: Human and social capital in the entrepreneurial process. *Journal of Socio-Economics, 32*(1), 17–36. doi:10.1016/S1053-5357(03)00009-X

Anderson, C. (2012). *Makers: the new industrial revolution.* Random House.

Anderson, C., Bieck, C., & Marshall, A. (2020). How business is adapting to COVID-19: Executive insights reveal post-pandemic opportunities. *Strategy and Leadership.* Advance online publication. doi:10.1108/SL-11-2020-0140

Anderson, J. C., & Wynstra, F. (2010). Purchasing higher-value, higher-price offerings in business markets. *Journal of Business-To-Business Marketing, 17*(1), 29–61. doi:10.1080/10517120903000363

Anderson, P., & Williams, C. (2008). *The conversation between statistics and social policy: When we listen, when we do not.* Dialogue for Development Lecture. Kingston, Jamaica: Planning Institute of Jamaica. doi:10.1080/02681102.2012.751571

Andersson, L. M., & Pearson, C. M. (1999). 'Tit for tat? The spiraling effect of incivility in the workplace. *Academy of Management Review, 24*(3), 452–471.

Andrews, R., Jilke, S., & Van de Walle, S. (2014). Economic strain and perceptions of social cohesion in Europe: Does institutional trust matter? *European Journal of Political Research, 53*(3), 559–579. doi:10.1111/1475-6765.12052

Angell, R. C. (1936). *The Family Encounters the Depression.* Scribner.

Anholon, R., & Sano, A. (2016). Analysis of critical processes in the implementation of Lean manufacturing projects using project management guidelines. *International Journal of Advanced Manufacturing Technology, 84*(9–12), 2247–2256. doi:10.100700170-015-7865-9

Anyanwu, J. C., & Salami, A. O. (2021). The impact of COVID-19 on African economies: An introduction. *African Development Review, 33*(1), 1–16. doi:10.1111/1467-8268.12531 PMID:34149237

Aoyagi, C., & Ganelli, G. (2015). Asia's quest for inclusive growth revisited. *Journal of Asian Economics, 40*, 29–46. doi:10.1016/j.asieco.2015.06.005

Arcieri, K. (2021, December 16). *US e-commerce sales set to maintain pandemic-fueled heights into 2022.* S&P Global Market Intelligence. Retrieved from: https://www.spglobal.com/marketintelligence/en/news-insights/latest-news-headlines/us-e-commerce-sales-set-to-maintain-pandemic-fueled-heights-into-2022-68009405

Argyris, C., & Schon, D. A. (1974). *Theory in practice: Increasing professional effectiveness.* Jossey-Bass.

Armstrong, K., Ahsan, M., & Sundaramurthy, C. (2018). Microfinance ecosystem: How connectors, interactors, and institutionalizers co-create value. *Business Horizons*, *61*(1), 147–155. doi:10.1016/j.bushor.2017.09.014

Ashley, M. (2021). *What are the Most In-Demand Skills for Graduates in 2021?* Retrieved from https://www.academic-courses.com/article/what-are-the-most-in-demand-skills-for-graduates-in-2021/

Asian Development Bank Outlook 2006. (2014, October 7). Retrieved from https://www.adb.org/projects/documents/asian-development-outlook-2006-tcr

Asian Development Bank. (2006). Asian Development Outlook 2006. Author.

Atkins, R., Cook, L., & Seamans, R. (2022). Discrimination in lending? Evidence from the Paycheck Protection Program. *Small Business Economics*, *58*(2), 843–865. doi:10.100711187-021-00533-1

Audretsch, D. B., Seitz, N., & Rouch, K. M. (2018). Tolerance and innovation: the role of institutional and social trust. *Eurasian Business Review, 8*(1), 71. Available at: http://search.ebscohost.com.proxy-cs.researchport.umd.edu/login.aspx?direct=true&db=edb&AN=128333469&site=eds-live

Audretsch, D. B., Belitski, M., & Desai, S. (2015). Entrepreneurship and economic development in cities. *The Annals of Regional Science*, 1–28.

Autor, D. & Salomons, A. (2018). *Is Automation Labour-Displacing? Productivity Growth, Employment, and the Labour Share.* National Bureau of Economic Research.

Aworanti, O. A. (2015). *Partnership in Technical, Vocational education and training (TVET) for National Development.* A lead paper presented at the 23rd Annual International conference of the Nigeria Vocational Association held at Yaba College of Technology, Lagos.

Ayatakshi-Endow, S., & Steele, J. (2021). Striving for balance: Women entrepreneurs in Brazil, their multiple gendered roles and Covid-19. *International Journal of Gender and Entrepreneurship*, *13*(2), 121–141. doi:10.1108/IJGE-09-2020-0142

Aziz, M. K., & Khan, N. L. B. M. A. (2015). *Regional course on statistics on informality: informal economy, work and employment – country report for Malaysia* [Country Report]. https://www.unsiap.or.jp/e-learning/el_material/3_Population/3_2_labor/ 1507_Informal/cr/MLY_cr.pdf

Azubuike, O. B., Adegboye, O., & Quadri, H. (2021). Who gets to learn in a pandemic? Exploring the digital divide in remote learning during the COVID-19 pandemic in Nigeria. *International Journal of Educational Research Open*, *2*, 100022. doi:10.1016/j.ijedro.2020.100022 PMID:35059664

Badawi, A. A. (2013). TVET and entrepreneurship skills. *Revisiting global trends in TVET: Reflections on theory and practice*, 275-308.

Bahrami, H., & Evans, S. (1995). Flexible Re-Cycling and High Technology Entrepreneurship. *California Management Review*, *37*, 62–89.

Bakas, F. E. (2017). Community resilience through entrepreneurship: The role of gender. *Journal of Enterprising Communities: People and Places in the Global Economy*, *11*(1), 61–77. doi:10.1108/JEC-01-2015-0008

Balcilar, M., Gupta, R., Ma, W., & Makena, P. (2019). *Income inequality and economic growth: A re-examination of theory and evidence.* Working Paper. University of Pretoria.

Bali, A. S., Capano, G., & Ramesh, M. (2019). Anticipating and designing for policy effectiveness. *Policy and Society*, *38*(1), 1–13. doi:10.1080/14494035.2019.1579502

Bama, H. K. N., & Nyikana, S. (2021). The Effects of COVID-19 on Future Domestic Travel Intentions in South Africa: A Stakeholder Perspective. *African Journal of Hospitality, Tourism and Leisure, 10*(1), 179–193. doi:10.46222/ajhtl.19770720-94

Bamkole, P., & Ibeku, S. (2020). Entrepreneurial Universities: A Case Study of the Pan Atlantic University, Lagos, Nigeria. In Entrepreneurial Universities (pp. 119-141). Springer.

Bandura, A. (1997). *Self-efficacy: The exercise of control.* Freeman.

Barmash, I. (1990, July 4). Federated's New Buying Strategy. *New York Times.*

Barnes, A., & Felts, T. (2020, September 26). New in KC: Why Jackie Nguyen hit the brakes on acting to open a mobile coffee café. *Startland News.* Retrieved from: https://www.startlandnews.com/2020/09/jackie-nguyen-cafe-ca-phe/

Barr, A., Henry-Nickie, M., & Broady, K. (2021, December 8). *The November jobs report shows Black women are leaving the laborforce.* https://www.brookings.edu/blog/the-avenue/2021/12/08/the-november-jobs-report-shows-black-women-are-leaving-the-labor-force/

Barr, M. S. (2008). *Policies to expand minority entrepreneurship: Closing comments.* Academic Press.

Barrett, T., Pizzico, M., Levy, B. D., Nagel, R. L., Linsey, J. S., Talley, K. G., Forest, C. R., & Newsletter, W. C. (2015). *A review of university maker spaces.* Georgia Institute of Technology. doi:10.18260/p.23442

Barringer, B. R., & Ireland, R. D. (2019). *Entrepreneurship: Successfully Launching New Ventures* (6th ed.). Pearson.

Barro, R. J. (2008). *Inequality and growth revisited* (No. 11). ADB Working paper series on regional economic integration.

Bartak, J., & Jabłoński, Ł. (2020). Inequality and growth: What comes from the different inequality measures? *Bulletin of Economic Research, 72*(2), 185–212. doi:10.1111/boer.12220

Bartik, A. W., Bertrand, M., Cullen, Z. B., Glaeser, E. L., Luca, M., & Stanton, C. T. (2020). *How are small businesses adjusting to COVID-19? Early evidence from a survey* (No. w26989). National Bureau of Economic Research. doi:10.3386/w26989

Bartik, A. W., Bertrand, M., Cullen, Z. B., Glaeser, E. L., Luca, M., & Stanton, C. (2020). The impact of COVID-19 on small business outcomes and expectations. *Proceedings of the National Academy of Sciences of the United States of America, 117*(30), 17656–17666. doi:10.1073/pnas.2006991117 PMID:32651281

Basuki, B., Widyanti, R., & Rajiani, I. (2021). Nascent entrepreneurs of millennial generations in emerging market of Indonesia. *Entrepreneurial Business and Economics Review, 9*(2), 151–165. doi:10.15678/EBER.2021.090210

Bates, T. (2011). Minority entrepreneurship. *Foundations and Trends in Entrepreneurship, 7*(3-4).

Bates, T. (1989). Small business viability in the urban ghetto. *Journal of Regional Science, 29*(4), 625–643. doi:10.1111/j.1467-9787.1989.tb01248.x

Bates, T. (1989). The changing nature of minority business: A comparative analysis of Asian, nonminority, and black-owned businesses. *The Review of Black Political Economy, 18*(2), 25–42. doi:10.1007/BF02895231

Bates, T. (1990). Entrepreneur human capital inputs and small business longevity. *The Review of Economics and Statistics, 72*(4), 551–559. doi:10.2307/2109594

Bates, T. (1995). Self-Employment Entry Across Industry Groups. *Journal of Business Venturing, 10*(2), 143–156. doi:10.1016/0883-9026(94)00018-P

Bates, T. (1995). Why do minority business development programs generate so little minority business development? *Economic Development Quarterly*, *9*(1), 3–14. doi:10.1177/089124249500900101

Bates, T. (1996). The financial capital needs of Black-owned businesses. *Journal of Developmental Entrepreneurship*, *1*(1), 1–15.

Bates, T. (1997). Unequal Qccess: Financial Institution Lending to Black-and White-Owned Small Business Start-Ups. *Journal of Urban Affairs*, *19*(4), 487–495. doi:10.1111/j.1467-9906.1997.tb00508.x

Bates, T., & Bradford, W. (2004). Analysis of venture-capital funds that finance minority-owned businesses. *The Review of Black Political Economy*, *32*(1), 37–46. doi:10.100712114-004-1017-z

Bates, T., & Robb, A. (2013). Greater access to capital is needed to unleash the local economic development potential of minority-owned businesses. *Economic Development Quarterly*, *27*(3), 250–259. doi:10.1177/0891242413477188

Baumeister, R. F., & Leary, M. R. (1995). The need to belong: Desire for interpersonal attachments as a fundamental human motivation. *Psychological Bulletin*, *117*(3), 497–529. doi:10.1037/0033-2909.117.3.497 PMID:7777651

Baumeister, R. F., Twenge, J. M., & Nuss, C. K. (2002). Effects of social exclusion on cognitive processes: Anticipated aloneness reduces intelligent thought. *Journal of Personality and Social Psychology*, *83*(4), 817–827. doi:10.1037/0022-3514.83.4.817 PMID:12374437

Baumeister, R. F., & Vohs, K. D. (2007). Self-Regulation, Ego Depletion, and Motivation. *Social and Personality Psychology Compass*, *1*(1), 115–128. doi:10.1111/j.1751-9004.2007.00001.x

Bawakyillenuo, S., Akoto, I. O., Ahiadeke, C., Aryeetey, E. B., & Agbe, E. K. (2013). *Tertiary education and industrial development in Ghana: Working paper.* Institute of Statistical, Social and Economic Research (ISSER): University of Ghana, Legon.

Beck, K. (2001). The Agile Manifesto. *Agile Alliance.* http://agilemanifesto.org/

Bell, D. (2000). Brown v. Board of Education: Forty-five years after the fact. *Ohio NUL Rev.*, *26*, 171.

Bell, D. (2018). Faces at the bottom of the well: The permanence of racism. Hachette UK.

Bell, D. A. JrBoard of Education and the Interest-Convergence Dilemma. (1980). Brown v. Board of Education and the interest-convergence dilemma. *Harvard Law Review*, *93*(3), 518–533. doi:10.2307/1340546

Bento, A., & Brown, T. N. (2021). Belief in systemic racism and self-employment among working blacks. *Ethnic and Racial Studies*, *44*(1), 21–38. doi:10.1080/01419870.2020.1737170

Berg, A., Ostry, J. D., Tsangarides, C. G., & Yakhshilikov, Y. (2018). Redistribution, inequality, and growth: New evidence. *Journal of Economic Growth*, *23*(3), 259–305. doi:10.100710887-017-9150-2

Beriso, B. S. (2021). Determinants of economic achievement for women entrepreneurs in Ethiopia. *Journal of Innovation and Entrepreneurship*, *10*(1), 1–14. doi:10.118613731-020-00141-5

Bernard, M. (2019). *The 10 Vital Skills You Will Need for The Future of Work.* Retrieved from https://www.forbes.com/sites/bernardmarr/2019/04/29/the-10-vital-skills-you-will-need-for-the-future-of-work/

Bertulfo, L. (2011), *Women and the Informal Sector.* Office of Development Effectiveness, Australian Government. https://dfat.gov.au/aid/how-wemeasure-performance/ode/ Documents/women-informal-economy-lota-bertulfo.pdf

Bester, M. (2017). Educating entrepreneurial mind-sets at a University of Technology: Curriculum enablers and constraints of selected programmes. *Journal for New Generation Sciences*, *15*(1), 188–206.

BeutellN.O'HareM.SchneerJ.AlsteteJ. (2019). Work-Family Issues Among Self-Employed Married Women. doi:10.2139/ssrn.3326543

Bhave, M. P. (1994). A process model of entrepreneurial creation. *Journal of Business Venturing*, *9*(3), 223–242. doi:10.1016/0883-9026(94)90031-0

Bhopal, R. (2004). Glossary of terms relating to ethnicity and race: For reflection and debate. *Journal of Epidemiology and Community Health*, *58*(6), 441–445. doi:10.1136/jech.2003.013466 PMID:15143107

Bican, P. M., & Brem, A. (2020). Digital Business Model, Digital Transformation, Digital Entrepreneurship: Is There A Sustainable "Digital"? *Sustainability*, *12*(13), 5239. doi:10.3390u12135239

Big Data. (2019). In *Wikipedia*. Retrieved from http:// en.wikipedia.org/ wiki/Bigdata

Biggs, R., Westley, F., & Carpenter, S. (2010). Navigating the Back Loop: Fostering Social Innovation and Transformation in Ecosystem Management. *Ecology and Society*, *15*(2), art9. Advance online publication. doi:10.5751/ES-03411-150209

Billett, S. (2014). The standing of vocational education: Sources of its societal esteem and implications for its enactment. *Journal of Vocational Education and Training*, *66*(1), 1–21. doi:10.1080/13636820.2013.867525

Blackman, A., Ibañez, A. M., Izquierdo, A., Keefer, P., Moreira, M. M., Schady, N., & Serebrisky, T. (2020). *La política pública frente al COVID-19: recomendaciones para América Latina y el Caribe* (Vol. 810). Inter-American Development Bank.

Blanchard, L., Zhao, B., & Yinger, J. (2008). Do lenders discriminate against minority and woman entrepreneurs? *Journal of Urban Economics*, *63*(2), 467–497. doi:10.1016/j.jue.2007.03.001

Blanchflower, D. G., Levine, P. B., & Zimmerman, D. J. (2003). Discrimination in the small-business credit market. *The Review of Economics and Statistics*, *85*(4), 930–943. doi:10.1162/003465303772815835

Blustein, D. L., Duffy, R., Ferreira, J. A., Cohen-Scali, V., Cinamon, R. G., & Allan, B. A. (2020). Unemployment in the time of COVID-19: A research agenda. *Journal of Vocational Behavior*, *119*, 103436. doi:10.1016/j.jvb.2020.103436 PMID:32390656

Boateng, G. O., Boateng, A. A., & Bampoe, H. S. (2014). Barriers to youthful entrepreneurship in rural areas of Ghana. *Global Journal of Business Research*, *8*(3), 109-119.

Boellstorff, T. (2019). The opportunity to contribute: Disability and the digital entrepreneur. *Information Communication and Society*, *22*(4), 474–490. doi:10.1080/1369118X.2018.1472796

Bogan, V., & Darity, W. Jr. (2008). Culture and entrepreneurship? African American and immigrant self-employment in the United States. *Journal of Socio-Economics*, *37*(5), 1999–2019. doi:10.1016/j.socec.2007.10.010

Bögenhold, D., & Klinglmair, A. (2015). Female Solo Self-Employment-Features of Gendered Entrepreneurship. *International Review of Entrepreneurship*, *13*(1).

Bone, J., Gonzalez-Uribe, J., Haley, C., & Laher, H. (2019). *The Impact of Business Accelerators and Incubators in the UK. Department for Business, Energy, and Industrial Strategy*. BEIS.

Bone, S. A., Christensen, G. L., & Williams, J. D. (2014). Rejected, shackled, and alone: The impact of systemic restricted choice on minority consumers' construction of self. *The Journal of Consumer Research*, *41*(2), 451–474. doi:10.1086/676689

Bonilla-Silva, E. (2006). *Racism without racists: Color-blind racism and the persistence of racial inequality in the United States*. Rowman & Littlefield Publishers.

Bonin, S., Singh, W., Suresh, V., Rashed, T., Uppaal, K., Nair, R., & Bhavani, R. R. (2021). A priority action roadmap for women's economic empowerment (PARWEE) amid COVID-19: A co-creation approach. *International Journal of Gender and Entrepreneurship*, *13*(2), 142–161. doi:10.1108/IJGE-09-2020-0148

Bottan, N., Hoffmann, B., & Vera-Cossio, D. (2020). The unequal impact of the coronavirus pandemic: Evidence from seventeen developing countries. *PLoS One*, *15*(10), e0239797. doi:10.1371/journal.pone.0239797 PMID:33027272

Bowlby, J. (1969). Attachment and Loss: Vol. 1. *Attachment*. Penguin.

Bowman, L., Rocco, T. S., Peterson, E., & Adker, W. A. (2009, May). Utilizing the lens of critical race theory to analyze stories of race. In *Proceedings of the 2009 Adult Education Research Conference* (pp. 36-41). Academic Press.

Bradbury, A. (2020). A critical race theory framework for education policy analysis: The case of bilingual learners and assessment policy in England. *Race, Ethnicity and Education*, *23*(2), 241–260. doi:10.1080/13613324.2019.1599338

Bradford, W. D. (2003). The wealth dynamics of entrepreneurship for black and white families in the U.S. *Review of Income and Wealth*, *49*(1), 89–116. doi:10.1111/1475-4991.00076

Braun, V., & Clarke, V. (2006). Using thematic analysis in psychology. *Qualitative Research in Psychology*, *3*(2), 77–101. doi:10.1191/1478088706qp063oa

Bremmer, I. (2020). Six prominent thinkers reflect on how the pandemic has changed the world. International Monetary Fund.

Briscese, G., Lacetera, N., Macis, M., & Tonin, M. (2020). *Compliance with COVID-19 social-distancing measures in Italy: the role of expectations and duration*. https://docs.iza.org/dp13092.pdf

Brooks, K. (2020). *Few minority business owners got Paycheck Protection Program loans, survey shows*. Retrieved June 2, 2020, from https://www.cbsnews.com/news/paycheck-protection-program-black-hispanic-business-owners-shut-out-survey/

Brush, C. G., & Gatewood, E. J. (2008). Women growing businesses: Clearing the hurdles. *Business Horizons*, *51*(3), 175–179. doi:10.1016/j.bushor.2008.01.007

Brush, C., Monti, D., Gannon, A., & Ryan, A. (2006). *Inner city entrepreneurs: Building ventures and expanding community ties*. Babson College, Frontiers of Entrepreneurship Research.

Bruyn, S. T. (1966). *The Human Perspective in Sociology*. Prentice-Hall.

Brzezinski, M. (2018). Income inequality and the Great Recession in Central and Eastern Europe. *Economic Systems*, *42*(2), 219–247. doi:10.1016/j.ecosys.2017.07.003

Bughin, J. (2018). *Skill Shift: Automation and the Future of the Workforce*. McKinsey Global Institute. Retrieved online https://www.mckinsey.com/featured-insights/future-of-work/skill-shift-automation-and-the-future-of-the-workforce

Bungau, C., Borza, A., & Aurel, C. A. U. S. (2018). Comparative studies of indicators defining entrepreneurship culture in Romania. *Acta Technica Napocensis-Series: Applied Mathematics. Mechanical Engineering*, *61*(3).

Burke, J. J. (2014). *Makerspaces: a practical guide for librarians* (Vol. 8). Rowman & Littlefield.

Burt, R. S. (1992). *Structural holes: The social structure of competition*. Harvard University Press. doi:10.4159/9780674029095

BusinessTech. (2020). *Ramaphosa on large vs small companies in South Africa, and how entrepreneurs are finding success in Covid-19.* Available from: https://businesstech.co.za/news/business/417795/ramaphosa-on-large-vs-small-companies-in-south-africa-and-how-entrepreneurs-are-finding-success-in-covid-19/

Buvinić, M., & Furst-Nichols, R. (2016). Promoting women's economic empowerment: What works? *The World Bank Research Observer, 31*(1), 59–101.

Bux, S., & van Vuuren, J. (2019). The effect of entrepreneurship education programmes on the development of self-efficacy, entrepreneurial intention and predictions for entrepreneurial activity. *Acta Commercii, 19*(2), 1–13. doi:10.4102/ac.v19i2.615

Caldeira, M. M., & Ward, J. M. (2003). Using resource-based theory to interpret the successful adoption and use of information systems and technology in manufacturing small and medium-sized enterprises. *European Journal of Information Systems, 12*(2), 127–141. doi:10.1057/palgrave.ejis.3000454

Camilleri, M. A. (2017). The Tourism Industry: An Overview. Doi:10.1007/978-3-319-49849-21

Camilleri. (2017). Corporate sustainability and responsibility: creating value for business, society and the environment. *Asian Journal of Sustainability and Social Responsibility, 2*(1), 59–74. doi:10.1186/s41180-017-0016-5

Campbell, G. (2010). Microfinancing the Developing World: How small loans empower local economies and catalyse neoliberalism's endgame. *Third World Quarterly, 31*(7), 1081–1090. doi:10.1080/01436597.2010.518785

Canlas, I. P., & Karpudewan, M. (2021). Teaching and environmentalism: A deduction from values, beliefs and norms in teaching disaster risk reduction in science. *Research in Science & Technological Education*, 1–22. doi:10.1080/02635143.2021.1978421

Caraballo, M. Á., Dabús, C., & Delbianco, F. (2017). Income inequality and economic growth revisited. A note. *Journal of International Development, 29*(7), 1025–1029. doi:10.1002/jid.3300

Carlson, L. E., & Sullivan, J. F. (2006). A Multi-Disciplinary Design Environment. *ASME 2006 International Design Engineering Technical Conferences and Computers and Information in Engineering Conference, 4c*, 835–840. 10.1115/DETC2006-99148

Carr, D. (1996). Two paths to self-employment? Women's and men's self-employment in the United States, 1980. *Work and Occupations, 23*(1), 26–53. doi:10.1177/0730888496023001003

Carroll, D. (2014). *Enhancement of the Business Environment in the South Mediterranean: National Seminar for Palestine.* The European Union's project for ENP South Countries, EUROPEAID/ 133918/C/SER/MULTI.

Carroll, N., & Conboy, K. (2020). Normalising the "new normal": Changing tech-driven work practices under pandemic time pressure. *International Journal of Information Management, 55*, 102186. doi:10.1016/j.ijinfomgt.2020.102186 PMID:32836643

Cassia, L., & Minola, T. (2012). Hyper-growth of SMEs: Toward a reconciliation of entrepreneurial orientation and strategic resources. *International Journal of Entrepreneurial Behaviour & Research, 18*(2), 179–197. doi:10.1108/13552551211204210

Catalyst for Growth. (2020). *The impact of Covid-19 on African SMMES operations.* Available from: https://www.goethe.de/resources/files/pdf208/c4g-the-impact-of-covid-19-on-african-smmes-operations-online.pdf

Caucutt, E. M., Guner, N., & Rauh, C. (2016). *Is marriage for White people? Incarceration and the racial marriage divide.* Unpublished paper, Department of Economics, Western University.

Cavalluzzo, K. S., Cavalluzzo, L. C., & Wolken, J. D. (2002). Competition, small business financing, and discrimination: Evidence from a new survey. *The Journal of Business*, *75*(4), 641–679. doi:10.1086/341638

Centre of Development Enterprise. (2020). *Impact of COVID-19 on small, medium and micro enterprises since lockdown.* Available from: http://www.nyda.gov.za/Portals/0/downloads/Impact%20of%20COVID_19%20on%20SMMEs_1000_Businesses_100Days%202020_10_01.pdf

Chacha. (2019). *Kenya Economic Update: Securing Future Growth - Policies to Support Kenya's Digital Transformation.* Kenya economic update, no. 20. Washington, DC: World Bank Group. https://documents.worldbank.org/curated/en/968481572468094731/Kenya-Economic-Update-Securing-Future-Growth-Policies-to-Support-Kenya-s-Digital-Transformation

Chair and lannony. (2018). *Youth Deprivation and the Internet in Africa.* Retrieved from https://researchictafrica.net/after-access-survey papers/2018/After_Access:_youth_and_digital_inequality_in_Africa.pdf

Chang, W. J., & Wyszomirski, M. (2015). What is arts entrepreneurship? Tracking the development of its definition in scholarly journals. *Artivate*, *4*(2), 33–31. doi:10.1353/artv.2015.0010

Channing, A., & Sherman, R. (2020). *Who Has Been Hit hardest by the South Africa's Lockdown: Working paper.* Braamfontein: The Conversation. https://theconversation.com/who-has-been-hit-hardest-by-south-africas-lockdown-we-found-some-answers-138481

Charlton, E. (2021). *40% of all projected job opportunities will be created in this sector. And it's not technology.* World Economic Forum. Retrieved from https://www.weforum.org/ agenda/2021/05/care-economy-emerging-job-opportunities/#:~:text=Shifting%20demographics%20are%20leading%20to,nursing%2C%20therapy%20and%20personal%20trainers

Chatterjee, S., Chaudhuri, R., Vrontis, D., & Basile, G. (2021). Digital transformation and entrepreneurship process in SMEs of India: a moderating role of adoption of AI-CRM capability and strategic planning. *Journal of Strategy and Management.*

Chen, M. A. (2012), *The Informal Economy: Definitions, Theories and Policies* [Working Paper No. 1]. Women in Informal Employment: Globalizing and Organizing (WIEGO). http://www.wiego.org

Chen, M. A. (2001). Women and Informality: A Global Picture, the Global Movement. *SAIS Review (Paul H. Nitze School of Advanced International Studies)*, *21*(1), 71–82. doi:10.1353ais.2001.0007

Chernenko, S., & Scharfstein, D. S. (2022). Racial disparities in the paycheck protection program (No.w29748). National Bureau of Economic Research.

Chernoff, A. W., & Warman, C. (2020). *COVID-19 and Implications for Automation.* National Bureau of Economic Research Working Papers 27249. Retrieved from: https://www.nber.org/system/files/working_papers/w27249/w27249.pdf

Cherns, A. (1976). The Principles of Sociotechnical Design. *Human Relations*, *29*(8), 783–792. doi:10.1177/001872677602900806

Chertkovskaya, E., Alakavuklar, O. N., Husted, E., & Rácz, M. (2020). Reconfiguring work and organizing for post-pandemic futures. *Ephemera*, *20*(4), 1–18.

Chesbrough, H. W. (2003). *Open Innovation.* Harvard Business Press.

Chiloane-Tsoka, G. E., & Mmako, N. M. (2014). Effects of migration and immigration on SMMEs: The case study of Diepsloot informal settlement, South Africa. *Problems and Perspectives in Management*, *12*(4), 377–383.

Chiteji, N. S., & Hamilton, D. (2002). Family connections and the black-white wealth gap among middle-class families. *The Review of Black Political Economy*, *30*(1), 9–28. doi:10.1007/BF02808169

Choudhury, S. R. (2020). *How technology helped Asian countries cope in the coronavirus pandemic.* CNBC Online. https://www.cnbc.com/2020/05/13/coronavirus-mckinsey-says-technology-helping-asia-cope-better.html

Christensen, C. M., & Raynor, M. E. (2003). *The Innovator's Solution: Creating and Sustaining Successful Growth.* Harvard Business School Press.

Chuang, L.-M. (2007). The Social Psychology of Creativity and Innovation: Process Theory (Pt) Perspective. *Social Behavior and Personality*, *35*(7), 875–888. doi:10.2224bp.2007.35.7.875

Chun, H. K., Comyn, P., & Moreno da Fonseca, P. (2021). *Skills development in the time of COVID-19: taking stock of the initial responses in technical and vocational education and training.* https://www.ilo.org/wcmsp5/groups/public/---ed_emp/---ifp_skills/documents/publication/wcms_766557.pdf

CIPE. (2021). *Effects of COVID-19 on Youth Entrepreneurs.* Available from: https://www.cipe.org/blog/2021/07/22/effects-of-covid-19-on-youth-entrepreneurs/

Citi G. P. S. Global Perspectives & Solutions (2020). *Closing the Racial Inequity Gaps: The Economic Cost of Racial Inequality in the U.S.* https://ir.citi.com/NvIUklHPilz14Hwd3oxqZBLMn1_XPqo5FrxsZD0x6hhil84ZxaxEuJUWmak51UHvYk75VKeHCMI%3D

Clare, E. (1999). *Exile and Pride: Disability, Queerness and Liberation.* South End Press.

Clarke, A., & MacDonald, A. (2019). Outcomes to partners in multi-stakeholder cross-sector partnerships: A resource-based view. *Business & Society*, *58*(2), 298–332. doi:10.1177/0007650316660534

Clark, R., Lusardi, A., Mitchell, O. S., & Davis, H. (2021). Factors contributing to financial well-being among Black and Hispanic women. *The Journal of Retirement*, *9*(1), 71–97. doi:10.3905/jor.2021.1.088

Clark, W. C., van Kerkhoff, L., Lebel, L., & Gallopin, G. C. (2016, April 26). Crafting Usable Knowledge for Sustainable Development. *Proceedings of the National Academy of Sciences of the United States of America*, *113*(17), 4570–4578. doi:10.1073/pnas.1601266113 PMID:27091979

Cluadia, S., Maritz, A., & Nguyen, Q. (2019). Entrepreneurial Ecosystems: A Holistic and Dynamic Approach. *Journal of Industry-University Collaboration*, *1*(2), 79–95. doi:10.1108/JIUC-03-2019-0007

Cockshaw, W. D., Shochet, I. M., & Obst, P. L. (2014). Depression and Belongingness in General and Workplace Contexts: A Cross-Lagged Longitudinal Investigation. *Journal of Social and Clinical Psychology*, *33*(5), 448–462. doi:10.1521/jscp.2014.33.5.448

Cohen, P. J., Lawless, S., Dyer, M., Morgan, M., Saeni, E., Teioli, H., & Kantor, P. (2016). Understanding adaptive capacity and capacity to innovate in social–ecological systems: Applying a gender lens. *Ambio*, *45*(S3), 309–321. doi:10.100713280-016-0831-4 PMID:27878535

Coleman, J. S. (1994). *Foundations of social theory.* Harvard University Press.

Coleman, S. (2005). The impact of human capital measures on firm performance: A comparison by gender, race and ethnicity. *The Journal of Entrepreneurial Finance*, *10*(2), 38–56.

Coleman, S. (2005). The Impact of Human Capital Measures on Firm Performance: A Comparison by Gender, Race and Ethnicity. *The Journal of Entrepreneurial Finance*, *10*(2), 38–56.

Coley, C., Sheshadri, S., Devanathan, S., & Bhavani, R. R. (2021). Contextualizing women's empowerment frameworks with an emphasis on social support: A study in rural, South India. *Community Work & Family*, 1–20. doi:10.1080/13668803.2021.1879021

Conyers, A., & Wright Fields, C. (2021). A Critical Race Theory Analysis of Institutional Racial Paralysis in Organizational Culture. *Public Integrity*, *23*(5), 484–495. doi:10.1080/10999922.2020.1832365

Corner, P., Singh, S., & Pavlovich, K. (2017). Entrepreneurial resilience and venture failure. *International Small Business Journal: Researching Entrepreneurship*, *35*(6), 687–708. doi:10.1177/0266242616685604

Cotnam, H. (n.d.). *Wash and fold: Pandemic forcing local laundromats out of business.* CBC. Retrieved from: https://www.cbc.ca/news/canada/ottawa/covid-19-laundry-dry-cleaning-pandemic-economic-pressure-1.6027247

COVID-19 Impact and the future of small business. (2021, March 19). *SCORE Association.* Retrieved from: https://www.score.org/blog/covid-19-impact-and-future-small-business

Cowley, S. (2022) *Little of the Paycheck Protection Program's $800 Billion Protected Paychecks.* Retrieved February 4, 2020 from, https://www.nytimes.com/2022/02/01/business/paycheck-protection-program-costs.html

Crenshaw, K., Gotanda, N., Peller, G., & Thomas, K. (1995). Critical race theory. The Key Writings that formed the Movement. Academic Press.

Cressey, D. R. (1953). *Other People's Money.* Free Press.

Creswell, J. W., & Poth, C. N. (2017). *Qualitative inquiry and research design: Choosing among five approaches.* Sage Publications.

Cross, J. C. (2000). Street vendors, modernity and postmodernity: Conflict and compromise in the global economy. *The International Journal of Sociology and Social Policy*, *20*(1/2), 29–51. doi:10.1108/01443330010789061

Crump, M. E. S. (2013). Black entrepreneurship: Formal versus informal economy exploitation. *Washington Business Research Journal*, *3*(1), 85–111.

Crump, M. E. S., Hill, N. J., & Tayor, P. G. (2017). Examining minority population and the impact of informal economy activity on collected revenues in U.S. cities. *Washington Business Research Journal*, *7*(1), 6–41.

Crump, M. E. S., Singh, R. P., & Wilbon, A. D. (2009). Assessing the black entrepreneurship literature: What's known, and who's informing? *Washington Business Research Journal*, *1*(1), 101–116.

Crump, M. E. S., Singh, R. P., Wilbon, A. D., & Gibbs, S. R. (2015). Socio-demographic differences of black versus white entrepreneurs. *Academy of Entrepreneurship Journal*, *21*(1), 115–129.

C-SPAN (Producer). (2020). *Books and Books Bookstore on the continued impact of COVID-19.* Retrieved from: https://www.c-span.org/video/?474512-1/books-books-bookstore-continued-impact-covid-19

Dahl, M. S., & Sorenson, O. (2009). The Embedded Entrepreneur. *European Management Review*, *6*(3), 172–181. doi:10.1057/emr.2009.14

Dana, L.-P., Tajpour, M., Salamzadeh, A., Hosseini, E., & Zolfaghari, M. (2021). The impact of entrepreneurial education on technology-based enterprises development: The mediating role of motivation. *Administrative Sciences*, *11*(4), 105. doi:10.3390/admsci11040105

Danes, S. M., Lee, J., Amarapurkar, S., Stafford, K., Haynes, G., & Brewton, K. E. (2009). Determinants of family business resilience after a natural disaster by gender of business owner. *Journal of Developmental Entrepreneurship*, *14*(04), 333–354. doi:10.1142/S1084946709001351

Darity, W. (2005). Stratification economics: The role of intergroup inequality. *Journal of Economics and Finance*, *29*(2), 144–153. doi:10.1007/BF02761550

Darity, W. A. Jr, Hamilton, D., & Stewart, J. B. (2015). A tour de force in understanding intergroup inequality: An introduction to stratification economics. *The Review of Black Political Economy*, *42*(1-2), 1–6. doi:10.100712114-014-9201-2

Davidsson, P., & Honig, B. (2003). The Role of Social and Human Capital Among Nascent Entrepreneurs. *Journal of Business Venturing*, *18*(3), 301–331. doi:10.1016/S0883-9026(02)00097-6

de Groot, H. L. F., de Dominicis, L., & Florax, R. J. G. M. (2008). Growth and Inequality: A Meta-Analysis. *Scottish Journal of Political Economy*, *55*(5), 654–682. doi:10.1111/j.1467-9485.2008.00470.x

de Lucas Ancillo, A., Teresa del Val Núñez, M., & Gavrila Gavrila, S. (2021). Workplace change within the COVID-19 context: A grounded theory approach. *Economic Research-Ekonomska Istraživanja*, *34*(1), 2297–2316. doi:10.1080/1331677X.2020.1862689

De Soto, H. (1989). *The other path: The invisible revolution in the third world.* Tauris.

De Stefano, V. (2015). The rise of the just-in-time workforce: On-demand work, crowdwork, and labor protection in the gig-economy. *Comp. Lab. L. & Pol'y J.*, *37*, 471.

De Wit, G., & De Kok, J. (2014). Do small businesses create more jobs? New evidence for Europe. *Small Business Economics*, *42*(2), 283–295. doi:10.100711187-013-9480-1

De', R., Pandey, N., & Pal, A. (2020). Impact of digital surge during Covid-19 pandemic: A viewpoint on research and practice. *International Journal of Information Management*, *55*, 102171. https://doi.org/10.1016/j.ijinfomgt.2020.102171

Dees, J. G. (2018). The Meaning of Social Entrepreneurship 1, 2. In *Case Studies in Social Entrepreneurship and Sustainability* (pp. 22–30). Routledge. doi:10.4324/9781351278560-5

Deichmann, U., Goyal, A., & Mishra, D. (2016). Will digital technologies transform agriculture in developing countries? *Agricultural Economics*, *47*(S1), 21–33. doi:10.1111/agec.12300

DeJaeghere, J., & Baxter, A. (2014). Entrepreneurship education for youth in sub-Saharan Africa: A capability approach as an alternative framework to neoliberalism's individualizing risks. *Progress in Development Studies*, *14*(1), 61–76. doi:10.1177/1464993413504353

Delgado, R., & Stefancic, J. (2017). Critical race theory. In *Critical Race Theory* (3rd ed.). New York University Press.

Dépelteau, F. (2018). Relational Thinking in Sociology: Relevance, Concurrence and Dissonance. In F. Dépelteau (Ed.), *The Palgrave Handbook of Relational Sociology*. Palgrave Macmillan. doi:10.1007/978-3-319-66005-9_1

Desai, S., Looze, J., & Pechenina, A. (2020). *Student Loans and Entrepreneurship: An Overview. Entrepreneurship Issue Brief. No. 5*. Ewing Marion Kauffman Foundation.

Dettling, L. J. (2017). *Recent Trends in Wealth-Holding by Race and Ethnicity: Evidence from the Survey of Consumer Finances.* Retrieved November 20, 2018, from https://www.federalreserve.gov/econres/notes/feds-notes/recent-trends-in-wealth-holding-by-race-and-ethnicity-evidence-from-the-survey-of-consumer-finances-20170927.htm

Di Crosta, A., Ceccato, I., Marchetti, D., La Malva, P., Maiella, R., Cannito, L., Cipi, M., Mammarella, N., Palumbo, R., Verrocchio, M. C., Palumbo, R., & Di Domenico, A. (2021). Psychological factors and consumer behavior during the COVID-19 pandemic. *PLoS One*, *16*(8), e0256095. doi:10.1371/journal.pone.0256095 PMID:34398916

Diniso, C. (2020). *Youth entrepreneurship in South Africa: A progressive review*. Available from: https://www.researchgate.net/publication/351249747_YOUTH_ENTREPRENEURSHIP_IN_SOUTH_AFRICA_A_PROGRESS_REVIEW

Diraditsile, K., & Maphula, P. (2018). Entrepreneurship as a mechanism for addressing youth unemployment in Botswana: A reality or idealism? *International Journal of Development and Sustainability*, *7*(3), 836–847.

Dladla, L. G. (2020). The Economics of the Covid-19 Pandemic and its Effects on Small Businesses in South Africa. *Asian Journal of Social Sciences Review*, *2*(2).

Doherty, E. (2012). *Broadband adoption and diffusion: a study of Irish SMEs* [PhD Thesis]. Ulster University Coleraine.

Dorado, S., Giles, D. E. Jr, & Welch, T. C. (2009). Delegation of coordination and outcomes in cross-sector partnerships: The case of service-learning partnerships. *Nonprofit and Voluntary Sector Quarterly*, *38*(3), 368–391. doi:10.1177/0899764008316055

Downing, J., & Daniels, L. (1992). *The growth and dynamics of women entrepreneurs in Southern Africa* [GEMINI Technical Report No. 47]. United States Agency for International Development.

Draxler, A. (2008). *New Partnerships for EFA: Building on Experience*: ERIC. http://efaidnbmnnnibpcajpcglclefindmkaj/viewer.html?pdfurl=https%3A%2F%2Ffiles.eric.ed.gov%2Ffulltext%2FED499733.pdf&clen=1247609

Dreher, A., & Schneider, F. (2010). Corruption and the shadow economy: An empirical analysis. *Public Choice*, *144*(1/2), 215–238. doi:10.100711127-009-9513-0

Dreyfus, H. L., & Dreyfus, H. L. (1980). *A Five-stage Model of the Mental Activities Involved in Directed Skill Acquisition*. Amsterdam University Press. doi:10.21236/ADA084551

Dreyfus, H., Dreyfus, S. E., & Athanasiou, T. (2000). *Mind over machine*. Simon and Schuster.

Drinkwater, S., Lashley, J. G., & Robinson, C. (2018). Barriers to enterprise development in the Caribbean. *Entrepreneurship and Regional Development*, *30*(9/10), 942–963. doi:10.1080/08985626.2018.1515821

DTI. (2013). *Youth Enterprise Development Strategy*. Available from: https://www.ilembechamber.co.za/wp-content/uploads/2017/12/Youth-EnterpriseDevelopment-Strategy-2013-2023.pdf

DTI. (2013). *Youth Enterprise Development Strategy*. Available from: https://www.ilembechamber.co.za/wp-content/uploads/2017/12/Youth-Enterprise-Development-Strategy-2013-2023.pdf

Dua, A., Ellingrud, K., Mahajan, D., & Silberg, J. (2020). *Which small businesses are most vulnerable to COVID-19—and when.* McKinsey & Company. Retrieved from: https://www.mckinsey.com/industries/public-and-social-sector/our-insights/us-small-business-recovery-after-the-covid-19-crisis

Dua, A., Mahajan, D., Oyer, L., & Ramaswamy, S. (2020). *US small-business recovery after the COVID-19 crisis.* McKinsey & Company. Retrieved from: https://www.mckinsey.com/industries/public-and-social-sector/our-insights/us-small-business-recovery-after-the-covid-19-crisis

Dube, K. (2021). Implications of COVID-19 Induced Lockdown on the South African Tourism Industry and Prospects for Recovery. *African Journal of Hospitality, Tourism and Leisure*, *10*(1), 270–287. doi:10.46222/ajhtl.19770720-99

Dubini, P. (1989). The Influence of Motivations and Environment on Business Start-Ups: Some Hints For Public Policies. *Journal of Business Venturing*, *4*(1), 11–26. doi:10.1016/0883-9026(89)90031-1

Duflos, E., & Imboden, K. (2004). The role of governments in microfinance. Academic Press.

Dunfey, T. S. (2019). *What is Social Change and Why Should We Care?* Southern New Hampshire University.

Dunn, T., & Holtz-Eakin, D. (2000). Financial capital, human capital, and the transition to self-employment: Evidence from intergenerational links. *Journal of Labor Economics*, *18*(2), 282–305. doi:10.1086/209959

Dyer, W. G., Nenque, E., & Hill, E. J. (2014). Toward a theory of family capital and entrepreneurship: Antecedents and outcomes. *Journal of Small Business Management*, *52*(2), 266–285. doi:10.1111/jsbm.12097

Dzeto, G. K. (2014). *Projecting Ghana into the real middle-income economy: the role of Technical, Vocational Training*. Parliamentary Briefing Paper, Friedrich Ebert Stiftung. http://library.fes.de/pdf-files/bueros/ghana/11300.pdf

Dzomonda, O., & Fatoki, O. (2019). The role of institutions of higher learning towards youth entrepreneurship development in South Africa. *Academy of Entrepreneurship Journal*, *25*(1), 1–11.

East Africa Development Ban. (2020). *How Rwanda is spurring a generation of women in technology*. Retrieved form https://etradeforall.org/news/adb-how-rwanda-is-spurring-a-generation-of-women-in-technology/?lang=es

Ebewo, P. E., Rugimbana, R., & Shambare, R. (2017). Effects of entrepreneurship education on students' entrepreneurial intentions: A case of Botswana. *Management Studies*, *5*(4), 278–289.

Economic and Social Commission for Asia and the Pacific. (2017). *Women's entrepreneurship: lessons and good practice*. United Nations Publication. https://www.unescap.org/sites/default/files/ASEAN%20women%E2%80%99s%20entrepreneurship%20case%20studies.pdf

Edgcomb, E. L., & Thetford, T. (2004). *The Informal Economy: Making it in Rural America*. Aspen Institute.

Edomwonyi, J., Osasogie, H., & Olaita, E. (2016). *Actualizing Sustainable High Standard of Quality in Nigerian TVET Programme Through Multi-Stakeholders Partnership*. Academic Press.

Ehrbeck, T., Pickens, M., & Tarazi, M. (2012). *Financially Inclusive Ecosystems: The roles of government today*. Academic Press.

Elahi, N., & Malik, Q. A. (2021). *Assessing the environmental and social obstacles to women entrepreneurs: a case study of Pakistan. In Women Empowerment and Well-Being for Inclusive Economic Growth*. IGI Global. doi:10.4018/978-1-7998-3737-4.ch006

Emery, F. (1959). *Some characteristics of sociotechnical systems*. Document # 527. London: Tavistock Institute.

Engel, A. (2018). Why Does Culture 'Eat Strategy For Breakfast'? *Forbes*. http://www. forbes.com/sites/forbescoaches-council/2018/11/20/why-does-culture-eat-strategy-for-breakfast

Erel, I., & Liebersohn, J. (2020). Does fintech substitute for banks? evidence from the paycheck protection program (No. w27659). National Bureau of Economic Research.

Eurostat Statistics Explained. (2021). *Culture statistics - cultural employment*. https://ec.europa.eu/eurostat/statistics-explained/index.php?title=Culture_statistics_-_cultural_employment

Fairlie, R. W. (2020). The Impact of Covid-19 on Small Business Owners: Evidence of Early-Stage Losses from the April 2020 Current Population Survey (No. w27309). National Bureau of Economic Research.

Fairlie, R. W., & Fossen, F. (2021). Did the $660 Billion Paycheck Protection Program and $220 Billion Economic Injury Disaster Loan Program Get Disbursed to Minority Communities in the Early Stages of COVID-19? (No. w28321). National Bureau of Economic Research.

Fairlie, R. W., & Robb, A. M. (2008). Race and entrepreneurial success. Academic Press.

Fairlie, R. (2020). The impact of COVID-19 on small business owners: Evidence from the first three months after widespread social-distancing restrictions. *Journal of Economics & Management Strategy*, *29*(4), 727–740. doi:10.1111/jems.12400 PMID:32904856

Fairlie, R. W. (1999). The absence of the African-American owned business: An analysis of the dynamics of self-employment. *Journal of Labor Economics*, *17*(1), 80–108. doi:10.1086/209914

Fairlie, R. W. (2004). Recent trends in ethnic and racial business ownership. *Small Business Economics*, *23*(3), 203–218. doi:10.1023/B:SBEJ.0000032031.28403.31

Fairlie, R. W. (2005). Entrepreneurship and earnings among young adults from disadvantaged families. *Small Business Economics*, *25*(3), 223–236. doi:10.100711187-003-6457-5

Fairlie, R. W. (2012). Immigrant entrepreneurs and small business owners, and their access to financial capital. *Small Business Administration*, *396*, 1–46.

Fairlie, R. W., & Fossen, F. M. (2020). *Defining opportunity versus necessity entrepreneurship: Two components of business creation*. Emerald Publishing Limited.

Fairlie, R. W., & Robb, A. M. (2007). Why are black-owned businesses less successful than white-owned businesses? The role of families, inheritances, and business human capital. *Journal of Labor Economics*, *25*(2), 289–323. doi:10.1086/510763

Fairlie, R. W., & Robb, A. M. (2009). Gender differences in business performance: Evidence from the Characteristics of Business Owners survey. *Small Business Economics*, *33*(4), 375–395. doi:10.100711187-009-9207-5

Fairlie, R. W., & Robb, A. M. (2014). *Race and entrepreneurial success black-, asian-, and white-owned businesses in the United States*. MIT Press.

Fairlie, R. W., Robb, A. M., & Hinson, D. (2010). *Disparities in Capital Access Between Minority and Non-minority-owned Businesses*. US Department of Commerce, Minority Business Development Agency.

Fairlie, R., & Desai, S. (2021). *National report on early-stage entrepreneurship in the United States: 2020*. Kauffman Indicators of Entrepreneurship, Ewing Marion Kauffman Foundation.

Farrell, K., & Farrell, L. C. (2001). *Entrepreneurial Age*. Allworth Press.

Fatoki, O., & Chindoga, L. (2011). An investigation into the obstacles to youth entrepreneurship in South Africa. *International Business Research*, *4*(2), 161–169. doi:10.5539/ibr.v4n2p161

Faulkner, S. L., & Trotter, S. P. (2017). Data saturation. In J. Matthes, S. C. Davis, & R. F. Potter (Eds.), The International Encyclopedia of Communication Research Methods (pp. 1–2). doi:10.1002/9781118901731.iecrm0060

Fayolle, A., & Gailly, B. (2015). The Impact of Entrepreneurship Education on Entrepreneurial Attitudes and Intention: Hysteresis and Persistence. *Journal of Small Business Management*, *53*(1), 75–93. doi:10.1111/jsbm.12065

Feagin, J. R., & Imani, N. (1994). Racial barriers to African American entrepreneurship: An exploratory study. *Social Problems*, *41*(4), 562–584. doi:10.2307/3096989

Fearnow, B. (2018, July 10). *Black Women Graduate With Most U.S. Student Loan Debt, Study Says*. https://www.newsweek.com/student-loans-pay-gap-college-debt-black-women-white-men-women-gender-gap-1016776

Federal Republic of Nigeria (FRN). (2013). *National Policy on Education*. NERDC Press.

Fehder, D. (2015). *Startup Accelerators and Ecosystem: Substitutes or Compliments?* Working paper. http://danielfehder.com/wpcontent/uploads/2015/10/Fehder_Accel_Ecosystem. pdf

Feigenbaum, E. (2020). *A New Desire, Authenticity and transparency supersede hard-sell aspirational marketing*. VMSD Magazine.

Fennell, S. (2010). Public-private partnerships and educational outcomes: New conceptual and methodological approaches. *RECOUP Working Paper, 37*(3). https://ceid.educ.cam.ac.uk/researchprogrammes/recoup/publications/workingpapers/WP37-PPP_and_Educational_Outcomes.pdf

Fetzer, T. R., Witte, M., Hensel, L., Jachimowicz, J., Haushofer, J., Ivchenko, A., ... Yoeli, E. (2020). *Global Behaviors and Perceptions at the Onset of the COVID-19 Pandemic* (No. w27082). National Bureau of Economic Research. doi:10.3386/w27082

Feyen, E., Frost, J., Gambacorta, L., Natarajan, H., & Saal, M. (2021). *Fintech and the digital transformation of financial services:Impliccations for market structure and Public Policy*. World Bank and BIS.

Fike, R. (2017). Adjusting for gender disparity in economic freedom and why it matters. In J. Gwartney, R. Lawson, & J. Hall (Eds.), *Economic Freedom of the World: 2017 Annual Report*. Fraser Institute.

Fineberg, H. V. (2014). Pandemic Preparedness and Response— Lessons from the H1N1 Influenza of 2009. *The New England Journal of Medicine, 370*(14), 1335–1342. doi:10.1056/NEJMra1208802 PMID:24693893

Forbes. (2016). *Black women are the fastest-growing group of entrepreneurs in the U.S.* Accessed from http://www.forbes.com/sites/clareoconnor/2016/02/17/inside-one-woman-investors-plan-to-get-black-female-founders-funding/#18614f132837

Forbes, K. J. (2000). A reassessment of the relationship between inequality and growth. *The American Economic Review, 90*(4), 869–887. doi:10.1257/aer.90.4.869

Forcher-Mayr, M., & Mahlknecht, S. (2020). Critical Entrepreneurship Education in General Education and TVET: Two Concepts of Practice in a South African Township. *Discourse and Communication for Sustainable Education, 11*(2), 65–84. doi:10.2478/dcse-2020-0019

Forman, J. (2007). Damschroder L Qualitative content analysis. In *Empirical methods for bioethics: A primer* (pp. 39–62). Emerald Group Publishing Limited. doi:10.1016/S1479-3709(07)11003-7

Foss, N. J. (2020b). Behavioral Strategy and the COVID-19 Disruption. *Journal of Management, 46*(8), 1322–1329. doi:10.1177/0149206320945015

Fowle, M. (2019). The entrepreneurial dream: Happiness, depression and freedom. *International Review of Entrepreneurship, 17*(3), 305–322.

Fox, M. (2021, May 19). *Here's how these small businesses pivoted to survive during the pandemic*. CNBC. https://www.cnbc.com/2021/05/19/heres-how-these-small-businesses-pivoted-to-survive-during-the-pandemic.html

Fox, Z., Zain, T., Thomas, L., & Palicpic, C. (2019, July 25). *Bank brand closures take greatest toll on majority-black areas*. Retrieved on June 2, 2020 from, https://www.spglobal.com/marketintelligence/en/news-insights/latest-news-headlines/bank-branch-closures-take-greatest-toll-on-majority-black-areas-52872925

Franck, A. K. (2012). Factors motivating women's informal micro-entrepreneurship. *International Journal of Gender and Entrepreneurship, 4*(1), 65–78. doi:10.1108/17566261211202981

Franken, R. E. (1998). *Human Motivation*. Books/Cole Publishing Company.

Frank, M. W. (2009). Inequality and growth in the United States: Evidence from a new state-level panel of income inequality measures. *Economic Inquiry, 47*(1), 55–68. doi:10.1111/j.1465-7295.2008.00122.x

Fraser, N. (2003). Social justice in the age of identity politics: Redistribution, recognition and participation. In N. Fraser & A. Honneth (Eds.), Redistribution. Academic Press.

Fratoe, F. A. (1988). Social capital of black business owners. *The Review of Black Political Economy*, *16*(4), 33–50. doi:10.1007/BF02892164

Freeman, M., Staudenmaier, P., Zisser, M., & Andresen, L. (2018). The prevalence and co-occurrence of psychiatric conditions among entrepreneurs and their families. *Small Business Economics*, *53*(2), 323–342. doi:10.100711187-018-0059-8

Frey, C., & Osborne, M. (2017, September 17). *The future of employment: How susceptible are jobs to computerization?* Oxford Martin School, University of Oxford.

Frey, C. B., & Osborne, M. A. (2013). *The future of employment: how susceptible are jobs to computerisation?* Oxford University Engineering Sciences Department and the Oxford Martin Programme on the Impacts of Future Technology.

Friedman, M. (1970). The Social Responsibility Of Business Is to Increase Its Profits. *New York Times*.

Fuller, J. B., Wallenstein, J. K., Raman, M., & de Chalendar, A. (2019). Your workforce is more adaptable than you think. *Harvard Business Review*, *97*(3), 118–126.

Fusch, P. I., & Ness, L. R. (2015). Are we there yet? Data saturation in qualitative research. *Qualitative Report*, *20*(9), 1408–1416. doi:10.46743/2160-3715/2015.2281

Gagnon, P. L. (2019). *Collaborative research on community engagement in TVET*. https://unevoc.unesco.org/home/UNEVOC+Publications/lang=en/akt=detail/qs=6145

Galvão, A. R., Marques, C. S., Ferreira, J. J., & Braga, V. (2020). Stakeholders' role in entrepreneurship education and training programmes with impacts on regional development. *Journal of Rural Studies*, *74*, 169–179. doi:10.1016/j.jrurstud.2020.01.013

Gamede, B. T., & Uleanya, C. (2019). Factors impacting entrepreneurship education in TVET colleges: A case of South Africa. *Journal of Entrepreneurship Education*, *22*(3), 1–12. https://www.proquest.com/scholarly-journals/factors-impacting-entrepreneurship-education-tvet/docview/2331183669/se-2?accountid=36534

García, J. J., Gee, G. C., & Jones, M. (2016). A critical race theory analysis of public park features in Latino immigrant neighborhoods. *Du Bois Review*, *13*(2), 397–411. doi:10.1017/S1742058X16000187

Garcia-Penalosa, C., & Turnovsky, S. J. (2006). Growth and income inequality: A canonical model. *Economic Theory*, *28*(1), 25–49. doi:10.100700199-005-0616-7

Gartner Inc. (2020, April 3). *Garner CFO survey reveals 74% intend to shift some employees to remote work permanently* [Press release]. Retrieved from: https://www.gartner.com/en/newsroom/press-releases/2020-04-03-gartner-cfo-surey-reveals-74-percent-of-organizations-to-shift-some-employees-to-remote-work-permanently2

Garvin, D. A. (1987). Competing on the eight dimensions of quality. *Harvard Business Review*.

Gawel, A. (2021). The gender-based attainment of education and female entrepreneurship: The European perspective. *Entrepreneurship and Sustainability Issues*, *8*(4), 403–417. doi:10.9770/jesi.2021.8.4(24)

Gawel, A., & Głodowska, A. (2021). On the relationship between economic dynamics and female entrepreneurship: Reflections for the visegrad countries. *Administrative Sciences*, *11*(3), 88. doi:10.3390/admsci11030088

Gaynor, T. S., & Wilson, M. E. (2020). Social vulnerability and equity: The disproportionate impact of COVID-19. *Public Administration Review*, *80*(5), 832–838. doi:10.1111/puar.13264 PMID:32836465

George, T. (2021). *Exploratory Research | Definition, Guide, & Examples* [Blog]. https://www.scribbr.com/methodology/exploratory-research/

George, G., Merrill, R. K., & Schillebeeckx, S. J. (2021). Digital sustainability and entrepreneurship: How digital innovations are helping tackle climate change and sustainable development. *Entrepreneurship Theory and Practice*, *45*(5), 999–1027. doi:10.1177/1042258719899425

Gerda, L. (1986). *The Creation of Patriarchy*. Oxford University Press.

Germak, A., & Robinson, J. A. (2013). Exploring the Motivation of Nascent Social Entrepreneurs. *Journal of Social Entrepreneurship*, *5*(1), 5–21. doi:10.1080/19420676.2013.820781

Gholami, M., & Al Tahoo, L. (2021). Investigating the Influence of Entrepreneurship on Entrepreneur's Life. *International Journal of Business Ethics and Governance*, 69-95.

Ghosh, N. (2021). De-mystifying the Role of Emotions in Decision-making Sciences- A new HRD indicator dimension. *International Journal of Human Capital and Information Technology Professionals*, *12*(4), 46–64. doi:10.4018/IJHCITP.2021100104

Ghosh, N., & Rajaram, G. (2015). Developing Emotional intelligence for Entrepreneurs: Role of entrepreneurship development programs. *South Asian Journal of Management*, *22*(4), 85–100.

Giandhari, J., Pillay, S., Wilkinson, E., Tegally, H., Sinayskiy, I., Schuld, M., Lourenço, J., Chimukangara, B., Lessells, R., Moosa, Y., Gazy, I., Fish, M., Singh, L., Sedwell Khanyile, K., Fonseca, V., Giovanetti, M., Carlos Junior Alcantara, L., Petruccione, F., & de Oliveira, T. (2021). Early transmission of SARS-CoV-2 in South Africa: An epidemiological and phylogenetic report. *International Journal of Infectious Diseases*, *103*, 234–241. doi:10.1016/j.ijid.2020.11.128 PMID:33189939

Gibb, A. (2008). Entrepreneurship and enterprise education in schools and colleges: Insights from UK practice. *International Journal of Entrepreneurship Education*, *6*(2), 1–48.

Gibbs, S. R., Mahone, C., & Crump, M. E. S. (2013). A framework for informal economy entry: Socio-spatial, necessity-opportunity, and structural-based factors. *Academy of Entrepreneurship Journal*, *20*(2), 61–85.

Gibson, H., & Rochelle, S. (2021). *Want to Build Better Leaders?* Focus on Mindset, Skills, Knowledge. Op-Ed Harvard Business School.

Gillborn, D. (2005). Education policy as an act of white supremacy: Whiteness, critical race theory and education reform. *Journal of Education Policy*, *20*(4), 485–505. doi:10.1080/02680930500132346

Gillborn, D. (2014, January). Racism as policy: A critical race analysis of education reforms in the United States and England. *The Educational Forum*, *78*(1), 26–41. doi:10.1080/00131725.2014.850982

Gines, D. (2017). *Black women business startups*. Retrieved November 20, 2018, from https://www.kansascityfed.org/~/media/40186481e0ce43a39255752080d4916b.ashx

Gines, D. (2018). *Black women business startups*. The Federal Reserve Bank of Kansas City.

Gkorezis, P., Kalampouka, P., & Petridou, E. (2013). The Mediating Role of Belongingness in the Relationship between Workplace Incivility and Thriving. *International Journal of Employment Studies*, *21*(2), 63–78.

Global Entrepreneurship Monitor (GEM). (2019). *GEM 2018/2019 global report*. Available at: https:// www.gemconsortium.org/report/gem-2018-2019-global-report

Gnanasambandam, C., Harrysson, M., Srivastava, S., & Wu, Y. (2017). *Product managers for the digital world*. McKinsey and Company. Retrieved from https:// www.mckinsey.com /industries /technology -media-and- telecommunications / our-insights/product-managers-for-the-digital-world

Gnyawali, D. R., & Fogel, D. S. (1994). Environments for Entrepreneurship Development: Key Dimensions and Research Implications. *Entrepreneurship Theory and Practice*, *18*(4), 43–46. doi:10.1177/104225879401800403

Golesorkhi, L.-Z., Fortson, G., Harder, K., & Riedmann, T. (2022). Centering community in COVID-19 responses: Refugee women's livelihoods in a global pandemic. *The International Journal of Sociology and Social Policy*, *42*(3/4), 289–297. doi:10.1108/IJSSP-07-2020-0332

Gompers, P. A., & Wang, S. Q. (2017). *Diversity in Innovation*. National Bureau of Economic Research.

Goodell, J. W. (2020). COVID-19 and finance: Agendas for future research. *Finance Research Letters*, *35*(1). Advance online publication. doi:10.1016/j.frl.2020.101512

Gordon, R. H. (2000). Taxation of capital income vs labour income: an overview. In S. Cnossen (Ed.), *Taxing Capital Income in the European Union: Issues and Options for Reform*. Oxford University Press.

Gotanda, N. (1991). A critique of our constitution is color-blind. *Stanford Law Review*, *44*(1), 1. doi:10.2307/1228940

Graham, L., Brown-Jeffy, S., Aronson, R., & Stephens, C. (2011). Critical race theory as theoretical framework and analysis tool for population health research. *Critical Public Health*, *21*(1), 81–93. doi:10.1080/09581596.2010.493173

Granja, J., Makridis, C., Yannelis, C., & Zwick, E. (2020). Did the Paycheck Protection Program hit the target? (No. w27095). National Bureau of Economic Research. doi:10.3386/w27095

Granovetter, M. (1985). Economic action and social structure: The problem of embeddedness. *American Journal of Sociology*, *91*(3), 481–510. doi:10.1086/228311

Greene, P. G., Hart, M. M., Gatewood, E. J., Brush, C. G., & Carter, N. M. (2003). Women entrepreneurs: Moving front and center: An overview of research and theory. *Coleman White Paper Series*, *3*(1), 1-47.

Gregori, P., & Holzmann, P. (2020). Digital sustainable entrepreneurship: A business model perspective on embedding digital technologies for social and environmental value creation. *Journal of Cleaner Production*, *272*, 122817. doi:10.1016/j.jclepro.2020.122817

Greiner, L. E. (1973). What managers think of participative leadership. *Harvard Business Review*, *51*(2), 111–117.

Griffin, O. H., & Cortes, S. (2006). A Learning Space of, by, and for Engineers: Virginia Tech's Joseph F. Ware, Jr. Advanced Engineering Laboratory. *ASME 2006 International Design Engineering Technical Conferences and Computers and Information in Engineering Conference*, 841–848. 10.1115/DETC2006-99205

Grigoli, F., Paredes, E., & Di Bella, G. (2017). *Inequality and Growth: A Heterogeneous Approach*. International Monetary Fund.

Gu, Y., & Wang, Z. (2021). Income Inequality and Global Political Polarization: The Economic Origin of Political Polarization in the World. *Journal of Chinese Political Science*. doi:10.1007/s11366-021-09772-1

Guillermo, V. (2008). What is the size of the pie? Measuring the informal economy in Latin America and the Caribbean. *Money Affairs*, *21*(2), 161–191.

Gulati, R. (2021). *Team Success Starts with the Individual—and with Love*. Op-Ed Harvard Business School.

Gulua, E. (2020). Trends. *Challenges and Orientations of HRM.*, *7*, 51–67. doi:10.46361/2449-2604.7.1.2020.51-67

Gupta, S. (2019). *Investigation of the barriers affecting innovation: A qualitative comparative study of Indian start-ups operating in high and low-to medium technology sectors* (Doctoral dissertation). Brunel University London.

Guragain, S. (2019, October 31). *Exploratory Research Design*. https://shyamguragain.com.np/exploratory-research-design/

Gurchiek, K. (2020, September 19). *Small businesses get creative to survive during the pandemic.* SHRM. https://www.shrm.org/hr-today/news/all-things-work/pages/small-businesses-get-creative-to-survive-during-the-pandemic.aspx

GuttermanA. (2020). Definitions and Types of Entrepreneurships. Available at SSRN. doi:10.2139/ssrn.3930375

Gwija, S., Eresia-Eke, C., & Iwu, C. (2014). Challenges and Prospects of Youth Entrepreneurship Development in a Designated Community in the Western Cape, South Africa. *The Journal of Behavioral Economics*, *6*, 10–20.

Haag, M. (2020, August 3). *One third of New York small businesses may close be gone forever.* Retrieved December 1, 2021 from: https://www.nytimes.com/2020/08/03/nyregion/nyc-small-businesses-closing-coronaviru s.html

Haan, H. C. (2006). Training for Work in the Informal Micro-Enterprise Sector: Fresh Evidence from Sub-Sahara Africa. UNESCO-UNEVOC, Springer.

Haas, R., Watson, J., Smith, K., Buonasera, T., Viviano, C., Southon, J., Chen, J., Noe, S., Parker, G., & Eerkens, J. (2020). Female hunters of the early Americas. *Science Advances*, *6*(45), abd0310. Advance online publication. doi:10.1126ciadv

Hakala, H., O'Shea, G., Farny, S., & Luoto, S. (2020). Re-storying the Business, Innovation and Entrepreneurial Ecosystem Concepts: The Model-Narrative Review Method. *International Journal of Management Reviews*, *22*(1), 10–32.

Hakura, M. D., Hussain, M. M., Newiak, M. M., Thakoor, V., & Yang, M. F. (2016). *Inequality, gender gaps and economic growth: Comparative evidence for sub-Saharan Africa.* International Monetary Fund.

Hallen, B., Bingham, C., & Cohen, S. (2016). *Do Accelerators Accelerate? The role of indirect learning in New Venture Development.* Academic Press.

Hamilton, L., & De Klerk, N. (2016). Generation Y Female students' motivation towards entrepreneurship. *International Journal of Business and Management Studies*, *8*(2), 50–65.

Hamlett, C. (2019). *The Adverse Effects of Technology in the Workplace.* Retrieved from https://smallbusiness.chron.com/adverse-effects-technology-workplace-22649.html

Hamza, S. (2021). *The Impact of New Technologies on Employment and the Workforce: What are the Implications for Developing Countries.* Especially in Africa.

Handcock, M. S., & Gile, K. J. (2011). Comment: On the concept of snowball sampling. *Sociological Methodology*, *41*(1), 367–371. doi:10.1111/j.1467-9531.2011.01243.x PMID:35095124

Hanna, D. (1988). *Designing organizations for high performance.* Addison Wesley.

Haq, A., & Safavian, M. (2013). *Are Pakistan's Women Entrepreneurs Being Served by the Microfinance Sector?: Are They Being Served by the Microfinance Sector?* World Bank Publications.

Harvard Kennedy Educator's Series. (2021). *Promoting Social Change through the private sector.* Retrieved January 2, 2022, from https://m.youtube.com/watch?v=W0GWqFeEu1A

Hauge, R. (2021, July). Photos: In your business at Curbside Bicycles. *The Cap Times.* Retrieved from: https://captimes.com/news/local/photos-in-your-business-at-curbside-bicycles/collection_4b2ab1cb-d67b-531d-ac34-2eed086d6173.html

Hayward, M., Forster, W., Sarasvathy, S., & Fredrickson, B. (2010). Beyond hubris: How highly confident entrepreneurs rebound to venture again. *Journal of Business Venturing*, *25*(6), 569–578. doi:10.1016/j.jbusvent.2009.03.002

Healy, J., Nicholson, D., & Pekarek, A. (2017). Should we take the gig economy seriously? *Labour & Industry: A Journal of the Social and Economic Relations of Work, 27*(3), 232–248. doi:10.1080/10301763.2017.1377048

Heathcote, J., Perri, F., & Violante, G. L. (2010). Unequal we stand: An empirical analysis of economic inequality in the United States, 1967–2006. *Review of Economic Dynamics*, *13*(1), 15–51. doi:10.1016/j.red.2009.10.010

Henderson, R. (2021, December 10). *How COVID-19 Has Transformed The Gig Economy*. Retrieved from https://www.forbes.com/sites/rebeccahenderson/2020/12/10/how-covid-19-has-transformed-the-gig-economy/?sh=194140826c99

Henderson, T. (2017). Why innovation is crucial to your organization's long-term success. *Forbes*.

Herring, C. (2004). Open for business in the black metropolis: Race, disadvantage, and entrepreneurial activity in Chicago's inner city. *The Review of Black Political Economy*, *31*(4), 35–57. doi:10.100712114-004-1009-z

Herrington, M., & Kew, P. (2016). *Global Entrepreneurship Monitor (GEM): South African Report 2015/16 – Is South Africa heading for an economic meltdown?* Available from: https://www.gemconsortium.org/news/Is%20South%20Africa%20headed%20for%20economic%20meltdown?

Herrington, M., & Kew, P. (2017). *Is there a change in attitude towards the small and medium business sector in South Africa?* Global Entrepreneurship Monitor. https://www.gemconsortium.org/file/open?fileId=50411

Herrington, M., & Coduras, A. (2019). The national entrepreneurship framework conditions in sub-Saharan Africa: A comparative study of GEM data/National Expert Surveys for South Africa, Angola, Mozambique and Madagascar. *Journal of Global Entrepreneurship Research*, *9*(1), 1–24. doi:10.118640497-019-0183-1

Herrington, M., & Kelley, D. (2012). *Global Entrepreneurship Monitor, African Entrepreneurship, Sub-Saharan African Regional Report*. International Development Research Centre.

Heshmati, A., Kim, J., & Wood, J. (2019). A Survey of Inclusive Growth Policy. *Economies*, *7*(3), 65. doi:10.3390/economies7030065

Hewing, M. (2014). The Playful Ingenuity of Potential Users in Collaboration: Enriched Compensation and Improvisation. *Collaboration with Potential Users for Discontinuous Innovation: Experimental Research on User Creativity*, 103-149. . doi:10.1007/978-3-658-03753-6-4

Hisrich, R. D., & Peters, M. P. (2002). Entrepreneurship (5th ed.). McGraw Hill/Irvin, Higher Education.

History.com Editors. (2010, March 4). *The Great Migration*. History.com. Retrieved January 5, 2022, from http://www.history.com/topics/black-history/great-migration

Hoang, C., Bernier, J., & Bard, C. (2016). How Federal, State, Local R&D Incentives Are Supporting Startups. *Chief Financial Officers (CFOs) Magazine*. Retrieved 2022, May 17 from: https://www.cfo.com/strategy/2016/07/federal-state-local-rd-incentives-supporting-startups/

Hoftijzer, M., Levin, V., Santos, I., & Weber, M. (2020). *TVET Systems' Response to COVID-19*. https://openknowledge.worldbank.org/bitstream/handle/10986/33759/TVET-Systems-response-to-COVID-19-Challenges-and-Opportunities.pdf?sequence=1&isAllowed=y

Holder, M., Jones, J., & Masterson, T. (2021). The early impact of COVID-19 on job losses among black women in the United States. *Feminist Economics*, *27*(1-2), 103–116. doi:10.1080/13545701.2020.1849766

Home. (2020, May 20). Retrieved from https://foundation.ifma.org/

Homi, K., & Cohen, J. (2018). *Using Big data and atrificial intelligence to accelerate global development*. Academic Press.

Honig, B. (1998). What determines success? examining the human, financial, and social capital of Jamaican microentrepreneurs. *Journal of Business Venturing*, *13*(5), 371–394. doi:10.1016/S0883-9026(97)00036-0

Horda, T. (2021). *A guide to future-oriented skills: Skills in demand to watch in the next five years.* https://hrforecast.com/a-guide-to-future-oriented-skills-skills-in-demand-to-watch-in-the-next-five-years/

Hornaday, R., & Wheatly, W. (1986). Managerial characteristics and the financial performance of small business. *Journal of Small Business Management*, *24*(2), 1–7.

Hotspot. (2021). *The Ultimate List of Marketing Statistics for 2021.* Retrieved from https://www.hubspot.com/marketing-statistics

Hou, Remøy, Jylhä, & Putte. (2021). An Investigation on Office-Based Workplace Modification During the COVID-19 Pandemic in the Netherlands. In *Proceedings of the 25th International Symposium on Advancement of Construction Management and Real Estate* (pp. 845-855). Springer.

Hou, H. C., Remøy, H., Jylhä, T., & Vande Putte, H. (2021). A study on office workplace modification during the COVID-19 pandemic in The Netherlands. *Journal of Corporate Real Estate*, *23*(3), 186–202. https://doi.org/10.1108/jcre-10-2020-0051

Hout, M., & Rosen, H. S. (2000). Self-employment, family background, and race. *The Journal of Human Resources*, *35*(4), 670–692. doi:10.2307/146367

Howard, J. (2021, December 31). *It won't be a pandemic forever. Here's what could be next.* CNN. Retrieved from: https://www.cnn.com/2021/12/31/health/covid-19-omicron-what-pandemic-end-might-look-like/index.html

Howell, S. T., Kuchler, T., Snitkof, D., Stroebel, J., & Wong, J. (2021). Racial Disparities in Access to Small Business Credit: Evidence from the Paycheck Protection Program (No. w29364). National Bureau of Economic Research.

Howlett, M.National Approaches to Theories of Instrument Choice. (1991). Policy instruments, policy styles, and policy implementation: National approaches to theories of instrument choice. *Policy Studies Journal: the Journal of the Policy Studies Organization*, *19*(2), 1–21. doi:10.1111/j.1541-0072.1991.tb01878.x

Howlett, M., & Ramesh, M. (1993). Patterns of policy instrument choice: Policy styles, policy learning and the privatization experience. *The Review of Policy Research*, *12*(1-2), 3–24. doi:10.1111/j.1541-1338.1993.tb00505.x

Huang, L. (2020). *Why women get less funding: Exploring the gender gap in venture capital investing.* https://carta.com/blog/why-women-get-less-funding/

Humphries, J. E., Neilson, C., & Ulyssea, G. (2020). *The Evolving Impacts of COVID-19 on Small Businesses Since the CARES Act Cowles Foundation.* Discussion Paper No. 2230, NYU Stern School of Business. Available at SSRN: https://ssrn.com/abstract=3584745

Huxham, C., & Hibbert, P. (2004). Collaborating to know? Interorganizational engagement and learning. *Advanced Institute of Management Research Paper*, (013). doi:10.2139/ssrn.1306956

Hwang, H., & Höllerer, M. A. (2020). The COVID-19 Crisis and Its Consequences: Ruptures and Transformations in the Global Institutional Fabric. *The Journal of Applied Behavioral Science*, *56*(3), 294–300. https://doi.org/10.1177/0021886320936841

IATA. (2020). *The impact of COVID-19 on aviation.* iata.org

Ibrahim, N. A., & Lucky, E. O. I. (2014). Relationship between entrepreneurial orientation, entrepreneurial skills, environmental factor and entrepreneurial intention among Nigerian students in UUM. *Entrepreneurship and Innovation Management Journal*, *2*(4), 203–213.

IDCRC-CRDI. (2020). *Boosting youth employment in Africa during and after the COVID-19 pandemic.* Available from: https://www.idrc.ca/en/research-in-action/boosting-youth-employment-africa-during-and-after-covid-19-pandemic

Igbo, C. A. (2006). Developing entrepreneurship through entrepreneurship education. *Journal of Home Economics Research*, (7), 50–54.

Iivari, N. (2020). Digital transformation of everyday life – How COVID-19 pandemic transformed the basic education of the young generation and why information management research should care? *International Journal of Information Management*, 55. doi:10.1016/j.ijinfomgt.2020.102183

Ikram, M., Shen, Y., Ferasso, M., & D'Adamo, I. (2021). Intensifying effects of COVID-19 on economic growth, logistics performance, environmental sustainability and quality management: Evidence from Asian countries. *Journal of Asia Business Studies*. doi:10.1108/JABS-07-2021-0316

IMF Working Paper. (2017). *The Informal Economy in Sub-Saharan Africa: Size and Determinants.* https://www.imf.org

Ince-Yenilmez, M. (2020). The Role of Socioeconomic Factors on Women's Risk of Being Exposed to Intimate Partner Violence. *Journal of Interpersonal Violence*, *37*(9-10), NP6084–NP6111. doi:10.1177/0886260520966668 PMID:33047645

Inman, K. (2016). *Women's resources in business start-up: A study of black and white women entrepreneurs*. Routledge. doi:10.4324/9781315276519

Institute of Development Studies. (2020). *Disability inclusive development; Kenya situational analysis, June 2020 Update.* https://opendocs.ids.ac.uk/opendocs/bitstream/handle/20.500.12413/15508/DID%20Kenya%20SITAN_June%20 2020.pdf?sequence=1

International Facility Management Association. (2020). *Pandemic manual – planning and responding to a global health crisis for facility management professionals*. Available at: https://foundation.ifma.org/ wp-content/uploads/2020/05/ IFMA-Foundation-Pandemic-Manual-FINAL.pdf

International Labour Office. (1972). *Employment, Incomes and Equality: A Strategy for Increasing Productive Employment in Kenya*. ILO.

International Labour Office. (2018). Women and Men in the Informal Economy: A Statistical Picture - Third edition. International Labour Office.

International Monetary Fund. (2020). *Access to Finance: Why Aren't Women Leaning In?* https://www.imf.org/external/pubs/ft/fandd/2020/03/pdf/africa-gender-gap-access-to-finance-morsy.pdf

Intracen.org. (2021). *COVID-19: The Great Lockdown and its Impact on Small Business - SMECO 2020 Executive Summary*. Available from: https://www.intracen.org/publication/SMECO2020/Ex-Summary

Intracen.org. (2021). *Lifting Ghana's youth entrepreneurs through the Ye! Boost Programme*. Available from: https://www.intracen.org/news/Lifting-Ghana-youth-entrepreneurs-through-the-Ye-Boost-Programme/

Ionesco-Sommers, E., & Tara Wa, A. (Eds.). (2022, February 11). *Diagnosing covid-19 impacts on entrepreneurship – exploring policy remedies for recovery.* InnLab. Retrieved April 5, 2022, from https://www.upo.es/inn-lab/eventos/ diagnosing-covid-19-impacts-on-entrepreneurship-e xploring-policy-remedies-for-recovery/?lang=en

Ismail, A., & Farooq, S. (2021). Business Ecosystem Framework for a Sustainable Microfinance Industry in Pakistan (PhD). University of the Punjab.

Ismail, A., Adnan, W. N., Masek, A., Hassan, R., Hashim, S., & Ismail, M. E. (2019). Effectiveness of entrepreneurship programmes in developing entrepreneurship skills towards quality TVET graduates. *Journal of Technical Education and Training*, *11*(1), 81–86. doi:10.30880/jtet.2019.11.01.010

Ismail, A., Farooq, S., & Ahmed, Z. (2020). Understanding the Functions of Microfinance Ecosystem: A Perspective of Microfinance Providers in Pakistan. *Paradigms*, *14*(2), 50–64.

Ivan, M., & Albu, R. G. (2014). A new model of Vocational Education and Training in Brasov County. *Bulletin of the Transilvania University of Brasov. Economic Sciences. Series V*, *7*(1), 77–84.

IWEC. (2018). *Uganda leads In the ration of women doing business*. Retrieved from https://www.iwecfoundation.org/news/uganda-leads-in-ratio-of-women-doing-business/

Jackson, J. T. (2009). Capitalizing on digital entrepreneurship for low-income residents and communities. *West Virginia Law Review*, *112*, 187.

Jackson, T. M., & Sanyal, P. (2019). Struggles and strategies of Black women business owners in the US. *Journal of Business Anthropology*, *8*(2), 228–249. doi:10.22439/jba.v8i2.5850

Jafari-Sadeghi, V., Dutta, D. K., Ferraris, A., & delGiudice, M. (2020). Internationalisation business processes in an under-supported policy contexts: Evidence from Italian SMEs. *Business Process Management Journal*, *26*(5), 1055–1074. doi:10.1108/BPMJ-03-2019-0141

Jansen, J., Veenstra, S., Zuurveen, R., & Stol, W. (2016). Guarding against online threats: Why entrepreneurs take protective measures. *Behaviour & Information Technology*, *35*(5), 368–379.

Jawad, M., Naz, M., & Maroof, Z. (2021). Era of digital revolution: Digital entrepreneurship and digital transformation in emerging economies. *Business Strategy & Development*, *4*(3), 220–228.

Jena, R. K. (2020). Measuring the impact of business management Student's attitude towards entrepreneurship education on entrepreneurial intention: A case study. *Computers in Human Behavior*, *107*, 106275. doi:10.1016/j.chb.2020.106275

Jenkins, A., Wiklund, J., & Brundin, E. (2014). Individual responses to firm failure: Appraisals, grief, and the influence of prior failure experience. *Journal of Business Venturing*, *29*(1), 17–33. doi:10.1016/j.jbusvent.2012.10.006

Jennings, J. E., & Brush, C. G. (2013). Research on women entrepreneurs: Challenges to (and from) the broader entrepreneurship literature? *The Academy of Management Annals*, *7*(1), 663–715. doi:10.1080/19416520.2013.782190

Jennings, N. S. (1994). Small-scale mining: a labour and social perspective. In A. J. Ghose (Ed.), *Small-Scale Mining: A Global Overview* (pp. 11–18). A.A. Balkema.

Jing, P., Huang, H., Ran, B., Zhan, F., & Shi, Y. (2019). Exploring the factors affecting mode choice Intention of autonomous vehicle based on an extended theory of planned behavior—A case study in China. *Sustainability*, *11*(4), 1155. doi:10.3390u11041155

Johnson, S., Kaufmann, D., & Zoido-Lobaton, P. (1998). Regulatory discretion and the unofficial economy. *The American Economic Review*, *88*(2), 387–392.

Jones, J. (2017). *The racial wealth gap: How African-Americans have been shortchanged out of the materials to build wealth*. Economic Policy Institute. http://epi.org

Kalidas, S., Magwentshu, N., & Rajagopaul, A. (2020). *How South African SMEs can survive and thrive post COVID-19*. Academic Press.

Kane, G. (2019). The Technology Fallacy. *Research Technology Management*, *62*(6), 44–49. https://doi.org/10.1080/08956308.2019.1661079

Karakaplan, M. U. (2021). This time is really different: The multiplier effect of the Paycheck Protection Program (PPP) on small business bank loans. *Journal of Banking & Finance*, *133*, 106223.

Kariv, D. (2011). Entrepreneurial Orientations of Women Business Founders from a Push/Pull Perspective: Canadians versus non-Canadians—A Multinational Assessment. *Journal of Small Business and Entrepreneurship*, *24*(3), 397–425. doi:10.1080/08276331.2011.10593546

Kasseeah, H., & Tandrayen-Ragoobur, V. (2014). Women in the informal sector in Mauritius: A survival mode. *Equality, Diversity and Inclusion*, *33*(8), 750–763. doi:10.1108/EDI-04-2013-0022

Kasseeah, H., & Tandrayen-Ragoobur, V. (2016). Ex-garment female workers: A new entrepreneurial community in Mauritius. *Journal of Enterprising Communities: People and Places in the Global Economy*, *10*(1), 33–52. doi:10.1108/JEC-08-2015-0042

Kasseeah, H., Thoplan, R., & Tandrayen-Ragoobur, V. (2014). Financial crisis and informal sector women entrepreneurs in Mauritius. *International Journal of Economics and Business Research*, *8*(2), 227–243. doi:10.1504/IJEBR.2014.064123

Kassis, L. (2014). *10 Years Forward – The Palestinian Tech Startup Scene*. LinkedIn Pulse. Retrieved from: https://www.linkedin.com/pulse/20140527081001-19548561-10-years-forward-the-palestinian-tech-startup-scene/

Kast, F. E., & Rosenzweig, J. E. (1973). *Contingency views of organization and management*. Science Research Associates.

Katare, B., Marshall, M. I., & Valdivia, C. B. (2021). Bend or break? Small business survival and strategies during the COVID-19 shock. *International Journal of Disaster Risk Reduction*, *61*, 102332.

Katrodia, A., & Sibanda, R. (2018). Challenges experienced by young entrepreneurs entering the small and medium enterprise sector (SME) in Rajkot region, Gujarat-India. *Academy of Entrepreneurship Journal*, *24*(4), 1–14.

Katznelson, I. (2005). *When affirmative action was white: An untold history of racial inequality in twentieth-century America*. WW Norton & Company.

Kazumi, T., & Kawai, N. (2017). *Institutional support and women's entrepreneurial self-efficacy*. Asia Pacific Journal of Innovation and Entrepreneurship.

Keeton, G. (2014). Inequality in South Africa. *The Journal of the Helen Suzman Foundation*, *74*(1), 26–31.

Kelley, D., Brush, C., Greene, P., Herrington, M., Ali, A., & Kew, P. (2014). *Special report: Women's Entrepreneurship*. Global Entrepreneurship Monitor.

Kelley, D., Majbouri, M., & Randolph, A. (2021). Black women are more likely to start a business than white men. *Harvard Business Review*.

Kew, J. (2015). *Africa's Young Entrepreneurs: Unlocking the Potential for a Brighter Future*. University of Cape Town, Development Unit for New Enterprise.

Key, M., Kenya, T., & Works, M. (2013). *Development of 21st Century Skills for Innovation and Enterprise: Exploring the role of Informal Learning Environments in the Development of Skills and Aptitudes for the Digital Creative Media Industries*. Report collated by Neil Butcher and Associates for GESCI January 2013.

Khalidi, R., Abugattas, L., Hinn, H., Hammoudah, W., Jamil, M., & Srouji. (2022). *Prospects for Development in Palestine 2021: Weathering the Storm, Mobilizing Together.* Palestine Economic Policy Research (MAS).

Khalidi, R., & Taghdisi-Rad, S. (2009). *The Economic Dimensions of Prolonged Occupation: Continuity and Change in Israeli Policy Towards the Palestinian Economy*. UNCTAD.

Khan, N., Kakabadse, N. K.-, & Skouloudis, A. (2021). Socio-ecological resilience and environmental sustainability: case of avocado from Mexico. *International Journal of Sustainable Development & World Ecology, 28*(8), 744–758. https://doi-org.mec.ezproxy.cuny.edu/10.1080/13504509.2021.1902419

Khatib, I., Tsipouri, L., Bassiakos, Y., & Haj-daoud, A. (2013). Innovation in Palestinian Industries: A Necessity for Surviving the Abnormal. *Journal of the Knowledge Economy*, *4*(4), 492–510. doi:10.100713132-012-0093-8

Khavul, S., Bruton, G. D., & Wood, E. (2009). Informal family business in Africa. *Entrepreneurship Theory and Practice*, *33*(6), 1219–1238. doi:10.1111/j.1540-6520.2009.00342.x

Kickul, J., Griffiths, M. D., Robb, C. C., & Gundry, L. (2021). All for one? The Paycheck Protection Program distribution disparity. *Journal of Entrepreneurship and Public Policy*.

Kidd & Kabare. (2019). *Social protection and Disability in Rwanda, working paper 2019, development pathways*. https://www.developmentpathways.co.uk/wp-content/uploads/2019/08/Social-Protection-and-Disability-in-Rwanda-Report-.pdf

Kiggundu, M. N. (2002). Entrepreneurs and entrepreneurship in Africa: What is known and what needs to be done. *Journal of Developmental Entrepreneurship*, *7*(3), 239–258.

Kim, & Vachon, S. (2016). Asian journal of sustainability and social responsibility Inaugural Editorial. *Asian Journal of Sustainability and Social Responsibility, 1*(1), 57–59. doi:10.1186/s41180-016-0006-z

Kimberly, M. (2021). *ICT industry full-time employment worldwide in 2019, 2020 and 2023*. Retrieved from http://www.ezwswmjk.com/statistics/1126677/it-employment-worldwide/

Kimberly, M. (2021). *Size of the cybersecurity market worldwide from 2021 to 2026 (in billion U.S. dollars)*. Retrieved from https:// www.statista.com/statistics/595182/ worldwide-security-as-a-service-market-size/

Kimmons, R., & Veletsianos, G. (2016). Education scholars' evolving uses of twitter as a conference backchannel and social commentary platform. *British Journal of Educational Technology*, *47*(3), 445–464. https://doi.org/10.1111/bjet.12428

Kim, P. H., Aldrich, H. E., & Keister, L. A. (2006). Access (not) denied: The impact of financial, human, and cultural capital on entrepreneurial entry in the United States. *Small Business Economics*, *27*(1), 5–22. doi:10.100711187-006-0007-x

King, N. (2004). Using templates in the thematic analysis of text. In C. Cassell & G. Symon (Eds.), Essential guide to qualitative methods in organizational research (pp. 257–270). London, UK: Sag. doi:10.4135/9781446280119.n21

Kirkwood, J. (2009). Motivational factors in a push-pull theory of entrepreneurship. *Gender in Management*, *24*(5), 346–364. doi:10.1108/17542410910968805

Kissi, E., Ahadzie, D. K., Debrah, C., & Adjei-Kumi, T. (2020). Underlying strategies for improving entrepreneurial skills development of technical and vocational students in developing countries: Using Ghana as a case study. *Education + Training*, *62*(5), 599–614. Advance online publication. doi:10.1108/ET-11-2019-0264

Kluev, A., Bagirova, A., & Zabokritskaya, L. (2017). Predprinimatel'skoe obrazovanie v universitetakh stranyu: masshtabyu, vidyu programm, balans kompetentsii [Entrepreneurial education in universities of the country: scope, types of curricula, balance of competencies]. *Sovremennaya konkurenciya*, 6-20.

Kocak, H., Kinik, K., Caliskan, C., & Aciksari, K. (2021). The Science of Disaster Medicine: From Response to Risk Reduction. *Medeniyet Medical Journal, 36*(4), 333–342. https://doi-org.mec.ezproxy.cuny.edu/10.4274/MMJ.galenos.2021.50375

Kochhar, R. (2021, March 18). *The Pandemic Stalls Growth in the Global Middle Class, Pushes Poverty Up Sharply.* Retrieved from https://www.pewresearch.org/global/2021/03/18/the-pandemic-stalls-growth-in-the-global-middle-class-pushes-poverty-up-sharply/

Kogut, C. S., & Mejri, K. (2021). Female entrepreneurship in emerging markets: challenges of running a business in turbulent contexts and times. *International Journal of Gender and Entrepreneurship*. doi:10.1108/IJGE-03-2021-0052

Köllinger, P., & Minniti, M. (2006). Not for lack of trying: American entrepreneurship in black and white. *Small Business Economics*, *27*(1), 59–79. doi:10.100711187-006-0019-6

Koloba, H., & Surujlal, J. (2021). Influence of demographic factors on self-employment intentions of university students. *Polish Journal of Management Studies*, *24*(2), 228–241. doi:10.17512/pjms.2021.24.2.14

Komunte, M. (2015). Usage of mobile technology in women entrepreneurs: A case study of Uganda. *The African Journal of Information Systems*, *7*(3), 3.

Korber, S., & McNaughton, R. (2017). Resilience and entrepreneurship: A systematic literature review. *International Journal of Entrepreneurial Behavior & Research*, *24*(7), 1129–1154. doi:10.1108/IJEBR-10-2016-0356

Kotter, J. P. (2012). Accelerate! *Harvard Business Review*, *90*(11), 44–52. PMID:23155997

Krathwohl, D. R., Bloom, B. S., & Masia, B. B. (1973). *Taxonomy of Educational Objectives, the Classification of Educational Goals. In Handbook II: Affective Domain*. David McKay Co., Inc.

KritiKoS. (2014). *Entrepreneurs and their impact on jobs and economic growth*. IZA World of Labor. Available from: https://wol.iza.org/articles/entrepreneurs-and-their-impact-on-jobs-and-economic-growth/long

Krogh, E., Hansen, T. N., Wendt, S., & Elkjaer, M. (2009). *Promoting Employment for Women as a Strategy for Poverty Reduction, Organization for Economic Cooperation and Development (OECD)*. Available at: www.oecd.org/dac/povertyreduction/43280489.pdf

Kroon, J. (2002). 'n Strategie vir entrepreneurskapontwikkeling in Suid-Afrika. *Tydskrif vir Geesteswetenskappe*, *42*(3), 215–223.

Kuckertz, A. (2021). Why we think we teach entrepreneurship-and why we should really teach it. *Journal of Entrepreneurship Education*, *24*(3), 1–7.

Kuester, S., & Arya, P. (2021). *State of the Palestinian Startup Ecosystem*. Startup Genome & Innovative Private Sector Development.

Küttim, M., Kallaste, M., Venesaar, U., & Kiis, A. (2014). Entrepreneurship education at university level and students' entrepreneurial intentions. *Procedia: Social and Behavioral Sciences*, *110*, 658–668. doi:10.1016/j.sbspro.2013.12.910

Kuznets, S. (1955). Economic Growth and Income Inequality. *The American Economic Review*, *45*(1), 1–28.

Kwagala, B., Wandera, S. O., Ndugga, P., & Kabagenyi, A. (2013). Empowerment, partner's behaviours and intimate partner physical violence among married women in Uganda. *BMC Public Health*, *13*(1), 1–10.

Kwon, S.-W., Heflin, C., & Ruef, M. (2013). Community Social Capital and Entrepreneurship. *American Sociological Review*, *78*(6), 980–1008. doi:10.1177/0003122413506440

La Barbera, F., & Ajzen, I. (2020). Control interactions in the theory of planned behavior: Rethinking the role of subjective norm. *Europe's Journal of Psychology*, *16*(3), 401–417. doi:10.5964/ejop.v16i3.2056 PMID:33680190

Lackéus, M. (2015). *Entrepreneurship in education: What, why, when, how.* Background paper.

Ladipo, M., Akhuemonkhan, I., & Raimi, L. (2013). *Technical Vocational Education and Training (TVET) as mechanism for Sustainable Development in Nigeria (SD): Potentials, Challenges and Policy Prescriptions.* Paper presented at the Presentation at CAPA International Conference, Banjul, Gambia.

Lakshmi Ratan, A., Roever, S., Jhabvala, R., & Sen, P. (2021). *Evidence Review of COVID-19 and Women's Informal Employment: A Call to Support the Most Vulnerable First in the Economic Recovery*. Bill & Melinda Gates Foundation.

Lang, J. (2020). *Covid-19 crisis a potential breeding ground for youth entrepreneurship in SA*. Available from: https://www.news24.com/citypress/voices/covid-19-crisis-a-potential-breeding-ground-for-youth-entrepreneurship-in-sa-20200611

Lardier, D. T., Reid, R. J., & Garcia, R. P. (2018). Validation of the Brief Sense of Community Scale among the youth of color from an underserved urban community. *Journal of Community Psychology*, *46*(8), 1062–1074. doi:10.1002/jcop.22091 PMID:30311964

Laspita, S., Breugst, N., Heblich, S., & Patzelt, N. (2012). Intergenerational transmission of entrepreneurial intentions. *Journal of Business Venturing*, *27*(4), 414–435. doi:10.1016/j.jbusvent.2011.11.006

Leach. (2021). Post-Pandemic transformation: How and why COVID-19 requires us to rethink development. *World Development*, 138. doi:10.1016/j.worlddev.2020.105233

Leach, F. (1996). Women in the Informal Sector: The Contribution of Education and Training. *Development in Practice*, *6*(1), 25–36. doi:10.1080/0961452961000157584

Leach, W. (1994). *Land of Desire*. Penguin Random House.

Leaders International. (2021). *Fast Forward Accelerator Program*. Retrieved 2021, November 17 from: https://leadersinternational.org/projects/fastforward-accelerator-programme/

Lean Enterprise Institute. (2020, July 14). *Target Cost*. Retrieved from Lean Enterprise Institute: https://www.lean.org/lexicon/target-cost

Lederer, A., & Oros, S. (2020). *Lending discrimination within the paycheck protection program.* Retrieved February 4, 2022, from http://arks.princeton.edu/ark:/88435/dsp01zk51vk84t

Ledgerwood, J., Earne, J., & Nelson, C. (2013). *The New Microfinance Handbook: A Financial Market System Perspective*. World Bank Publications. doi:10.1596/978-0-8213-8927-0

Ledgerwood, J., & Gibson, A. (2013). The evolving financial landscape. In J. E. J. Ledgerwood & C. Nelson (Eds.), *The New Microfinance Handbook: A Financial Market System Perspective* (pp. 15–48). World Bank Publications. doi:10.1596/9780821389270_CH01

Lee, N. (2018). Inclusive Growth in cities: A sympathetic critique. *Regional Studies*, *53*(3), 424–434. https://doi.org/10.1080/00343404.2018.1476753

Lee, N. (2019). Inclusive Growth in cities: A sympathetic critique. *Regional Studies*, *53*(3), 424–434. doi:10.1080/00343404.2018.1476753

Lee, W. (2019). Character-based lending for micro business development: Empirical insights into conceptualizing character. *Journal of Small Business and Entrepreneurship*, 1–16. doi:10.1080/08276331.2019.1701256

Legg-Jack, D. W. (2014). *Employability skills of Technical College graduates: A case for Government Technical College (GTC) in Ahoada Rivers State Nigeria* (Masters). University of KwaZulu-Natal, Durban, South Africa. http://hdl.handle.net/10413/12688

Legg-Jack, D. W. (2018). *Technical and vocational education and training (TVET) provision in Nigerian technical colleges: exploring the relevance, effectiveness and efficiency (REE) of stakeholder partnerships using community-based participatory action research (CBPAR)* (Doctoral dissertation). University of KwaZulu-Natal, Durban, South Africa. https://researchspace.ukzn.ac.za/handle/10413/18199

Lemann, N. (1992). *The Promised Land: The great black migration and how it changed America*. Vintage Books.

Leshilo, A., & Lethoko, M. (2017). The contribution of youth in Local Economic Development and entrepreneurship in Polokwane municipality, Limpopo Province. *Skills at Work: Theory and Practice Journal*, *8*(1), 45–58.

Letteiri & Lyons. (2020). *Understanding the Paycheck Protection Program*. Briefs and Blogs, Economic Innovation Group.

Levin, A., Lin, C. F., & Chu, C. S. J. (2002). Unit root tests in panel data: Asymptotic and finite-sample properties. *Journal of Econometrics*, *108*(1), 1–24. doi:10.1016/S0304-4076(01)00098-7

Levy, F. (2002). *Apex institutions in microfinance*. Retrieved from https://www.cgap.org/sites/default/files/CGAP-Occasional-Paper-Apex-Institutions-in-Microfinance-Jan-2002.pdf

Lewis, L., & Patrinos, A. H. (2012). *Impact evaluation of private sector participation in education*. The World Bank: CfBT Education Trust.

Li, G., Pervaiz, S., & He, Q. (2021). *Can universities be a gleam of hope during COVID-19? Entrepreneurial intentions approach for academia in Pakistan*. Paper presented at the Frontiers in Education.

Libecap, G. D. (2003). Introduction. In G. D. Libecap (Ed.), *Issues in Entrepreneurship (Advances in the Study of Entrepreneurship, Innovation and Economic Growth, 14)* (pp. ix–xvii). Emerald Group Publishing Limited. doi:10.1016/S1048-4736(02)14010-0

Libombo, D. B., & Dinin, A. (2015). Entrepreneurship education in the context of developing countries: Study of the status and the main barriers in Mozambican higher education institutions. *Journal of Developmental Entrepreneurship*, *20*(3), 1–26. doi:10.1142/S108494671550020X

Light, I. (1980). *Ethnic Entrepreneurship in America*. University of California Press.

Liguori, E. W., & Pittz, T. G. (2020). Strategies for small business: Surviving and thriving in the era of COVID-19. *Journal of the International Council for Small Business*, *1*(2), 106–110.

Liguori, E., & Winkler, C. (2020). From Offline to Online: Challenges and Opportunities for Entrepreneurship Education Following the COVID-19 Pandemic. *Entrepreneurship Education and Pedagogy*, *3*(4), 346–351. doi:10.1177/2515127420916738

Liñán, F. (2008). Skill and value perceptions: How do they affect entrepreneurial intentions? *The International Entrepreneurship and Management Journal*, *4*(3), 257–272. doi:10.100711365-008-0093-0

Lindesmith, A. R. (1947). *Opiate Addiction*. Principa.

Lindner, J. (2020). *Entrepreneurial learning for TVET institutions: A practical guide*. UNESCO Publishing.

Liu, Y., Lee, J. M., & Lee, C. (2020). The challenges and opportunities of a global health crisis: The management and business implications of COVID-19 from an Asian perspective. *Asian Business & Management*, *19*(3), 277–297.

Lock, S. (2021). *Global tourism industry - statistics & facts*. Retrieved November 19, 2021, from https://www.statista.com/topics/962/global-tourism/#dossierKeyfigures

Lofstrom, M., & Bates, T. (2013). African Americans' pursuit of self-employment. *Small Business Economics*, *40*(1), 73–86. doi:10.100711187-011-9347-2

Lofstrom, M., Bates, T., & Parker, S. C. (2014). Why are some people more likely to become small-businesses owners than others: Entrepreneurship entry and industry-specific barriers. *Journal of Business Venturing*, *29*(2), 232–251. doi:10.1016/j.jbusvent.2013.01.004

Looze, J., & Desai, S. (2020). Economic Engagement of Mothers: Entrepreneurship, Employment, and the Motherhood Wage Penalty. *Employment, and the Motherhood Wage Penalty.*

Looze, J., & Desai, L. (2020). *Challenges along the Entrepreneurial Journey: Considerations for Entrepreneurship Supporters*. Ewing Marion Kauffman Foundation.

Lopez, G. R. (2003). The (racially neutral) politics of education: A critical race theory perspective. *Educational Administration Quarterly*, *39*(1), 68–94. doi:10.1177/0013161X02239761

Loss, L. (2019). *Tourism has generated 20% of total world employment since 2013.* Retrieved November 10, 2021, from https://www.tourism-review.com/tourism-industry-is-the-pillar-of-economy-news11210

Love, I., & Zicchino, L. (2006). Financial development and dynamic investment behavior: Evidence from panel VAR. *The Quarterly Review of Economics and Finance*, *46*(2), 190–210. doi:10.1016/j.qref.2005.11.007

Luckwaldt, J. H. (2017). *These Skills Are Most Likely to Be Automated Out of the Human Workforce* Retrieved from https:// www.payscale.com/ career-advice/skills-likely- automated-human-workforce/

Luke, R. (2020). The impact of COVID-2019 on transport in South Africa. *Journal of Transport and Supply Chain Management*, *14*, 1. doi:10.4102/jtscm.v14i0.545

Lund, S., Madgavkar, A., Manyika, J., Smit, S., Ellingrud, K., Meaney, M., & Robinson, O. (2021). *The future of work after COVID-19.* McKinsey Global Institute.

Lundberg, M., & Squire, L. (2003). The simultaneous evolution of growth and inequality. *Economic Journal (London)*, *113*(487), 326–344. doi:10.1111/1468-0297.00127

Lyttelton, T., Zang, E., & Musick, K. (2020). *Gender Differences in Telecommuting and Implications for Inequality at Home and Work.* Yale University. doi:10.2139srn.3645561

Maclean, R. (2011). Key Issues and Research Challenges for TVET: Bridging the gap between TVET research and the needs of policy makers. *NORRAG NEWS, Towards a New Global World of Skills Development*, 125-127.

Madeira, A., Palrao, T., & Mendes, A. S. (2021). The Impact of Pandemic Crisis on the Restaurant Business. *Sustainability*, *13*(1), 1–13. doi:10.3390u13010040

Maheshwari, P., Gokhale, A., Agarwal, N., Makena, A., & Borthakur, S. (2019). *The global landscape of gender lens investing*. Academic Press.

Maina, S. W. (2012). *Factors influencing the development of youth entrepreneurship in Ongata Rongai Township, Kajiado County, Kenya* (Doctoral dissertation). University of Nairobi, Kenya.

Maity, A. K., Rakshit, P., & Ghosh, C. S. (2016). *Shifting trends in the microfinance ecosystem.* Retrieved from PwC: https://www.pwc.in/publications/2016/shifting-trends-in-the-microfinance-ecosystem.html

Majola, J. E. P. (2017). *The impact of entrepreneurial capital on the performance of youth-owned enterprises in South Africa* (Doctoral dissertation).

Majumdar, S., & Partridge, M. D. (2009). *Impact of economic growth on income inequality: A regional perspective* (No. 319-2016-9872). Academic Press.

Maloney, W. F. (2004). Informality revisited. *World Development, 32*(7), 1159–1178. doi:10.1016/j.worlddev.2004.01.008

Man, T. W. Y. (2019). Nurturing entrepreneurial competencies through university-based entrepreneurship centers: a social constructivist perspective. In *Seminal Ideas for the Next Twenty-Five Years of Advances*. Emerald Publishing Limited. doi:10.1108/S1074-754020190000021006

Marom, D., Robb, A., & Sade, O. (2016). *Gender dynamics in crowdfunding (kickstarter): evidence on entrepreneurs, investors, deals and taste-based discrimination.* Social Science Research Network Paper 2442954.

Marr, A., & Tubaro, P. (2012). Global financial partnerships in microfinance: India, Peru and Tanzania. *Revista Iberoamericana de Estudios de Desarrollo, 1*(1), 28–57. doi:10.26754/ojs_ried/ijds.35

Marte, J. (2021, April 14). *Asian-American businesses suffer outsized pandemic toll.* Reuters. https://www.reuters.com/business/finance/asian-american-businesses-suffer-outsized-pandemic-toll-2021-04-14/

Martínez-Rodríguez, I., Quintana-Rojo, C., & Gento, P., & Callejas-Albinana, F. E. (2021). Public policy recommendations for Promoting female entrepreneurship in Europe. *The International Entrepreneurship and Management Journal*, 1–28.

Martins, F. S. & Serra, F. A. R. (2018). Secondary Data in Research – Uses and Opportunities. *Revista Ibero-Americana de Estratégia. 17*(1), 1-4. . doi:10.5585/ijsm.v17i4.2723

Martin, W., Welch, B. A., Sandefur, J., & Pan, R. (2006). African American small business owners' attitudes toward business training. *Journal of Small Business Management, 44*(4), 577–591. doi:10.1111/j.1540-627X.2006.00192.x

Mason, C., & Brown, R. (2014). *Entrepreneurial ecosystems and growth-oriented entrepreneurship.* Final report to OECD. https://www.oecd.org/cfe/leed/Entrepreneurial-ecosystems.pdf

Maurer, R. (2017). *Candidates Choose Jobs Because of Company Culture.* https://www.shrm.org/resourcesandtools/hr-topics/talent-acquisition/pages/candidates-choose-jobs-company-culture.aspx

Mayasari, Y., & Chandra, T. (2020). Social capital for knowledge management system of the creative industry. *Journal of Enterprising Communities: People and Places in the Global Economy, 14*(4), 481–494. doi:10.1108/JEC-01-2020-0008

Mbuya, M. J.-M. (2022). *Youth entrepreneurship in South Africa: A progress review.* Academic Press.

McCaffry, R., & Topsail, N. (2014, December 12). *The Integrated Reporting System: A new ... Integrated reporting in the Public Sector.* Retrieved February 12, 2022, from https://www.researchgate.net/publication/304997679_The_integrated_reporting_system

McClure, J., & Brown, J. (2008). Belonging at work. *Human Resource Development International, 11*(1), 3–17. doi:10.1080/13678860701782261

McGinnis, D. (2020). *What Is the Fourth Industrial Revolution?* Available from: https://www.salesforce.com/blog/what-is-the-fourth-industrial-revolution-4ir/

McGrath, S. (2012). Vocational education and training for development: A policy in need of a theory? *International Journal of Educational Development, 32*(5), 623–631. doi:10.1016/j.ijedudev.2011.12.001

McKibbin, W., & Fernando, R. (2020). The economic impact of COVID-19. *Economics in the Time of COVID-19, 45*(10.1162).

McKinsey & Company. (2020). *How South African SMEs can survive and thrive post COVID-19.* Available from: https://www.mckinsey.com/featured-insights/middle-east-and-africa/how-south-african-smes-can-survive-and-thrive-post-covid-19

McMillan, D. W., & Chavis, D. M. (1986). Sense of Community: A Definition and Theory. *Journal of Community Psychology, 14*(1), 6–23. doi:10.1002/1520-6629(198601)14:1<6::AID-JCOP2290140103>3.0.CO;2-I

Mehta, R. K., Mehta, D., & Mehta, N. K. (2012). Lean Manufacturing Practices: Problems and Prospects. *Annals of the Faculty of Engineering Hunedoara - International Journal of Engineering, 10*(3), 119–124.

Meier, T. R. (2020). *Black Communications and learning to read: Building on children's linguistic and cultural strengths.* Routledge. doi:10.4324/9781003064442

Meister, J. C., & Brown, R. H. (2020). 21 HR jobs of the future. *Harvard Business Review.*

Melkani, E., Singh, K., & Mehta, M. (2021). Productivity of rural women through entrepreneurship intervention. *International Journal of Education and Management Studies, 11*(1), 7–12.

Mercer, E. (2021). *How to Adapt to Changes at Work with Technology.* Retrieved from https://smallbusiness. chron.com/adapt- changes- work-technology- 30901.html

Mertineit, K.-D. (2013). *TVET for a Green Economy.* GIZ. https://www.enterprise-development.org/wp-content/uploads/TVET_Green_Economy.pdf

Mervosh, S., Lu, D., & Swales, V. (2020, April). See which states and cities have told residents to stay at home. *The New York Times.* Retrieved from: https://www.nytimes.com/interactive/2020/us/corona stay-at-home-order.html

Meyer, K., Prashantham, S., & Xu, S. (2021). Entrepreneurship and the Post-COVID-19 Recovery in Emerging Economies. *Management and Organization Review, 17*(5), 1–18. doi:10.1017/mor.2021.49

Meyer, N. (2017). *South Africa's youth unemployment dilemma: Whose Baby is it anyway?* Academic Press.

Mhlanga, D., & Ndhlovu, E. (2020). Socio-economic implications of the COVID-19 pandemic on smallholder livelihoods in Zimbabwe. doi:10.20944/preprints202004.0219.v1

Milanovic, B. (2016). Global Inequality in This Century and the Next. In *Global inequality: A new approach for the age of globalization.* Harvard University Press. doi:10.4159/9780674969797-006

Millis, V., Perez-Timermans, B., & Sakurai, H. (2018). *Special Study-Credit Lines - Lending through financial intermediaries.* Retrieved from European Bank- United Kingdom file:///E:/Downloads/credit-lines.pdf

Mills, C. K., & Battisto, J. (2020). Double jeopardy: COVID-19's concentrated health and wealth effects in Black communities. Federal Reserve Bank of New York.

Mills, Q. T. (2013). *Cutting along the color line: Black Barbers and Barber Shops in America.* Univ. of Pennsylvania Press.

Minai, M. S., & Raza, S., bin Hashim, N. A., Zain, A. Y. M., & Tariq, T. A. (2018). Linking entrepreneurial education with firm performance through entrepreneurial competencies: A Proposed Conceptual framework. *Journal of Entrepreneurship Education, 21*(4), 1–9.

Mjadu, G. (2018). *How to address common entrepreneurial challenges in SA.* Available from: https://www.news24.com/citypress/voices/how-to-address-common-entrepreneurial-challenges-in-sa-20180626

Moffatt, M. (2020, June 25). *An Economic Introduction to the Japanese Keiretsu System.* Retrieved from Thought Company: https://www.thoughtco.com/intro-to-the-japanese-keiretsu-economics-system-1148018

Mohamed, N. (2020). *Top 5 Takeaways on the importance of entrepreneurship.* Available from: https://dcid.sanford.duke.edu/importance-of-entrepreneurship/

Mohammed, A.-M., & Paleologos, E. (2021). *Social Sustainability. Social Sustainability - an overview | ScienceDirect Topics.* Retrieved January 2, 2022, from https://www.sciencedirect.com/topics/engineering/social-sustainability

Mohrman, S., & Winby, S. (2018). Working toward sustainable development: Consulting to the ecosystem. In Research in organization change and development 26 (pp. 1–45). London: Emerald.

Molina-López, M., Tejeiro Koller, M., Rubio-Andrés, M., & González-Pérez, S. (2021). Never too late to learn: How education helps female entrepreneurs at overcoming barriers in the digital economy. *Sustainability, 13*(19), 11037.

Momen, M. N. (2020). Multi-stakeholder partnerships in public policy. In W. Leal Filho, A. Azul, L. Brandli, P. Özuyar, & T. Wall (Eds.), *Partnerships for the goals. Encyclopedia of the UN sustainable development goals* (pp. 1–9). Springer. doi:10.1007/978-3-319-71067-9_50-1

Monckton, P. (2021, December 10). This is why millions of people are posting black squares on Instagram. *Forbes.* Retrieved January 2, 2022, from https://www.forbes.com/sites/paulmonckton/2020/06/02/blackout-tuesday-instagram-black-squares-blackouttuesday-theshowmustbepaused/?sh=7d9df7b02794

Moore, M.-L., & Westley, F. (2011, January 18). *Surmountable chasms: Networks and Social Innovation for Resilient Systems. Ecology and Society.* Retrieved December 20, 2021, from https://www.ecologyandsociety.org/vol16/iss1/art5/

Morales-Alonso, G., Vila, G. A., Lemus-Aguilar, I., & Hidalgo, A. (2020). Data retrieval from online social media networks for defining business angels' profile. *Journal of Enterprising Communities: People and Places in the Global Economy, 14*(1), 57–75. doi:10.1108/JEC-10-2019-0095

More than Green. (2016). *What's cultural sustainability? More than Green. What's cultural sustainability?* Retrieved January 2, 2022, from https://m.youtube.com/watch?v=gyIrvEZ2vXY

Morgan, G. (1986). *Images of organization.* Sage Publications.

Morgan, J. (2017). *The employee experience advantage: How to win the war for talent by giving employees the workspaces they want, the tools they need, and a culture they can celebrate.* John Wiley & Sons.

Morrar, R. (2019). Innovation in the MENA region. *IEMed Mediterranean Yearbook 2019.*

Morrar, R., & Baba, S. (2022). Social Innovation in Extreme Institutional Contexts: The Case Of Palestine. Management Decision. doi:10.1108/MD-11-2020-1528

Morrar, R. (2018). Development of Key Performance Indicators and Impact Assessment for Research and Development (R&D) Sector in Palestine. *Review of Economics and Business Administration, 2*(2), 41–65.

Morrar, R., & Abdelhadi, M. (2016). Obstacles of Innovation in Palestine. *Journal of Inspiration Economy, 3*(2), 53–64.

Morrar, R., Abdeljawad, I., Jabr, S., Kisa, A., & Younis, M. Z. (2019). The Role of Information and Communications Technology (ICT) in Enhancing Service Sector Productivity in Palestine: An International Perspective. *Journal of Global Information Management, 27*(1), 47–65. doi:10.4018/JGIM.2019010103

Morrar, R., Amara, M., & Syed Zwick, H. (2022). The Determinants of Self-Employment Entry of Palestinian Youth. *Journal of Entrepreneurship in Emerging Economies, 14*(1), 23–44. doi:10.1108/JEEE-06-2020-0184

Morrar, R., & Arman, H. (2020). The Transformation Role of a Third Actor Within the Triple Helix Model-the Case of Palestine. *Innovation (Abingdon),* 1–21. doi:10.1080/13511610.2020.1828045

Morrar, R., & Sultan, S. (2020). The Donor-Driven Model and Financial Sustainability: A Case Study from Palestinian Non-Government Organizations. *Cosmopolitan Civil Societies: An Interdisciplinary Journal*, *12*(2/3), 20–35. doi:10.5130/ccs.v12.i2-3.6771

Morrar, R., & Syed Zwick, H. (2021). Determinants and Wage Penalty of Qualification Mismatches: The Case of Palestine. *Journal of Education and Work*, *34*(4), 504–517. doi:10.1080/13639080.2021.1943331

Moser, C. (1989). Gender planning in the Third World: Meeting practical and strategic gender needs. *World Development*, *17*(11), 1799–1825. doi:10.1016/0305-750X(89)90201-5

Mpisi, N. (2020, July 1). *The Importance of Stakeholder Relationships in Developing Business Opportunities for Entrepreneurs*. The Innovation Hub. https://www.theinnovationhub.com/press-room-media/thought-leadership-articles/innovation-articles/the-importance-of-stakeholder-relationships-in-developing-business-opportunites-for-entrepreneurs--nws682

Mudassir, H. (2022). *COVID-19 Will Fuel the Next Wave of Innovation*. Retrieved from https://www.entrepreneur.com/article/347669

Mukherjee, D. (2016). Informal economy in emerging economies: Not a substitute but a complement! *International Journal of Business & Economic Development*, *4*(3), 16–27.

Mukirae, S. N. (2005). *Income generating activities and their contribution to the provision of teaching-learning resources in National Polytechnics in Kenya*. Academic Press.

Mulas, V., Qian, K., Garza, J., & Henry, S. (2018). *Tech Startup Ecosystem in West Bank and Gaza*. The World Bank.

Mullen, C. (2021, April 14). *Women of color drive new business growth during pandemic*. https://www.bizjournals.com/bizwomen/news/latest-news/2021/04/minority-women-drive-business-growth-in-pandemic.html?page=all

Munson, B. (2018). *Video will account for 82% of all internet traffic by 2022, Cisco says*. https://www.fiercevideo.com/video/video-will-account-for- 82-all-internet- traffic-by-2022-cisco-says

Mustafa, F., Khursheed, A., Fatima, M., & Rao, M. (2021). Exploring the impact of COVID-19 pandemic on women entrepreneurs in Pakistan. *International Journal of Gender and Entrepreneurship*, *13*(2), 187–203. doi:10.1108/IJGE-09-2020-0149

Mutwiri, N., & Kimutai, C. (2021). *Social-Legal Environment and Women Participation in the Securities Market in Kenya*. Academic Press.

Mwakilama, E. P. (2021). *Support more students with innovative business ideas*. Available from: https://www.universityworldnews.com/post.php?story=20210926110903106

Myers, S., & Chan, P. (2017). *Stuck from the Start; The Financial Challenges of Low- and Moderate-Income African-American Entrepreneurs in the South*. https://prosperitynow.org/files/PDFs/07-2017_stuck_from_the_start.pdf

Myers, S., & Chan, P. (2017, July). Stuck from the Start: The Financial Challenges of Low-and Moderate-Income African-American Entrepreneurs in the South. *Prosperity Now*.

Nagaj, R., & Žuromskaite, B. (2014). Tourism in the Era of Covid-19 and Its Impact on the Environment. *Energies*, *14*(7), 2000. Advance online publication. doi:10.3390/en14072000

Naguib, R., & Jamali, D. (2015). Female entrepreneurship in the UAE: A multi-level integrative lens. *Gender in Management*, *30*(2), 135–161. doi:10.1108/GM-12-2013-0142

Nah, F. F. H., & Siau, K. (2020). COVID-19 Pandemic – Role of Technology in Transforming Business to the New Normal. *Lecture Notes in Computer Science*, 585–600. doi:10.1007/978-3-030-60152-2_43

Narula, R. (2020). Policy opportunities and challenges from the COVID-19 pandemic for economies with large informal sectors. *Journal of International Business Policy*, *3*(3), 302–310. doi:10.105742214-020-00059-5

Nasir, M., Iqbal, R., & Akhtar, C. (2019). Factors affecting growth of women entrepreneurs in Pakistan. *Pakistan Administrative Review*, *3*(1), 35–50.

National Federation of Independent Business. (2020). *COVID-19 Small business survey Part 1: Impact on Small Business.* Retrieved from: https://www.nfib.com/covid-surveys/

National Federation of Independent Business. (2020). *COVID-19 Small business survey Part 11: PPP, EIDL, unemployment, insurance, the economy.* Retrieved from: https://www.nfib.com/covid-surveys/

National Federation of Independent Business. (2020). *COVID-19 Small business survey Part 12: PPP, EIDL, the economy, payment deferrals.* Retrieved from: https://www.nfib.com/covid-surveys/

National Federation of Independent Business. (2020). *COVID-19 Small business survey Part 2: Small Business Employers in Crisis.* Retrieved from: https://www.nfib.com/covid-surveys/

Navarro-García, A., & Coca-Pérez, J. L. (2014). Antecedents and Consequences of Entrepreneurial Orientation of Spanish Exporting SMEs in Time of Crisis. In *Entrepreneurship, Innovation and Economic Crisis* (pp. 21–29). Springer. doi:10.1007/978-3-319-02384-7_3

Ndofirepi, T. M. (2020). Relationship between entrepreneurship education and entrepreneurial goal intentions: Psychological traits as mediators. *Journal of Innovation and Entrepreneurship*, *9*(1), 2. doi:10.118613731-020-0115-x

Nelson, J. (2020). *Promoting Social Change Through the Private Sector.* Harvard Kennedy School. https://www.hks.harvard.edu/more/about/leadership-administration/deans-office/deans-d iscussions/how-can-private-sector-promote

Neumark, D., Wall, B., & Zhang, J. (2011). Do Small Businesses Create More Jobs? New Evidence for the United States from the National Establishment Time Series. *The Review of Economics and Statistics*, *93*(1), 16–29. doi:10.1162/REST_a_00060

New York City Small Business Services. (2022). https://www1.nyc.gov/site/sbs/businesses/black-entrepreneurs-nyc.page

Newman, K. S. (2009). *No shame in my game: The working poor in the inner city.* Vintage.

Nicola, M., Alsafi, Z., Sohrabi, C., Kerwan, A., Al-Jabir, A., Iosifidis, C., Agha, M., & Agha, R. (2020). The socio-economic implications of the coronavirus pandemic (COVID-19): A review. *International Journal of Surgery*, *78*, 185–193. doi:10.1016/j.ijsu.2020.04.018 PMID:32305533

Nijkamp, P. (2003). Entrepreneurship in a Modern Network Economy. *Regional Studies*, *37*(4), 395–405. doi:10.1080/0034340032000074424

Nolan, B., & Maitre, B. (2008). Economic growth and income inequality: setting the context. In *Quality of life in Ireland* (pp. 27–41). Springer. doi:10.1007/978-1-4020-6981-9_3

Nopper, T. K. (2010). Colorblind racism and institutional actors' explanations of Korean immigrant entrepreneurship. *Critical Sociology*, *36*(1), 65–85. doi:10.1177/0896920509347141

Nowell, L. S., Norris, J. M., White, D. E., & Moules, N. J. (2017). Thematic analysis. *International Journal of Qualitative Methods, 16*(1). doi:10.1177/1609406917733847

Nowell, L., Norris, J., White, D., & Moules, N. (2017, October 2). *Thematic Analysis: Striving to Meet the Trustworthiness Criteria.* Retrieved December 20, 2022, from https://journals.sagepub.com/doi/10.1177/1609406917733847

Nowiński, W., Haddoud, M. Y., Lančarič, D., Egerová, D., & Czeglédi, C. (2019). The impact of entrepreneurship education, entrepreneurial self-efficacy and gender on entrepreneurial intentions of university students in the Visegrad countries. *Studies in Higher Education*, *44*(2), 361–379. doi:10.1080/03075079.2017.1365359

Nsengimana, S. (2017). *Challenges to women entrepreneurship in Kigali, Rwanda* (Doctoral dissertation). Cape Peninsula University of Technology.

Nwafor. (2021). The effectiveness of Blockchain Smart Contracts in Reshaping the Business landscape in Nigeria. *Business Law Review*, *42*(4), 195–200.

Nwanko, S. (2005). *African Entrepreneurship in the UK. Report of the Leverhulme Study*. University of East London.

NYDA. (2020). *COVID-19 crisis funding support for South Africa businesses*. Available from: http://www.nyda.gov.za/Portals/0/Downloads/Covid%20Funding%20Resources%20for%20SA%20Businesses%207-4-2020.pdf

O'Brien, R. L. (2012). Depleting capital? Race, wealth and informal financial assistance. *Social Forces*, *91*(2), 375–396. doi:10.1093fos132

O'Connor, C. M., Anoushiravani, A. A., DiCaprio, M. R., Healy, W. L., & Iorio, R. (2020). Economic recovery after the COVID-19 pandemic: Resuming elective orthopedic surgery and total joint arthroplasty. *The Journal of Arthroplasty*, *35*(7), S32–S36. doi:10.1016/j.arth.2020.04.038 PMID:32345566

O'Reilly, C., & Binns, A. J. M. (2019). The Three Stages of Disruptive Innovation: Idea Generation, Incubation, and Scaling. *California Management Review*, *61*(3), 49–71. doi:10.1177/0008125619841878

Ober, C. (2020, April 6). *Bmore Art*. Retrieved from All Masks Are Not Created Equal: Washable, Antimicrobial Masks Made in Baltimore: https://bmoreart.com/2020/04/all-masks-are-not-created-equal-washable-antimicrobial-masks-made-in-baltimore.html

Obschonka, M., & Stuetzer, M. (2017). Integrating psychological approaches to entrepreneurship: The Entrepreneurial Personality System (EPS). *Small Business Economics*, *49*(1), 203–231. doi:10.100711187-016-9821-y

OECD. (2017). *Entrepreneurship at a Glance 2017*. OECD Publishing.

OECD. (2018). *Bridging the Digital gender divide, Include, Upskill, Innovate*. Retrieved form https://www.oecd.org/digital/bridging-the-digital-gender-divide.pdf

OECD. (2020). *OECD policy responses to coronavirus (COVID-19) - SME policy responses – OECD overview*. Available at https://www.oecd.org/coronavirus/en/

OECD. (2020). *OECD Policy responses to coronavirus: Building back better- a sustainable resilient recovery after COVID-19*. Retrieved from https://www.oecd.org/coronavirus/policy-responses/building-back-better-a-sustainable-resilient-recovery-after-covid-19-52b869f5/

OECD. (2020). *Supporting Young Entrepreneurs through the COVID-19 Crisis: What's Next?* Available from: https://www.oecd.org/cfe/leed/OECD_Webinar_Youth_Entrepreneurship_Policy_and_COVID-19_SUMMARY.pdf

OECD. (2021). An in-depth analysis of one year of SME and entrepreneurship policy responses to COVID-19: lessons learned for the path to recovery. In *OECD SME and Entrepreneurship Papers*. OECD Publishing.

OECD. (2021). *OECD Policy Responses to Coronavirus (COVID-19), One year of SME and entrepreneurship policy responses to COVID-19: Lessons learned to "build back better"*. Available from: https://www.oecd.org/coronavirus/policy-responses/one-year-of-sme-and-entrepreneurship-policy-responses-to-covid-19-lessons-learned-to-build-back-better-9a230220/

Oestmann, S., & Dymond, A. C. (2001). Telecentres – experiences, lessons and trends, in the commonwealth of learning. In Telecentre: Case studies and key issues. Vancouver, Canada: The Commonwealth of Learning.

Ogbolu, M. N. (2015). Relationship Between Legitimacy and Intended Patronage: One Size Fits All? *Journal of Business Diversity*, *15*(1).

Okwelle, P. C., & Wordu, C. C. R. (2014). Public-Private Partnership in Education: A Strategy for Improving Quality of Vocational-Technical Education Programme in Nigeria: A Case Study of Rivers State. *Journal of Education and Practice*, *5*(35), 180–183.

Oliver, M. L., & Shapiro, T. M. (1995). Black Wealth/White. *Wealth: A New Perspective on.*

Omar, H. (2013). *An Unlikely Setting: Hasan Omar Walks Us Through One of the Up-and-Coming*. Academic Press.

Omer, W., & Aljaaidi, K. (2020). The association of entrepreneurial education and support with entrepreneurial intention at Northern Boarder University: the case of students from College of Business Administration. *Entrepreneurship and Sustainability Issues, 8*(1), 555-572. Retrieved from https://EconPapers.repec.org/RePEc:ssi:jouesi:v:8:y:2020:i:1:p:555-572

Omoto, A. M., & Packard, C. D. (2016). The power of connections: Psychological sense of community as a predictor of volunteerism. *The Journal of Social Psychology*, *156*(3), 272–290. doi:10.1080/00224545.2015.1105777 PMID:27064179

Omri, A., Frikha, M. A., & Bouraoui, M. A. (2015). An empirical investigation of factors affecting small business success. *Journal of Management Development*, *34*(9), 1073–1093. doi:10.1108/JMD-07-2013-0088

Onuoha, G. (2007). Entrepreneurship, *AIST. International Journal (Toronto, Ont.)*, *10*(1), 20–32.

Open Source Medical Supplies. (2020, July 4). *Open Source Medical Supplies*. Retrieved from Open Source Medical Supplies: https://opensourcemedicalsupplies.org/?fbclid=IwAR11eW3ODq9aeBu2CwTA6pWqGNdRTLtTfhAUzQaTXYWCLv-erRKhCi95rL0

Open Works Baltimore. (2019). *About Us*. https://www.openworksbmore.org/about-us/

Organisation for Economic Co-operation and Development (OECD). (2019). *Regions in Industrial Transition: Policies for People and Places*. OECD Regional Development Studies, OECD Publishing. . doi:10.1787/c76ec2a1-en

Orobia, L. A., Tusiime, I., Mwesigwa, R., & Ssekiziyivu, B. (2020). *Entrepreneurial framework conditions and business sustainability among the youth and women entrepreneurs. Asia Pacific Journal of Innovation and Entrepreneurship.*

Ortega Carpio, M. L., Martinez-Cousinou, G., & Morales-Fernández, E. J. (2018). Transformative Volunteerism: An Inventory of NGDO Volunteers' Motivations. *Human Service Organizations, Management, Leadership & Governance*, *42*(1), 33–52. doi:10.1080/23303131.2017.1363103

Osman, I., Ho, T. C., & Carmen Galang, M. (2011). The relationship between human resource practices and firm performance: An empirical assessment of firms in Malaysia. *Business Strategy Series*, *12*(1), 41–48. doi:10.1108/17515631111100412

Otioma, C., Madureira, A. M., & Martinez, J. (2019). Spatial analysis of urban digital divide in Kigali, Rwanda. *GeoJournal*, *84*(3), 719–741.

Oum, S. O., & Wexler, A. (2022, February 7). *Economic impact of covid-19 on PEPFAR countries*. KFF. Retrieved February 12, 2022, from https://www.kff.org/global-health-policy/issue-brief/economic-impact-of-covid-19-on-pepfar-countries/

Oviawe, J. I. (2010). Repositioning Nigerian youths for economic empowerment through entrepreneurship education. *European Journal of Educational Studies*, *2*(2), 113–118.

Pacetti, E. G. (2016). *The Five Characteristics of an Inclusive Economy: Getting Beyond the Equity-Growth Dichotomy.* The Rockefeller Foundation. Retrieved from: https://www.rockefellerfoundation.org/blog/five-characteristics-inclusive-economy-getting-beyond-equity-growth-dichotomy/

Pager, D., & Shepherd, H. (2008). The sociology of discrimination: Racial discrimination in employment, housing, credit, and consumer markets. *Annual Review of Sociology, 34*(1), 181–209. doi:10.1146/annurev.soc.33.040406.131740 PMID:20689680

Palestine's Information and Communications Technology Incubator (PICTI). (2018). *About Us.* Retrieved 2021, December 3 from: https://picti.ps/

Palia, D. (2016). Differential access to capital from financial institutions by minority entrepreneurs. *Journal of Empirical Legal Studies, 13*(4), 756–785. doi:10.1111/jels.12132

Pallagst, K., Fleschurz, R., & Said, S. (2017). What Drives Planning in a Shrinking City? Tales from Two German and Two American Cases. *The Town Planning Review, 88*(1), 15–28. doi:10.3828/tpr.2017.3

Palmer, R. (2007). Skills development, the enabling environment and informal micro-enterprise in Ghana. *Compare: A Journal of Comparative Education, 37*(4), 565. doi:10.1080/03057920701541927

Panda, S. (2018). Constraints faced by women entrepreneurs in developing countries: Review and ranking. *Gender in Management, 33*(4), 315–331. doi:10.1108/GM-01-2017-0003

Panizza, U. (2002). Income inequality and economic growth: Evidence from American data. *Journal of Economic Growth, 7*(1), 25–41. doi:10.1023/A:1013414509803

Pan, J., & Zhou, W. (2015). How do employees construe their career success: An improved measure of subjective career success. *International Journal of Selection and Assessment, 23*, 45–58. doi:10.1111/ijsa.12094

Pantano, E., Pizzi, G., Scarpi, D., & Dennis, C. (2020). Competing during a pandemic? Retailers' ups and downs during the COVID-19 outbreak. *Journal of Business Research, 116*, 209–213. doi:10.1016/j.jbusres.2020.05.036 PMID:32501307

Papulová, Z., & Papula, J. (2015). Entrepreneurship in the Eyes of the Young Generation. *Procedia Economics and Finance, 34*, 514–520. doi:10.1016/S2212-5671(15)01662-7

Parasuraman, A., Zeithaml, V. A., & Berry, L. L. (1988). Servqual: A multiple-item scale for measuring consumer perceptions of service quality. *Journal of Retailing, 64*(1), 12–23.

Park, H. Y., & Cho, I. H. (n.d.). *Creativity and the Market for Entrepreneurs in ICT Industry.* Academic Press.

Park, K., & Ki-Woong, P. (2011). ACCENT: Cognitive cryptography plugged compression for SSL/TLS-based cloud computing services. *Journal of ACM Transactions on Internet Technology, 11*(2), 7. doi:10.1145/2049656.2049659

Pascoe, E. A., & Richman, L. S. (2009). Perceived discrimination and health: A meta-analytic review. *Psychological Bulletin, 135*(4), 531–554. doi:10.1037/a0016059

Pasmore, W. A. (2001). Action research in the workplace: The socio-technical perspective. In P. Reason & H. Bradbury (Eds.), *Handbook of action research: Participative inquiry and practice* (pp. 38–48). Sage.

Paul, J.H., Shoemaker, Krupp, S., & Howland, S., X. (2013). Strategic Leadership: The Essential Skills. *Harvard Business Review.* PMID:23390746

Paycheck Protection Program: Loan Forgiveness And Other Challenges: Hearing before the Committee On Small Business United States House Of Representatives, 116th Cong. 12 (2020) (testimony of Dr. Rich Coleman, DVM)

PCBS. (2020). *Palestinian Labour Force Survey 2020*. Retrieved from: https://www.pcbs. gov.ps/Downloads/book2562.pdf

Pearson, C. M., & Porath, C. L. (2005). On the nature, consequences, and remedies of workplace incivility: No time for "nice"? Think again. *The Academy of Management Executive*, *19*(1), 7–18. doi:10.5465/ame.2005.15841946

Peery, D. (2011). The colorblind ideal in a race-conscious reality: The case for a new legal ideal for race relations. *Nw. JL & Soc. Pol'y*, *6*, 473.

Pennings, J. M. (1982). The Urban Quality of Life and Entrepreneurship. *Academy of Management Journal*, *25*(1), 63–79.

Perera, R. (2017). *The PESTLE analysis*. Nerdynaut.

Pesaran, M. H. (2007). A simple panel unit root test in the presence of cross-section dependence. *Journal of Applied Econometrics*, *22*(2), 265–312. doi:10.1002/jae.951

Peter, M., & Tim, G. (2011). *The NIST Definition of Cloud Computing*. Computer Security Division Information Technology Laboratory, National Institute of Standards and Technology Gaithersburg. Retrieved from https://csrc.nist.gov/publications/detail/sp/800-145/final

Petersen, I., & Kruss, G. (2021). Universities as change agents in resource-poor local settings: An empirically grounded typology of engagement models. *Technological Forecasting and Social Change*, *167*, 120693. doi:10.1016/j.techfore.2021.120693

Piketty, T., Yang, L., & Zucman, G. (2019). Capital accumulation, private property, and rising inequality in China, 1978–2015. *The American Economic Review*, *109*(7), 2469–2496. doi:10.1257/aer.20170973

Pinet, M., Phiona, S., & Youn, A. (2021). *Advancing youth-centred digital ecosystems in Africa in a post-Covid-19 world. ODI Working paper*. ODI. https://odi.org/en/publications/advancing-youth-centred-digital-ecosystems-in-africa-in-a-post-covid-19-world/

Ployhart, R. E., & Moliterno, T. P. (2011). Emergence of the human capital resource: A multilevel model. *Academy of Management Review*, *36*(1), 127–150. doi:10.5465/amr.2009.0318

Poor, M. A. (2014). *2014 Maryland Poverty Profile*. Retrieved from Catholic Charities of Maryland: http://www.catholiccharities-md.org/public-policy/2014-map-poverty-profiles.pdf

Porter, M. E., & Blaxill, M. (1997). Inner cities are the next retailing frontier. *Wall Street Journal*.

Porter, M. E. (2005). More tales of the inner city. *Inc.*, *27*(6), 86–89.

Portes, A. (1998). Social capital: Its origins and applications in modern sociology. *Annual Review of Sociology*, *24*(1), 1–24. doi:10.1146/annurev.soc.24.1.1

Portuguez Castro, M., & Gómez Zermeño, M. G. (2021). Being an entrepreneur post-COVID-19 – resilience in times of crisis: A systematic literature review. *Journal of Entrepreneurship in Emerging Economies*, *13*(4), 721–746. doi:10.1108/JEEE-07-2020-0246

Powell, J. A., Menendian, S., & Ake, W. (2019). *Targeted universalism: Policy & practice. Haas Institute for a Fair and Inclusive Society*. University of California.

Pressman, J. L., & Wildavsky, A. (1984). *Implementation: How great expectations in Washington are dashed in Oakland; Or, why it's amazing that federal programs work at all, this being a saga of the Economic Development Administration as told by two sympathetic observers who seek to build morals on a foundation* (Vol. 708). Univ of California Press.

ProjectDiane. (2020). *The State of Black & LatinxWomen Founders*. Digitalundivided. https://www.projectdiane.com/

Purkayastha, D., Tripathy, T., & Das, B. (2020). Understanding the ecosystem of microfinance institutions in India. *Social Enterprise Journal*, *16*(3), 243–261. doi:10.1108/SEJ-08-2019-0063

Quality Assurance Agency for Higher Education (QAA). (2012). *Enterprise and Entrepreneurship Education*. Guidance for UK Enterprise Education Providers.

Quarterly Labour Force Survey. (2021). *Quarterly Labour Force Survey (QLFS) – Q3:2021*. Statistics South Africa. Retrieved 10 May 2022, from https://www.statssa.gov.za/?p=14957

Radebe, T. N. (2019). The challenges/barriers preventing the South African youth in becoming entrepreneurs: South African overview. *Journal of Economics and Behavioral Studies*, *11*(4 (J)), 61–70. doi:10.22610/jebs.v11i4(J).2921

Radhakrishnan, S. (2008). Examining the 'global' Indian middle class: Gender and culture in the Silicon Valley/Bangalore Circuit. *Journal of Intercultural Studies (Melbourne, Vic.)*, *29*(1), 7–20. doi:10.1080/07256860701759915

Radipere, S. (2012). South African university entrepreneurship education. *African Journal of Business Management*, *6*(44), 11015–11022. doi:10.5897/AJBM12.410

Raffaelli, R. L. (2020). *Reinventing Retail: The Novel Resurgence of Independent Bookstores*. Working paper 20-068. Harvard Business School. Retrieved from: https://www.hbs.edu/ris/Publication%20Files/20-068_c19963e7-506c-479a-beb4-bb339cd293ee.pdf

Raimi, L., & Akhuemonkhan, I. A. I. A. (2014). Has Technical Vocational Education and Training (TVET) impactedon Employability and National Development? *The Macrotheme Review: A Multidisciplinary Journal of Global Macro Trends*, *3*(2), 129-145.

Ramadani, V. (2015). The Woman Entrepreneur in Albania: An Exploratory Study on Motivation, Problems and Success Factors. *Journal of Balkan & Near Eastern Studies*, *17*(2), 204–221. doi:10.1080/19448953.2014.997488

Ramadani, V., Dana, L., Gërguri-Rashiti, S., & Abazi-Alili, H. (2015). *The profile of female entrepreneurs in the Republic of Macedonia. In Female Entrepreneurship in Transition Economies: Trends and Challenges*. Palgrave Macmillan.

Ramos, A. G. (2020). *The New Sciences Organizations*. University of Toronto Press.

Rasheed, H. S. (2004). Capital access barriers to government procurement performance: Moderating effects of ethnicity, gender and education. *Journal of Developmental Entrepreneurship*, *9*(2), 109–126.

Rastogi, N. I. T. A. N. K., & Trivedi, M. K. (2016). PESTLE technique–a tool to identify external risks in construction projects. *International Research Journal of Engineering and Technology*, *3*(1), 384–388.

Ratten, V. (2016). Female entrepreneurship and the role of customer knowledge development, innovation outcome expectations and culture on intentions to start informal business ventures. *International Journal of Entrepreneurship and Small Business*, *27*(2/3), 262. doi:10.1504/IJESB.2016.073977

Ratten, V. (2021). Coronavirus (Covid-19) and entrepreneurship: Cultural, lifestyle and societal changes. *Journal of Entrepreneurship in Emerging Economies*, *13*(4), 747–761. doi:10.1108/JEEE-06-2020-0163

Ratten, V., & Dana, L. P. (2017). Gendered perspective of indigenous entrepreneurship. *Small Enterprise Research*, *24*(1), 62–72. doi:10.1080/13215906.2017.1289858

Ratten, V., & Usmanij, P. (2021). Entrepreneurship education: Time for a change in research direction? *International Journal of Management Education*, *19*(1), 100367.

Rawat, P. S. (2014). Patriarchal Beliefs, Women's Empowerment, and General Well-being. *Vikalpa*, *39*(2), 43–56. doi:10.1177/0256090920140206

Report, P. W. C. (2015). *Will the shift in global economic power continue*. Retrieved from https://www.pwc.com/gx/en/issues/the-economy/assets/world-in-2050-february-2015.pdf

Reuben, L., & Queen, P. (2015). Capital constraints and industry mix implications for African-American business success. *The Review of Black Political Economy*, *42*(4), 355–378. doi:10.100712114-015-9210-9

Reynolds, P. D., Carter, N. M., Gartner, W. B., & Greene, P. G. (2004). The prevalence of nascent entrepreneurs in the United States: Evidence from the Panel Study of Entrepreneurial Dynamics. *Small Business Economics*, *23*(4), 263–284. doi:10.1023/B:SBEJ.0000032046.59790.45

Rezaei, S., Goli, M., & Dana, L. P. (2014). Beyond legal entrepreneurship: The case of Austria. *International Journal of Entrepreneurship and Small Business*, *21*(2), 202. doi:10.1504/IJESB.2014.059473

Rheault, M., & Tortora, B. (2008). *Nigeria: Drivers and challenges of entrepreneurship*. www.gallup.com/poll/106345/nigeria-drivers-challenges-entrepreneurship.aspx

Rhodes, C., & Butler, J. S. (2004). Understanding self-perceptions of business performance: An examination of black American entrepreneurs. *Journal of Developmental Entrepreneurship*, *9*(1), 55–71.

Rhyne, B. M. (2021, September). *New business applications in the US hit historic heights last year.* World Economic Forum. Retrieved from: https://www.weforum.org/agenda/2021/09/new-business-applications-in-the-us-hit-historic-highs-last-year/

Ribeiro, D., & Montoro-Sánchez, M. Á. (2011). Introduction: The challenges of defining and studying contemporary entrepreneurship. *Canadian Journal of Administrative Sciences*, *28*(3), 297–301. doi:10.1002/cjas.217

Richardson, C., & Pisani, M. J. (2012). *The Informal and Underground Economy of the South Texas Border*. University of Texas Press. doi:10.7560/739277

Rini, D. L., & Hamonangan Tambunan, T. T. (2021). Inclusive Economic Growth of Indonesia and Its Determinants-Recent Evidence with Provincial Data. *Asian Journal of Interdisciplinary Research*, 85–100. doi:10.34256/ajir2118

Ritesh, M. (2018). Solidity Programming Essentials: A beginner's guide to build smart contracts for Ethereum and blockchain. Packt Publishing Ltd.

Ritter, T., & Pedersen, C. (2020). Analyzing the impact of the coronavirus crisis on business models. *Industrial Marketing Management*, *88*, 214–224. doi:10.1016/j.indmarman.2020.05.014

Robb, A. M. (2002). Entrepreneurial performance by women and minorities: The case of new firms. *Journal of Developmental Entrepreneurship*, *7*(4), 383–398.

Robinson, J., Blockson, L., & Robinson, S. (2005). *African American women entrepreneurs and firm growth: New theoretical directions at the intersection of race, gender, and firm growth*. Babson College, Frontiers of Entrepreneurship Research.

Rocco, T. S., & Gallagher, S. J. (2004). Discriminative justice: Can discrimination be just? *New Directions for Adult and Continuing Education*, *2004*(101), 29–41. doi:10.1002/ace.126

Rodrik, D. (2000). Growth versus Poverty Reduction: A Hollow Debate. *Finance & Development*, *37*(4), 8–9.

Roebroek, S. (2017). *The Effect of Human Capital, Support Systems and cultural support of the Performance of an entrepreneurial Ecosystem: An Empirical Study on the Entrepreneurial Ecosystem in Europe*. Available at: https://scripties.uba.uva.nl/document/655274

Rogers, C. D., Gent, M. J., Palumbo, G. M., & Wall, R. A. (2001). Understanding the growth and viability of inner-city businesses. *Journal of Developmental Entrepreneurship*, *6*(3).

Rogerson, C. M. (2020). COVID-19 and Tourism Spaces of Vulnerability in South Africa. *Journal of Hospitality. Tourism and Leisure*, *9*(4), 382–401. doi:10.46222/ajhtl.19770720-26

Rogerson, C. M., & Rogerson, J. M. (2020). COVID-19 tourism impacts in South Africa: Government and industry responses. *Geo Journal of Tourism and Geosites*, *31*(3), 1083–1091. doi:10.30892/gtg.31321-544

Rohit, A. (2021). *Credit Scores and Average Earnings of Women- Owned Businesses Rose, Yet Loan Approvals Lagged in 2020*. https://www.forbes.com/sites/rohitarora/2021/03/25/credit-scores-and-average-earnings-of-women-owned-businesses-rose-yet-loan-approvals-lagged-in-2020/?sh=bdde22b2c804

Rolle, J., & Kisato, J. (2019). The future of work and entrepreneurship for the underserved. *The Business & Management Review*, *10*(2), 224–234.

Roose, N., & Bishnoi, K. (2012). *Defining an Ecosystem for Social Finance* Master Dissertation. The FletcherSchool, TuftsUniversity.

Rose, M. (2012). Rethinking remedial education and the academic-vocational divide. *Mind, Culture, and Activity*, *19*(1), 1–16. doi:10.1080/10749039.2011.632053

Rosyadi, S., Kusuma, A. S., Fitrah, E., Haryanto, A., & Adawiyah, W. (2020). The multi-stakeholder's role in an integrated mentoring model for SMEs in the creative economy sector. *SAGE Open*, *10*(4). doi:10.1177/2158244020963604

Rowling, M. (2021*). Research shows COVID-19 did not stop clean energy jobs from rising*. Thomson Reuters Foundation in collaboration with World Economic Forum. Retrieved from https://www.weforum.org/ agenda/ 2021/10/renewable-energy-jobs-grew-globally-2020-covid-19

Rudiger, K., Peris-Ortiz, M., & Blanco-Gonzales, A. (2014). *Entrepreneurship, Innovation and Economic Crisis, Lessons for Research, Policy and Practice*. Springer. doi:10.1007/978-3-319-02384-7

Ruef, M. (2010). Entrepreneurial groups. In *Historical Foundations of Entrepreneurship Research*. Edward Elgar Publishing. doi:10.4337/9781849806947.00020

Ruiz, N. G., Horowitz, J. M., & Tamir, C. (2020, July 1). *Many Black and Asian Americans say they have experienced discrimination amid the COVID-19 outbreak*. Pew Research Center. Retrieved from: https://www.pewresearch.org/social-trends/2020/07/01/many-black-and-asian-americans-say-they-have-experienced-discrimination-amid-the-covid-19-outbreak/

Saad, S. K. (2020, July 17). *How celsious, an eco-friendly laundromat, pivoted during the pandemic*. Bustle. https://www.bustle.com/life/small-business-salutes-celsious-laundromat-founders-pivot-coronavirus

Saadia, Z. (2020). *We need a global reskilling revolution – here's why*. Retrieved from https://www.weforum.org/agenda/2020/01/reskilling-revolution-jobs-future-skills/

SABC News. (2020). *SA musician finds innovative ways to engage supporters*. Available from: https://www.sabcnews.com/sabcnews/sa-musician-finds-innovative-ways-to-engage-supporters/

Sadeq, T., & Hamed, M. (2011). *Policies to Promote Female Entrepreneurship in the Palestinian Territory*. Working paper, Palestine Economic Policy Research Institute (MAS).

Saeed, A., Kersten, W., & Abdelaziz, B. (2019). Sustainable product purchase: Does information about product sustainability on social media affect purchase behavior? *Asian Journal of Sustainability and Social Responsibility*, *4*(1), 1–18. https://doi.org/10.1186/s41180-019-0029-3

Sahlman, W. A. (1990). The structure and governance of venture-capital organizations. *Journal of Financial Economics, 27*(2), 473–521.

Saldaña, J. (2015). *The coding manual for qualitative researchers* (3rd ed.). Sage Publications.

Sambo, W. (2016). Factors affecting youth entrepreneurship development in Kibera district, Kenya. *Problems and Perspectives in Management, 14*(3), 154–161. doi:10.21511/ppm.14(3-1).2016.02

Sami Ur Rehman, M., Shafiq, M. T., & Afzal, M. (2021). Impact of COVID-19 on project performance in the UAE construction industry. *Journal of Engineering, Design and Technology, 20*(1), 245–266. doi:10.1108/JEDT-12-2020-0481

Sampson, R. J., & Wilson, W. J. (2005). Toward a theory of race, crime and urban inequality. In S. L. Gabbidon & H. T. Greene (Eds.), *Race, crime, and justice: A Reader*. Routledge: Taylor & Francis, Inc.

SAMSHA. (2018). *Sustainability Planning: Cultural Considerations*. Retrieved January 2, 2022, from https://m.youtube.com/watch?v=80POEiA-WDQ

Sanders, J. M., & Nee, V. (1996). Immigrant self-employment: The family as social capital and the value of human capital. *American Sociological Review, 61*(2), 231–249. doi:10.2307/2096333

SansaN. A. (2020). Analysis for the Impact of the COVID-19 to the Petrol Price in China. doi:10.2139/ssrn.3547413

Santos, G., Marques, C. S., & Ferreira, J. J. (2018). A look back over the past 40 years of female entrepreneurship: Mapping knowledge networks. *Scientometrics, 115*(2), 953–987. doi:10.100711192-018-2705-y

Saptono, A., Wibowo, A., Widyastuti, U., Narmaditya, B. S., & Yanto, H. (2021). Entrepreneurial self-efficacy among elementary students: The role of entrepreneurship education. *Heliyon, 7*(9), e07995. doi:10.1016/j.heliyon.2021.e07995 PMID:34585012

Sarnoff, I. (1960). Psychoanalytic theory and social attitudes. *Public Opinion Quarterly, 24*(2), 251–279. doi:10.1086/266948

Satalkina, L., & Steiner, G. (2020). Digital entrepreneurship and its role in innovation systems: A systematic literature review as a basis for future research avenues for sustainable transitions. *Sustainability, 12*(7), 2764.

Sathiabama, K. (2010). *Rural Women Empowerment and Entrepreneurship Development*. esocialsciences.com

Saunders, B., Sim, J., Kingstone, T., Baker, S., Waterfield, J., Bartlam, B., Burroughs, H., & Jinks, C. (2018). Saturation in qualitative research: Exploring its conceptualization and operationalization. *Quality & Quantity, 52*(4), 1893–1907. doi:10.100711135-017-0574-8 PMID:29937585

Schaltegger, S., & Wagner, M. (2011). Sustainable entrepreneurship and sustainability innovation: Categories and interactions. *Business Strategy and the Environment, 20*(4), 222–237.

Schimperna, F., Nappo, F., & Marsigalia, B. (2022). Student Entrepreneurship in Universities: The State-of-the-Art. *Administrative Sciences, 12*(1), 5. Advance online publication. doi:10.3390/admsci12010005

Schiuma, G., & Carlucci, D. (2018). Managing strategic partnerships with universities in innovation ecosystems: A research agenda. *Journal of Open Innovation, 4*(3), 25. doi:10.3390/joitmc4030025

Schlag, M., & Melé, D. (2020). Building Institutions for the Common Good. The Practice and Purpose of Business in an Inclusive Economy. *Humanist Manag J, 5,* 1–6. doi:10.1007/s41463-020-00092-9

Schlosser, K. (2020, April 14). *Startup founder Jane Park 'pivots with purpose' as gift wrap maker Tokki shifts to face masks.* GeekWire. https://www.geekwire.com/2020/startup-founder-jane-park-pivots-purpose-gift-wrap-maker-tokki-shifts-face-masks/

Schneider, F. (2005). The size of shadow economies in 145 countries from 1999 to 2003. *The Brown Journal of World Affairs*, *11*(2), 113–129.

Schøtt, T., Kew, P., & Cheraghi, M. (2015). *Future Potential: A GEM perspective on youth entrepreneurship.* Available from: https://portal.findresearcher.sdu.dk/en/publications/future-potential-a-gem-perspective-on-youth-entrepreneurship

Schumpeter, J. A. (1965). Economic Theory and Entrepreneurial History. In H. G. Aitken (Ed.), *Explorations in enterprise*. Harvard University Press.

Scott, P. (2017). *These are the jobs most at risk of automation according to Oxford University: Is yours one of them?* Retrieved from https:// www.telegraph.co.uk/ news/2017/09/27/jobs-risk-automation-according-oxford-university-one/

Seema, Choudhary, & Saini. (2021). Effect of Job Satisfaction on Moonlighting Intentions: Mediating Effect of Organizational Commitment. *European Research on Management and Business Economics*, *27*(1). doi:10.1016/j.iedeen.2020.100137

Seetharaman, P. (2020). Business models shifts: Impact of Covid-19. *International Journal of Information Management*, *54*, 1–4. doi:10.1016/j.ijinfomgt.2020.102173 PMID:32834338

Seo, H. J., Kim, H., & Lee, Y. S. (2020). The Dynamic Relationship between Inequality and Sustainable Economic Growth. *Sustainability*, *12*(14), 5740. doi:10.3390u12145740

Seshie-Nasser, H. A., & Oduro, A. D. (2018). Women-owned businesses and household welfare. *International Journal of Gender and Entrepreneurship*, *10*(4), 310–331. doi:10.1108/IJGE-01-2018-0001

Shahnaz, D. (2021). The Risks Not Taken: Building Inclusive Markets for Under-served Communities. In *Generation Impact*. Emerald Publishing Limited. doi:10.1108/978-1-78973-929-920200008

Shane, S. (2003). *A general theory of entrepreneurship: The individual-opportunity nexus*. Edward Elgar. doi:10.4337/9781781007990

Shane, S. A. (2008). *The illusions of entrepreneurship: The costly myths that entrepreneurs, investors, and policy makers live by*. Yale University Press.

Shane, S. A., & Venkataraman, S. (2000). The promise of entrepreneurship as a field of research. *Academy of Management Review*, *25*(1), 217–226. doi:10.5465/amr.2000.2791611

Shantz, A., Wang, J., & Malik, A. (2018). Disability status, individual variable pay, and pay satisfaction: Does relational and institutional trust make a difference? *Human Resource Management*, *57*(1), 365–380. doi:10.1002/hrm.21845

Sharma, G. D., Thomas, A., & Paul, J. (2021). Reviving tourism industry post-COVID-19. *Tourism Management Perspectives*, *37*(1), 67–72. doi:10.1016/j.tmp.2020.100786 PMID:33391988

Sharma, K. (2012). Role of women in informal sector in India. *Journal of the Humanities and Social Sciences*, *4*(1), 29–36. doi:10.9790/0837-0412936

Sharma, L. (2018). Entrepreneurial intentions and perceived barriers to entrepreneurship among youth in Uttarakhand state of India: A cross-cultural investigation across genders. *International Journal of Gender and Entrepreneurship*, *10*(3), 243–269. doi:10.1108/IJGE-02-2018-0009

Shepherd, D. A. (2020). COVID 19 and entrepreneurship: Time to pivot? *Journal of Management Studies*, *57*(8), 1750–1753. doi:10.1111/joms.12633

Sheridan, K., Halverson, E. R., Litts, B., Brahms, L., Jacobs-Priebe, L., & Owens, T. (2014). Learning in the Making: A Comparative Case Study of Three Makerspaces. *Harvard Educational Review*, *84*(4), 505–531. doi:10.17763/haer.84.4.brr34733723j648u

Shi, C., Liao, L., Li, H., & Su, Z. (2022). Which urban communities are susceptible to COVID-19? An empirical study through the lens of community resilience. *BMC Public Health*, *22*(1), 1–15. https://doi-org.mec.ezproxy.cuny.edu/10.1186/s12889-021-12419-8

Shipton, D. (2021). Knowing the goal: An inclusive economy that can address the public health challenges of our time. *Journal of Epidemiology and Community Health*, *75*(11), 1129–1132. https://doi.org/10.1136/jech-2020-216070

Shoba, S. (2020). *How young entrepreneurs are surviving the pandemic*. Available from: https://www.dailymaverick.co.za/article/2020-07-23-how-young-entrepreneurs-are-surviving-the-pandemic/

Shrivastava, S., & Shrivastava, R. (2013). Role of entrepreneurship in economic development: With special focus on necessity entrepreneurship and opportunity entrepreneurship. *International Journal of Management and Social Sciences Research*, *2*(2), 1–5.

Siegel, M. (2020). Racial disparities in fatal police shootings: An empirical analysis informed by critical race theory. *BUL Rev.*, *100*, 1069.

Silverman, D. (2006). *Interpreting Qualitative Data: Methods for Analysing Talk, Text and Interaction* (3rd ed.). Sage Publications.

Simon Kemp. (2018). *Digital 2020: Rwanda*. https://datareportal.com/reports/digital-2020-rwanda?rq=Rwanda%20intern

Simon, R., & McGinty, T. (2014, March 14). *Loan Rebound Misses Black Businesses. Fewer SBA-Backed Loans Go To Black Borrowers*. https://www.wsj.com/articles/no-headline-available-1394831256

Sims, L., & Robbennolt, S. (2020, December). *Racial and Ethnic Inequity in SBA Lending Patterns, 2010-2020*. Retrieved on June 2, 2020, from https://prosperitynow.org/resources/racial-and-ethnic-inequity-sba-lending-patterns-2010-2020

Sindabiwe, P., & Mbabazi, D. (2014). Triad Problematic of Youth Entrepreneurship. *Voices from University Students*, *1*(6), 463.

Sinek, S. (2017). *Understanding Empathy* [Video]. YouTube. https://www.youtube.com/watch?v=RyTQ5-SQYTo

Singh, R. P., & McDonald, G. (2004). *Reasons for pursuing new venture creation: Differences between black and white nascent entrepreneurs*. 2004 Academy of Management Meeting, New Orleans, LA.

Singh, V. K. (2020). *Policy and Regulatory Changes for a Successful Startup Revolution: Experiences from the Startup Action Plan in India*. ADBI Working Paper 1146. Tokyo: Asian Development Bank Institute.

Singh, R. P., & Crump, M. E. S. (2007). Educational attainment: A key factor for improving the lagging rate of black entrepreneurship. *The Review of Black Political Economy*, *34*(2), 217–229. doi:10.100712114-008-9011-5

Singh, R. P., Crump, M. E. S., & Zu, X. (2009). Family matters: Examining how self-employed blacks and whites differ in having self-employed parents. In M. V. Bradshaw & P. T. Carrington (Eds.), *Entrepreneurship and its Economic Significance, Behavior and Effects* (pp. 1–20). Nova Science Publishers.

Singh, R. P., & Hills, G. E. (2003). *Recognizing opportunities vs. deciding to become an entrepreneur: A test of Bhave's model. In Research at the Marketing/Entrepreneurship Interface*. University of Illinois at Chicago.

Singh, R. P., Knox, E. L., & Crump, M. E. S. (2008). Opportunity recognition differences between black and white nascent entrepreneurs: A test of Bhave's model. *Journal of Developmental Entrepreneurship*, *13*(1), 59–75. doi:10.1142/S1084946708000855

Siqueira, A. C. O., & Bruton, G. D. (2010). High-technology entrepreneurship in emerging economies: Firm informality and contextualization of resource-based theory. *IEEE Transactions on Engineering Management*, *57*(1), 39–50.

Skeggs, B. (1997). *Formations of Class and Gender: Becoming Respectable*. Sage Publications.

Small Business Association. (2021). *What's New with Small Business?* Retrieved from: https://www.sba.gov/sites/default/files/Whats_New_With_Small_Business.pdf

Smeeding, T. (2012). *Income, wealth, and debt and the Great Recession. Report*. The Russell Sage Foundation and the Stanford Center on Poverty and Inequality.

Smith, B. (2016). Intersectionality Discrimination and Substantive Equality: A comparative and Theoretical perspective. *The Equality Rights review*, (16).

Smith, D. (2010). The Role of Entrepreneurship in Economic Growth. *Undergraduate Economic Review*, *6*(1). Available from: https://digitalcommons.iwu.edu/cgi/viewcontent.cgi?article=1064&context=uer

Smith-Hunter, A. E., & Boyd, R. L. (2004). Applying theories of entrepreneurship to a comparative analysis of white and minority women business owners. *Women in Management Review*, *19*(1), 18–28. doi:10.1108/09649420410518403

Sol6rzano, D. G., & Yosso, T. J. (2002). Critical race methodology: Counter-storytelling as an analytical framework for education research. *Qualitative Inquiry*, *8*(1), 23–44. doi:10.1177/107780040200800103

Solt, F. (2020). Measuring Income Inequality Across Countries and Over Time: The Standardized World Income Inequality Database. *Social Science Quarterly*, *101*(3), 1183–1199. doi:10.1111squ.12795

Soni, S. (2021). *Covid horror: Thousands of micro, small businesses in India are on sale right now*. Financial Express. Retrieved from: https://www.financialexpress.com/industry/sme/msme-eodb-covid-horror-covid-horror-thousands-of-micro-small-businesses-in-india-are-on-sale-right-now/2339616/

Sonobe, T., Takeda, A., Yoshida, S., & Truong, H. T. (2021). *The Impacts of the COVID-19 Pandemic on Micro, Small, and Medium Enterprises in Asia and Their Digitalization Responses. ADBI Working Paper 1241*. Asian Development Bank Institute. Available https://www.adb.org/publications/impacts-covid-19-pandemic-msme-asia-their-digitalizationresponses

Sousa, M. J., & Almeida, M. D. R. (2014). Entrepreneurial skills development. *Recent Advances in Applied Economics*, 135-139.

South Africa, S. M. E. (2020). *The best time to start a business is now - 10 plus business ideas for youth*. Available from: https://smesouthafrica.co.za/10-plus-business-ideas-for-youth/

Sowell, T. (1991). Cultural Diversity: A World View. *American Enterprise (Washington, D.C.)*, *2*(3), 44–55.

Spriggs, W., & Williams, R. (2000). What do we need to explain about African American unemployment? In R. Cherry & W. R. Rogers III, (Eds.), *Prosperity for all? The economic boom and African Americans* (pp. 188–207). Russell Sage Foundation.

Srigley, K. (2005). "In case you hadn't noticed!": Race, Ethnicity, and Women's Wage-Earning in a Depression-Era City. *Labour/Le Travailleur, 55*, 69-106.

Srinivasan, N. (2015). Mobile Applications: A Game Changer for Rural Women Entrepreneurs? In Unveiling Women's Leadership. Palgrave Macmillan.

Stack, C. B. (2008). *All our kin: Strategies for survival in a black community*. Basic Books.

Stam, E. (2015). Entrepreneurial Ecosystems and Regional Policy: A Sympathetic Critique. *European Planning Studies*, *23*(9), 1759–1769. doi:10.1080/09654313.2015.1061484

Statista. (2021). *Worldwide installations of industrial robots from 2004 to 2020, with a forecast through 2024.* https://www.statista.com/statistics /264084/worldwide-sales-of-industrial-robots

Statistics South Africa (STATS SA). (2020). *Tourist accommodation.* Retrieved September 7, 2021, from http://www.statssa.gov.za/publications/P6410/P6410May2020.pdf

Steinmetz, C. (2021, September 24). Why Jackie Nguyen is planning a permanent stop, safe space for Café Cà Phê in Columbus Park. *Starland News.* Retrieved from: https://www.startlandnews.com/2021/09/cafe-ca-phe-columbus-park/

Stenholm, P., Acs, Z. J., & Wuebker, R. (2013). Exploring Country-Level Institutional Arrangements on the Rate and Type of Entrepreneurial Activity. *Journal of Business Venturing*, *28*(1), 176–193. doi:10.1016/j.jbusvent.2011.11.002

Stephan, U., Zbierowski, P., Pérez-Luño, A., &Klausen, A., (2021). *Entrepreneurship during the Covid-19 Pandemic: A global study of entrepreneurs' challenges, resilience, and well-being.* KBS Covid-19 Research Impact Papers, No. 4.

Stephan, U., Uhlaner, L. M., & Stride, C. (2015). Institutions and Social Entrepreneurship: The Role of Institutional Voids, Institutional Support, and Institutional Configurations. *Journal of International Business Studies*, *46*(3), 308–331. doi:10.1057/jibs.2014.38

Stephens, S., Cunningham, I., & Kabir, Y. (2021). Female entrepreneurs in a time of crisis: Evidence from Ireland. *International Journal of Gender and Entrepreneurship*, *13*(2), 106–120. doi:10.1108/IJGE-09-2020-0135

Steyaert, C., & Katz, J. (2004). Reclaiming the Space of Entrepreneurship in Society: Geographical, Discursive and Social Dimensions. *Entrepreneurship and Regional Development*, *16*(3), 179–196. doi:10.1080/0898562042000197135

Stiglitz, J. E. (2013). Society Endangers Our Future. New York: WW Norton & Company.

Strack, R., Kaufman, E., Kotsis, A., Sigelman, M., Restuccia, D., & Taska, B. (2019). *What's Trending in Jobs and Skills.* Retrieved from https://www.bcg.com/publications/2019/what-is-trending-jobs-skills

Strandh, V., & Eklund, N. (2018). Emergent groups in disaster research: Varieties of scientific observation over time and across studies of nine natural disasters. *Journal of Contingencies and Crisis Management*, *26*(3), 329–337. doi:10.1111/1468-5973.12199

Struyven, D., George-Joseph, G., & Milo, D. (2021). *Black Womenomics: Investing in the Underinvested.* Goldman Sachs Research https://www.goldmansachs.com/insights/pages/black-womenomics-f/black-womenomics-report.pdf

Stukas, A. A., Snyder, M., & Clary, E. G. (2016). Understanding and encouraging volunteerism and community involvement. *The Journal of Social Psychology*, *156*(3), 243–255. doi:10.1080/00224545.2016.1153328 PMID:27064177

Sucheran, R. (2021). Preliminary Economic Impact of the COVID-19 pandemic on the Hotel Sector in South Africa. *African Journal of Hospitality, Tourism and Leisure*, *10*(11), 115–130. doi:10.46222/ajhtl.19770720-90

Suhaimi, N. H. B. M., Al Mamun, A., Zainol, N. R., Nawi, N. C., Permerupan, Y., & Malarvizhi, C. A. (2016). Characteristics of informal micro-entrepreneurs in Malaysia. *Mediterranean Journal of Social Sciences*, *7*(2), 128.

Sune, L. (2020). *The Palestinian Startups Scene.* LinkedIn Pulse. Retrieved from: https://www.linkedin.com/pulse/palestinian-startups-scene-laure-sune/

Surbhi, S. (2017). Difference between exploratory and descriptive research. *Key Differences.* https://keydifferences.com/difference-between-exploratory-and-descriptive-research.html

Suri, R. (2010). *It's about time: The competitive advantage of quick response manufacturing.* CRC Press. doi:10.1201/EBK1439805954

Sytch, M., & Greer, L. L. (2021, February 2). *Is Your Organization Ready for Permanent WFH?* Retrieved from https://hbr.org/2020/08/is-your-organization-ready-for-permanent-wfh

Tabosa, F. J. S., & de Carvalho, P. U. (2017). Brazil, 1981-2013: the effects of economic growth and income inequality on poverty. Commission for Latin America and the Caribbean, 153.

Tafotie, R. (2020). *Fostering Digital Financial Services in Africa: a case of embracing*. SSRN.

Tagicakiverata, I. W. (2012). *TVET in Fiji: attitudes, perceptions and discourses* [Unpublished PhD Thesis]. University of Newcastle.

Takei, K. (2016). *The production of skills for the agricultural sector in Tanzania: the alignment of the provision of technical, vocational education and training with the demand for workforce skills and knowledge for rice production*. University of Sussex. http://hdl.voced.edu.au/10707/416180

Tandrayen-Ragoobur, V., & Kasseeah, H. (2012b). Unveiling the profile of women entrepreneurs in the small island economy of Mauritius. *Interdisciplinary Journal of Contemporary Research in Business*, *4*(4), 437–449.

Tan, K. S., Chong, S. C., Lin, B., & Eze, U. C. (2010). Internet based ICT adoption among SMEs: Demographic versus benefits, barriers, and adoption intention. *Journal of Enterprise Information Management*, *23*(1), 27–55.

Tanzi, V., & Chu, K. Y. (Eds.). (1998). *Income distribution and high-quality growth*. Mit Press.

Tapper, M. (2013). Emerging viral diseases and infectious disease risks. *Haemophilia*, *12*(1), 3–7. PMID:16445811

Technologies, B. G. (2020) *What's Trending in Jobs and Skills*. Retrieve from https:// www.burning-glass.com/ research-project/ bcg-trending-jobs-skills/

TED Talks. (2016). *The Power of Culture in Driving Sustainability*. Retrieved February 11, 2022, from https://m.youtube.com/watch?v=vDZHbP_tgDY

Terrell, F., & Terrell, S. L. (1993). Level of cultural mistrust as a function of educational and occupational expectations among black students. *Adolescence*, *28*(111), 573–578. PMID:8237544

Thapa Karki, S., & Xheneti, M. (2018). Formalizing women entrepreneurs in Kathmandu, Nepal. *The International Journal of Sociology and Social Policy*, *38*(7–8), 526–541. doi:10.1108/IJSSP-12-2017-0166

Thapa Karki, S., Xheneti, M., & Madden, A. (2021). To formalize or not to formalize: Women entrepreneurs' sensemaking of business registration in the context of Nepal. *Journal of Business Ethics*, *173*(4), 687–708.

The megaphone of main street: The impact of COVID-19. (2020). *SCORE Association*. Retrieved from: https://s3.amazonaws.com/mentoring.redesign/s3fs-public/Sept2020-SCORE-Megaphone-Covid-021221.pdf

The World Bank. (2020, September). *Survey reveals extent of the fallout from the pandemic on micro, small, and medium enterprises in Nepal*. Retrieved from: https://www.worldbank.org/en/news/press-release/2020/09/23/survey-reveals-extent-of-the-fallout-from-the-pandemic-on-micro-small-and-medium-enterprises-in-nepal

Thornton, G. (2021). Hotel industry: Navigating the impact of COVID-19. Surviving, adapting, and preparing for the new normal. *Japan-Hospitals*, *10*, 5–9.

Tinkler, J. E., Ku, M. C., Whittington, K. B., & Davies, A. R. (2015). Gender and venture capital decision making: The effects of technical background and social capital on entrepreneurial evaluations. *Social Science Research*, *51*(1), 1–16.

Tong, A., Sainsbury, P., & Craig, J. (2007, December). Consolidated criteria for reporting qualitative research (COREQ): A 32-item checklist for interviews and focus groups. *International Journal for Quality in Health Care*, *19*(6), 349–357. doi:10.1093/intqhc/mzm042

Toyota Industries Corporation. (2020, June 24). *History*. Retrieved from Toyota-Industries: https://www.toyota-industries.com/company/history/

Trading Economics. (2019). *South Africa Youth Unemployment Rate*. Available from: https://tradingeconomics.com/south-africa/youth-unemployment-rate

Trist, E. L. (1981). *The evolution of socio-technical systems: A conceptual framework and an action research program*. Ontario Quality of Working Life Center, Occasional paper.

Tshabalala, M., & Beharry-Ramraj, A. (2021). Examining the 4th Industrial Revolution and South Africa Youth Entrepreneurship Linkage to Covid 19: Opportunities and Challenges. *Gender & Behaviour*, *19*(1), 17204–17218.

Tundui, H. P., & Tundui, C. S. (2021). Marriage and business performance: The case of women-owned micro and small businesses in Tanzania. *Journal of Entrepreneurship in Emerging Economies*, *13*(5), 1287–1308. doi:10.1108/JEEE-06-2020-0202

Tunio, M. N., Chaudhry, I. S., Shaikh, S., Jariko, M. A., & Brahmi, M. (2021). Determinants of the Sustainable Entrepreneurial Engagement of Youth in Developing Country—An Empirical Evidence from Pakistan. *Sustainability*, *13*(14), 7764. doi:10.3390u13147764

Twigg, J. (2015). *Disaster Risk Reduction* (Vol. 9). Humanitarian Policy Group. http://bvpad.indeci.gob.pe/doc/pdf/esp/doc2601/doc2601-contenido.pdf

Tyagarajan, T. (2019). To Prepare for Automation, Stay Curious and Don't Stop Learning. *Harvard Business Review*. https://hbr.org/2019/10/to-prepare-for-automation-stay-curious-and-dont-stop-learning

U.S. Bureau of Labour Statistics. (2021). *Advertising, Promotions, and Marketing Managers*. Retrieved from https://www.bls.gov/ooh/ management/ advertising- promotions- and- marketing- managers.htm

Ughetto, E., Rossi, M., Audretsch, D., & Lehmann, E. E. (2020). Female entrepreneurship in the digital era. *Small Business Economics*, *55*(2), 305–312. doi:10.100711187-019-00298-8

UK Commission for Employment and Skills. (2015). *UK Commission for Employment and Skills (UKCES) annual report and accounts for financial year 2014 to 2015*. Retrieved from https://www.gov.uk/government /publications / uk-commission-for-employment-and-skills-annual-report-and-accounts-2014-to-2015

Umar, I. Y., & Ma'aji, A. S. (2010). Repositioning the facilities in technical college workshops for efficiency: a case study of North Central Nigeria. *Journal of STEM Teacher Education, 47*(3), 62-85. https://ir.library.illinoisstate.edu/jste/vol47/iss3/6

UN Dept Economic and Social Affairs. (2021, October 25). *First Global Webinar for the Voluntary National Reviews*. Retrieved February 2, 2022, from https://sustainabledevelopment.un.org/content/documents/29441Summary_First_Global_Webinar_2022_VNRs.pdf

UNCDF. (2020). *Youth Entrepreneurs Engaging in the Digital Economy: The Next Generation*. Available from: https://www.undp.org/publications/youth-entrepreneurs-engaging-digital-economy-next-generation

UNCTAD. (2014). *United Nations Conference on trade and development*. https://unctad.org/system/files/official-document/dtlstict2013d2_en.pdf

UNCTAD. (2020). *Equipping East Africa women Digital entrepreneurs with skills thrive*. Retrieved form https://unctad.org/news/equipping-east-african-women-digital-entrepreneurs-skills-thrive

UNCTAD. (2020). *Uganda Science, technology & Policy review*. Retrieved from https://unctad.org/system/files/official-document/dtlstict2020d4_en.pdf

UNCTAD. (2021). *Economic Costs of the Israeli Occupation for the Palestinian People: Poverty in the West Bank Between 2000 and 2019*. UNCTAD.

UNDP. (2020). *Youth Entrepreneurs and COVID-19*. Available from: https://www.za.undp.org/content/south_africa/en/home/presscenter/articles/2020/youth-entrepreneurs-and-covid-19.html

UNESCO. (2003). *Implementing the UNESCO/ILO recommendations concerning technical and vocational education and training: Final report of the Sub-Regional Seminar for West Africa*. UNESCO/ILO. https://unesdoc.unesco.org/images/0014/001438/143822e.pdf

UNESCO. (2004). *UNESCO international experts meeting: Learning for work, citizenship and sustainability. Final report*. UNESCO.

UNESCO. (2010). *Guidelines for TVET Policy Review*. https://unesdoc.unesco.org/ark:/48223/pf0000187487

UNESCO. (2020). *COVID-19 impact on education*. United Nations Educational, Scientific and Cultural Organization. Available at: https://en.unesco.org/covid19/educationresponse

UNESCO. (2021). *Fighting COVID-19 through digital innovation and transformation*. Available from: https://en.unesco.org/covid19/communicationinformationresponse/digitalinnovation

Unite, M. (2020, July 14). *FAQ*. Retrieved from Makers Unite: https://mdmakersunite.org/participate/process

United Nations Conference on Trade and Development (UNCTAD). (2012). *The Palestinian economy: Macroeconomic and trade policymaking under occupation*. UNCTAD/GDS/APP/2011/1.

United Nations Conference on Trade and Development. (2020). *COVID-19 and tourism*. Retrieved September 5, 2021, from https://unctad.org/system/files/official-document/ditcinf2020d3_en.pdf

United Nations Educational Scientific and Cultural Organisation (UNESCO). (2016). *Unpacking Sustainable Development Goal 4: Education 2030 – Guide*. https://unesdoc.unesco.org/images/0024/002463/246300E.pdf

United Nations. (2020, September). *SDG indicators*. United Nations. Retrieved December 15, 2021, from https://unstats.un.org/sdgs/report/2020/

United Nations. (2021, May 28). *Home. Sustainable development knowledge platform. Business and Industry Group Major Group - HLPF 2021 // Sectoral Paper*. Retrieved January 2, 2022, from https://sustainabledevelopment.un.org/

United States Census Bureau. (2022). *Small Business Pulse Survey*. Retrieved from: https://portal.census.gov/pulse/data/

United States Department of Labor. (2020, July 14). *Occupational Safety and Health Administration*. Retrieved from Personal Protective Equipment: https://www.osha.gov/personal-protective-equipment

Unnikrishnan, S., & Blair, C. (2019). *Want to Boost the Global Economy by $5 Trillion? Support Women as Entrepreneurs*. BCG Publications.

UNTWO. (2021). *2020: Worst year in tourism history with 1 billion fewer international arrivals*. Retrieved November 19, 2021, from https://www.unwto.org/news/2020-worst-year-in-tourism-history-with-1-billion-fewer-international-arrivals

US Census. (2012). https://www.census.gov/quickfacts/NY

Uzunidis, D., Boutillier, S., & Laperche, B. (2014). The entrepreneur's 'resource potential'and the organic square of entrepreneurship: Definition and application to the French case. *Journal of Innovation and Entrepreneurship*, *3*(1), 1–17. doi:10.1186/2192-5372-3-1

Vaal University. (2020). *Uber who? Kasi catering to the townships*. Available from: https://www.vut-research.ac.za/uber-who-kasi-catering-to-the-townships/

Valcke, B., Van Hiel, A., Van Assche, J., Van Roey, T., Onraet, E., & Roets, A. (2020). The Need for Inclusion: The relationships between Relational and Collective inclusion needs and psychological well-and ill-being. *European Journal of Social Psychology*, *50*(3), 579–596. doi:10.1002/ejsp.2641

Valdez, Z. (2008). The effect of social capital on White, Korean, Mexican and Black business owners' earnings in the US. *Journal of Ethnic and Migration Studies*, *34*(6), 955–973. doi:10.1080/13691830802211265

Valles, B. G., & Villalpando, O. (2021). A critical race policy analysis of the school-to-prison pipeline for Chicanos. In *Handbook of critical race theory in education* (pp. 394–403). Routledge. doi:10.4324/9781351032223-34

Van de Ven, A., & Stam, E. (2019). Entrepreneurial Ecosystem Elements. *Small Business Economics*, *56*, 809–832.

Van De Ven, H. (1993). The Development of an Infrastructure For Entrepreneurship. *Journal of Business Venturing*, *8*(3), 211–230. doi:10.1016/0883-9026(93)90028-4

Van den Broeck, A. (2010). Capturing autonomy, competence, and relatedness at work: Construction and initial validation of the Work-related Basic Need Satisfaction scale. *Journal of Occupational and Organizational Psychology*, *83*(4), 981–1002. doi:10.1348/096317909X481382

Van Nuys, A. (2019). *New LinkedIn Research: Upskill Your Employees with the Skills Companies Need Most in 2020*. Retrieved from https://www.linkedin.com/business/learning/blog/learning-and-development/most-in-demand-skills-2020

Varpio, L., Paradis, E., Uijtdehaage, S., & Young, M. (2020). The distinctions between theory, theoretical framework, and conceptual framework. *Academic Medicine*, *95*(7), 989–994. doi:10.1097/ACM.0000000000003075 PMID:31725464

Venkatesh, V. (2000). Determinants of Perceived Ease of Use: Integrating Control, Intrinsic Motivation, and Emotion into the Technology Acceptance Model. *Information Systems Research*, *11*(4), 342–365.

Venkatesh, V., Morris, M., Davis, G., & Davis, F. (2003). User Acceptance of Information Technology: Toward a Unified View. *Management Information Systems Quarterly*, *27*(3), 425–478.

Villaseca, D., Navío-Marco, J., & Gimeno, R. (2021). Money for female entrepreneurs does not grow on trees: Start-ups' financing implications in times of COVID-19. *Journal of Entrepreneurship in Emerging Economies*, *13*(4), 698–720.

Vining, A. R., & Boardman, A. E. (2008). Public-private partnerships in Canada: Theory and evidence. *Canadian Public Administration*, *51*(1), 9–44. doi:10.1111/j.1754-7121.2008.00003.x

Vohra-Gupta, S., Kim, Y., & Cubbin, C. (2021). Systemic racism and the Family Medical Leave Act (FMLA): Using critical race theory to build equitable family leave policies. *Journal of Racial and Ethnic Health Disparities*, *8*(6), 1482–1491. doi:10.100740615-020-00911-7 PMID:33211249

Von Kutzschenbach, M., & Daub, C. H. (2021). Digital Transformation for Sustainability: A Necessary Technical and Mental Revolution. In *New Trends in Business Information Systems and Technology* (pp. 179–192). Springer.

Vossenberg, S. (2013). Women Entrepreneurship Promotion in Developing Countries: What explains the gender gap in entrepreneurship and how to close it. *Maastricht School of Management Working Paper Series, 8*(1), 1-27.

Vujica Herzog, N., & Tonchia, S. (2014). An Instrument for Measuring the Degree of Lean Implementation in Manufacturing. *Strojniski Vestnik. Jixie Gongcheng Xuebao, 60*(12), 797–803. https://doi-org.proxy-cs.researchport.umd.edu/10.5545/sv-jme.2014.1873

Wahba, M. (2010). Vocational technical education and development. In *Vocational technical education and development.* http://www.nigerianbestforum.com/blog

Wahiba, N. F., & El Weriemmi, M. (2014). The relationship between economic growth and income inequality. *International Journal of Economics and Financial Issues., 4*(1), 135.

Walby, S. (1990). *Theorising Patriarchy.* Blackwell.

Walstad, W. B., & Kourilsky, M. L. (1998). Entrepreneurial attitudes and knowledge of black youth. *Entrepreneurship Theory and Practice, 23*(2), 5–18. doi:10.1177/104225879802300201

Wang, J., & Zhang, D. H. (2021). *The cost of banking deserts: racial disparities in access to PPP lenders and their implications.* Retrieved February 4, 2022, from https://davidzhang.scholar.harvard.edu/files/dhz/files/geographyppp.pdf

Wang, Q., & Richardson, L. (2021). Fostering Art and Cultural Entrepreneurship in Underserved Communities: A Case of Newark, NJ. *Journal of Planning Education and Research.*

Wang, S. (2012). *The Legal Frameworks of Technical and Vocational Education and Training (TVET) from International Level to National Level of China.* Academic Press.

Wardynski, D. J. (2019). *What Are the Effects of Technology on Human Interaction?* Brainspire. https://www.brainspire.com/blog/what-are-the-effects-of-technology-on-human-interaction

Warström, J. (2020). *Why Leaders Must Listen.* And Not Just Hear, Forbes.

Watkins, A. (2021, November 8). Violent Year in New York and Across U.S. as Pandemic Fuels Crime Spike. *The New York Times.* https://www.nytimes.com/2020/12/29/nyregion/nyc-2020-crime-covid.html

Watson, A., Lupton, D., & Michael, M. (2021). The COVID digital home assemblage: Transforming the home into a work space during the crisis. *Convergence (London), 27*(5), 1207–1221. https://doi.org/10.1177/13548565211030848

Watson, J. (2002). Comparing the performance of male- and female-controlled businesses: Relating outputs to inputs. *Entrepreneurship Theory and Practice, 26*(3), 91–100. doi:10.1177/104225870202600306

Watters, J. J., Hay, S., Dempster, N., & Pillay, H. (2013). School industry partnerships: an innovative strategy for vocational education. *Proceedings of the ECER VETNET Conference 2013.* https://eprints.qut.edu.au/63684/

WBAL. (2020, March 24). *People with 3D printers wanted to help make face shields for hospital workers.* WBAL TV News 11. Baltimore, MD: Hearst Broadcast Group.

WDI. (2020a). *World Development Indicators.* The World Bank.

Webb, A., McQuaid, R., & Rand, S. (2020). Employment in the informal economy: Implications of the COVID-19 pandemic. *The International Journal of Sociology and Social Policy, 40*(9/10), 1005–1019. doi:10.1108/IJSSP-08-2020-0371

Webb, J. W., Tihanyi, L., Ireland, R. D., & Sirmon, D. G. (2009). You say illegal, I say legitimate: Entrepreneurship in the informal economy. *Academy of Management Review, 34*(3), 492–510. doi:10.5465/amr.2009.40632826

WEF. (2021). *World Economic Forum.* Retrieved from https://www.weforum.org/agenda/2021/11/digital-entrepreneurship-africa-botswana-women-gender-equality/

Weiler, S., Silverstein, J., Chalmers, K., Lacey, E., Rogers, W., & Widner, B. (2003). Understanding the retail business potential of inner cities. *Journal of Economic Issues*, *37*(4), 1075–1105. doi:10.1080/00213624.2003.11506643

Wenting, R., Atzema, O., & Frenken, K. (2011). Urban Amenities and Agglomeration Economies? The Locational Behaviour and Economic Success of Dutch Fashion Design Entrepreneurs. *Urban Studies (Edinburgh, Scotland)*, *48*(7), 1333–1352. doi:10.1177/0042098010375992

Werbner, P. (2001). Metaphors of spatiality and networks in the plural city: A critique of the ethnic conclave economy debate. *Sociology*, *35*(3), 671–693. doi:10.1177/S0038038501000347

WGI. (2020b). *Worldwide Governance Indicators*. The World Bank.

Whaley, A. L. (2001). Cultural mistrust and mental health services for African Americans: A review and metanalysis. *The Counseling Psychologist*, *29*(4), 513–531. doi:10.1177/0011000001294003

Whaley, A. L. (2004). Ethnicity/race, paranoia, and hospitalization for mental health problems among men. *American Journal of Public Health*, *94*(1), 78–82. doi:10.2105/AJPH.94.1.78 PMID:14713702

Wilczynski, V. (2015). Academic maker spaces and engineering design. In American Society for Engineering Education (Vol. 26, p. 1). doi:10.18260/p.23477

Williams, R. (2019). *To Know Us is to Love Us: Developing a Culture of Data-Informed Inclusivity*. https://makethedata.org/2019/12/06/to-know-us-is-to-love-us-developing-a-culture-of-data-informed-inclusivity/

Williams, C. C. (2008). Beyond necessity-driven versus opportunity-driven entrepreneurship: A study of informal entrepreneurs in England, Russia and Ukraine. *International Journal of Entrepreneurship and Innovation*, *9*(3), 157–166. doi:10.5367/000000008785096647

Williams, C. C. (2019). Tackling undeclared work in the European Union: An evaluation of government policy approaches. *UTMS Journal of Economics (Skopje)*, *10*(2), 135–147.

Williams, C. C., & Krasniqi, B. (2017). Evaluating the individual- and country-level variations in tax morale. *Journal of Economic Studies (Glasgow, Scotland)*, *44*(5), 816–832. doi:10.1108/JES-09-2016-0182

Williams, C. C., & Nadin, S. (2010). The commonality and character of off-the-books entrepreneurship: A comparison of deprived and affluent urban neighbourhoods. *Journal of Developmental Entrepreneurship*, *15*(03), 1–14. doi:10.1142/S1084946710001592

Williams, C. C., & Round, J. (2008). Retheorizing the nature of informal employment: Some lessons from Ukraine. *International Sociology*, *23*(3), 367–388. doi:10.1177/0268580908088896

Williams, C. C., & Shahid, M. S. (2016). Informal entrepreneurship and institutional theory: Explaining the varying degrees of (in)formalization of entrepreneurs in Pakistan. *Entrepreneurship and Regional Development*, *28*(1-2), 1–25. doi:10.1080/08985626.2014.963889

Williams, D., & Kluev, A. (2014). The entrepreneurial university: Evidence of the changing role of universities in modern Russia. *Industry and Higher Education*, *28*(4), 271–280. doi:10.5367/ihe.2014.0212

Williams, M. (2001). In whom we trust: Group membership as an effective context for trust development. *Academy of Management Review*, *26*(3), 377–396. doi:10.5465/amr.2001.4845794

Williams, R., & Klugh, E. (2017). Creating a University Driven "Ingepreneurial" Ecosystem in West Baltimore: A Strategy for Rust Belt Revitalization. *Metropolitan Universities Journal.*, *28*(2), 103–123. Advance online publication. doi:10.18060/21510

Willis, W. (2020). Take a Seat at Oregon's Kitchen Table: Adapting Targeted Universalism for Broad and Deep Civic Engagement. *National Civic Review*, *108*(4), 16–26.

Wilmoth, D. (2021, March). *The Effects of the COVID-19 Pandemic on Small Businesses*. US Small Business Administration Office of Advocacy.

Wilson, N. (2020). *Iconic hotels Mount Grace in Magaliesburg & Durban's Edward to close: Times Live*. Retrieved September 7, 2021, from https://www.timeslive.co.za/news/southafrica/2020-06-19-marriott-international-shuts-iconic-mount-grace-hotel-inmagaliesburg/

Wilson, F., Marlino, D., & Kickul, J. (2004). Our entrepreneurial future: Examining the diverse attitudes and motivations of teens across gender and ethnic identity. *Journal of Developmental Entrepreneurship*, *9*(3), 177–197.

Wolfgang, F., Francoise, M.-N., Indermit, G., Benedecte, B., & Facundo, P. (2021). *South Africa accelerating job creation*. Available from: https://blogs.worldbank.org/africacan/south-africa-after-covid-19-accelerating-job-creation

Women in Informal Employment, Globalizing, and Organizing (WIEGO). (2020). *Counting the World's Informal Workers: A Global Snapshot*. WIEGO. https://www.wiego.org/sites/default/files/resources/files/WIEGO-Global-Statistics-Snapshot-Pamphlet-English-2019.pdf

Wong, E. L. Y., Ho, K. F., Wong, S. Y. S., Cheung, A. W. L., Yau, P. S. Y., Dong, D., & Yeoh, E. K. (2020). Views on Workplace Policies and its Impact on Health-Related Quality of Life During Coronavirus Disease (COVID-19) Pandemic: Cross-Sectional Survey of Employees. *International Journal of Health Policy and Management*. doi:10.34172/ijhpm.2020.127

World Bank Group. (2019). Kenya Digital Economy Assessment. Summary Report. Washington, DC: World Bank.

World Bank Group. (2020, September 1). *Five things you need to know about social sustainability and inclusion*. World Bank.

World Bank. (2010). *The worlds bank in Eastern and Southern Africa*. https://www.worldbank.org/en/region/afr/eastern-and-southern-africahttps://www.worldbank.org/en/region/afr/eastern-and-southern-africa

World Bank. (2016). *Women, Business and the Law*. International Bank for Reconstruction and Development/The World Bank.

World Bank. (2018). *The Digital Economy for Africa Initiative*. https://www.worldbank.org/en/programs/all-africa-digital-transformation

World Bank. (2019). *Accelerating Poverty reduction in Africa: In Five Charts*. https://www.worldbank.org/en/region/afr/publication/accelerating-poverty-reduction-in-africa-in-five-charts

World Bank. (2019). *Kenya economic Update Accelerating Keya's Digital economy*. Retrieved form https://www.worldbank.org/en/country/kenya/publication/kenya-economic-update-accelerating-kenyas-digital-economy

World Bank. (2020). *Ease of Doing Business in West Bank and Gaza*. World Bank Group.

World Bank. (2020a). *World Bank Injects $104 Million to Strengthen Skills Development Programs in Mozambique*. https://www.worldbank.org/en/news/press-release/2020/09/08/world-bank-injects-104-million-to-strengthen-skills-development-programs-in-mozambique

World Bank. (2020b). *Additional Financing of the Women Entrepreneurship Development Project (WEDP)*. World Bank. https://documents1.worldbank.org/curated/en/103061607914878676/text/Ethiopia-Women-Entrepreneurship-Development-Project-Additional-Financing.txt

World Bank. (2021). *Economic Monitoring Report to the Ad hoc Liaison Committee*. World Bank Group.

World Bank. (2021). *Unlocking the potential of women entrepreneurs in Uganda: a brief of policy interventions*. https://openknowledge.worldbank.org/bitstream/handle/10986/36220/Unlocking-the-Potential-of-Women-Entrepreneurs-in-Uganda-A-Brief-of-Policy-Interventions.pdf?sequence=1&isAllowed=y

World Economic Forum. (2018). *10 skills you'll need to survive the rise of automation*. Retrieved from https: // www.weforum.org/ agenda/ 2018/07/the-skills-needed-to- survive-the-robot-invasion-of-the-workplace

World Economic Forum. (2020). *Discovering the real impact of COVID-19 on entrepreneurship*. Available from: https://www.weforum.org/agenda/2020/06/how-covid-19-will-change-entrepreneurial-business/

World Economic Forum. (2020). Jobs of Tomorrow Mapping Opportunity in the New Economy. Author.

World Economic Forum. (2020). *The Reskilling Revolution: Better Skills, Better Jobs, Better Education for a Billion People by 2030*. https://www.weforum.org/press/2020/01/the-reskilling-revolution-better-skills-better-jobs-better-education-for-a-billion-people-by-2030/

World Health Organization (WHO). (2020). *Coronavirus disease (COVID-19)*. Available from: https://www.who.int/health-topics/coronavirus#tab=tab_1

World Health Organization. (2020). *Coronavirus disease 2019 (COVID-19) situation report – 43*. Available at: www.who.int/docs/default-source/coronaviruse/situation-reports/20200303-sitrep43-covid-19.pdf?sfvrsn=2c21c09c_2

Wu, A., Song, D., & Yang, Y. (2020). Untangling the effects of entrepreneurial opportunity on the performance of peasant entrepreneurship: The moderating roles of entrepreneurial effort and regional poverty level. *Entrepreneurship and Regional Development*, *32*(1-2), 112–133.

Xheneti, M., Karki, S. T., & Madden, A. (2019). Negotiating business and family demands within a patriarchal society – the case of women entrepreneurs in the Nepalese context. *Entrepreneurship and Regional Development*, *31*(3–4), 259–278. doi:10.1080/08985626.2018.1551792

Xiao, Y., Becerik-Gerber, B., Lucas, G., & Roll, S. C. (2021). Impacts of Working From Home During COVID-19 Pandemic on Physical and Mental Well-Being of Office Workstation Users. *Journal of Occupational and Environmental Medicine*, *63*(3), 181–190. https://doi.org/10.1097/JOM.0000000000002097

Yamoah, F. A., & Johnson, C. (2020). Minding the Gaps in British Ethnic Entrepreneurship and Commercial History: From the Genesis to the 21st Century. *Journal of Historical Sociology*, *33*(4), 614–627. doi:10.1111/johs.12296

Yang, K. M., & Pisani, M. J. (2018). When informality meets formality: Evidence from China. *Chinese Management Studies*, *12*(1), 184–201. doi:10.1108/CMS-03-2017-0055

Yin, R. K. (2009). How to do better case studies. In *The SAGE handbook of applied social research methods* (Vol. 2, pp. 254–282). Sage.

Young, N. (1998). *The structure and substance of African American entrepreneurial networks: Some preliminary findings*. Babson College, Frontiers of Entrepreneurship Research.

Youth Co. Lab. (2020). *Impact of COVID-19 on Youth Entrepreneurs in Indonesia*. Available from: https://www.unicef.org/indonesia/media/8236/file

Zagelmeyer, S., & Gollan, P. (2012). Exploring terra incognita: Preliminary reflections on the impact of the global financial crisis upon human resource management. *International Journal of Human Resource Management*, *23*, 3287-3294. . doi:10.1080/09585192.2012.689158

Zahra, S. A. (2007). Contextualizing Theory Building in Entrepreneurship Research. *Journal of Business Venturing*, *22*(3), 443–452.

Zahra, S. A., Wright, M., & Abdelgawad, S. G. (2014). Contextualization and the Advancement of Entrepreneurship Research. *International Small Business Journal*, *32*(5), 479–500. doi:10.1177/0266242613519807

Zainol, N. R., & Al Mamun, A. (2018). Entrepreneurial competency, competitive advantage and performance of informal women micro-entrepreneurs in Kelantan, Malaysia. *Journal of Enterprising Communities: People and Places in the Global Economy*, *12*(3), 299–321. doi:10.1108/JEC-11-2017-0090

Zaw, K., Bhattacharya, J., Price, A., Hamilton, D., & Darity Jr, W. (2017). Women, race and wealth. *Research Brief Series, 1*(1), 1-4.

Zeeshan, M. (2021, March 4). *COVID-19 Threatens to Waste India's Demographic Dividend.* Retrieved from https://thediplomat.com/2021/03/covid-19-threatens-to-waste-indias-demographic-dividend/

Zucman, G. (2019). Global wealth inequality. *Annual Review of Economics*, *11*(1), 109–138. doi:10.1146/annurev-economics-080218-025852

About the Contributors

Jo-Ann Denise Rolle holds a PhD in Economics from Howard University. Dr. Rolle has served as the Dean of the School of Business at Medgar Evers College, City University of New York (CUNY) for the past 8 years. Dean Rolle has a history of success, she served in the U.S. Government and I.B.M. before her academic career. She served as CEO of a university; as a Chief Academic Officer; and as a Business School Dean at two universities. She launched two entrepreneurial Centers and many entrepreneurship programs. She has been recognized as a Top 25 Influential African American Women in Business. She has delivered Keynote speeches and workshops to include the U.N. She is a Price-Babson Symposium for Entrepreneurship Educators fellow, Administrative Fellow, Harvard University, Member of the Economic Club of New York, and Fellow of Centre for Business & Economic Research and President of the HBCU Business Deans Roundtable.

Micah Crump holds a PhD in management and entrepreneurship from Morgan State University. He is a professor of business at Medgar Evers College in Brooklyn, New York, USA. He holds an MBA from Morgan State University and a BS degree from Coppin State University. He has taught more than 10,000 MBA, Executive MBA, and undergraduate business and entrepreneurship students at Howard, Morgan State, Coppin State, Jackson State, and Medgar Evers College. He served as entrepreneurship trainer for small business development centers in Washington, DC and Jackson, Mississippi, and as faculty advisor to student entrepreneurship organizations and startup bootcamps throughout the U.S. He is a McNair Scholar and member of multiple societies. He served in the U.S. military and the U.S. federal government, and has run several businesses. Dr. Crump has implemented innovative new entrepreneurship activities and curricula at Howard University, Jackson State University, and Medgar Evers College.

* * *

Iris Billy is a serial entrepreneur with a passion for entrepreneurship, education and coaching small business owners. Dr. Billy is no stranger to entrepreneurship, having spent over ten (10) years as a business owner. Prior to starting her consultancy business, Dr. Billy spent 15 years in the financial industry in the areas of banking, treasury, cash management and financial analysis for a diverse range of organizations, including small business startups; large corporations; private sector; non-profits; government agencies. In this role, Dr. Billy was responsible for funding, treasury analysis and cash management. After the financial crash of 2008 Dr. Billy saw the need and importance of small business ownership and start-up developments. Drawing on her many years' experience in financial industry, management and entrepreneurship Dr. Billy now focuses mainly on lecturing on financial literacy/credit and funding startups. Dr. Iris Billy is the principal consultant with Iris Billy Consultancy Services, founder of 5013c

SIRI'S H.O.P.E. (Helping Others Pursue Excellence) In her organizational role, Dr. Billy coordinates/manages all aspects of providing consultancy services, including coaching, mentoring and advising on change management to individuals and corporations. In her 501c3 role she provides young women and women with mentoring and professional development to assist them in making life changing decisions. A big believer in entrepreneurship, Dr. Billy supports and today regularly guest lectures on entrepreneurship at seminars and workshops with an emphasis on Women Entrepreneurship. Dr. Billy is a successful small business coach who has carved a niche with helping women make the transition from homemakers to successful entrepreneurs. Dr. Billy started her entrepreneurship coaching role in 2013 because she saw the need to help other women deal with the sometimes overwhelming prospect of starting a new business while still running a household. Today Dr. Billy offers a wide range of coaching programs and services – from individual coaching, to seminars and keynote speeches geared towards women and minority entrepreneurs Dr. Billy is a published author, public speaker, advisor to minority and women businesses, corporations, institutions, immigrants, non-profit and worker organizations. Dr. Billy graduated from Mercy College, NY and holds a B.S. in Business Administration, a Master Science in Organizational Leadership and graduated with a PhD. in Organizational Leadership/Management. She recently graduated with a Master Science in Criminal Justice (Social Justice) and is currently in her second year of Law program with a concentration in Criminal Justice. Dr. Billy is a College Professor with a senior City of NY (CUNY) college and has been teaching for fifteen (15) years. Dr. Billy is a generalist and strategic thinker, with expertise in management/leadership, entrepreneurship, economic development, and diversity management.

Nigel Chiweshe is a lecturer at the University of KwaZulu-natal. He is currently pursuing Doctoral studies specialising in Marketing with a focus on motivations for luxury brand consumption by deluxe aspirers. He also lectures Responsible & Sustainable Management Principles, Technology Management at the undergraduate level and Entrepreneurship Innovation and Venture Creation, at the Honours level and Contemporary Marketing at the Masters level. Through his engagement with the disciplines of management, marketing and entrepreneurship, Nigel has developed a keen interest in social enterprises, sustainability practices in SMMEs and luxury branding. He is currently involved in mentoring youth entrepreneurs, communities of practice in youth entrepreneurship, book editorship and research in social enterprises in the 4th Industrial Revolution.

Vikiana Clement, a graduate from Barnard, Columbia University undergrad and New York University grad, and a New York Times Scholar, has served as a corporate software engineer for two decades. She created interactive gaming platforms that use motion assessment and virtual reality to incorporate STEM and social-emotional learning. She is the recipient of NSF (national science foundation) grants for her software. She has been the lead technical developer, designer, and software architect for renowned companies. She advocates for closing the educational gap within the STEM sciences for underserved youths through innovative program creation.

Ericka Covington is an Assistant Professor of Management at Coppin State University's College of Business. She has a Doctor of Business Administration with a concentration in Leadership. Dr. Covington is a dynamic business expert and an accomplished leader with a wealth of expertise in leading national marketing initiatives for a major Fortune 500 company and has facilitated numerous trainings on management and effective leadership to corporate professionals. She earned her Bachelor of Arts from University of Maryland in the area of Criminal Justice and Master of Science in Criminal Justice Administration from Coppin State University. Dr. Covington has also worked as a parole and probation officer with the State of Maryland and has interned extensively with the Baltimore City State's Attorney's Office, The Office of the Public Defender, and served as a Victim Witness Coordinator in Montgomery County. While experienced in the areas of business and organizational leadership, her passion for social justice and her concern for her home town of Baltimore, gave rise to her research evaluating fluctuating leadership styles within the Baltimore City Police Department and how styles may influence the motivation of patrol officers. Her other areas of research interest include: sustainable business development in urban communities, and using leadership styles to develop effective organizational practices. Dr. Covington is an associate editor for the Journal of Leadership and Management and has served as a reviewer for the Eastern Academy of Management. She is a member of Delta Sigma Theta Sorority, Incorporated and lives in Owings Mills with her husband and two sons.

Sadia Farooq is an assistant professor at University of the Punjab. She has more than twenty years of teaching experience with active involvement in research as an educationist and researcher. Her areas of interest include microfinance, sustainability, stock market and behavioral finance, and hospitality.

Jeff Fuchs has been a lean practitioner for 27 years. His experience includes automotive, aerospace, machining, and energy industries, in roles including plant manager, quality manager, engineering director, and lean champion. He has managed numerous activities in non-profits and government offices designed to improve performance and enhance employee satisfaction. At Neovista Consulting, he focuses on operational excellence, leadership development, organizational culture, and lean transformation across all industries. For eleven years, Jeff served as Executive Director of a lean consortium helping organizations build cultures of continuous improvement using Lean Thinking techniques. He is a lean trainer, improvement facilitator, leadership coach, and strategic advisor. Jeff has been deeply involved in the national Lean Certification program. He is Lean Bronze, Silver, and Gold Certified. He is a member of the Lean Certification Oversight Committee jointly managed by the Association for Manufacturing Excellence, the Shingo Institute, and the Society of Manufacturing Engineers, and is past Committee Chairman. Jeff received his bachelor's degree in aerospace engineering from West Point. He is a combat veteran of the first Gulf War, and studies team and organizational leadership. He is an examiner for both the Shingo Institute's Shingo Prize and the AME Excellence Award. For four years, Jeff chaired the State of Maryland's Manufacturing Advisory Commission, and he currently serves on the Board of Directors of Open Works, a Baltimore maker space, community resource and small business incubator.

Nitu Ghosh, Associate Professor in the School of Management Studies, REVA University, is a dynamic instructor and thought – leader. She has been awarded the Doctorate of Philosophy in Management Studies and possesses a degree in M.B.A. with HR specialization, P.G.D.M., B.Ed, UGC-NET. She has an industry experience of 4 years and teaching experience of over 10 years. Having presented more than 25 papers in International and National conferences, she has successfully presented 6 research papers in International Conferences in IIMs and is the author of a book on Workplace Ethics. Dr. Nitu Has couple of publications in SCOPUS and web of science journals. One of her papers on "Emotional Intelligence and entrepreneurship development has been published in the South Asian Journal of Management, an ABDC listed journal. She has 20 research publications in international journals and conference publications. Besides, she has actively participated in more than 20 Faculty Development Programmes and Workshops. Presently, she is also a trainer and consultant in career management, personality and soft skills development.

Adem Gök is currently employed in Department of Economics at Kırklareli University, Turkey as an associate professor. He received his bachelor degree in economics from Boğaziçi University in 2008 and master degree in economics (English) from Marmara University in 2012. He holds a Ph.D in economics (English) from Marmara University since 2016. His research area includes foreign direct investment, growth and development, economics of governance, environmental economics, economics of education and financial economics.

Priscilla Harrison is a Professor of Project Management at Campbellsville University and Colorado State University-Global Campus. She is a certified project manager with a Project Management Professional (PMP) certification from PMI and has extensive background mentoring and working with underserved communities in the Houston area. She is also the co-author for the book chapter of "Women Entrepreneurs and Disparities during Pre and Post COVID Pandemic Era: Women Entrepreneurs" for the book titled "Sustainability and the Future of Work and Entrepreneurship for the Underserved. Dr. Harrison has been teaching in higher education for several years and is a passionate guide, facilitator, and mentor challenging her students, stretching their horizons, and helping them become excited about looking over the next academic or practitioner hill to climb. Dr. Harrison and her husband, Glenn, are the parents of two grown daughters and reside in The Woodlands, Texas.

Will Holman is a sought-after expert regarding design and makerspaces. His publications include Guerilla Furniture Design: How to Build Lean, Modern Furniture with Salvaged Materials, "How a Baltimore makerspace is encouraging trust between local residents, businesses, and institutions "in the Brookings Institutions Placemaking Postcards Series, "Makerspaces and the Future of Work" in Taking Action: Positioning Low-Income Workers to Succeed in a Changing Economy" edited by the Hatcher Group for the Annie E. Casey Foundation, "Alternatives to the Atelier: Makerspaces and Design Education" in Design School: After Boundaries and Disciplines edited by Paul A. Rodgers and Craig Bremner, the Make Magazine "Made in Baltimore Series, and many more. His speaking engagements include conferences, panels, expert testimony and other events across the nation. Prior to his role at Open Works, Will worked as an architectural designer, carpenter, artist's assistant, cabinetmaker, furniture designer, and educator. He lives in an old house in Baltimore with his wife Amanda and daughter Annie. His primary interest is in expanding access to the means of production through writing, community development, and open-source design.

Aisha Ismail is a researcher working in the field of finance, her areas of interest are corporate finance, microfinance and distance learning. She is currently working on microfinance by taking an ecosystem perspective that can benefit underserved communities and more specifically women entrepreneurs working in under-served communities.

Carolyne Jebiwott Kimutai is a Lecturer within the Department of Accounting and Finance, Kenyatta University. She holds a PhD in Finance and is a Certified Public Accountant (CPA-K). She specializes in Sustainable Corporate Finance and Entrepreneurial Finance. ORCHID: https://orcid.org/0000-0001-6199-5257.

Dagogo William Legg-Jack is a Postdoctoral Research Fellow at Walter Sisulu University, Nelson Mandela Drive, Mthatha, Eastern Cape, South Africa. He obtained his PhD in Technology Education, and has served as a teacher in high schools in Nigeria, where he taught Technology-based subject. He has also functioned as a lecturer in the Department of Metal Work Technology, School of Secondary Education (Technical), Federal College of Education (Technical), Omoku, Rivers State, Nigeria for several years. In South Africa, he has also served as a lecturer in the Department of Technology Education, at the University of KwaZulu-Natal. Dr Legg-Jack's research project supervision experience spans across different levels of higher education institutions namely, the National Certificate of Education (NCE) in Federal College of Education (Technical), Omoku, and Bachelor of Education (B. Ed) of the same institution in affiliation with the University of Nigeria, Nssuka. Moreover, he has participated in seminars and conferences both within and outside South Africa and has published articles in peer-reviewed journals that focus on skills development, poverty reduction, Education Technology, Teacher development as well as wealth creation among others.

Soolakshna Lukea-Bhiwajee is currently Senior Lecturer at the University of Technology, Mauritius where she has been working for 20 years. She holds a Bachelor of Commerce and a Masters in Personnel Management from the University of Pune, India. Her research and publication interests are in the fields of social sustainability, sustainable HRM and the public Sector. Dr. Bhiwajee is the recipient of numerous research grants awarded by the Mauritius Research and Innovation Council and the Higher Education Commission in Mauritius.

Rabeh Morrar received his Ph.D. in Innovation Economy from Lille 1 University for Science and Technology, Lille, France in 2011. He joined An-Najah National University, Palestine, as assistant professor in Economics and was Economics Department head, 2011 to 2015. Between May 2018 to June 2019, he has worked as senior researcher in Centre of International Development at Northumbria University, UK. Afterward, he received a postdoctoral in Social Innovation. Since 2021, Dr. Morrar has become the director of research at the Palestine Economic Policy Research Institute-MAS. His current research interests include Knowledge Economy, Innovation Economy, Palestinian Economy, and Sustainable Development. Dr. Morrar is a Fellow of the Economic Research Forum (ERF), Arab Council for the Social Sciences (ACSS), Turkish Economic Research Forum, American Economic Association (AEA), and Middle East Economic Association (MEEA). He published more than 20 articles in an international peer-reviewed journals, and many other reports and policy papers at local and international levels.

Nathan Mwenda Mutwiri is a Lecturer within the Department of Accounting and Finance, Kenyatta University. He holds a PhD in Finance, Masters of Science in Finance, Bachelors of Commerce, Bachelors of Laws and is a Certified Public accountant (CPA-K). He specializes in Financial Markets, Corporate Governance, entrepreneurship and Law. ORCHID: https://orcid.org/0000-0002-9158-320X.

Nompumelelo Sindiswa Nqoko is an avid researcher in the field of Entrepreneurship. Her research focus is on entrepreneurship education and youth entrepreneurship.

Nitisha Purusram Dhondee currently works as Culture Officer at the Ministry of Arts and Cultural Heritage of the Republic of Mauritius and part-time Research Assistant at the University of Technology, Mauritius. She holds a rich academic background. She completed her degree in Psychology, in 2010, at the University of Pune, India. She completed a dual Master in Business Administration, specializing in Human Resource Management and IT & ITES, in 2012, at the University of Pune, India. She completed her Master in Public Administration and Governance, in 2017, at the Sun Yat-Sen University, China. Her Master Project on the Disability Employment Policy in Mauritius obtained excellent grade and she received the "Best Master Thesis" award and the "Excellent Master Student" award by the Sun Yat-Sen University, China. She hopes to pursue her Phd in the areas of social and public policy in the near future. Her areas of interests include Management, Social Policy, Cross-Culturalism, Public Policy and Public Administration.

Andrisha Beharry Ramraj, lecturer at the University of KwaZulu-Natal, holds a PhD in Management studies majoring in management, leadership and governance. Further to this she holds a Diploma in Higher Education. In 2004 and 2005 she received NRF scholarships to complete her Honours and Masters degrees respectively. She has presented at local and international conference in the areas of Management, Leadership, Marketing, Global Business and Entrepreneurship. She has published in the fields of Leadership, Entrepreneurship, Human Resources and Business Management. She recently published book chapters on entrepreneurial suitability and employee wellness across the globe. In 2016 and 2017 she received best presentation awards for best paper delivered at conferences, she serves on the Teaching and Learning committee within the University of KwaZulu Natal (UKZN) and served as the Bachelor of Business Administrator Programme Manager (Self-Funding Teaching Programme) for a one term. She teaches across levels within the Discipline of Management and Entrepreneurship, from entry level to masters level. She is keen on developing undergraduate curriculum transformation within the discipline. Redesigning curricular to suite the dynamics of the modern world enabling sustainability is fast becoming her passion. Having realised her desire for higher education, Dr Beharry served as an expert advisor for the Student Society of Entrepreneurship (CAVE) based at UKZN. Additional to this she now shares her expertise as a research expert for the Centre of Entrepreneurship.

Fuad Rayyan is an independent researcher and practitioner in international development and political economics, with a special interest in Palestine and the Middle East and North Africa (MENA) region.

Yosmayra Reyes, a graduate from Columbia University and undergrad from New York University, is a licensed clinical social worker focusing on creating and implementing targeted community initiatives. She is a recipient of an NSF (national science foundation) grant for co-creating an educational interactive gaming platform that uses motion assessment and virtual reality to incorporate STEM and social-emotional learning. She advocates for increasing mental health literacy and incorporating into daily practice.

Pratigya Sigdyal is an Assistant Professor of Management at California State University, Bakersfield. She earned her PhD from the University of North Texas. Her research interests are in the area of mindfulness, mental health, and employee wellbeing.

Clarice Tate is Vice President of Quality and Systems Assurance of Peregrine Global Services. Peregrine provides programmatic assessment services, online instructional modules used to develop business acumen and essential soft skills, and a variety of leadership development services. In 2017, Clarice brought her range of experiences, skills, and knowledge to support quality assurance at Peregrine Global Services. A firm believer in the process of continuous improvement, Clarice sustains quality metrics to ensure constant improvement of Peregrine's services and operations. With more than 20 years of combined experience in the public and private sectors, including nonprofit organizations and formerly owning her own insurance business, Clarice's management skills and passion for business successfully supported her career change into education. Clarice has been globally recognized and honored as teacher of the year in 2012 for her work in Baltimore City Public Schools as a secondary educator by the Network for Teaching Entrepreneurship (NFTE). Her work at Coppin State University continues to be recognized for the successful outcomes in higher education with notable success in accreditation management for leading Coppin's initial accreditation of their business school programs with "no conditions; no notes". Through her experience, Clarice has developed expertise in curriculum and instruction, accreditation management, business and academic consulting, research, program administration, and continuous quality improvement system design and processes. Clarice is best known for her strategic thinking and planning abilities, and as such, she is an invaluable member of Peregrine's Leadership team. Clarice Tate holds a Master of Education from Coppin State University and a Master of Business Administration from the University of Maryland, Robert H. Smith School of Business. Clarice has an unparalleled enthusiasm for education, service, entrepreneurship, and innovation, and her passion is ever-present as she leads.

Rand Taweel is an Assistant Researcher at the Palestine Economic Policy Research Economic. She has BA in Economics and International Politics from Middlebury College.

Ronald (Ron) Coleman Williams is an associate professor of management and founding director of the Center for Strategic Entrepreneurship with 35 years of experience in higher education, 25 of which have been at the Coppin State University (CSU) College of Business. He also served as interim dean from 2013 until 2017. In 2016, Dr. Williams established a formal relationship between CSU and Open Works Baltimore, a 34K sq. ft makerspace. This groundbreaking relationship is the first of its kind in the nation and led to a role as principal investigator in the 2019 "Turning Makerspaces into Greater Places: An Organizational Assessment and Economic Impact Study of Open Works" (www.GreaterSpacesAnd-Places.com), another significant innovation as the first comprehensive organizational assessment and economic impact study of a makerspace. He further contributed to the understanding of makerspace value in 2020 as principal investigator in the case study of Open Works' application of Lean Manufacturing principles during the initial months of the Covid-19 global pandemic, producing over 28,000 face shields in 56 days for over 100 clients. Immediately before the 2015 unrest in Baltimore, Dr. Williams coined the phrase "ingepreneurship" (inge… as in ingenuity) in a 2017 Metropolitan Journal article entitled "Creating a University Driven 'Ingepreneurial' Ecosystem in West Baltimore: A Strategy for Rust Belt Revitalization." The concept describes a framework for improving the socio-economic well-being of underrepresented communities and aligns with his work as academic advisor to the Manufacturing Workforce Development Industry & Inclusion Study (a joint research project by The Century Foundation and Urban Manufacturing Alliance), development of the recently approved Certificate in Entrepreneurship and Innovation, and development of a trust-climate assessment instrument for collaborative economic development across cultural and geographic divides. He is also the faculty advisor of award-winning student teams in local and national innovation competitions. Dr. Williams holds a Ph.D. in management and organization from George Washington University with concentrations in organization behavior & development and the management of science, technology, & innovation; a master's degree in human resource development from Johns Hopkins University in Baltimore, Maryland; and a bachelor's degree with majors in psychology, social science, and education from the University of Tampa in Tampa, Florida. He also serves on the AAAS HBCU Making & Innovation Advisory Board, the Open Works Board of Directors, and as chair of the Urban Manufacturing Alliance Board of Directors.

Index

www.ingramcontent.com/pod-product-compliance
Lightning Source LLC
LaVergne TN
LVHW081250011026
849162LV00006BA/1268